From the Library of

Julia Christensen Hughes

MANAGING HUMAN RESOURCES

CANADIAN EDITION

MONICA BELCOURT
ASSOCIATE PROFESSOR OF
ADMINISTRATIVE STUDIES
YORK UNIVERSITY, TORONTO

ARTHUR W. SHERMAN, JR.
PROFESSOR OF PSYCHOLOGY
CALIFORNIA STATE UNIVERSITY, SACRAMENTO

GEORGE W. BOHLANDER
PROFESSOR OF MANAGEMENT
ARIZONA STATE UNIVERSITY

SCOTT A. SNELL
ASSOCIATE PROFESSOR OF BUSINESS
PENNSYLVANIA STATE UNIVERSITY

Nelson Canada

I(T)P An International Thomson Publishing Company

Toronto • Albany • Bonn • Boston • Cincinnati • Detroit • London • Madrid • Melbourne
Mexico City • New York • Pacific Grove • Paris • San Francisco • Singapore • Tokyo • Washington

I(T)P
International Thomson Publishing
The ITP logo is a trademark under licence

© Nelson Canada
A division of Thomson Canada Limited, 1996

Published in 1996 by
Nelson Canada
A division of Thomson Canada Limited
1120 Birchmount Road
Scarborough, Ontario M1K 5G4

Original U.S. Edition published by South-Western College Publishing. Copyright 1996.

Canadian Cataloguing in Publication Data

Main entry under title:

Managing human resources

Canadian ed.
ISBN 0-17-605557-6

1. Personnel management.   I. Belcourt, Monica Laura,
date .

HF5548.M35 1995   658.3   C95-932750-9

Publisher	Jacqueline Wood
Senior Editor	Rosalyn Steiner
Project Coordinator	Edward Ikeda
Senior Production Coordinator	Carol Tong
Art Director	Stuart Knox
Cover Design	Sylvia Vander Schee
Cover Art	*Arena in Arles* by Vincent Van Gogh.
	Hermitage Museum, St. Petersburg, Russia/Superstock.
Lead Composition Analyst	Zenaida Diores

Printed and bound in Canada

1 2 3 4 (BBM) 98 97 96 95

To Cristy Libunao, the best home-support system a working mother ever had

To my wife, Leneve Sherman, and to our children, Judy, Beverly, and Sandy

To my wife, Ronnie Bohlander, and to our children, Ryan and Kathryn

To my wife, Marybeth Snell, and to our children, Sara, Jack, and Emily

BRIEF CONTENTS

Contents

PART 6 INTERNATIONAL HUMAN RESOURCES MANAGEMENT AND HR AUDITS

PART 2 MEETING HUMAN RESOURCES REQUIREMENTS

PART 6   INTERNATIONAL HUMAN RESOURCES MANAGEMENT AND HR AUDITS

Authors

Monica Belcourt

Monica Belcourt is Associate Professor, Administrative Studies at Atkinson College, York University, Toronto. She has an extensive and varied background in Human Resources Management. After receiving an undergraduate degree in psychology from the University of Manitoba, Winnipeg, she joined the Public Service Commission of Canada as a staffing officer. She has worked in most functional areas of HR, including Manager of HR Development at the National Film Board, Manager of Consumer Services for the Quebec region of Consumer and Corporate Affairs, and Director of Personnel for CP Rail.

Dr. Belcourt alternated working in HR with graduate work, and has an M.A. in Organizational Psychology from York University, an M.Ed. in Adult Education from the University of Ottawa, and a Ph.D. in Management from York University. She has taught graduate and undergraduate courses in management and HR at Concordia University, McGill University, Université du Québec à Montréal, and York University. Currently, she heads one of the largest undergraduate HR programs in Canada. As well, she has extensive experience as a speaker at seminars and conferences.

Dr. Belcourt's research interests include entrepreneurship and human resources. She has published over 50 articles since receiving her Ph.D. in 1986. She is Series Editor for the Nelson Canada Series in Human Resources Management, and co-author of one of the books in the series *Performance Management through Training and Development*. Dr. Belcourt founded and is Editor for "The Research Forum," a monthly column for the *Human Resources Professional Magazine*.

Active in many professional associations and not-for-profit organizations, she has served as Vice-President, Publications, and Chair, HR Division of the Administrative Sciences Association of Canada, and Chair of the Senate Committee on Teaching and Learning. Currently, she is on the board of CIBC Insurance and HRPAO (the Human Resources Professional Association of Canada). She is Founding Director of the Human Resources Research Institute.

Arthur W. Sherman, Jr.

Arthur W. Sherman, Jr., is Professor of Psychology, California State University, Sacramento. During most of his academic career he has taught undergraduate and graduate courses in organizational psychology, personnel psychology, human resources management, psychological testing, and professional development in psychology. Dr. Sherman has served as a personnel consultant to several organizations, including the Department of Consumer Affairs of the State of California and the Social Security Administration. He has been a participant in seminars and workshops, for twelve consecutive years as a lecturer in the management development program conducted by the CSUS School of Business Administration for the federal government. For over twenty years he had a private practice as a licensed psychologist specializing in career counselling.

During World War II and the Korean War, Dr. Sherman served in the U.S. Air Force as a Personnel Classification Officer, as an Aviation Psychologist, and as head of a proficiency test development unit for the Airman Career program. Later he was active in the planning of the psychology curriculum at the U.S. Air Force Academy.

As an undergraduate, Dr. Sherman attended Oberlin College and Ohio University, receiving an A.B. in psychology from Ohio University. He received an A.M. from Indiana University and a Ph.D. in industrial and counselling psychology for the Ohio State University. His professional affiliations include the American Psychological Association, the Society for Industrial and Organizational Psychology, and the Academy of Management.

He has been an author of this book since its beginning as well as *Personnel Practices of American Companies in Europe*, published by the American Management Association.

George W. Bohlander

George W. Bohlander is Professor of Management at Arizona State University. He teaches undergraduate, graduate, and executive development programs in the field of human resources and labour relations. His areas of expertise include employment law, training and development, work teams, public policy, and labour relations. He is the recipient of five outstanding teaching awards at ASU and has received the Outstanding Undergraduate Teaching Excellence Award given by the College of Business at ASU.

Dr. Bohlander is an active researcher and author. He has published over 40 articles and monographs covering various topics in the human resources area ranging from labour-management cooperation to employee productivity. His articles appear in such academic and practitioner journals as *Labor Studies Journal, Personnel Administrator, Labor Law Journal, Journal of Collective Negotiations in the Public Sector, Public Personnel Management, National Productivity Review, Personnel, and Employee Relations Law Journal.*

Before beginning his teaching career, Dr. Bohlander served as Personnel Administrator for General Telephone Company of California. His duties included recruitment and selection, training and development, equal employment opportunity, and labour relations. He was very active in resolving employee grievances and in arbitration preparation. Dr. Bohlander continues to be a consultant to both public- and private-sector organizations, and he has worked with such organizations as the U.S. Postal Service, Kaiser Cement, McDonnell Douglas, Arizona Public Service, American Productivity Center, Rural Metro Corporation, and Del Webb. Dr. Bohlander is also an active labour arbitrator. He received his Ph.D. from the University of California at Los Angeles and his M.B.A. from the University of Southern California.

Scott A. Snell

Scott A. Snell is Associate Professor of Business Administration at Penn State University. During his career Dr. Snell has taught courses in human resource management, principles of management, and strategic management to undergraduates, graduates, and executives. He is actively involved in executive education and serves as Faculty Director for Penn State's Strategic Leadership Program as well as faculty leader for programs in Human Resources, Developing Managerial Effectiveness, Engineer/Scientist as Manager, and Managing the Global Enterprise. Dr. Snell also serves as Director of Research for Penn State's Institute for the Study of Organizational Effectiveness.

As an industry consultant, Professor Snell has worked with companies such as Arthur Andersen, AT&T, GE, IBM, and Shell Chemical to redesign human resource systems to cope with changes in the competitive environment. His specialization is the realignment of staffing, training, and reward systems to complement technology, quality, and other strategic initiatives. Recently, his work has centred on the development of transitional teams in global network organizations.

Dr. Snell's research has been published in the *Academy of Management Journal, Human Resource Management Review, Industrial Relations, Journal of Business Research, Journal of Management, Journal of Managerial Issues, Personnel Administrator, Strategic Management Journal,* and *Working Woman.* In addition, Dr. Snell is on the editorial boards of *Journal of Managerial Issues, Digest of Management Research,* and *Journal of Quality Management.* He is author of two books, *Management: Building Competitive Advantage,* with Thomas S. Bateman (Irwin Publishing), and *Strategic Human Resource Management* (Austin Press).

He holds a B.A. in Psychology from Miami University, as well as M.B.A. and Ph.D. degrees in Business Administration from Michigan State University. His professional associations include the Strategic Management Society, Academy of Management, and the Society for Human Resource Management.

· ·

In today's rapidly changing world of business, managers, supervisors, and human resource management professionals must be able to anticipate and respond to problems before they occur. Meeting challenges head-on and using human resources (HR) effectively are critical to the success of any work organization. To ensure effectiveness, HR policies and procedures must be placed into a comprehensive program that managers can follow in their day-to-day interactions with employees.

Managing Human Resources, Canadian edition, emphasizes the role managers and supervisors play in determining the success of the HR program. While the focus is on the HR role of managers, we do not exclude the impact and importance of the HR department's role—the responsibility for developing, coordinating, and enforcing policies and procedures relating to HR functions.

Our intent is to appeal to the diverse interests and career goals of your students. We recognize that at some point in their careers the majority of students will occupy a managerial position, while few will become members of the HR department staff. Whether the reader becomes a manager, an HR staff member, or is employed in other areas of the organization, *Managing Human Resources* provides a functional understanding of HR programs to enable students to see how HR affects all employees, the organization, the community, and the larger society.

As we approach the close of the twentieth century, those of us who have studied work organizations are gratified to observe the increased attention and recognition given to human resources and their management. The HR manager has achieved a status equal to that of managers in charge of such major functions as marketing, production, and finance. Top management has become aware that HR managers can play a vital role in determining the success of an organization.

The role of HR managers is no longer viewed as limited to service functions such as recruiting and selecting employees. Today they assume an active role in the strategic planning and decision making at the upper echelons of their organizations. Their contributions to the achievement of organizational objectives have finally earned them the recognition they deserve. Their contributions in the past signal even greater potential for the future.

We recognize the manager's changing role and emphasize current issues and real-world problems and the policies and practices of HRM used to meet them. As authors, we present a realistic picture of HR management as it is today and offer suggestions as to how it contributes to greater productivity and employee satisfaction.

Features of this Text

Integrated Learning System. The text and supplements are organized around the learning objectives presented at the beginning of each chapter. Numbered icons identifying the objectives appear next to the material throughout the text and in the Instructor's Resource Guide and Test Bank where each objective is fulfilled. When students need further review to meet a certain objective, they can quickly identify the relevant material by simply looking for the icon. This integrated structure creates a comprehensive teaching and testing system.

Greater emphasis on current issues and problems of the actual business world establishes a clear understanding of working relationships within today's organizations. Each chapter contains an interview with a functional Canadian expert. These interviews, highlighted in "Reality Check," provide not only a validation that the concepts presented in the chapter are applied in real organizations, but also illustrate some of the current issues that practitioners are facing. References and examples of the policies and practices of hundreds of organizations show HR concepts in action in the business world today.

Some of these issues are not resolved, as the situations discussed in "Ethics in HRM" illustrate. Human resource management is an evolving field, and as such, some policies and practices are still being debated. By exposing students to these ethical questions, we hope to increase their ability to think critically about HR. References and examples of the policies and practices of hundreds of organizations show HR concepts in action in the business world today.

Increased attention to the impact of internal and external environments upon HR activities demonstrates how HR plays a key role in all business activities.

Expanded discussions cover major current issues such as:

- Conflict resolution
- Diversity in the workplace
- Employee empowerment
- Employee teams
- Global perspective of HR
- HR in small businesses
- Total-quality management

Many "Highlights in HRM" boxes present the student with up-to-date, real-world examples from a variety of large and small organizations. Greater use of charts depicting trends further clarifies these concepts for the student.

Eighteen cases reinforce critical thinking skills and problem-solving techniques. Name, organization, and subject indexes provide valuable reference sources.

In order to make the material more meaningful for students, we have included a section entitled "Career Counsel" at the end of each chapter. One goal of this feature is to provide a means for students to apply material learned in the chapter to their personal lives, thus increasing the possibility of deeper and longer learning. A second goal is to help the students prepare a career plan containing important elements such as résumé preparation, values assessment, and salary negotiation tactics.

Designed to facilitate understanding and retention of the material presented, each chapter contains several of the following items.

- Learning objectives listed at the beginning of each chapter provide the basis for the integrated learning system. Icons for identifying the learning objectives appear throughout the text material.
- Key terms appear in boldface and are defined in margin notes next to the text discussion. The key terms are also listed at the end of the chapter.
- Figures. An abundance of graphic materials, flow charts, and summaries of research data provide a visual, dynamic presentation of concepts and HR activities. All figures are systematically referenced in the text discussion.

- "Highlights in HRM." This popular boxed feature provides real-world examples of how organizations perform HR functions. Highlights are introduced in the text discussion and include topics such as small businesses and international issues.
- Illustrations. Captioned photographs and carefully selected cartoons reinforce points made in the text and maintain student interest.
- Summary. A paragraph or two for each learning objective provides a brief review of the chapter.
- Discussion questions following the chapter summary offer an opportunity to focus on major points in the chapter and to stimulate critical thinking and discussion.
- Cases present current HRM issues in a real-life setting that encourages student consideration and critical analysis.
- Notes and References. Each chapter includes references from academic and practitioner journals and books. Author notes cite some historical information as well as personal observations and experiences.

Organization of the Text

This book is organized into six parts and eighteen chapters covering the following major topics:

Part 1. Human Resources Management in Perspective
The Role of Human Resources Management, The Environment for Human Resources Management, Equity and Diversity

Part 2. Meeting Human Resources Requirements
Human Resources Planning, Job Requirements, Recruitment, Selection

Part 3. Developing Effectiveness in Human Resources
Training, Career Development, Appraising and Improving Performance

Part 4. Implementing Compensation and Security
Managing Compensation, Incentive Compensation, Employee Benefits, Health and Safety

Part 5. Strengthening Employee-Management Relations
The Dynamics of Labour Relations, Collective Bargaining, Contract Administration

Part 6. International Human Resources Management and HR Audits
International Human Resources Management and Auditing the HRM Program

Supplementary Materials

All printed supplementary materials were prepared by the text authors to guarantee full integration with the text. Multimedia and additional text supplements were prepared by experts in those fields.

Instructor's Resource Guide. For each chapter in the textbook, the resource guide contains the following:

- Chapter synopsis and learning objectives.
- A very detailed lecture outline, based on the textbook chapter outline, complete with notes on the transparencies and transparency masters.
- An annotated list of audiovisual materials pertinent to the chapter's subject matter and available from various sources.
- Answers to the end-of-chapter discussion questions in the textbook.
- Analysis of the end-of-chapter cases in the textbook.

Multicolour Transparencies and Transparency Masters. Also available with this edition is a set of multicolour transparencies. Only a few of these transparencies duplicate the figures in the textbook. The set of masters includes each chapter's learning objectives, outline, and other useful information.

Test Bank and Computerized Test Bank. The test bank has been expanded to include 1800 test questions. Each test bank chapter includes a matrix table that classifies each question according to type and learning objective. There are true/false, multiple-choice, and essay items for each chapter, arranged by learning objective. Page references from the text are included. Each objective question is coded to indicate whether it covers knowledge of key terms, understanding of concepts and principles, or application of principles.

Human Resource Manager CD-ROM from The Institute for the Learning Sciences, Northwestern University. This new interactive multimedia CD-ROM-based simulation uses personnel information for a fictitious company to allow students to interact with managers as they make decisions, just as an HR manager would on issues of productivity, morale, and profits. The program covers five years, including one year of history and four years of work time. Students advance one month at a time as they learn how to manage people throughout the employee life cycle.

Video. Part-opener videos sourced from real companies as well as professionally produced, short video segments developed from business features on CNBC, the cable business news network. The tape is accompanied by an instructor's guide, which includes descriptions of the segments and other information designed to help you integrate the videos with the text material. Use them to introduce a topic, cover lecture material, or stimulate discussion.

Applications in Human Resource Management: Cases, Exercises, and Skill Builders, 3d Edition, by Stella M. Nkomo, Myron D. Fottler, and R. Bruce McAfee. This text supplement includes 75 new and updated cases, experiential exercises, skill builders, and term projects. These activities will supplement many of the topics covered in *Managing Human Resources,* Canadian edition.

The Mescon Group's Performance Through Participation (PTP) Series. This series of flexible instructional modules allows students to learn through experiential

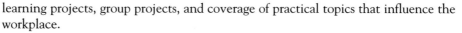

learning projects, group projects, and coverage of practical topics that influence the workplace.

With the purchase of every copy of this text, students will receive a special shrink-wrapped issue of *The Globe and Mail's* **Report on Business** magazine.

Acknowledgments

The manuscript of this work was reviewed at various stages of its development by a great number of our peers across Canada, and we wish to thank those who shared their insights and their constructive criticism. Among them are Thomas Kilpatrick, St. Clair College; Doug Bicknell, University of Saskatchewan; Diana White, Seneca College; Normand Fortier, University of Ottawa; Gordon Hayward, Northern Alberta Institute of Technology; Jed Fisher, University of Alberta.

We appreciate the efforts of the Market and Product Development Team at Nelson Canada who helped develop and produce this text. They include Jackie Wood, Edward Ikeda, Rosalyn Steiner, Carol Tong, and Zenaida Diores.

In particular, we thank Deborah Zinni, the research associate who worked relentlessly to obtain Canadian examples, statistics, and sources for the adaptation. She was responsible for 16 of the 18 interviews with the experts in Reality Checks. Her creative efforts, 18-hour days, and extensive HR contacts within Canada contributed significantly to the text.

As always, my husband, Michael, and my sons, Marc and Brooker Belcourt, have been both understanding and supportive of my work.

We are indebted to our wives—Leneve Sherman, Ronnie Bohlander, and Marybeth Snell—who have contributed in so many ways to this book over the years. They are always sources of invaluable guidance and assistance. Furthermore, by their continued enthusiasm and support, they have made the process a more pleasant and rewarding experience. We are most grateful to them for their many contributors to this publication, to our wives, and to our families.

Monica Belcourt
York University, Toronto

Arthur W. Sherman, Jr.
California State University, Sacramento

George W. Bohlander
Arizona State University

Scott A. Snell
The Pennsylvania State University

Part 1

Human Resources Management in Perspective

The three chapters in Part 1 provide an overview of the field of human resources management. Chapter 1 describes the development of HR management, including the programs and policies required for HR departments to succeed. Chapter 2 discusses both the internal and the external factors that affect the supervision of an organizations' human resources. It reviews the important demographic changes in the Canadian workforce and discusses how organizations are evolving to meet the demands of today's employees. Chapter 3 is concerned with federal and provincial employment equity legislation that influences how managers must treat present and prospective employees. The emerging issue of diversity management is introduced. As managers and supervisors understand the environment of managing employees, they are in a better position to utilize these valuable organizational resources effectively.

one objective
Cite the reasons for studying human resources management (HRM).

two objective
Describe the major forces in the development of HRM.

three objective
List the characteristics of HRM that enable us to refer to it as a profession.

four objective
Identify the principal elements of an HR program and their importance in managing HR.

five objective
Describe the various responsibilities of the HR department and the nature of its relationship with other departments.

six objective
Describe the types of changes that are forecast for HRM.

Chapter 1

The Role of Human Resources Management

If an organization is to achieve its goals, it must not only have the required resources, but it must also use them effectively. The resources available to a manager are human, financial, physical, and informational.[1] While human resources (HR) have always been critical to the success of any firm, they have assumed an increasingly greater importance that is being recognized inside and outside work organizations.

Human resources services typically include individuals with a wide variety and range of knowledge, skills, and abilities who are expected to perform job activities in a manner that contributes to the attainment of organizational goals. How effectively employees contribute to the firm depends in large part upon the quality of the HR program (including staffing, training, compensation, and other functions) as well as the ability and eagerness of management—from the CEO to first-line supervisors—to create an environment that fosters the effective use of human resources.

Why Study Human Resources Management (HRM)?

objective

Anyone who embarks on a course of specialized study typically wonders about its relevance to his or her interests and goals. The answer to the question "Why study HRM?" should become apparent as we explore the importance of HR management and examine the contribution that it can make to an organization.

The Importance of HRM

Personnel management
Basic functions of selection, training, compensation, etc., in the management of an organization's personnel.

Human resources management (HRM)
Extension of the traditional requirements of personnel management, which recognizes the dynamic reaction of personnel functions with each other and with the strategic and planning objectives of the organization.

For many decades such responsibilities as selection, training, and compensation were considered basic functions constituting the area historically referred to as **personnel management**. These functions were performed without much regard for how they related to each other. From this narrow view we have seen the emergence of what is now known as human resources management. **Human resources management (HRM)**, as it is currently perceived, represents the extension rather than the rejection of the traditional requirements for managing personnel effectively. An understanding of human behaviour and skill in applying that understanding are still required. Also required are knowledge and understanding of the various personnel functions performed in managing human resources, as well as the ability to perform them in accordance with organizational objectives. An awareness of existing economic, social, and legal constraints upon the performance of these functions is also essential. Attention will be given to these constraints in the next chapter.

HRM, as it is practised today, recognizes the dynamic interaction of personnel functions with each other and with the objectives of the organization. Most important, it recognizes that HR planning must be coordinated closely with the organization's strategic and related planning functions. As a result, efforts in HRM are being directed toward providing more support for the achievement of the firm's competitive goals.

HRM: Current Challenges

According to a survey of HR managers conducted by Andrew Templer, University of Windsor, and James Ladouceur, St. Clair College, Ontario, the most challenging HR issues are (1) the flexibility to manage change, diversity, and strategic planning; (2)

education, training, and development, and (3) recruitment of talent and productivity of human resources. Generating efficiency is the most current concern. Respondents felt that training and development would help achieve this goal, as well as the objective of maintaining a supply of motivated workers.[2] International companies face increased global competition. One may expect to see emerging in the future new issues and challenges that require appropriate action. Evolving business and economic factors forge changes in the HR field requiring that preparation for change be a continual process.[3]

The Role of the HR Department

Top management generally recognizes the contributions that the HR program can make to the organization and thus expects HR managers to assume a broader role in the overall organizational strategy. Thus HR managers must remember the bottom line if they are to fulfil their role. In an award-winning study, Mark Huselid has demonstrated conclusively that investment in sophisticated HR practices contributes to greater financial performance and productivity as well as to reduced turnover.[4]

In the process of managing human resources, increasing attention is being given to the personal needs of the participants. Thus throughout this book we will not only emphasize the importance of the contributions that HRM makes to the organization but also give serious consideration to its effects on the individual and on society.

Increasingly, employees and the public at large are demanding that employers demonstrate greater social responsibility in managing their human resources. Complaints that some jobs are devitalizing the lives and injuring the health of employees are not uncommon. Charges of discrimination against women, minorities, the physically disabled, and aboriginals with respect to hiring, training, advancement, and compensation are being levelled against some employers. Issues such as the rising costs of health benefits and alternative work schedules are concerns that many employers must address.

The HR Role of Managers and Supervisors

Students who are now preparing for careers in organizations will find that the study of HRM will provide a background of understanding that will be valuable in managerial and supervisory positions. Although HR managers have the responsibility for coordinating and enforcing policies relating to the HR functions, *all managers and supervisors are responsible for performing these functions in their relations with subordinates*. It is in such positions of authority that the majority of students using this book will be employed. This book is therefore oriented to help them in managing subordinates more effectively, whether they become first-line supervisors or chief executive officers. Discussions concerning the role of the HR department can serve to provide one with a better understanding of the functions performed by this department. A familiarity with the role of the HR department should help one to cooperate more closely with the department's staff and to utilize more fully the assistance and services available from this source.

We should recognize that the present status of HRM was achieved only after years of evolutionary development. We hope that this chapter will help readers not only to understand the forces that have contributed to this program but also to become more aware of the forces today that will have an effect on it in the future.

objective

The Development of Human Resources Management

HRM, at least in a primitive form, has existed since the dawn of group effort. Certain HR functions, even though informal in nature, were performed whenever people came together for a common purpose. During the course of this century, however, the processes of managing people have become more formalized and specialized, and a growing body of knowledge has been accumulated by practitioners and scholars. An understanding of the events contributing to the growth of HRM (see Figure 1-1) can provide a perspective for contemporary policies and practices.

In the discussion that follows, the major trends will be noted and some of the events described. While most of the books and articles cited in the Notes and References section (at the end of each chapter) are current, the reader should always be aware that the philosophy and practices reflected in contemporary HRM have evolved from a history encompassing several decades.

The Factory System

During the 19th century, the development of mechanical power made possible a factory system of production. The concentration of workers in factories served to focus public attention on their conditions of employment, which were often unhealthy and hazardous. During the early to mid-1900s, laws were passed in several provinces to regulate hours, to establish minimum wages, and to regulate working conditions that affect employee health and safety. It was also at this time that laws were enacted to provide payments for injuries suffered in industrial accidents. Eventually, as the result of legislation and collective bargaining, employment conditions began to improve.

The Mass Production System

Mass production was made possible by the availability of standardized and interchangeable parts designed to be used in assembly-line production. With this system came improvements in production techniques and the use of labour-saving machinery and equipment. The accompanying increases in overhead costs and wage rates, however, forced companies to seek ways of using production facilities and labour more efficiently. Frederick W. Taylor's work stimulated the scientific management movement.

Scientific management
Substitution of exact scientific investigation and knowledge for the old individual judgment or opinion of either the worker or the boss.

According to Taylor, **scientific management** required accurate performance standards based on objective data gathered from time studies and other sources. These standards provided a basis for rewarding the superior workers financially and for eliminating the unproductive ones. Taylor's approach was in sharp contrast to the then-prevailing practice of attempting to gain more work from employees by threatening them with the loss of their jobs.[5]

FIGURE 1-1   *Important Events in the Development of HRM*

YEAR	EVENT
1827	Boot and Shoe Workers in Montreal is the first union recorded in Canada.
1827	First Occupation Group of Printers organize in Quebec City for the purpose of regulating wages in their trade, caring for their sick, and providing social and recreational aid for their members.
1850–1870	Unionism develops quickly in Canada during this period due to the rapid progress of the trade union movement in Great Britain and the United States.
1872	First strike in Canada takes place in Hamilton, Ontario, where printers strike for a nine-hour day. Union leaders are jailed for conspiracy.
1872	Government passes legislation that frees unions from liability under common law for conspiracy in restraint of trade.
1881	Beginning of Frederick W. Taylor's work in scientific management at the Midvale Steel Plant.
1880–1910	A number of union associations are formed. The Knights of Labour first local Canadian assembly organize with total membership at 16,000. Labour Congress of Canada (TLC) and Canadian Federation of Labour (CFL) are founded.
1920	First text in personnel administration, by Ordway Tead and Henry C. Metcalf.
1920s	Women begin entering workforce to handle managerial paperwork.
1922	Formation of province-wide federation of Catholic unions known as Confédération des travailleurs catholiques du Canada (CTCC).
1924	Point method of job evaluation developed by the National Electric Manufacturers' Association and the National Metal Trades Association.
1927	Hawthorne studies begun by Mayo, Roethlisberger, and Dickson.
1927	All-Canadian Congress of Labour (ACCL) established.
1930s	Government passes legislation dealing with minimum wages and the right to join a union. This legislation helps shape the present role of personnel departments by adding legal obligations.
1935	Establishment of the Congress of Industrial Organizations (CIO) in the United States. Their monies are pumped into Canada to aid its labour movement.
1938	CIO established in Canada.
1940	ACCL renamed CCL.
1940	Unemployment Insurance Commission established.
1948	Industrial Relations and Disputes Investigation Act passed to allow permanent framework for compulsory bargaining. Role of personnel grows in importance due to increased bargaining activities and postwar recruitment and training demands.
1956	TLC, CIO, and CTCC merge.
1960–1970	Additional legislation passed with respect to working conditions, wage levels, safety, health, and other benefits.

YEAR	EVENT
1965	Public Service Alliance of Canada (PSAC) established.
1965	Canadian Union of Public Employees (CUPE) established, making it the largest union in Canada.
1967	Public Servants Staff Relations Act gives federal employees the option of arbitration or strike to settle disputes.
1977	Canadian Human Rights Act passed (effective March 1978), paving the way for pay equity in several provinces and employment equity for federal contractors. Ontario legislation follows.
1985	Increased emphasis on employee participation and involvement in organizational decision making to improve productivity and competitive position.
1990	Human Resources Professionals Association of Ontario receives approval under Bill Pr70 to grant the designation CHRP (Certified Human Resources Professional), the first HR accreditation program in North America.
1990s	Emergence of the human resources professional as business partner; increased use of contract employees with more flexible working arrangements to meet family needs; greater awareness of diversity in workforce and society; more emphasis on global HRM practices.

Though the work remained hard, legislation in the early 1900s improved the safety for many factory workers.

Among his contemporaries in this movement were Frank B. Gilbreth and his wife Lillian M. Gilbreth,[6] Henry L. Gantt, and Harrington Emerson.[7] Lillian Gilbreth was one of the first women to gain an international reputation as a management consultant.

Contributions of Industrial/Organizational Psychology

By the early 1900s, some of the knowledge and research from the field of psychology was beginning to be applied to the management of personnel. One of the best-known pioneers in industrial psychology was Hugo Münsterberg. His book *Psychology and Industrial Efficiency* (1913) called attention to the contributions that psychology could make in the areas of employment testing, training, and efficiency improvement.[8]

Many psychologists whose work before World War I had been largely theoretical and experimental followed Münsterberg's lead by making practical contributions to the personnel field in business and industry. Walter Dill Scott received acclaim for his early work in the rating of sales personnel and for his classic book in personnel management, which he co-authored with Robert C. Clothier.[9]

James McKeen Cattell, another pioneer, is noted for his test-development activities and for his leadership in establishing the Psychological Corporation (1921), an organization that offers personnel services.[10] These services include publishing and distributing employment tests and conducting validation studies for employers; the latter activity has become a very important aspect of HRM. A contemporary of Cattell, Walter Van Dyke Bingham gained prominence as an author of books on interviewing and aptitude testing that were widely used by personnel practitioners.[11]

Over the years, industrial/organizational psychology has broadened its scope and has become one of the major areas of psychology. A separate division of the Canadian Psychological Association known as the Society for Industrial and Organizational Psychology has more than 3,500 members who are academic and professional practitioners in the field.[12]

The Hawthorne Studies

Hawthorne studies
Experiments conducted in the 1920s to determine what effect hours of work, periods of rest, and lighting may have upon worker fatigue and productivity.

Begun in the 1920s, the **Hawthorne studies** were an effort to determine what effect hours of work, periods of rest, and lighting might have on worker fatigue and productivity. These experiments constituted one of the first cooperative industry/university research efforts. As the studies progressed, however, it was discovered that the social environment could have an equivalent if not greater effect on productivity than the physical environment.

Conducted by Elton Mayo, Fritz J. Roethlisberger, and W.J. Dickson at the Western Electric Company's Hawthorne Works, these studies were a pioneering endeavour to examine factors affecting productivity.[13] While there has been considerable controversy over interpretation of the findings, HR specialists generally agree that the Hawthorne studies had a very important role in the development of HRM.[14] The studies spurred efforts to humanize the workplace and to find more sensitive ways to motivate workers. Out of the interviewing techniques used by the Hawthorne researchers grew the nondirective approach to counselling, which recognizes the importance of feelings—something that until that time was generally considered inappropriate in employment situations.

It is interesting to note that what the Hawthorne studies revealed about human relations had been anticipated some years earlier by the sociologist Mary Parker Follett. In her writings, she continually emphasized the important role of informal groups in work situations.[15]

The Human Relations Movement

Human relations movement
Movement that focused attention on individual differences among employees and on the influence that informal groups may have upon employee performance and behaviour.

Along with the work of Kurt Lewin at the National Training Laboratories, the Hawthorne studies helped to give rise to the **human relations movement** by providing new insights into human behaviour.[16] This movement focused attention on individual differences among employees and on the influence that informal groups may have upon employee performance and behaviour. It also focused attention on the necessity for managers to improve their communications and to be more sensitive to the needs and feelings of their subordinates. Furthermore, the movement emphasized the need for a more participative and employee-centred form of supervision. The reader will observe later that various principles and practices currently applied in employee involvement, work teams, and employee empowerment grew out of the work of researchers and practitioners of the human relations movement.

Contributions of the Behavioural Sciences

Behavioural sciences
Various disciplines of psychology, sociology, anthropology, social economics, political science, linguistics, and education.

As the human relations movement evolved, it became broader in scope. The understanding of human behaviour was enhanced by contributions not only from the traditional disciplines of psychology, sociology, and anthropology, but also from social economics, political science, linguistics, and education. More important, the interrelationships of these various disciplines became more widely recognized, so that they are now referred to collectively as the **behavioural sciences.**

The behavioural science approach is oriented toward economic objectives, concerned with the total climate or milieu, and consistent with the development of interpersonal competence. It stresses a humanistic approach and the use of groups and participation in the achievement of organizational objectives, including the management of change.[17] All of these issues of importance to managers are discussed throughout the text.

Growth of Governmental Regulations

Prior to the 1930s, employer relations with employees and with their labour organizations were subject to very few federal or provincial laws and regulations. However, political pressures for social reform created by the Depression of the 1930s gave rise to both federal and provincial legislation affecting these relations. Federal and provincial regulations have expanded to the point where they govern the performance of virtually every HR function.

Important federal legislation and major court decisions affecting HRM activities will be cited throughout this book. While emphasis must necessarily be given to federal laws and regulations, the reader should be aware that HR managers and supervisors are also responsible for compliance with all provincial and local laws and regulations that govern work environments. Their requirements are often more stringent than federal laws. Although employers are often critical of the demands these laws and regulations impose on their operations, most legislation is a response to employers' lack of social responsibility as manifested in their poor treatment of employees in the past.

Increased Specialization of HR Functions

Initially, the management of human resources was limited largely to hiring, firing, and recordkeeping, functions carried out by managerial and supervisory personnel. Eventually, clerical personnel were employed to assist in keeping records relating to hours worked and to payroll.

By the 1940s, the typical personnel department in a medium-sized or large firm included individuals with specific training and/or experience to carry out these specialized functions.[18] The major functions performed in organizations today are shown in Figure 1-2, which provides an overview of the functions that will be discussed in detail in this book. (At the end of this chapter, we will outline the order in which we will study the functions.)

Increasing Emphasis on Strategic Management

We have mentioned the fact that top management expects HR managers to assume a broader role in overall organizational strategy. HRM in the 1990s should play a vital role in creating and sustaining the competitive advantage of an organization. In order to carry out their expanded role, many HR professionals will therefore need to acquire new competencies. These competencies are summarized below.

1. *Business capabilities.* HR professionals will need to know the business of their organization thoroughly. This requires an understanding of its economic and financial capabilities.
2. *State-of-the-art HRM practices.* HR professionals will be the organization's behavioural science experts. In areas such as staffing, development, appraisal, rewards, organizational design, and communication, HR professionals should develop competencies that keep them abreast of developments.
3. *Management of change process.* HR professionals will have to be able to manage change processes so that HR activities are effectively merged with the business needs of the organization.

The ability to integrate business, HRM, and management of change is essential.[19] By helping their organization build a sustained competitive advantage through HRM and by learning to manage many activities well, HR professionals will become strategic business partners. Many of the most forward-looking CEOs are seeking top HR managers who can report directly to them and help them address key issues. Highlights in HRM 1 illustrates what Digital, a decentralized high-technology computer company with 62,000 employees worldwide, including approximately 700 HR professionals, is doing to meet the challenges it faces in the future in carrying out its global HRM functions.

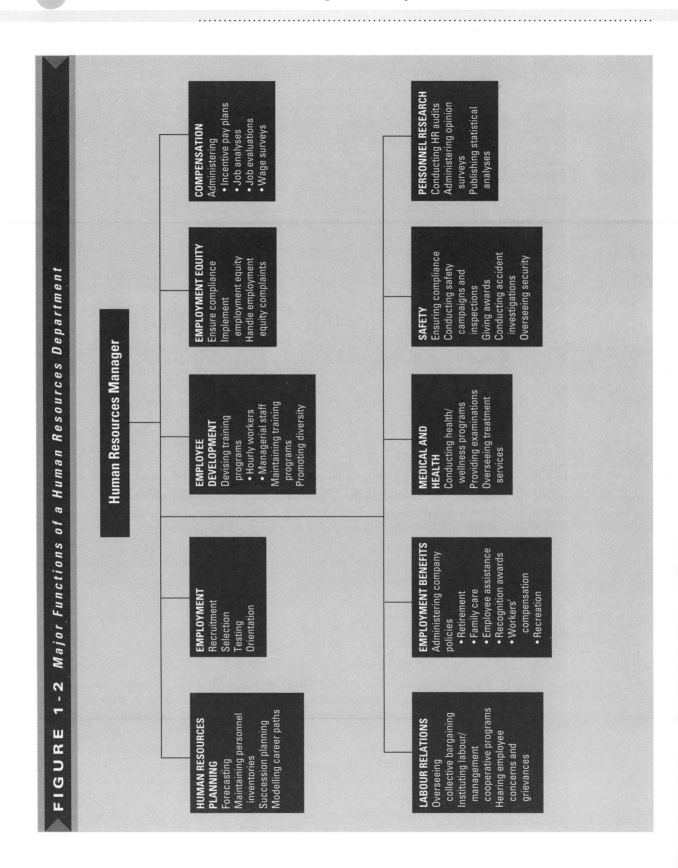

FIGURE 1-2 *Major Functions of a Human Resources Department*

Human Resources Manager

HUMAN RESOURCES PLANNING
Forecasting
Maintaining personnel inventories
Succession planning
Modelling career paths

EMPLOYMENT
Recruitment
Selection
Testing
Orientation

EMPLOYEE DEVELOPMENT
Devising training programs
• Hourly workers
• Managerial staff
Maintaining training programs
Promoting diversity

EMPLOYMENT EQUITY
Ensure compliance
Implement employment equity
Handle employment equity complaints

COMPENSATION
Administering
• Incentive pay plans
• Job analyses
• Job evaluations
• Wage surveys

LABOUR RELATIONS
Overseeing collective bargaining
Instituting labour/management cooperative programs
Hearing employee concerns and grievances

EMPLOYMENT BENEFITS
Administering company policies
• Retirement
• Family care
• Employee assistance
• Recognition awards
• Workers' compensation
• Recreation

MEDICAL AND HEALTH
Conducting health/wellness programs
Providing examinations
Overseeing treatment services

SAFETY
Ensuring compliance
Conducting safety campaigns and inspections
Giving awards
Conducting accident investigations
Overseeing security

PERSONNEL RESEARCH
Conducting HR audits
Administering opinion surveys
Publishing statistical analyses

HRM highlights

1   HRM AT DIGITAL LOOKS TO THE FUTURE

One way to conceive of the human resources professional of the future is as an architect of *organization*, *programs*, and *information management*, who at the same time maintains and values the earlier work functions.

As an *organizational architect*, the human resources professional would:

- Address globalization of management teams and international awareness
- Adapt design for temporary project/work organization teams and drive transformation of working and management teams
- Create multiple methods to manage new work environments across all employee levels
- Develop stress-management methods relating to shortened time to market and technology curves
- Invent and implement optimal communications to provide direction and manage an organizational culture that provides psychological safety in times of rapid change.

In the role of programs architect, the HR manager would:

- Create programs to address use of temporary labour
- Design cooperative training ventures with local and federal government
- Promote skill transitioning that addresses obsolescence
- Respond humanely to redeployment and change management tactics.

All of these functions involve identifying the people issues—to obtain and develop the human resources necessary to competitive business practices—and at the same time addressing longer-term issues. Creative programs can prevent a reactive approach and contribute to competitive advantage. This role encourages HR professionals to be activists, to address situations before they become problems that result in productivity loss.

As information management architect, the HR professional would use current computer systems and artificial intelligence to create business models and simulations to:

- Plan and administer compensation programs
- Provide simulations of organization design options
- Track development
- Manage succession.

The information management architect must be able to assess and manipulate information necessary for management decision making, allow for on-line benefits changes, and provide more information for employee decision making. These kinds of applications could free up time from other HR professionals for consultation and employee contact.

Source: Betty Bailey, "Ask What HR Can Do for Itself," *Personnel Journal* 70, no. 7 (July 1990): 37. Reprinted with permission of *Personnel Journal*, Costa Mesa, CA. All rights reserved.

Professionals improve and broaden their expertise through seminars.

three

Professionalization of Human Resources Management

objective 3

Because of the changes occurring in the workforce and its environment, HR managers can no longer function simply as technical specialists who perform the various HRM functions. Instead, they must concern themselves with the total scope of HRM and its role within the firm and society as a whole. Therefore, HR managers today should be professionals with respect to both their qualifications and their performance.

One of the characteristics of a profession is the development through research and experimentation of an organized body of knowledge. This knowledge is exchanged through conferences, seminars, and workshops sponsored by professional associations. The latest information in the field is communicated through the literature published by the professional associations, as well as by various nonprofit organizations and educational institutions. Other characteristics of a profession include the establishment of a code of ethics and of certification requirements for its members. HRM exhibits all these characteristics.

Professional Associations and Certification

Today a number of professional organizations represent general, as well as specialized, areas of HRM. The professional association with the largest membership—more than 7,000—is the Human Resources Professionals Association of Ontario (HRPAO). HRPAO offers workshops, seminars, dinner speakers, and an annual conference. The Association publishes a source book and *Human Resources Professional Magazine*. While Ontario has the largest HR membership, nearly every province has an association of HR practitioners. These associations are affiliated through the Canadian Council of Human Resources Associations (CCHRA), representing more than 15,000 practitioners across the country. Their mission is to provide a national and international collective voice on human resources issues and to establish core standards for the human resources profession.

Other leading professional associations in the field include the Canadian Public Personnel Managers Association, International Personnel Management Association, the International Personnel Management Association for Personnel Women, the American Management Association (AMA), and the Conference Board (CB). AMA and CB are prominent nonprofit organizations that provide publications and educational services relating to HRM and other functional areas. Organizations that represent specialized areas of interest include the Society of Human Resource Planners, the Canadian Association of Human Resource Systems Professionals, Canada Recruiters' Guild, the Association of Canadian Pension Management, the Canadian Compensation Association, the Canadian Industrial Relations Association, the International Foundation of Employee Benefit Plans, the Ontario Society for Training and Development, the Association for Industrial Research, and the Society for Industrial and Organizational Psychology of the Canadian Psychological Association. For professors in the field, there is the Human Resources Division of the Administrative Sciences Association of Canada, the Industrial Relations Division of the Learneds, and the Personnel and Human Resources Division of the Academy of Management.[20] All of these organizations sponsor meetings and workshops that promote the professional growth of their members. They also provide opportunities for contact with other organizations, including government agencies.

Certification
Recognition of having met certain professional standards.

The professionalization of a field generally leads to some form of **certification** for practitioners to enhance their status and to recognize their competency. Certification criteria vary between provinces but generally include related professional HR experience; an approved study program with courses in finance, labour economics, organizational behaviour, and human resources management; and various HR functional courses. Those provinces with associations and certification programs are listed in Figure 1-3. Under the umbrella organization of the Canadian Council of Human Resources Associations, practitioners who have received certification in one province will have that designation recognized in all member provinces.

To qualify for certification in Ontario, an applicant must provide verification of course work and pass a written competency examination to demonstrate mastery of knowledge. The certifications and membership, which must be renewed every year, serve largely to indicate the qualifications of recipients. In addition to the CHRP (Certified Human Resources Professional) certification for generalists in HRM, there are other certifying agencies with specific certification designations in the areas of compensation, employee benefits, and training and development (see Figure 1-3). As the reputations of these programs grow and become more widely recognized by top management, certification may become an important qualification for individuals seeking positions in HRM.[21]

> **FIGURE 1-3** *Certification Options in Human Resources Management*

CERTIFICATION IN HUMAN RESOURCES MANAGEMENT		CERTIFICATION IN HR SPECIALITIES
Canadian Public Personnel Management Association	CPPMA	Canadian Compensation Association: CCP-Certified Compensation Professional and CBP-Certified Benefits Professional
B.C. Human Resources Management Association	CHRP	Ontario Society for Training and Development (CTDP): Certified Training and Development Professional
Greater Victoria Human Resources Management Association	CHRP	
Human Resources Institute of Alberta	CHRP	
Human Resources Management Association of Manitoba	CHRP	
Human Resources Professionals Association of Ontario	CHRP	
Canadian Payroll Association	CPA	

Code of Ethics

It is typical for professional associations to develop a code of ethics that members are expected to observe. The code shown in Highlights in HRM 2 was developed by HRPAO. Many large corporations have their own code of ethics to govern corporate relations with employees and the public at large.

Adherence to a code often creates a dilemma for professionals, including those in HRM. As one HR professional asked, "With an observation toward profitable business, whom do HR professionals service? Who is the client—management or the individual employees? In the course of serving the employees and management and maintaining respect and regard for human values, whose needs are paramount? What happens when—as is frequently the case in HR work—the confidential issues of management and/or the employees are in conflict?[22] These and similar questions are not easy to answer. Each chapter in this text includes an Ethics in HRM feature, which poses an ethical question centred on the topic of the chapter and highlights the dilemmas faced by HRM professionals as they try to meet the sometimes conflicting goals of expediency, efficiency, and ethics. The code of ethics may provide a basis for HR professionals to evaluate their plans and their actions.

The HR staff is, of course, concerned with monitoring ethics in its own operations. More recently, however, HR departments have been given a greater role in communicating the firm's values and standards, monitoring compliance with its code of ethics, and enforcing the standards throughout the organization. Many firms have ethics committees and ethics ombudsmen to provide training in ethics to employees. The general objectives of ethics training are stated in Highlights in HRM 2.

**2   HUMAN RESOURCES PROFESSIONALS
ASSOCIATION OF ONTARIO**

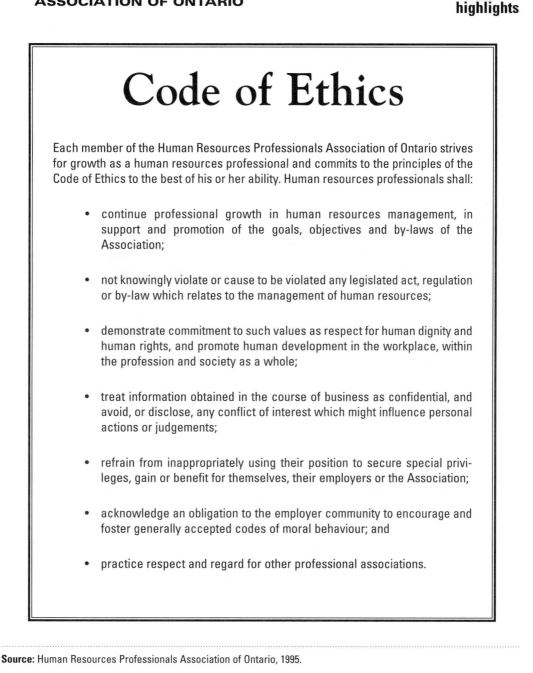

Code of Ethics

Each member of the Human Resources Professionals Association of Ontario strives for growth as a human resources professional and commits to the principles of the Code of Ethics to the best of his or her ability. Human resources professionals shall:

- continue professional growth in human resources management, in support and promotion of the goals, objectives and by-laws of the Association;

- not knowingly violate or cause to be violated any legislated act, regulation or by-law which relates to the management of human resources;

- demonstrate commitment to such values as respect for human dignity and human rights, and promote human development in the workplace, within the profession and society as a whole;

- treat information obtained in the course of business as confidential, and avoid, or disclose, any conflict of interest which might influence personal actions or judgements;

- refrain from inappropriately using their position to secure special privileges, gain or benefit for themselves, their employers or the Association;

- acknowledge an obligation to the employer community to encourage and foster generally accepted codes of moral behaviour; and

- practice respect and regard for other professional associations.

Source: Human Resources Professionals Association of Ontario, 1995.

The Code of Ethics for members of HRPAO was adopted to promote and maintain the highest standards of personal conduct and professional standards among its members. Adherence to this code is required for membership in the Association and serves to assure public confidence in the integrity and service of human resource management professionals.

The ultimate goal of ethics training is to avoid unethical behaviour, adverse publicity, and potential lawsuits, and to gain a strategic advantage. To achieve these objectives, two approaches are frequently used: (1) developing employee awareness of ethics in business; and (2) drawing attention to potential ethical issues to which an employee may be exposed.[23]

Professional Literature

Personal development in any profession requires knowledge of the current literature in the field. A number of periodicals contain articles on general or specialized areas of interest in HRM. Some of the more important journals students and practitioners should be familiar with are shown in Figure 1-4.

FIGURE 1-4 *Some Important Professional Journals*

Benefits Canada
Canadian Employment Safety & Health Guide
Canadian HR Reporter
Canadian Industrial Relations and Personnel Development
Canadian Labour Law Reporter
Compensation and Benefits Review
Computers in Personnel
Education and Psychological Measurement
Ergonomics
Focus on Employment and Equality Rights
Group and Organization Studies
HR Focus
HR Magazine
HR News
Human Resource Management
Human Resource Planning
Human Resources Management in Canada
Human Resources Management Review

Human Resources Professional
International Journal of Human Resources Management
International Journal of Selection and Assessment
Journal of Applied Psychology
Journal of Labour Research
Journal of Management
Journal of Staffing and Recruitment
Labour Studies Journal
Monthly Labour Review
National Productivity Review
Personnel
Personnel Journal
Personnel Psychology
Public Personnel Management
Supervisory Management
Training
Training and Development Journal

> ## ETHICS IN HRM
>
> ### "PEOPLE WHO FIT IN, PLEASE"
>
> Placement agencies are used by many employers to hire temporary help, contract help, seasonal help, and other personnel needed immediately and/or for short-term duration. Placement agencies tend to specialize in niche labour markets such as secretarial help, computer experts, labourers, or executives. These agencies have inventories of qualified candidates, amassed through contacts in the sector or solicited through general advertisement. Two events have cast shadows on their methods, and draw attention to the problems of making a profit, making sure people fit, and doing what is legal and right.
>
> In 1992, a survey of the staffing practices of 10 agencies in Toronto revealed that 6 of them agreed to send only Caucasians to interviews, a direct contravention of human rights legislation. Ten employment agencies were contacted by the Canadian Civil Liberties Association and all but four were willing to refer only white candidates for jobs. Pollsters told the agencies that they represented an American firm and asked if the agency would be prepared to refer "whites only." These practices draw attention to the ethical dilemma of doing what is legal, what is right, and what clients, who pay the bills, want.
>
> Should laws be passed requiring that only certified HR professionals be allowed to recruit and select?
>
> **Source:** V. Galt, "Agencies still refer whites only," *The Globe and Mail* (September 8, 1992).

Other periodicals that cover the general field of business and management often contain articles pertaining to HRM. Among these are *Academy of Management Executive, Academy of Management Journal, Academy of Management Review, Business Horizons, Business Week, California Management Review, Canadian Business Quarterly, Canadian Journal of Administrative Studies, European Management Journal, Fortune, The Globe and Mail Report on Business, Harvard Business Review, Journal of Business Ethics, Management Review, Business Week,* and *Worklife.*

The vast number of books and articles being published on HRM makes it virtually impossible even to locate, let alone read, all of the literature in the field. Consequently, students and practitioners will find four references invaluable in locating those books and articles they may have time to read and those with the most pertinent information. One is *Personnel Management Abstracts,* which contains abstracts from journals and books and an index of periodical literature.[24] The second is *Work Related Abstracts,* organized into broad categories with a cumulative guide to specific subjects, organizations, and individuals.[25] The third is *Human Resources Abstracts* (an international information service), which provides abstracts of current literature from more than 250 sources.[26] The fourth is *Business Periodicals Index*, which provides a broader coverage of subjects and periodicals.[27] Also, the reader should not overlook various computerized compilations of periodical literature that are available in most libraries. Two major sources are the Dialogue Data Base System, which includes ABI/INFORM and CBCA (Canadian Business and Current Affairs). ABI/INFORM is also available on CD ROM, and CBCA is also available in print. Both ABI/INFORM and CBCA contain an index to business information and sometimes provide brief summaries of significant articles.

Research Organizations

Throughout this book many of the findings from the efforts of a number of different research organizations and individuals will be reported. The primary function of these organizations is to conduct research and to make their findings available to all who are interested in them. Many such organizations may be found at universities. Probably the largest university research centre in the behavioural sciences is the Institute for Social Research at the University of Michigan. Its three divisions, the Survey Research Centre, the Research Centre for Group Dynamics, and the Centre for Political Studies, have together published over 5,000 books, articles, and reports.

A number of Canadian universities have centres for the study of labour and industrial relations, including the Applied Social Science Research Centre at York University, and the Guelph Centre for Occupational Research Inc. Other research centres are located at Laurier, UBC, and Queen's. Organizations sponsored by industry, such as the Conference Board of Canada, publish research studies that benefit managers in HRM.

Commerce Clearing House (CCH) and Prentice-Hall (PH) also conduct surveys relating to HRM policies and practices. Survey results from these organizations may be found in loose-leaf volumes that contain a wealth of information about policies and practices as well as the legal aspects of HRM. The student of HRM should become familiar with the various CCH and PH publications that are updated regularly. These volumes are available in many college and university libraries, city libraries, and the libraries of the larger work organizations.

Academic Training

With so much attention focused on the behavioural sciences during the 1960s and 1970s, the subject of HRM suffered from neglect at some colleges and universities. Since then, however, equal employment opportunity, international HRM, employee rights, concern for productivity, cost of employee benefits, and other current issues have rekindled interest in HRM courses and in HRM as a major field of study. Indeed, in some business programs, HRM is a mandatory course, along with finance and marketing.

In the past, many HR professionals entered the field with degrees in liberal arts and sciences and perhaps a few business courses taken as electives. However, as certification requirements and other factors became essential for professional status, a bachelor's degree and even a master's degree in business have become more important.

In addition to business courses, students planning careers in HRM should take courses in such areas as personnel and organizational psychology, industrial sociology, labour economics, and industrial engineering. A knowledge of human resources information systems and software is essential for administering, processing, and reporting personnel data to gauge the performance of HR programs. While learning about the uses of computers, future HR professionals should become knowledgeable in research design and in the use of statistics in research.

objective

Programs for Managing Human Resources

An HR program constitutes the overall plan for managing HR and for guiding managers and supervisors in decisions relating to their subordinates. It establishes the objectives, policies, procedures, and budget pertaining to the HR functions to be performed. Although HR managers are responsible for coordinating and enforcing policies relating to HR functions, responsibility for performing these functions rests with all managers and supervisors within an organization.

Objectives

HR objectives
Goals to be achieved in the area of HRM.

HR policies
Guides to the actions required to achieve HR objectives.

HR objectives are determined by the organization's objectives as a whole. More and more, HR objectives are reflecting the increasing social responsibilities of firms, which include not only traditional responsibilities to customers, employees, and shareholders but also responsibilities to the community and the total society. Creating employment opportunities for the disadvantaged and providing a favourable work environment and greater financial security represent but a few ways in which firms can exercise greater social responsibility.

Employers focus on abilities when selecting employees.

Policies

Closely related to HR objectives are **HR policies** that serve to guide the actions required to achieve these objectives. Policies provide the means for carrying out the management processes and as such are an aid to decision making. Like objectives, they may be idealistic or realistic, general or specific, flexible or inflexible, qualitative or quantitative, broad or narrow in scope. However, while objectives determine what is to be done, policies explain how it is to be done.

Need for Policies
Carefully developed policies are vital to HRM because employees are sensitive to any differences, no matter how slight, in the treatment they may receive compared with others. The quickest way to impair employee efficiency and morale is for a manager to show favouritism in decisions such as those relating to vacations, schedules, raises and promotions, overtime, or disciplinary action. Decisions can be made more rapidly and more consistently if policies relating to

highlights

3   VOLKSWAGEN CANADA POSITIVE DISCIPLINE PROGRAMME

Positive Discipline is a method of attempting to solve employee problems before they develop into serious situations. It treats employees as adults and emphasizes turning inappropriate behaviour around instead of punishing employees every time they do something wrong. Positive Discipline relies on coaching and counselling as a front line method of helping employees identify inappropriate behaviour and suggests ways of turning that behaviour around. Positive Discipline allows supervisors to treat their fellow employees in a fair and consistent manner. While it is expected that most employees will respond to coaching and counselling, for those employees who still do not correct their behaviour or are involved in an incident so serious that coaching or counselling is deemed inappropriate, there are steps in place to impress upon every employee the seriousness of their actions and the consequences of continued poor behaviour. A general outline of the programme is contained herein.

There are 5 general methods used in the Positive Discipline Programme:
> **Coaching and Counselling**
> **Step One - Verbal reminder**
> **Step Two - Written Warning**
> **Step Three - Decision Making**
> **Step Four - Termination**

There are three categories of work rule violations:
> **Work Performance**
> **Attendance**
> **Misconduct**

There are three degrees of severity of workplace violations:
> **Minor**
> **Major**
> **Grave**

There are two other major ingredients of the Positive Discipline Programme:
> **Praise**
> **Goal Setting**

Guidelines
- The Union, if requested, may be involved in every step of the discipline process, but must be involved in Step One and higher.
- An employee may, under certain circumstances, be sent home with or without pay pending an investigation into the incident. The Union should be involved in any investigation into serious incidents.

- Counselling should be the preferred method of correcting behaviour when a problem first appears.
- Praise should be used often, whenever an employee has corrected a potential problem, had a step deactivated, performed beyond his/her normal duties, or any other time the supervisor feels it is appropriate. This praise should be done both verbally and in writing.
- Goal setting should be used at every step in the disciplinary process in order to ensure both the supervisor and the employee know exactly what is expected of them.
- This programme is aimed at those very few employees who insist on conducting themselves in an inappropriate manner. The vast majority of our employees may never have to encounter the various steps of this programme.

Time Limits
The time periods in which satisfactory performance must be maintained before a disciplinary step in considered inactive are:

Step 1	6 months
Step 2	9 months
Step 3	12 months

Note
This quick reference guide is meant to give you a brief overview of the programme and should not be considered to be the total programme or have all the answers. For a full explanation of the programme, please refer to the Positive Discipline Programme manual.

Workplace Violations
- For an employee with no active discipline on record, the appropriate level of discipline for each degree of seriousness is set out below:
  Minor - Verbal reminder or written warning
  Major - Written warning or decision-making leave
  Grave - Decision-making leave or discharge

- A range of disciplinary responses is provided here as specific incidents may vary in severity. These work rule violations are not intended to be a total list. Discipline may be imposed for offences not included above.

Violations	*Relative Degree of Seriousness*
AWOL (1 day - including scheduled overtime shifts)	Minor
Lateness	Minor
Safety Rule Violations	Minor
Failure to report injury/accident	Minor
Inexcused absences	Minor
Unauthorized distribution of literature	Minor
Leaving workstation early, or without authorization	Minor
Creating or contributing to unsanitary conditions	Minor
Reading on the job	Minor

Extended coffee/lunch breaks	Minor
Soliciting	Minor
Insufficient quantity	Minor
Excessive waste	Minor
Verbal abuse (profanity)	Minor
Smoking in unauthorized areas	Minor
Insubordination	Major
Sleeping on the job	Major
Leaving plant early or without permission	Major
Reporting for work in an unfit condition	Major
AWOL (2 days)	Major
Excessive error	Major
Poor quality	Major
Assault or threat of assault	Grave
Sexual/Workplace assault	Grave
Work refusal (except OHSA)	Grave
Illegal weapons on premises	Grave
Possession, distribution, consumption of alcohol or drugs on company property	Grave
Theft	Grave
Fighting	Grave
Deliberate destruction of company property	Grave
Misrepresentation, altering, or forging company, medical or WCB forms	Grave
Initiating, encouraging or participating in a walkout or work stoppage	Grave
Violations of safety rules that could inflict serious consequences	Grave
AWOL (3 days or more)	Grave

Source: Donald McQuirter, Manager Human Resources, Volkswagen Canada, Inc. September 1995.

these and other subjects have been formulated and communicated throughout the organization.

Formulation of Policies

The formulation of HR policies for approval by top management should be a cooperative endeavour among managers, supervisors, and members of the HR staff. In some cases it may be important to have employees' input. Policy committees facilitate the pooling of experience and knowledge. Participation by operating managers is particularly essential because they are often more familiar with the specific areas in which problems arise, and also because their cooperation is required for policy enforcement. On the other hand, the manager and staff of the HR department have the responsibility for exercising leadership in formulating policies that are consistent with overall organizational objectives. They also must make certain that these policies are compatible with current economic conditions, collective bargaining trends, and laws and regulations at the federal, provincial, and municipal levels.

Written Policy Statements

Organizations can make their HR policies more authoritative by putting them in writing. To strengthen their effectiveness, these statements, which may be compiled into a policy manual, should include the reasons the policy is needed. Written policy statements can serve as invaluable aids in orienting and training new personnel, administering disciplinary action, and resolving grievance issues with employees and their unions. When distributed to employees, these policy statements can provide answers to many questions that might otherwise have to be referred to supervisors. A sample policy statement is provided in Highlights in HRM 3 on page 22.

In recent years, HR policy statements as well as employee handbooks have assumed the force of a legal contract between employer and employee. Just as employers refer to policy statements as a basis for their personnel actions, employees now cite company failure to adhere to established policies as a violation of their rights. It is therefore advisable for firms to insert a disclaimer or waiver in employee manuals to the effect that the contents of the manual do not constitute a contract. The disclaimer should be prominently placed, not buried in a footnote. Wording the manual carefully (avoiding "always" and "never," for example), using a conversational tone rather than legalistic jargon, and having an outside labour counsel check the manual can help in avoiding problems.

Procedures

HR procedures
Prescribed sequence of steps to be followed in carrying out HR policies.

HR procedures serve to implement policies by prescribing the chronological sequence of steps to follow in carrying out the policies. Procedures relating to employee selection, for example, might provide that individuals first be required to complete an application form, followed by an interview with an HR office representative. Grievances, promotions, transfers, and wage adjustments likewise must be administered according to established procedure in order to avoid the problems resulting from oversights. For example, as a step in the disciplinary procedure, the failure to give an employee written warning of a violation might prevent the firm from discharging the employee for a second violation.

HR procedures, like HR policies, must be treated as means to an end, not as ends in themselves. As we mentioned earlier, when firms become more bureaucratic, complaints may be raised about excessive red tape, inflexibility, and impersonality in making HR decisions. Unfortunately, when procedures become too detailed or numerous, they can impair rather than further the interests of the firm and its employees. To avoid this hazard, procedures must be reviewed periodically and modified to meet changing conditions.

Throughout this book the discussion of policies and procedures for the various HRM functions will reflect what is typical of the large or medium-sized firm. In smaller organizations, HRM is often carried out on an informal basis and attention to policies and formal procedures may vary considerably. Since most federal laws governing work organizations apply to large firms, small organizations have greater latitude in the way they manage their employees and perform HR activities. The reader should also be aware that our descriptions of the implementation of various HR policies are probably closer to the ideal than to what is typically found in many firms.

Human Resources Information Systems

HR information system (HRIS)
Network of procedures, equipment, information, people, and information management to provide data for purposes of control and decision making.

Effective HRM requires an **HR information system (HRIS)** to provide current and accurate data for purposes of control and decision making. The system is composed of procedures, equipment, information, methods to compile and evaluate information, the people who use the information, and information management.

The use of HRIS was enhanced by advancements in computer technology. According to one survey conducted in 1993, computers are used in virtually all areas in human resources, from nearly 100 percent utilization in payroll management to 15 percent in grievance management.[28] Computers are used not only for storage and retrieval of information but for broader applications. These applications include production of basic reports, HR calculations, long-range forecasting and strategic planning, career/promotion planning, and evaluation of HR policies and practices—a topic discussed further in Chapter 2.

A well-designed HRIS can serve as the main management tool in the alignment of HR department goals with the goals of long-term strategic planning. As HR issues have been increasingly recognized as critical factors in strategic planning decisions, the ability of the HRIS to quantify, analyze, and model change has enhanced the status of the HRIS in many organizations. Global competition is putting increasing pressure on managers to make better and faster decisions. HR information technology can improve HRM and contribute to the competitive advantage.[29]

In addition to the major uses of computer technology, with a PC, the HR professional can take advantage of a variety of information services. An on-line service designed especially for HR departments is the HR On-line, which provides up-to-the-minute information in several categories, including news, research, software, and services, covering all disciplines of HRM.

In developing an effective HRIS, a firm must address privacy issues in advance. A data-privacy policy can make the HRIS a positive factor in employee relations rather than a mistrusted disseminator of sensitive personnel information.

The Budget

HR budget
Financial plan and a control for the expenditure of funds necessary to support the HR program.

Statements relating to objectives, policies, and procedures, or to a program as a whole can be meaningful only if they are supported financially through the budget. An **HR budget** is both a financial plan and a control for the expenditure of funds necessary to support the HR program. As such, it is one of the best indicators of management's real attitude toward the program. Thus, while a firm's selection policy may be to hire only fully qualified applicants to fill vacancies, its ability to observe this policy will depend on whether it budgets enough money to screen applicants carefully. Securing adequate funds for the HR budget further requires the HR staff to be able to convince top management that the HR program is cost-effective and is producing results.

Evaluating the Human Resources Program

Just as financial audits are conducted, audits or evaluations of the HRM program should be conducted periodically to assure that its objectives are being accomplished. Audits typically involve analyzing data relative to the program, including employee turnover, grievances, absences, accidents, and similar indicators. Special attention is usually given to assessing compliance with laws and regulations governing various specific areas such as equal employment opportunity and safety and health. A comprehensive audit should encompass all aspects of the HR function as performed by both the HR department and the operating or line managers.

Companies such as Xerox Canada and the Bank of Montreal are concerned with benchmarking HRM practices, that is, measuring their results against practices in other firms. One good source of information about these practices is the *Human Resource Effectiveness Report* co-sponsored by SHRM and the Saratoga Institute. In 1992, Saratoga released its first *Best Practices Report*. The report revealed that departments that had high levels of HR effectiveness cultivated communication, interdependence, strategy and planning, commitment, customer focus, continued improvement, risk taking, and culture consciousness and relationships.[30]

The Human Resources Department

objective

We observed earlier that the HR manager is assuming a greater role in top-management planning and decision making. This trend reflects a growing awareness of the contributions that HRM can make to the success of the firm. Although managerial personnel at all levels are engaged in HRM activities, the top manager of the HR department has the primary responsibility for developing a program that will help the firm to meet its HRM objectives.

Responsibilities of the Human Resources Manager

Since the early 1960s, federal and provincial legislation and court decisions have had a major influence on HR policies and practices. More recently, concern for productivity improvement, employee desires for balancing family and job demands, and the desire of workers for more equitable treatment have added to the responsibilities of the HR manager. These influences have thus required HR managers not only to be more knowledgeable about many issues, but also to be more versatile in handling several activities. The major activities for which an HR manager is typically responsible are as follows:

   1. *Policy initiation and formulation.* Proposal and drafting of new policies or policy revisions to cover recurring problems or prevent anticipated problems. Ordinarily, these are proposed to the senior executives of the firm, who actually issue the policy.

2. *Advice*. Counselling and advising line managers. The HR staff is expected to be fully familiar with HR policy, labour agreements, past practice, and the needs and welfare of both the firm and the employees in order to develop sound solutions to problems.
3. *Service*. Activities of HR administration such as recruiting, selection, testing, planning of training programs, grievance hearings, and so forth.
4. *Control*. Monitoring performance of line departments and other staff departments to ensure conformity with established HR policy, procedures, and practice.

The HR manager's authority in carrying out these activities is restricted to staff authority (policy initiation and formulation and advice giving) and functional authority (service and control). Within the scope of functional authority, the HR manager generally has the right and is expected to issue policies and procedures for HR functions (i.e., selection, training, performance evaluation, and so on) throughout an organization. The only line authority the HR manager has is over subordinates in his or her department. Reality Check provides the reader with a better understanding of the variety of activities in the typical day of a generalist HR manager.

In-House Consultants

A major contribution that the HR department staff can make to the firm is to serve as in-house consultants to the managers and supervisors of other departments. Alerting top management to contemporary issues and changes within society that affect the firm is also an important responsibility. Closely related is the responsibility of monitoring new developments taking place in the HR field and, when feasible, getting top management to adopt them.

Any consultation provided by the HR staff must be based on managerial and technical expertise. Furthermore, it should be concerned with the operating goals of the managers and supervisors who are their consulting clients and should help them to make firm decisions. These managers and supervisors must be convinced that the HR staff is there to assist them in increasing their productivity rather than to impose obstacles to their goals. This requires not only the ability to consider problems from the viewpoint of the line managers and supervisors, but also skill in communicating with these individuals.[31]

Outside Consultants and Outsourcing

HR managers often go outside the organization for professional assistance from qualified consultants. These consultants are hired to solve a variety of HR problems. In the past, most of the firms specialized in one or two areas of expertise, though many have broadened their expertise in order to meet the expanding needs of their clients more effectively. The areas for which consultants are used most frequently are pension plans, executive recruitment, health and welfare plans, psychological assessment, wage and salary administration, job evaluation, and executive compensation. When using the services of a consultant, it is important to select an experienced, reputable individual, to educate him or her about the corporate environment, and to have a clear understanding of what the consultant is to do.[32]

REALITY CHECK

A GENERALIST HR MANAGER AT CANADIAN TIRE

Meet Rob Turner, MBA, Senior Director, HR Services, Home Office for Canadian Tire Corporation—he's an example of the new regime of human resource professional generalist who embraces customer service as a way of life.

Turner and his team of human resource consultants and administrators stalk the halls of Canadian Tire's Home Office, taking care of their clients on the retail side of life. Turner is responsible for the tactical side of the strategic plan, ensuring that HR programs and practices meet the goals of CTC and are delivered effectively. The "team" to which he constantly refers is positioning human resources as a business partner. Gone are the days of shuffling papers. The 1990s demand that HR be an integral part of the business.

Turner and his team meet the needs of their clients by starting the day at 7:30 a.m. or earlier. As Turner boards the train for work, he scans the paper for local and international news. He needs to understand the business environment in which CTC is working and the moves of the competition. On arrival at work, he scans his electronic mail to respond quickly to the needs of his clients. He uses technology as a tool wherever he can. After the mail messages are completed, he scans his electronic newspaper for more information on the business environment.

"Every Friday morning, I sit in on a marketing strategy meeting with my senior cohorts for about two hours," says Turner. "These meetings are the key to understanding what is happening on the business side, and our 'partners' need to hear how human resources can help."

"To be successful today, the HR professional must possess a strong business sense in addition to the standard HR training available out there. A lot can be said for on-the-job-training in these business areas." Turner believes in cross-training. For instance, one of his HR consultants is going to a line job where she will gain more analytical skills before returning in a few years to HR. Another will be trading positions with one of the organizational development specialists so that both can learn new skills.

Today's agenda begins with a performance appraisal of one of the HR consultants. This lasts from 9:00 to 10:30 a.m. In preparation for the appraisal, Turner seeks information from the rest of the team and the clients they assist. He encourages open dialogue and together they chart a course of development. "From 10:30 until 11:30 a.m., I will meet with my team and the organizational development specialist to do a post-mortem on this year's performance appraisal program," says Turner.

From 11:30 until noon, Turner returns to the e-mail to check and return calls. "Today, I need to prepare an announcement for the other HR divisions to advise them about a new structural change within my division and new duties for some members of my team. We are installing a computerized résumé-tracking system and the workload will change."

Noon rolls around and Turner meets with a functional manager of another department, as is his custom a few days a week. These lunches are essential to learning more about the business. Turner tries to understand the other departments as much as he can so that HR can assist them with their needs, both today and in the future. However, today's lunch is a little different. "Two days ago, the vice-president of this department called me and asked if I would meet with this manager. There is going to be a restructuring going on and this individual is not going to be part of the new team. The VP has asked me to try and find out how the individual is feeling since he may open up more to me than to his direct manager."

Turner returns at about 1:30 p.m. for a meeting with the occupational health and safety nurse to discuss absenteeism trends and possible options to decrease the figures. "Our absenteeism rates are in line, but you can always improve on your successes."

At 2:30 p.m. Turner returns to the screen and responds to more calls. When booking his meetings, he tries not to book things back-to-back, especially within his own department. The needs of the client must come first and if it means cancelling an appointment with departmental members, then the team understands fully.

It's 3:00 p.m. and the team meets again to discuss the restructuring of the department. Roles will change and one of the HR assistants will be taking on more of the HR consultant role due to the changes in the résumé-tracking program.

At 4:00 p.m. Turner decides it's time to walk the halls. It's part of his management philosophy to do this. "Sitting behind your desk is a luxury," he says. "You need to be visible and on the front line." He walks down the hall and pops his head into an office to comment on the manager's successful business venture. The manager looks up, smiles, and says, "Got a minute? I'm having difficulty with some of my warehousing staff and I could use your advice." Turner is ready to respond to his client. They sit and discuss the matter for 30 minutes. The manager has the information and advice she needs and is ready to speak to her people and resolve the issue. Another satisfied customer.

Turner speaks to a few more people and heads back to his office for a 4:30 p.m. interview concerning a divisional manager position. Using behavioural interviewing techniques, he speaks with the candidate until about 5:30.

Once more Turner scans his mail and prepares for the next day. Tomorrow he is meeting with the president to review a list of proposed stock option holders—these are the stars that CTC wants to develop for future management positions. Turner will add some final touches to the proposal at home that evening. "We want to let them know that we're there to help them develop their skills, but in the end they choose their own career paths."

Turner also needs to meet with the new president of a subsidiary, Canadian Tire Acceptance Limited. "This president also holds a dual function as VP of Diversified Business. We're going to meet to discuss how HR can help them achieve their mandate. They will need to act as a change agent in the future, and we need to work out how we are going to accomplish that as a group. I'll be briefing him on the strengths of his team and their development plans."

As Turner heads home at 6:15 p.m., he reflects on the day's successes and ponders how the team could have performed better.

Source: Interviewed by Deborah M. Zinni, June 1995.

Outsourcing
Practice of contracting with outside vendors to handle specified HR functions.

In recent years, **outsourcing**—the practice of contracting with outside firms to handle some of the HR functions previously performed in-house—has become a trend at companies of all sizes. A recent survey of 927 firms by the Wyatt Company shows that 32 percent of employers already outsource some or all of the administration of the HR and benefit programs.

Unlike one-time vendor contracts, outsourcing contracts require months of study and negotiation to make certain that all the major and minor issues have been carefully examined and resolved. When outsourcing is used, the vendors are actually integrated into the firm. In a comprehensive article, Sunoo and Laabs provide detailed instructions on how to proceed in making outsourcing arrangements.[33]

Department Organization

In a small firm, the HR department may consist only of a manager and a few assistants. In a larger firm, many additional staff members may be required. Increased size eventually leads to the establishment of departmental units.

The relative contribution of each function will help determine the need for specialization. For example, changes in the legal environment have forced many firms to establish a unit to oversee and coordinate equal employment opportunity efforts. When a firm becomes unionized, a separate unit is likely to be established to oversee the labour relations function.

objective

HRM in the Future

During the 1990s, HRM has been in the throes of a radical transformation. According to a study by IBM and the consulting firm of Towers Perrin and another by the SHRM Foundation—as well as many articles by respected scholars—the HR functions are being transformed into a significant management function. Where HR departments fail to recognize their responsibilities to become vital members of the management team, line managers are reaching out to take control and ownership of the various HR functions.[34]

The IBM–Towers Perrin study (1992), conducted in twelve countries with 2,961 individuals including line executives, HR executives, faculty, and consultants, provides valuable information on the new and potentially stronger role of HRM in work organizations. Looking to the year 2000, both line and HR executives agree that a proactive and strategically oriented HR function will be critical. Almost all respondents see the need for a dramatic movement from centralized and functionally organized HR units to more flexible and decentralized units. This will necessitate more supervisory involvement in HR activities.

In the IBM–Towers Perrin study, the respondents were asked about various attributes of the HR role through a series of six paired alternative choices (shown in Figure 1-5). The response clearly shows that the current HR roles are not what they should be in the year 2000. Figure 1-6 shows how much the existing roles differ from those described for 2000. What it ultimately shows is a new role model for the HR department and its functions. The study itself shows that both line and HR executives support the concept of shared responsibilities between line managers and HR managers and that the single greatest attribute of the HR staff will be the ability to educate and influence line managers on HR issues.[35]

An earlier study prepared for the Society of Human Resource Management was conducted to determine what pressures organizations face today, what they must do to remain competitive, what the role of HR is in providing a competitive advantage, and how this role is changing. A leading question in the survey was "What distinguishes superior HR performance from average performance?" The study found a clear link between an organization's level of success and the effectiveness of its HR leadership.

Over the course of the study, more than 20 CEOs and 50 practitioners participated in determining the role they expect HR to play in meeting competitive and organizational challenges. This information was obtained to create the Senior-Level

FIGURE 1-5 *Alternative Attributes of the HR Role*

Concentrate on operational matters	Participate in strategic planning matters
Respond to management's view of needed changes	Proactively create and manage change
Assume full responsibility for the management of all human resources	Advise and counsel line management, who takes responsibility for HR
Focus on individual employees	Focus on teams and groups of employees
Focus on internal business needs	Actively address societal issues
Represent the views and concerns of employees	Represent the views and concerns of management

Source: Towers Perrin, *Priorities for a Competitive Advantage, an IBM–Towers Perrin Study* (New York: Towers Perrin, 1992), 20. Reproduced with permission.

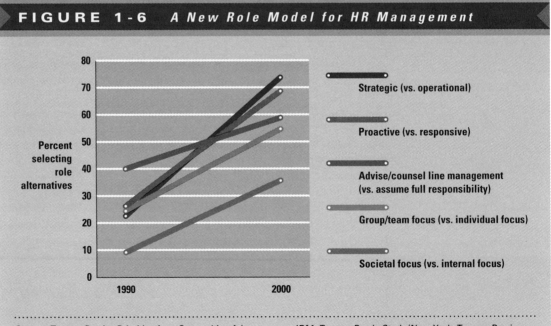

FIGURE 1-6 *A New Role Model for HR Management*

Percent selecting role alternatives

- Strategic (vs. operational)
- Proactive (vs. responsive)
- Advise/counsel line management (vs. assume full responsibility)
- Group/team focus (vs. individual focus)
- Societal focus (vs. internal focus)

Source: Towers Perrin, *Priorities for a Competitive Advantage, an IBM–Towers Perrin Study* (New York: Towers Perrin, 1992), 21. Reproduced with permission.

HR Competency Model shown in Figure 1-7. The purpose of this model is to define and describe the competencies required of superior HR leaders from the perspective of both CEOs and HR practitioners.[36] Study the individual competencies within each of the five clusters: goal and action management, functional and organizational leadership, influence management, business knowledge, and HR technical proficiency.

While the HR competency model was prepared as guidance for HR leaders and those who aspire to such positions, the knowledge and skills within the individual clusters can be used as a guide by anyone who wishes to succeed in a work organization or as an entrepreneur.

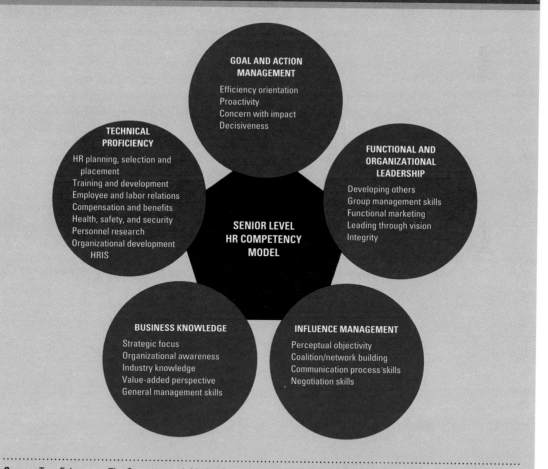

FIGURE 1-7 *Competency Clusters and Individual Competencies*

GOAL AND ACTION MANAGEMENT

Efficiency orientation
Proactivity
Concern with impact
Decisiveness

FUNCTIONAL AND ORGANIZATIONAL LEADERSHIP

Developing others
Group management skills
Functional marketing
Leading through vision
Integrity

TECHNICAL PROFICIENCY

HR planning, selection and placement
Training and development
Employee and labor relations
Compensation and benefits
Health, safety, and security
Personnel research
Organizational development
HRIS

SENIOR LEVEL HR COMPETENCY MODEL

BUSINESS KNOWLEDGE

Strategic focus
Organizational awareness
Industry knowledge
Value-added perspective
General management skills

INFLUENCE MANAGEMENT

Perceptual objectivity
Coalition/network building
Communication process skills
Negotiation skills

Source: Tom E. Lawson, *The Competency Initiative Standards of Excellence for Human Resource Executives* (Alexandria, Va., SHRM Foundation, 1990), 25. Used with permission from the Society for Human Resource Management, Alexandria, Va. Copyright, 1989.

Organization of the Text

This book is divided into six parts. In Part 1 we show why and how the various HRM functions have evolved and examine the different environments that must be considered. The rights of employees are discussed in Chapter 3, early in the text, because of the impact that issues such as employment equity have on all HRM functions. The chapters in Part 2 focus on the way that the HR requirements are met through human resources planning, analyzing job requirements, recruiting personnel, and selecting those individuals who are most likely to be successful. Once individuals are hired, it is necessary to provide training, to assist in their career development, and to appraise their performance on the job. These topics are discussed in Part 3.

In Part 4 we study the importance of implementing compensation and providing economic, physical, and emotional security for employees. Part 5, Enhancing Employee–Management Relations, discusses the dynamics of labour relations, collective bargaining, and contract administration. While these activities are typically handled by specialists in labour relations, all managers must be alert to the constraints of employee–management agreements.

The last part of the book—Part 6—contains a chapter on international HRM. The rapid growth of global enterprises in recent years demands that managers have an understanding of the types of differences that one encounters in operations outside one's homeland. The topic of the final chapter is the auditing of the HRM program. As with other organizational programs, there should be formal procedures for determining the extent to which HR objectives are being met.

A name index, an organization index, and a subject index follow.

SUMMARY

HRM represents a new concept of and approach to performing personnel functions. It still requires the performance of those personnel functions that have evolved over the years in response to emerging needs. However, instead of treating these functions as separate and distinct, HRM considers them interrelated parts of a management system that must be integrated closely with strategic organizational planning. Accordingly, HR managers are becoming more involved in the decision making of top management in a wide variety of issues and problems. Knowledge of HRM is important for individuals who will occupy managerial and supervisory roles since they will also perform HR functions.

The present status of HRM was achieved only after years of evolutionary development. During the 19th century, the factory system of production enabled products to be manufactured more cheaply than before. The concentration of workers in factories focused public attention on the need for better working conditions and greater consideration for employee health and safety. This period saw the emergence of an objective and systematic approach to improving worker efficiency known as scientific management. By the early 1900s, some of the knowledge and research from the field of psychology was beginning to be applied to the management of personnel.

Since the late 1920s, several forces have contributed significantly to the HRM movement. The Hawthorne studies were influential in humanizing the workplace and the human relations movement focused attention on individual differences and informal groups. As the human relations movement evolved, it became broader in scope and included the various behavioural sciences, focusing on the achievement of organizational objectives. During this period, political pressures gave rise to federal and provincial legislation affecting HRM. Increasingly, there is specialization of HR functions and an emphasis on strategic management.

HRM may be referred to as a profession because it has the following characteristics: (1) it is based upon an organized body of knowledge developed through research and experimentation, (2) the knowledge is disseminated through publications and professional meetings, (3) professional associations promote the professional growth of their members, (4) various types of certification allow practitioners to increase their competency, and (5) the various HRM professional associations have developed codes of ethics that their members are expected to observe.

A code of ethics focuses attention on ethical values and provides a basis for HR professionals to evaluate their plans and their actions. HR departments have been given a greater role in communicating the organization's values and standards and in monitoring compliance with its code of ethics.

The principal elements of an HR program are objectives, policies, and procedures. HR objectives are determined by the organization's objectives as a whole. Policies serve to guide the actions required to achieve these objectives. HR policies must be compatible with current economic conditions, collective bargaining trends, and laws and regulations at all levels. HR procedures implement policies by prescribing the steps to follow in carrying out the policies. Statements relating to objectives, policies, and procedures can be meaningful only if they are supported financially by the budget. It is important that the HRM program be audited periodically to assure that its objectives are being accomplished.

The HR department is responsible for policy initiation and formulation; counselling and advising line managers; providing services such as recruiting, selection, and planning of training programs; and monitoring the performance of line and staff departments to ensure conformity with established HR policy and procedures. The HR manager's authority in carrying out these activities is restricted to staff authority and functional authority. HR managers often use the services of outside consultants and, more recently, they have outsourced some of the HR functions to vendors on a long-term basis.

HRM is in the midst of a radical transformation. Line managers are reaching out to take control of the HR functions where HR departments fail to recognize their responsibilities. Comprehensive research studies have shown that a proactive, strategically oriented function is critical. Both line and HR executives support the concept of shared responsibility between line and HR managers. An HR competency model emphasizes goal and action management, functional and organizational leadership, influence management, business knowledge, and HR technical proficiency.

KEY TERMS

behavioural sciences	HR procedures
certification	human relations movement
Hawthorne studies	human resources management (HRM)
HR budget	outsourcing
HR information system (HRIS)	personnel management
HR objectives	scientific management
HR policies	

DISCUSSION QUESTIONS

1. In what respects does HRM differ from the traditional approach of personnel management?
2. Why is HRM playing an increasingly important role in organizations?
3. What specific HRM responsibilities do line managers and supervisors have?
4. HRM is referred to as a profession. On what basis can this statement be made?
5. Explain why policy statements are needed and describe the manner in which they should be disseminated.
6. What should be the role of the HR staff in its relations with personnel outside the HR department?
7. Of those functions performed in HRM, which do you consider to be most important? State your reasons.

CASE: The Business of HR at IBM

HR departments are typically viewed by management personnel as cost centres rather than as profit-generating centres. Until a major restructuring of International Business Machines (IBM) in 1992, its HR department was no exception to this rule. At that time IBM was divided into thirteen separate divisions, each with increased autonomy. While not one of the thirteen new divisions, HR was restructured into a more autonomous organization and a separate company known as Workforce Solutions (WFS) was formed. In the process, hundreds of IBM HR professionals joined WFS—all with impressive academic credentials and training, in-depth HR experience, industry association involvement, and dedication to quality and customer satisfaction.

With the formation of WFS, HR personnel were retained in the major divisions of IBM to provide advice and counsel and to report to line management as they always had. HR strategy, responsibility, and decision making remains in the major divisions. WFS is designed to deliver quality programs and services that support the HR strategies, plans, and functions of the major divisions. Every line still has an HR department, but now it serves only the advise and counsel function. At IBM there are approximately 700 employees (about 575 HR professionals and about 125 staff members at WFS).

WFS is headquartered in Westchester County, New York; operating nationwide, it provides, for a charge, the following programs and services to IBM companies:

- Human resource research and consulting services
- Leadership development programs
- Workforce diversity programs
- Equal opportunity programs and compliance monitoring
- Resources planning services
- Compensation and benefits programs
- Recruiting and employment services
- Occupational health services
- Relocation programs
- International assignment services
- Employee involvement and suggestion programs
- Testing and assessment services.

The results have been excellent: HR services delivered at a lower cost, enhancement of the commitment to HR, flexibility and responsiveness to customer needs, streamlining of HR processes, and innovative HR programs for the workplace. WFS innovations include introduction of a world-class employee suggestion program, design of cost-saving medical plan changes, establishment of centralized employee-benefits support using state-of-the-art technology, and increased employee involvement in the organization through incentive pay programs.

While WFS was primarily designed to provide quality, cost-effective service to the IBM community of businesses, its services are now available to outside organizations.

Source: IBM brochure, "Workforce Solutions," and Jennifer J. Laabs, "HR Becomes a Separate Business at IBM," *Personnel Journal* 72, no. 4 (April 1993): 25–29.

Questions
1. How can the WFS concept make an HR program more cost-effective?
2. What effect is the availability of a WFS type of organization likely to have on HR personnel in their advising and counselling roles?
3. Do you foresee other companies developing similar ventures? Why or why not?

Getting Ready

Most students are worried legitimately about their jobs and career prospects. **Career Counsel** is a feature at the end of each chapter designed to help students prepare for a career and manage their working lives. The assessment exercises are designed to encourage introspection and self-discovery. We encourage the reader to complete the exercises and compile them into a separate career planning workbook. A by-product of completing these assignments will be increased retention of the chapter material. The exercises to be completed are:

Chapter 1:   Getting Ready

Chapter 2:   Self-Employment

Chapter 3:   Wrongs versus Rights

Chapter 4:   Life Planning

Chapter 5:   Your Dream Job

Chapter 6:   Job-Search Strategies

Chapter 7:   Resumé Preparation

Chapter 8:   Training Lists

Chapter 9:   Assessing Values

Chapter 10:   Performance Feedback

Chapter 11:   Compensation in Your Career

Chapter 12:   Assessing Your Incentives

Chapter 13:   Flexible Benefits

Chapter 14:   Job Stress Management

Chapter 15:   Conflict Management Styles

Chapter 16:   Salary Negotiation Tactics

Chapter 17:   Culture Quiz

Chapter 18:   Auditing and Benchmarking the Career Plan

Get ready by purchasing a binder and labelling it *Career Planning Workbook*. This could be your first step on a journey of self-discovery.

NOTES AND REFERENCES

1. Andrew J. DuBrin and R. Duane Ireland, *Management & Organization*, 2nd ed. (Cincinnati: South-Western, 1993), 6–8. See also Lee Dyer, ed., *Human Resource Management—Evoking Roles and Responsibilities* (Washington, DC: Bureau of National Affairs, 1988).

2. A.J. Templer and J.D. Ladouceur, "Northern Exposure: Can Canadian Human Resources Managers Meet the Challenges of the '90s?" *Human Resources Professional* (June/July 1994): 14–18.

3. Charlene Marmer Solomon, "Managing the HR Career in the '90s," *Personnel Journal* 73, no. 6 (June 1994): 62–76; see also Shannon Peters Talbott, "How HR Keeps Current in Century-Old Companies," *Personnel Journal* 37, no. 10 (October 1994): 86–94.

4. Mark A. Huselid, "Documenting the HR's Effect on Company Performance," *HR Magazine* 39, no. 1 (January 1994): 79–85. See also George C. Tokesky and Joanne F. Kornides, "Strategic HR Management Is Vital," *Personnel Journal* 73, no. 12 (December 1994): 115–17.

5. Frederick W. Taylor, "What Is Scientific Management?" in *Classics in Management*, ed. Harwood F. Merrill (New York: American Management Association, 1960), 80. See also Edwin A. Locke, "The Ideas of Frederick W. Taylor: An Evaluation," *Academy of Management Review* 7, no. 1 (January 1982): 14–24. See also Hindy Lauer Schacter, "Frederick Winslow Taylor and the Idea of Worker Participation: A Brief against Easy Administrative Dichotomies," *Administration and Society* 21, no. 1 (May 1989): 20–30; and Charles D. Wrege and Ronald G. Greenwood, *Frederick W. Taylor, Father of Scientific Management: Myth and Reality* (Homewood, IL: Business One Irwin, 1991).

6. For the collected works of the Gilbreths, see William R. Spriegel and Clark E. Myers, eds., *The Writings of the Gilbreths* (Homewood, IL: Richard D. Irwin, 1953). For many years Dr. Lillian Gilbreth combined a career as a management consultant with that of a homemaker and the mother of twelve children, who her husband alleged were "cheaper by the dozen." For an entertaining account of the lives of Lillian and Frank Gilbreth as parents, see Frank B. Gilbreth, Jr., and Ernestine Gilbreth Carey, *Cheaper by the Dozen* (New York: Grosset & Dunlap, 1948).

7. Harrington Emerson, *The Twelve Principles of Efficiency* (New York: The Engineering Magazine Co., 1913). See also Alex W. Rathe, ed., *Gantt on Management* (New York: American Management Association, 1961).

8. Hugo Münsterberg, *Psychology and Industrial Efficiency* (Boston: Houghton Mifflin, 1913).

9. Walter Dill Scott and Robert C. Clothier, *Personnel Management: Practices and Point of View* (New York: A.W. Shaw, 1923). See also Edmund C. Lynch, *Walter Dill Scott, Pioneer in Personnel Management* (Austin: Bureau of Business Research, University of Texas, 1968), 2223.

10. For extensive references to Cattell, see Ernest R. Hilgard, ed., *American Psychology in Historical Perspective* (Washington, DC: American Psychological Association, 1978). The address of the Psychological Corporation is 555 Academic Court, San Antonio, TX 78204-0952.

11. Walter Van Dyke Bingham and Bruce Victor Moore, *How to Interview* (New York: Harper & Brothers, 1931). See also Bingham, *Aptitudes and Aptitude Testing* (New York: Harper & Brothers, 1937).

12. For a comprehensive view of the many aspects of organizational psychology, see the special issue of *American Psychologist* 45, no. 2 (February 1990) edited by Lynn R. Offermann and Marilyn K. Gowing.

13. F.J. Roethlisberger and W.J. Dickson, *Management and the Worker* (Cambridge, MA: Harvard University Press, 1939).

14. John G. Adair, "The Hawthorne Effect: A Reconsideration of the Methodological Artifact," *Journal of Applied Psychology* 69, no. 2 (May 1984): 334–345. This article includes a comprehensive bibliography of articles that contain critiques and reinterpretations of the Hawthorne experiments. See also Berkeley Rice, "The Hawthorne Defect: Persistence of a Flawed Theory," *Psychology Today* 16, no. 2 (February 1982): 70–74.

15. For an appreciation of Mary Parker Follett's contributions, see Elliot M. Fox, "Mary Parker Follett: The Enduring Contribution," *Public Administration Review* 28, no. 6 (November–December 1968): 520–529.

16. Kurt Lewin, *The Research Centre for Group Dynamics* (New York: Beacon House, 1947). See also Alfred J. Marrow, *The Practical Theorist: The Life and Work of Kurt Lewin* (New York: Basic Books, 1969).

17. Harold M.F. Rush, *Behavioral Science: Concepts and Management Application*, Personnel Policy Study No. 216 (New York: National Industrial Conference Board, 1969), 2.

18. Harold E. Burtt, *Principles of Employment Psychology*, rev. ed. (New York: Harper & Brothers, 1942), 62–66. Author's note: One of Burtt's former doctoral students, Frank Stanton, president emeritus of CBS Inc., honoured his professor's 100th birthday April 26, 1990, by donating US$1.25 million to Ohio State University to establish the Harold E. Burtt Chair in Industrial Psychology. As an author of ten books and a university professor for over 40 years, Dr. Burtt (1890–1991) had widespread influence in the area of personnel and industrial psychology.

19. David Ulrich, Wayne Brockbank, and Arthur Yeung, "HR Competencies in the 1990s," *Personnel Administrator* 34, no. 11 (November 1989): 91–93.

20. Addresses of these associations may be found in the latest edition of the *Encyclopedia of Associations* (Detroit, MI: Gale Research), available in most libraries.

21. Carolyn Wiley, "The Certified HR Professional," *HR Magazine* 37, no. 8 (August 1992): 77–84.

22. Fran A. Wallace, "Walking a Tightrope: Ethical Issues Facing HR Professionals," *Personnel* 62, no.6 (June 1985): 32–36.

23. Susan J. Harrington, "What Corporate America is Teaching about Ethics," *The Executive* V, no. 1 (February 1991): 21–30. See also Alan Weis, "Seven Reasons to Examine Workplace Ethics," *HR Magazine* 36, no. 3 (March 1991): 69–74; Paul G. Kaponya, "March to a Different Drummer," *HR Magazine* 37, no. 4 (April 1992): 66–68; Bernard J. Reilly, *Business Horizons* 33, no. 6 (November–December 1990): 23–27; and Michael R. Hyman, Robert Skipper, and Richard Tansey, "Ethical Codes Are Not Enough," *Business Horizons* 33, no. 2 (March–April 1990): 15–22.

24. Issued quarterly, *Personnel Management Abstracts* includes abstracts of articles and recent books, a subject and author index of articles, and a list of journals abstracted with addresses of publishers.

25. Issued monthly, *Work Related Abstracts* extracts significant information from over 250 management, labour, government, professional, and university publications.

26. *Human Resources Abstracts* is published quarterly in March, June, September, and December by Sage Periodicals Press.

27. *Business Periodicals Index* is published monthly (except August) by the H.W. Wilson Company.

28. Gutri, L., "Desperately Seeking HRIS: High Technology Continues to Tempt, Seduce and Disappoint Its HR

Partners," *HR Professional* 11, no. 1 (January/February 1994).

29. Scott A. Snell, Patricia Pedigo, and George M. Krawiec, "Managing the Impact of Information Technology on Human Resources Management," Chapter 9 in Geral R. Ferris, Sherman D. Rosen, and Darold T. Barnum, eds., *Handbook of Human Resources Management* (Oxford, U.K.: Blackwell Publishers, 1994). See also Samuel Greengard, "How Technology Is Advancing HR," *Personnel Journal* 72, no. 9 (September 1993): 80–90; Renae Broderick and John W. Boudreau, "Human Resource Management, Information Technology, and the Competitive Edge," *Academy of Management Executive* 6, no. 2 (May 1992): 7–17.

30. Linda Thornburgh, "The White Knight of HR Effectiveness," *HR Magazine* 37, no. 11 (November 1992): 67–78.

31. "Building a Customer-Oriented HR Department," *HR Magazine* 36, no. 10 (October 1991): 64–66.

32. Robert S. Seeley, "HR Redesigns to Optimize Effectiveness," *HR Magazine* 37, no. 11 (November 1992): 44–46; Peter Rosik, "Four Ways to Profit from Consultants," *HR Magazine* 37, no. 11 (November 1992): 77–85.

33. Brenda Paik Sunoo and Jennifer J. Laabs, "Winning Strategies for Outsourcing Contracts," *Personnel Journal* 73, no. 3 (March 1994): 69–78.

34. Randall S. Schuler, "Repositioning the Human Resource Function," *Academy of Management Executive* 4, no. 3 (August 1990): 49–60.

35. Towers Perrin, *Priorities for a Competitive Advantage, an IBM–Towers Perrin Study* (New York: Towers Perrin, 1992).

36. Tom E. Lawson, *The Competency Initiative Standards of Excellence for Human Resource Executives* (Alexandria, VA: SHRM Foundation, 1990).

one
objective

Explain why managers should be concerned with the external and internal environments of their organizations.

two
objective

Explain how technological changes affect employee jobs and HRM.

three
objective

Describe the federal regulatory system as it pertains to HRM.

four
objective

Identify the major demographic trends that influence HRM.

five
objective

Explain how an organization's concern about quality is reflected in its approach to HRM.

six
objective

Identify the elements of a strong organizational culture.

Chapter 2
The Environment for Human Resources Management

An HRM *program functions in a complex environment comprising several elements both inside and outside the firm. In order to have an effective HR program, HR managers must give careful attention to all aspects of the environment. Rapid changes are occurring within society and therefore in the environment within which organizations operate. These changes present challenges that require early solutions if an HR program is to be successful and make its full contribution to the organization and to all its members. One specific example well known to most of us is the declining number of middle-manager jobs, coupled with a growing number of baby boomers competing for those positions. Other issues such as unemployment, the influx of immigrants, the education and skills gap, the adoption of advanced technology, and lifestyle adjustments for dual-career couples all have significant implications for HRM.*

From the broadest perspective, HRM balances the needs of the organization with the realities of the internal and external environments. In this chapter, we will consider the kinds of changes that are anticipated and their effects on HRM. How to improve an organization's internal environment is one of the major challenges confronting employers today, so we will give special emphasis to ways the internal environment can be changed to improve the quality of work life. Reality Check provides the reader with an overview of what some futurists envision for the management of human resources.

Elements of an Organization's Environment

objective

Environment
The conditions, circumstances, and influences that affect the organization's ability to achieve its objectives.

External environment
The environment that exists outside an organization.

Environmental scanning
Analyzing the environment and the changes occurring within it.

Issues management
Process by which managers keep abreast of current issues and bring organizational policies in line with prevailing public opinion.

The **environment** of an organization consists of the conditions, circumstances, and influences that affect the firm's ability to achieve its objectives. Figure 2-1 shows that every organization exists in an environment that has both external and internal components. It also illustrates that both the external and the internal environment are composed of five elements: physical, technological, social, political, and economic. As shown by the arrows, the five elements of the external environment influence how HR functions will be performed. The internal environment influences both HR policies and procedures and the individuals who make up the workforce of the organization. One could further argue that performance of the HR functions also has some influence on the external environment. In fact, more than a decade ago, the president of the Conference Board of Canada observed: "For an increasing number of HR executives, their role goes beyond the sensing and interpreting of the impact of the environment on the firm. For them it is equally important to participate in and influence the environment."[1]

The External Environment

The environment that exists outside the firm, the **external environment**, has a significant impact on HRM policies and practices. It helps to determine the values, attitudes, and behaviour that employees bring to their jobs. This is why many organizations engage in **environmental scanning**, which involves analyzing the environment and changes occurring within it. The purpose here is to determine the environment's possible impact on organizational policies and practices. Another closely related practice is **issues management**, by which managers attempt to keep abreast of current issues. This may include bringing the organization's policies in line with prevailing public opinion.

. . . .

REALITY CHECK

THE FUTURE OF MANAGING HUMAN RESOURCES

David Foote, Economics Professor, University of Toronto
Organizations are shaped like triangles, with a limited number of positions at the top. The great bulge of baby boomers, now in their 40s, are pushing at the peak of this triangle, resulting in too many middle managers. This great bulge of people born between 1947 and 1960 looks like a rectangle. We all know what happens when you try to push a rectangle up a triangle. The organizational response has been to downsize or to flatten the triangle. This reduces vertical movement, but increases lateral movement. The organizational challenge is to provide new challenges in current jobs or retraining to new jobs, or to move people out who will start their own businesses.

Peter Drucker, Management Thinker
The productivity of the knowledge worker will be the key challenge in the postcapitalist world. Knowledge workers and service workers account for about 75 percent of the workforce in all developed countries. About one third of all capital investment has gone into technology to handle data and information: faxes, computers, electronic mail, etc. A great amount of service work includes clerical jobs such as data processing, billing, etc. This production work looks similar to factory production work, but the flow of information has to be organized differently. For example, nurses and sales representatives do a a lot of things, such as filling out forms, which do not contribute to their main tasks of patient care and selling. Identifying knowledge work that contributes directly to productivity is one challenge. Measuring and rewarding service and knowledge workers, based on their productivity, is another.

. . . .

Sources: David Foote [Triangles, Rectangles, and Workaholics: Who's Minding the Workforce?] interviewed by Peter Gzowski for *Morningside* (transcript of interview appears in *The Globe and Mail*, April 11, 1995); Peter F. Drucker, *Post Capitalist Society*, Harper Business, 1993.

Physical Element

The major defining characteristic of Canada is its physical environment. The physical element of the external environment includes the geography, climate, and other physical characteristics of the area in which the organization is located. Canada is the world's largest country, covering 9,198,687 square kilometres but containing less than 1 percent of the world's population. We are proud of the fact that we have the world's longest undefended border, but this means that Halifax is closer to England than to Vancouver and that it is cheaper to fly from Montreal to Paris than to Calgary. Eighty-five percent of Canada's population is positioned within

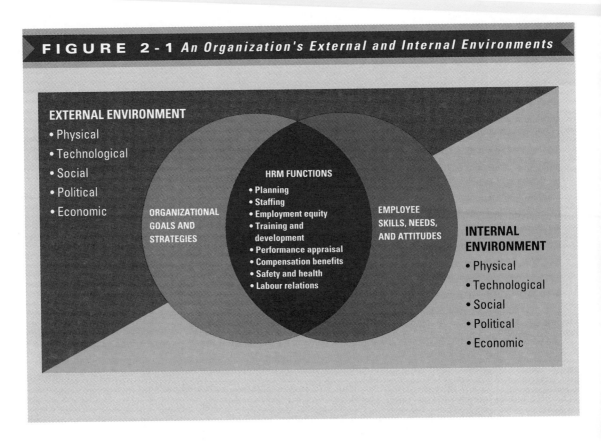

FIGURE 2-1 *An Organization's External and Internal Environments*

EXTERNAL ENVIRONMENT
- Physical
- Technological
- Social
- Political
- Economic

ORGANIZATIONAL GOALS AND STRATEGIES

HRM FUNCTIONS
- Planning
- Staffing
- Employment equity
- Training and development
- Performance appraisal
- Compensation benefits
- Safety and health
- Labour relations

EMPLOYEE SKILLS, NEEDS, AND ATTITUDES

INTERNAL ENVIRONMENT
- Physical
- Technological
- Social
- Political
- Economic

200 kilometres of the Canada–U.S. border. Because of its geographic expanse, Canada has had an enormous amount of economic development devoted to transportation and communication systems. Canadian National Railways, Air Canada, and the Trans-Canada Highway are all examples of government-sponsored developments. Canada's vast size also means that human resource managers in Halifax must wait until nearly 1 p.m. to talk to a candidate in Victoria. In addition, the length and severity of Canadian winters can make the scheduling of certain types of work more difficult.

Physical surroundings can help or hinder a firm's ability to attract and retain employees. Housing, commuting, and living costs can vary from one location to another and can have a significant impact on the compensation employees will expect. Recent population shifts to the West Coast and to small towns and rural areas can be attributed, at least in part, to the desire of migrants to work and live in what they perceive to be a more desirable physical environment. For example, the Bureau of the Census projects that the population in the Yukon will increase about 33 percent between 1993 and 2016. In Quebec, the population is expected to increase about 16 percent, while a 20 percent increase has been predicted for Ontario. The lowest increase (14.3 percent) will be experienced in Nova Scotia.[2] Ironically, the population shifts have created, and will continue to create, congestion, pollution, and other problems of growth in the areas to which people are moving.

Geographic shifts in the population alter the demand for and the supply of workers in local job markets. Organizations that depend on scientists and engineers, for example, pay particular attention to geographic regions where they can recruit "knowledge workers." Cities such as Kanata, Mississauga, and the Waterloo-Kitchener hub are among the best for finding high-tech talent. Vancouver has over 500 software developers, with annual growth rates of 30 percent. Japanese firms such as Hitachi, Sharp, and Matsushita, and Canadian firms like Oracle, Astra, and Corel, locate close to this high-tech talent.

Technological Element

objective

We live in an extremely competitive age. Only through technological innovation can firms develop new products and services and improve existing ones in order to stay competitive. Technology also provides a basis for an organization to attain the productivity and quality it needs to gain a competitive advantage. One study reported that, from 1986 to 1991, the proportion of employees working with computers rose from 15 percent to 57 percent.[3]

Advancements in computer technology have enabled firms to take advantage of the information explosion. With computers, unlimited amounts of data can be stored, retrieved, and used in a wide variety of ways, from simple recordkeeping to controlling complex equipment. In our everyday living we see bank tellers, airline reservation clerks, and supermarket cashiers using computers to perform their jobs. At the bank's automated teller machine and at the library's computerized card catalog we become computer operators ourselves.

Less visible are the systems that monitor employees' speed, efficiency, and accuracy. Companies such as Bell Canada, American Express, and automotive manufacturers use sophisticated devices to measure employee work output.[4] But while large businesses and computer firms tout computerized monitoring as an effective means of improving productivity, the computerized control systems used for this purpose have been linked to increased stress, loss of job privacy rights, health risks, and job dissatisfaction among employees. Supporters argue that such systems improve the consistency, clarity, and objectivity of performance measurement and so are an improvement over stressful, subjective evaluations by human supervisors.

The introduction of advanced technology affects the number of employees as well as the skills they need on the job. In particular, technological advancements have tended to reduce the number of jobs that require little skill and to increase the number of jobs that require considerable skill. In general, this transformation is referred to as a shift from "touch labour," where employee responsibilities are limited to only physical execution of work, to "**knowledge workers,**" where their responsibilities expand to include a richer array of activities such as planning, decision making, and problem solving.[5] In many cases, current employees can be retrained to assume new roles and responsibilities. However, those employees who are displaced also require retraining. We thus experience the paradox of having pages and pages of newspaper advertisements for applicants with technical or scientific training while several hundred thousand job seekers without such training register for work with employment agencies.

Because of the implications of advanced technology for HRM, the HR manager should play a major role in planning for its implementation. In the new era, employees are increasingly viewed as assets to be fully utilized rather than as costs to be

Knowledge workers

Employees whose responsibilities include a rich array of activities such as planning, decision making, and problem solving.

DAVE CARPENTER..

"OPEN THE DOOR, CLAYTON— YOU KNEW IT WAS INEVITABLE..."

Reprinted with permission of Dave Carpenter

minimized. Communication with employees clearly plays a crucial role, as management must demonstrate a real commitment to supporting change through staffing, training, job redesign, and reward systems.[6]

HR can play an important role in helping line managers cope with the organizational changes caused by new technology. HR can, for example, identify methods for introducing new technology that minimize disruption and disarm the threat perceived by employees. In addition, HR can provide guidance to line managers in ensuring that the right technological skills are identified and sought in new employees, as well as in developing technology-literacy training programs. HR can also identify and evaluate the changes in organizational relationships brought about by new technology. Finally, HR should work with line managers to develop new structures that use technology to improve service, increase productivity, and reduce costs.[7]

Information technology has, of course, changed the face of HR in organizations around the world. In the United Kingdom alone, several companies have made significant changes in their HR systems. Smith Kline Beecham, for example, has developed a news service based on voice-mail technology that is available to all its employees. The London Underground has developed a computer-based training program to help staff with evacuation procedures in the event of fire. The Miller Group, the largest privately owned construction company in Britain, has automated its process for determining profit-based bonuses. British Gas has computerized its employee suggestion system to automatically log suggestions, check for duplicates, statistically analyze the database, produce letters, and manage other aspects of reporting. Finally, Britain's North West Regional Health Authority has developed an information system that receives data from each health authority's personnel database and presents aggregated information for senior line managers. Each of these examples shows that technology is changing the face of HRM: altering the methods of collecting employment information, speeding up the processing of that data, and improving the process of internal and external communication.[8]

Social Element

Increasingly, employers are expected to demonstrate a greater sense of responsibility toward employees and toward society as a whole. Employees, furthermore, are expecting the same rights and benefits on the job that they enjoy as members of society. Health-care, retirement, and safety issues, for example, represent just a few of the important areas where organizations must balance economic and social concerns. Employers who fail to accept this fact are encountering difficulties with their employees. In addition, employers are being constrained by legislation and court decisions that support their employees' rights in the workplace.

objective

Many employees today are less obsessed with the acquisition of wealth and now view life satisfaction as more likely to result from balancing the challenges and rewards of work with those in their personal lives. Though most people still enjoy work, and want to excel at it, they also appear to be seeking ways of living that are less complicated but more meaningful. These new lifestyles cannot help but have an impact on the way employees must be motivated and managed. Consequently, HRM has become more complex than it was when employees were concerned primarily with economic survival.[9]

Organizational changes place new demands on families by changing the roles of parents.

Political Element

Governments have a significant impact on HRM. Each of the functions performed in the management of human resources—from employee recruitment to termination—is in some way affected by laws and regulations established at the provincial and federal levels. Indeed, 70 percent of human resource respondents in one survey cited changing regulatory requirements as a major factor altering their external business environment. This pressure for labour market regulation with respect to layoffs, hours, benefits, and minimum-wage laws is due in part to the uncertainty created by global and corporate restructuring. A second factor is the composition of the workforce, resulting in laws such as employment and pay equity.[10]

As mentioned earlier, managers must follow all laws and government regulations—federal, provincial, and local—relating to HRM. In this book, however, we will emphasize the common elements of provincial laws and regulations, because the legislation impacting HR activities is, for the most part, mandated by the provinces.

Federally regulated employment is subject to employment interpretation under the Canada Labour Code, while provincial legislation applicable to employment relates to health and safety, workers' compensation, employment standards, pay equity, and employment equity. While not every province has pay equity or employment equity regulations, human rights legislation derives its power from the Constitution and, as such, is applicable throughout Canada.

Today's manager must understand the regulatory system in order to function effectively within the network of various agencies, directives, reviews, regulations, and determinations. Figure 2-2 shows that regulation begins with social and political problems that prompt lawmakers to pass laws empowering agencies to take regulatory actions that, in turn, trigger management responses. Finally, the courts oversee the process by settling disputes between the litigating parties.

To complicate matters further, the courts and management may differ in terms of how they interpret the legislation. To keep abreast of the latest interpretations, most managers find it advisable to read various publications or consult labour lawyers. We will refer in this book to laws and court decisions that are currently viewed as having a major influence on HRM. Be aware, however, that each week brings news of pending legislation and court decisions that may change the course of HRM policies and practices.

Economic Element

The economic environment has a profound influence on business in general and on the management of human resources in particular. Economic conditions often dictate whether a firm will need to hire or lay off employees. They also affect an employer's ability to increase employees' pay and/or benefits. While economic recessions can force the curtailment of operations in the private sector, they may have the opposite effect in the public sector. Unemployment generated by a recession usually necessitates the expansion of agencies that provide welfare and other social services. Expanding federal programs to combat a recession normally means that these agencies need more employees to supervise the programs. However, most governments in Canada are engaged in a cost-reduction strategy, with downsizing as the primary method of reducing costs.

Economists have long argued that a critical determinant of economic growth is the quality and quantity of inputs such as labour, private- and public-sector capital, and knowledge. Canadian productivity growth has been steadily declining since the late 1970s, dropping from 2.5 percent to under .5 percent.[11] Put in perspective, this decline is significant: had our growth rate been as high from 1970 to present as it was from 1900 to 1970, our current standard of living would be at least 25 percent higher than it is today. Productivity rates remain a concern for Canadians, because until we can improve productivity we cannot improve real incomes.[12] A large part of the drop in productivity growth is the result of technological change that has not yet paid off. As Robert Solow, Nobel Prize winner for Economics, noted, "We see the computer age everywhere but in the productivity statistics."[13] With respect to the U.S. productivity rate, contrary to some suspicions, Japan's productivity rate is less than 70 percent of that of the United States, and productivity in Germany is only about 80 percent of that of the United States.[14]

As seen in Figure 2-3, Canadian manufacturing firms have lost the labour cost advantage they had over their American counterparts during the 1980s. The

FIGURE 2-2   *The Regulatory Model*

ISSUES	LAWS	AGENCIES	REGULATORY ACTIONS	MANAGEMENT RESPONSES

SOCIAL
Economic
  problems
Social conflict
Preventable
  catastrophes
 	
POLITICAL
Parties
Interest groups
Constituency
  opinion
Lobbyists
	Acts of
	  Parliament
	
	Queen
	  (Governor
	  General)
	
	Federal—P.M.
	
	House of
	  Commons
	
	Senate
	
	Provincial
	  Premier
	
	Local Mayor
		Federal,
		  provincial,
		  municipal
		  departments
		Boards
		Central
		  agencies
		Crown
		  corporations
		Independent
		  commissions
		Task forces
			Rulings
			Written
			  regulations
			Complaint
			  investigations
			Inspections
			Technical
			  assistance
			Lawsuits
				Planning
				  compliance
				  strategies
				Auditing
				  personnel
				  practices
				Altering
				  personnel
				  practices
				Negotiating
				  with agencies
				Defending
				  lawsuits
				Supervising,
				  training,
				  rewording,
				  and
				  disciplining
				  employees
				Lobbying for
				  policy change

	Constitution
	"Supreme law
	  of land"
		CANADIAN COURT SYSTEMS
		Federal Courts
		  Supreme
		  Court
		  Federal Court
		  of Canada
		Provincial
		  Courts
		  Court of
		  Appeal
		  Court of
		  Justice
		  (criminal,
		  family, and
		  civil)
			Opinions and
			  decisions	

Source: Randy G. Hoffman, Victor S. MacKinnon, Janice E. Nicholson, and James C. Simeon, *Public Administration: Canadian Materials* (North York, ON: Captus Press, 1993).

FIGURE 2-3	*Compensation Costs for Manufacturing Production*		
COUNTRY	**1975**	**1985**	**1991**
Canada	100	100	100
United States	110	120	89
European Community	87	120	89
Japan	53	60	83
Asian NICs	9	15	24
Mexico	n.a.	15	13

Note: Compensation costs include pay for time worked, other direct pay, and employers, expenditures on public and private benefit plans.

Source: G. Betcherman, K. McMullen, N. Leckie, and C. Caron, *The Canadian Workplace in Transition* (Kingston, ON: IRC Press, Queen's University, 1994).

comparisons with other countries show dramatically that we cannot compete on a pure cost basis.

These comparisons are important, as we now live in a global economy. Competition and cooperation with foreign companies have become increasingly important focal points for business since the early 1980s. About 45 percent of the top 400 companies in Canada (excluding financial institutions) are foreign owned. Nations such as Japan, Germany, France, Taiwan, Brazil, and South Korea represent both formidable rivals and important partners in our transformation to a global economy. In every country of the world, political leaders are under pressure to provide jobs for their unemployed, and not just jobs but "decent" jobs that will provide the standard of living to which their citizens aspire. These jobs can be created only if employers are able to compete successfully in the domestic and foreign markets. The North American Free Trade Agreement (NAFTA), for example, was created to establish a free-trade zone between Mexico, Canada, and the United States. (Plans are underway to include Argentina and other South American countries by the beginning of the next century.) Proponents of NAFTA argue that the agreement will remove impediments to trade and investment, thereby creating jobs. But opponents of NAFTA fear that jobs will be lost to Mexico, where wages are lower.[15] Canada's economy is highly dependent on trade, which accounts for more than half of our gross domestic product, almost triple the proportion in the United States,[16] our major trading partner. The U.S. and Canadian economies are so intertwined that "when the United States sneezes, Canada gets a cold."

Figure 2-4 shows fluctuations in Canadian unemployment rates from 1980 to June 1995. When our economy is healthy, companies hire more workers to fill demand, and unemployment rates fall. But the economic picture is neither simple nor completely predictable. Perennially successful corporations, such as NorTel,

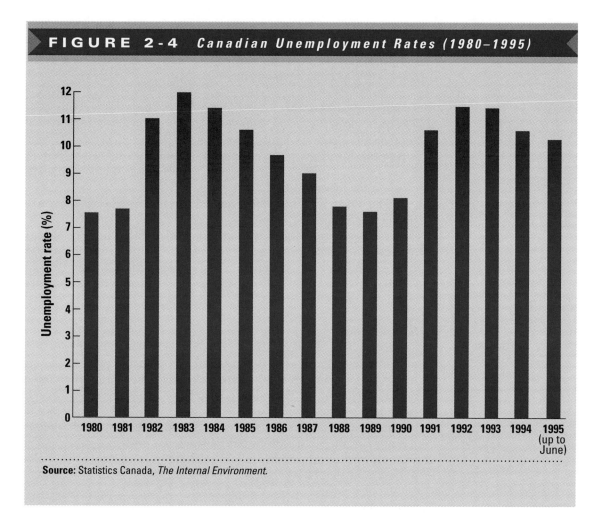

FIGURE 2-4 *Canadian Unemployment Rates (1980–1995)*

Source: Statistics Canada, *The Internal Environment.*

CBC, IBM, and Bank of Canada undergoing profound change, still are laying off employees to compete better in a global economy.

The Internal Environment

Internal environment (organizational climate)
The environment that exists within an organization.

The environment that exists within an organization is known as the **internal environment,** or **organizational climate.** Like the external environment, the internal environment consists of physical, technological, social, political, and economic elements. These elements affect and are affected by the policies, procedures, and employment conditions that managers oversee. Therefore, the program developed for managing human resources must take into account the internal as well as the external environment.

Physical Element
The physical element of the internal environment includes such factors as air quality, temperature, noise, dust, radiation, and other conditions affecting employee

health and safety. Employees are increasingly aware of the health and safety aspects of their work settings, and legislation is evolving to address these concerns. In addition, organizations are monitoring conditions such as air quality in order to ensure a comfortable working environment.

Technological Element

The technological element of the internal environment relates closely to the physical element. It consists of the layout of the workplace; the process by which the work is performed; and the tools, equipment, and machinery used to perform the work. These factors, in turn, determine both the way work is processed and the requirements of the jobs performed.

The way in which work is organized affects interpersonal relations and interaction among employees within a work area. It influences the formation of informal work groups and the degree of cooperation or conflict among employees. More and more, technological systems are being integrated with the social systems of an organization, creating what is referred to as a **sociotechnical system**. Under this system, which is discussed more fully in Chapter 5, job design is based on human as well as technological considerations.[17]

Sociotechnical system

Environment in which the technical and social systems are integrated so that job design is based on human as well as technological considerations.

Social Element

The social element reflects the attitudes and behaviours of managers and employees, individually and in groups. Because of their influential place in the organizational hierarchy, top managers play an extremely important role in determining the quality of the social element. The rules and regulations they devise, the concern they have for employees, the rewards and support they provide, and the tolerance they have for varying opinions are major factors in determining the organizational climate. In recent years, there has been considerable interest in "the corporate culture." We will examine later in this chapter how the culture influences the type of climate as well as the course that HRM will take.

Political Element

Politics is an important social process found in all organizations. Organizational politics, of course, has the potential for being helpful or harmful to organizations and individuals. There are several tactics used in organizational politics. These include attacking or blaming others, using (or withholding or distorting) information, building images, building support for ideas, praising others, creating power coalitions, associating with the influential, and performing services or favours to create obligations. Which of these tactics an individual will use depends on that individual's nature or disposition and on the particular situation confronting him or her.

Power is the capacity to influence the behaviour of others. The degree of power that managers possess is determined in part by where they fit into the formal organization structure, the number of subordinates they supervise, and the authority delegated to them. Power may also be derived from personal expertise and from informal leadership skills.

Power is an important aid in HRM. It can provide a means of gaining the type of performance and behaviour desired of employees. As noted in Chapter 1, two recent studies, one by the Society for Human Resource Management (SHRM) and the other by IBM–Towers Perrin, suggest that HR departments must play a more active role in influencing change in their firms. This means having both the political power and leadership capabilities to overcome resistance to change.[18] Companies such as AT&T, Exxon, and Pepsico have designed programs to ensure that HR executives develop these types of competencies. The more power HR managers have in their organizations, the more successful they will be in getting other managers to carry out their own HR responsibilities and to comply with established policies and procedures.

In order to build a broad base of influence, HR managers should learn to adopt the perspective and language of business and focus on the bottom line. Too often HR managers view themselves as performing strictly a service function. Once HR managers establish themselves as business partners, they become more involved in strategic matters shaping the business.[19]

Economic Element

The economic element of a firm's internal environment reflects the organization's financial condition. The more favourable this condition, the more financial resources the organization will have to support its human resources, including employee compensation and benefits. Furthermore, when the financial health of a firm is strong, there is a tendency to expand HRM activities such as training and development, employee assistance programs, and recreational activities. If the organization is growing, there is the possibility of expansion leading to employee recruitment, selection, and orientation. Conversely, when financial resources are low, an organization tends to reduce its HR budget and to cut back the HR services it offers to its employees.

objective

Changes That Challenge Managers of Human Resources

In the preceding section, we briefly mentioned some of the environmental changes that may precipitate changes in an HR program. Increasingly, HR managers are involved in issues management directed toward early identification of trends that may require adjustments in HR policies and procedures. Beginning in the fall of 1986, SHRM began an organizational effort known as the Issues Management Program. After reviewing the trends and patterns of development of more than 200 specific issues, SHRM identified five basic areas where change is occurring. These five areas are shown in Highlights in HRM 1. The goals of the departments of SHRM are now directly related to these areas so that the Society can provide the services most relevant to the needs of its members.

A Canadian survey of HR managers supported SHRM findings. The study, conducted by Andrew Templer, University of Windsor, and James Ladouceur, St. Clair College, reported that HR managers saw as current concerns flexibility to manage change; diversity and strategic planning; recruitment of talent; and productivity of human resources and training as a means to achieving efficiencies.[20]

In our discussion of changes that challenge managers, we will incorporate key issues from the SHRM Issues Management Program under the following categories: demographic changes, job trends, cultural changes, and total quality management.

1   CURRENT ISSUES IN HUMAN RESOURCES MANAGEMENT

Employer/Employee Rights

This is clearly an important and growing area of debate and concern. To some degree, it reflects the shift in employer/employee negotiations from the bargaining table to the courtroom, as organizations and individuals attempt to define rights, obligations, and responsibilities. Among the many specific issues covered in this broad area are

- Job as an entitlement
- Employment at will
- Privacy (testing)
- Whistle-blowing
- Mandated benefits
- Plant closing notification
- Right to know
- Comparable worth
- Right to manage
- AIDS

Work and Family Relationships

There is a new and important perception that the individual at work is not "detached" from family concerns and responsibilities. Due, in part, to the rapid increase of women in the workplace, as well as a growing interest in and concern with the family, there is increasing demand for recognition and support of family-related employee concerns. Among the issues in this area are

- Day care
- Child-care leave
- Alternative work plans
- Elder care
- Parental leave
- Cafeteria plans
- Mandated benefits

Education/Training/Retraining

As organizations trim personnel and gear up for the tough competition within the global economy, the skills and competence of the available pool of employees are becoming a pivotal issue. This issue spans the range of skill development from the earliest stages of the education experience to the challenges of retraining an aging workforce. If "human resources are our most important asset," it is here that the investments must be made if that asset is to be productive. Among the key issues in this area are

- Literacy
- Employee education/training
- Management development
- Plant closings
- Dropout prevention
- Retraining
- Industry obsolescence

Changing Demographics

The next twenty years will bring a constant aging of the workforce. This has major implications for all aspects of human resource management as it alters traditional experience and expectations regarding the labour pool. Among the issues in this area are

- Shrinking pool of entry-level workers
- Retirement health benefits funding
- Social security
- "Plateauing" and motivation

- Increasing number of "nonpermanent/contract" employees
- Elder care
- Pension fund liabilities

Productivity/Competitiveness

The calls for increased productivity, quality, and competitiveness will only grow in intensity over the coming years. A persistent trade deficit and continued successes in the global market of our international competitors will serve to intensify the quest for a more productive workforce. Among the issues in this area are

- Productivity improvement
- Worker participation
- Foreign Competition
- Mergers
- Quality programs and measurement
- Incentive/performance pay
- Globalization
- Downsizing

Source: Catherine Downes Bower and Jeffrey J. Hallett, "Issues Management at ASPA," *Personnel Administrator* 34, no. 1 (January 1989): 40–43. Reprinted with the permission of *HR Magazine* (formerly *Personnel Administrator*), published by the Society for Human Resource Management, Alexandria, Va.

Demographic Changes

Among the most significant challenges to managers are the demographic changes occurring in Canada. Because they affect the workforce of an employer, these changes—in population growth, in age and gender distribution of the population, and in education trends—are important topics for discussion. According to Frank Doyle, General Electric's vice-president for external and industrial relations, demographic changes "will turn the professional human resources world on its ear." Jean Fraser, vice-president of employee relations at American Express, echoes these views but adds, "We're not just sitting around and waiting for demographic changes to take place. To us, the year 2000 is already here."[21]

Population Growth

Population growth is the single most important factor governing the size and composition of the labour force. The Canadian labour force totalled about 12.6 million in 1995 and is expected to grow by less than 1 percent annually until the year 2016, although in 1994 growth was 2.1 percent.[22]

Of course, Canadian workers will continue to be a diverse group. Canada admits more immigrants per capita than any other country. The United Nations declared Toronto the most multiculturally diverse city in the world, thus serving as the milestone that moves us from a bicultural past to a multicultural future.[23] By the year 2001, most people entering the workforce will be women, visible minorities, aboriginals, and people who are physically challenged.[24]

The arrival of immigrants also has significant implications for the labour force. Figure 2-5 shows the distribution of population by ethnic origin in Canada for 1991. Prior to 1960, 90 percent of the immigrants who came to Canada were European born; today that figure is 25 percent. The remaining 75 percent of immigrants were born in Asia and the Middle East (48%), Central and South America (10%), Caribbean (6%) Africa (6%), the United States (4%), and Oceania (1%).[25] Most companies are aware that diversity issues are critical to the future success of their companies.[26]

To accommodate the shift in demographics, many organizations have increased their efforts to recruit and train a more diverse workforce.[27] Organizations such as the Bank of Montreal, CIBC, Connaught Laboratories, and the federal government have made it a priority to employ a workforce that represents the communities in which they operate. (See Chapter 3 for a discussion of the management of diversity.) Figure 2-6 illustrates the projected representations of visible minorities in urban centres across Canada.

Age Distribution of the Population

Past fluctuations in the birthrate are producing abrupt changes in the makeup of major Canadian labour-force groups. The number of younger (15–24) workers fell from a high of 4.7 million in 1981 to 3.8 million in 1991. This downward trend is expected to continue until 2016.[28]

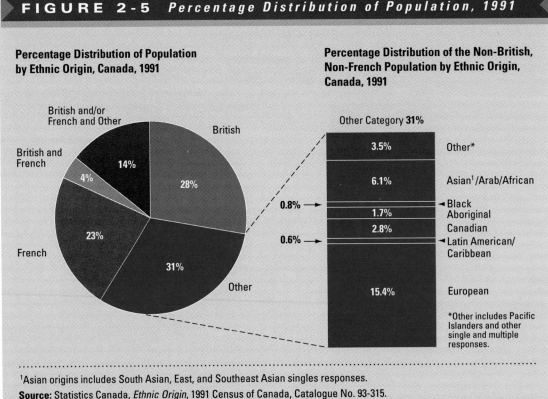

FIGURE 2-5 *Percentage Distribution of Population, 1991*

Percentage Distribution of Population by Ethnic Origin, Canada, 1991

Percentage Distribution of the Non-British, Non-French Population by Ethnic Origin, Canada, 1991

British and/or French and Other
British
British and French 14%
4%
28%
French
23%
31%
Other

Other Category **31%**
3.5% Other*
6.1% Asian[1]/Arab/African
0.8% → ◄ Black
1.7% Aboriginal Canadian
2.8% ◄ Latin American/
0.6% → Caribbean
15.4% European

*Other includes Pacific Islanders and other single and multiple responses.

[1]Asian origins includes South Asian, East, and Southeast Asian singles responses.

Source: Statistics Canada, *Ethnic Origin*, 1991 Census of Canada, Catalogue No. 93-315.

FIGURE 2-6   *Visible Minorities in Urban Centres*

| | ACTUAL | | | | PROJECTED | | | |
	1986	%	1991	%	1996	%	2001	%
Metro Toronto	588,000	17.3	961,000	25.2	1.47 mil	35.1	2.11 mil	44.6
Vancouver	230,000	16.9	378,000	23.8	578,000	30.8	830,000	39.3
Edmonton	72,000	9.3	119,000	14.1	182,000	19.8	260,000	25.0
Calgary	73,000	10.9	119,000	16.0	182,000	20.4	260,000	25.0
Winnipeg	49,000	8.0	80,000	12.2	122,000	17.9	147,000	20.6
Montreal	205,000	7.1	336,000	10.8	512,000	15.0	737,000	19.9
Ottawa-Hull	51,000	6.3	83,000	9.3	126,000	12.5	182,000	16.0
Halifax	15,000	5.1	26,000	8.2	40,000	11.2	57,000	13.5
Regina	8,000	4.4	13,000	6.8	20,000	9.6	25,000	11.0
Victoria	14,000	5.5	21,000	7.3	32,000	9.0	45,000	10.7

Source: Canadian Advertising Foundation.

Older workers find greater job satisfaction as they acquire new skills.

The number of older workers (55 and above) will decline through the mid-1990s, then start to rise sharply as the baby boomers themselves approach retirement age. By 2010, 16 percent of Canadians will be over age 65. The proportion of seniors is increasing rapidly as the baby boomers reach this age bracket. With the anticipated decline in younger workers and the increase in seniors, employers will have no other choice than to tap the labour pool of seniors. Many firms with a primary interest in this younger age group—such as fast-food restaurants and other retail establishments—can expect to see the population from which they draw part-time workers, as well as customers, shrink throughout most of the 1986–2000 period.[29]

Despite the fact that the pool of younger workers is shrinking and labour shortages loom ahead, public policy can discourage the employment of older workers beyond traditional retirement age, regardless of substantial evidence of the value of their training and experience. Some employers, however, are making positive efforts to attract more older workers, especially those who have taken early retirement, by expanding the number of part-time hours available and offering sabbaticals and job sharing. McDonald's, for example, places a great deal more emphasis on hiring retirees and other older workers as an alternative for dealing with the coming youth shortage.[30] John Snodgrass, president of the Days Inn hotel chain, argues that "Corporate America is walking past an unbelievable resource of talent—reliable, trained, educated."

But there are a number of barriers to overcome before firms can succeed in making continued employment attractive to older workers. Many employers fall victim to the myth that older people don't want to work or are incapable of it. There is a continuing need to counteract this and other inaccurate perceptions of the older worker.[31] Older workers, for example, have significantly lower accident rates and absenteeism than younger workers. Further, they tend to report higher job-satisfaction scores. And while some motor skills and cognitive abilities may start to decline (starting around age 25), most individuals find ways to compensate for this fact so that there is no discernible impact on their performance.

There is an old cliché that "You can't teach an old dog new tricks." Probably we should revise this to say, "You can't teach an old dog the same way you teach a puppy." To address the fact that seniors learn in different ways, McDonald's, a heavy recruiter of older workers, has developed its McMasters program in which newly hired seniors work alongside experienced employees so that in a matter of four weeks, they can be turned loose to work on their own. The training program is designed to help seniors "unlearn" old behaviours while acquiring new skills. One survey of over 400 HR practitioners indicated that they had active strategies for dealing with an older workforce: wellness programs (43%), using retirees on special projects (42%), hiring retirees as consultants (39%), elder-care information and referral (20%), pension benefits for part-time workers (18%), elder-care counselling (5%), gradual retirement (3%), rehearsal retirement (2%), retiree job banks (6%) and the reduction of early-retirement incentives (3%).[32]

Imbalance in the age distribution of our labour force has significant implications for employers. At Algoma Steel, for example, the average age of employees is almost 48 years. On the other hand, those who constitute the population bulge are experiencing greater competition for advancement from others of approximately the same age. This situation challenges the ingenuity of managers to develop career patterns for members of this group and to motivate their performance. In addition, providing pension and social security benefits for this group when they reach retirement age early in the next century will present a very serious problem for employers and society. Because of the drop in the birthrate following the baby boom, the labour force available to support the retirees will be smaller. The solutions to this and other problems created by the imbalance in the age distribution of our labour force will require long-range planning on the part of both organization and government leaders.

Gender Distribution of the Workforce

Women make up approximately 45 percent of the workforce. While the number will continue to climb close to 50 percent, this increase will be slower than in previous years. The increase of women in the labour force is a trend that organizations continue to recognize. Employers are under constant pressure to ensure equality for women with respect to employment, advancement opportunities, and compensation. They also need to accommodate working mothers and fathers through parental leaves, part-time employment, flexible work schedules, job sharing, telecommuting, and child-care assistance. More and more, benefit programs are being designed to meet the needs of the two-wage-earner family.

Because more women are working, employers are more sensitive to the growing need for policies and procedures to eliminate sexual harassment in the workplace. Some organizations have special orientation programs to acquaint all personnel with the problem and to warn potential offenders of the consequences. Many employers are demanding that managers and supervisors enforce their sexual-harassment policy vigorously. (The basic components of such policies will be presented in Chapter 3.)

Typically, sexual harassment involves one individual taking advantage of another. However, instead of a single individual being charged with harassment, there are an increasing number of cases in which the whole environment is seen as the source of sexual harassment. Characteristic of the "chilly climate" syndrome are risqué jokes, pornographic magazines, slides in video presentations, and pinup posters. While some employers argue that it isn't always easy to define what constitutes an environment of sexual harassment, a spokesman for DuPont says that, to be safe, "We tell people: It's harassment when something starts bothering somebody."[33]

Rising Levels of Education

In recent years, the educational attainment of the Canadian labour force has risen dramatically. Currently, more than three out of four Canadians aged 20–24 have attained at least high school. Ontario has the most people in this age category with secondary school, while Quebec has the largest percentage of people with trade and other nonuniversity qualifications. Nova Scotia has the largest percentage of university graduates.[34] The emphasis on education is expected to continue; Figure 2-7 shows the average payoff in earnings from education.

For the past few decades, the most secure and fastest-growing sectors of employment have been in those areas requiring higher levels of education. For example, three of the four fastest-growing occupational groups are (1) executive, administrative, and managerial occupations; (2) professional specialty occupations; and (3) technicians and related support occupations—occupations that generally require the highest levels of education and skill.[35]

On the other hand, opportunities for high-school dropouts will be increasingly limited. At the same time, university graduates may find that to be employed will require taking a job that does not fully utilize the knowledge and skills they acquired in university. For example, a recent political science graduate who has found employment in a department store as a sales clerk says, "It's all right to pay the bills, but it's not what I want to do forever." In the current economy, thousands of well-qualified

FIGURE 2-7   *Impact of Education on Earnings*

HIGHEST LEVEL OF SCHOOLING	EARNINGS
Less than grade 9	$25,077
Grade 9–13, no certificate	$27,289
Grade 9–13, certificate	$28,919
Trade certificate or some university	$32,850
University degree	$49,861

Source: *Earnings of Canadians* (Ottawa: Statistics Canada, Ministry of Industry, Science and Technology, Cat. No. 96-317 E).

people are underemployed.[36] To compensate their employees for this lack of parity, employers must try harder to improve the quality of work life. We will discuss some suggested improvements later in the chapter.

It is important to observe that while the educational level of the workforce has continued to rise over the past several decades, the number of students graduating with degrees in science and engineering is very low compared to other disciplines. A number of studies suggest that there will be a shortage of engineers and scientists by the year 2000. Although women now make up nearly half of the labour force, less than 2 percent of them are engineers and scientists. Even further, while visible minorities are expected to make up approximately 20 percent of the labour force by the turn of the century, and while 18 percent of them have university degrees compared to 11 percent of the majority, their unemployment rates are higher.[37]

There is a widening gap between the educated and noneducated. At the lower end of the educational spectrum, many employers are having to cope with individuals who are functionally illiterate—i.e., unable to read, write, calculate, or solve problems at a level that enables them to perform even the simplest technical tasks. One study found that 16 percent of adult Canadians have limited reading skills and cannot face most daily demands alone.[38] The traditional reason for rejecting candidates for entry-level positions—lack of experience—has been replaced by inadequate reading and writing skills.[39] Cavendish Farms, one of North America's largest frozen-food corporations, was one firm that realized many of its employees lacked the necessary training to cope with the technology of the 1990s. The employees lacked basic computer skills and were having difficulty understanding the more complicated service manuals. Literacy training was needed.[40]

Clearly, there is much work to be done. Modernization makes basic skill deficiencies that much more noticeable, and many believe that without immediate action, we are running down a path toward a national crisis. To rectify the situation, both private- and public-sector organizations are working together. Many organizations and educational institutions are establishing much-needed partnerships to ensure that future employees have the skills they need for work. Sears and IBM, for example, have begun developing apprenticeship-type programs that combine academic and vocational instruction with on-the-job training. (See Chapter 8 for a discussion of apprenticeship programs.)

A related problem is technological illiteracy. In Ottawa, Ontario, a coalition of high-technology businesses and educators launched the Partners Summer Institute for high-school teachers as part of a larger program that is encouraging students to pursue technologically oriented careers. IBM alone has spent more than $60 million since 1982 working with Canadian educational institutions to help bolster technological skills.[41]

Canadian companies spend approximately $4 billion annually on training and development; about half of this amount is spent proportionately by U.S. firms. A study by Michael Porter of Harvard University warned that unless Canada invests in training and education in the workplace, Canadians will face a declining standard of living in the future. Aware that training impacts not only standards of living but also competitive advantage, Canadian human resource directors view employees as important assets and are very supportive of the need for training. Indeed, the most profitable companies among those rated as one of the 100 best companies to work for in Canada spend the most money on training per employee. The result is that training budgets are increasing at a higher rate than inflation and the use of training staff and consultants is increasing.[42]

Job and Occupational Trends

Government studies show that as incomes and living standards have risen, the desire for services has grown more rapidly than the desire for goods. As a result, employment in service-producing industries has increased faster than employment in goods-producing industries. Furthermore, imports of foreign-made goods have been limiting the growth of goods-producing industries.

Increase in Service Jobs

The service sector consists of services, public administration, finance, insurance, real estate, trade, transportation communications, and other utilities. As seen in Figure 2-8, employment in the service sector is growing. The goods sector, consisting of agriculture, primary industries, manufacturing, and construction, continued to post a steady decline. Governments at all levels are downsizing, and this reduction will impact the growth rate of the service sector. However, economists predict that as Canadians look for alternative means of self support, and as more companies contract out work, the growth in community, business, and personal services will offset this decline. Self-employment represents about 15 percent of the workforce but accounted for about 25 percent of the overall employment growth in 1994. Three-quarters of this growth was attributable to women.[43]

The federal government and other forecasters are extremely reluctant to predict future job openings. Most rely on extrapolations from present occupational patterns, which are not useful for students who are planning careers requiring ten to fifteen years of education and training.

Since there are proportionately larger numbers of clerical and service jobs at the lower pay levels, special effort may be required to attract and retain employees in these jobs. Career ladders will be needed to enable the more capable employees to

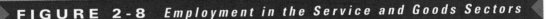

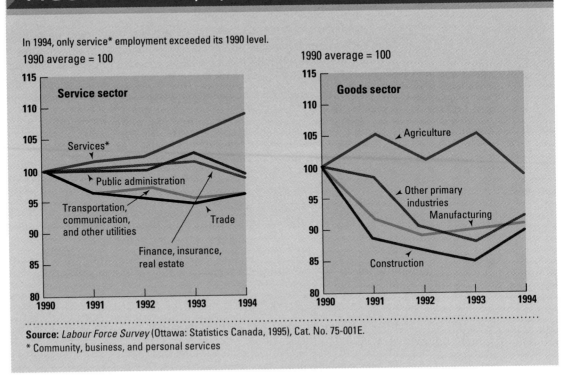

FIGURE 2-8 *Employment in the Service and Goods Sectors*

In 1994, only service* employment exceeded its 1990 level.

1990 average = 100

Service sector

1990 average = 100

Goods sector

Source: *Labour Force Survey* (Ottawa: Statistics Canada, 1995), Cat. No. 75-001E.
* Community, business, and personal services

advance and to provide greater psychological rewards for those unable to do so. On the other hand, for professional, technical, and managerial jobs, employers will have to develop recruiting and selection programs appropriate to the type of applicants being sought. Effective HR planning that involves career ladders and development programs will be essential to help employees reach these positions through internal promotion.

Jobs in High-Technology Industries

High technology is often touted as the source of new employment opportunities to help replace jobs lost in declining "smokestack" industries. Although they are growing faster than the average for all sectors, and particularly for the manufacturing sector, high-tech industries such as computers, bioengineering, and telecommunications have accounted for only a small proportion of new jobs through 1995. The greatest increases in high-tech industries are projected to be in computer and data-processing services.[44]

Despite changes and fluctuations in various industries and occupations, most jobs that become available through the year 2005 will be through replacement needs. Replacement openings occur as individuals leave occupations, through transfer, promotion, retirement, and the like. As a consequence, basic industries will continue to be an important sector in the Canadian economy.

HR managers are interested in these job trends because of their effects on all of the HRM functions. For example, given that visible minorities and women are increasing their share of the labour force, HR managers frequently analyze how each group is represented in both fast-growing and slow-growing occupations. Women, for example, are fairly well represented in fast-growing occupations such as health services but are also represented in some slow-growth occupations such as secretarial, computer processing, and financial-records processing. For visible minorities, the data are less encouraging, particularly given their higher levels of education. Corporate efforts to employ more people from the designated groups are discussed in Chapter 3.

Use of Contingency Employees

Many organizations are using more contingency employees—temporaries, part-timers, contract labour, and the like—to effectively handle extra workloads without committing themselves to providing permanent employment or benefits. By using contingency workers and dealing with agencies such as Olsten or Kelly Services, organizations can have the benefit of finding individuals who have been screened and trained. The fact that the number of people employed by temporary-help agencies in Canada increases annually is an indicator of their value to employers. More specifically, temporary or part-time jobs accounted for 17 percent of total employment in Canada. The number of part-time workers more than doubled from 988,000 in 1975 to 2.1 million in 1993.[45] The situation in Canada reflects the American scene. Manpower, with 600,000 employees, is now the largest private employer in the United States—with 200,000 more employees than General Motors and over 300,000 more employees than IBM.[46]

Freelancers are a new breed of employee who work directly for the employer through contract arrangements, including self-employment, contract, part-time, and anything exclusive of traditional full-time employment. Statistics Canada estimates that 30 percent of Canadians with paid jobs fall into this category, and forecasts that their numbers will increase. Tom Peters likens the freelance work experience to that of a team engaged in the production of a movie in which a collection of actors, make-up artists, designers, and others assemble for one project and then disperse.[47] The adaptability of employees to these short-term assignments is a concern, as outlined in Ethics in HRM.

The use of contingency workers is not restricted to low-level clerical jobs. Many of these workers are scientists, bankers, lawyers, and executives. Retired executives who still want to work only a few months of the year, genuine freelancers who prefer short-term assignments, and displaced executives who face a long waiting period make up this group. Some of these individuals are eventually hired full-time, but most are employed for several months and then move on to some other work. In many cases, the assignments can help them make contacts, gain new experience, and get a lead on future openings.[48]

Telecommuting

Telecommuting
Use of microcomputers, networks, and other communications technology such as fax machines to do work in the home that is traditionally done in the workplace.

One of the more recent changes and potentially the most far-reaching is telecommuting. **Telecommuting** is the use of microcomputers, networks, and other communications technology such as facsimile (fax) machines to do work in the home that is traditionally done in the workplace. As technology becomes both more

> **ETHICS IN HRM**

NONSTANDARD WORK

The job-for-life norm is gone, and the current employment trend of nonstandard work may be as important as the Industrial Revolution. To some, like Jean White and Cameron Sobolik, this is an exciting time. White, a former legal secretary in her 60s, is a consultant on industrial quality standards. She does everything from writing technical documents to developing software to running workshops—all on contract. Sobolik, a computer programmer in his 20s, says that one company can't expose him to everything that's out there and that a job description is limiting; therefore, he moonlights. These brain workers find better pay and more satisfying work as contractors.

People with marketable skills are helping redefine what a career means. This movement has been triggered by organizations engaged in downsizing efforts and contracting-out strategies. Companies are moving toward just-in-time employees, that is, hiring only the people they need for the limited time they are needed.

However, for many employees who like security, structure, and rules, this revolution is frightening. Being on contract often means the loss of benefits and a social network. To protect themselves, the self-employed may form associations to provide these benefits, to pool training, and to engage in teamwork on certain projects.

Organizations that employ mainly contract employees may also lose. Companies may forego loyalty to the corporate vision, the strength that comes from working together over long periods, and the resultant experience curve. Also, there is an acknowledgment that a competitive advantage comes from investing in employees in lifelong learning and involving and empowering them.

These two visions—investing deeply in employees or using just-in-time-employees—are obviously at odds. Which is the better system for employees and employers?

Sources: R. Williamson, "The Jobless Recovery," *The Globe and Mail*, January 15, 1995; and J. Raymond, "Worth Repeating: Credo's in Conflict," *The Globe and Mail*, November 11, 1993, B2.

sophisticated and user-friendly, employees can hook up with their offices and perform their tasks while still remaining miles away.

Not all jobs lend themselves to at-home work, but many do: travel agent, architect, writer, salesperson, data-entry clerk, insurance agent, real-estate agent, bookkeeper, accountant, computer programmer, word-processing secretary, engineer, and others. Numerous organizations, including the Royal Bank, the Bank of Montreal, and Bell Canada, have developed some sort of telecommuting policy.

What potential benefits do HR managers see in telecommuting? The most common responses of over 100 HR managers were decreased production costs, increased employee satisfaction, and increased productivity.[49] Yet despite the increasing use and value of telecommuting, managers may not feel comfortable supervising a telecommuting employee. Managers of telecommuters must be innovative thinkers and risk takers. According to Jack Nilles, who coined the term telecommuter, "The major obstacle to telecommuting in the last 15 years has been conservative management with industrial revolution mind-sets."[50] Many employers have been reluctant to consider telecommuting because they fear they will lose control if employees are not physically present. When Continental Corporation rolled out a series of programs including telecommuting and job sharing, many were sceptical. However, within fifteen months of initiating the program, the company found that productivity jumped 15 percent and that the voluntary employee turnover rate had been cut to less than 5 percent, better than a 50 percent improvement.[51]

Ironically, many employers now report that there is a tendency for telecommuters to become workaholics. In choosing telecommuters, organizations should try to fill the positions with people whose jobs have not required interaction with others, who have been with the organization for some time, who have the appropriate psychological characteristics to work at home, and who above all are self-starters. Preparing managers to supervise employees who are not physically present is a special requirement for success. Managers have to work harder at planning and communicating with their telecommuting subordinates, and they have to be clearer about their objectives. Ultimately, the key to putting together a successful telecommuting program is to have quality HR leadership guiding and managing the process.

Cultural Changes

The attitudes, beliefs, values, and customs of people in a society are an integral part of their culture. Naturally, their culture affects their behaviour on the job and the environment within the organization, influencing their reactions to work assignments, leadership styles, and reward systems. Like the external and internal environments of which it is a part, culture is undergoing continual change. HR policies and procedures therefore must be adjusted to cope with this change.

Employee Rights

Over the past few decades, federal legislation has radically changed the rules for management of employees by granting them many specific rights. Among these are laws granting the right to equal employment opportunity (Chapter 3), union representation if desired (Chapters 15 and 16), a safe and healthful work environment (Chapter 14), a pension plan that is fiscally sound (Chapter 13), equal pay for men and women performing essentially the same job (Chapter 11), and privacy in the workplace.

Concern for Privacy

HR managers and their staffs, as well as line managers in positions of responsibility, generally recognize the importance of discretion in handling all types of information about employees. Since the passage, in 1982, of Canada's Privacy Act, which protects the indiscriminate use of personal data, increased attention to privacy has been evident.

Employer responses to the issue of information privacy vary widely. A number of companies have policies that limit the disclosure of personal data by having employees sign a form allowing the company to confirm personal information requests from creditors. Forms that require employees to self-identify as visible minorities have led to concerns over the confidentiality and accuracy of the data collected. The privacy and protection of information stored on an organization's data base is an ongoing concern.

Changing Attitudes Toward Work

Changing attitudes toward authority have become prevalent in today's labour force. Employees increasingly expect to exercise certain freedom from management control without jeopardizing their job security or chances for advancement. They are more demanding, more questioning, and less willing to accept the "I'm the boss" approach.

Another well-established trend is for employees to define success in terms of personal self-expression and fulfilment of potential on the job, while still receiving adequate compensation for their efforts. A greater proportion of the workforce now strives for challenging jobs. More people are also seeking rewarding careers and multiple careers rather than being satisfied with just having a job.

Workers also seem to value free time more than they did in earlier decades. Many polls report that North Americans feel they have less free time than they once did. Contrary to their reported feelings, however, a use-of-time project at the University of Maryland's Survey Research Centre found that people today actually have more free time than ever before. Men have 40 hours of free time a week and women have 39 hours. ("Free time" is defined as what is left over after subtracting the time people spend working and commuting to work, taking care of their families, doing housework, shopping, sleeping, eating, and engaging in other personal activities.) According to the report, free time has increased because women are doing much less housework than they did several decades ago and because the number of actual work hours that workers record in their daily diaries—not the number of "official" hours of work—has fallen significantly for both men and women. The findings, however, do hide much individual variation. Working parents, especially, are under severe time pressures. On balance, though, more people are gaining free time than are losing it.[52]

Personal and Family Life Orientation

We noted earlier that HRM has become more complex than it was when employees were concerned primarily with economic survival. Today's employees have greater expectations from society and from their employment. In many cases, having time to develop a satisfying personal life and pursue cultural and other nonwork-related interests is valued by workers today as much as having a full-time job.[53] Employers are thus being forced to recognize the fact that as individuals strive for a greater balance in their lives, organizations will have to alter their attitudes and their HRM policies to satisfy employee desires.

Work and the family are connected in many subtle and not-so-subtle social, economic, and psychological ways. Because of the new forms that the family has taken—e.g., the two-wage-earner and the single-parent family—work organizations find it necessary to provide employees with more flexibility and options. "Flexibility" is a broad term and may include unconventional hours, day care, part-time work, job sharing, maternity leave, parental leave, executive transfers, spousal involvement in career planning, assistance with family problems, and telecommuting. These issues have become important considerations for all managers. Some of the most progressive companies, such as Warner Lambert, Royal Bank, Apple Canada, Bank of Montreal, and Bell Canada, promote flexibility throughout their organizations.[54] In general, these companies calculate that accommodating individual needs and circumstances is a powerful way to attract and retain top-calibre people.

The Toronto-based law firm of Minden Gross Grafstein & Greenstein is counting community work and other non-billable activities as part of reaching billable targets.[55] There are acknowledged costs, however. In professional firms, such as accounting and law, career paths and promotion sequences are programmed in a lockstep manner. Time away from work can slow down—and, in some cases, derail—an individual's career advancement.

objective

Human Resources and Total Quality Management

The annual growth in output per worker averaged approximately 1 percent between 1985 and 1993. In recent years, productivity in basic manufacturing operations has improved slightly. Following a cycle of downsizing, the forging of new union agreements, and the closing or modernization of obsolete plants, this trend should continue.[56]

Intense international competition has forced Canadian organizations to enhance quality, as well as productivity, to regain their competitive edge.[57] **Total quality management (TQM)** is a set of principles and practices whose core ideas include doing things right the first time, striving for continuous improvement, and understanding customer needs. Through TQM initiatives, companies such as Weston Foods and Standard Aero have substantially improved productivity and bolstered their competitive advantage. However, quality programs are certainly no panacea. Unfortunately, too many organizations view quality as a quick fix. As a consequence, 75 percent of all quality programs begun in 1982 had been discontinued by 1986.[58] Further, the number of applications for the Malcolm Baldrige National Quality Award peaked in 1991 and has fallen sharply ever since. If quality initiatives are to work, an organization must make major changes in its philosophy, its operating mechanisms, and its HR programs.

A survey asked 307 executives from *Fortune* 1000 companies and 308 executives from smaller firms (twenty-plus employees) to rate the importance of eight quality-improvement techniques. Those techniques that stressed human factors—employee motivation, change in corporate culture, and employee education—received higher ratings than those emphasizing processes or equipment. Organizations known for

Total quality management (TQM)

A set of principles and practices whose core ideas include doing things right the first time, striving for continuous improvement, and understanding customer needs.

product and service quality strongly believe that employees are the key to that quality. They believe that proper attention to employees will naturally improve quality and productivity.[59] In other words, they believe that HRM is the most promising strategy for reversing the productivity slide. Figure 2-9 shows how organizations tend to change their HR practices to support quality initiatives.[60]

To test the validity of this belief that HRM is instrumental for improving quality and productivity, two researchers designed an empirical study. The study was conducted at two autonomous divisions of a large service-recreation corporation, each with a separate profit centre. Using a list of activities the company believed to be important and a set of critical employee-attitude statements, an employee-opinion survey was developed and administered. The results showed that when a firm is committed to good HR department programs and activities, employees will see this commitment in a positive manner and attitudes will be affected, thus contributing to organizational effectiveness in many ways. These findings add empirical support to the literature and other reported HR surveys.[61]

The fact that many organizations in North America have found it difficult to compete successfully with those in Japan has stimulated interest in uncovering differences between the two countries. Cultural and sociological differences between Japanese and North American workers may explain to some extent why workers in Japan are credited with being more productive and more dedicated to their work. For example, the Japanese tradition in the larger companies of providing lifetime employment and avoiding layoffs, even at a financial sacrifice, has generated a sense of loyalty and commitment to employers among Japanese workers. In addition, evidence suggests that Japanese workers tend to identify more than North American workers with their employers and their employers' goals. However, they tend to be very similar to North American workers with respect to their dedication to the work ethic or to doing a decent job.[62]

One of the keys to the increased productivity of Japanese workers lies in the coordinated efforts of individuals—through interdependence, collaboration, and teamwork. Teamwork has also become one of the mainstays in manufacturing and service firms.[63] Levi Strauss, for example, has converted one facility from assembly lines to modular manufacturing teams. Sewing-machine operators, rather than acting as "living extensions of their machines," now work as a self-managed team to coordinate scheduling, maintenance, and troubleshooting. As a result, Levi Strauss has reduced the time it takes to get out a 60-pair bundle of jeans from six days to one. Equally important is the concern for quality, and here the company has lowered its defect rate from 3.9 percent to 1.9 percent.[64]

Another philosophy borrowed from the Japanese is employee management, which rests on respect for the worker's intelligence and need for self-esteem. Some Japanese subsidiaries, such as Nissan and GM-Toyota, have been able to apply this philosophy to the management of their North American employees. These companies have translated the philosophy into action by encouraging their workers to participate in decision making and to identify with company goals.

Many organizations have adopted certain aspects of Japanese management practices to their advantage. It should be observed, however, that the Japanese business and management system is undergoing significant changes. Lifetime employment, seniority-based promotion systems, and company-wide unions—all characteristic of Japanese-style management—have recently been called into serious question.

FIGURE 2-9   *The Evolution of a Total-Quality HR Paradigm*

HUMAN RESOURCE CHARACTERISTICS	TRADITIONAL PARADIGM	TOTAL-QUALITY PARADIGM
Corporate culture	Individualism Differentiation Autocratic leadership Profits Productivity	Collective efforts Cross-functional work Coaching/enabling Customer satisfaction Quality
Communications	Top-down	Top-down Horizontal, lateral; Multidirectional
Voice and involvement	Employment-at-will Suggestion systems	Due process Quality circles Attitude surveys
Job design	Efficiency Productivity Standard Procedures Narrow span of control Specific job descriptions	Quality Customization Innovation Wide span of control Autonomous work teams Empowerment
Training	Job-related skills Functional, technical Productivity	Broad range of skills Cross-functional Diagnostic, problem-solving Productivity and quality
Performance measurement and evaluation	Individual goals Supervisory review Emphasize financial performance	Team goals Customer, peer, and supervisory review Emphasize quality and service
Rewards	Competition for individual merit increases and benefits	Team/group-based awards Financial rewards, financial and nonfinancial recognition
Health and safety	Treat problems	Prevent problems Safety and wellness programs Employee assistance
Selection/promotion Career development	Selected by manager Narrow job skills Promotion based on individual accomplishment Linear career path	Selected by peers Problem-solving skills Promotion based on group facilitation Horizontal career path

Source: Richard Blackburn and Benson Rosen, "Total Quality and Human Resources Management: Lessons Learned from Baldrige Award-Winning Companies," *Academy of Management Executive* 7, no. 3 (1993): 51; Reproduced with permission.

Quality of Work Life

Quality of work life (QWL)

The extent to which work is rewarding and free of anxieties and stresses

Improving a firm's external environment is, to a large extent, beyond an employer's control. However, improving the organization's internal environment is definitely within the realm of an employer's influence. A major challenge confronting employers today is that of improving the **quality of work life (QWL)**. This challenge stems not only from the need to meet foreign competition but also from the demographic and cultural changes that have just been discussed.

Many of our largest private and public organizations are making changes to try to improve the QWL of their employees. These efforts consist of looking for ways to make work more rewarding and reduce anxieties and stresses in the work environment. Several different approaches are being used, including restructuring work organization and job design, increasing employee involvement in shaping the organization and its functions, and developing an organizational culture that will encourage members to behave in ways that will maximize productivity, strengthen human relationships, meet employee expectations, and sustain desired attitudes and beliefs.[65]

Work Organization and Job Design

If quality is to be improved, there is no better place to start than with the way work is organized and the way jobs are designed. Since each industry and its jobs present special problems to be solved, it is possible to present only some general prescriptions. Jacquie Mansell and Tom Rankin of the Ontario Quality of Working Life Centre have developed criteria for designing organizational structures and processes, including jobs, for high QWL. These criteria are presented in Highlights in HRM 2. We will discuss specific ways of making jobs more meaningful and more satisfying in Chapter 5. Other aspects of job design and such work arrangements as job rotation, flexible working hours, and job sharing that contribute to QWL will also be discussed in that chapter.

Empowerment and Participative Management

Participative management

A system of management that enables employees to participate in decisions relating to their work and employment conditions, thereby creating a psychological partnership between management and employees.

Essential to TQM is employee empowerment and the development of **participative management**. By involving employees in decisions relating to their work and employment conditions, firms can create a solid psychological partnership with employees. Unfortunately, at times efforts to provide a more participative environment are resisted by managers and viewed with suspicion by employees. Nevertheless, empowerment and participation are realities of today's business environment. Enlightened organizational leaders recognize that basic changes in relations between employers and employees are essential.[66] Many are also convinced that bringing workers into the decision-making process offers the best opportunity to improve quality and productivity. If only for reasons of survival, both sides must recognize that they have a mutual interest in working together to reduce costs and avoid becoming victims of foreign and domestic competition. Thus there is a strong incentive to work jointly to reduce costs and improve quality. Caterpillar and General Motors, through their QWL programs, are making substantial progress in providing avenues for employee input.

HIGHLIGHTS IN HRM

HRM
highlights

2 STRUCTURES AND PROCESSES FOR A HIGH-QUALITY WORKING LIFE

1. Decisions are made at the lowest level possible. *Self-regulation* for individuals and groups is a primary goal.
2. Individuals or integrated groups of workers are responsible for a *whole job.* People do not work on fragmented, meaningless tasks.
3. The *potential* (technical and social) of individuals, of groups, and of the overall organization is developed to the fullest.
4. Hierarchies are minimized and *artificial barriers do not exist* between people or between functions.
5. *Quality and quality control* are built directly into the primary production system.
6. *Safety and health* are built directly into the total system.
7. Support systems and structures promote and support *self-regulation, integration, and flexibility.* For example, information systems provide immediate feedback directly to those who need the information in order to perform their job; information is not used to retain power or to police others.
8. *Problems are resolved on the basis of joint control and shared responsibility* between all groups. Structures and processes for the sharing of decision-making powers are guaranteed at all levels in the organization.

Source: Jacquie Mansell and Tom Rankin, *Changing Organizations: The Quality of Working Life Process* (Toronto, ON: Ontario Quality of Working Life Centre, September 1983), 10–11. Reproduced with permission of the authors.

Supportive Organizational Culture

Over the years, much has been written about firms such as 3M, Procter & Gamble, and Hewlett-Packard that are noted for the quality of their products and services and their relationships with people both outside and inside the organization. These companies are well known for the attention they give to HR and the work environments they have created and nurtured. The credo of Johnson & Johnson, reproduced in Highlights in HRM 3, conveys the attitudes characteristic of these companies.

In the past decade, **organizational culture** has been viewed as an intangible but real and important factor in determining the organizational climate. The conventional wisdom about culture is that it is "the glue that holds the organization together." Organizational culture is defined as the shared philosophies, values, assumptions, beliefs, expectations, attitudes, and norms that knit an organization together. It may also be defined as "the way things are done around here."[67] For example, everyone at Hewlett-Packard knows that employees are expected to be

Organizational culture
The shared philosophies, values, assumptions, beliefs, expectations, attitudes, and norms that knit an organization together.

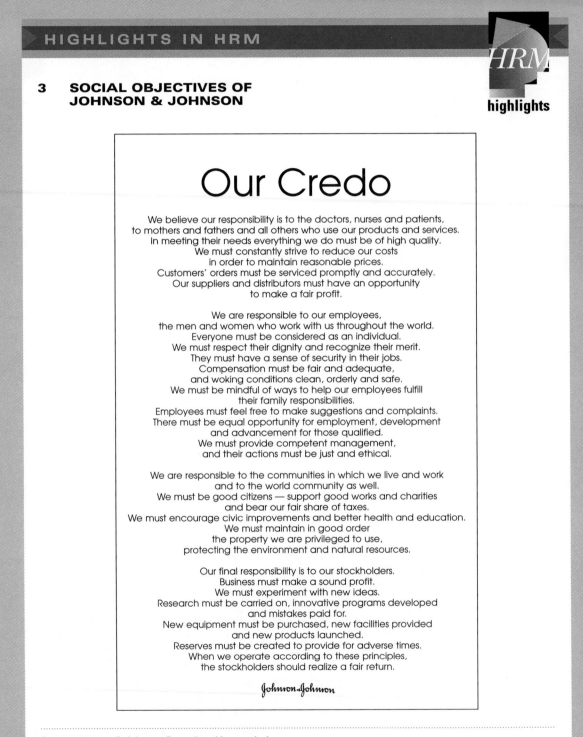

3 SOCIAL OBJECTIVES OF JOHNSON & JOHNSON

Our Credo

We believe our responsibility is to the doctors, nurses and patients,
to mothers and fathers and all others who use our products and services.
In meeting their needs everything we do must be of high quality.
We must constantly strive to reduce our costs
in order to maintain reasonable prices.
Customers' orders must be serviced promptly and accurately.
Our suppliers and distributors must have an opportunity
to make a fair profit.

We are responsible to our employees,
the men and women who work with us throughout the world.
Everyone must be considered as an individual.
We must respect their dignity and recognize their merit.
They must have a sense of security in their jobs.
Compensation must be fair and adequate,
and woking conditions clean, orderly and safe.
We must be mindful of ways to help our employees fulfill
their family responsibilities.
Employees must feel free to make suggestions and complaints.
There must be equal opportunity for employment, development
and advancement for those qualified.
We must provide competent management,
and their actions must be just and ethical.

We are responsible to the communities in which we live and work
and to the world community as well.
We must be good citizens — support good works and charities
and bear our fair share of taxes.
We must encourage civic improvements and better health and education.
We must maintain in good order
the property we are privileged to use,
protecting the environment and natural resources.

Our final responsibility is to our stockholders.
Business must make a sound profit.
We must experiment with new ideas.
Research must be carried on, innovative programs developed
and mistakes paid for.
New equipment must be purchased, new facilities provided
and new products launched.
Reserves must be created to provide for adverse times.
When we operate according to these principles,
the stockholders should realize a fair return.

Johnson & Johnson

Source: Johnson & Johnson. Reproduced by permission.

innovative. Everyone at Mary Kay Cosmetics knows the philosophy of the chair emeritus of the board, Mary Kay Ash:

> *People come first at Mary Kay Cosmetics—our beauty consultants, sales directors and employees, our customers, and our suppliers. We pride ourselves as a "company known for the people it keeps." Our belief in caring for people, however, does not conflict with our need as a corporation to generate a profit. Yes, we keep our eye on the bottom line, but it's not an overriding obsession. To me, P and L doesn't only mean profit and loss— it also means people and love.*[68]

In her book *Mary Kay on People Management*, Ash describes how managers can develop an organizational culture and provide leadership that is based on the golden rule. Unlike most management books, which are written by and for men, her book is written for women and men who aspire to be effective managers.[69]

An increasing number of larger firms, including Bank of Montreal, are receiving widespread acclaim for their supportive cultures. While each of these companies has its own unique culture, team spirit is a characteristic they all share. In addition to what observers have noted about these and other companies, the findings from two research studies of employees show a positive correlation between employees' perception of being valued and cared about by the firm and (1) conscientiousness in carrying out conventional job responsibilities, (2) expressed emotional involvement in the organization, and (3) innovative work for the organization, even in the absence of anticipated reward or personal recognition.[70]

Elements of culture. Terrence Deal and Allan Kennedy made an exhaustive study of the organizational literature from the 1950s to the early 1980s to understand better the elements that make up a strong culture. They found five elements, which they describe as follows:

1. *Business environment.* Each organization carries on certain kinds of activities—e.g., selling, inventing, conducting research. Its business environment is the single greatest influence in shaping its culture.
2. *Values.* These are basic concepts and beliefs that define "success" in concrete terms for employees—e.g., "If you do this, you too will be a success."
3. *Heroes.* People who personify the culture's values provide tangible role models for employees to follow. Organizations with strong cultures have many heroes.
4. *Rites and rituals.* The systematic and programmed routines (rituals) of day-to-day life in the organization show employees the kind of behaviour that is expected of them and what the organization stands for.
5. *Cultural network.* Through informal communication the corporate values are spread throughout the firm.[71]

A strong culture not only spells out how people are to behave, it also enables people to feel better about what they do, causing them to work harder.

Keeping culture contemporary. We observed earlier in this chapter that there are many changes taking place in our society that affect HRM. Organizations with strong cultures must be able to adapt to these changes and at the same time retain their basic philosophy. And organizations must find ways to keep their cultures current—that is, support efforts to adapt to changes in the competitive environment. IBM, for example, is making feverish attempts to be more flexible and responsive in order to compete with foreign and domestic competition. When Louis Gerstner was brought in as the company's new CEO, he noted that fixing a "broken culture" is the most crucial—and difficult—part of a corporate transformation. To revamp the culture, Gerstner is working to encourage cooperation among divisions, as well as to foster trust and teamwork. Left unchecked, managers and employees over time may become risk-averse and turf-conscious. To stay on top, Gerstner argues that he must eliminate unnecessary bureaucracy and infuse the firm with "china breakers," employees with innovative ideas who challenge the status quo.[72]

Intrapreneurs
Employees who remain in the organization but are given freedom to create new products, services, and/or production methods.

Along these lines, other organizations have also pushed hard to encourage employees to become entrepreneurs or innovators on the job. Since they remain in the employ of the firm but are given freedom to create new products, services, and production methods, these innovative workers are referred to as **intrapreneurs**. G. Pinchot defines this people-based approach to innovative management as allowing "entrepreneurs ... freedom and incentive to do their best in small groups within large corporations."[73] Often the results of such activities lead to the organization of a new division or subsidiary. Among the better-known divisions or subsidiaries devoted to intrapreneurship are the Colgate Venture Company, General Foods' Culinova Unit, and Scott Paper's Do-It-Yourself Group.[74]

Employers are beginning to recognize that if the spirit of intrapreneurism is to exist beyond the lifespan of a fad, it must be nurtured. Not only should intrapreneurs be given special recognition, but incentives and rewards should be customized on an individual basis. To quote one writer, "A major roadblock to the nurturing of intrapreneurs is often the compensation manager whose traditional interests are control and consistency."[75]

The challenge for management in the coming decades will be to maintain a balance between the fact of rapid change and the need for stability. Since the focus of managers is on human performance and everything that affects it, they should not lose sight of their responsibility to keep the culture open and flexible.

SUMMARY

one
objective

The internal and external environments of an organization can have a significant impact on the productivity of its human resources and on their management. For this reason, managers must be aware of the impact these environments—and the changes occurring within them—may have on their programs. The failure of management in many organizations to anticipate and cope effectively with these changes is one of the principal causes for the declining rate of productivity growth.

two
objective

Technology influences both the number of employees needed as well as the skills they require. This has the effect of reducing the number of jobs for "touch labour" and increasing the number of jobs for "knowledge workers." HR must take a leadership role in helping managers cope with technological change, identifying the skills needed of employees, training new employees, and retraining current employees. Technology has also changed HRM by altering the methods of collecting employment information, speeding data-processing efforts, and improving the process of internal and external communication.

objective

The regulatory system begins with social and political problems that prompt lawmakers to pass laws. These laws then empower agencies such as the Human Rights Commission, and the Workers' Compensation Board to ensure compliance. These agencies make certain that management has initiated actions that bring their practices under compliance with the law. In those cases where compliance is not met, courts oversee the process of settling disputes between the parties involved.

objective

While changes are taking place in many areas that affect HRM, those related to demographics include the rising number of minorities and immigrants, the aging workforce and decreasing number of 16- to 24-year-olds, the influx of women in the workforce, and the education and skills gap.

objective

To improve quality and increase productivity, many organizations have begun to rethink their approaches to human resource management. These efforts include an emphasis on teamwork, job design, empowerment and participative management, and the building of a supportive organizational culture. All of these efforts reflect the increasing responsiveness of employers to the changes that affect the management of their human resources.

objective

The elements of organizational culture include the business environment, values and beliefs that define success; heroes and role models; rites and rituals that show employees the kind of behaviour expected; and an informal communications network through which organizational values are spread throughout the firm.

KEY TERMS

environment	knowledge workers
external environment	organizational culture
environmental scanning	participative management
internal environment	quality of work life (QWL)
(organizational climate)	sociotechnical system
intrapreneurs	telecommuting
issues management	total quality management (TQM)

1. What impact will the growing proportion of women and the rising level of education in the workforce have on HRM?
2. What are some of the issues employers may encounter with respect to government regulation of HRM?
3. What are some of the jobs that can be performed by telecommuting? How is telecommuting likely to affect superior–subordinate relationships?
4. How do employee demands for more rights affect HRM?
5. It is generally recognized that today's employees are seeking a more balanced lifestyle. What effect does this have on HR policies and procedures?
6. Describe the culture of an organization with which you have been associated. What are its values, who are its heroes, and what rites and rituals does it use to reinforce the culture?
7. What can the management of an organization do to encourage intrapreneuring?
8. What is your opinion concerning the governmental regulation of HRM? Do you consider the amount of regulation to be excessive? Insufficient? About right? What would your viewpoint be if you were an employer? A union leader?

CASE: The High-Performance Workplace

HR managers have witnessed many changes in the last two decades. Since the late 1970s, economic performance has deteriorated, productivity is down, income growth is down, and general employment security is down. Manufacturing jobs are declining, while jobs in the service sector are increasing. Business competition within Canada and globally has increased, and managers identify this competition as their number one concern. Information technology has not only changed the ways in which we do work, but the type of workers that organizations need to employ. The labour force is now composed of more women, more visible minorities, more senior workers, and more highly educated baby boomers.

Paradoxically, organizations are reporting shortages of highly skilled workers, at the same time as they are developing downsizing options to deal with employee surpluses. Workplace innovations demand the commitment of empowered, participating employees with deep training, but employer outsourcing and contracting out has never been higher.

In studies conducted by the Industrial Relations Centre at Queen's University, two HRM strategies were reported as a response to these turbulent changes. One path—the low labour–low cost path—has been undertaken by most organizations in the survey. The goal of this approach is the reduction of costs, both labour and nonlabour. Firms employing this strategy lay off workers, do not engage in skills training, and employ nonstandard workers.

A second (and emerging) path is the high-performance model. It builds on Michael Porter's differentiation strategy in which an organization seeks to compete through product innovation, quality, service, and specialization. Characteristic of this approach is a flexible work organization, a commitment to training, employee involvement and participation in decision making, and policies to promote the sharing of benefits and risks. The studies found some tentative links between this path and firm performance.

Source: G. Betcherman, K. McMullen, N. Leckie, and C.Caron, *The Canadian Workplace in Transition,* (Kingston, ON: IRC Press, Queen's University, 1994).

Questions
1. What are the advantages and limitations of both the low labour–low cost path and the high performance model?
2. Why is the high performance model not more widely diffused in Canada?
3. What is the role of the union within each strategy?

Self-Employment

Labour market statistics demonstrate that more and more people are working in nonstandard employment relationships, such as contract work and part-time work. Additionally, the number of people starting small businesses is increasing, particularly among women and in the service sector. Therefore, it is likely that at some point in your career you will be self-employed.

Some people dream about becoming entrepreneurs, not because of the economic restructuring factors cited above, but because they want control of their own destinies. Should you consider self-employment? The following quiz will help you determine if you have the characteristics most often associated with entrepreneurs.

PART A: Personality Traits
Rate yourself on the items listed below using the following scale:

–2	Disagree Strongly
–1	Disagree
0	Neutral or Don't Know
+1	Agree
+2	Strongly Agree

Characteristic:

	–2	–1	0	+1	+2
1. I have a high need to achieve.					
2. I believe that effort and energy are more important that fate or luck in determining my future.					
3. I am not easily defeated and I rarely give up.					
4. I see opportunities, not problems.					
5. I really value independence.					
6. I prefer moderate risks.					
7. I want control over my own destiny.					
8. I am determined.					
9. I don't like being controlled by others.					
10. I have a lot of energy.					
TOTAL					

PART B: Sociological Factors
Indicate which of the following apply to you:

Factor:

1. My father was self-employed.

2. I or my parents are immigrants.

3. I had a role model who was an entrepreneur.

4. I am the first born (or only child) in my family.

5. I am a member of a minority group.

6. I had a serious displacement experience while growing up. (family bankruptcy, death of a parent, political upheaval or war, etc.)

7. I was self-employed as a teenager.

TOTAL

	Yes	No

Scoring:
Part A lists the personality traits possessed by entrepreneurs. The scoring range is from minus 20 to plus 20. The more positive your score, the more you are like an entrepreneur. Part B lists the demographic and sociological factors found to be part of many entrepreneurs' backgrounds. The more "yes's" you note, the more your background resembles that of entrepreneurs.

Note: These scales do not predict success or failure as an entrepreneur.

....

Sources: M. Belcourt, "Variables Influencing Entrepreneurial Activity," *Proceedings, Administrative Sciences Association of Canada*, Vol. 3, No. 5, 1982; M. Belcourt, "Sociological Correlates of Entrepreneurship," *Journal of Small Business Management*, Vol. 4, No. 3 (Winter), 1987a; M. Belcourt, "The Family Incubator Model of Entrepreneurship," *Journal of Entrepreneurship and Small Business*, Vol. 5, No. 3 (Winter), 1988–89.

NOTES AND REFERENCES

1. James R. Nininger, "Human Resource Priorities in the 1980s," *Canadian Business Review* 7, no. 4 (Winter 1980): 11.

2. M.V. George, M.J. Norris, F. Nault, S. Loy, and S.Y. Dai, "1991 Census Mobility and Migrations," *Statistics Canada Technical Reports* (Ottawa: Ministry of Industry, Science and Technology, 1995), 1–103, Cat No. 92–326E.

3. K. McMullen, N. Leckie, and C. Caron, *Innovation at Work: The Workplace Technology Survey 1980–91*, HRM Project Series (Kingston, ON: IRC Press, Queen's University, 1993).

4. Gary T. Marx and Sanford Sherizen, "Corporations That Spy on Their Employees," *Business and Society Review* 60 (Winter 1987): 32–37; Rebecca Grant and Christopher Higgins, "Monitoring Service Workers via Computer: The Effect on Employees, Productivity, and Service," *National Productivity Review* 8, no. 2 (Spring 1989): 101–112; Marco A. Monsalve and Arlene Triplett, "Maximizing New Technology," *HR Magazine* (March 1990): 85–87.

5. James W. Dean, Jr., and Scott A. Snell, "Integrated Manufacturing and Job Design: Moderating Effects of Organizational Inertia," *Academy of Management Journal* 34, no. 4 (1991): 776–804. See also Walter Kiechel, III, "How We Will Work in the Year 2000," *Fortune*, May 17, 1993, 38–52.

6. Scott A. Snell and James W. Dean, Jr., "Integrated Manufacturing and Human Resource Management: A Human Capital Perspective," *Academy of Management Journal* 35, no. 3 (1992): 467–504.

7. Marco A. Monsalve and Arlene Triplett, "Maximizing New Technology," *HR Magazine* (March 1990): 85–87.

8. Colin Richards-Carpenter, "Bright Ideas from Systems Users," *Personnel Management* (February 1992): 19–20.

9. Brian Dumaine, "Why Do We Work?" *Fortune*, December 26, 1994, 196–204; and Myron Magnet, "You Don't Have to Be a Workaholic," *Fortune*, August 9, 1993, 64. See also Marlys Harris, "What's Wrong with This Picture?" *Working Woman* (December 1990): 72–76; and Charlene Marmer Solomon, "Managing the Baby Busters," *Personnel Journal* (March 1992): 52–59.

10. G. Betcherman, K. McMullen, N. Leckie, and C. Caron, *The Canadian Workplace in Transition* (Kingston, ON: IRC Press, Queens' University, 1994).

11. R.G. Lipsey, D.D. Purvis, G.R. Sparks, and P.O. Steiner *Economics* (New York: Harper & Row, 1982), 233.

12. *Canada, Jobs and Growth: Building a More Innovative Economy* (Ottawa: Minister of Supply and Services Canada, 1994), 8–9, Cat. No. C2–254.

13. John W. Mayo, "The U.S. Economic Outlook: A Turn for the Better?" *Survey of Business* (Winter 1993): 16–20. See also Evangelos O. Simos and John E. Triantis, eds., "International Economic Outlook," *Journal of Business Forecasting* (Spring 1993): 30–37.

14. Mayo, "U.S. Economic Outlook"; Simos and Triantis, "International Economic Outlook."

15. "North American Free Trade Agreement," *HR Magazine* (December 1991): 85–86. See also "The Mexican Worker," *Business Week*, April 19, 1993, 84–92.

16. Canada, "Jobs and Growth," 8.

17. Alistair Mant, "Putting Humanity Back into Human Resources," *Personnel Management* (January 1992): 24–27.

18. "The Competency Initiative: Standards of Excellence for Human Resource Executives," Society for Human Resource Management Foundation (1990). See also "Priorities for Competitive Advantage" in A 21st Century Vision: A Worldwide Human Resource Study, an IBM study conducted by Towers Perrin (1992); and Stephenie Overman, "Reaching for the 21st Century," *HR Magazine* (April 1992): 61–63.

19. Donna Brown, "HR Is the Key to Survival in the '90s," *HR Magazine* (March 1991): 5–6.

20. A.Templer and J. Ladouceur, "Northern Exposure: Can Canadian HR managers meet the challenges in the 90's?" *Human Resources Professional* (June/July 1994), 14–18.

21. William H. Miller, "A New Perspective for Tomorrow's Workforce," *Industry Week* (May 6, 1991): 7–8.

22. E.B. Akeyeampong, "The Labour Market: Year End Review" *Perspectives* (Spring 1995), Statistics Canada, Cat. No. 75–001E.

23. J. Berridge, "Is Toronto Different from US Cities? Was It Planned That Way?" *The Globe and Mail*, April 10, 1995, A13.

24. R. Lattimer, "Managing Workforce Diversity: Problems Similar in Canada and U.S.," *Towers Perrin Focus* (Spring 1993): 9–10.

25. J. Badets and T.W.L. Chui, "Canada's Changing Immigrant Population: Focus on Canada" (Ottawa: Statistics Canada, Ministry of Industry, Science and Technology, 1994), Cat. No. 96–311E.

26. *Workforce 2000* (Toronto: Hudson Institute Canada and Towers Perrin, 1993).

27. Anthony Redwood, "Human Resources in the 1990s," *Business Horizons* (January/February 1990): 6–12.

28. D. Kerr, D. Larivee, P. Greenhalgh, "Children and Youth: An Overview" (Ottawa: Statistics Canada, Ministry of Industry, Science and Tourism, 1994), 1, 5, 74, Cat. No. 96–320E.

29. "Tomorrow's Jobs," *Occupational Outlook Handbook*, 1992–1993 edition (Washington, DC: Bureau of Labor Statistics, bulletin no. 2400, May 1992), 8–14.

30. Redwood, "Human Resources in the 1990s."

31. Nancy J. Perry, "Workers of the Future," *Fortune*, Spring/Summer 1991, 68–72.

32. *Workforce 2000*.

33. Joseph Pereira, "Women Allege Sexist Atmosphere in Offices Constitutes Harassment," *The Wall Street Journal*, February 10, 1988, 23; Louise F. Fitzgerald, "Sexual Harassment: Violence against Women in the Workplace," *American Psychologist* (October 1993): 1070–1076; and Ronni Sandroff, "Sexual Harassment: The Inside Story," *Working Woman* (June 1992): 47–78.

34. J. Gartley, *Earnings of Canadians* (Ottawa: Statistics Canada, Ministry of Industry, Science and Technology, 1994) Cat. No. 96–317E.

35. Ronald E. Kutscher, "Outlook 1990–2005: Major Trends and Issues," *Occupational Outlook Quarterly* (Spring 1992): 2–5.

36. B. McKenna, "Rough Road Ahead for Unemployed Youth," *The Globe and Mail*, January 14, 1993, B1.

37. "Occupation," *1991 Census of Canada* (Ottawa: Statistics Canada, Ministry of Industry, Science and Technology, 1993), 7; and A. Mitchell, "Members of Minorities Hold More Degrees," *The Globe and Mail*, June 14, 1995, A1, A6.

38. G. Montigny, K. Kelly, and S. Jones, "Adult Literacy in Canada: Results of a National Study, Part I" (Ottawa: Statistics Canada, Labour and Household Surveys Division, Ministry of Industry, Science and Technology, 1991), 1–46.

39. Workplace 2000.

40. H.S. Horne, "Literacy in the Workplace," *Atlantic Lifestyle Business* 6, no. 3: 17–19.

41. Anita K. Ross, "IBM Canada's Involvement in Education," *Canadian Business Review* 17, no. 3 (Autumn 1990): 21–23.

42. M. Belcourt and P. Wright, *Managing Performance throughout Training and Development* (Scarborough, ON: Nelson Canada, 1995), 9, 11.

43. Akyeampong, "The Labour Market."

44. "Tomorrow's Jobs."

45. N. Noreau, "Involuntary Part-Timers," *Perspectives on Labour and Income* (Ottawa: Statistics Canada, Autumn 1994) 25–30, Cat. No.75–001E.

46. Jaclyn Fierman, "The Contingency Workforce," *Fortune*, January 1994, 30–36. See also Michael R. Losey, "Temps: They're Not Just for Typing Anymore," *Modern Office Technology* (August 1991): 58–59; Louis S. Richman, "CEOs to Workers: Help Not Wanted," *Fortune*, July 12, 1993, 42–43; and Linda Dickens, "Part–Time Employees: Workers Whose Time Has Come?" *Employee Relations* 14, no. 2 (1992): 3–12.

47. R. Williamson, "Tradition Giving Way to World of Freelancers," *The Globe and Mail*, January 15, 1995, B1, B4.

48. C. Howard, "Short Term Jobs Attract Three Kinds of Executives," *The Globe and Mail*, March 28, 1995, A24.

49. Barbara J. Risman and Donald Tomaskovic–Devey, "The Social Construction of Technology: Microcomputers and the Organization of Work," *Business Horizons* 32, no. 3 (May–June 1989): 71–75.

50. Lynne F. McGee, "Setting Up Work at Home," *Personnel Administrator* 33, no. 12 (December 1988): 58–62.

51. John Mascotte, "Business Is Still Structured Like Fourth Grade," *Business Week*, June 28, 1993, 86; Barbara J. Farrah and Cheryl D. Dagen, "Telecommuting Policies That Work," *HR Magazine* (July 1993): 64–71. See also "Vanishing Offices," *The Wall Street Journal*, June 4, 1993, A1.

52. John P. Robinson, "Time's Up," *American Demographics* 11, no. 7 (July 1989): 33–35. See also Dumaine, "Why Do We Work?"

53. Harris, "What's Wrong with This Picture?" See also Patricia Sellers, "Don't Call Me a Slacker," *Fortune*, December 12, 1994, 180–196.

54. T. McCallum, "The Old 'Seven to Three': Restructured Work Weeks Enable Employees to Strike a Healthy Balance between Work and Family," *Human Resources Professional*, 12, no. 4 (June 1995): 12–14. See also M. Gibb-Clark, "Leaves of Absence Gaining Popularity," *The Globe and Mail*, March 30, 1992, B4.

55. "Quality of Life and a Law Career?" *The Financial Post*, October 31, 1991, 16.

56. D. Galarneau and J.P. Maynard, "Measuring Productivity," *Perspectives on Labour and Income* (Ottawa: Statistics Canada, Spring 1995), 26–32, Cat. No. 75–001E.

57. R. Krishnan, A.B. Rami Shani, R.M. Grant, and R. Baer, "In Search of Quality Improvement: Problems of Design and Implementation," *Academy of Management Executive* (November 1993): 7–20.

58. Thomas A. Stewart, "Allied-Signal's Turnaround Blitz," *Fortune*, November 30, 1992, 72–76.

59. Y.K. Shetty, "The Human Side of Product Quality," *National Productivity Review* 8, no. 2 (Spring 1989): 175–182. See also Rosabeth Moss Kanter, Barry A. Stein, and Todd Jick, *The Challenge of Organizational Change—How People Experience It and Manage It* (New York: Free Press, 1991).

60. Richard Blackburn and Benson Rosen, "Total Quality and Human Resources Management: Lessons Learned from Baldrige Award-Winning Companies," *Academy of Management Executive* 7, no. 3 (1993): 49–66.

61. George W. Bohlander and Angelo J. Kinicki, "Where Personnel and Productivity Meet," *Personnel Administrator* 33, no. 9 (September 1988): 122–130.

62. Richard G. Linowes, "The Japanese Manager's Traumatic Entry into the United States: Understanding the American-Japanese Cultural Divide," *Academy of Management Executive* (November 1993): 21–40.

63. Jon R. Katzenbach and Douglas K. Smith, *The Wisdom of Teams: Creating the High Performance Organization* (Cambridge, MA: Harvard Business School, 1993).

64. Perry, "Workers of the Future."

65. Robert T. Golembiewski and Ben-chu Sun, "QWL Improves Worksite Quality: Success Rates in a Large Pool of Studies," *Human Resource Development Quarterly* 1, no. 1 (Spring 1990): 35–43. See also "Evolution of the Workplace: Reich Presses Worker Involvement," *USA Today*, July 28, 1993, 4B.

66. Brian O'Reilly, "The New Deal: What Companies and Employees Owe One Another," *Fortune*, June 13, 1994, 44–52.

67. An interesting technique for studying an organization's culture is outlined in W. Jack Duncan, "Organizational Culture: 'Getting a Fix' on an Elusive Concept," *Academy of Management Executive* 3, no. 3 (August 1989): 229–236.

68. Mary Kay Ash, *Mary Kay on People Management* (New York: Warner Books, 1984), xix. See also Mary Kay Ash, *Mary Kay* (New York: Harper & Row, 1981); Richard E. Hattwick, "Mary Kay Ash," *The Journal of Behavioral Economics* 16 (Winter 1987): 61–69; and Alan Farnham, "Mary Kay's Lessons in Leadership," *Fortune*, September 20, 1993, 68–77.

69. Ash, *Mary Kay on People Management*, xviii–xix.

70. Kenneth Labich, "Hot Company, Warm Culture," *Fortune*, February 27, 1989, 74–78; John Huey, "Wal–Mart—Will It Take Over the World?" *Fortune*, January 30, 1989, 52–61. See also Robert Eisenberger, Peter Fasolo, and Valerie Davis-LaMastro, "Perceived Organizational Support and Employee Diligence,

Commitment, and Innovation," *Journal of Applied Psychology* 75, no. 1 (1990): 51–59.

71. Terrence E. Deal and Allan A. Kennedy, *Corporate Cultures: The Rites and Rituals of Corporate Life* (Reading, MA: Addison-Wesley, 1982), 7. See also Benjamin Schneider, ed., *Organizational Climate and Culture* (San Francisco: Jossey-Bass, 1990).

72. Patricia Sellers and David Kirkpatrick, "Can This Man Save IBM?" *Fortune*, April 19, 1993, 63–67.

73. G. Pinchot, "Intrapreneurialism for Corporations," *The Futurist* (February 1984): 82–83. See also Peter F. Drucker, *Innovation and Entrepreneurship—Practice and Principles* (New York: Harper & Row, 1985); and Philip R. Harris, *Management in Transition* (San Francisco: Jossey-Bass, 1985), Chapter 3. For an interesting biography of probably America's greatest intrapreneur, see Stuart W. Leslie, *Boss Kettering—Wizard of General Motors* (New York: Columbia University Press, 1983).

74. Ronald Alsop, "Consumer-Product Grants Relying on 'Intrapreneurs' in New Ventures," *The Wall Street Journal*, April 22, 1988, A25.

75. Kirkland Ropp, "Bringing Up Baby: Nurturing Intrapreneurs," *Personnel Administrator* 32, no. 6 (June 1987): 92–96. See also W. Jack Duncan, Peter M. Guites, Andrew C. Ruchs, and T. Douglas Jacobs, "Intrapreneurship and the Reinvention of the Corporation," *Business Horizons* 31, no. 3 (May-June 1988): 16–21.

Chapter 3

Equity and Diversity in Human Resources Management

After studying this chapter, you should be able to

objective one
Discuss the employment status of the four designated groups.

objective two
Identify and describe the major laws affecting employment equity and explain how they are enforced.

objective three
Describe pay equity and strategies for implementing it.

objective four
Discuss the Employment Equity Act in terms of its origins, its purpose, and its continued enforcement.

objective five
Describe how employment equity is implemented within organizations.

objective six
Discuss reverse discrimination, sexual harassment, and mandatory retirement as employment equity issues.

objective seven
Explain and give examples of diversity management.

Employment equity

The employment of individuals in a fair and nonbiased manner.

W ithin *the field of HRM, perhaps no topic has received more attention during the last decades than employment equity.* **Employment equity**, *or the treatment of employed individuals in a fair and nonbiased manner, has attracted the attention of the media, the courts, practitioners, and legislators. Employment equity legislation affects all aspects of the employment relationship. When managers ignore the legal aspects of HRM, they risk incurring costly and time-consuming litigation, negative public attitudes, and damage to organization moral.*

Employment equity is not only a legal topic; it is also an emotional issue. It concerns all individuals regardless of their sex, race, religion, age, national origin, colour, or position in an organization. Supervisors should be aware of their personal biases and how these attitudes can influence their dealings with subordinates. It should be emphasized that covert, as well as blatantly intentional, discrimination in employment is illegal.

The legislation governing employment equity will be emphasized in this chapter. The organizational response to this legislation is described. Compliance with employment equity has evolved into the management of diversity as a means to optimizing the utilization of human capital within organizations.

objective

Employment Equity

Central to Canada's economic growth and prosperity in a highly competitive global marketplace will be a barrier-free environment in which all Canadians can fully explore and develop their career potential. Labour-force statistics, described in Chapter 2, indicated changing patterns of immigration, the rising labour-force participation rates of women, and an aging population with a proportionally higher incidence of disabilities. Women, visible minorities, and persons with disabilities make up over 60 percent of Canada's labour force, and their numbers continue to rise. The designated group members entering Canada's labour pool constitute a vital resource, and their full participation in the workplace will be fundamental to an organization's ability to understand and respond to the needs of a rapidly changing marketplace. As a society, we have moved beyond principle to imperative in ensuring equal access to employment opportunities.[1]

Equity by definition means fairness or impartiality. In a legal sense, it means justice based on the concepts of ethics and fairness and a system of jurisprudence administered by courts and designed primarily to mitigate the rigours of common law. There are four **designated groups** in Canada that have not received equitable treatment in employment.

Designated groups

Women, visible minorities, aboriginal peoples, and persons with disabilities who have been disadvantaged in employment.

Status of Designated Groups

Women, aboriginal peoples, visible minorities, and persons with disabilities face significant but different disadvantages in employment. Some of these include high unemployment, occupational segregation, pay inequities, and limited opportunities for career progress.

Women tend to be concentrated in occupations that are accorded lower status and pay. In 1986, women constituted 44 percent of the total workforce but were not equally represented in all occupations. For example, they held only 17 percent of upper-level manager positions. Women were also underrepresented in skilled crafts and trades occupations, where they made up 8 percent of the workforce. In comparison, 14 percent of the semiskilled manual occupations and 29 percent of other manual occupations were held by women. Conversely, almost 80 percent of all clerical workers and 61 percent of all service workers were women.[2]

The numbers of young aboriginal workers will increase dramatically in the 1990s, and in western Canada will account for a substantial portion of labour market growth. However, many aboriginals face major employment barriers, which may be compounded by low educational achievement and lack of job experience, as well as language and cultural barriers. In urban centres, many aboriginal workers are concentrated in low-paying, unstable employment.

The unemployment rate for employable persons with disabilities is 20 percent, compared to the national unemployment rate of 10 percent. Persons with disabilities face attitudinal barriers, physical demands that are unrelated to actual job requirements, and inadequate access to the technical and human support systems that would make productive employment possible. Employers seek to redress attitudinal barriers by focusing on abilities, not disabilities, as illustrated in Highlights in HRM 1.

Visible minority groups vary in their labour-force profiles and in their regional distributions. Studies have shown that Latin Americans and Southeast Asians experience lower than average incomes, higher rates of unemployment, and reduced access to job interviews, even for those persons with the same qualifications as other candidates. Black Nova Scotians have faced disadvantages in employment for many years. The unemployment rate of blacks is higher in Nova Scotia (25 percent) than in any other province except Prince Edward Island, where a small number of blacks reside. Systemic barriers that have a negative employment impact on visible minorities can include culturally biased aptitude tests, lack of recognition of foreign credentials, and excessive levels of language requirements. Recent statistics indicate that although visible minorities, 75 percent of whom are immigrants, possess higher educational achievements, they also have the highest unemployment rates.[3]

Between 1987 and 1990, women and visible minorities fared best in federally regulated organizations. Figure 3-1 shows that the workforce representation of women increased by nearly 3 percent while that of members of visible minorities increased by 5 percent over the same four-year period.

Benefits of Employment Equity

Employment equity makes good business sense since it contributes to the bottom line by broadening the base of qualified individuals for employment, training, and promotions, and by helping employers to avoid costly human rights complaints. Some of the benefits derived from implementing employment equity include enhanced means to attract and keep the best-qualified employees, which results in greater access to a broader base of skills; enhanced employee morale resulting from special measures employed such as flexible work schedules or work sharing; and improved corporate image in the community.[4]

In Canada, the Charter of Rights, the federal Canadian Human Rights Act, and pay equity and employment equity acts are the governing pieces of legislation dealing with employment equity.

HRM highlights

1 FOCUS ON ABILITIES

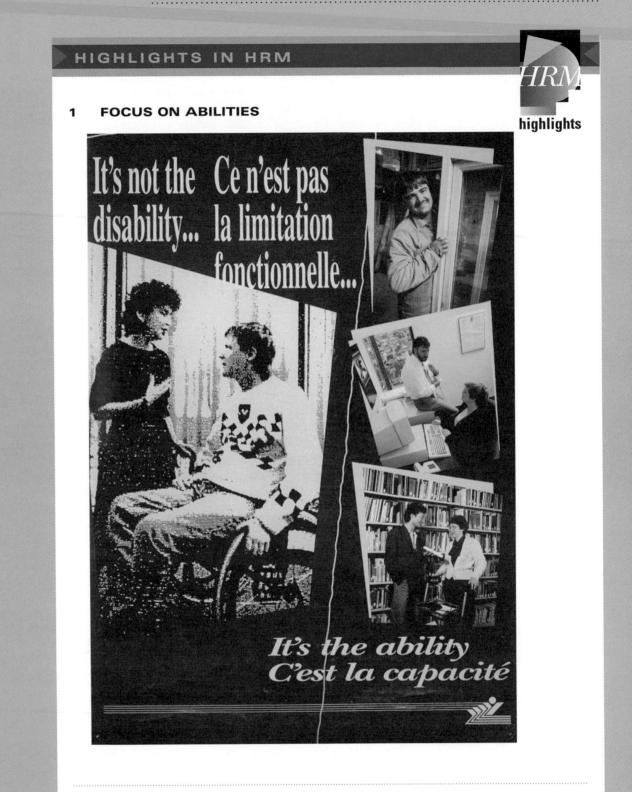

Source: Reproduced with permission of the Minister of Supply and Services.

> ### FIGURE 3-1   *Representation of Designated Groups in the Labour Force*

	REPRESENTATION IN THE CANADIAN LABOUR FORCE	REPRESENTATION IN THE WORKPLACE UNDER EE ACT, 1990	PERCENTAGE CHANGE, 1987–1990
Women	44.0	43.74	2.81
Aboriginal peoples	2.1	0.85	0.19
People with disabilities	5.4	2.39	0.80
Members of visible minorities	6.3	7.09	2.09

Source: *Statistical Summary, Employment Equity Act, 1987–1990,* Employment Equity Branch, Employment and Immigration Canada.

objective

The Legal Framework

The Charter of Rights and Freedoms

The Constitution Act of 1982, which contains the Canadian Charter of Rights and Freedoms, is the cornerstone of equity legislation. The Charter guarantees some fundamental rights to every Canadian, including:

- Fundamental freedoms (s. 2) that comprise the standard rights of freedom of speech, press, assembly, association and religion;
- Democratic rights (ss. 3 to 5), covering franchise rights;
- Mobility rights (s. 6), concerning the right to move freely from province to province for the purposes of residence and/or employment;
- Legal rights (ss. 7 to 14), conferring standard procedural rights in criminal proceedings;
- Equality rights (s. 15), guaranteeing no discrimination by law on grounds of race, ethnic origin, colour, religion, sex, age, or mental and physical ability; and
- Language rights (ss. 16 to 23).[5]

Although the Charter has offered many Canadians an opportunity in terms of their own individual rights and responsibilities, it has also been a source of disappointment. The enactment of the Charter created high expectations on the part of various groups, particularly unions, which believed that, under Section 2, all employees would have a fundamental right to associate and, furthermore, to bargain collectively and to strike. However, in 1987 the Supreme Court of Canada, in making its ruling on a challenge of federal public-sector laws that imposed compulsory arbitration for the right to strike, back-to-work legislation, and wage-restraint legislation, declared that Section 2 of the Charter does not include the right to bargain collectively and to strike. In the Court's view, these were not fundamental freedoms, but rather statutory rights created and regulated by the legislation. As a result of this ruling, governments can weaken the collective bargaining process by limiting salary increases, legislating strikers back to work, and imposing compulsory arbitration.

Canadian Human Rights Act (CHRA)

The Canadian Human Rights Act was passed by Parliament on July 14, 1977, and became effective March 1978. The Act proclaims:

> *every individual should have an equal opportunity with other individuals to make for himself or herself the life that he or she is able and wishes to have, consistent with his or her duties and obligations as a member of society, without being hindered in or prevented from doing so by discriminatory practices based on race, national or ethnic origin, colour, religion, age, sex or marital status, or convictions for an offence for which a pardon has been granted or by discriminatory employment practices based on physical handicap.*[6]

The Act applies to all federal government departments and agencies, to crown corporations, and to other business and industries under federal jurisdiction such as banks, airlines, railway companies, and insurance and communications companies.

For those areas not covered under federal jurisdiction, protection is available under provincial human rights laws. Provincial laws, although very similar to federal ones, do differ from province to province. All the provinces and the two territories have a human rights act or code, and each has jurisdiction prohibiting discrimination in the workplace.

The prohibited grounds of discrimination in employment include race, religion, sex, age, national or ethnic origin, physical handicap, and marital status (see Figure 3-2 for a complete listing). Employers are permitted to discriminate if employment preferences are based on a **bona fide occupational qualification (BFOQ)** or BFOR (bona fide occupational requirements). A BFOQ is justified if the employer can establish necessity for business operations. In other words, differential treatment is not discrimination if there is a justifiable reason. For example, adherence to the tenets of the Roman Catholic Church was deemed a BFOQ for employment as a teacher in a Roman Catholic school.[7] Business necessity is a practice that includes the safe and efficient operation of an organization. There is an ongoing debate as to whether male guards should be allowed to work in female prisons.

Bona fide occupational qualification (BFOQ)
A justifiable reason for discrimination based on business reasons of safety or effectiveness.

Enforcement of the Canadian Human Rights Act

The Canadian Human Rights Commission (CHRC) deals with complaints concerning discriminatory practices covered by the Canadian Human Rights Act. The CHRC may choose to act on its own if it feels there are sufficient grounds for a finding of discrimination. It also has the power to issue guidelines interpreting the Act. Highlights in HRM 2 summarizes the CHRC enforcement procedures.

Individuals have a right to file a complaint if they feel they have been discriminated against. (The CHRC may refuse to accept a complaint if it has not been filed within a prescribed period of time, if it is deemed trivial, or if it was filed in bad faith.) The complainant must first complete a written report describing the discriminatory action. A CHRC representative reviews the facts and determines if the claim

FIGURE 3-2   *Prohibited Grounds of Discrimination in Employment by Jurisdiction*

PROHIBITED GROUNDS OF DISCRIMINATION	FEDERAL	ALTA.	BC	MAN.	NB	NFLD.	NS	ONT.	PEI	QUE.	SASK.	NWT	YUKON
Race	•	•	•	•	•	•	•	•	•	•	•	•	•
Colour	•	•	•	•	•	•	•	•	•	•	•	•	•
Ethnic or national origin	•	•		•	•	•	•	•	•	•		•	•
Creed or religion	•	•	•	•	•	•	•	•	•	•	•	•	•
Sex	•	•	•	•	•	•	•	•	•	•	•	•	•
Marital status	•	•	•	•	•	•	•	•	•	•	•	•	•
Age	•	18+	46–65	•	19+	19–65	40–65	18–65	•	•	18–65	•	•
Mental handicap	•	•		•	•	•	•	•	•	•		•	•
Physical handicap	•	•	•	•	•	•	•	•	•	•	•	•	•
Pardoned offence	•											•	
Record of criminal conviction			•					•		•			•
Harassment[1]	•	•		•	•		•	•	•	•	•	•	•
Sexual orientation	•			•		•				•			
Language										•			

[1] The federal, Ontario, Quebec, and Yukon statutes ban harassment on all proscribed grounds. Manitoba prohibits sexual harassment.

Source: H.C. Jain and P.C. Wright, eds., *Trends and Challenges in Human Resource Management* (Scarborough, ON: Nelson Canada, 1994), 73.

is legitimate. Once a complaint has been accepted by the CHRC, an investigator is assigned to the case in order to gather more facts, from both the individual and the accused. The investigator submits a report to the CHRC recommending a finding of either substantiation or nonsubstantiation of the allegation. If the allegation is substantiated, a settlement may be arranged in the course of the investigation. If the parties are unable to reach agreement, a human rights tribunal consisting of up to three members may be appointed to further investigate the complaint. If the tribunal finds that a discriminatory practice did take place, or that the victim's feelings or self-respect have suffered as a result of the practice, it may order the person or organization responsible to compensate the victim. Former employees of Majestic Electronics received $300,000 in compensation because they were harassed after they refused to obey the racist and sexist orders of the company president.[8]

Any person who obstructs an investigation or a tribunal, or fails to comply with the terms of a settlement, can be found guilty of an offence that may be punishable by a fine and/or jail sentence. If the guilty party is an employer or an employee organization, the fine might be as high as $50,000 and up to $5000 for individuals.[9]

The Enforcement of Provincial Human Rights Laws

Provincial human rights laws are enforced in a manner very similar to that used in the federal system. The major difference between the two systems is that, at the federal level, federally regulated organizations tend to be larger and have more sophisticated HR systems and policies as well as more experienced HR professionals. At the provincial level, the employers tend to be small and medium-sized businesses, many of which lack an HR professional who is knowledgeable about human rights legislation. Employers and employees alike may have little experience in matters of discrimination.

The majority of cases are resolved at the investigation stage. If no agreement can be reached, the case is presented to the province's human rights commission. The members of the commission study the evidence and then submit a report to the minister in charge of administering human rights legislation. The minister may appoint an independent Board of Inquiry, which has similar powers as a tribunal at the federal level. Failure to comply with the remedies prescribed by the Board of Inquiry may result in prosecution in provincial court. Individuals may be fined between $500 and $1000, and organizations or groups between $1000 and $10,000. These levies may vary across provinces.

objective

Pay Equity

As a result of a 1978 amendment to the Canadian Human Rights Act, pay equity became enacted as law. Pay equity law makes it illegal for employers to discriminate against individuals on the basis of job content. The goal of pay equity is to eliminate the historical wage gap between men and women and to ensure that the salary ranges reflect the value of work performed. For example, the average income of males who worked full-time in 1992 was $39,468, while women's average earnings were only $28,350. By province, the female to male earnings ratio ranged from 80.1 percent in Prince Edward Island to 66.0 percent in Nova Scotia.[10] Figure 3-3 shows that while the pay differentials between males and females has narrowed over the last two decades, women working full-time earn only 72 percent of what men earn.

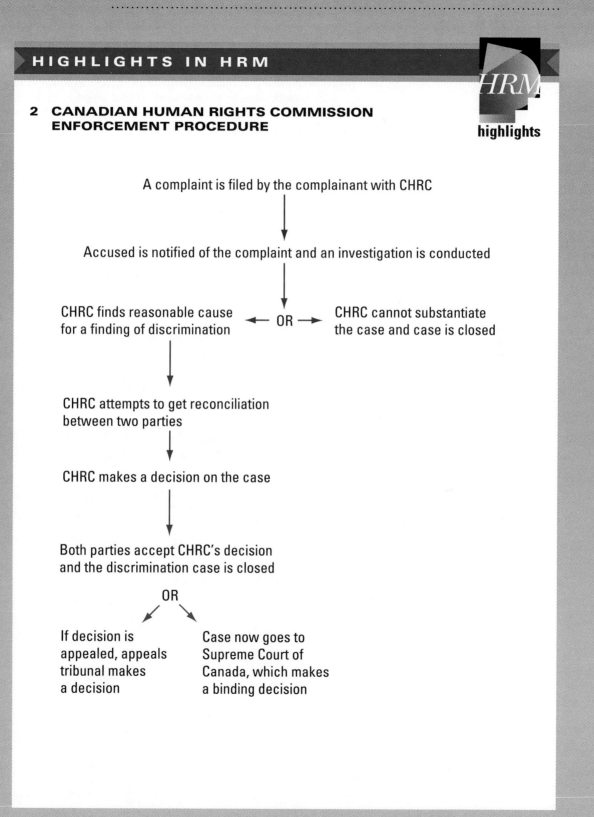

HIGHLIGHTS IN HRM

HRM
highlights

2 CANADIAN HUMAN RIGHTS COMMISSION ENFORCEMENT PROCEDURE

A complaint is filed by the complainant with CHRC

Accused is notified of the complaint and an investigation is conducted

CHRC finds reasonable cause for a finding of discrimination ← OR → CHRC cannot substantiate the case and case is closed

CHRC attempts to get reconciliation between two parties

CHRC makes a decision on the case

Both parties accept CHRC's decision and the discrimination case is closed

OR

If decision is appealed, appeals tribunal makes a decision

Case now goes to Supreme Court of Canada, which makes a binding decision

By definition, pay equity means equal pay for work of equal value. It is based on two principles. The first is equal pay for equal work.[11] Male and female workers must be paid the same wage rate for doing identical work. The second principle is equal pay for similar or substantially similar work (equal pay for work of comparable worth). This means that male and female workers must be paid the same wage rate for jobs of a similar nature that may have different titles (e.g., "nurse's aide" and "orderly").

Implementation of pay equity is based on comparing the work of female-dominated job classes to the value of work performed by males. Comparisons require the use of a gender-neutral, unbiased comparison system to evaluate the jobs in an establishment.[12] Comparisons must be based on the amount and type of skill, effort, and responsibility needed to perform the job and on the working conditions in which it is performed. The comparison must be done in such a way that the characteristics of "male" jobs, such as heavy lifting or "dirty" working conditions, are valued fairly in comparison to the characteristics of "female" jobs, such as manual dexterity or caring for others.[13]

The federal pay equity legislation applies to that section of the workforce under its jurisdiction and covers all organizations regardless of number of employees. The federal pay equity system is complaint-based, meaning that complaints can be raised by an employee, a group of employees, or a bargaining agent.[14]

The most comprehensive provincial pay equity legislation was instituted in Ontario, where employers were required to conduct job evaluations and implement

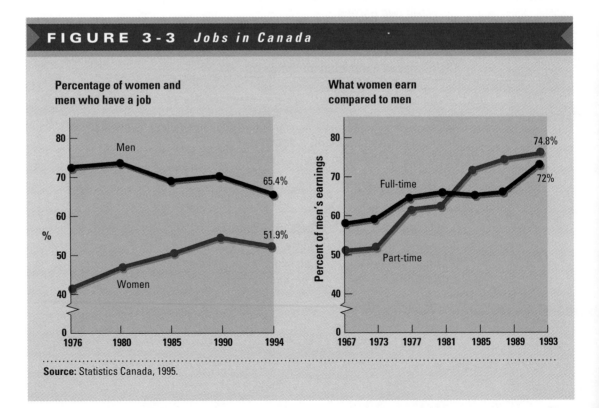

FIGURE 3-3 *Jobs in Canada*

Percentage of women and men who have a job

What women earn compared to men

Source: Statistics Canada, 1995.

pay equity. Both the provincial civil service and the private sector were bound by this legislation, although organizations with fewer than twenty employees are fully exempted and organizations with 10 to 99 employees are not required to conduct formal job evaluations.[15] A more comprehensive review of pay equity is provided in Chapter 11.

objective

An Act Respecting Employment Equity (Federally Regulated Companies)

The Royal Commission on Equality in Employment (Abella Commission), chaired by then Ontario Judge Rosalie Silberman Abella,[16] reviewed the employment practices of federal crown and government-owned corporations. Its report, tabled in 1984, made recommendations on how four traditionally disadvantaged groups—women, aboriginal peoples, members of visible minorities, and people with disabilities—could be brought into the mainstream of Canada's labour force. The report recommended that legislation be enacted to cover all federally regulated employers and urged provincial governments to consider developing compatible legislation. To reach employees who did not fall under federal jurisdiction, the report further recommended that a contract compliance program be included for organizations that did business with the federal government.

The Abella Commission also stressed that data collection and reporting should be an important component of compliance, since the success of an employment equity program would be measured by results. Data were to be collected on new hires, promotions, terminations, layoffs, part-time work, and other conditions of employment. Also recommended were enforceable requirements and the creation of an independent, well-resourced overseer.

In response to the findings of the Abella Commission, the federal government introduced the Employment Equity Act in 1986.

The Employment Equity Act

Employers and crown corporations that have 100 employees or more and that are regulated under the Canada Labour Code must implement employment equity and report on their results. Employer obligations are specified in Section 4 of the Employment Equity Act.

> *An employer shall, in consultation with such persons as have been designated by the employees to act as their representative or, where a bargaining agent represents the employees, in consultation with the bargaining agent, implement employment equity by:*
>
> *a) identifying and eliminating each of the employer's employment practices, not otherwise authorized by a law, that results in employment barriers against persons in designated groups; and*
>
> *b) instituting such positive policies and practices and making such reasonable accommodation as will ensure that persons in designated groups achieve a degree of representation in the various positions of employment with the employer that is at least proportionate to their representation:*
> *i. in the work force,*

ii. or in those segments of the work force that are identifiable by qualifications, eligibility or geography and from which the employer may reasonably be expected to draw or promote employees.[17]

The concept of employment equity is rooted in the wording of federal and provincial employment standards legislation, human rights codes, and the Canadian Charter of Rights and Freedoms. Employment equity involves the identification and removal of systemic barriers to employment opportunities that adversely affect women, visible minorities, aboriginal peoples, and persons with disabilities. Employment equity also involves the implementation of special measures and reasonable accommodation. The purpose of the Act is further defined under Section 2:

To achieve equality in the workplace so that no person shall be denied employment opportunities or benefits for reasons unrelated to ability and in the fulfilment of that goal, to correct the conditions of disadvantage in employment experienced by women, aboriginal peoples, persons with disabilities and persons who are, because of their race or colour, in a visible minority in Canada by giving effect to the principle that employment equity means more than treating persons in the same way but also requires special measures and the accommodation of differences.[18]

All employers who are federally regulated are required to implement an employment equity plan under the Federal Contractors Program. (For a list of this program's implementation criteria, see Highlights on HRM 3.) The legislation is further extended to contractors who bid for goods and services contracts with the federal government valued at $200,000 or more, and who employ 100 persons or more. To assist in the process, the federal government provides professional consulting services on the implementation of employment equity to employers throughout Canada. Federally regulated employers must prepare an annual Employment Equity Plan (with goals and timetables), and retain for at least three years each plan and all records that were used to prepare their annual report.

Administration and Enforcement of the Employment Equity Act

The Employment Equity Branch of Employment and Immigration Canada (EIC) is responsible for the administration of both the Employment Equity Act— also known as the Legislated Employment Equity Program (LEEP)—and the Federal Contractors Program (FCP). Although enforcement of the Employment Equity Act is not clearly defined, the Canadian Human Rights Commission (CHRC) is mandated under the Canadian Human Rights Act[19] to prohibit discrimination in the establishments of federally regulated businesses.[20]

EIC has developed regulations, documentation, and procedures with respect to the filing of annual reports. It plays an educative and consultative role in assisting employers to develop and implement employment equity programs. EIC's ability to enforce the development and implementation of employment equity plans extends mainly to moral suasion. Nearly all employers have complied with statistical reporting requirements. Only a handful have been levied small fines by courts for failing to file reports before deadlines.[22]

HRM
highlights

3   IMPLEMENTATION CRITERIA OF THE FEDERAL CONTRACTORS PROGRAM

1. Communication by the organization's CEO to employees, unions and/or employee associations of the commitment to achieve equality in employment through the design and implementation of an employment equity plan.
2. Assignment of senior personnel with responsibility for employment equity.
3. Collection and maintenance of information on the employment status of designated-group employees by occupation and salary levels and in terms of hiring, promotion and termination in relation to all other employees.
4. Analysis of designated-group representation within the organization in relation to their representation in the supply of qualified workers from which the contractor may reasonably be expected to recruit employees.
5. Elimination or modification of those human resource policies, practices and systems, whether formal or informal, shown to have or likely to have an unfavourable effect on the employment status of designated-group employees.
6. Establishment of goals for the hiring, training and promotion of designated-group employees. Such goals will consider projections for hiring, promotions, terminations, layoffs, recalls, retirements and, where possible, the projected availability of qualified designated-group members.
7. Establishment of a work plan for reaching each of the goals in 6 above.
8. Adoption of special measures where necessary to ensure that goals are achieved, including the provision of reasonable accommodation as required.
9. Establishment of a climate favourable to the successful integration of designated-group members within the organization.
10. Adoption of procedures to monitor the progress and results achieved in implementing employment equity.
11. Authorization to allow representatives of the Canada Employment and Immigration Commission access to the business premises and to the records noted in 3 above in order to conduct on-site compliance reviews for the purpose of measuring the progress achieved in implementing employment equity.[21]

Source: Employment Equity and Immigration Canada, Federal Contractors Program, Information for Suppliers. Reproduced with permission from the Minister of Supply and Services, 1995.

The Implementation of Employment Equity within Organizations

Implementing employment equity in an organization follows the precepts of any change management program. Therefore, successful implementation must employ strategic planning that must be incorporated into an overall business strategy. The Federal Contractor's Program outlined in Highlights in HRM 3 provides a good overview of what a plan should incorporate. The process involves six main steps: senior management commitment, data collection and analysis, employment systems review, establishment of a workplan, implementation, and a follow-up process that includes evaluation, monitoring, and revision.

Step 1: Senior Management Commitment

Commitment to an employment equity plan necessitates a top-down strategy. A more supportive culture is created when the CEO or owner-operator publicly introduces written policy describing the organization's commitment to employment equity. This policy must be strategically posted throughout the organization and sent to each employee. Highlights in HRM 4 demonstrates the commitment Amdahl Canada Limited has made to its employment equity effort.

Since an employment equity policy statement may raise many questions, it is important to be thorough in this process in order to keep concerns to a minimum. The policy statement should be supplemented with a communiqué explaining what employment equity is, the rationale for the program, and its implications for present and future employees. Assurances must be given at this time that all information provided will be treated confidentially and will not be used to identify individuals other than for the purpose of employment equity program activities. The communiqué should also list the names of persons responsible for administering the program and outline any planned activities the employer may deem necessary to establish the program (e.g., analysis of the workforce or of policies and procedures).

Communication tools may include periodic information sessions, workplace posters, departmental or small group meetings conducted by line management, or newsletters or other vehicles such as videos, brochures, orientation, training programs, employee handbooks and memos from the union. An innovative approach to communications was taken at Centre de recherché industrielle du Québec (CRIQ), where employees decided to create a video to demonstrate that seemingly harmless comments and attitudes can have devastating consequences for designated group members. Their goal was to sensitize people without lecturing or pointing fingers. The employees acted, selected the music, directed, and produced the video, entitled *Moi ... des préjugés? (Me ... prejudiced?)*. The video depicts the experiences of a black man, a person who is deaf, and a woman who are all seeking employment with a company, and who are confronted with opinions and attitudes that have everything to do with prejudice and nothing to do with the requirements of the job.[23]

Assignment of accountable senior staff. Senior management must place the responsibility for employment equity in the hands of a senior manager, a joint labour–management committee, and an employment equity advisory committee with mechanisms for union consultation (or, in non-unionized settings, for consul-

HIGHLIGHTS IN HRM

4   AMDAHL LIMITED STATEMENT OF EMPLOYMENT EQUITY

HRM highlights

All employees of Amdahl Limited are entitled to a work environment within which individuals are treated with respect, provided with equality of opportunity based on merit and kept free of discrimination and harassment.

This commitment to employees and candidates for employment applies to all aspects of the employment relationship, including recruitment, work assignment, training opportunities, compensation, promotions, transfers and terminations.

Individuals in their employment relationship will not be unlawfully discriminated against or harassed for any reason such as their race, religion, creed, sex, marital status, age, natural/ethnic origin, political belief or handicap.

Each employee is responsible for adhering to the spirit and content of this Statement. Violations of this policy constitute unacceptable behaviour and will be subject to appropriate corrective action.

Management is committed to addressing and resolving employee concerns associated with the rights described in this statement.

D.B. McGlaughlin
President

Source: Charles Shrzan, Director, Human Resources, Amdahl Limited, August 1995. Printed with permission.

tation with designated employee representatives). They must designate line management responsibility and accountability. Anyone given responsibility for employment equity must be knowledgeable about the problems and concerns of designated groups; have the status and ability needed to gain the cooperation of employees at all levels in the organization; have access to financial and human resources required to conduct planning and implementation functions; have sufficient time to devote to employment equity issues; monitor and be in a position to report to the CEO on the results of employment equity measures; and be prepared to serve as the employment equity contact person with federal and provincial government agencies.

Among the employment areas committee members may be required to review are employment practices, advertising and recruitment policies, company-sponsored training, the organization of work schedules and facilities, and systems for promotion to management positions. While committees are usually given responsibility for making recommendations and reporting on issues, ultimate authority usually rests with senior management.

Employers covered by the Employment Equity Act are legally obligated to consult with designated employee representatives or, in unionized settings, with bargaining agents. Consultation means that the employer must supply sufficient information and opportunity to employee representatives or bargaining agents to enable them to ask questions and submit advice on the implementation of employment equity.

The labour movement in Canada generally supports the concept of employment equity, so long as unions are fully informed and involved from the beginning with respect to an employer's planning process. This makes sense considering that unions are the legitimate representatives of employee interests in unionized settings. Supportive mechanisms for the achievement of employment equity have been reported by the Human Resources Department of Canada.[24] Family-friendly policies such as parental leave, child-care provisions, and flexible hours have been successfully negotiated between many employers and unions.

Step 2: Data Collection and Analysis

The development of an internal workforce profile is an important tool in employment equity planning. Without this information an organization would not be able to determine where it stands relative to the internal and external workforce. Profiles must be based on both stock data and flow data. **Stock data** provide a snapshot of the organization. They show where members of designated groups are employed in the organization, at what salaries and status, and in what occupations on a particular date. **Flow data** refer to the distribution of designated groups in applications, interviews, hiring decisions, training and promotion opportunities, and terminations. They provide information on the movement of employees into and through the organization. Examples of stock and flow data relating to hiring and terminations, as well as to occupational groupings and promotions, are found in Figure 3-4.

Most of the information necessary for equity planning (e.g., salary, sex, access to benefits, seniority status, occupational and career history within the organization) is contained in existing personnel files. Information pertaining to the distribution of members of designated groups in the employer's organization must be accumulated by the employer through a self-identification process. Under the Employment Equity Act, employers may gather data on designated groups members as long as employees voluntarily agree to be identified or identify themselves as members of designated groups, and as long as the data are used only for employment equity planning or reporting purposes.

Creating a climate of trust in the management of the program is a major challenge. Employers can encourage participation and confidence in the program by providing focused employment equity training to managers and by providing oppor-

Stock data
Data showing the status of designated groups in occupational categories and compensation level.

Flow data
Data that provide a profile of the employment decisions affecting designated groups.

FIGURE 3-4   *Representation of Designated Groups*

	% share of hirings (1990)	% increase in share of hiring (1987–90)	% share of promotions (1990)	% increase in share of promotions (1987–90)	% share of terminations (1990)	Net Effect— hirings and terminations (1987–90)
Women	42.68	5.33	58.09	7.04	41.20	17,153
Aboriginal persons	1.44	0.83	0.83	0.24	1.12	483
People with disabilities	1.33	0.67	2.84	1.40	1.98	(1,240)
Members of visible minorities	10.87	5.63	11.09	4.07	6.84	(10,834)

Source: *Statistical Summary, Employment Equity Act, 1987–1990,* Employment Equity Branch, Employment and Immigration Canada.

tunities for managers to be recognized for their contributions to the development and administration of effective employment equity strategies. Companies such as Pratt & Whitney have introduced equity and diversity training for their supervisors.[25]

If an employer administers a self-identification questionnaire, confidentiality and a clear commitment at senior levels to the concept of employment equity should be communicated. Having employees self-identify is crucial to the success of the program, but problems may occur with self-identification. Under some provincial employment equity acts, terms like "aboriginal" or "racial minority" are not defined. Some employees, who have "hidden" disabilities such as epilepsy or partial deafness, may not wish to label themselves for fear of future discriminatory treatment. Some minorities, such as aboriginals, have never disclosed their ethnic origins for similar reasons.

If many of the nonvisible disabled employees do not identify themselves as disabled, then the program might be designed to recruit more disabled employees, leaving another segment of the employee population underrepresented. Thus because inaccurate data was accumulated on one group, the other group will not benefit from the employment equity efforts. An additional concern is that individuals with disabilities may need some form of accommodation to help them perform their jobs better. If they do not self-identify, they have denied themselves of certain basic rights.

A self-identification form should contain:

- an explanation of the employer's employment equity policy, the purpose of the employment equity program, and the need for the information requested;

- an indication that the information supplied will be confidential and will be used only for employment equity purposes by those persons identified as responsible for the program;
- the categories for self-identification, with brief explanations and examples;
- an indication that the form has been reviewed by the relevant human rights agency;
- space for comments and suggestions; and
- the name of the contact person for information and suggestions.[26]

An example of a self-identification form used by the City of Calgary appears in Highlights in HRM 5.

Once the personal-information forms have been completed, all occupations within an organization must be cross-referenced to the National Occupational Classification (NOC)—formerly Standard Occupational Classification (SOC)—manual created by Statistics Canada for use in statistical surveys and for other purposes. Personal-information data are organized according to four-digit NOC classifications. To build a workforce profile, employers should first refer to the four-digit unit group and then determine in which one the job belongs. For example, secretaries and stenographers are classified in unit group 4111, which in turn can be assigned to the "clerical workers" group.

To assist employers in the storage of data and in report writing, the Employment Equity Computerized Reporting System (EECRS) has been designed. Other organizations that use relational data bases and more integrated computer systems design may use other software packages to consolidate the EIC reports.

A full workforce analysis can be generated once all the information has been loaded and the reports are complete. This utilization analysis will include a distribution of designated group members according to occupations and salary levels throughout the organization. Comparisons will show which designated groups exhibit **underutilization** and which groups exhibit **concentration** in specific occupations or levels, in proportion to their numbers in the labour market.[27]

Step 3: Employment Systems Review

"Employment systems" or "employment practices" are the means by which employers carry out such personnel activities as recruitment, hiring, training and development, promotion, job classification and salary level decisions, discipline and termination. Some of these practices are found in personnel manuals and collective agreements, while others remain more informal and based on traditional practices.

An important legal principle is that employers are accountable even when discrimination is the unintended result of employment systems that block the progress of particular groups of employees or potential employees for reasons unrelated to qualifications, merit, or business requirements. This unintentional discrimination is referred to as systemic discrimination.

Systemic barriers in employment practices. **Systemic discrimination** refers to the exclusion of members of certain groups through the application of employment policies or practices based on criteria that are not job-related or required for the safe and efficient operation of the business. Systemic discrimination can create legal concerns for an organization. Many employment barriers are usually hidden, unintentionally,

Underutilization
Term applied to designated groups that are not utilized or represented in the employer's workforce proportional to their numbers in the labour market.

Concentration
Term applied to designated groups whose numbers in a particular occupation or level are high relative to their numbers in the labour market.

Systemic discrimination
The exclusion of members of certain groups through the application of employment policies or practices based on criteria that are not job-related.

> HIGHLIGHTS IN HRM

5   SELF-IDENTIFICATION FORM, CITY OF CALGARY

highlights

EMPLOYMENT EQUITY IDENTIFICATION

In keeping with The City of Calgary's employment equity initiatives and outreach program, we ask that applicants provide us with the following information. Your answers are confidential, will only be used to collect data and will not affect your eligibility as an applicant as hiring decisions are based on the merit principle. Please note: the Alberta Human Rights Commission has reviewed these questions and found them acceptable.

Completion of this section is considered OPTIONAL and VOLUNTARY.

LAST NAME	GIVEN NAME	COMPETITION NUMBER
		| | | | | – | | | |

Please check the appropriate box.

Are you:

☐ Male   ☐ Female

☐ White (Caucasian)

☐ A visible minority (Black, Chinese, South Asian, etc.)

☐ Aboriginal (Canadian Indian, Metis, Inuit)

☐ Person with a disability (mobility, vision, hearing impaired, etc.)

Source: City of Calgary, Self-Identification Form, August 1995. Printed with permission.

> ### FIGURE 3-5 *Employment Practices*
>
> | EXAMPLES OF SYSTEMIC BARRIERS | EXAMPLES OF POSSIBLE SOLUTIONS |
> |---|---|
> | 1. Recruitment practices that limit applications from designated groups, e.g., word of mouth, internal hiring policies. | Word of mouth could be supplemented by calls to community organizations representing designated groups or to the local Canada Employment Centre. |
> | 2. Physical access which restricts those who are mobility impaired, e.g., no ramps, heavy doors, narrow passageways. | Facility upgrading. |
> | 3. Job descriptions and job evaluation systems which undervalue the work of positions traditionally held by women. | Rewrite job descriptions, rationalize evaluation systems, provide special training for supervisors. |
> | 4. A workplace environment that does not expressly discourage sexual or racial harassment. | Issue a company policy against these practices, with guidelines and follow-up through appraisal and discipline procedures, and develop complaint and problem-solving mechanisms for an employee to use. |
>
> **Source:** *Employment Equity: A Guide for Employers*, Employment and Immigration Canada, Cat. No. 143-5-91, May 1991, p. 19. Reproduced with permission from the Minister of Supply and Services, 1995.

in the rules and procedures and even the facilities that employers provide to manage their human resources. (See Figure 3-5 for examples of systemic barriers, along with possible solutions.) Inequity can result if these barriers encourage or discourage individuals based on their membership in certain groups rather than on their ability to do a job that the employer needs done. In *Colfer v. Ottawa Board of Commissioners of Police* (1979), the human rights tribunal found that a police-force policy that stipulated height and weight requirements was discriminatory, since it precluded most women from joining the force.[28]

Another example of systemic discrimination would occur when an employer's workforce represents one group in our society and the company recruits new employees by posting job vacancies within the company or by word of mouth among the employees. This recruitment strategy is likely to generate a candidate similar to those in the current workforce, thereby unintentionally discriminating against other groups of workers in the labour market. A better approach might be to vary recruitment methods by contacting outside agencies and organizations.

Employment practices to be reviewed may include job classifications and descriptions, recruitment processes, training and development, performance evaluation systems, promotions and upward mobility, levels of compensation, access to benefits, termination processes, discipline procedures, facilities (building design/barrier-free access), and access to assistance.

The usual test for identifying systemic barriers involves using the following criteria to assess the policy:

- Is it job-related?
- Is it valid? (i.e., does it, or the required qualification, have a direct relationship to job performance?)
- Is it consistently applied?
- Does it have adverse impact? (i.e., does it affect members of designated groups more than those in dominant groups?)
- Is it a business necessity?
- Does it conform to human rights and employment standards legislation?[29]

If the employee profiles indicate that certain types of people are underrepresented, then special measures may be undertaken to correct this imbalance.

Special measures and reasonable accommodation. Special measures are initiatives designed to accelerate the entry, development, and promotion of designated group members from among the interested and qualified workforce. For example, some special measures may include targeted recruitment or special training initiatives aimed primarily at correcting, over a specified period of time, employment inequities stemming from past discrimination. These measures are intended to hasten the achievement of fair representation in an employer's workforce of the four designated groups.

Reasonable accommodation deals with the adjustment of employment policies and practices so that no individual is denied benefits, disadvantaged for employment opportunities, or blocked from carrying out the essential components of a job because of race, colour, sex, or disability. Human rights tribunals across Canada have placed employers under a duty to demonstrate a degree of flexibility in meeting the reasonable needs of employees. It is no longer acceptable for employers to simply assume that all employees will "fit in" no matter what their special needs. Employers must find the means to alter systems to meet the needs of their employees as long as this does not cause "undue hardship to the employer." Reasonable accommodation may include redesigning job duties, adjusting work schedules, providing technical, financial, and human support services, and upgrading facilities. The City of Toronto developed award-winning facilities in its Barrier Free Access program, which was designed to allow accessible passage to persons with disabilities throughout City facilities.

Reasonable accommodation benefits all employees. The provision of allowances for child-care expenses when employees take company-sponsored courses not only removes a barrier that blocks many women but may also assist any employee with sole parenting responsibilities. The flexible work schedules adopted by some companies in northern Canada benefit aboriginal employees who are prepared to work unusual hours in exchange for significant breaks away from the work site in order to take part in traditional hunting and fishing activities. Many other employees also benefit from these flexible work schedules.

Reasonable accommodation
Attempt by employers to adjust the working conditions or schedules of employees with disabilities or religious preferences.

Special arrangements should be made to accommodate persons who may be visually impaired, illiterate, or unfamiliar with the English language with tools such as Braille forms, confidential interviews, or translation.

Step 4: Establishment of a Workplan

The workforce analysis and the review of employment systems will provide the employer with a useful base from which to develop a workplan with realistic goals and timetables. A narrative statement or summary of the conclusions drawn from the examination of the workforce analysis forms part of the employment equity workplan. The summary should include any restrictions faced in hiring due to collective agreements, staff movements, or the need for specialized skills in a particular profession. The identification of restrictions helps to form an overall employment equity strategy.

The plan should be considered a working tool designed to achieve results. It is a document that describes how proposed actions are to be achieved. The plan should be an integral part of the organization's overall operational plans, and must include:

- numerical goals with time frames;
- explanations about the proposed improvement in the hiring, training, and promotion of the four designated groups to increase their representation and improve their distribution throughout the organization;
- descriptions of specific activities to achieve the numerical goals; and
- an outline of monitoring and evaluation procedures to follow program implementation.

Numerical goals must be realistic numbers related to the workforce analysis. The goals must catalogue opportunities for hiring, training, and promotion, and must demonstrate a valid effort to correct underrepresentation or concentration of all designated groups in specific occupations or occupational categories. Nonnumerical goals include activities such as implementation of barrier-free design, targeted recruitment and advertising, modification of employment policies or practices, and provision of developmental training.

The overall goal for an organization is to achieve a representative workforce. An organization's workforce is representative when it reflects the demographic composition of the external workforce. A nonrepresentative workforce is an indicator of the need for evaluation and action to remove the barriers that block or discourage certain groups from employment and advancement. Workplan initiatives in conjunction with special measures and reasonable accommodation should contribute to the overall success of this goal.

Step 5: Implementation

The implementation of employment equity is idiosyncratic in that no two plans will be the same. Each strategy should be designed to meet the needs of the particular organization. The success of plan implementation depends on senior management's commitment to the process, how the roles and responsibilities are defined, what resources are available, the effectiveness of the communications strategy, the acceptance of plan initiatives and objectives, and the availability of training. The plan, in essence a living document, will be affected by the changes in the internal and external environment throughout the implementation period. Therefore, its strategies may be modified or eliminated when results are not achieved or if resource restraints or economic conditions necessitate a different strategy. The implementation is guided and monitored by those responsible and accountable for its outcome.

Step 6: Evaluation, Monitoring, and Revision

By monitoring progress, the employer will be able to evaluate the overall success of the equity initiatives used to achieve a representative workforce as well as respond to organizational and environmental changes. Annual progress reports provided to all employees communicate initiatives and achievements. Interim reports on special projects heighten program visibility and acceptance in addition to promoting management commitment and accountability.

The monitoring activity is an essential component in the planning cycle. Only through monitoring can an employer determine whether goals are being attained and problems resolved, whether new programs are succeeding, and whether strategies have been effective. If the employer finds, upon review of the program, that there are negative results, alterations to the existing plan must be made with new goals. In this regard, the planning process is evolutionary because the achievement of employment equity involves organizational changes and builds on experience.

Other Employment Equity Issues

Reverse Discrimination

Reverse discrimination
Giving preference to members of designated groups to the extent that nonmembers become the subjects of discrimination.

In pursuing employment equity, employers may be accused of **reverse discrimination,** or giving preference to members of the designated groups to the extent that nonmembers believe they are suffering discrimination. When these charges occur, organizations are caught between attempting to correct past discriminatory practices and handling present complaints alleging that HR practices are unfair. It is exactly this catch-22 that makes employment equity controversial. The Ontario College of Art has adopted a policy of hiring only women for the next ten years to correct a preponderance of men on its faculty.[30] Several male applicants have complained that they should be interviewed and that the best person be given the job. Ethics in HRM describes the concerns of white males who feel that they are victims of reverse discrimination.

Sexual Harassment

Sexual harassment
Unwelcome advances, requests for sexual favours, and other verbal or physical conduct of a sexual nature in the working environment.

According to the Canadian Advisory Council on the Status of Women, only four of every ten Canadian women who suffer **sexual harassment** at work take any formal action, and only one out of every two women believe that a complaint would be taken seriously in their workplace.[31] To deal with the growing number of complaints regarding sexual harassment, many organizations are developing policies to deal with sexual harassment in the workplace. Sexual situations in the work environment are not new to organizational life. Sexual feelings are a part of group dynamics, and people who work together may come to develop these kinds of feelings for one another. Unfortunately, these encounters are often unpleasant and unwelcome, as evidenced by the many reported instances of sexual harassment.

The Ontario Human Rights Code identifies three kinds of sexual harassment:

1. When someone says or does things to you of a sexual nature and you do not want or welcome it. This includes behaviour that a person should know you

REVERSE DISCRIMINATION

"White, Male and worried" is the title of an article in *Business Week* that describes the unease Caucasian males feel with respect to the issue of employment equity. White males feel that they are being passed over for jobs and promotions in favour of less-qualified candidates. They complain of being blamed for everything, including all historical injustices. They are feeling threatened.

One bank manager responsible for identifying barriers to women's advancement received hate mail and was thrown out of some offices. People were saying to her: "Please stop. We have enough problems. There aren't enough jobs for the men, and you're talking about giving women more jobs and better jobs."

According to white males, members of designated groups are sometimes hired on the basis of the quota system, not the qualifications system. Merit is the heart of the employment equity issue. Are white males the invisible victims of employment equity?

Sources: D. Flavelle, "Teaching Chiefs How to Bank on Women Workers," *The Toronto Star*, May 10, 1995, E1, E3; and "White, Male and Worried," *Business Week,* January 31, 1994, 50–55.

do not want or welcome. For example, your supervisor makes you feel uncomfortable by talking about sex all the time. When you show that you do not welcome or want the remarks or actions, the Human Rights Code says that the person must stop doing those things right away.

2. A person who has authority or power to deny you something such as a promotion or a raise makes sexual suggestions or requests that you do not want or welcome. For example, your teacher says you must have sex with him or her or you will not pass the course. Even if you do not complain about a sexual suggestion or request, it can still be sexual harassment unless it is clear that you welcome or want it.

3. A person with authority or the power to deny you something important punishes you or threatens to do something to you for refusing a sexual request. For example, your employer fires you, or threatens to fire you, because you refuse to go on a date.

Figure 3-6 illustrates various types of sexual harassment and their frequency of occurrence as reported in a recent study.

York University has developed a comprehensive program for the purpose of dealing with issues about sexual harassment. To augment its program it has published

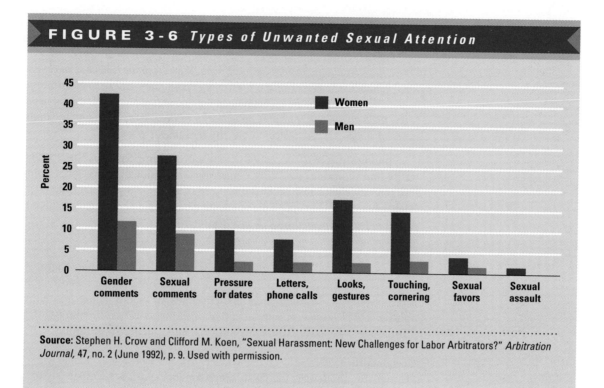

FIGURE 3-6 *Types of Unwanted Sexual Attention*

Source: Stephen H. Crow and Clifford M. Koen, "Sexual Harassment: New Challenges for Labor Arbitrators?" *Arbitration Journal*, 47, no. 2 (June 1992), p. 9. Used with permission.

a booklet entitled *Sexual Assault and Harassment on Campus*, which is intended for students and employees. This booklet explains safety tips for women and men, a definition of sexual harassment, and other forms of harassment.[32] A pamphlet entitled *Sexual Harassment and You: What Every Student Should Know* is made available to any interested person. York's policy states:

> *York University strives to provide an environment wherein all students, faculty and staff are able to learn, study, teach and work, free from sexual harassment.*
>
> *Sexual harassment is:*
>
> 1. *Unwanted sexual attention of a persistent or abusive nature, made by a person who knows or ought reasonably to know that such attention is unwanted;*
> 2. *The making of an implied or express promise of reward for complying with a sexually oriented request;*
> 3. *The making of an implied or express threat or reprisal, in the form of actual reprisal or in the denial of opportunity, for refusal to comply with a sexually oriented request;*
> 4. *Sexually oriented remarks and behaviour which may reasonably be perceived to create a negative psychological and emotional environment for work and study.*

Incidents of sexual harassment shall be investigated and dealt with by the University in accordance with guidelines and procedures put in place for that purpose from time to time.

Students, faculty and staff who, it is determined, have sexually harassed another member(s) of the University community will be subject to discipline and sanctions as are appropriate in the circumstances, including but not limited to discipline and sanctions provided for in Presidential Regulations (in the case of students), and relevant collective agreements.[33]

Important to the success of sexual-harassment policies is the need for confidentiality and a method for filing complaints. Without organizational commitment to zero tolerance with respect to harassment, the policy would be rendered meaningless. Highlights in HRM 6 presents some suggestions for an effective policy to minimize sexual harassment in the work environment.[34]

Mandatory Retirement

Age is a prohibited ground of discrimination under the Human Rights Act, and yet employees are forced to retire at age 65. The Supreme Court recently upheld mandatory retirement, arguing that its elimination would cause monumental social upheaval.[35] However, provinces can abolish mandatory retirement within their own jurisdictions. To date, Alberta, Manitoba, and Quebec have done so.

Conclusion

Despite the challenges facing it, employment equity is so much a part of organizational plans that, even when the legislation that guides it is threatened, employers indicate that they will keep equity alive.

"Regardless of any legislative requirement, [employment equity] is a good business decision for us," says Robert Rochon, Director of Employment Equity for National Grocer Co. Ltd. "When you consider the changing face of Canada, it just makes good business sense to reflect the customers that you serve."[36] Other companies such as North American Life Assurance, Cathham's Union Gas Ltd., and Wellesley Hospital publicly support equity.

Having had a number of years of experience with employment equity legislation, mostly at the federal level, companies are ready to move to the next phase of their plans to embrace the overall concept of diversity.

objective

Managing Diversity

Diversity management
The optimization of an organization's multicultural workforce in order to reach business objectives.

Managing diversity goes beyond Canadian employment equity legislation's four designated groups in addressing the need to create a fair work environment. The terms "diversity management" and "employment equity" are often used interchangeably, but there are differences. **Diversity management** is voluntary, employment equity is not. Managing diversity is a broader, more inclusive concept encompassing such factors as religion, personality, lifestyle, and education. By managing diversity, organizations hope to gain a strategic and competitive advantage by helping all employees perform to their full potential.[37]

The City of Toronto led by example in 1994 when it recognized "non-Christian City of Toronto staff" by giving them two days of paid time off for religious holidays

HIGHLIGHTS IN HRM

6 BASIC COMPONENTS OF AN EFFECTIVE SEXUAL HARASSMENT POLICY

1. Develop a comprehensive organization-wide policy on sexual harassment and present it to all current and new employees. Stress that sexual harassment will not be tolerated under any circumstances. Emphasis is best achieved when the policy is publicized and supported by top management.
2. Hold training sessions with supervisors to explain their role in providing an environment free of sexual harassment, and proper investigative procedures when charges occur.
3. Establish a formal complaint procedure in which employees can discuss problems without fear of retaliation. The complaint procedure should spell out how charges will be investigated and resolved.
4. Act immediately when employees complain of sexual harassment. Communicate widely that investigations will be conducted objectively and with appreciation for the sensitivity of the issue.
5. When an investigation supports employee charges, discipline the offender at once. For extremely serious offences, discipline should include penalties up to and including discharge. Discipline should be applied consistently across similar cases and among managers and hourly employees alike.
6. Follow up on all cases to ensure a satisfactory resolution of the problem.

if they agreed to work Christmas Day and Good Friday (Christian holidays) at straight time. Councillor Kyle Rae stated, "I think there will be many members of our work force who will be thankful that we've acknowledged there is diversity in the workplace and they will be treated not as second-class citizens but as equals."[38]

Organizations such as CN, Bank of Montreal, and Warner-Lambert are pioneers in this new philosophy. According to Marie Tellier, Canadian National's assistant vice-president of employment equity,

> the hiring and development and good management of a diverse workforce whose values and expectations are different from their managers is no longer an option—it is an economic necessity. By the year 2000, 70 to 80 per cent of new arrivals on the work market will be women and non-whites. In this context, diversity management is not merely a legal obligation, whereby we would try to integrate target groups, but rather a necessity imposed by market laws, by competition and by the need to be the best to survive."[39]

Statistics show that the ethnocultural profile of Canada has been changing since the 1960s, and will continue to change dramatically over the next twenty years. Figure 3-7 shows the projection of ethnic groups to the year 2006. Between

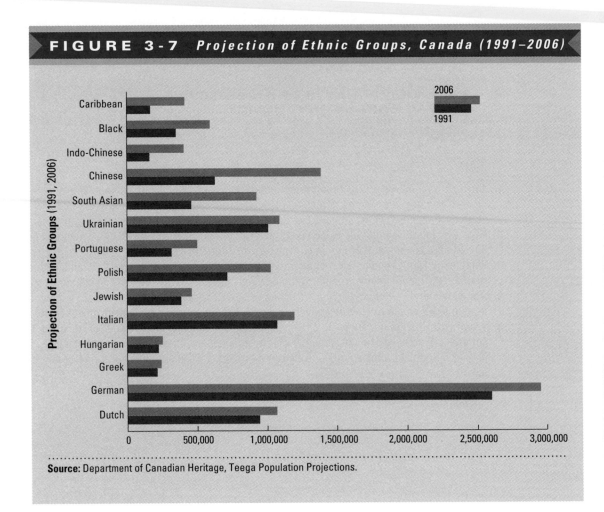

FIGURE 3-7 *Projection of Ethnic Groups, Canada (1991–2006)*

Source: Department of Canadian Heritage, Teega Population Projections.

1986 and 1991, census figures show that the proportion of the population reporting ethnic origins other than British/French/Canadian increased by 20 percent while the number of people reporting a mother tongue other than English or French grew by 10 percent. The top six nonofficial languages (i.e., neither French nor English) spoken by Canadians in 1991 were Italian, the Slavic languages, German, Chinese, the South Asian languages, and Spanish.[40]

CEOs in Canada recognize that ethnic groups possess expertise such as language skills, knowledge of foreign cultures and business practices, and natural trade links with overseas markets that can be used to capture market share in emerging economies and "new" Canadian markets.[41] Ebco, a manufacturing company in Richmond, British Columbia, which has won awards for excellence in race relations, is doing business in Germany and Taiwan because it was able to tap the networks and skills of its employees, who traced their origins to 48 different countries. Besides the business reasons for hiring ethnic groups, the spending power of these groups is another motivating factor. In 1991, the spending power in Canada's visible minorities was estimated at $76 billion, a figure expected to rise to $300 billion by 2001.[42]

Chung Kwong Cheung, winner of a contest sponsored by the National Movement for Harmony in Canada to promote racial understanding, was able to capture the essence of the new face of Canada.[44]

Edgar Ware, ethnocultural business manager at Digital Equipment of Canada, says, "We have an obligation to the cultural fabric. We want to look like the people we sell to."[43] Digital's goal is to balance a diversity strategy with the organization's business plan.

In addition to the moral issues surrounding diversity, there is a critical economic need for Canada to increase its share of world trade and expand its trade portfolio. In 1994, 84 percent of our export market was dominated by the United States, Japan, and the United Kingdom. If Canadian business continues to rely heavily on these markets, our export growth and standard of living may not keep pace with other international markets.[45] Third World countries with emerging markets will require new investments in infrastructure, public systems, and productive capital. Given the multicultural background of many of its workers, Canada is in an excellent position to be able to provide these services.[46] Canadian companies such as NorTel, SNC-Lavaline, and many other consulting engineering firms have already begun to tap the potential of these emerging markets.

Creating an Environment for Success

Transforming an organizational culture into a culture that embraces diversity can be a complex and lengthy process. Diversity initiatives should be taken slowly so that everyone can understand that this change is an evolutionary process and that expectations should be realistic. Individuals must fully understand the time, effort, commitment, and risk involved and the requirements of a systematic approach.[47]

Leadership is one of the most important variables in an organization's ability to successfully incorporate the value of diversity into its business strategy. Eighty-six percent of respondents in a recent Conference Board of Canada survey indicated that responsibility rested with human resources.[48] The initiative should not be perceived as a human resource program or policy, but rather as a business imperative. In the words of Prem Benimadhu, vice-president of human resources research for the Conference Board, "building a racially and culturally diverse work force has been perceived as a human resources issue. But as long as it is, it's not going to be in the mission statement of organizations."[49] Only 6 percent of firms surveyed by the Conference Board study mentioned ethnic and cultural diversity in their mission statements.

Diversity initiatives must be directly linked to the business objectives/goals of the most senior level of management to ensure employee. Figure 3-8 demonstrates how the Bank of Montreal weaves its program into the fabric of the organization, as does this chapter's Reality Check.

Organizations seeking to incorporate the value of diversity into their corporate philosophy must incorporate appropriate internally and externally focused communications. For example, the National Bank of Canada participates annually in Montreal's "La semaine des communautés culturelles," a week dedicated to the celebration of Montreal's multiculturalism. The bank believes that its visible demonstrations of commitment to ethnocultural diversity within the community it serves help raise the bank's profile.[50] Rogers Communications, a Canadian pioneer in diversity management, issued a corporate statement to communicate its commitment to diversity, expressed in Highlights in HRM 7.

Cross-functional teams established to drive the diversity initiative are used successfully as communication vehicles by many leading-edge organizations. Toronto's Sunnybrook Health Science Centre has implemented a Patient Diversity Task Force to examine and report on the barriers faced by their patients, residents,

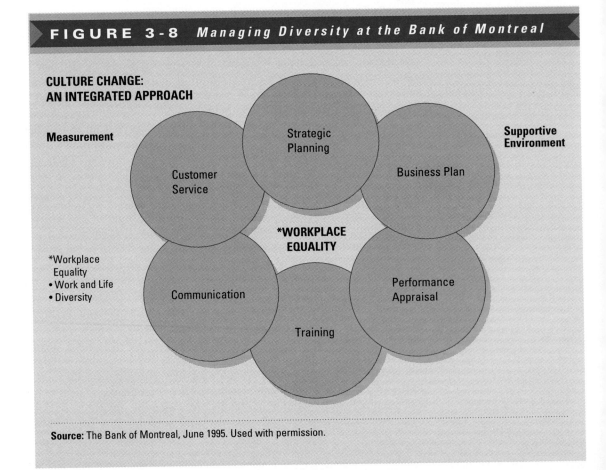

FIGURE 3-8 *Managing Diversity at the Bank of Montreal*

CULTURE CHANGE: AN INTEGRATED APPROACH

Measurement

Supportive Environment

Strategic Planning

Business Plan

Customer Service

*WORKPLACE EQUALITY

Performance Appraisal

Communication

Training

*Workplace Equality
• Work and Life
• Diversity

Source: The Bank of Montreal, June 1995. Used with permission.

REALITY CHECK

THE BANK OF MONTREAL

The Bank of Montreal, well-known throughout the Canadian marketplace as an exemplary leader in diversity and equality issues, won the Catalyst Award for promoting women's careers. It was the first time a Canadian organization has won the award. (Catalyst recognizes the outstanding achievements in employment equity of organizations in North America.) Johanne Totta, Vice-President, Workplace Equality, spearheads the equity campaign from her Montreal and Toronto offices.

"One of the keys to our success is the ability to integrate our programs into the fabric of the organization. In other words, it does not become the flavour of the month. We have to really understand the issues in each of our communities across the country. We promote qualified people into senior positions, people who can make a difference and who understand their communities. In one aboriginal community, our vice-president is an aboriginal with ties to his community. Working closely with the elders, he is able to find out what is going on in his business community and in that way he can better serve their needs. What might be successful in an aboriginal community might not work the same way in another community.

"To ensure that goals are met, the whole aspect of 'diversity and equality' is linked to the annual business plan. The managers are expected to understand their communities in which they provide service, so they are expected to monitor their environments and look for ways to service the communities with the appropriate staff. You can't do the right thing for the wrong reasons, so specific training is provided on how to build diversity into the business plan. As an initial step in the process, the managers must develop a plan considering the demographics and then continually build on the plan. By providing a supportive environment, managers are able to achieve the performance measurements expected. Managers must be accountable to the program through their performance appraisal.

"Communication of our program and achievements is a major component. Successes are reported through a video called '875 Live.' (The term '875' is the form number for our inter-office memo.) All branches get the good news every couple of months. On a quarterly basis, the president also reports on equality initiatives. We use a National and Regional Advisory Council to learn about issues. The National Advisory Council consists of senior executives who meet to discuss the results of the business plan and ensure the plan is aggressive enough and achievable. The Regional Advisory Councils are made up of people from diversified backgrounds, including senior and junior representatives. The advisory councils are the channels whereby we find out what's really happening. We had an instance where one manager wanted everyone to go on flextime. However, the intent is not to force people to go on a program that does not meet their needs. Through the council we were able to rectify this issue.

"The ultimate goal is to meet the customer's needs. We have to understand not only their language but their culture. For example, when we set up the Asian banking strategy, we introduced a hotline number for our customers. Just before it was introduced, one of our Asian executives pointed out that we had assigned a lot of number fours. We did not realize that the number four was not acceptable to the Asian community, so we changed it immediately. To ensure our branches are more inviting to our aboriginal communities, we use earth tones and aboriginal artifacts.

"When our efforts toward advancement of women began in 1990, we only had 6 percent of women in executive positions; today we have 16 percent. This was achieved as a result of a Task Force on the Advancement of Women. One of the keys in any of our task forces is to repudiate myths. For example, with women, myths such as "they have babies and quit," "they're too young or too old," "they just need more education," and "they don't have the right stuff" have often been used. We made efforts to show that those statements were not true. When we compared the ages of both groups, we found them to be about the same for both women and men. We also proved that although women have babies, they also had longer service records than men at the bank at every level except senior management.

"Through our strategic plan and our annual business plan, we will continue to maintain momentum, identify new issues as they arise, and survey to see if the culture is changing in any one of our business communities. It is important to remove all barriers and enhance diversity so that the program is fair to everyone. Workplace equality includes not only diversity—it also considers work and life. Providing programs that offer flexibility and opportunity to meet the needs of our employees will ultimately result in meeting the needs of our customers."

Source: Interview by Deborah M. Zinni, July 1995.

and families.[51] Other organizations seek to raise the awareness of ethnocultural diversity. Some of these initiatives are outlined in Highlights in HRM 8.

Training is essential to the success of diversity implementation. A number of companies including Imperial Oil and Connaught Laboratories have incorporated diversity training. Cultural etiquette is an important aspect of diversity training that aims to explain the differences, or diversity, in people. In a booklet entitled *Cultural Etiquette: A Guide for the Well-Intentioned*, Amoja Three Rivers explains "that bad cultural manners do not necessarily mean that someone is a bad person, but that they just don't know any better."[52] Later in the booklet, the author presents some common cultural myths:

- A large radio/tape player is a boom-box or a stereo. It is not a "ghetto blaster."
- Everybody can blush, bruise, tan, and get sunburned. Everybody.
- Not all people with dreadlocks are from Jamaica. They are also not necessarily Rastafarians, nor are they drug dealers or "militants."
- Columbus didn't discover diddly-squat. Millions of Native Americans have known for countless generations that what they were living on was land, and where it was—was right here.[53]

Of even greater importance than training is the need to incorporate elements of diversity into all core training programs and to tailor those elements to meet the needs of specific business units or groups of employees.[54]

An added advantage of implementing a diversity initiative is the impact on employee retention. Retention of well-qualified and skilled employees is an important goal considering the amount of resources, both in time and money, spent on recruiting and hiring new employees. In 1992, Canadian organizations spent an average of 28 hours recruiting a new management and professional employee, 42 hours recruiting a new executive, and 20 hours recruiting a new technical/supervisory employee.[55] Maintaining a balanced and diversified workforce during periods of downsizing continues to be a major challenge.

Much the same as is required under employment equity, an overall review of policies and employment practices must be considered. To achieve those results, the

> **HIGHLIGHTS IN HRM**
>
> **7   ROGERS COMMUNICATIONS
> DIVERSITY MANAGEMENT PROGRAM**
>
> **MISSION STATEMENT**
> - Rogers employees are our single most important asset and we need to ensure that we continue to attract the highest qualified candidates to fill our current and future business needs.
> - We must create an environment that celebrates the diversity of our workforce and accommodates individual needs to maximize staff morale and productivity.
> - A diverse workforce will position us to take advantage and develop our business in the diverse markets and communities we serve.
> - All Rogers business units need to continually seek opportunities that ensure Diversity Management plan initiatives are realistic and achievable.
>
> **Source:** Courtesy of Colleen Quinn, Director, Staffing and Planning, Rogers Communications.

use of an employee attitude survey may prove beneficial in finding areas of systemic or perceived discrimination. The evaluation criteria used most often by Canadian organizations are surveys of staff attitudes, increases in promotions for minority employees, reduction in turnover of minority employees, reduction in number of harassment suits, recruitment statistics for minorities, and improvements in productivity.[56]

A final element in achieving success is to monitor progress and provide qualitative and quantitative evidence of change. For example, all salaried employees at Levi Strauss & Co. (Canada) Ltd. are evaluated during their performance appraisal on their ability to meet both business and aspirational goals. Aspirational goals are based on the company's core values, which include valuing diversity, ethical management practices, new behaviours, recognition, communications, and empowerment. These aspirations are the shared values and behaviours that will drive the company toward its mission of "sustained responsible commercial success."[57] Measuring management's performance related to diversity initiatives will instil those values in the minds of all employees and demonstrate that changes and valuing diversity are part of day-to-day business. Key to achieving success in diversity objectives are setting an example and creating an atmosphere that respects and values differences. Canadian organizations have recognized the competitive advantage gained by embracing diversity within their business strategies.

HIGHLIGHTS IN HRM

8 DIVERSITY AT WORK

When Apple Computer was about to market a piece of audio software called "Moof," it came close to offending 1.7 billion potential consumers in the growing computer markets of India and the Middle East. Moof was a phonetic combination of a "moo" and a "woof." Mentioning the word "cowdog" could have proved offensive to both Hindus (to whom cows are sacred) and Muslims (to whom dogs are filthy creatures).

Quebecor Printing Inc. won a $10-million deal in the Caribbean because of one employee who was a Jamaican immigrant. Lester Garnett knew the Caribbean local markets. Mr. Garnett was able to match the region's needs with Quebecor expertise to open up a new market for the Canadian company. As a result, telephone directories for Trinidad, Bermuda, and the Bahamas are printed in Canada.

Warner-Lambert Canada has promotional material printed in Korean and hired an Asian representative to establish an initial contact with the current and potential accounts due to the high involvement with Korean small retailers in Toronto.

Caisse populaire Desjardin Cartierville has hired staff to provide service in nine languages—French, English, German, Arabic, Italian, Creole, Spanish, Portuguese, and Armenian. Select marketing and promotional material has been translated into each of these languages. Regular information seminars are held to welcome new immigrants to the caisse system, and the caisse is an active participant in several ethnoculturally oriented communication organizations.

Sources: C.L. Taylor, "Dimensions of Diversity in Canadian Business: Building a Business Case for Valuing Ethnocultural Diversity," *The Conference Board of Canada, Report 143-95*, April 1995, 11; J. Schilder, "The Rainbow Connection: Employers Who Promote Diversity May Discover a Pot of Gold, " *Human Resources Professional* (April 1994): 13–15; and M. Gibb-Clark, "The Payoff Is Global," *The Globe and Mail*, May 16, 1995, B14.

SUMMARY

one objective

Employment equity refers to the employment of individuals in a fair and non-biased manner. Four groups in Canada—women, visible minorities, aboriginals, and persons with disabilities— tend to be concentrated in a few occupations that are accorded lower status and pay.

two objective

The Canadian Human Rights Act applies to all federally governed departments and agencies, and all organizations incorporated under federal jurisdiction. The Act prohibits discrimination on the basis of such grounds as race, religion, sex, age, national or ethnic origin, physical handicap, and marital status. The Canadian Human Rights Commission enforces the Act through a formal complaint procedure.

Pay equity is an amendment to the Canadian Human Rights Act that makes it illegal for employers to discriminate against individuals on the basis of job content. By definition, pay equity means equal pay for work of equal value.

The Employment Equity Act requires all federally regulated employers to prepare an employment equity plan.

The implementation of employment equity involves six steps: senior management support, data collection and analysis, an employment system review, establishment of a workplan, implementation, strategy, and a follow-up process that includes monitoring, reviewing, and revision.

Reverse discrimination, sexual harassment, and mandatory retirement are among the employment equity issues undergoing continued debate.

Managing diversity not only incorporates but goes beyond employment equity. The goal of diversity management is to optimize the utilization of an organization's multicultural workforce in order to realize strategic advantage.

three objective
four objective
five objective
six objective
seven objective

KEY TERMS

bona fide occupational qualification (BFOQ)

concentration

designated groups

diversity management

employment equity

flow data

reasonable accommodation

reverse discrimination

sexual harassment

stock data

systemic discrimination

underutilization

DISCUSSION QUESTIONS

1. Explain why employment equity is needed in organizations. What are the arguments for and against it?
2. List the prohibited grounds of discrimination. How does the CHRC deal with complaints under the Canadian Human Rights Act?
3. Describe the process involved in implementing an employment equity plan. How would you evaluate its success?

4. After receiving several complaints of sexual harassment, the HR department of a city library decide to establish a sexual harassment policy. What should be included in the policy? How should it be implemented?

5. Describe the ways in which an organization can optimize the use of a multicultural workforce.

CASE: Workplace Harassment

Jeans and Comfort is one of the many chain stores seen in just about every shopping mall. It is long and narrow, with change rooms at the back. All the different varieties of jeans hang on display racks in the middle of the store, with stacks on the shelves of each side wall. In one store, a new manager named George had started two months ago. He was in his early 30s, very big and muscular, loud and friendly. George had made many suggestive comments to Gina, an employee, when they were alone. But he would always laugh after he said anything. Gina thought this meant that he was just joking around, so she didn't complain.

It was usually quiet in the mornings at Jeans and Comfort, and this being a Tuesday morning in the second week of January made it even more so. Only Gina and George were working this morning's shift. George started making comments about how girls " with nice butts," like Gina, would look much more tempting if they'd wear a pair of tight jeans. Gina felt uncomfortable and responded by saying that it was a good thing she'd worn a pair of pleated, baggy corduroys. She said she didn't want to be known for how her body looked in a pair of Levi's three sizes too small.

A few seconds later, a woman walked in looking for sweaters. Gina helped her find the right sizes and colours. George watched. When the customer went into the change room to try some on, George came up close behind Gina and squeezed her buttocks. She was startled and shocked. She quickly moved away from George. Before she could think of anything to say, the customer had emerged from the change room. By the time Gina had finished ringing in the customer's purchase, George had left.

It wasn't until her shift had ended that Gina regained control of her anger and was ready to talk with George. She told him that he was a jerk. She also said that if there was ever a repeat of what happened that morning, she would scream rape. When she was finished, George started talking very loudly, saying that he wanted her to stop making advances toward him and that he had a steady girlfriend. By then, everyone in the store was staring. Gina was so emotionally overwrought that she quit.

Source: H. Jain and P.C. Wright, eds., *Trends and Challenges in Human Resources Management* (Scarborough, ON: Nelson Canada, 1994), 426.

Questions

1. In many incidents like this, the female employee quits. Did she have any other choice? Why? Why not?

2. Was Gina sexually harassed? Where does sexual harassment begin? Discuss.

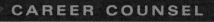

Wrongs versus Rights

During a job interview, many students have faced some of the following questions:

- How old are you?
- Where do you come from? Where were you born?
- You speak English well. What is your mother language?
- Are you married?
- Are you planning on having children?

Tempted as you might be to proclaim your rights ("That question is illegal, and I don't have to answer it!"), you still want the job. How, then, should you answer the above questions?

The correct response is to demonstrate your willingness and ability to do the job, but without revealing any information (related to the prohibited grounds) that may prejudice the interview. So, if you are asked if you have children, you could reply that you are available for any overtime work required and for short assignments out of town. Develop some responses to these difficult questions you might encounter.

NOTES AND REFERENCES

1. Prem Benimadhu and Ruth Wright, "Implementing Employment Equity: A Canadian Experience," *Conference Board of Canada Report 94-92,* December 1992, 1.
2. Dorothy Lipovenko, "Women Face Poverty, Study Says," *The Globe and Mail,* April 18, 1995, A10.
3. J. Badets and T.W.L. Chu, "Canada's Changing Immigrant Population: Focus on Canada," Statistics Canada, Ministry of Industry, Science, and Technology, Cat. No. 96-311E, 1994.
4. *Employment Equity: A Guide for Employers,* Employment and Immigration Canada, May 1991, 9, Cat. No. LM-143-5-91.
5. Victor S. Mackinnon, "The Canadian Charter of Rights and Freedoms," in *Public Administration: Canadian Materials* (North York: Captus Press, 1993), 179–180.
6. Canadian Human Rights Act, Canadian Human Rights Commission, 1978, Paragraph 2, Subsection (a).
7. A.P. Aggarwal, *Sex Discrimination: Employment Law and Practices* (Toronto: Butterworths Canada, 1994).
8. "Firm Pays $300,000 in Racial Harassment Settlements," *Human Resources Management in Canada,* Report Bulletin No. 72 (Scarborough, ON: Prentice-Hall Canada, February 1989), 1–2.
9. Canadian Human Rights Act, Paragraph 46, Section 2(a), (b).
10. "Earnings Gap Narrows," *Worklife* 9, no. 4 (1994): 17.
11. Russel J.G. Juriansz, "Equal Pay Legislation and Ontario's New Pay Equity Act" (Toronto: Blake, Cassels & Graydon), 3–5.
12. Susan Riggs, "Comparing Apples and Oranges: Job Evaluations," *Worklife* 8, no. 1 (1991): 7–10.
13. "Achieving Pay Equity First Goal, But through Co-operation: Commissioner," *Pay Equity Commission Report* 1, no. 1 (March 1988): 6.
14. Morley Gunderson and Roberta Edgecombe Robb, "Equal Pay for Work of Equal Value: Canada Experience," *Advances in Industrial and Labour Relations* 5 (1991): 151–168. See also John G. Kelly, *Pay Equity Management* (Toronto: CCH Canadian Ltd., 1988), 45–54.
15. Gunderson and Robb, "Equal Pay for Work of Equal Value."
16. Judge Rosalie Silberman Abella, Commissioner, *Equality in Employment: A Royal Commission Report* (Ottawa: Supply and Services Canada, 1984), 9.
17. Section 4, Employment Equity Act, 1986.
18. Section 2, Employment Equity Act, 1986.
19. Canadian Human Rights Act, S.C. 1976-77, c. as amended.
20. R.G.L. Fairweather, Canadian Human Rights Commission, The Standing Committee on Legal and Constitutional Affairs, May 29, 1986, 10.
21. Employment Equity and Immigration Canada, Federal Contractors Program, Information for Suppliers.
22. *Employment Equity Act Annual Report 1991,* Employment and Immigration Canada, Employment Equity Branch, 2.
23. *Towards Equity: 1993 Merit Awards,* Human Resources Development Canada, Employment Equity Branch, June 1994, 17–18.
24. *Workplace Innovations Overview—1994,* Bureau of Labour Information, Human Resources Development Canada, 1–84.
25. *Towards Equity: 1993 Merit Awards,* 11–12.
26. *Employment Equity: A Guide for Employers,* 17.
27. Ibid, 18.
28. Aggarwal, *Sex Discrimination.*
29. *Employment Equity: A Guide for Employers,* 19.
30. J. Coutts, "OCA to Hire Women for Next 10 Years," *The Toronto Star,* January 9, 1990, A13.
31. "Sexual Harassment," *CACSW Fact Sheet,* Canadian Advisory Council on the Status of Women, March 1993.
32. Dale Hall and Siobhan McEwan, *Sexual Assault and Harassment on Campus,* York University Sexual Harassment Education and Complaint Centre, York University.
33. *Sexual Harassment and You: What Every Student Should Know,* Sexual Harassment Education and Complaint Centre, York University, 1986.
34. For a good review of sexual harassment policy, see Dana S. Connell, "Effective Sexual Harassment Policies: Unexpected Lessons from Jacksonville Shipyards," *Employee Relations Law Journal* 17, no. 2 (Autumn 1991): 191–205.
35. "Supreme Court Upholds Mandatory Retirement," *Human Resources Management in Canada,* Report Bulletin no. 95 (Scarborough, ON: Prentice-Hall Camada, January 1991), 1–2.
36. Kelly Toughill, "Firms Back Equity: To Some It's 'Good Business' Despite Harris' Vow to Scrap It," *The Toronto Star,* June 21, 1995, A2.
37. Christine L. Taylor, "Dimensions of Diversity in Canadian Business: Building a Business Case for Valuing Ethnocultural Diversity," *Conference Board of Canada Report 143-95,* April 1995, 1.
38. Paul Moloney, "Toronto Okays Non-Christian Holidays for Staffers," *The Toronto Star,* May 17, 1995, A6.
39. Jennie Constantinides, "Diversity Management: At CN, the 'Token' Will Be Broken," *Human Resources Professional* 7, no. 4 (April 1991): 29–30.
40. Taylor, "Dimensions of Diversity in Canadian Business, 3.
41. Ibid.

42. Jana Schilder, "The Rainbow Connection: Employers Who Promote Diversity May Discover a Pot of Gold," *Human Resources Professional* 11, no 3 (April 1994): 13–15.

43. Ibid.

44. Lindsay Scotton, "We Are the World: The Many Faces of Canada Come Together on Winning Images in a Contest to Depict Racial Harmony," May 19, 1995, B3. See also "Logo & Poster Design Exhibition," *Voices of Harmony* 1, no. 1 (Summer 1995): 1–7.

45. Doug Nevison, "Profiting in the Pacific Rim: Can Canada Capture Its Share?" *Conference Board of Canada, Report 117-94,* 1994.

46. World Bank, 1993.

47. R. Roosevelt Thomas, Jr., "Beyond Race and Gender," *AMACOM,* 1991, 34.

48. Taylor, "Dimensions of Diversity in Canadian Business," 13.

49. John Spears, "The Many Colours of Money: Diversity Boosts Profit, Firms Told," *The Toronto Star,* May 9, 1995.

50. Taylor, "Dimensions of Diversity in Canadian Business, 15.

51. *Continuing In-Patient Focused Care Excellence,* Sunnybrook Community and Public Affairs, Sunnybrook Health Science Centre, Toronto, April 1995.

52. Amoja Three Rivers, *Cultural Etiquette: A Guide for the Well-Intentioned,* Market Wimmin, 1991, p. 1.

53. Ibid., 7–8.

54. Claudine Kapel, "Variation Is the Theme: Organizations That Value Diversity Glimpse Profits in Improved Productivity," *Human Resources Professional* 1, no. 3 (April 1994): 9–12.

55. *Compensation Planning Outlook,* Conference Board of Canada, 1992.

56. Taylor, "Dimensions of Diversity in Canadian Business."

57. Ibid., 18.

Part 2

Meeting Human Resources Requirements

The four chapters in Part 2 focus on HR staffing concerns. Chapter 4 discusses human resources planning and methods for dealing with employee shortages or surpluses. Chapter 5 deals with establishing job requirements and designing jobs that are both technologically efficient and psychologically satisfying to employees. Chapter 6 examines recruitment methods. Chapter 7 is concerned with the many issues involved in selecting employees whose personal characteristics fit with the requirements of the job. When these four interrelated HR functions are performed effectively, the organization will have developed jobs that are meaningful to employees and will have acquired a workforce capable of contributing to organizational success.

objective one *Identify the advantages of integrating human resource planning and strategic planning.*

objective two *Describe the basic approaches to human resource planning.*

objective three *Outline the options available to employers when employee shortages are forecasted.*

objective four *Delineate the alternatives for dealing with employee surpluses.*

objective five *Identify the consequences of workforce reductions.*

Chapter 4

Human Resources Planning

In earlier chapters, we stressed that the structure of an organization and the design of the jobs within it affect the organization's ability to reach its objectives. These objectives, however, can be achieved only through the efforts of people. It is essential, therefore, that jobs within the organization be staffed with personnel who are qualified to perform them. Meeting these staffing needs requires effective planning for human resources.

Human Resources Planning

objective

Human resources planning (HRP)
The process of anticipating and making provision for the movement of people into, within, and out of an organization.

Human resources planning (HRP) is the process of anticipating and making provision for the movement of people into, within, and out of an organization. Its purpose is to deploy these resources as effectively as possible, *where* and *when* they are needed, in order to accomplish the organization's goals. Other more specific purposes of HRP include anticipating labour shortages and surpluses, providing more employment opportunities for the designated groups, and mapping out employee training programs. In fact, HRP provides a launching point for almost all of the activities that are subsumed under HRM.

The most significant role played by HR planners occurs when organizations consider restructuring options. The types of decisions available to employers are discussed in this chapter.

Importance of Human Resources Planning

Consider these facts:

- The Canadian labour force will grow by less than 1 percent each year between 1993 and 2016.
- Approximately 80 percent of the new labour force entrants will be aboriginal people, visible minorities, women, and people with disabilities.[1]
- The average age of the workforce will be in the 40s by the year 2000. Over 16 percent of Canadians will be over 65 in 2010.[2]
- The five occupations expected to experience faster-than-average growth are natural, computer, and maths scientists; technicians; and sales and marketing people.[3]
- Nearly 18 percent of the workforce is composed of part-timers.[4] Over 1.5 million households included a member who operated a business from home, which represents 14.7 percent of all households.[5]
- Over one million Canadians are functionally illiterate, representing 7.5 percent of the workforce.[6]

These dramatic shifts in the composition of the labour force require that HR managers become more involved in HRP. Each of these changes affects employee recruitment while requiring additional HRP in the areas of employee selection, training, compensation, and motivation. Although planning has always been an essential process of management, increased emphasis on HRP provides the foundation for establishing an effective HRM program and for coordinating the HRM functions being performed within it. See Highlights in HRM 1 for a description of how Ault Foods Limited uses the HR plan as the driver for its other HR programs.

HIGHLIGHTS IN HRM

1   USING THE HR PLAN—AULT FOODS LTD.

Ault Foods Limited, with revenues of $1.3 billion and 3000 employees, has established strong linkages between strategic planning and human resources management. This is accomplished in three stages:

- Developing an understanding with the employees of the current realities that the business is facing.
- Vision-based planning that answers three questions: Where do we want the business to be? Where are we now? What few (one to five) areas of leverage are we going to focus on to close the gap?
- Linking the HR initiatives to the strategic development of the company and its subunits.

Broadly speaking, the organization engages cross sections of employees in an attempt to clearly understand the appropriate financial measures for the company, as well as the current reality of the business environment in which it finds itself. This usually incorporates (but is not limited to) an assessment of economic value added (EVA) as a primary financial measure, a clear determination of the business (not people) competencies required to be successful, and, lastly, the development of possible scenarios that could positively or negatively affect the business in the near to moderate term.

Having completed this stage, employees at all levels meet to review this information and to participate in a vision-based planning process. This meeting is designed to illuminate fully the current reality of the company (or appropriate subunit), and to allow participants to determine what the future will be and, more specifically, to agree on the one to five major areas of leverage that will represent the focus of investment and resourcing for the period. An example of leverage would be an investment or in research and development or in information technology.

Having established these areas of leverage, the HR function must partner at the highest level and throughout the organization to ensure that both the HR programs and developments are aligned with and meeting the needs of the business plans.

The link to planning is so critical to the HR function that business planning at Ault Foods Limited is a partnership between the financial planners and HR function. Vision-based planning, as well as certain aspects of scenario planning and core-competence determination, are either supported by or wholly managed by HR professionals. The circular process of business planning always establishes links through performance management, employee enrolment, and compensation practices.

The outputs are the long-range strategy, which forecasts over a three- to five-year horizon, and the comprehensive business plan, which incorporates the detailed action plans, budgets, targets, and contingencies for a fiscal year period. This, in turn, influences the short- and long-term HR planning initiatives, which drive the performance management process, variable compensation programs, training and development plans, succession planning, reskilling initiatives, and other HR initiatives throughout the company.

Source: Personal correspondence with Larry Morden, Senior Vice President, Ault Foods Limited, June 1995.

As one HR vice-president noted, "The scope and mission of the HR function will be under pressure to change and be responsive to market conditions, international competitive pressures, and business readjustments."[7] HRP becomes especially critical when organizations consider mergers, the relocation of plants, downsizing, or the closing of operating facilities.

An organization may incur several intangible costs as a result of inadequate HRP or the lack of HRP. For example, inadequate HRP can cause vacancies to remain unstaffed. The resulting loss in efficiency can be costly, particularly when lead time is required to train replacements. Situations also may occur in which employees are laid off in one department while applicants are hired for similar jobs in another department. This may cause overhiring and result in the need to lay off those employees who were recently hired. Finally, lack of HRP makes it difficult for employees to make effective plans for career or personal development. As a result, some of the more competent and ambitious ones may seek other employment where they feel they will have better career opportunities.

HRP and Strategic Planning

As organizations plan for their future, HR managers must be concerned with meshing HRP with strategic business planning.[8] At the broadest level, strategic planning addresses the question "What business are we in?" HRP, on the other hand, addresses the question "What skills are needed for success in this business?" Through strategic planning, organizations set major objectives and develop comprehensive plans to achieve those objectives.[9] This involves making primary resource allocation decisions, including those pertaining to structure, key processes, and the interrelationships among human resources. One element of strategic planning is determining if people are available, internally or externally, to carry out the organization's goals. An increasingly important component is the separation decisions caused by organizational restructuring.

HRP and strategic planning become effective when there is a reciprocal and interdependent relationship between them. In this relationship, the top-management team recognizes that strategic planning decisions affect—and are affected by—HR functions.[10] The HR department and its activities are viewed as credible and important along with other management functions such as production, marketing, service, and finance. HR managers must not only recognize the potential contribution they can make to organizational growth and development, they must be proactive in developing HR programs and policies that foster the organization's strategic mission.[11] This positive linkage occurs when the HR manager becomes a member of the organization's management steering committee or strategic planning group. Once this interactive and dynamic structure exists, HR managers are recognized as contributing strategic planners alongside other top managers.[12] An example of this integration is featured in Reality Check.

IBM has been a forerunner in the integration of HRP and strategic planning. Within IBM's manufacturing and product development businesses, the corporation's HR department develops a five-year HR strategic plan and a two-year tactical plan based on tentative business goals. These goals are formulated only after IBM conducts an internal and external analysis of the company's strengths and weaknesses. Major business decisions are not approved until the vice-president of HR concurs with the business plan.[13]

A HUMAN RESOURCE PLAN AT SUN LIFE OF CANADA

Wendy Yule, Director of Organization Development for Sun Life of Canada, is continually involved in strategic planning of human resources. "Having the right resources in place to make change happen is key. We are constantly looking at how our business is changing, and at ongoing trends. We want to ensure that we can anticipate the human resources needs of our business," says Yule. She belongs to professional associations, such as the Human Resources Planning Society and the Canadian Human Resource Planners, that assist her with this forecasting challenge. "We are constantly reading about new issues and trends, attending seminars and breakfast meetings. We listen to our business units to hear how their businesses are changing and jointly seek strategies to meet their needs."

Sun Life of Canada integrates its HR planning process very tightly with overall strategic planning. Each July all vice-presidents, including the VP of HR, meet to develop the strategic plan. Collectively, they develop an issue and response list, based on short- and long-term business needs. Each business unit is responsible for developing its own plan. An HR consultant reports directly to the VP of each business unit, with a dotted line relationship to the VP of HR. One part of the planning process is succession planning, that is, ensuring that the right resources are in place to achieve company objectives. The plan is then sent to the Executive Office for review and final approval in January.

A very difficult task is predicting what the organizational changes will be. "We are currently working on some very proactive business systems changes which have required us to hire more staff," says Yule. "But in two or three years from now, what will we do with that staff? We are starting to plan now and trying to identify other possible opportunities for those people."

Key to our success in HR planning is our conservative approach. "We are able to evolve because we avoid fads. Questions like 'What are our needs?' and 'What can we learn from this trend?' are considered before we do anything. It has to work in our culture."

Source: Interview with Deborah M. Zinni, May 1995.

Highlights in HRM 2 illustrates how Texas Instruments has integrated HRP and strategic planning. This effort earned them the Society for Human Resource Management's Optimas Award.

HRP and Environmental Scanning

Environmental scanning is the systematic, regular monitoring of the major external forces influencing the organization.[14] In theory, HRP requires an integration of the environment with all of the HRM functions. As the IBM example illustrates, the HRP process will be integrated with the strategic planning process through environmental scanning. This procedure is necessary because any strategies developed must be consistent with those environmental trends and contemporary issues that may

2   INTEGRATION OF HRP AND STRATEGIC PLANNING AT TEXAS INSTRUMENTS

Because Texas Instruments comprises five distinct business divisions, several of which operate internationally, human resources programs that might work well for one division could be a disaster for another. To complicate matters, any changes implemented throughout the company require the support and input of the leaders of the various divisions.

Addressing this problem has been a major effort during the past two decades, resulting in a variety of approaches.

Human resources began to establish management action teams in the late '70s. The teams were measured quarterly based on: an attitude survey; HR assessment; fair employment model results; communication; and turnover. Not all objectives were achieved and the programs didn't relate to actual business elements.

In the late '80s, the human resources function began to take a look at where it wanted to be by the year 2000. Human resources' vision for the future was a company that provided an environment of open communication and mutual trust for its work force of empowered employees.

The effort began with an analysis from a business perspective. There was a deliberate decision to get away from the old pattern in which HR developed policy and then tried to sell it to every business in the organization. The resulting structure represents a significant change from the way human resources has operated in the past.

A policy committee was formed that represented a joint venture between two teams of management, having the operating people on one team and the human resources people on the other. Every business in the organization is represented on the teams, and representation is also global: The presidents of the European, Asian and Japanese operations are all members of the committee.

Bellwether decisions are being made by this policy committee on all agenda issues basic to the culture of the organization, moving it from being seniority-based to being performance-based. The result is a set of HR policies and programs that all divisions can buy into. The HR department implements these policies and programs.

People costs represent 55 percent of operating costs in the U.S., so the company must ensure that everything possible is done to develop its people to their highest potential and use them to the best advantage. This effort has helped Texas Instruments to remain competitive in the tough high-tech industry.

The human resources function at Texas Instruments has excelled in providing service to the company by ensuring that its policies and programs are responsive to individual needs of the businesses in the organization.

have an impact on the organization. HRP, in turn, must anticipate the possible impact of these strategies upon HRM.

Organizations can select any number of environmental factors to scan; however, the following five are monitored most frequently:

1. Economic factors (including general and regional conditions and competition trends).
2. Technological changes (including robotics and office automation).
3. Political/legislative issues (including laws and administrative rulings).
4. Social concerns (including child care and educational priorities).
5. Demographic trends (including age, composition, and literacy of the workforce).

The labour force trends listed earlier, for example, illustrate the importance of monitoring demographic changes in the population as a part of HRP. Such changes can affect the composition and performance of an organization's workforce. These changes are important because employment equity plans must take into account the demographic composition of the population in the area where the organization is located. The Bank of Montreal has been a leader in the integration of HRP and strategic planning, realizing that the bank's employees must reflect its customers. The bank's strategic plan incorporated equal opportunity as a strategic goal.[15]

Furthermore, with a "maturing" workforce, HRP must consider the many implications of this demographic fact on recruitment and replacement policies. McDonald's and other fast-food chains, for example, have made a stronger effort in recent years to hire older workers.

Elements of Effective HRP

objective

HR managers follow a systematic process, or model, when undertaking HRP, as shown in Figure 4-1. The three key elements of the process are forecasting demand for labour, performing supply analysis, and balancing supply and demand considerations. Careful attention to each factor will help either top managers or supervisors to meet their staffing requirements.

Forecasting Employee Demand

A key component of HRP is forecasting the *number* and *type* of people needed to meet organizational objectives. A variety of organizational factors—including competitive strategy, technology, structure, and productivity—can influence the demand for labour. For example, as noted in Chapter 2, utilization of advanced technology is generally accompanied by less demand for low-skilled workers and more demand for knowledge workers. External factors such as business cycles (economic and seasonal trends) can also play a role. Revenue Canada, for example, relies heavily on temporary employees between January and May when tax returns are received for processing. For other organizations, the drivers of labour demand may not be quite so predictable.

Forecasting is frequently more an art than a science, providing inexact approximations rather than absolute results. The ever-changing environment in which an

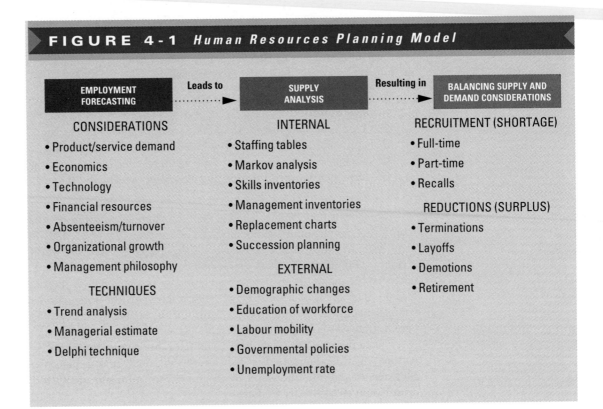

FIGURE 4-1 *Human Resources Planning Model*

EMPLOYMENT FORECASTING	Leads to →	SUPPLY ANALYSIS	Resulting in →	BALANCING SUPPLY AND DEMAND CONSIDERATIONS
CONSIDERATIONS		**INTERNAL**		**RECRUITMENT (SHORTAGE)**
• Product/service demand		• Staffing tables		• Full-time
• Economics		• Markov analysis		• Part-time
• Technology		• Skills inventories		• Recalls
• Financial resources		• Management inventories		**REDUCTIONS (SURPLUS)**
• Absenteeism/turnover		• Replacement charts		• Terminations
• Organizational growth		• Succession planning		• Layoffs
• Management philosophy		**EXTERNAL**		• Demotions
TECHNIQUES		• Demographic changes		• Retirement
• Trend analysis		• Education of workforce		
• Managerial estimate		• Labour mobility		
• Delphi technique		• Governmental policies		
		• Unemployment rate		

organization operates contributes to this problem. For example, estimating changes in product or service demand is a basic forecasting concern, as is anticipating changes in national or regional economics. A hospital anticipating internal changes in technology, organization, or administration must consider these environmental factors in its forecasts of staffing needs. Also, the forecasted staffing needs must be in line with the organization's financial resources.

There are two approaches to HR forecasting: quantitative and qualitative. When concentrating on human resource needs, forecasting is primarily quantitative in nature and in large organizations is accomplished by highly trained specialists. Quantitative approaches to forecasting can employ sophisticated analytical models, although forecasting may be as informal as having one person who knows the organization anticipate future HR requirements. Organizational demands will ultimately determine which technique to use. Regardless of the method, however, forecasting should not be neglected even in relatively small organizations.

Quantitative Approaches

Quantitative approaches to forecasting involve the use of statistical or mathematical techniques; they are the approaches used by theoreticians and professional planners. One example is **trend analysis**, which forecasts employment requirements based on some organizational index and is one of the most commonly used approaches for projecting HR demand.[16]

Trend analysis
A quantitative approach to forecasting labour demand based on an organizational index such as sales.

FIGURE 4-2 *Example of Trend Analysis of HR Demand*

YEAR	BUSINESS FACTOR (Sales in thousands)	LABOUR PRODUCTIVITY (Employees/sales)	HUMAN RESOURCE DEMAND (Number of employees)
1989	$2,351	.07	164
1990	$2,613	.09	235
1991	$2,935	.12	352
1992	$3,306	.10	330
1993	$3,613	.09	325
1994	$3,748	.09	337
1995	$3,880	.08	310
1996*	$4,095	.08	328
1997*	$4,283	.08	343
1998*	$4,446	.07	311

* projected figures

Trend analysis is typically done by following several steps. First, select an appropriate *business factor*. This should be the best available predictor of human resource needs. Frequently, sales or value added (selling price minus costs of materials and supplies) are used as predictors in trend analysis. Second, plot a historical trend of the business factor in relation to number of employees. The ratio of employees to the business factor will provide a *labour productivity ratio* (e.g., employees per dollar of sales). Third, compute the productivity ratio for at least the past five years. Fourth, calculate human resource demand by multiplying the business factor by the productivity ratio. Finally, project human resource demand out to the target year. This procedure is summarized in Figure 4-2 for a housing contractor.

Other, more sophisticated statistical planning methods include modelling or multiple-predictive techniques. Whereas trend analysis relies on a single factor (e.g., sales) to predict employment needs, the more advanced methods combine several factors, such as interest rates, gross national product, disposable income, and sales, to predict employment levels. Because of the high costs of developing these forecasting methods, they are used only by large organizations in relatively stable industries such as transportation, communications, and utilities.

Qualitative Approaches

In contrast to quantitative approaches, qualitative approaches to forecasting are less statistical, attempting to reconcile the interests, abilities, and aspirations of individual employees with the current and future staffing needs of an organization. In both large and small organizations, HR planners may rely on experts who assist in preparing forecasts to anticipate staffing requirements. **Management forecasts** are the

Management forecasts
The opinions (judgments) of supervisors, department managers, or other knowledgeable about the organization's future employment needs.

opinions (judgments) of supervisors, department managers, experts, or others knowledgeable about the organization's future employment needs.

Another forecasting method, the *Delphi technique*, attempts to decrease the subjectivity of forecasts by soliciting and summarizing the judgments of a preselected group of individuals. The final forecast thus represents a composite group judgment. The Delphi technique requires a great deal of coordination and cooperation in order to ensure satisfactory forecasts. This method works best in organizations where dynamic technological changes affect staffing levels.

Ideally, HRP should include the use of both quantitative and qualitative approaches. In combination, the two approaches serve to complement each other, providing a more complete forecast by bringing together the contributions of both the theoreticians and the practitioners.

Supply Analysis

Once an organization has forecast its future requirements for employees, it must then determine if there are sufficient numbers and types of employees available to staff anticipated openings. Supply analysis will encompass two sources—internal and external.

Internal Labour Supply

An internal supply analysis may begin with the preparation of staffing tables. **Staffing tables** are a pictorial representation of all organizational jobs along with the numbers of employees currently occupying those jobs and future employment requirements. Another technique, called Markov analysis, shows the percentage (and actual number) of employees who remain in each job from one year to the next, as well as the proportions of those who are promoted, demoted, transferred, or exit the organization. As shown in Figure 4-3, **Markov analysis** can be used to track the pattern of employee movements through various jobs and develop a transition matrix for forecasting labour supply.

In conjunction with quantitative techniques that forecast the number of employees, **skill inventories** can also be prepared that list each employee's education, past work experience, vocational interests, specific abilities and skills, compensation history, and job tenure. Of course, confidentiality is a vital concern in setting up any such inventory. Nevertheless, well-prepared and up-to-date skill inventories allow an organization to quickly match forthcoming job openings with employee backgrounds. Organizations like DuPont Canada and Hewlett-Packard (Canada) Ltd. use computers and special programs to perform this task.[17] When data are gathered on managers, these inventories are called *management inventories*.

Both skill and management inventories can be used to develop employee **replacement charts**, which list current jobholders and identify possible replacements should openings occur. Figure 4-4 shows an example of how an organization might develop a replacement chart for the executives in one of its divisions. Note that this chart provides information on the current job performance and promotability of possible replacements. As such, it can be used side by side with other pieces of information for **succession planning**—the process of identifying, developing, and tracking key individuals so that they may eventually assume top-level positions.

Staffing tables
Pictorial representation of all organizational jobs along with the numbers of employees currently occupying those jobs and future (monthly or yearly) employment requirements.

Markov analysis
Method for tracking the pattern of employee movements through various jobs.

Skill inventories
Files of education, experience, interests, skills, etc., that allow managers to quickly match job openings with employee backgrounds.

Replacement charts
Listings of current jobholders and persons who are potential replacements if an opening occurs.

Succession planning
The process of identifying, developing, and tracking key individuals for executive positions.

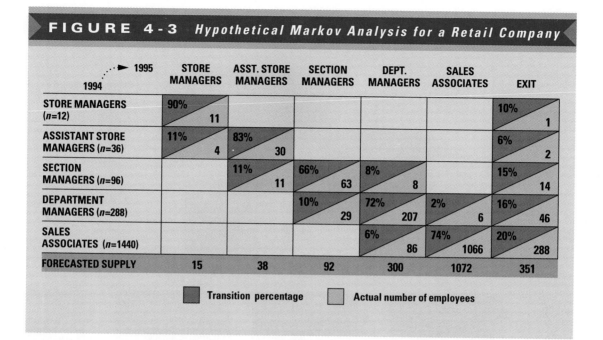

FIGURE 4-3 *Hypothetical Markov Analysis for a Retail Company*

1994 → 1995	STORE MANAGERS	ASST. STORE MANAGERS	SECTION MANAGERS	DEPT. MANAGERS	SALES ASSOCIATES	EXIT
STORE MANAGERS (*n*=12)	90% 11					10% 1
ASSISTANT STORE MANAGERS (*n*=36)	11% 4	83% 30				6% 2
SECTION MANAGERS (*n*=96)		11% 11	66% 63	8% 8		15% 14
DEPARTMENT MANAGERS (*n*=288)			10% 29	72% 207	2% 6	16% 46
SALES ASSOCIATES (*n*=1440)				6% 86	74% 1066	20% 288
FORECASTED SUPPLY	15	38	92	300	1072	351

■ Transition percentage   □ Actual number of employees

General Electric Canada engages in an HR planning process that emphasizes succession planning. Each year, all salaried employees are encouraged to participate in an accomplishment summary and development review. The employees describe their achievements, developmental needs, and career interests. Their managers appraise their performance and outline employee development needs and career prospects. Then the CEO and VP of HR review all Code 1 employees—those considered to be most promotable. These employees are registered as replacements or backups for all key posts. Candidates from other divisions are also registered if the fit seems good.[18]

External Labour Supply

When an organization lacks an internal supply of employees for promotions, or when it is staffing entry-level positions, managers must consider the external supply of labour. As noted in Chapter 2, many factors influence labour supply, including demographic changes in the population, national and regional economics, education level of the workforce, demand for specific employee skills, population mobility, and governmental policies. National and regional unemployment rates are often considered a general barometer of labour supply.

Fortunately, labour market analysis is aided by various published documents. Unemployment rates, labour force projection figures, and population characteristics are reported by various government agencies. The Canadian Employment and Immigration Commission (CEIC) analyzes labour markets to determine the supply and demand of Canadian labour. Information about supply and demand, both short and long term, is published in a variety of sources. For example, the Ford Occupational Forecast Program (COFOR) analyzes long-term labour market

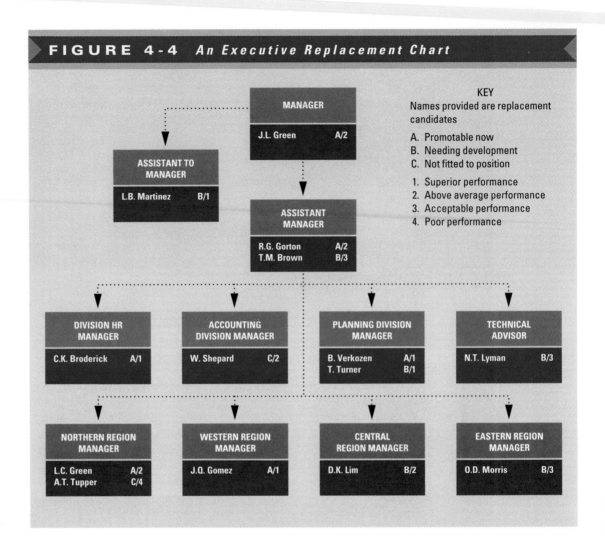

FIGURE 4-4 *An Executive Replacement Chart*

projections on a national and provincial basis. A model called the Canadian Disaggregated Interdepartmental Econometric Model (CANDIDE), developed by the Economic Council of Canada, provides a medium-term forecast of labour market trends. CANDIDE allows users to input "what if" scenarios. Another forecasting model, the Canadian Occupational Projection System (COPS), analyzes labour supply and demand by occupation over a ten-year period. The Microelectronics Simulation Model (MESIM) is a computerized supplement to COPS. The impact of technology on the composition of occupations is incorporated in MESIM. Chambers of commerce and individual provincial development and planning agencies also may assist with labour market analysis.

Balancing Supply and Demand Considerations

HRP should strive for a proper balance not only between forecasting techniques and their application, but also between the emphasis placed on *demand considerations* and that placed on *supply considerations*. Demand considerations are based on forecasted trends in business activity. Supply considerations involve the determination of where and how candidates with the required qualifications are to be found to fill vacancies. Because of the difficulty in locating applicants for the increasing number of jobs that require advanced training, this aspect of planning is receiving more attention. Greater planning effort is also needed in recruiting members of protected classes for managerial jobs and technical jobs that require advanced levels of education.

objective

Labour Shortages

According to demographic studies, Canada has neither the necessary population growth nor the right proportions of students entering technical and engineering schools to meet the predicted demand.[19] The result will be labour shortages in particular occupations, and this will impact the strategic plans within certain industries.

In an effort to meet the demand for labour, companies have several staffing possibilities, including hiring full-time employees, having employees work overtime, recalling those laid off, and using temporary employees. One Statistics Canada survey found that about 20 percent of dual-earner couples were working 90 hours or more between them.[20]

Downsizing, or rightsizing, also means that alternate ways of meeting needs for labour will have to be devised. One strategy may be to retain a small core of permanent employees, plus a fluctuating number and type of less permanent quasi-employment relationships.[21] Some ways of obtaining labour include temporary agencies, freelance professionals, part-time employees, employee leasing, subcontracting of work, and at-home workers. Employee–employer bonds are weakening along the dimensions of physical proximity, administrative control, and duration of employment.[22] Some of these employment options are discussed in the chapter on recruitment.

Many people are able to work at home because of special arrangements they have negotiated with their employers.

However, when HRP shows a surplus of jobholders, organizations may use terminations, work sharing, layoffs, or demotions or else rely on attrition (a gradual reduction of employees through resignations, retirements, or deaths) to achieve workforce balance. Because a large number of employers are restructuring their organizations, thus causing the separation of tens of thousands of workers, the options for dealing with these surplus workers are described in more detail in the following section.

Labour Surpluses

In recent years, a host of organizations have undertaken the extremely painful task of downsizing and restructuring. In a survey of 164 large companies in Canada, 80 percent reported downsizing at least once since 1988.[23] **Restructuring** refers to any major change that occurs within an organization, and that may be the result of acquisitions, retrenchments, mergers, leveraged buyouts, divestiture, plant closures or relocations, or bankruptcies. Restructuring almost always results in cutbacks, downsizing, or consolidations.

Either because of economic or competitive pressures, organizations have found themselves with too many employees or with employees who have the wrong kinds of skills. In an effort to reconcile supply and demand considerations, companies such as Safeway, CBC, Petro-Canada, Nortel, and CN Rail have eliminated literally thousands of jobs. Indeed, the federal government is laying off 20,000 employees, the largest mass layoff in Canadian history.[24] These cuts are not simply restricted to hourly workers. Technical, professional, and managerial positions are being eliminated at an unprecedented rate.[25] Furthermore, the layoffs are not simply a result of a stagnant economy. In many cases, downsizing is part of a longer-term process of restructuring to take advantage of new technology, corporate partnerships, and cost minimization.

There are several options available to employers when it comes to dealing with surplus employees: layoffs, attrition, and termination.

Layoff Strategies

Employee layoff decisions are usually based on seniority and/or ability. In some organizations, especially those with labour agreements, seniority may be the primary consideration. In other organizations, such factors as current skills and ability to learn may take precedence over seniority in determining layoffs.

In the case of unionized organizations, the criteria for determining an employee's eligibility for layoff are typically set forth in the collective agreement. As a rule, seniority on the job receives significant weight in determining which employees are laid off first. Similar provisions in the collective agreement provide for the right of employees to be recalled for jobs they are still qualified to perform. Organizational policy, as well as provisions in the collective agreement, should therefore establish and define clearly the employment rights of each individual and the basis upon which layoff selections will be made and re-employment effected. The rights of employees during layoffs, the conditions concerning their eligibility for recall, and their obligations in accepting recall should also be clarified. It is common for collective agreements to preserve the re-employment rights of employees laid off for periods of up to two years, providing that they do not refuse to return to work if recalled sooner.

objective

Restructuring
Any major change that occurs within an organization and that may be the result of acquisitions, retrenchments, mergers, leveraged buyouts, divestiture, plant closures or relocations, or bankruptcies.

While it has become customary for employers to recognize seniority in unionized employees, nonunion employees are not always given the same consideration. Due to the demand for a technically skilled workforce, the ability of employees to change jobs and learn new skills, in addition to performance and competencies, is given a great deal of weight in the layoff decision. The most important reason for using seniority as a basis for layoffs is the objective nature of the decision: number of years of work, not perception of ability, is the basis for the decision. The system is fair, and employees themselves can calculate their own probability of being employed.

One of the major disadvantages of overemphasizing seniority is that the less competent employees receive the same rewards and security as the more competent ones. The seniority system ignores talent and effort. The payroll is also higher than under other systems, because more experienced workers tend to earn more money. Also, the practice of using seniority as the basis for deciding which workers to lay off may well have a disproportionate impact on women and minority workers, who often have less seniority than other groups.

In cases where economic conditions have brought about layoffs, employees who were let go while in good standing may be recalled to their jobs when the economic outlook brightens and job openings occur. However, in many cases these new job openings require a different set of skills than the one they replaced. Identifying individuals for these jobs may be accomplished by searching among previous employees or among current employees who can be transferred. Frequently it requires searching externally in the broader labour market.

Within the layoff strategy are several work-reduction options: reduced workweek, reduced shifts, or transfers to related companies. Under the reduced workweek, employees work about 20 to 30 hours per week. This option allows the organization to retain a skilled workforce, lessen the financial and emotional impact of a full layoff, and at the same time reduce the costs of production. Some organizations have worked out arrangements so that unemployment insurance benefits make up most of the difference of the lost wages. However, it is sometimes difficult to predict how much work is available each week; in addition, overhead fixed costs such as rent and administration continue, independent of the number of hours worked.

Reduced shift work is based on a similar concept of reducing costs through the reduction of number of hours worked. Some plants operate three shifts a day and may shut down the midnight to 8:00 a.m. shift to save money. General Motors of Canada eliminated the second shift at its assembly plant in Ste. Thérèse, Quebec, throwing 1400 employees out of work.[26] Another approach is to reduce the number of operators per shift. These decisions depend on the type of operation. For continuous runs, such as those that occur in papermaking plants, the choice would be to reduce employees per shift. For clothing manufacturers, which produce in batches, the better option would be to drop one shift.

In some rare cases, organizations can transfer laid-off employees to a sister company. For example, when Dylex closed its Town and Country stores, more than 500 of its 600 laid-off Ontario employees were placed in other Dylex chain stores.[27] Shell Canada has even contacted other organizations that are in the hiring mode. Some Shell employees are re-employed within days of the layoff. Bell Canada, in the midst of laying off 5,000 employees, revamped its training courses to emphasize employability. Layoffs are the fastest way to achieve workforce reduction; attrition is the slowest.

Attrition

The natural departure of employees from organizations through quits, retirements, and deaths.

Hiring freeze

A policy in which departing employees are not replaced.

Attrition Strategies

Some organizations have adopted a no-layoff policy. These firms view people as their most important asset, and recognize that their competencies and attitudes are valuable and cannot be easily replaced. They prefer to reduce the workforce through attrition. **Attrition** refers to the "natural" departure of employees through quits, retirements, and deaths. The turnover rates of an organization vary greatly by industry and by occupation. For example, university professors rarely quit, while turnover among fast-food workers can reach 100 percent a year. Most organizations can easily estimate the numbers of people who will leave the organization, and so can slowly reduce the workforce through natural means.

Attrition must be supplemented by other practices. Hiring freezes are usually implemented at the same time as the organization adopts a strategy of workforce reduction through attrition. A **hiring freeze** means that organizations will not hire new workers as planned, or will hire only in areas critical to the success of the organization. Sometimes, the practice is to not replace the worker who has left or been fired.

These practices have several advantages. Organizations can control and predict compensation expenses. But the savings go beyond the salaries and benefits redeemed from departing employees. Take, for example, the costs of employing a manager earning $60,000 a year. Her benefits probably cost another $20,000. However, the costs of replacing her would include recruitment costs ($5000), paperwork and time in hiring costs ($1000), orientation and training expenses ($7000), and office supplies and space ($10,000). Thus, the organization can save significantly by not replacing workers.

However, the disadvantages are significant. Present employees may be overburdened with the work of those who left; their skills may not match the skill set of the departed worker; and, of course, no new skills or ideas are infiltrating the organization. The major disadvantage of reduction through attrition is that the organization cannot control who leaves and who stays. Thus, valuable employees may be retiring, while less needed ones are still on the job. And the process takes a very long time compared to layoffs, which can be accomplished in days.

Some organizations attempt to accelerate attrition by offering incentives to employees to leave. These incentives include cash bonuses for people to leave during a specified time, accelerated or early retirement benefits, and free outplacement services. However, the buyout process must be carefully managed. Employees with valuable skills who can easily find another job may be the first to cash in. Key people in key positions should not be targeted for this program. Another disadvantage is that buyouts require a great deal of money up-front, which might contravene the goal of cost reduction. For example, Ontario Hydro paid out millions in buyouts for a few thousand employees. The buyout fiasco at Safeway Canada is described in Highlights in HRM 3. Employers must be cautious when extending offers of early retirements. An older worker recently was awarded $250,000 plus benefits in a wrongful dismissal suit, because he was forced to accept the "voluntary" early retirement option.[28]

In order to sustain a no-layoffs policy, some organizations ask for volunteers to transfer into divisions where employee shortages are occurring. This causes other problems. For example, highly competent employees who have years of experience, expertise, and contacts in one position may not be as productive in another division. Skill match is a recurrent problem. Mandatory transfers allow the employer to match

HIGHLIGHTS IN HRM

3   BUYOUT BACKFIRES!

In an attempt to cut $45 million in payroll, Canada Safeway Ltd. offered a buyout package of up to $35,000 if its Alberta employees quit the company, but the offer backfired when more than half of the chain's workers in the province applied for the package. Safeway had estimated that up to 2,000 employees would accept the offer, by the April 30th deadline. Instead, between 4000 and 5000 employees applied. The buyout offer was negotiated under an agreement with the United Food and Commercial Workers union. They are now negotiating with the union to devise a way to retain some part-time workers who applied for the buyout.

Source: "News Briefs," *Human Resources Management in Canada* (Scarborough: Prentice-Hall Canada, 1993).

employee skills with vacant positions more accurately. There may be associated morale problems as individuals move into jobs or divisions they do not like, or leave their team and its working style. Union contracts may forbid or inhibit these types of transfers.

Another practice, which is extremely rare in Canada but emerging in the United States, is the worker loan-out program. Recognizing that the downsizing may be temporary, or that the policy of no-layoffs is sacrosanct, organizations might prefer to loan employees to other (noncompeting) organizations for temporary assignments. For example, IBM pays its employees for up to two years while they work in schools or charitable institutions. These loans, while apparently expensive, actually have some economic incentives. Because organizations keep their employees, there are no costs associated with severance pay, rehiring, and training. Employees return with new skills, ideas, and contacts. The goodwill generated in the community and among employees may result in free press and publicity.

If the surplus of employees is deemed to be permanent, terminations may be the only option.

Termination Strategies

Termination is a practice initiated by an employer to separate an employee from the organization permanently. Termination is different from firing, in which an employee is released for causes such as poor performance, high absenteeism, or unethical behaviour. The purpose of termination is to reduce the size of the workforce, thus saving money.

Termination
Practice initiated by an employee to separate an employer from the organization permanently.

HIGHLIGHTS IN HRM

4 SURVIVAL IN THE NEXT MILLENNIUM

The 1990s credo is the 50-50 rule: If you are over 50 years of age and make more than $50,000 your job is at risk. "We don't go out to lunch, we're afraid the doors will be blocked when we get back," says one anxious manager. About one-fifth of job losses occur at the management level. Loyalty is out; it is not reciprocated by the organization. In fact, companies may not want loyal, that is, obedient and rule-minded employees. They may require employees who are ready to push the boundaries of the organization, not be dominated or intimidated by them. Loyalty is to the profession, and it means developing different attitudes toward employment. Some suggestions are:

- Develop portable skills. Invest in training in negotiation or general management skills.
- Build outside networks. Be a member of a professional association. Attend conferences. Be aware of trends in your industry by reading all trade magazines, business sections of the newspapers, not just the company reports. Belong to volunteer organizations and other social networks. All these strategies will serve you well should you need to search for a job.
- Plan for transitions. Assume that you will not be employed by one organization for a lengthy time period. Save money for these transition periods. Identify industries where your portable skills could be useful. For example, if you have always worked in marketing, consider how these skills might be useful in the not-for-profit sector of social marketing, such as the Participaction effort of Health and Safety Canada.

Sources: C. Heckcher, *White Collar Blues, Management Loyalties in an Age of Corporate Restructuring* (Toronto: Harper Collins, 1995); "Monkeys in the Middle," *The Globe and Mail*, May 9, 1995, B10.

A termination strategy begins with the identification of employees who are in positions that are no longer considered useful or critical to the company's effectiveness. Then the managers of these employees are contacted about redeployment or termination options. Next the employee is told the news, with varying degrees of advance notice. CIBC gives three-months' notice, allows the employee and the manager to prepare a redeployment plan, and allows up to six months for retraining and repositioning.[29] At CIBC, the emphasis is on retaining competent employees whose jobs have been eliminated; the title of the program, Employment Continuity, reflects this strategy.

Employees should be concerned about their own marketability (i.e. employability). Some suggestions for surviving rightsizing are given in Highlights in HRM 4.

Employers cannot terminate without some form of compensation to the employee. **Severance pay**, a lump-sum payment given to terminated employees, is

Severance pay
A lump-sum payment given to terminated employees.

> ## ▶ HIGHLIGHTS IN HRM
>
>
> **HRM**
> **highlights**
>
> ### 5   EASING TERMINATION SHOCK
>
> Any manager who has terminated an employee will describe it as one of the worst experiences in his or her working life. Some have reported sleepless nights, stomach pains, and inability to work. There is no way to mitigate the emotional distress for the supervisor who has to terminate an employee he or she knows well. However, some experts have suggested ways in which tensions can be eased and employee retaliation reduced:
>
> 1. Plan the termination interview early in the week, so that the employee can start an action plan with the outplacement service during the week.
> 2. Make sure the date does not correspond with important dates (such as birthdays) for the employee. Recently, an employee was terminated on "take your daughter to work day." The shock and bitterness of being terminated in front of his daughter, and leaving his office with her carrying his box of belongings, has resulted in a lawsuit.
> 3. Make the interview short (less than fifteen minutes). State the reasons clearly and firmly, establishing that the decision is final, and clearly communicate all aspects of the severance package (preferably in writing).
> 4. Tell the employee the next steps and, if possible, give him or her the name of the outplacement counsellor.
>
> **Source:** Adapted from Phyllis Macklin and Lester Minsuk, "Ways to Ease Dismissal Dread," *HR Magazine* (November 1991).

calculated on the basis of years of service and salary. The legal minimum varies by province. For example, a clerk making $500 a week with eight years service would receive about $4000 in severance pay. Some additional severance-pay benefits might include continued medical and dental coverage, and insurance for a specified time period. These payments, if accepted by the employee, would immediately discharge the employer from any further obligation. Most employers now make reference to "ballpark," "reasonable range," or "reasonable offer" court decisions.[30] The ballpark approach gives some degree of certainty to appropriate layoff notice and compensation, and thus helps employees avoid costly court battles.

Some organizations adopt "golden parachutes," a form of severance pay, to protect their employees (particularly executives) from the downsizing effects of mergers, acquisitions, and leveraged buy-outs. Golden parachutes are guarantees by the employer that detail the compensation and benefits employees will receive in

ETHICS IN HRM

DOWNSIZING OR DUMBSIZING?

Numerous reports suggest that about two-thirds of companies that downsize simultaneously hire people with the same skills. Indeed, one company rehired its terminated workers to return to do the same jobs under inflated contractual arrangements. For the duration of the contract, the employees were receiving severance payments. What would the shareholders and owners say about the effectiveness of these human resource planners?

More important, how would the terminated employees feel knowing that while they were launching an often fruitless search for work, their previous company was hiring people with highly similar skills? The planning of workforce reductions must be done carefully and sensitively because the impact on employees is overwhelming.

termination situations. Golden parachutes encourage managers to work actively with the company during a restructuring, and reduce the possibility of legal challenges upon termination. But they are costly.

Outplacement services

The provision of services such as stress and career counselling, financial advice, and assistance in finding another job to a terminated employee.

Many organizations soften the blow of termination by offering **outplacement services**. This service, most often offered by agencies external to the corporation, eases the impact of termination by providing terminated employees with stress counselling, financial advice, career counselling, and assistance in locating another job. The job-search support might include office space, telephones and secretarial support, vocational testing, résumé writing, and feedback on interviewing skills.[31]

Some suggestions for managing the termination process are presented in Highlights in HRM 5 on page 143.

objective

Evaluating Restructuring

A 1993 survey uncovered over 500 articles dealing with downsizing.[32] However, very few even touched on its consequences. This section examines the consequences of downsizing on finances, organization climate, and public image.

Finances

A 1994 survey of hundreds of companies revealed that about half reported improved earnings, but only a third said productivity or customer service improved. Two-thirds had to hire at the same time as the layoffs because they were losing skills they needed to keep.[33] The ethics involved in terminating and hiring at the same time are discussed in Ethics in HRM.

Investors generally react negatively to an announcement of layoffs or large-scale reductions in the workforce.[34] A large-scale study of organizations in Atlantic Canada concluded that downsizing fails to meet financial goals because workforce reduction results in considerable people costs and the remaining personnel are less productive.[35]

Climate

Study after study shows the following effects of downsizing: surviving employees become narrow-minded, self-absorbed, and risk averse; morale sinks; productivity drops; and survivors distrust management.[36] Internally, all forms of restructuring are likely to generate fear, anxiety, and hostility. Early retirement programs and other soft attrition strategies are likely to be interpreted with less resentment than massive terminations. The organization can assume that employees anxious about the next round of terminations will suffer many stress symptoms, including reduced performance, depression, and proneness to error. The Atlantic Canada study referred to above concluded that employee commitment and morale decreased while conflict increased.

These reactions underline the growing awareness of a problem associated with restructuring: survivor sickness. Survivor sickness is a range of emotions that can include violation, betrayal, guilt, detachment, and depression. An expert in corporate downsizing, speaking to managers at a Conference Board of Canada meeting, used a family metaphor to describe the emotional impact of downsizing: "Imagine a family that seems to be functioning and suddenly the parents tell the four kids that they can no longer afford to support two of them. The next day at breakfast, nobody talks about the ones who have left. The father talks about how 'this will make us closer-knit, but you will have to take on your brother's chores.' "[37] Organizations such as Amdahl Canada recognize the existence of survivor sickness, and in a recent downsizing allocated 25 percent of the strategy to the "management of mourning," that is, mitigating the inevitable pain by communicating with honesty, directness, and respect toward fired employees.[38] The remaining 75 percent of the strategy was targeted at revitalization.

Public Image

Terminations have the most adverse impact on public perception. While layoffs are seen as temporary and attrition as benevolent, terminations are interpreted as cold and unfeeling, especially if the terminations affect competent employees with long tenure. Indeed, one expert speaking to the Calgary Personnel Association said the downsizing has driven the final nail into the coffin of company loyalty.[39] Baby boomers feel a loyalty to professions, not companies, after watching their loyal parents lose the security of lifelong employment.

However, a contrarian view suggests that the era of "entitlement" is over. The attitude that regular raises, scheduled promotions, and a secure job for life were the rights of every worker has been replaced by the attitude that workers must take responsibility for their own employability by continually earning their jobs and retraining.[40]

SUMMARY

objective

As organizations plan for their future, top management and strategic planners must recognize that strategic planning decisions affect—and are affected by—HR functions. On the one hand, HRP plays a reactive role in making certain the right number and type of employees are available to implement a chosen business plan. On the other hand, HRP can proactively identify and initiate programs needed to develop organizational capabilities upon which future strategies can be built.

objective

HRP is a systematic process that involves forecasting demand for labour, performing supply analysis, and balancing supply and demand considerations. Forecasting demand requires using either quantitative or qualitative methods to identify the number and type of people needed to meet organizational objectives. Supply analysis involves determining if there are sufficient employees available within the organization to meet demand and also determining whether potential employees are available on the job market. Reconciling supply and demand requires a host of activities including internal and external recruitment.

objective **objective** **objective**

Organizations have many options when faced with shortages or surpluses of labour. Employee shortages can be solved through leasing, outsourcing, overtime, and contract or temporary hires. Employee surpluses can be lessened through layoffs, attrition, and terminations, although the effectiveness of these strategies is under attack.

KEY TERMS

attrition

hiring freeze

human resources planning (HRP)

management forecasts

Markov analysis

outplacement services

replacement charts

restructuring

trend analysis

termination

staffing tables

severance pay

skill inventories

succession planning

DISCUSSION QUESTIONS

1. Identify the three key elements of the human resources planning model, and discuss the relationship among them.
2. Distinguish between the quantitative and the qualitative approaches to forecasting the need for human resources.
3. Delineate the advantages and disadvantages of downsizing through layoffs, attrition, and termination.
4. **a.** If you were a manager responsible for terminating your employees, describe how you would prepare for the termination interview.
   b. If you were an employee about to be terminated, what kind of assistance would you want your employer to provide?

CASE: The Federal Government

The federal government is engaging in the largest mass layoff in Canadian history. Twenty thousand employees will be affected. Some of the departments announcing cuts are Transport (16,000), Natural Resources (9,000), Public Works (5,200), and Human Resources (5,000).

Everyone is scrambling. Most workers do not know who will be affected. Even the president of the Public Service Alliance of Canada (PSAC) does not know which of his 165,000 workers will be terminated. (The Treasury Board, which is responsible for downsizing the civil service, has refused to release names for fear of violating the Privacy Act.) The president of the PSAC complained to reporters, "We are in a hell of a position trying to find these people so we can provide them assistance or even guidance and advice. At the same time, because of that fear mentality that's out there, some of the individuals are saying that 'if I go to the union that might hurt my chances of keeping my job.' It's absolutely ridiculous what's going on out there and it's another reason why we need more time."

The PSAC faces the difficult task of protecting its employees from the effects of a proposed bill (C-76) that would override the key job-security provisions of the union's labour contracts. Under the old legislation, government employees have the right to another job in the public service if their positions are eliminated. The new legislation gives public employees whose jobs are terminated 60 days to choose between a generous buyout, a chance at another job, or early retirement.

The government expects about 15,000 workers to take the buyout and another 4,000 (over age 50) to accept early retirement programs. The buyouts will cost $1 billion. In a novel twist, the PSAC wants to open up the incentive package so that affected workers who do not want to leave the government can swap their packages with employees who *want* to leave but whose positions are not terminated. Many workers in the Ministry of Transport will be transferred to the soon-to-be privatized airports and ports.

Government workers have good reason to worry. According to psychologists, people who work in huge organizations do not develop a network of external contacts that may lead to new jobs. Their skills are very narrow because of the volumes of work. For example, a clerk in the government might spend his or her entire year processing a form unique to the government. Many of these individuals have worked for only one employer and have no job-search skills. Public perceptions about the easy working life of civil servants may work against their employability. And while they are waiting for the axe to fall, they are expected to continue to work.

Source: This case was developed from information contained in newspapers, including *The Globe and Mail*, May 2, 1995, A13, and May 26, 1995, A1.

Questions

1. What downsizing strategies has the federal government adopted? What are the limitations of these strategies?
2. What should the government do to help laid-off workers find new jobs?
3. What should the government do to manage survivor sickness?
4. If you were a federal employee about to be laid off, what would you do to optimize your chances of re-employment?

Life Planning

This chapter is about planning. The first step in HR planning is to work with the senior management team to delineate organizational objectives or goals from which HR goals can be derived. Similarly, the first step in career planning is to delineate life plans from which career plans can be derived. The purpose of the exercise in this chapter is to start you thinking about your goals in life. So, find a quiet place where you will not be interrupted and allocate 30 minutes to think about the most important question: what do you want to do with your life? To help you do this, write down your answers to the following questions.

1. In two minutes, write down everything you want to do or accomplish in your lifetime.

_____

_____

_____

_____

_____

_____

_____

_____

_____

_____

_____

_____

_____

_____

_____

_____

_____

_____

2. In two minutes, write down everything you want to do or accomplish in the next THREE years.

_____

_____

_____

_____

_____

_____

_____

_____

_____

_____

_____

_____

_____

_____

3. Now, assume you have a brain tumour and will die within six months. What would you do with the last six months of your life?

_____

_____

_____

_____

_____

_____

Take your answers on these lists, and put them all on one list. Look them over. Assign an A to all those items that are most important to you. Assign a B to those items that come next in significance. Put a C beside all the rest.

The next step in priority setting is ranking. Consider those items that you have marked A. Choose the most important and put a #1 beside it. You now have your most important life goal. Find your #2, #3 (etc.) goals within the A's. Repeat this ranking exercise for the B's and C's. You now have a life plan.

NOTES AND REFERENCES

1. Shayda Kassam, "The Changing Face of the Workforce," *Plant Engineering & Maintenance* (Winter/Spring 1994): 12.

2. David Gillians, "Looking Ahead to the Year 2010," *Canadian Shareowner* 7 (September/October 1993): 16–17. See also M.V. George, J.J. Norris, F. Nault, S. Loh and J.S. Dai, "Population Projections for Canada, Provinces and Territories, 1993–2016," *Population Projections*, Demography Division, Statistics Canada, Ministry of Industry, Science and Technology, December 1994.

3. Shimon L. Dolan and Randall S. Schuler, *Human Resource Management: The Canadian Dynamic* (Scarborough: Nelson Canada, 1994), 105.

4. Drew Hasselback, "Jobless Rate Drops but Job Growth Falls: Unemployment Decline No Cause for Celebration," *The Toronto Star*, May 6, 1995.

5. "Working at Home," *The Globe and Mail*, April 10, 1995, B6.

6. "Literacy and Business: An Economic Challenge for the 90's" *Canadian Business Review* 18 no. 1 (Spring 1991): 13–15.

7. James W. Walker and Gregory Moorhead, "CEOs: What They Want from HRM," *Personnel Administrator* 32, no. 12 (December 1987): 51

8. James W. Walker, "Human Resource Planning, 1990s Style," *Human Resource Planning*, 13, no. 4 (1990): 229–240. See also Patrick Wright and G. McMahan, "Theoretical Perspectives for Strategic Human Resource Management," *Journal of Management* 18 (1992): 295–320.

9. A.D. Chandler, Jr., *Strategy and Structure: Chapters in the History of American Industrial Enterprise* (Cambridge, MA: MIT Press, 1962). See also R.E. Miles and C.C. Snow, *Organization Strategy, Structure, and Process* (New York: McGraw-Hill, 1978).

10. Dave Ulrich, "Strategic and Human Resource Planning: Linking Customers and Employees," *Human Resource Planning* 15, no. 2 (1992): 47–62. See also William E. Fulmer, "Human Resource Management: The Right Hand of Strategy Implementation," *Human Resource Planning*, 12, no. 4 (1990): 1–11.

11. Charles C. Snow and Scott A. Snell, "Staffing as Strategy," in N. Schmitt, W.C. Borman, and Associates, eds., *Personnel Selection in Organizations* (San Francisco: Jossey-Bass Publishers, 1993), 448–480.

12. Walker, "Human Resource Planning, 1990s Style."

13. "Human Resources Managers Aren't Corporate Nobodies Anymore," *Business Week*, December 2, 1985, 59.

14. R.S. Schuler, "Scanning the Environment: Planning for Human Resource Management and Organizational Change," *Human Resource Planning* 12, no. 4 (1989).

15. M.N. Martinez, "Equality Effort Sharpens Bank's Edge," *Human Resources Magazine* 4, no. 1 (January 1995): 38–43.

16. W.F. Cascio, *Applied Psychology in Personnel Management*, 4th ed. (Englewood Cliffs, NJ: Prentice Hall, 1991).

17. Tricia McCallum, "Beauty and the Hi-Tech Beast," *Human Resources Professional* 8, no. 4 (April 1992): 19–21.

18. Stuart Foxman, "Corporate Contenders," *Human Resources Professional* 10, no. 8 (September 1993): 17–19.

19. J. Schilder, "Trial by Hire," *Human Resources Professional* 11, no. 2 (March 1994): 21–23.

20. M. Gibb-Clark, "Jobs Keeping Couples Apart," *The Globe and Mail*, June 2, 1995, A1.

21. C. Fisher, "Current and Recurrent Challenges in HRM," *Journal of Management* 14, no. 2 (1989): 157–180.

22. J. Pfeiffer and J.N. Baron, "Taking the Workers Back Out: Recent Trends in the Structuring of Employment," *Research in Organizational Behaviour* 10 (1988): 257–303.

23. "Downsizing on the Decline," *Human Resources Professional* 11, no. 8 (October 1994): 6.

24. Barrie McKenna, "Axe Falls on Civil Service Jobs," *The Globe and Mail*, May 16, 1995, A1–2.

25. Jaclyn Fierman, "The Contingency Workforce," *Fortune*, January 24, 1994, 30–36; Ronald Henkoff, "Getting Beyond Downsizing," *Fortune*, January 10, 1994, 58–64; Susan Caminiti, "What Happens to Laid-Off Managers?" *Fortune*, June 13, 1994, 68–78; Del Jones, "Kodak to Eliminate 10,000 Jobs by '96," *USA Today*, August 19, 1993, B1; Tim Jones, "Retooling Unleashes Huge Wave of Layoffs," *Chicago Tribune*, June 22, 1994.

26. G. Keenan, "GM Slashing 1,400 Quebec Jobs," *The Globe and Mail*, June 3, 1995, B1.

27. Linda Gutri, "Survivor Skills," *Human Resources Professional* 9 no. 3 (March 1993): 13–15.

28. Anneli Legault, "Aging Disgracefully," *Human Resources Professional* 10, no. 11 (December 1993): 10–11.

29. David McCabe, "Improvising the Future," *Human Resources Professional* 10, no. 11 (December 1993): 17–19.

30. Malcolm MacKillop, "Ballpark Justice," *Human Resources Professional* 11, no. 7 (September 1994): 10–11.

31. William Soukup, Miriam Rothman, and Dennis Brisco, "Outplacement Services: a Vital Component of Personnel Policy," *SAM Advanced Management Journal* (Autumn 1987): 19–23.

32. W. Cascio, "Downsizing? What Do We Know? What Have We Learned?" *The Executive*, no. 7 (1993): 95–104.

33. Margot Gibb-Clark, "Survivors Also Suffer in Downsizing: Expert," *The Globe and Mail*, May 23, 1995, B5.

34. D. Worrell, W. Davidson, and V. Sharma, "Layoff Announcements and Shareholder Wealth," *Academy of Management Journal* 34 (1991): 662–678.

35. T. H. Wagar, "Downsizing or Dumbsizing? Possible Consequences of Permanent Workforce Reduction," *Proceedings of the Administrative Sciences Association of Canada Annual Conference* Vol. 15, No. 9, Human Resources Division, Halifax, 1994.

36. Cascio, "Downsizing?" 95–104.

37. Gibb-Clark, "Survivors Also Suffer in Downsizing," B5.

38. Gutri, "Survivor Skills," 13–15.

39. Bruce Tucker, "Downsizing Has Killed Loyalty," *Human Resources Management in Canada*, Report Bulletin 124 (Scarborough, Prentice Hall, June 1993), 124.

40. Chris Lee, "After the Cuts," *Training* 29, no. 7 (July 1992): 17–23.

Chapter 5

Job Requirements

After studying this chapter you should be able to

one
objective

Discuss the relationship of job requirements to the performance of HRM functions.

two
objective

Describe the methods by which job analysis typically is completed.

three
objective

Explain the various sections of job descriptions.

four
objective

List the factors that must be taken into account in designing a job.

five
objective

Describe the different quality-of-work-life programs.

six
objective

Discuss the job characteristics that motivate employees.

seven
objective

Explain the different adjustments in work schedules.

In previous chapters, we discussed the effects of the external and internal settings on HR managers. The interaction between an organization and its environment has important implications for internal organization and structure. For example, as the organization interacts with its environment, it will organize human resources to achieve specific objectives and perform different functions. The organization will formally group the activities to be done by its human resources into basic units. These basic units of the organization structure are referred to as **jobs**.

In this chapter, we will discuss how jobs may be designed so as to best contribute to the objectives of the organization and at the same time satisfy the needs of the employees who are to perform them. The value of job analysis, which defines clearly and precisely the requirements of each job, will be stressed. We will emphasize that these job requirements provide the foundation for making objective and legally defensible decisions in managing human resources. The chapter concludes by reviewing several innovative job design techniques that increase employee job satisfaction while improving organizational performance.

The Role and Importance of Jobs

Job
A group of related activities and duties.

Position
The different duties performed by, and responsibilities associated with, a single employee.

Work must be divided into manageable units and ultimately into jobs that can be performed by employees. A **job** consists of a group of related activities and duties. Ideally, the duties of a job should consist of natural units of work that are similar and related. They should be clear and distinct from those of other jobs to minimize misunderstanding and conflict among employees and to enable employees to recognize what is expected of them. For some jobs, several employees may be required, each of whom will occupy a separate position. A **position** consists of the different duties performed by, and responsibilities associated with, a single employee. In a city library, for example, four employees (four positions) may be involved in reference work, but all of them have only one job (reference librarian).

Role of Jobs in the Organization

Within an organization, each job is designed to facilitate the achievement of the organization's objectives. This is accomplished by coordinating the contents of jobs in order to perform particular functions or activities. Since all organizations experience change, individual jobs and the relationships between jobs should be continually studied to ensure an efficient work arrangement. Furthermore, delineation of jobs within the organization facilitates the division of work. If the duties of one job are made clear and distinct from those of other jobs, it is less likely that any activity required to be performed within the organization will be neglected or duplicated.

During recent years, the contribution that jobs make to organizational success has become an important new concern of managers. The cause of this concern is the effect that unproductive job duties and responsibilities have on organizational productivity. Restrictive work rules and inflexible job duties contribute to the "productivity gap" between North American and European and Asian manufacturing industries. Therefore, it is not surprising that approaches like job redesign, the increased use of employee work teams, and flexible work schedules are touted as significant new means to improve worker productivity and organizational performance.

Changing Role of Jobs in Society

The creation of jobs contributes to the economic prosperity of a community or a country as a whole. Yet according to one study, the last years of this century will bring new developments in technology, international competition, demography, and other factors that will alter the country's job structure.[1] Manufacturing jobs will continue to decline and new jobs in service industries will demand much higher skill levels. The future workplace will need employees with strong skills in communications and mathematical and technical knowledge. Unfortunately, a large number of new job entrants will lack the qualifications needed to perform successfully in the growth occupations. This situation, unless corrected, portends a shift of jobs from Canada to those countries able to provide a well-trained workforce and, consequently, a likely decline in the standard of living.[2] As Chapter 8 (on training) discusses, organizations like Bell Canada and Bruncor are establishing training programs to upgrade employee skills.

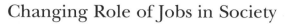

objective

Relationship of Job Requirements and HRM Functions

Job requirements
The duties, tasks, and responsibilities that make up a job.

Job requirements are the duties, tasks, and responsibilities that make up a job. Not surprisingly, job requirements influence many of the HR functions that are performed as a part of managing employees. When job requirements are modified in any way, it may be necessary to make corresponding changes in HRM activities.

Recruitment

Job specification
Statement of the needed knowledge, skills, and abilities of the person who is to perform the job.

Before they can find capable employees for an organization, recruiters need to know the job specifications for the positions they are to fill. A **job specification** is a statement of the knowledge, skills, and abilities required of the person performing the job. In the HR department for the City of Calgary, Alberta, the job specification for senior equity consultant includes the following:

1. Appropriate university degree, preferably at the Master's level.
2. Four to five years of corporate management experience.
3. Working knowledge of employment equity, human rights legislation, statistical analysis, investigative procedures, and organizational development.[3]

Because job specifications establish the qualifications required of applicants for a job opening, they serve an essential role in the recruiting function. These qualifications typically are contained in the notices of job openings. Whether posted on organization bulletin boards or included in help-wanted advertisements or employment agency listings, job specifications provide a basis for attracting qualified applicants and discouraging unqualified ones.

Selection

Job description
Statement of the tasks, duties, and responsibilities associated with a job.

In addition to job specifications, HR recruiters and supervisors will use job descriptions to select and orient employees to jobs. A **job description** is a statement of the tasks, duties, and responsibilities associated with a job.

Job specifications must not discriminate against designated groups.

In the past, job specifications used as a basis for selection sometimes bore little relation to the duties to be performed under the job description. Examples of such non-job-related specifications abounded. Applicants for the job of labourer were required to have a high-school diploma. Firefighters were required to be at least six feet tall. And applicants for the job of truck driver were required to be male. These kinds of job specifications served to discriminate against members of certain designated groups, many of whom were excluded from these jobs.

Employers must be able to show that the job specifications used in selecting employees for a particular job relate specifically to the duties of that job. In 1984, Lewington, Moran, and Leuszler brought charges of discrimination against the Vancouver fire department. The Fire Department argued that successful candidates must be at least five foot nine to be considered for employment. The Human Rights Board that heard the case could not find any correlation between the height of a firefighter and injuries or efficiencies or capacity to perform the job. The Vancouver Fire Department was found in violation of the Human Rights Act.[4] An organization must be careful to ensure that managers with job openings do not hire employees based on "individualized" job requirements that satisfy personal whims but bear little relation to successful job performance.

Training and Development

Any discrepancies between the knowledge, skills, and abilities (often referred to as KSA) demonstrated by a jobholder and the requirements contained in the description and specification for that job provide clues to training needs. Also, career development as a part of the training function is concerned with preparing employees for advancement to jobs where their capacities can be utilized to the fullest extent possible. The formal qualification requirements set forth in high-level jobs serve to indicate how much more training and development are needed for employees to advance to those jobs.

Performance Appraisal

The requirements contained in the description of a job provide the criteria for evaluating the performance of the holder of that job. The results of performance appraisal may reveal, however, that certain requirements established for a job are not completely valid. As we have already stressed, these criteria must be specific and job-related. If the criteria they use to evaluate employee performance are vague and not job-related, employers may find themselves being charged with discrimination.

Compensation Management

In determining the rate to be paid for the performance of a job, the relative worth of the job is one of the most important factors. This worth is based on what the job demands of an employee in terms of skill, effort, and responsibility, as well as the conditions and hazards under which the work is performed. The systems of job evaluation by which this worth may be measured are discussed in Chapter 11.

objective

Job Analysis

Job analysis

Process of obtaining information about jobs by determining the duties, tasks, or activities associated with those jobs.

Job analysis is sometimes called the cornerstone of HRM because the information it collects serves so many HRM functions. **Job analysis** is the process of obtaining information about jobs by determining the duties, tasks, or activities associated with those jobs. The procedure involves undertaking a systematic investigation of jobs by following a number of predetermined steps specified in advance of the study.[5] When completed, job analysis results in a written report summarizing the information obtained from the analysis of 20 to 30 individual job tasks or activities.[6] HR managers will use these data to develop job descriptions and job specifications. These documents, in turn, will be used to perform and enhance the different HR functions such as the development of performance appraisal criteria or the content of training classes. The ultimate purpose of job analysis is to improve organizational performance and productivity. Figure 5-1 illustrates how job analysis is performed, including the functions for which it is used.

In contrast to job design, which reflects subjective opinions about the ideal requirements of a job, job analysis is concerned with objective and verifiable information about the actual requirements of a job. The job descriptions and job specifications developed through job analysis should be as accurate as possible if they are to be of value to those who make HRM decisions. These decisions may involve any of the HR functions, from recruitment to termination of employees.

The Job Analyst's Responsibilities

Conducting job analysis is usually the primary responsibility of the HR department. If this department is large enough to have a division for compensation management, job analysis may be performed by members of that division. For example, in the HR department of Dofasco Inc. of Hamilton, job analysis is performed by the section titled Compensation.

Staff members of the HR department who specialize in job analysis have the title of job analyst or personnel analyst. Since the job carrying this title requires a high degree of analytical ability and writing skill, it sometimes serves as an entry-level job for college graduates who choose a career in HRM. The job description for a specialist in human resources, shown in Figure 5-2, is taken from the *National Occupational Classification*.

Although job analysts are the personnel primarily responsible for the job analysis program, they usually enlist the cooperation of the employees and supervisors in the departments where jobs are being analyzed. It is these supervisors and employees who are the sources of much of the information about the jobs. If at all possible, these

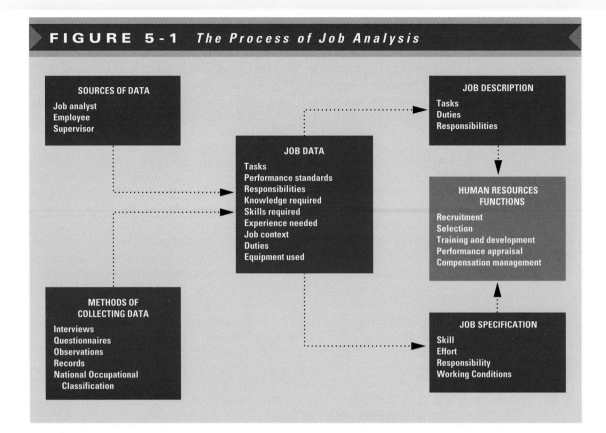

FIGURE 5-1 *The Process of Job Analysis*

supervisors and employees may be asked to prepare rough drafts of the job descriptions and specifications the job analysts need.

Gathering Job Information

Job data may be obtained in several ways. The more common methods of studying jobs are interviews, questionnaires, observation, and diaries.

Interviews
The job analyst may question individual employees and supervisors about the job under review.

Questionnaires
The job analyst may circulate carefully prepared questionnaires to be filled out individually by jobholders and supervisors. These forms will be used to obtain data in the areas of job duties and tasks performed, purpose of the job, physical setting, and the following requirements for performing the job:

1. *Skill*: experience, knowledge, education.
2. *Effort*: mental/physical demands and volume of work.
3. *Responsibility*: accountability, accuracy, supervision of others.

FIGURE 5-2 *Specialists in Human Resources*

Specialists in Human Resources develop, implement and evaluate human resources and labour relations policies, programs and procedures and advise managers and employees on personnel matters. Specialists in Human Resources are employed throughout the private and public sectors, or may be self-employed.

Examples of titles classified in this unit group

Business Agent, Labour Union
Classification Officer
Classification Specialist
Compensation Research Analyst
Conciliator
Consultant, Human Resources
Employee Relations Officer

Employment Equity Officer
Human Resources Research Officer
Job Analyst
Labour Relations Officer
Mediator
Union Representative
Wage Analyst

Main duties

Specialists in Human Resources perform some or all of the following duties:

- Develop, implement and evaluate personnel and labour relations policies, programs and procedures
- Advise managers and employees on the interpretation of personnel policies, benefit programs and collective agreements
- Negotiate collective agreements on behalf of employers or workers, and mediate labour disputes and grievances
- Research and prepare occupational classifications, job descriptions and salary scales
- Administer benefit, employment equity and affirmative action programs and maintain related record systems.
- Co-ordinate employee performance and appraisal programs
- Research employee benefit and health and safety practices and recommend changes or modifications to existing policies.

Employment requirements

- A university degree or college diploma in a field related to personnel management, such as business administration, industrial relations, commerce or psychology

or

  Completion of a professional development program in personnel administration is required.
- Some experience in a clerical or administrative position related to personnel administration may be required.

Additional information

- Progression to management positions is possible with experience.

Classified elsewhere

- *Human Resources Managers* (0112)
- *Personnel and Recruitment Officers* (1223)
- *Personnel Clerks* (1442)
- *Professional Occupations in Business Services to Management* (1122)
- Training officers and instructors (in 4131 *College and Other Vocational Instructors*)

Source: Employment and Immigration Canada, *National Occupational Classification*, Cat. No. MP 53-25/1-1992-E (Ottawa: Ministry of Supply and Services, 1992).

    4. *Working conditions*: danger, exposure to accident and/or health hazards, physical environment/surroundings.

Equipment and materials may also be included.

Observation

The job analyst may learn about the jobs by observing and recording on a standardized form the activities of jobholders. Videotaping jobs for later study is an approach used by some organizations.

Diaries

Jobholders themselves may be asked to keep a diary of their work activities during an entire work cycle. Diaries are normally filled out at specific times of the work shift (e.g., every half-hour or hour) and maintained for a two- to four-week period.

Controlling the Accuracy of Job Information

If job analysis is to accomplish its intended purpose, the job data collected must be accurate. Care must be taken to ensure that all important facts are included. A job analyst should watch out for employees who tend to exaggerate the difficulty of their jobs in order to inflate their egos (and their paycheques). Ethics in HRM highlights such a case. When interviewing employees or reviewing their questionnaires, the job analyst must look for any responses that do not agree with other facts or impressions the analyst has received. Furthermore, when job information is collected from employees, a representative group of individuals should be surveyed.

    Whenever a job analyst doubts the accuracy of information provided by employees, he or she should obtain additional information from them, from their supervisors, or from other individuals who are familiar with or perform the same job. It is common practice to have the descriptions for each job reviewed by the jobholders and their supervisors. The job description summaries contained in the *National Occupational Classification* can also serve as a basis for the job analyst's review.

    Finally, the traditional approach to job analysis assumes a static job environment. However, as jobs change, job analysis data becomes inaccurate. Outdated job analysis information can hinder an organization's ability to be flexible and adapt to change. Downsizing, computerization, the demands of small organizations, or the need to respond to global changes alter the nature of jobs and the characteristics of individuals needed to successfully perform them. Therefore, a "future-oriented" approach to job analysis is recommended when organizations anticipate rapid change.[7]

The *NOC* and Job Analysis

Commonly referred to as the *NOC*, the *National Occupational Classification* is compiled by the federal government. The *NOC* contains standardized and comprehensive descriptions of about 25,000 occupational titles. The purpose of the *NOC* is to compile, analyze, and communicate information about occupations. This information may be used for employment equity, human resource planning, and occupational supply and demand forecasts or analyses.

> ### ETHICS IN HRM
>
> ### INFLATION
>
> At some point in your working life, you will be asked to describe your job, perhaps by answering questions on a form or being interviewed by a job analyst. Most employees have a reasonable expectation that their answers will affect their lives in significant ways. The information obtained may be used to reclassify the job to either a higher or lower pay level. Most employees believe that working standards may change—and the employer will expect them to work faster or to do more—although that is not the goal of job analysis.
>
> As a result of these beliefs and expectations, employees have a vested interest in "inflating" the job description by making the job sound very important and very difficult. Thus, night clerks in hotels become auditors and receptionists become executive assistants. Making a job sound more important than it is may reflect an employee's sincere belief in the significance of his or her contribution, or an attempt to lobby for higher pay.

The *NOC* is a composite of the Canadian labour market, and has helped to bring about a greater degree of uniformity in the job titles and descriptions used by employers in different parts of the country. This uniformity has facilitated the movement of workers from regions that may be experiencing widespread unemployment to areas where employment opportunities are greater. The *NOC* code numbers facilitate the exchange of statistical information about jobs, and are useful in reporting research in the HR area, in vocational counselling, and in charting career paths through job transfers and/or advancements.

The *NOC* replaces the Canadian Classification and Dictionary of Occupations (CD) and the closely related 1980 Standard Occupational Classification (SOC) system prepared by Statistics Canada. It represents a new structure for analyzing and understanding the labour market, and reflects occupational changes that have occurred over the past two decades. Companies that formerly used CD or SOC codes will find it necessary to cross-reference to the *NOC* counterparts.[8]

Approaches to Job Analysis

The systematic and quantitative definition of job content that job analysis provides is the foundation of many HRM practices, serving to justify job descriptions and other HRM selection procedures. It should be emphasized that a major goal of modern job analysis is to help the organization establish the *job-relatedness* of its selection requirements. Therefore, these procedures help both large and small employers to meet their legal obligations under human rights employment standards and/or pay equity and employment equity legislation as prescribed by each province. Several different job analysis approaches are used, each with specific advantages and disadvantages. Three of the more popular methods are functional job analysis, the position analysis questionnaire system, and the critical incident method.

Functional Job Analysis

Functional job analysis (FJA)

Quantitative approach to job analysis that utilizes a compiled inventory of the various functions or work activities that can make up any job and that assumes that each job involves three broad worker functions: (1) data, (2) people, and (3) things.

The **functional job analysis (FJA)** approach utilizes an inventory of the various types of functions or work activities that can constitute any job. FJA thus assumes that each job involves performing certain functions. Specifically, there are three broad worker functions that form the bases of this system: (1) data, (2) people, and (3) things. These three categories are subdivided to form a hierarchy of worker-function scales as shown in Figure 5-3. The job analyst, when studying the job under review, will indicate the functional level for each of the three categories (e.g., "copying" under "DATA") and then reflect the relative involvement of the worker in the function by assigning a percentage figure to each function (i.e., 50 percent to "copying"). This is done for each of the three areas, and the three functional levels must equal 100 percent. The end result is a quantitatively evaluated job. FJA can easily be used to describe the content of jobs and to facilitate the writing of job descriptions and specifications; it is used as a basis for the *Dictionary of Occupational Titles* (*DOT*) code, the U.S. equivalent of *NOC*.

FIGURE 5-3 *Difficulty Levels of Worker Functions*

DATA (4TH DIGIT)	PEOPLE (5TH DIGIT)	THINGS (6TH DIGIT)
0 Synthesizing	0 Mentoring	0 Setting-up
1 Coordinating	1 Negotiating	1 Precision working
2 Analyzing	2 Instructing	2 Operating-controlling
3 Compiling	3 Supervising	3 Driving-operating
4 Computing	4 Diverting	4 Manipulating
5 Copying	5 Persuading	5 Tending
6 Comparing	6 Speaking-signalling*	6 Feeding-offbearing
	7 Serving	7 Handling
	8 Taking instructions—Helping	

*Hyphenated factors are single factors.

Source: U.S. Department of Labour, Employment and Training Administration, *Revised Handbook for Analyzing Jobs* (Washington, DC: U.S. Government Printing Office, 1991).

The Position Analysis Questionnaire System

The **position analysis questionnaire (PAQ)** is a quantifiable data collection method covering 194 different worker-oriented tasks. Using a five-point scale, the PAQ seeks to determine the degree, if any, to which the different tasks, or job elements, are involved in performing a particular job. The 194 different elements are grouped into the six divisions shown in Figure 5-4.[9]

A sample page from the PAQ covering eleven elements of the Information Input Division is shown in Figure 5-5. The person making an analysis with this questionnaire would rate each of the elements using the five-point scale shown in the upper right-hand corner of the sample page. The results obtained with the PAQ are quantitative and can be subjected to statistical analysis. The PAQ also permits dimensions of behaviour to be compared across a number of jobs and permits jobs to be grouped on the basis of common characteristics.

Critical Incident Method

The objective of the **critical incident method** is to identify critical job tasks. Critical job tasks are those important duties and job responsibilities performed by the jobholder that lead to job success. Information about critical job tasks can be collected through interviews with employees or supervisors or through self-report statements written by employees.

Suppose, for example, that the job analyst is studying the job of reference librarian. The interviewer will ask the employee to describe the job on the basis of what is done, how the job is performed, and what tools and equipment are used. The reference librarian may describe the job as follows:

> *I assist patrons by answering their questions related to finding books, periodicals, or other library materials. I also give them directions to help them find materials within the building. To perform my job I may have to look up*

Position analysis questionnaire (PAW)

Questionnaire covering 194 different tasks which, by means of a five-point scale, seeks to determine the degree to which different tasks are involved in performing a particular job.

Critical incident method

Job analysis method by which important job tasks are identified for job success.

FIGURE 5-4   *Divisions and Number of Job Elements in the*

DIVISION	NUMBER OF JOB ELEMENTS
Information input (where and how does the worker get the information used in the job)	35
Mental processes (what reasoning, decision making, planning, etc., are involved in the job)	14
Work output (what physical activities do the workers perform, and what tools or devices do they use)	49
Relationships with other persons (what relationships with other people are required in the job)	36
Job context (in what physical and social contexts is the work performed)	19
Other job characteristics	41

FIGURE 5-5   *A Sample Page from the Position Analysis Questionnaire*

INFORMATION INPUT

		Extent of Use (U)
	NA	Does not apply
	1	Nominal/very infrequent
	2	Occasional
	3	Moderate
	4	Considerable
	5	Very substantial

1   **INFORMATION INPUT**

1.1   Sources of Job Information

Rate each of the following items in terms of the extent to which it is used by the worker as a source of information in performing his job.

1.1.1   Visual Sources of Job Information

1 U   Written materials (books, reports, office notes, articles, job instructions, signs, etc.)

2 U   Quantitative materials (materials which deal with quantities or amounts, such as graphs, accounts, specifications, tables of numbers, etc.)

3 U   Pictorial materials (pictures or picturelike materials used as *sources* of information, for example, drawings, blueprints, diagrams, maps, tracings, photographic films, x-ray films, TV pictures, etc.)

4 U   Patterns/related devices (templates, stencils, patterns, etc., used as *sources* of information when *observed* during use; do *not* include here materials described in item 3 above)

5 U   Visual displays (dials, gauges, signal lights, radar scopes, speedometers, clocks, etc.)

6 U   Measuring devices (rulers, calipers, tire pressure gauges, scales, thickness gauges, pipettes, thermometers, protractors, etc., used to obtain visual information about physical measurements; do *not* include here devices described in item 5 above)

7 U   Mechanical devices (tools, equipment, machinery, and other mechanical devices which are sources of information when *observed* during use or operation)

8 U   Materials in process (parts, materials, objects, etc., which are *sources* of information when being modified, worked on, or otherwise processed, such as bread dough being mixed, workpiece being turned in a lathe, fabric being cut, shoe being resoled, etc.)

9 U   Materials *not* in process (parts, materials, objects, etc., not in the process of being changed or modified, which are *sources* of information when being inspected, handled, packaged, distributed, or selected, etc., such as items or materials in inventory, storage, or distribution channels, items being inspected, etc.)

10 U   Features of nature (landscapes, fields, geological samples, vegetation, cloud formations, and other features of nature which are observed or inspected to provide information)

11 U   Man-made features of environment (structures, buildings, dams, highways, bridges, docks, railroads, and other "man-made" or altered aspects of the indoor or outdoor environment which are *observed* or *inspected* to provide job information; do not consider equipment, machines, etc., that an individual uses in his work, as covered by item 7).

Source: E.J. McCormick, P.R. Jeanneret, and R.C. Mecham, *Position Analysis Questionnaire*, copyright 1979 by Purdue Research Foundation, West Lafayette, IN 47907. Reprinted with permission.

materials myself or refer patrons to someone who can directly assist them. Some individuals may need training in how to use reference materials or special library facilities. I also give library tours to new patrons. I use computers and a variety of reference books to carry out my job.

After the job data are collected, the analyst will then write separate task statements that represent important job activities. For the reference librarian, one task statement might be "Listens to patrons and answers their questions related to locating library materials." Typically the job analyst will write five to ten important task statements for each job under study. The final product will be written task statements that are clear, complete, and easily understood by those unfamiliar with the job. The critical incident method is an important job analysis method since it teaches the analyst to focus on employee behaviours critical to job success.

objective

Job Descriptions

As previously noted, a job description is a written description of a job and the types of duties it includes. Since there is no standard format for job descriptions, they tend to vary in appearance and content from one organization to another. However, most job descriptions will contain at least three parts: the job title, a job identification section, and a job duties section. If the job specifications are not prepared as a separate document, they are usually stated in the concluding section of the job description. Highlights in HRM 1 shows a job description for an HR employment assistant. This sample job description includes both job duties and job specifications, and should satisfy most of the job information needs of managers who must recruit, interview, or orient a new employee.

The Job Title

Selection of a job title is important for several reasons. First, the job title lends psychological importance and status to the employee. For instance, "sanitation expert" is a more appealing title than "garbage collector." Second, if possible, the title should provide some indication of what the duties of the job entail. Titles like "meat inspector," "electronics assembler," "salesperson," and "engineer" obviously hint at the nature of the duties of these jobs. The job title also should indicate the relative level occupied by its holder in the organizational hierarchy. For example, the title "junior engineer" implies that this job occupies a lower level than that of "senior engineer." Other titles that indicate the relative level in the organizational hierarchy are "welder's helper" and "laboratory assistant."

Certain kinds of job titles should be avoided altogether. For example, a series of identical titles with qualifiers, such as "inventory clerk I" and "inventory clerk II," makes it difficult to distinguish one job from another.[10] Job titles qualified by the terms "man" or "woman" are also being discarded to avoid the implication that the jobs can be performed only by members of one gender. Thus, a postman is now a postal worker; and a steward or a stewardess, a "flight attendant."

The Job Identification Section

The job identification section of a job description usually follows the job title. It includes such items as the departmental location of the job, the person to whom the jobholder reports, and the date the job description was last revised. Sometimes it also

HIGHLIGHTS IN HRM

1 JOB DESCRIPTION FOR AN EMPLOYMENT ASSISTANT

Job Identification

JOB TITLE: Employment Assistant

Division:	Western Region
Department:	Human Resources Management
Job Analyst:	Virginia Sasaki
Date Analyzed:	09-01-95
Wage Category:	Exempt
Report to:	HR Manager
Job Code:	11-17
Date Verified:	11-12-95

Brief Listing of Major Job Duties

JOB STATEMENT

Performs professional human resources work in the areas of employee *recruitment* and *selection, testing, orientation, transfers,* and maintenance of employee human resources files. May handle special assignments and projects in *Employment Equity/Pay Equity, employee grievances, training,* or *classification and compensation.* Works under general supervision. Incumbent exercises initiative and independent judgment in the performance of assigned tasks.

Essential Duties and Responsibilities

ESSENTIAL FUNCTIONS

1. Prepares recruitment literature and job advertisements for applicant placement.
2. Schedules and conducts personal interviews to determine applicant suitability for employment. Includes reviewing mailed applications and résumés for qualified personnel.
3. Supervises administration of testing program. Responsible for developing or improving testing instruments and procedures.
4. Presents orientation program to all new employees. Reviews and develops all materials and procedures for orientation program.
5. Coordinates division job posting and transfer program. Establishes job posting procedures. Responsible for reviewing transfer applications, arranging transfer interviews, and determining effective transfer dates.
6. Maintains a daily working relationship with division managers on human resource matters, including recruitment concerns, retention or release of probationary employees, and discipline or discharge of permanent employees.
7. Distributes new or revised human resources policies and procedures to all employees and managers through bulletins, meetings, memorandums, and/or personal contact.
8. Performs related duties as assigned by the human resource manager.

(continued)

Job Specifications abd Requirements

JOB SPECIFICATIONS

1. Four-year university degree with major course work in human resources management, business administration, or industrial psychology; OR a combination of experience, education, and training equivalent to a degree in human resources management.
2. Considerable knowledge of principles of employee selection and assignment of personnel.
3. Ability to express ideas clearly in both written and oral communications.
4. Ability to independently plan and organize one's own activities.
5. Knowledge of human resource computer applications desirable.

contains a payroll or code number, the number of employees performing the job, the number of employees in the department where the job is located, and the *NOC* code number. The "Statement of the Job" usually appears at the bottom of this section and serves to distinguish the job from other jobs—something the job title may fail to do.

Essential Functions Section
The statements covering job duties are typically arranged in order of importance. These statements should indicate the weight, or value, of each duty. Usually, but not always, the weight of a duty can be gauged by the percentage of time devoted to it. The statements should stress the responsibilities all the duties entail and the results they are to accomplish. It is general practice also to indicate the tools and equipment used by the employee in performing the job.

Job Specifications
As stated earlier, the personal qualifications an individual must possess in order to perform the duties and responsibilities contained in a job description are compiled in the job specification. Typically the job specification covers two areas: (1) the skill required to perform the job, and (2) the physical demands the job places upon the employee performing it.

Skills relevant to a job include education or experience, specialized training, personal traits or abilities, and manual dexterities. The physical demands of a job refer to how much walking, standing, reaching, lifting, or talking must be done on the job. The condition of the physical work environment and the hazards employees may encounter are also among the physical demands of a job.

Problems with Job Descriptions

HR managers consider job descriptions a valuable tool for performing HRM functions. Nevertheless, several problems are frequently associated with these documents, including the following:

1. They are often poorly written, providing little guidance to the jobholder.
2. They are not updated as job duties or specifications change.

3. They may violate federal or provincial legislation by containing specifications not related to job success.

4. The job duties they include may be written in vague rather than specific terms.

5. They can limit the scope of activities of the jobholder.

Some of these problems are being addressed by new approaches to job analysis, outlined in Reality Check.

Writing Clear and Specific Job Descriptions

When writing a job description, it is essential to use statements that are terse, direct, and simply worded. Unnecessary words or phrases should be eliminated. Typically the sentences that describe job duties begin with a verb in its present tense, with the implied subject of the sentence being the employee performing the job. The term "occasionally" is used to describe those duties that are performed once in a while. The term "may" is used in connection with those duties performed only by some workers on the job.

Even when set forth in writing, job descriptions and specifications can still be vague. To the consternation of many employers, however, today's legal environment has created what might be called an "age of specifics." Human rights legislation requires that the specific performance requirements of a job be based on *valid* job-related criteria. Personnel decisions that involve either job applicants or employees and are based on criteria that are vague or not job-related are increasingly being challenged successfully. Managers of small businesses, where employees may perform many different job tasks, must be particularly concerned about writing specific job descriptions.

When preparing job descriptions, managers must be aware of human rights legislation. Written job descriptions must match the requirements of the job. Position descriptions may need to be altered to meet "reasonable accommodation." Reasonable accommodation is used most frequently to match religious or disability needs. The 1992 case *Renaud v. British Columbia School Board* made it clear that reasonable accommodation for religious reasons is valid.[11] Job descriptions written to meet the needs for reasonable accommodation reduce the risk of discrimination. The goal is to match and accommodate human capabilities to job requirements. For example, if the job requires the jobholder to read extremely fine print, to climb ladders, or to memorize stock codes, these physical and mental requirements should be stated within the job description.

The Value of Written Job Requirements

Spelling out job requirements in job descriptions and job specifications is essential in order for members of the HR staff to perform their duties. Job descriptions, in particular, are of value to both the employees and the employer. From the employees' standpoint, job descriptions can be used to help them learn their job duties and to remind them of the results they are expected to achieve. From the employer's standpoint, written job descriptions can serve as a basis for minimizing the misunderstandings that occur between supervisors and their subordinates concerning job requirements. They also establish management's right to take corrective action when the duties covered by the job description are not performed as required.

JOB ANALYSIS AT HAY McBER

The nature of job analysis is changing, as competency based models are gaining strength in Canadian workplaces. As we focus on people, the development of job descriptions, which consider the abilities, knowledge, and skill of our "job contributors," is predominating. A job used to be a piece of paper outlining what was expected of jobholders—nothing less, nothing more. Today, we are seeing that piece of paper change to address the needs of a changing workforce and workplace expectations.

Dr. Charles Bethell-Fox, vice-president of Hay McBer's Human Resources Planning and Development practice in New York and Toronto, works closely with organizations to help them manage change via development of effective work processes and competencies aligned with strategic business needs.

Dr. Bethell-Fox says, "When we look at what is changing in the workplace, we see that the traditional job and the nature of work are not what they used to be. People who work for organizations increasingly find themselves performing work that may not be covered in a job description. People are working in teams, and the demands in terms of skills and knowledge,change as the project changes. Functional silos are breaking down and cross-functional teams are becoming the norm. We have also seen a delayering in organizations where a part of the hierarchy, particularly middle management, is being taken away. What that means for people and jobs is that they don't fit into tidy slots within the organization."

When we try to capture what people do in their jobs it is important to look at what they bring to the work situation. Knowing what they are able to do determines what they can get involved with, what strengths they bring to the team, how they can contribute. For example, look at the technical support who knows about a content area such as information systems. He or she is asked to work on project teams to supply a particular type of skill the team requires. Then he or she may also be asked to work on a different team with different groups of people and contribute other types of knowledge.

In addition, organizations are becoming increasingly focused on customers as a means of gaining a competitive advantage. "If you want competitive advantage, you need to leverage all internal resources to the greatest degree," states Bethell-Fox. As a jobholder, if you have a particular strength you don't want to be positioned in the organization in such a way that the organization cannot gain maximum competitive advantage from your strength. The old hierarchical structures used to foster people working within functional silos, but today you want people working together. When you combine the skills of Person A with those of Person B, the two together may meet the customer or market needs that could not have been achieved had you not built on the combined strengths of your people. "If people are working this way, based on what they can contribute, how can we talk about a job as if it fits into one part of the organization?" asks Bethell-Fox.

Looking at what people bring to their roles—their abilities, knowledge, and skills—is important because it helps you to understand what they can contribute to the team. Bethell-Fox goes on to state, "If the measures of what an individual brings to an organization are accurate and reliable, you are in a better position to assess people and can better put them on teams where they will be able to maximize their contributions."

Clearly, job descriptions must still contain a clear description of accountabilities. But we also need to capture what competencies are expected in the job and how the person needs to do the job.

For example, when we say that the individual must have this five years of management experience, this tells us little about what is expected. If instead we state that the individual must be able to generate a high level of teamwork and achievement, the expectations become clearer—we can almost visualize what is expected.

Bethell-Fox further states, "If people are to maximize their contribution to the organization we need to have a clear understanding of the competencies that will deliver *superior* results. To deal with that we have devised are called 'Just Noticeable Difference' (JND) competency measurement scales. On these scales, different behavioural indicators of any one competency are organized into an ascending scale where behaviours known to deliver progressively higher levels of job output and performance appear at progressively higher levels on each scale."

Once the right competencies have been identified for a job or job family, the scales can be used to specify the level of behaviour required to deliver superior performance. Then current jobholders and job applicants can be assessed against the scales to measure how well their demonstrated levels of competency match the requirements for superior performance. For those who do not meet the right competencies, training can be provided.

Different levels of competency lead to different jobholders doing the same job in different ways and, in effect, thereby doing different jobs. For example, one jobholder might be a willing participant in the team, doing his or her share of the work. Another person in the same job, however, might demonstrate more proactive team behaviours, such as actively soliciting input from other team members or taking action to calm down conflicts among other team members. Effectively, these two people are doing two different jobs because of the competencies they demonstrate. In this way, competencies define what a job means.

In closing, one of the advantages of looking at things with a competency-based point of view is that if you have a clear understanding of the competencies that drive superior performance in a role then you can integrate a whole range of human resource applications around the competency framework. In other words, selection, training and development, performance management, and even pay systems can all be built around the competency framework. This adds significant value by ensuring that you now have multiple HR programs all pointed in the same direction and closely aligned with the business strategy.

Source: Interview with Deborah M. Zinni, June 1995.

Job Design

objective

Job design
Outgrowth of job analysis that improves jobs through technological and human considerations in order to enhance organization efficiency and employee job satisfaction.

An outgrowth of job analysis, **job design** is concerned with structuring jobs in order to improve organization efficiency and employee job satisfaction. The design of a job should reflect both technological and human considerations. It should facilitate the achievement of organizational objectives and the performance of the work that the job was established to accomplish. At the same time, the design should recognize the capacities and needs of those who are to perform it.

As Figure 5-6 illustrates, job design is a combination of four basic considerations: (1) the organizational objectives the job was created to fulfil; (2) industrial engineering considerations, including ways to make the job technologically efficient; (3) human engineering concerns, including workers' physical and mental capabili-

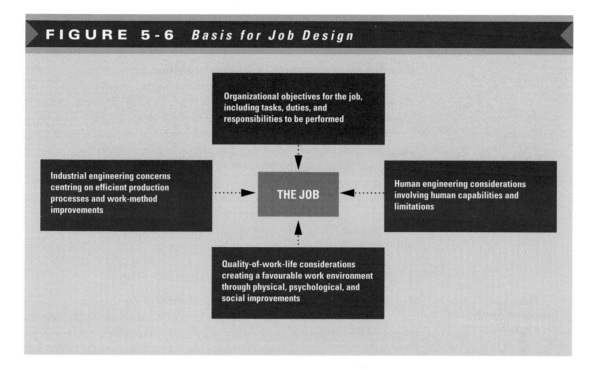

FIGURE 5-6 *Basis for Job Design*

Organizational objectives for the job, including tasks, duties, and responsibilities to be performed

Industrial engineering concerns centring on efficient production processes and work-method improvements

THE JOB

Human engineering considerations involving human capabilities and limitations

Quality-of-work-life considerations creating a favourable work environment through physical, psychological, and social improvements

ties; and (4) quality-of-work-life changes. Quality-of-work-life considerations in job design or redesign are reflected in contemporary programs. Three of the more popular programs are job enrichment, job enlargement, and employee teams, all of which are discussed later in the chapter.

Industrial Engineering Considerations

Industrial engineering
A field of study concerned with analyzing work methods and establishing time standards.

The study of work is an important contribution of the scientific management movement. **Industrial engineering,** which evolved with this movement, is concerned with analyzing work methods and establishing time standards. Specifically, it involves both analyzing the elements of the work cycle that compose a particular job activity and determining the time required to complete each element. This may include eliminating any seemingly duplicate processes in the work cycle, or it may involve combining the tasks of two employees.

Development of Time Standards

Identifying and timing the elements in a work cycle are generally the responsibilities of the industrial engineering staff. They study the work cycle to determine which, if any, of its elements can be modified, combined, rearranged, or eliminated to reduce the time needed to complete the cycle.

To establish time standards, the industrial engineering staff measures and records the time required to complete each element in the work cycle, using a stopwatch or work sampling techniques. By combining the times for each element, they determine the total time required. This time is subsequently adjusted to allow for the skill and effort demonstrated by the observed worker and for interruptions that may occur in performing the work. The adjusted time becomes the time standard for that particular work cycle. This standard then provides an objective basis for evaluating and improving employee performance and for determining incentive pay.

Benefits and Limitations of Industrial Engineering

Since jobs are created primarily to enable an organization to achieve its objectives, the efficiency goals of industrial engineering cannot be ignored. Industrial engineering does constitute a disciplined and objective approach to job design. Unfortunately, the concern of industrial engineering for improving efficiency and simplifying work methods may cause the human considerations in job design to be neglected. What may be improvements in job design and efficiency from an engineering standpoint can sometimes prove to be psychologically unsound. For example, the assembly line with its simplified and repetitive tasks embodies sound principles of industrial engineering, but these tasks are often not psychologically rewarding for those who must perform them. Thus, to be effective, job design must also provide for the satisfaction of human needs.

Human Engineering Considerations

Human engineering

An interdisciplinary approach to designing machines and systems that can be easily and efficiently used by human beings.

Human engineering attempts to accommodate the human capabilities and deficiencies of those who are to perform a job. It is concerned with adapting the entire job system—the work, the work environment, the machines, the equipment, and the processes—to match human characteristics. In short, it seeks to fit the machine to the person rather than the person to the machine. Also referred to as *human factors engineering*, *ergonomics*, and *engineering psychology*, human engineering attempts to minimize the harmful effects of poor work design that otherwise may cause product defects, damage to equipment, or even the injury or death of employees.

Machine design must take into consideration the physical ability of operators to use the machines and to react through vision, hearing, and touch to the information that the machines convey. The National Aeronautics and Space Administration (NASA) widely employed the principles of human engineering to improve the visual and auditory display of information through dials, instruments, and indicators on the space shuttle *Discovery*. Designing equipment controls to be compatible with both the physical characteristics and reaction capabilities of the people who must operate them and the environment in which they work is increasingly important in the design of work systems. At General Motors of Canada's newly designed transmission plant in Windsor, Ontario, mechanical assists have been installed throughout workstations to insulate the operators from force factors. These ergonomically designed assists use articulating arms to help operators ward off the potentially strain-causing force of the heavy parts they may be lifting, pushing, or pulling.[12] While human engineering ordinarily focuses on what is the best arrangement for a large percentage of workers, it can also aid in the design of jobs for specific groups such as the physically challenged or the elderly.[13]

Job Design and the Problem of Overspecialization

Organizations typically combine similar duties and tasks into a job to facilitate the selection, training, and supervision of personnel who are to perform it. In doing so, organizations may unintentionally create jobs that are monotonous to perform. The employees performing such jobs face a problem referred to as "overspecialization."

The complex array of instruments aboard the space shuttle *Discovery*.

Recognizing the problems created by overspecialization, some employers have initiated programs to consolidate the duties of several jobs under a single title. For example, the jobs of typist, receptionist, and file clerk might be consolidated under the single title of "administrative assistant." This process is essentially one of enlarging the job duties of employees to relieve the boredom and feeling of low achievement that overspecialization creates.

Behavioural Considerations

Management thought pertaining to job design has evolved from preoccupation with work simplification, standardization, and division of labour to concerns about human needs in job performance. This change has been caused in part by the limitations of overspecialization and industrial engineering noted earlier. Another major challenge confronting employers today is that of improving the quality of work life (QWL). In large and small organizations, efforts are under way to use job design to improve the well-being of employees while also improving organizational productivity. These efforts consist of making work more rewarding psychologically and reducing anxieties and stresses of the work environment. They include job enrichment programs, changes in job characteristics, creation of employee participation teams, and adjustments in traditional work schedules.

Job Enlargement

Job enlargement Efforts to increase the number and variety of tasks in a job in order to offer additional variety to the jobholder.

Job enlargement, sometimes referred to as the *horizontal loading* of jobs, consists of increasing the number and variety of tasks a job includes. The tasks that are added are similar to current job duties; however, the new duties relieve boredom by offering additional variety to the jobholder. For example, a salesclerk's job may be enlarged by having that individual perform inventory control, merchandise returns, or shipping and receiving duties.

Job Rotation

Employees participate in job rotation when they do entirely different jobs on a rotating schedule. For example, employees working for an airline could be trained in reservations/sales, in-flight services (flight attendant), and ramp service work. Organizations may allow employees to rotate between jobs on a daily, weekly, or monthly basis depending on organizational needs or the seniority of the employee.

Job Enrichment

Job enrichment

Any effort that makes work more rewarding or satisfying by adding more meaningful tasks and duties to a job.

Any effort that makes work more rewarding or satisfying by adding more meaningful tasks to an employee's job is called **job enrichment**. Originally popularized by Frederick Herzberg, job enrichment is touted as fulfilling the high motivational needs of employees, such as self-fulfilment and self-esteem, while achieving long-term job satisfaction and performance goals.[14] Job enrichment, or the *vertical expansion* of jobs, may be accomplished by increasing the autonomy and responsibility of employees.[15] Herzberg discusses five factors for enriching jobs and thereby motivating employees: achievement, recognition, growth, responsibility, and performance of the whole job versus only parts of the job. For example, managers can use these five factors to enrich the jobs of employees by

- increasing the level of difficulty and responsibility of the job;
- allowing employees to retain more authority and control over work outcomes;
- providing unit or individual job performance reports directly to employees;
- adding to the job new tasks that require training and growth; and
- assigning individuals specific tasks, thus enabling them to become experts.

These factors allow employees to assume a greater role in the decision-making process and become more involved in planning, organizing, directing, and controlling their own work. Vertical job enrichment can also be accomplished by organizing workers into teams and giving these teams greater authority for self-management.

In spite of the benefits to be achieved through job enrichment, it must not be considered a panacea for overcoming production problems and employee discontent. Job enrichment programs are more likely to succeed in some jobs and work situations than in others. They are *not* the solution to such problems as dissatisfaction with pay, with employee benefits, or with employment insecurity. Moreover, not all employees object to the mechanical pacing of an assembly line, nor do all employees seek additional responsibility or challenge. Some prefer routine jobs because they can let their minds wander while performing their work.

Furthermore, managerial attitudes can be a factor that limits the success of a job enrichment program.[16] Granting employees more job responsibility and allowing them to make job decisions once made by supervisors can be demotivating and unsettling to managers. First-level managers who feel threatened with the possible loss of their jobs can be formidable sources of resistance to change. This point is well illustrated by a statement made to one of the authors of this text at the completion of a job enrichment program: "Now that you've enriched the jobs of my employees, what's left for me to do?" Moreover, in organizations where supervisors hold low opinions of participative decision making, this may discourage employees from participating in the redesign of work.

Job Characteristics

Job design studies explored a new field when behavioural scientists focused on identifying various job dimensions that would improve simultaneously the efficiency of organizations and the job satisfaction of employees. Perhaps the theory that best exemplifies this research is the one advanced by Richard Hackman and Greg Oldham.[17] Their **job characteristics model** proposes that three psychological states of a jobholder result in improved work performance, internal motivation, and lower absenteeism and turnover. The motivated, satisfied, and productive employee is one who (1) experiences *meaningfulness* of the work performed, (2) experiences *responsibility* for work outcomes, and (3) has *knowledge of the results* of the work performed. Achieving these three psychological states serves as reinforcement to the employee and is a source of internal motivation to continue doing the job well. As Hackman and Oldham state,

> *The net result is a self-perpetuating cycle of positive work motivation, powered by self-generated rewards, that is predicted to continue until one or more of the three psychological states is no longer present, or until the individual no longer values the internal rewards that derive from good performance.*[18]

Hackman and Oldham believe that five core job dimensions produce the three psychological states. As Figure 5-7 illustrates, three of these job characteristics foster meaningful work, while one contributes to responsibility and one to knowledge of results. The five job characteristics are as follows:

1. *Skill variety.* The degree to which a job entails a variety of different activities that demand the use of a number of different skills and talents by the jobholder.
2. *Task identity.* The degree to which the job requires completion of a whole and identifiable piece of work, that is, doing a job from beginning to end with a visible outcome.
3. *Task significance.* The degree to which the job has a substantial impact on the lives or work of other people, whether in the immediate organization or in the external environment.
4. *Autonomy.* The degree to which the job provides substantial freedom, independence, and discretion to the individual in scheduling the work and in determining the procedures to be used in carrying it out.
5. *Feedback.* The degree to which carrying out the work activities required by the job results in the individual being given direct and clear information about the effectiveness of his or her performance.[19]

It is important to realize that each of the five job characteristics affects employee performance differently. Therefore, employees will experience the greatest motivation when all five characteristics are present, since the job characteristics combine to produce the three psychological states. Since the works of Hackman and Oldham and Herzberg are similar, suggestions for redesigning jobs through job enrichment also apply to the job characteristics model.

The job characteristics model appears to work best when certain conditions are met. One of these conditions is that employees must have the psychological desire for the autonomy, variety, responsibility, and challenge of enriched jobs. When this

Job characteristics model

Job design that purports that three psychological states (experiencing meaningfulness of the work performed, responsibility for work outcomes, and knowledge of the results of the work performed) of a jobholder result in improved work performance, internal motivation, and lower absenteeism and turnover.

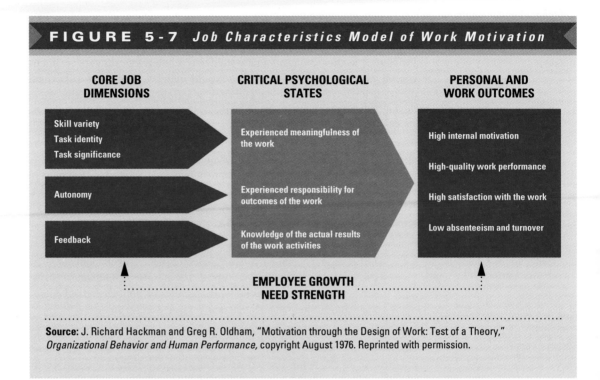

FIGURE 5-7 Job Characteristics Model of Work Motivation

CORE JOB DIMENSIONS	CRITICAL PSYCHOLOGICAL STATES	PERSONAL AND WORK OUTCOMES
Skill variety Task identity Task significance	Experienced meaningfulness of the work	High internal motivation
Autonomy	Experienced responsibility for outcomes of the work	High-quality work performance High satisfaction with the work
Feedback	Knowledge of the actual results of the work activities	Low absenteeism and turnover

EMPLOYEE GROWTH NEED STRENGTH

Source: J. Richard Hackman and Greg R. Oldham, "Motivation through the Design of Work: Test of a Theory," *Organizational Behavior and Human Performance,* copyright August 1976. Reprinted with permission.

personal characteristic is absent, employees may resist the job redesign effort. In addition, job redesign efforts almost always fail when employees lack the physical or mental skills, abilities, or education needed to perform the job. Forcing enriched jobs on individuals lacking these traits can result in frustrated employees.

Employee Involvement Teams

A logical outgrowth of job enrichment and the job characteristics model has been the growth of **employee involvement teams**. Teams are groups of employees who assume a greater role in the production or service process.[20] Teams provide a forum through which employees can express their beliefs about daily operations or identify and solve organizational problems. Involvement can include joint decision making in which employees are encouraged to share their knowledge to resolve operations concerns. Inherent in the concept of employee involvement is the belief that employees, not managers, are in the best position to contribute to workplace improvements.

Team members often acquire multiple skills that enable them to perform a variety of job tasks. Kelly Butt, Senior Vice-President of Information Services of London Life, wanted her employees to increase their ability to contribute to the results of the business units they served. With the involvement of her employees, she transformed the group into a professional services team—the PIT crew (Performance Improvement Team). Likened to the Indy 500, PIT has become more responsive to the needs of the teams and leader, as well as more professional and adaptable. Based on fifteen success factors, assessments have shown an increase in performance of about 15 percent.[21]

Employee involvement teams

Teams of employees offering production or service suggestions to improve organizational performance.

Employee involvement teams incorporate the motivational factors of job enrichment and the core job dimensions from the job characteristics model to produce a work environment that is intrinsically fulfilling to employees. One key ingredient of teams is their ability to foster among all team members a sense of ownership, involvement, and responsibility for completing the assigned tasks. Additionally, teams can foster feelings of employee empowerment, an important component of total quality management.[22]

Adjustments in Work Schedules

Another form of job design is to alter the normal workweek of five eight-hour days in which all employees begin and end their workday at the same preset time. Employers may depart from the traditional workday or workweek in their attempt to improve organizational productivity and morale by giving employees increased control over the hours they work. The more common alternative work schedules include the four-day workweek, flextime, and job sharing.

The Four-Day Workweek

Under the four-day workweek (or compressed workweek), the number of days in the workweek is shortened by lengthening the number of hours worked per day. This schedule is best illustrated by the four-day, 40-hour week, generally referred to as 4/10 or 4/40. Employees working a four-day workweek might work ten hours a day, Monday through Thursday. Although the 4/10 schedule is probably the best known, other compressed arrangements include reducing weekly hours to 38 or 36 hours or scheduling 80 hours over nine days (9/80), taking one day off every other week.[23]

Organizations that operate batch processing systems (e.g., oil companies like Shell Oil) use shorter workweeks to coordinate work schedules with production schedules. Compressed workweeks may assist with scheduling arrangements by improving plant and equipment utilization. The keying of work schedules to processing time for a specific operation rather than to a standard workweek reduces startup and closedown time and often results in higher weekly output.

Two of the strongest advantages of the compressed work schedule are that it accommodates the leisure-time activities of employees and facilitates the employee's scheduling of medical, dental, and other types of personal appointments. Other advantages include the improvement of employee job satisfaction and morale, reduced absenteeism, and the facilitation of recruitment.

The major disadvantage of the compressed workweek involves provincial legislation regarding overtime. Various provinces have stringent rules requiring the payment of overtime to nonsupervisory employees who work in excess of the prescribed workweek. Another disadvantage of the compressed workweek is that it increases the amount of stress experienced by supervisors. There is no apparent problem of employee fatigue associated with working ten-hour days, nor is there a loss of coordination of work activities between departments.

Flextime

Flextime, or flexible working hours, permits employees the option of choosing daily starting and quitting times provided they work a certain number of hours per day or week. With flextime, employees are given considerable latitude in scheduling their

Flextime
Flexible working hours that permit employees the option of choosing daily starting and quitting times provided they work a set number of hours per day or week.

work. However, there is a "core period" during the morning and afternoon when *all* employees are required to be on the job.

Some variations of flextime allow employees to work as many or as few hours per day as they desire, so long as the total hours worked per week meet the minimum specified by management, usually 40 hours. Flexible working hours are most common in service-type organizations—financial institutions, government agencies, or other organizations with large clerical operations. The head office of Manulife Financial has found that flextime provides many advantages for employees throughout the organization. Highlights in HRM 2 illustrates the flextime schedule used by Manulife Financial.

Flextime provides both employees and employers with several advantages. By allowing employees greater flexibility in work scheduling, employers can reduce some of the traditional causes of tardiness and absenteeism. Employees can adjust their work to accommodate their particular lifestyles and, in doing so, gain greater job satisfaction.[24] Employees can also schedule their working hours for the time of day when they are most productive. In addition, variations in arrival and departure times can help reduce traffic congestion at the peak commuting hours. In some cases, employees require less time to commute, and the pressures of meeting a rigid schedule are reduced.

From the employer's standpoint, flextime can be most helpful in recruiting and retaining personnel. It has proved invaluable to organizations wishing to improve service to customers or clients by extending operating hours. Bruncor, a telecommunications company, uses flextime to keep its business offices open for customers who cannot get there during the day. Research demonstrates that flextime can have a positive impact on the performance measures of reliability, quality, and quantity of employee work.[25]

There are, of course, several disadvantages to flextime. First, it is not suited to some jobs. It is not feasible, for example, where specific workstations must be staffed

Flextime alleviates the burden of rush hour traffic on many employees.

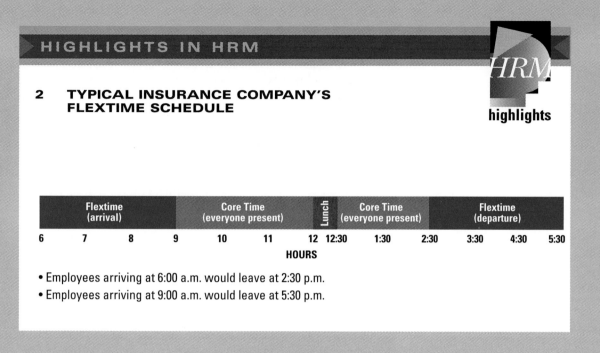

2 TYPICAL INSURANCE COMPANY'S FLEXTIME SCHEDULE

Flextime (arrival)				Core Time (everyone present)			Lunch	Core Time (everyone present)			Flextime (departure)		
6	7	8	9	10	11	12	12:30	1:30	2:30	3:30	4:30	5:30	

HOURS

- Employees arriving at 6:00 a.m. would leave at 2:30 p.m.
- Employees arriving at 9:00 a.m. would leave at 5:30 p.m.

at all times. Second, it can create problems for supervisors in communicating with and instructing employees. Flextime schedules may also force these supervisors to extend their workweek if they are to exercise control over their subordinates. Finally, keeping premises open for a longer period will increase energy consumption, resulting in higher costs for the employer.

Job Sharing

The arrangement whereby two part-time employees perform a job that otherwise would be held by one full-time employee is called job sharing. Job sharers usually work three days a week, "creating an overlap day for extended face-to-face conferencing."[26] Their pay is three-fifths of a regular salary; however, job sharers usually take on additional responsibilities beyond what the original job would require. Companies that use job sharing are primarily in the legal, advertising, and financial-services businesses. Companies such as Information Systems Management Corporation, London Life, and Great West Life use job sharing. Employers note that without job sharing two good employees might otherwise be lost.

Job sharing is suited to the needs of families where one or both spouses desire to work only part-time. It is suited also to the needs of older workers who want to phase into retirement by shortening their workday. For the employer, the work of part-time employees can be scheduled to conform to peaks in the daily workload. Job sharing can also limit layoffs in hard economic times. A final benefit is that employees engaged in job sharing have time off during the week to accommodate personal needs, so they are less likely to be absent.

Job sharing does have several problems, however. Employers may not want to employ two people to do the work of one because the time required to orient and train a second employee constitutes an added burden. They may also want to avoid prorating the employee benefits between two part-time employees. This problem may be reduced, however, by permitting the employees to contribute the difference between the health insurance (or life insurance) premiums for a full-time employee and the pro rata amount the employer would otherwise contribute for a part-time employee. The key to making job sharing work is good communications between partners who use a number of ways to stay in contact—phone calls, written updates, electronic mail, and voice mail.

A variation of job sharing is work sharing. A work-sharing program permits all employees in the organization to shorten their workweeks (usually under 32 hours) while continuing to receive normal employee benefits. Work sharing is used almost exclusively to reduce the harmful effects of extensive layoffs due to poor economic conditions.

Shift Work

In order to meet various service requirements, some industries, such as transportation, communications, and health care, must provide continuous operations. For economic reasons, some businesses (e.g., refinery operations) must maintain 24-hour production schedules. Employees working in these organizations are subject to round-the-clock work schedules, or shift work. The most common shift schedules are days (7 a.m. to 3 p.m.), evenings (3 p.m. to 11 p.m.), and nights (11 p.m. to 7 a.m.). Employees doing shift work may have their shifts rotated on a daily, weekly, or monthly basis. Rotating employees through the different shifts permits everyone to share in the favoured daytime hours. Employees can be assigned to shifts by management; in unionized organizations, the seniority rights of employees will dictate their ability to choose their work hours.

SUMMARY

Job requirements reflect the different duties, tasks, and responsibilities contained in jobs. Job requirements, in turn, influence HR functions performed by managers such as recruitment, selection, training and development, performance appraisal, compensation, and various labour relations activities.

Job analysis data may be gathered using one of several collection methods—interviews, questionnaires, observations, or diaries. Other more quantitative approaches include use of the functional job analysis approach, the position analysis questionnaire, and the critical incident method. HRM decisions on employment, performance appraisal, and promotions must be based on specific criteria that are job-related. These criteria can be determined objectively only by analyzing the requirements of each job.

The format of job descriptions varies widely, often reflecting the needs of the organization and the expertise of the writer. As a minimum, job descriptions should contain a job title, a job identification section, and a job duties section. A job specification section also may be included. Job descriptions should be written in clear and specific terms with consideration given to their legal implications.

Job design is a combination of four basic considerations: Industrial engineering concerns that involve analyzing work methods and establishing time standards; human engineering considerations that accommodate human capabilities and limitations to job tasks; behavioural considerations that make jobs more psychologically rewarding; and quality-of-life concerns that foster a favourable work environment through physical, psychological, and social job improvements.

To improve the internal environment of organizations and thereby increase productivity, greater efforts are being made by many organizations to enhance the quality of work life. These efforts include the establishment of job enrichment programs that offer opportunities for employees to experience achievement, responsibility, growth, and recognition in performing their jobs, thus giving them greater job satisfaction. Job enlargement programs reduce boredom by introducing variety into the job. This is accomplished by giving the jobholder additional and different tasks to perform. Job rotation programs allow employees to perform entirely different jobs on a selected schedule. Employee involvement teams allow employees to make suggestions to improve operations and services, thereby increasing their commitment to the organization.

In the job characteristics model, five job factors contribute to increased job performance and satisfaction—skill variety, task identity, task significance, autonomy, and feedback. All factors should be built into jobs since each factor influences different employee psychological states. When jobs are enriched through the job characteristics model, then employees experience more meaningfulness in their jobs, acquire more job responsibility, and receive direct feedback regarding the tasks they perform.

Changes in work schedules—which include the four-day workweek, flextime, and job sharing—permit employees to adjust their work periods to accommodate their particular lifestyles. Employees can choose from among these HR techniques to accommodate their diverse needs while at the same time fostering organizational effectiveness.

KEY TERMS

critical incident method

employee involvement teams

flextime

functional job analysis (FJA)

human engineering

industrial engineering

job

job analysis

job characteristics model

job description

job design

job enlargement

job enrichment

job requirements

job specification

position

position analysis questionnaire (PAQ)

DISCUSSION QUESTIONS

1. What does job analysis entail? Who within an organization participates in the job analysis process?
2. Clearly differentiate between job analysis, job descriptions, and job specifications.
3. Selection, performance appraisal, and similar decisions must be based on job-related criteria. What are the implications for job analysis?
4. To what extent, if any, can the absence of formal job descriptions contribute to employee dissatisfaction?
5. As a project, prepare a description of a job at which you are currently working or have worked. Develop specifications listing the minimum qualifications required for the job. How do the qualifications required for the job compare with your own qualifications? Are/were you underemployed or overemployed?
6. Considering your present job, or a recent job, how would you incorporate into the position the five job characteristics that motivate employees? Could all five characteristics be included?
7. As a small business employer, explain how nontraditional work schedules might make it easier for you to recruit employees.
8. Assume the role of a supervisor. What are the advantages and disadvantages you see with flextime?

CASE: Job Design, Saturn Style

Industry experts agree that Saturn Corporation, a General Motors subsidiary, has made a remarkable impact on the automobile market. Consider these facts. In 1991, Saturn sold more cars per dealer than any other manufacturer, including Honda, the leader for the previous two years. It was the first time in fifteen years that a U.S. car claimed the number one spot. Furthermore, 70 percent of Saturn buyers would have bought a non-GM car as their second choice. For 1991, Saturn placed sixth among all makes in the degree of satisfaction buyers had with the sales and delivery experience. Only luxury models like Lexus, Cadillac, or Mercedes-Benz outpaced Saturn.

Saturn did not achieve these results by resorting to traditional production methods. Saturn uses state-of-the-art manufacturing and job design techniques, including industrial engineering, ergonomics, and behavioural considerations. For example, workers stand on soft birch-wood floors instead of hard concrete. Cars pass through the assembly line on hydraulic lifts called "skillets," which allow employees to raise or lower the cars to the employee's height. Employees are allowed to ride the platform and take up to six minutes to finish tasks correctly. (On traditional assembly lines, employees are given less than one minute to complete their individual duties.) Industrial engineers videotape employees in action, looking for wasted motion. In one instance, employees were saved one-third of the steps walking to and from cars, thereby conserving employee energy.

Saturn managers agree, however, that the introduction of employee involvement teams is a key feature of the company's success. Teams are the basic organizational building block at Saturn. On the production floor, employees are formed into teams of five to fifteen people who manage themselves. Each team elects a leader called a *work-team counsellor*. Teams make decisions regarding scheduling, hiring, budgeting, and various production and quality concerns. Decisions are made by consensus, which requires a 70 percent "agreement rate" and a 100 percent "support rate" once a decision is reached.

Teams monitor themselves to ensure maximum efficiency. For example, one team member may check scrap and receive weekly reports on employee waste. Team members know the cost of parts and can calculate the added expense of wasted materials. Interestingly, each team forecasts yearly the amount of resources it plans to use in the coming year. Teams receive monthly breakdowns on budgeted items, even including telephone bills.

Above shop-floor teams are groups of employees called work-unit module advisers. Advisers serve as troubleshooters and coordinators for all work teams within each of three business units—powertrain, body system, and vehicle systems. The entire Saturn complex is overseen by the manufacturing advisory committee, which is composed of union and management representatives from each of the business units. At the pinnacle is the Strategic Action Committee (SAC), which is responsible for developing long-range planning and policy making for the company.

Questions
1. What arguments could be advanced both for and against the use of employee involvement teams?
2. At Saturn, since team members are responsible for hiring decisions, what job specifications would be important for the hiring of employees?

Your Dream Job

You have read about the factors that contribute to job satisfaction. Now, put down your pen, close your eyes, and dream about the ideal job. Use your imagination. What is your vision of the ideal job for you? This exercise is an important tool to help you shape your future. Using the format below, write a job description for your dream job.

Job Title

Summary

Essential Functions

Job Specifications

NOTES AND REFERENCES

1. *Workplace 2000: Work and Workers for the 21st Century*, Executive Summary (Washington, DC: U.S. Department of Labor, n.d.): 1; see also "The New World of Work," *Business Week*, October 17, 1994, 76–87.

2. For a good review of workforce trends, see "Tomorrow's Jobs," *Occupational Outlook Handbook*, 1992–93 ed. (Washington, DC: Bureau of Labor Statistics, Bulletin No. 2450, May 1992), 8.

3. Personal correspondence with Beth Ordoman, The City of Calgary Personnel Services Department, May 5, 1995.

4. *Canadian Human Rights Reporter/Le Babillard Canadien des Droits de la Personne*, vol. 6, 1985.

5. George T. Milkovich and Jerry M. Newman, *Compensation*, 4th rev. ed. (Homewood, IL: Irwin, 1993), 61; see also Ronald A. Ash, "Job Analysis in the World of Work," in Sidney Gall, ed., *The Job Analysis Handbook for Business, Industry, and Government* (New York: John Wiley and Sons, 1988), 3.

6. Richard Henderson, *Compensation Management*, 6th ed. (Englewood Cliffs, NJ: Prentice-Hall, 1993).

7. Bob Cardy and Greg Dobbins, "Job Analysis in a Dynamic Environment," *News* (Academy of Management, Human Resources Division) 16, no. 1 (Fall 1992): 4; see also Benjamin Schneider and Andrea Marcus Konz, "Strategic Job Analysis," *Human Resource Management* 28, no. 1 (Spring 1989): 51–63.

8. Employment and Immigration Canada, *National Occupational Classification*, Cat. No. MP 53-25-1-1993E (Ottawa: Minister of Supply and Services, 1993).

9. Milkovich and Newman, *Compensation*, 68.

10. Jai V. Ghorpade, *Job Analysis: A Handbook for the Human Resource Director* (Englewood Cliffs, NJ: Prentice-Hall, 1988), 97–98.

11. Paul Weinberg, "Labour Law Overview," *Canadian Lawyer*, March 1995, 36–43.

12. Personal correspondence with Dan Cerovec, Transmission Plant, GM of Canada, Windsor, Ontario, May 1995.

13. Bob Filipczak, "Adaptive Technology for the Disabled," *Training* 30, no. 3 (March 1993): 23–29.

14. For Herzberg's original article on job enrichment, see Frederick Herzberg, "One More Time: How Do You Motivate Employees?" *Harvard Business Review* 46, no. 2 (January–February 1968): 53–62.

15. Abraham A. Maidani, "Comparative Study of Herzberg's Two-Factor Theory of Job Satisfaction among Public and Private Sectors," *Public Personnel Management* 20, no. 4 (Winter 1991): 441–448.

16. Dean B. McFarlin, Paul D. Sweeney, and John L. Cotton, "Attitudes Toward Employee Participation in Decision-Making: A Comparison of European and American Managers in a United States Multinational Company," *Human Resource Management* 31, no. 4 (Winter 1992): 363–383.

17. For the original article on the job characteristics model, see J. Richard Hackman and Greg R. Oldham, "Motivation through the Design of Work: Test of a Theory," *Organizational Behaviour and Human Performance* 16, no. 2 (August 1976): 250–279.

18. Ibid., 256.

19. Ibid., 257–258.

20. Richard J. Magjuka, "The 10 Dimensions of Employee Involvement," *Training and Development Journal* 47, no. 4 (April 1993): 61–67.

21. Drew Davison, "Transformation to a High Performance Team," *Canadian Business Review* 21, no. 3 (Autumn 1994): 18, 19, 23.

22. John H. Dobbs, "The Empowerment Environment," *Training and Development Journal* 47, no. 2 (February 1993): 55–57.

23. Jon L. Pierce and Randall B. Dunham, "The 12-Hour Work Day: A 48-Hour, Eight-Day Week," *Academy of Management Journal* 35, no. 5 (December 1992): 1086–1098.

24. Charles S. Rogers, "The Flexible Workplace: What Have We Learned?" *Human Resource Management* 31, no. 3 (Fall 1992): 183–199; see also David A. Ralston, "How Flextime Eases Work/Family Tensions," *Personnel* 67, no. 8 (August 1990): 45–48; and Sue Shellenbarger, "Employees Take Pains to Make Flextime Work," *The Wall Street Journal*, August 18, 1992, B1.

25. Sue Shellenbarger, "More Companies Experiment with Workers Schedules," *The Wall Street Journal*, January 13, 1994, B1; see also *American Society for Personnel Administration and Commerce Clearing House Survey*, June 26, 1987, 4.

26. Sue Shellenbarger, "Two People, One Job: It Really Can Work," *The Wall Street Journal*, December 7, 1994, V1; see also Alan Deutschman, "Pioneers of the New Balance," *Fortune*, May 20, 1991, 61, 64, 68.

After studying this chapter you
should be able to

one
objective

*Explain the advantages
and disadvantages of
recruiting from within the
organization.*

two
objective

*Explain the advantages
and disadvantages of
external recruitment.*

three
objective

*Describe how recruitment
activities are integrated
with equal employment
initiatives.*

Chapter 6

Human Resources
Recruitment

*O*nce the HR planning function is fulfilled, then the staffing of the organization must be completed through the recruitment process. Employment recruiting has acquired a new importance for managers with the emergence of a new economy based on service and technology. Employers are finding it increasingly difficult to find qualified applicants to fill jobs. Employers cannot rely upon solicited applications to fill openings. Changing employment conditions mandate that managers consider a variety of recruitment alternatives to attract the right employees to the organization. The methods of attracting applicants will be discussed in this chapter.

objective

Recruiting Within the Organization

Recruitment is the process of locating and encouraging potential applicants to apply for existing or anticipated job openings. During this process, efforts are made to inform the applicants fully about the qualifications required to perform the job and the career opportunities the organization can offer them. Whether or not a particular job vacancy will be filled by someone from within the organization or from outside will, of course, depend upon the availability of personnel, the organization's HR policies, and the requirements of the job to be staffed.

Advantages of Recruiting from Within

Most organizations try to follow a policy of filling job vacancies above the entry-level position through promotions and transfers. By filling vacancies in this way, an organization can capitalize on the investment it has made in recruiting, selecting, training, and developing its current employees.

Promotion-from-within policies at CIBC as well as at Canada Mortgage and Housing Corporation have contributed to both companies' overall growth and success.[1] Promotion serves to reward employees for past performance and is intended to encourage them to continue their efforts. It also gives other employees reason to anticipate that similar efforts by them will lead to promotion, thus improving morale within the organization. This is particularly true for members of the designated groups who have encountered difficulties in finding employment and have often faced even greater difficulty in advancing within an organization. Most organizations have integrated promotion policies as an essential part of their employment equity programs.

If an organization's promotion policy is to have maximum motivational value, employees must be made aware of it. The following is an example of a policy statement that an organization might prepare:

> *"Promotion from within" is generally recognized as a foundation of good employment practice, and it is the policy of our museum to promote from within whenever possible when filling a vacancy. The job vacancy will be posted for five calendar days to give all qualified full- and part-time personnel an equal opportunity to apply.*

While a transfer lacks the motivational value of a promotion, it sometimes can serve to protect employees from layoff or to broaden their job experiences. Furthermore, the transferred employee's familiarity with the organization and its operations can eliminate the orientation and training costs that recruitment from the outside would entail. Most important, the transferee's performance record is likely to be a more accurate predictor of the candidate's success than the data gained about outside applicants.

Methods of Locating Qualified Job Candidates

The effective use of internal sources requires a system for locating qualified job candidates and for enabling those who consider themselves qualified to apply for the opening. Qualified job candidates within the organization can be located by computerized record systems, by job posting and bidding, and by recalling those who have been laid off.

Computerized Record Systems

Computers have made possible the creation of data banks that contain the complete records and qualifications of each employee within an organization. Apple Canada, for example, has developed a computer program named HR-Link that allows managers to access information.[2] Similarly, NorTel has developed a résumé tracking system that allows managers to query an on-line data base of résumés. Similar to the skills inventories mentioned earlier, these information systems allow an organization to screen its entire workforce in a matter of minutes to locate suitable candidates to fill an internal opening. These data can also be used to predict the career paths of employees and to anticipate when and where promotion opportunities may arise. Since the value of the data depends on how current the data are, the record system must include provisions for recording changes in employee qualifications and job placements as they occur.

Job Posting and Bidding

Job posting and bidding

Posting vacancy notices and maintaining lists of employees looking for upgraded positions.

Organizations may communicate information about job openings through a process referred to as **job posting and bidding**. This process consists largely of posting vacancy notices on bulletin boards, but may include use of designated posting centres, employee publications, special-announcement handouts, direct mail, and public-address messages. Du Pont Canada has a job- posting computerized system. As postings become vacant, they can be accessed by employees. Employees are encouraged to assume ownership and responsibility for their own career development. They are expected to apply for positions that they believe will support their career interests and direction.[3]

The system of job posting and bidding can provide many benefits to an organization. However, these benefits may not be realized unless employees believe the system is being administered fairly. Therefore, to reap the full advantages of job posting, organizations should follow the administrative guidelines for job posting and bidding programs presented in Highlights in HRM 1.

Furthermore, job bidding is more effective when it is part of a career development program in which employees are made aware of opportunities available to them within the organization. For example, HR departments may provide new employees with literature on job progression that describes the lines of job advancement, training requirements for each job, and skills and abilities needed as they move up the job-progression ladder.

1   ELEMENTS OF AN EFFECTIVE JOB POSTING AND BIDDING PROCEDURE

1. Establish and widely distribute applicant elegibility requirements for employees wishing to use the bidding procedure.
2. Develop job notices that are complete, including the job's essential functions and responsibilities and any special (unusual) tasks that must be performed.
3. List the minimum abilities, skills, experience, education, or special knowledge needed by applicants.
4. Communicate the availability of jobs to all affected employees. Use several notice methods if possible.
5. Establish posting periods and state any filing constraints if appropriate.
6. Develop an applicant-review procedure and feedback system that employees will accept.
7. Establish an appeals procedure for those employees wishing to challenge selection decisions.

Limitations of Recruiting from Within

Sometimes certain jobs at the middle and upper levels that require specialized training and experience cannot be filled from within the organization and must be filled from the outside. This is especially common in small organizations. Also, for certain openings it may be necessary to hire individuals from the outside who have gained from another employer the knowledge and expertise required for these jobs.

Even though HR policy encourages job openings to be filled from within the organization, potential candidates from the outside should be considered in order to prevent the inbreeding of ideas and attitudes. Applicants hired from the outside, particularly for certain management positions, can be a source of new ideas and may bring with them the latest knowledge acquired from their previous employers. Indeed, excessive reliance upon internal sources can create the risk of "employee cloning." Furthermore, it is not uncommon for firms in competitive fields such as high technology to attempt to gain secrets from competitors by hiring away their employees.

objective

Recruiting Outside the Organization

Unless there is to be a reduction in the workforce, a replacement from outside must eventually be found to fill a job left vacant when the jobholder moved to a new slot

HIGHLIGHTS IN HRM

highlights

2   BATTING A THOUSAND

The recruitment methods of major baseball clubs are well known—that is, we all know the process by which the players positions are staffed. But how does a small (if very public) organization such as the Blue Jays recruit administrative staff?

The Blue Jays are a $100-million-a-year business, but employ only 70 full-time people in the office. Recruitment is very straightforward. They receive about 1,000 unsolicited résumés a year, because people are very attracted by the glamour of working for a baseball team. But recruitment from outside occurs very rarely ... only two to three full-time staff a year. This is because the Blue Jays have an outstanding retention rate. Forty percent of their employees have worked for them for more than fifteen years.

And they have a policy of promoting from within. Their current Assistant General Manager started off as a part-time ticket seller. The Manager of Promotions began his career in the mailroom. The Blue Jays use head-hunting firms for some executive-level positions. Baseball is a compelling sport, and this excitement helps considerably in recruiting at any level in the Club.

Source: Ken Mark "Batting a Thousand," *Human Resources Professional* 11, no. 2 (March 1994): 13–15.

in the organization. Thus, when the president or CEO of the organization retires, a chain reaction of promotions may subsequently occur. This creates other managerial openings throughout the organization. The question to be resolved, therefore, is not whether to bring people into the organization, but rather at which level they are to be brought in.

In the past few years, organizations such as Air Canada and the CBC have brought in outsiders to be their new CEOs. In fact, an astounding 31 percent of *Fortune* 500 companies that replaced their CEOs in 1993, did so by hiring executives from outside their companies. In many of these cases, hiring someone from the outside was seen as essential for revitalizing the organizations.[4]

All entry-level positions must attract candidates from the external labour market. Highlights in HRM 2 describes how the Blue Jays recruit at various levels in their organization.

The Labour Market

Labour market
The area from which applicants are to be recruited.

The **labour market**, or the area from which applicants are to be recruited, will vary with the type of job to be filled and the amount of compensation to be paid for the job. Recruitment for executive or technical jobs requiring a high degree of knowledge and skill may be national or even international in scope. Most colleges and universities, for example, conduct national employment searches to fill top administrative positions. Recruitment for jobs that require relatively little skill, however, may encompass a relatively small geographic area. The reluctance of people to relocate may cause them to turn down offers of employment, thereby eliminating them from employment consideration beyond the local labour market. However, by offering an attractive level of compensation and by helping to defray moving costs, employers may induce some applicants to move.

The ease with which employees can commute to work will also influence the boundaries of the labour market. Insufficient public transportation or extreme traffic congestion on the streets and freeways can limit the distance employees are willing to travel to work, particularly to jobs with low pay. Also, population migration from the cities to the suburbs has had its effect on labour markets. If suitable employment can be obtained near where they live or if they can work at home (see Chapter 2), many suburbanites are less likely to accept or remain in jobs in the central city.

Outside Sources of Recruitment

The outside sources from which employers recruit will vary with the type of job to be filled. A computer programmer, for example, is not likely to be recruited from the same source as a machine operator. Trade schools can provide applicants for entry-level positions, though these recruitment sources are not as useful when skilled employees are needed.[5]

The condition of the labour market may also help to determine which recruiting sources an organization will use. During periods of high unemployment, organizations may be able to maintain an adequate supply of qualified applicants from unsolicited résumés alone. A tight labour market, one with low unemployment, may

In January 1995 thousands of people lined up for hours in bitter cold to apply for a limited number of potential jobs at a GM plant in Oshawa, Ontario.

force the employer to advertise heavily and/or seek assistance from local employment agencies. How successful an organization has been in reaching its employment equity goals may be still another factor in determining the sources from which to recruit. Typically an employer at any given time will find it necessary to utilize several recruitment sources.

Several studies have suggested that an employee's recruitment source can affect that employee's subsequent tenure and job performance with an organization.[6] In general, applicants who find employment as "walk-ins" or through referral by a current employee tend to remain with the organization longer and have higher-quality performance than those employees recruited through the formal recruitment sources of advertisements and employment agencies. Informal recruiting sources may also yield higher selection rates than formal sources. Employers are cautioned, however, that relying on only one or two recruitment sources to secure job applicants could have an adverse effect on the designated groups.

Advertisements

One of the most common methods of attracting applicants is through advertisements. While newspapers and trade journals are the media used most often, radio, television, billboards, posters, and even sound trucks have also been utilized. Advertising has the advantage of reaching a large audience of possible applicants. An advertisement, in this economy, will draw between 300 to 500 applicants, of which about a dozen will be good matches.[7] Some degree of selectivity can be achieved by using newspapers and journals directed toward a particular group of readers. Professional journals, trade journals, and publications of unions and various fraternal or nonprofit organizations fall into this category.

As Highlights in HRM 3 illustrates, the preparation of recruiting advertisements not only is time-consuming, but also requires creativity in developing design and message content. Well-written advertisements highlight the major assets of the position while showing the responsiveness of the organization to the job and career needs of the applicants. Also, there appears to be a correlation between the accuracy and completeness of information provided in advertisements and the recruitment success of the organization. Among the information typically included in advertisements is that the recruiting organization is an *equal opportunity employer*.

Advertising can sometimes place a severe burden on an organization's employment office. Even though the specifications for the openings are described thoroughly in the advertisement, many applicants who know they do not meet the job requirements may still be attracted. They may apply with the hope that the employer will not be able to find applicants who meet the specifications. An extreme example of this occurred in January 1995 when 26,000 people lined up to apply for available positions at GM in Oshawa.[8]

Public Employment Agencies

The Human Resource Centres of Canada are responsible for administrating the unemployment insurance program and can be found in most communities. Individuals who become unemployed must be registered at one of these offices and be available for "suitable employment" in order to receive their unemployment insurance commission cheques. Employers can call and place job postings with the centres. Applicants can access the Employment Telemessage system via the tele-

highlights

3 EFFECTIVE ADVERTISING

Working As A Team

building success

At Toyota Motor Manufacturing Canada Inc., teamwork is the driving force behind our success. Through working together to produce the best quality vehicle for our customers, Toyota team members share a commitment to safety, total quality and productivity. The world-famous Toyota Production System, a philosophy of continuous improvement, and ongoing training enables each team member to work towards their highest potential.

MANAGER
HEALTH & SAFETY

This position, reporting to the General Manager, Human Resources, at our Cambridge, Ontario Automotive Manufacturing facility, requires a strong leader with the skills and expertise to plan, develop and implement leading programs and training initiatives. An experienced manager and team player with a proven "continuous improvement mind-set", your professional qualifications include a minimum B.Sc., Industrial Hygiene certification and at least ten years of progressive experience, including five years of Health & Safety management experience in an operations/manufacturing environment. It goes without saying that you have excellent interpersonal and communication skills and a thorough knowledge of all applicable legislation.

Competitive compensation, including relocation assistance to the Cambridge, Ontario area, is offered. To apply, please forward a detailed resume and salary expectations, in confidence, to: **The Bedford Consulting Group Inc., Bedford House, 60 Bedford Road, Toronto, Ontario M5R 2K2. Fax (416) 963-9998.**

We appreciate the interest of all applicants and advise only those selected for an interview will be contacted.

TOYOTA ENDORSES THE PRINCIPLES OF EQUAL OPPORTUNITY

> ## ETHICS IN HRM
>
> ### SOURCING STRATEGIES
>
> Placement agencies find qualified applicants through many sources. One way of knowing who is qualified and active in the field is to scan the notices of appointments and promotions in the newspaper. Some placement agencies retain lists of these appointees in order to contact them a couple of years later in order to determine if they are interested in transferring to another organization. Some placement officers even have been accused of raiding — that is, contacting people whose names appear in the paper or in company telephone books and asking them if they know of any qualified candidates for a certain position. Incredibly, the position under discussion requires the same type of qualifications that they themselves possess. Is this ethical?

phone or review on-line information at the centre itself. There is also a national job bank that lists information about jobs across the country. Most of these jobs require specialized skills. Expanded services will include access to community sites such as libraries and town halls, and new self-serve electronic disks located in convenient places throughout each community.

CEC can also help applicants plan for their future by providing career information that will assist them in determining their next step in finding work or upgrading their skills. Information about prospective employers, interesting occupations, salaries, working conditions, education and training requirements, and growth opportunities can be obtained by talking to a CEC staff member, reviewing relevant publications, or accessing the on-line data base.

Group workshops are also held for those who may have the qualifications for a job but are unsure of how to go about finding one. Additionally, other subjects may include job-search strategies and job-finding clubs. If applicants require additional training or upgrading to help match their skills to a job in the local market, CEC has a number of programs to help. For instance, they offer classroom and on-the-job training, work internships, and income assistance.[9]

The system that lists positions available within the Public Service Commission (PSC) is called Info-Tel. The CEC and PSC systems offer position information within the immediate vicinity. Applicants can access the information via their telephone system and then apply directly to the employer.[10]

Private Employment Agencies

Charging a fee enables private employment agencies to tailor their services to the specific needs of their clients. It is common for agencies to specialize in serving a

EXECUTIVE SEARCH AT SPENCER STUART

Manon Vennat, Chair and Managing Director of the Montreal office of Spencer Stuart, one of the world's largest executive recruitment firms, deals only with the recruitment and placement of senior managers. Her fields of expertise, grounded by her experience and interests, are high-technology companies, consumer packaged goods, financial services, and cultural institutions. Vennat's work experience ranges from the federal government to high-tech firms. She serves on the boards of several private and not for profit firms, and at one time, served as President of the Montreal Board of Trade.

Vennat says, "There is more strategizing than one would assume in this business. You can't work for everyone. For example, I have to choose which financial institutions I will work for. In terms of ethics, you cannot recruit a president that you have placed, and we have a corporate hands-off policy of two years, an industry standard. This policy is worldwide and can extend to the various divisions of our client organizations, depending on the size. So I have to choose to work only with senior management in one or two divisions and head office of a major group."

The process of executive placement begins with a strategizing phase, so that when the call comes a strategic choice can be made. Indeed, at this point, it is important to be well informed about the industry climate. A lot of annual reports are at the recruiters' s fingertips. The next step is to meet with the client and listen to the needs and basic requirements of the position. A proposal is then prepared, outlining the strategy, the costs and the time frame of the search. If these conditions are agreeable to the client, Vennat then meets with many of the subordinates and colleagues associated with the vacant position in order to get a feel for the culture. She says, "I am working for two people: the client and the candidate. You cannot be a body snatcher. You have to care about the candidate's career. I want him or her to know the skeletons in the closet, and have as few surprises as possible. Also, candidates are fragile during this process, because they are being judged and they may not be chosen." Then, a complete description of the mandate, context, challenge, and responsibilities prepared. This document is given to serious candidates.

Sourcing is done in several ways. "We contact industry deans: people who are senior enough to know which people are good. We also have a data bank of thousands of names of people we know from around the world. Ninety-eight percent of the people we place are not looking for jobs. We also consult directories of directors and general information services like Info Globe. And of course, I consult my own network from community life, corporate life and politics."

The client then receives in-depth CV's and interview notes. Interviews are organized, after which the client chooses a candidate. Extensive reference checking occurs. "We talk to the immediate supports and subordinates, the peers, the clients, and as many people as far back as we can go. These references are provided to the company. We then assist in negotiating the contract and follow up with the candidate and the client." The entire process can take up to nine months, depending on the location of the position, the nature of the industry, and the pool of candidates.

Manon Vennat finds this a fascinating occupation, asserting, "At this level, it is fabulously interesting. These people have achievements. I love to learn how they've learned and built their careers. There is tremendous variety. In my job, the result of a search is a walking report, rather than a document on a sheet. The candidate has an impact—on share prices, or a new product launch. All kinds of things happen and are reported in the news. There is great satisfaction in having made a good match."

specific occupational area or professional field. A number of agencies provide access to employment for designated groups. For example, the Canadian Council for Aboriginal Business runs an employment agency called Aboriginal Choice Placement Services for clerical, technical, and engineering positions. Depending upon who is receiving the most service, the fee may be paid by either the employer or the job seeker or both. It is not uncommon for private employment agencies to charge an employer a 25 to 30 percent fee, based on the position's annual salary, if it hires an applicant found by the agency.

Private employment agencies differ in the services they offer, their professionalism, and the calibre of their counsellors. If counsellors are paid on a commission basis, their desire to do a professional job may be offset by their desire to earn a commission. Thus, they may encourage job seekers to accept jobs for which they are not suited. Or they may use unauthorized sources, such as the company's internal telephone directory to identify people working in the fields. One management consultant advises,

> *Take the time to find a recruiter who is knowledgeable, experienced, and professional. Discuss openly your philosophies and practices with regard to recruiting strategies, including advertising, in-house recruiting, screening procedures, and costs for these efforts. Find a recruiter who is flexible and who will consider your needs and wants.*[11]

Executives Search Firms

In contrast to public and private employment agencies, which help job seekers find the right job, executive search firms (often called *head-hunters*) help employers find the right person for a job. They seek out candidates with qualifications that match the requirements of the positions their client firm is seeking to fill. Executive search firms do not always advertise in the media for job candidates, nor do they accept a fee from the individual being placed.

The fees charged by search firms may range from 30 to 50 percent of the annual salary for the position to be filled. For the recruitment of senior executives, this fee is paid by the client firm whether or not the recruiting effort results in a hire. It is for this practice that search firms receive the greatest criticism.

Nevertheless, as noted earlier, it is an increasingly common occurrence that new chief executive officers (CEOs) are brought in from outside the organization. A large number of these new CEOs are placed in those positions through the services of an executive search firm. Since high-calibre executives are in short supply, a significant number of organizations, including City of Mississauga, the Government of Alberta, and Timberwest Forest Limited, use search firms to fill their top positions.

Educational Institutions

Educational institutions typically are a source of young applicants with formal training but with relatively little full-time work experience. High schools are usually a source of employees for clerical and blue-collar jobs. Community colleges, with their various types of specialized training, can provide candidates for technical and semi-professional jobs. These institutions can also be a source of applicants for a variety of white-collar jobs, including those in the sales and retail fields. Some management-trainee jobs are also staffed from this source. One such program with specialized training is Humber College in Etobicoke, Ontario. The Human Resource Management postgraduate program offers a wide range of courses, leading to a certificate in HRM. Program Coordinator Pat Goodman feels that "the success of the program lies in its integrated approach: teaching professionals with industry experience and work/study components." Organizations such as the Bank of Montreal, Brantford General Hospital, and Blackcomb Resorts in Whistler, B.C., have employed students on their work placements.[12]

For technical and managerial positions, colleges and universities are generally the primary source. However, the suitability of college graduates for open positions often depends on their major field of study. Organizations seeking applicants in the technical and professional areas, for example, are currently faced with a shortage of qualified candidates. To remedy an alarming shortage of qualified manufacturing engineers and to reduce the $30,000 recruitment cost per engineer, Newbridge Networks Corp. of Ottawa, Ontario, has gone back to school. This company sends its engineers from Ottawa to Halifax to present case studies to engineering students, and to look at the cream of the crop of graduating engineers of the Technical University of Nova Scotia.[13]

To attract graduates in areas of low supply, HR managers are employing other innovative recruitment techniques such as work-study programs, internships, low-interest loans, and scholarships. Writing on the subject of educational assistance programs, one professional journal noted that "the object is to ensure the company meets its personnel needs by targeting potential employees at a younger age, and nurturing their educational—and professional—development through college and even high school."[14]

Some employers fail to take full advantage of college and university resources because of a poor recruitment program. Consequently, their recruitment efforts fail to attract many potentially good applicants. Another common weakness is the failure to maintain a planned and continuing effort on a long-term basis. Furthermore, some recruiters sent to college campuses are not sufficiently trained or prepared to talk to interested candidates about career opportunities or the requirements of specific openings. Attempts to visit too many campuses instead of concentrating on selected institutions and the inability to use the campus placement office effectively are other recruiting weaknesses. Mismanagement of applicant visits to the plant or company headquarters and the failure to follow up on individual prospects or to obtain hiring commitments from higher management are among other mistakes that have caused employers to lose well-qualified prospects. A well-managed recruitment and selection program for university graduates operated by the federal government is described in the next chapter.

Nepotism
A preference for hiring relatives of current employees.

Employee Referrals

The recruitment efforts of an organization can be aided by employee referrals, or recommendations made by current employees. HR managers have found that the quality of employee-referred applicants is normally quite high, since employees are generally hesitant to recommend individuals who might not perform well. The effectiveness of this recruitment effort can be increased by paying commissions to employees when they make a successful "recruitment sale." Other recruitment incentives used by organizations include complimentary dinners, discounts on merchandise, all-expense-paid trips, and free insurance.[15]

Negative factors associated with employee referrals include the possibility of inbreeding and the violation of employment equity guidelines. Since employees and their referrals tend to have similar backgrounds, employers who rely heavily on employee referrals to fill job openings may intentionally or unintentionally screen out, and thereby discriminate against, members of designated groups. Furthermore, organizations may choose not to employ relatives of current employees. The practice of hiring relatives, referred to as **nepotism**, can invite charges of favouritism, especially in appointments to desirable positions.

Unsolicited Applications and Résumés

Many employers receive unsolicited applications and résumés from individuals who may or may not be good prospects for employment.[16] Even though the percentage of acceptable applicants from this source may not be high, it is a source that cannot be ignored. In fact, it is often believed that individuals who on their own initiative contact the employer will be better employees than those recruited through college placement services or newspaper advertisements.

Good public relations dictates that any person contacting an organization for a job be treated with courtesy and respect. If there is no possibility of employment in the organization at present or in the future, the applicant should be tactfully and frankly informed of this fact. Telling applicants, "Fill out an application, and we will keep it on file," when there is no hope for their employment is not fair to the applicant.

Professional Organizations

Many professional organizations and societies offer a placement service to members as one of their benefits. Listings of members seeking employment may be advertised in their journals or publicized at their national meetings. A placement centre is usually established at national meetings for the mutual benefit of employers and job seekers.

Labour Unions

Labour unions can be a principal source of applicants for blue-collar and some professional jobs. Some unions, such as those in the maritime and construction industries, maintain hiring halls that can provide a supply of applicants, particularly for short-term needs. Employers wishing to use this recruitment source should contact the local union under consideration for employer eligibility requirements and applicant availability.

Temporary Help Agencies

The temporary services industry is one of the fastest-growing recruitment sources. Temporary services will be one of the strongest employers through the 1990s.[17] Companies such as Imperial Oil Ltd., International Forest Products, and SaskTel use temps extensively. Because the use of temps is increasing, agencies have improved their ability to recruit, train, and retain qualified personnel. Small business managers use temporary help when they cannot justify hiring a full-time employee, such as for vacation fill-ins, during peak work periods, and as a replacement during an employee's maternity leave or sick leave.

Temporary employees, however, are being used more and more to fill positions once staffed by permanent employees. At Hydro-Québec, for example, "long-term temporary" has replaced permanent hires as a staffing practice. Employees are hired on one-to-three-year terms. This practice is growing because temporaries can be laid off quickly, and with less cost, when work lessens. Some companies use a *just-in-time staffing* approach where a core staff of employees is augmented by a trained and highly skilled supplementary workforce.[18] The use of temporaries thus becomes a viable way to maintain proper staffing levels. Also, the employment costs of temporaries are often lower than those of permanent employees because temps are not provided with benefits and can be dismissed without excessive termination expenses. Used predominantly in office clerical positions, temporaries are becoming more and more common in legal work, engineering, computer programming, and other jobs requiring advanced professional training.[19]

One Toronto-based recruitment agency reported that one-fifth of his business is devoted to this "contract" market, a good portion of which are displaced executives. These former managers, armed with retirement or severance packages, can make a reasonable living working about 60 to 80 percent of their former full-time hours.[20] The drawbacks of contract employees is that their commitment to the company is lower than that of a regular employee, and confidentiality conflicts if their next assignment is with a competitor.

Outsourcing

Unlike temporary help agencies, which supply workers only for limited periods, employee-leasing companies place their employees with subscribers on a permanent basis. Minacs Group, based in Pickering, Ontario, is a large independently owned employer of temporary and contract personnel. On behalf of its clients, it runs several mailrooms, data processing areas, and marketing departments with 350 full-time employees and 400 active temporary employees.[21] General Motors of Canada and Molson Breweries Ltd. use outsourcing because of the advantages: cost, convenience, flexibility, and added expertise.

The outsourcing company performs all the HR duties of an employer—hiring, payroll, performance appraisal, benefits administration, and other day-to-day HR activities—and in return is paid a placement fee of normally 5 to 10 percent of payroll cost.[22] Some leasing companies charge payroll cost plus a fixed fee per employee that might be $5 to $25 per week.[23]

Improving the Effectiveness of External Recruitment

With all of the uncertainties inherent in external recruiting, it is sometimes difficult to determine whether or not an organization's efforts to locate promising talent are effective and/or cost-efficient. However, there are several things the HR department can do to maximize the probability of success. These include calculating yield ratios on recruiting sources, training organizational recruiters, and conducting realistic job previews.

Yield ratio

The percentage of applicants from a recruitment source that make it to the next phase of the selection process.

Yield Ratios

Yield ratios help indicate which recruitment sources are most effective at producing qualified job candidates. Quite simply, a **yield ratio** is the percentage of applicants from a particular source that make it to the next stage in the selection process. For example, if 100 résumés are obtained from an employment agency, and 17 of these applicants are invited for an on-site interview, the yield ratio for that agency would be 17 percent (17/100). This yield ratio can then be recalculated for each subsequent stage in the selection process (e.g., after the interview, final offer, etc.) resulting in a cumulative yield ratio. By calculating and comparing yield ratios for each recruitment source, it is possible to find out not only which sources produce qualified applicants, but which sources are the most cost-effective.

Organizational Recruiters

Who performs the recruitment function depends mainly on the size of the organization. For large employers, professional HR recruiters are hired and trained to find new employees. In smaller organizations, recruitment may be done by an HR generalist; or if the organization has no HR position, recruitment may be carried out by managers and/or supervisors. At companies like Steelcase Canada Ltd., members of work teams take part in the selection of new team members.[24]

Regardless of who does the recruiting, it is imperative that these individuals have a good understanding of the knowledge, skills, abilities, experiences, and other characteristics required for the job. All too often, new persons in the HR department may be given a recruitment assignment before they have been given interview training or before they fully understand the job or even the values and goals of the organization.

It is important to remember that recruiters have an influence on applicants' job decisions. Recruiters are often a main reason applicants select one organization over another. One study showed that recruiters may have significant impacts on perceived job attractiveness, regard for job and company, and intention to accept a job.[25] Therefore, choosing personable, enthusiastic, and competent recruiters would seemingly have an impact on the success of an organization's recruitment program.

Realistic Job Previews

Realistic job preview (RJP)

Informing applicants about all aspects of the job, including both its desirable and undesirable aspects.

Another way organizations may be able to increase the effectiveness of their recruitment efforts is to provide job applicants with a **realistic job preview (RJP)**. An RJP informs applicants about all aspects of the job, including both its desirable and undesirable facets. In contrast, a typical job preview presents the job only in positive terms. The RJP may also include a tour of the working area combined with a discussion of any negative health or safety considerations. Proponents of the RJP believe that applicants who are given realistic information regarding a position are more likely to remain on the job and be successful, because there will be fewer unpleasant surprises. In fact, since 1980 a number of research studies on RJP report these positive results:

- Improved employee job satisfaction
- Reduced voluntary turnover
- Enhanced communication through honesty and openness
- Realistic job expectations.[26]

Like other HR techniques, however, RJPs must be tailored to the needs of the organization and should include a balanced presentation of positive and negative job information.[27]

Recruitment of Designated Group Members

In meeting their legal obligation to provide equal employment opportunity, employers often develop a formal employment equity program. An essential part of any employment equity policy must be an effort to recruit members of the designated groups. The steps that Employment Equity Commission recommends for organizations to follow in developing such a program were discussed in Chapter 3.

Recruitment of Women

Women constitute the largest group of workers in Canada, at about 45 percent. It is estimated that women will dominate the growth rate in the workforce by the year 2000, making up about two-thirds of this growth.[28] However, even with the large numbers of women in the labour force, employers today often have difficulty in recruiting women for clerical, secretarial, and other jobs in which they have traditionally been employed. Furthermore, women still encounter barriers to landing the better-paying jobs that have been traditionally performed by men or in rising to positions of top managerial responsibility.

Contrary to a once-common belief, most women do not go to work merely to "get out of the house" or to fulfil psychological needs. It is essential for employers to recognize that a majority of women, like men, work because of economic necessity. In recent years, over 60 percent of all women in the workforce have been responsible for supporting themselves, and three out of five of them are heads of households. These women have the employment disadvantage of having completed, on average, fewer years of school than married women not in the workforce, and they are concentrated in lower-skilled, lower-paying jobs.[29]

A major employment obstacle for women is the stereotyped thinking that persists within our society. For example, a recent study comparing male and female personality types concluded that females are still viewed as possessing fewer characteristics of the "ideal" manager profile.[30] Still another barrier has been that women in the past were not as likely as men to have professional training and preparation for entrance or advancement into management positions. This situation is changing, however, with a significant increase in the enrollment of women in programs leading to degrees in management. In addition, more women are enrolling in management seminars and certification programs that will further prepare them for higher managerial positions.

Recruitment of Visible Minorities

The 1982 Canadian Charter of Rights and to a large extent human rights and employment equity legislation have enabled many members of visible minority groups to realize some improvement in their social and economic well-being. A 1992 study conducted for the Canadian Advertising Foundation estimated that by the year 2001, nearly one-fifth of Canada's labour force will be visible minorities. This study anticipated that visible minorities will have earnings 9 percent greater than the white population, due in part to higher levels of education.[31]

Unless visible minorities can be retained within an organization, employment equity programs are likely to prove ineffective. If visible minority employees are to be retained, they, like any employees, must be made to feel welcome in their jobs, as well as to feel that their efforts contribute to the success of the organization.[32]

Many organizations develop specialized recruitment material in order to contact and attract members of the designated groups. For example, the Government of Canada has prepared for students in educational institutions a brochure entitled *A Pathway for Young Aboriginals of Canada*.[33] The message contained in the brochure is twofold: stay in school and consider a future career in the federal public service.

Recruitment of Persons with Disabilities

Persons with disabilities make up almost 14 percent of the Canadian population, but the percentage employed in the workforce is much less.[34] These individuals are often rejected for employment because of the mistaken belief that there are no jobs within an organization that they might be able to perform effectively. Fears that the disabled might have more accidents or that they might aggravate existing disabilities have also deterred their employment. The lack of special facilities for physically impaired persons, particularly those in wheelchairs, has been a further employment restriction. However, physical obstructions are being eliminated as employers are making federally legislated improvements to accommodate disabled workers.

Efforts to eliminate discrimination in hiring, promotion, and compensation of people with disabilities are expected to increase. Thanks to federal regulations, many companies are beginning to recognize that physical disabilities may constitute limitations only with respect to certain job requirements. An employee in a wheelchair

The elimination of physical obstructions for disabled workers allows this employee to pursue his career.

who might not be able to perform duties that involve certain physical activities may be quite capable of working at a bench or a desk. Some employers have even found ways to use workers' disabilities to an advantage. The U.S. Air Force, for example, estimates that the work of five blind inspectors of jet engine blades saves it several millions of dollars a year. Their keen sense of touch enables them to spot minor defects on blades that, if installed in a jet engine, might lead to mechanical failure and even the loss of life.

Advantages of Employing with Persons Disabilities

Among the most frequently cited advantages of employing disabled persons are their dependability, superior attendance, loyalty, and low turnover. Employers often find workers with disabilities to be more intelligent, better motivated, and better qualified than their nondisabled counterparts. However, the superior performance attributed to workers with disabilities could also be the result of hidden biases toward them. These biases may cause employers to require that persons with disabilities be overqualified for an entry-level job and to avoid promoting them above it.

Recruitment of Older Persons

There is a definite trend by organizations toward hiring older persons. The move has come as a result of changing workforce demographics and a change in the attitudes of employers and employees. Organizations realize that older workers have proven employment experience, have job "savvy," and are reliable employees. Older individuals are an excellent recruitment source to staff part-time and full-time positions that are hard to fill.

As the demand for skilled employees increases, organizations are offering flexible work schedules and additional training to attract older workers.[35] McDonald's has been employing older workers for a number of years with great success as measured by productivity and reduced turnover. No longer can organizations pursuing an effective employment strategy ignore older persons as a potential recruitment source.

► SUMMARY ◄

objective

Employers usually find it advantageous to fill by means of internal promotion as many openings as possible above the entry level. By recruiting from within, an organization can capitalize on previous investments made in recruiting, selecting, training, and developing its current employees. Further, internal promotions can reward employees for past performance and send a signal to other employees that their future efforts will pay off. However, potential candidates from the outside should occasionally be considered in order to prevent the inbreeding of ideas and attitudes.

objective

Filling jobs above the entry level often requires managers to rely upon outside sources. These outside sources are also utilized to fill jobs with special qualifications, to avoid excessive inbreeding, and to acquire new ideas and technology. Which outside sources and methods are used in recruiting depends on the recruitment goals of the organization, the conditions of the labour market, and the specifications of the jobs to be filled.

objective

Employment equity legislation encourages employers to exert a positive effort to recruit and promote members of designated groups so that their representation at all levels within the organization will approximate their proportionate numbers in the labour market. These efforts include recruiting not only those members who are qualified, but also those who can be made qualified with reasonable training and assistance.

KEY TERMS

job posting and bidding

labour market

nepotism

realistic job preview (RJP)

yield ratio

DISCUSSION QUESTIONS

1. What are the comparative advantages and disadvantages of filling openings from internal sources?
2. Describe the relationships between the recruitment function and the functions of selection, performance appraisal, and compensation management.
3. In what ways do executive search firms differ from the traditional employment agencies?
4. Explain how realistic job previews (RJPs) operate. Why do they appear to be an effective recruitment technique?
5. Discuss some of the employment problems faced by members of the designated groups.

CASE: British Airways

British Airways (BA) has the largest centralized commercial recruitment operation in the United Kingdom, recruiting nearly 5,000 people each year. A team of only 90 people, supported by a mainframe computer system, have the rather arduous task of handling 72,000 applications, 13,000 job applicants, and 169,000 unsolicited inquires—all for a workforce of 50,000 employees.

At the beginning of the 1990s, senior human resource executives at BA took significant steps to deal with changes they had observed in the labour market. For some time, it was becoming increasingly difficult to find skilled recruits in areas such as information technology, finance, and engineering. In addition, there had been a clear downturn in the supply of skilled young people. All of these trends were occurring side by side with an increase, driven by business growth, in demand for skilled labour.

The widening gap between supply and demand led to the creation of a recruitment marketing team within BA. The primary purpose of the team was to ensure consistency in the promotion of BA as a first-choice employer and to extend the company's customer-focused approach to the recruitment field.

The team's first priority was to apply some basic customer service principles to the recruitment operation as a whole. Having identified that there were, in fact, two customers for recruitment—external applicants and line managers—the team drew up basic guidelines and targets for measuring the quantity, quality, timing, and cost of services provided to each. Within career services, measures were developed to ensure excellent response to telephone inquiries (e.g., answer all calls within twenty seconds) and graduate recruitment (e.g., acknowledge receipt of a candidate's application within three days).

In addition to establishing quality standards, four different training programs were also developed for line managers to help increase their understanding of the recruitment marketplace, emphasize the importance of equal opportunity in recruitment, as well as improve their basic skills in assessment and selection. This training was a crucial element of BA's strategy of meeting the needs of the airline while simultaneously reducing the head count in the recruitment department itself. As a consequence of the reorganization and training, many of the traditional HR functions were handed over to line managers themselves.

In order to promote BA as a first-choice employer, the company worked with Barkers Advertising to develop a recruitment advertising style that was consistent with the company's £40 million advertising budget. The philosophy was to convey a consistent corporate message while targeting different niches, especially for positions that were difficult to fill.

In their efforts to promote BA as first choice among employers, the recruitment department made special efforts to maintain a delicate balance between projecting the genuine opportunities of working for a company of the size and diversity of British Airways and the tendency to paint too rosy a picture of the realities of life within a large corporation. This was seen as especially important since retaining talented employees in a diminishing labour market was perhaps more important than attracting them in the first place.

These efforts at BA are indicative of the company's overall effort to build a more flexible and capable workforce. Flexibility and capability are two vital ingredients in the company's strategy to become a world-class carrier in the airline industry.

Source: This case is a summary of an article written by Chris Wyche, "British Airways Flies the Marketing Flag," *Personnel Management* (October 1990): 125–127.

Questions

1. What is the relationship between strategy, human resource planning, and recruitment at British Airways?
2. Do you agree with BA's decision to shift responsibility for recruitment and selection over to line managers? Explain.
3. What else could British Airways do to attract qualified candidates?

Job-Search Strategies

In this chapter, you have read about the many ways in which employers search for qualified applicants. But there are ways in which potential employees can find qualified employers. These techniques, commonly referred to as *job-search strategies*, have been compiled from a variety of sources. Your career planning will benefit from an understanding of these strategies, which are described briefly below.

Job Search Strategy #1

Review the material you have prepared on your life goals (Chapter 4), and your dream job (Chapter 5). Based on the information generated from these exercises, identify a few jobs and a few sectors in which you would like to find employment. Try to develop generic rather than specific or narrow employment objectives. For example, broaden the goal of "grade-school teacher" to "teaching young children in any situation" or "communicating with children." By enlarging the goal, you will not restrict yourself to searching for a job at the local elementary school, but will widen the search to educational publishing houses, youth television stations, youth centres, private tutoring organizations, camps, and so forth.

Job-Search Strategy #2

Once you have identified several jobs or careers of interest to you, such as investment banking or advertising, obtain a lot of information about the field. There are two main ways to do this. First, visit the library and ask the librarian for materials that describe the duties and education requirements associated with these jobs. Ask also for any trade journals. Access the data base and search for newspaper articles on the sector or on the companies hiring in the job categories that interest you. Note the names of people who are active in the field.

Second, interview people who work in the field. These names can be generated by informing all your friends and relatives about your job search, and asking for names of people. Phone the industry or professional associations and ask them if they could give you names of people willing to talk about their jobs. Cold-call the names gleaned from the library search. In these interviews, do not ask for a job—ask for information. Then send a thank you letter. If there is any possibility of a job, the interviewers know you are interested and will contact you.

Job-Search Strategy #3

Searching for a job is a job. Manage your project. Set goals such as "five calls a day" or "read two trade magazines" this week. Track your work by organizing a contact list such as:

Name	Referral	Source	Call Interview	Thank you Letter
1.				
2.				
3.				
4.				
5.				

Track your information gathering by listing the source and key points. You may need this type of information in future interviews.

Job-Search Strategy #4

At this point, armed with information about your interests and industry/employer needs, contact a potential employer about a job. How do you do this effectively? According to one expert, the least effective ways to find a job are to use computer banks or registers (4% success rate); answer local newspaper ads (5–24%); approach private employment agencies (5–24%); respond to ads in trade journals (7%); and mail out your résumé (8%). The most effective ways are to research an employer and target your search (86%); apply directly to an employer without research (47%); ask friends and relatives for leads (30%); and use your college or university placement service.

The most important step you can take is to research the employer for whom you wish to work. Ask friends, go back to the library, read trade journals and business reports, including the company's annual report. Then write a covering letter explaining what you can contribute to the organization. Include a résumé, tailored specifically for that job or employer. (The next chapter will teach you how to write different types of résumés).

The most critical factor in a covering letter is understanding the needs of the organization and what you can do for it using your skills and experience. Two examples:

> I noted in the *Fashion Trade Magazine* that your organization is expanding into Canada and planning to open four stores. I can help you. I have opened and managed a retail store ....
>
> The *Report on Business* article in which you were interviewed indicated that your organization is focusing on customer service as a competitive advantage. I have significant experience in training personnel to meet service objectives ....

The use of these strategies will increase the probability of your finding employment in a field of your choice.

Sources: R.N. Bolles, *The 1995 What Colour Is Your Parachute?* (Berkeley, CA: Consolidated Printers Inc., 1995); J. Noble, *The Elements of Job Hunting* (Holbrook, MA: Bob Adams Inc., 1991).

NOTES AND REFERENCES

1. Jana Schiler, "The New Darwinian Workplace," *Human Resources Professional* 11, no. 6 (August 1994): 9–11. See also Leslie Goodson, "The Mentor Model," *Human Resources Professional* 8, no. 3 (March 1992): 19–22.

2. Kenneth Duff, "HR–Link: An HRIS from Apple Canada," *Personnel* 6, no. 5 (May 1990): 6–14.

3. Tricia McCallum, "Beauty and the Hi-Tech Beast," *Human Resources Professional* 8, no. 4 (April 1992): 19–21.

4. Brian Dumaine, "What's So Hot about Outsiders?" *Fortune*, November 29, 1993, 63–67.

5. L. Amante, "Help Wanted: Creative Recruitment Tactics," *Personnel* 66, no. 10 (1989): 32–36. See also R. Wayne Mondy, Robert M. Noe, and Robert E. Edwards, "Successful Recruitment: Matching Sources and Methods," *Personnel* 64, no. 9 (September 1987): 42–46.

6. Jean Powell Kirnan, John A. Farley, and Kurt F. Geisinger, "The Relationship between Recruiting Source, Applicant Quality, and Hire Performance: An Analysis by Sex, Ethnicity, and Age," *Personnel Psychology* 42, no. 2 (Summer 1989): 293–308. See also David F. Caldwell and A. Austin Spivey, "The Relationship between Recruiting Source and Employee Success: An Analysis by Race," *Personnel Psychology* 36, no. 1 (Spring 1983): 67–72.

7. Jana Schiler, "Trial by Hire," *Human Resources Professional* 11, no. 2 (March 1994): 21–23

8. Deirdre McMurdy, "How Bad Can It Get?" *Macleans*, January 23, 1995, 26–27.

9. *Unemployed? How Your Canada Employment Centre Can Help with Your Job Search*, Employment and Immigration Canada, Programs and Services, LM 196–11–92.

10. "Info Tel: A Service for the Job Seeking Public," *Public Service Commission of Canada*, Ottawa, 94-11-30.

11. Donald A. Levenson, "Needed: Revamped Recruiting Services," *Personnel* 65, no. 7 (July 1988): 52. See also J.A. Breaugh, *Recruitment: Science and Practice* (Boston: PWS-Kent, 1992).

12. Personal correspondence with Pat Goodman and Toby Fletcher, Humber College, May 1995.

13. Susan Lightstone, "Why Newbridge Goes to School," *The Globe and Mail*, May 2, 1995, B16.

14. Holly Rawlinson, "Scholarships Recruit Future Employees Now," *Recruitment*, a supplement of *Personnel Journal* (August 1988): 14.

15. Allan Halcrow, "Employees Are Your Best Recruiters," *Personnel Journal* 67, no. 11 (November 1988): 42–49.

16. For an excellent article on the contents of job résumés, see William H. Holly, Jr., Early Higgins, and Sally Speights, "Résumés and Cover Letters," *Personnel* 65, no. 12 (December 1988): 49–51.

17. Michael R. Losey, "Temps: They're Not Just for Typing Anymore," *Modern Office Technology* (August 1991): 58–59. See also Louis S. Richman, "CEOs to Workers: Help Not Wanted," *Fortune*, July 12, 1993, 42–43; and "The Temporary Services: A Lasting Impact on the Economy," *Personnel Administrator* 33, no. 1 (January 1988): 60–62.

18. Frank N. Liguori, "Get ready for Just-in-Time Staffing," *Chief Executive* (April 1993): 30–32; see also William E. Gruer and Herff L. Moore, "Staffing a Company with the Just-in-Time Employee," *Industrial Management* (January/February 1992): 31–32.

19. Linda Dickens, "Part-Time Employees: Workers Whose Time Has Come?" *Employee Relations* 14, no. 2 (1992): 3–12; see also Jack L. Simonetti, Nick Nykodym, and Louella M. Sell, "Temporary Employees," *Personnel* 65, no. 8 (August 1988): 52.

20. David McCabe, "Improvising the Future," *Human Resources Professional* 10, no. 11 (December 1993): 17–19.

21. Tricia McCallum, "The Minacs Touch," *Human Resources Professional* 11, no. 5 (June/July 1994): 21–22.

22. Virginia Gibson, "Staffing Alternatives for Today's Business Needs," *HR Focus* (March 1992): 11; see also Howard E. Potter, "Getting a New Lease on Employees," *Management Review* 78, no. 4 (April 1989): 28–31.

23. Paul N. Keaton and Janine Anderson, "Leasing Offers Benefits to Both Sides," *HR Magazine* (July 1990): 53–58; see also "Give Your Employees a Break—by Leasing Them," *Business Week*, August 14, 1989, 135.

24. "Two Visions of Teamwork," *Canadian Business Review* (Autumn, 1994): 21.

25. Michael M. Harris and Laurence S. Fink, "A Field Study of Applicant Reactions to Employment Opportunities: Does the Recruiter Make a Difference?" *Personnel Psychology* 40, no. 1 (Winter 1987): 781. See also G.N. Powell, "Applicant Reactions to the Initial Employment Interview: Exploring Theoretical and Methodological Issues," *Personnel Psychology* 44 (1991): 67–83.

26. Patricia Buhler, "Managing in the 90s: Hiring the Right Person for the Job," *Supervision* (July 1992): 21–23.

27. John P. Wanous, "Installing a Realistic Job Preview: Ten Tough Choices," *Personnel Psychology* 42, no. 1 (Spring 1989): 117–133.

28. Dorothy Lipovenko, "Women Face Poverty, Study Says," *The Globe and Mail*, April 18, 1995, A10.

29. Ibid.

30. Kenneth P. Carson, "Effects of Applicant Gender and Trait Characteristics on Selection Decision Behaviour and Outcome," unpublished manuscript, September 1989, 1–14. See also Madeleine E. Heilman, Caryn J.

Block, Richard F. Martell, and Michael C. Simon, "Has Anything Changed? Current Characterizations of Men, Women, and Managers," *Journal of Applied Psychology* 74, no. 6 (December 1989): 935–942.

31. Belinda Morin and Robert Lattimer, "Managing Work Force Diversity: Problems Similar in Canada and U.S.," *Towers Perrin Focus* (Spring 1993): 9–10.

32. Jennifer J. Laabs, "Affirmative Outreach," *Personnel Journal* (May 1991): 86–93. See also Wendy Hickey, "Balancing Act: Coordinated Strategy, Commitment Critical to Wooing Minority Staffers," *Advertising Age*, July 29, 1991, 13.

33. *Communiqué: Perspectives in Staffing*, Public Service Commission of Canada, November 1993, Ottawa.

34. Employment Equity Commission, *Opening Doors: A Report on the Employment Equity Consultations* (Ottawa: Ministry of Citizenship, 1995), 1080.

35. Benson Rosen and Thomas H. Jerdee, "Investing in the Older Worker," *Personnel Administrator* 34, no. 4 (April 1989): 70–74. See also David V. Lewis, "Make Way for the Older Worker," *HR Magazine* 36, no. 5 (May 1990): 75–77; Walter Kiechel III, "How to Manage Older Workers," *Fortune*, November 5, 1990, 183–186; and "The Rising Tide of Older Workers," *Nation's Business*, September 1992, 22–23.

After studying this chapter you
should be able to

one
objective

*Explain the objectives of
the personnel selection
process.*

two
objective

*Identify the various
sources of information
used for personnel
selection.*

three
objective

*Explain the value of
different types of
employment tests.*

four
objective

*Discuss the different
approaches to conducting
a selection interview.*

five
objective

*Describe the various
decision strategies for
selection.*

Chapter 7

Selection

Selection

The process of choosing individuals who have the relevant qualifications to fill existing or projected job openings.

The recruiting process typically yields a number of applicants whose qualifications must be measured against the requirements of the job. **Selection** is the process of choosing individuals who have the relevant qualifications to fill existing or projected job openings. Selecting from among applicants inside or outside the organization is a major HR function with far-reaching effects.

Today greater attention is being given to the selection process than ever before. With the increasing emphasis being placed on the human side of competitiveness, making correct hiring decisions is of crucial importance to an organization. Individuals hired after thorough screening against carefully developed job specifications learn their job tasks readily, are productive, and generally adjust to their jobs with a minimum of difficulty. As a result, both the individual and the organization benefit from a careful selection process.

The greatest impetus to improve the selection process may have come from human rights legislation and court decisions, discussed in Chapter 3. What was once the exclusive concern of the employment office may now be carried into the courtroom. Among other factors affecting selection are scarcity of labour supply in high-technology labour markets, increasing geographic immobility of career couples, and changing staffing needs due to promotion and turnover.[1] Where the job tenure of employees is protected by a collective agreement, there is an additional incentive for management to have sound selection policies and procedures since it is usually more difficult to discharge unsatisfactory employees who have such protection.

While the selection program typically is the responsibility of the HR department, managerial and supervisory personnel in all the departments of an organization also have an important role in the selection process. The final decision in hiring is usually theirs. It is important, therefore, that managers understand the objectives and policies relating to selection. They should also be thoroughly trained in the most effective and acceptable approaches for evaluating applicants and should be motivated to use them.

objective

Matching People and Jobs

Those responsible for making selection decisions should have adequate information upon which to base them. Information about the jobs to be filled, knowledge of the ratio of job openings to the number of applicants, and as much relevant information as possible about the applicants themselves are essential for making sound decisions.

Use of Job Specifications

In Chapter 5, we discussed the process of analyzing and developing specifications for jobs. Such factors as skill, effort, responsibility, and physical demands provide the basis for determining what types of information should be obtained from the applicant, from previous employers, or from other sources. The job specifications also form the basis for the administration of any applicable employment tests. Research has demonstrated that complete and unambiguous job information reduces the influence of racial and sex stereotypes and helps the interviewer to differentiate between qualified and unqualified applicants.

Ordinarily, the managers and supervisors in an organization are well acquainted with the requirements pertaining to skill, physical demands, and other factors for jobs in their respective departments. Interviewers and other members of the HR department who participate in selection should maintain a close liaison with the various departments so that they can become thoroughly familiar with the jobs.

The Selection Process

In most organizations, selection is a continuous process. Turnover inevitably occurs, leaving vacancies to be filled by applicants from inside or outside the organization or by individuals whose qualifications have been assessed previously. It is common to have a waiting list of applicants who can be called when permanent or temporary positions become open.

The number of steps in the selection process and their sequence will vary not only with the organization but also with the type and level of jobs to be filled. Each step should be evaluated in terms of its contribution. The steps that typically make up the selection process are shown in Figure 7-1. Not all applicants will go through all of these steps. Some may be rejected after the preliminary interview, others after taking tests, and so on.

As shown in Figure 7-1, organizations use several different means to obtain information about applicants. These include application blanks, interviews, tests, and background investigations. Regardless of the method used, it is essential that it conform to accepted ethical standards, including privacy and confidentiality, as well as legal requirements. Above all, it is essential that the information obtained be sufficiently reliable and valid.

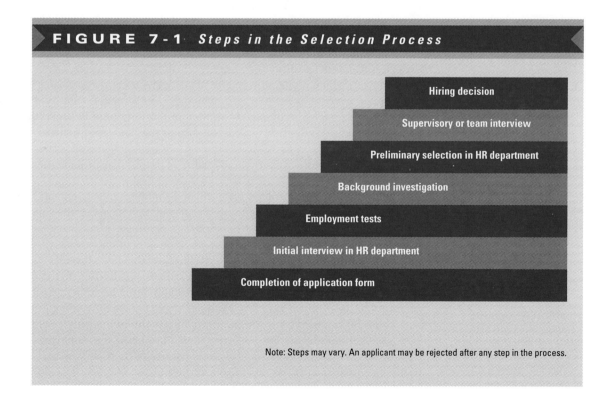

FIGURE 7-1 *Steps in the Selection Process*

Hiring decision

Supervisory or team interview

Preliminary selection in HR department

Background investigation

Employment tests

Initial interview in HR department

Completion of application form

Note: Steps may vary. An applicant may be rejected after any step in the process.

Obtaining Reliable and Valid Information

The degree to which interviews, tests, and other selection procedures yield comparable data over a period of time is known as **reliability**. For example, unless interviewers judge the capabilities of a group of applicants to be the same as they did yesterday, their judgments are unreliable (i.e., unstable). Likewise, a test that gives widely different scores when it is administered to the same individual a few days apart is unreliable.

Reliability also refers to the extent to which two or more methods (interviews, tests, etc.) yield similar results or are consistent. Interrater reliability—agreement between two or more raters—is one measure of a test's consistency. Unless the data upon which selection decisions are based are reliable, in terms of both stability and consistency, they cannot be used as predictors.

In addition to having reliable information pertaining to a person's suitability for a job, the information must be as valid as possible. **Validity** refers to *what* a test or other selection procedure measures and *how well* it measures it. In the context of personnel selection, validity is essentially an indicator of the extent to which data from a procedure (interview, test, etc.) are related to or predictive of job performance or some other relevant criterion. Like a new medicine, a selection procedure must be validated before it is used. There are good reasons for validating a procedure. First, validity is directly related to increases in employee productivity, as we will demonstrate later. Second, employment equity concepts emphasize the importance of validity in selection procedures.[2] Although we commonly refer to "validating" a test or interview procedure, validity in the technical sense refers to the inferences made from the use of a procedure, not the procedure itself.

Among the recognized approaches to validation are criterion-related validity, content validity, and construct validity.

Criterion-Related Validity

The extent to which a selection tool predicts or significantly correlates with important elements of work behaviour is known as **criterion-related validity**. Performance on a test, for example, is compared to actual production records, supervisory ratings, training outcomes, and other measures of success that are appropriate to each type of job. In a sales job, for example, it is common to use sales figures as a basis for comparison. In production jobs, quantity and quality of output may provide the best criteria of job success.

There are two types of criterion-related validity, concurrent and predictive. **Concurrent validity** involves obtaining criterion data at about the same time that test scores (or other predictor information) are obtained from *current employees*. For example, a supervisor is asked to rate a group of clerical employees on the quantity and quality of their performance. Within a few days these employees are given a clerical aptitude test that is then validated. **Predictive validity**, on the other hand, involves testing *applicants* and obtaining criterion data *after* they have been on the job for some indefinite period. For example, applicants are given a clerical aptitude test, which is then filed away for later study. After the individuals have been on the job for several months, supervisors, who should not know the employees' test scores, are asked to rate them on the quality and quantity of their performance. Test scores are then compared with the supervisors' ratings.

Reliability
The degree to which interviews, tests, and other selection procedures yield comparable data over a period of time.

Validity
The accuracy of measurement obtained by a test or other selection procedure.

Criterion-related validity
The extent to which a selection tool predicts or significantly correlates with important elements of work behaviour.

Concurrent validity
Criterion data are obtained from current employees at about the same time that test scores (or other predictor information) are obtained.

Predictive validity
Testing applicants and obtaining criterion data after they have been on the job for some indefinite period.

Cross-validation
Verifying the results obtained from a validation study by administering a test or test battery to a different sample (drawn from the same population).

Regardless of the method used, cross-validation is essential. **Cross-validation** is a process in which a test or test battery is administered to a different sample (drawn from the same population) for the purpose of verifying the results obtained from the original validation study.

Correlational methods are generally used to determine the relationship between predictor information such as test scores and criterion data. The correlation scatterplots in Figure 7-2 illustrate the difference between a selection test of zero validity (A) and one of high validity (B). Each dot represents a person. Note that in scatterplot A there is no relationship between test scores and success on the job; in other words, the validity is zero. In scatterplot B, those who score low on the test tend to have low success on the job, whereas those who score high on the test tend to have high success on the job, indicating high validity. In actual practice we would apply a statistical formula to the data to obtain a coefficient of correlation referred to as a validity coefficient. Correlation coefficients range from 0.00, denoting a complete absence of relationship, to +1.00 and to −1.00, indicating a perfect positive or perfect negative relationship, respectively.

A thorough survey of the literature shows that the averages of the maximum validity coefficients are 0.45 where tests are validated against *training* criteria and 0.35 where tests are validated against job *proficiency* criteria. These figures represent the predictive power of single tests.[3] A higher validity may be obtained by combining two or more tests or other predictors (interview, biographical data, etc.), using the appropriate statistical formulas. The higher the overall validity, the greater the chances of hiring individuals who will be the better performers. The criterion-related

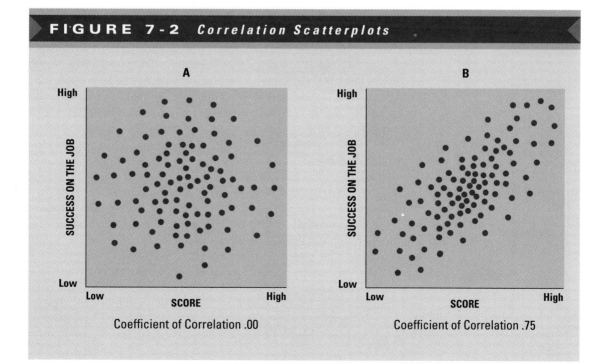

FIGURE 7-2 *Correlation Scatterplots*

A

B

Coefficient of Correlation .00

Coefficient of Correlation .75

method is generally preferred to other validation approaches because it is based on empirical data.

For several decades, personnel psychologists believed that validity coefficients had meaning only for the specific situation (job and organization). More recently, as a result of several research studies—many involving clerical jobs—it appears that validity coefficients can often be generalized across situations, hence the term **validity generalization**. Where there are adequate data to support the existence of validity generalization, the development of selection procedures can become less costly and time-consuming. The process involves analyzing jobs and situations and, on the basis of these analyses, consulting tables of generalized validities from previous studies using various predictors in similar circumstances. It is advisable for organizations to employ the services of an industrial/organizational psychologist experienced in test validation to develop the selection procedures.[4]

Validity generalization
The extent to which validity coefficients can often be generalized across situations.

Content Validity

Where it is not feasible to use the criterion-related approach, often because of limited samples of individuals, the content method is used. **Content validity** is assumed to exist when a selection instrument, such as a test, adequately samples the knowledge and skills needed to perform a particular job.

The closer the content of the selection instrument to actual work samples or behaviours, the greater the content validity. For example, a public service examination for accountants has high content validity when it requires the solution of accounting problems representative of those found on the job. Asking an accountant to lift a 30-kilogram box, however, is a selection procedure that has content validity only if the job description indicates that accountants must be able to meet this requirement.

Content validity is the most direct and least complicated type of validity to assess. It is generally used to evaluate job knowledge and skill tests, to be described later. Unlike the criterion-related method, content validity is not expressed in correlational terms. Instead, an index that indicates the relationship between the content of the test items and performance on the job is computed from evaluations of a panel of experts.[5] While content validity does have its limitations, it has made a positive contribution to job analysis procedures and to the role of expert judgment in sampling and scoring procedures.

Content validity
The extent to which a selection instrument, such as a test, adequately samples the knowledge and skills needed to perform a particular job.

Construct Validity

The extent to which a selection tool measures a theoretical construct, or trait, is known as **construct validity**. Typical constructs are intelligence, mechanical comprehension, and anxiety. They are in effect broad, general categories of human functions that are based on the measurement of many discrete behaviours. For example, the Bennett Mechanical Comprehension Test consists of a wide variety of tasks that measure the construct of mechanical comprehension.

Measuring construct validity requires showing that the psychological trait is related to satisfactory job performance and that the test accurately measures the psychological trait. There is a lack of literature covering this concept as it relates to employment practices, probably because it is difficult and expensive to validate a construct and also show how it is job-related.[6]

Construct validity
The extent to which a selection tool measures a theoretical construct or trait.

The strength of these two workers was tested before they were hired.

objective

Sources of Information about Job Candidates

Many sources of information are used to provide as reliable and valid a picture as possible of an applicant's potential for success on the job. The selection process at the Bay, described in the Reality Check, illustrates the use of the most important sources. In this section, we will study the potential contributions of application forms, biographical information blanks, background investigations, ability tests, lie detector tests, honesty tests, and medical examinations. Because interviewing plays such a major role in selection and because testing presents unique challenges, there will be expanded discussions of these sources of information later in the chapter. Assessment centres, which are often used in managerial selection, will be discussed in Chapter 9.

Application Forms

Most organizations require application forms to be completed because they provide a fairly quick and systematic means of obtaining a variety of information about the applicant. As with interviews, the Canadian Human Rights Commission and the courts have found that many questions asked on application forms disproportionately discriminate against females and minorities and often are not job-related. For example, an Ontario board of inquiry found that a security firm, which required applicants to fill out a form that asked for information regarding place of birth, complexion, eye and hair colour, discriminated against a former police officer from Guyana because of his race and place of origin.[7] Application forms, therefore, should be developed with great care and revised as often as necessary. Because of differences in provincial legislation, organizations operating in more than one province will find it difficult to develop one form that can be used nationally. Note that it is discriminatory to ask for a photograph with a résumé, for the obvious reason that the photo could be used to determine such characteristics as age, sex, and race.

SELECTION AT THE BAY

Canada's oldest corporation and the largest department store retailer is the Hudson's Bay Company, operating as The Bay and Zellers, which was established in 1670. Tina Peacock, Human Resources Manager for the Merchandise Services & Corporate Offices, has been with Hudson's Bay for over twenty years. She contributes to the overall achievement of goals by effectively using selection methods to identify key potential candidates for positions such as merchandising buyers and financial and systems managers.

"In addition to succession planning, we follow established trends, such as growth in our business units, turnover, and performance results, in order to identify those positions that may become vacant during the year. Through a number of training programs provided in-house, we are able to fill our positions internally. In fact, 80 percent are staffed from internal promotions. For the other 20 percent, we hire externally. As a proactive measure in anticipation of those openings, we run recruiting ads so that we always have a 'stable' of competent candidates," states Peacock.

"It is important that we work closely with the managers because they know what is needed to run their business," says Peacock. "My role is to provide them with qualified candidates who possess the basic job knowledge with the right competencies to work in our fast-paced, changing environment. For instance, a number of managers are tapped into the marketplace so they are able to get the ball rolling by identifying candidates in the industry before an ad is placed. Our role is to prescreen those candidates to ensure they have the attributes needed to successfully perform in our environment.

"We work very closely with an ad agency to assist us in preparing the ad and to provide advice on the marketing strategies of where and when to place the ad. They save you a lot of time, especially when they understand your business." Peacock adds further, "Running our ads for a particular position it yields us other qualified candidates for other positions we had not counted on.

"Many of our ads yield as many as 250 résumés. Based on the competencies required for a position, we prescreen the résumés. It is not uncommon for me to receive over 50 phone calls per day when an ad is running. If I can delegate some of those calls, I do; however, if they have asked me for something specific, I make an effort to call them back because "they are our customers and they are important to us," states Peacock. "Once I have determined a short list , I then conduct a pretty thorough telephone interview before bringing in any candidates. Questions regarding salary expectations, any information that may be missing on the résumé, and some very job specific questions are reviewed. We are always looking to improve our systems. Our next ad will incorporate a 'Voice Response System' has been developed internally by our Information Services Department. Candidates who wish to apply to an ad will be asked to call our system and respond to some basic job related questions. At the end of the session, the candidate will be advised if they possess the basic requirements of the job and whether they should apply to this position.

"The questions we ask during the face-to-face interview are open-ended questions that look for behavioural attributes specific to the competencies and key job requirements. For example, we want the candidate to demonstrate how they have gone about performing their job duties in the past. For those candidates who proceed to a final interview, we ask each of them to complete a Communications Survey. Using an outside consultant, we have developed a Prediction Performance Program Profile that has identified benchmark attributes for our buyers, merchandising trainees, and store managers. The results are graphed and compared against the benchmark. This profile is not used as a basis for determining whether we should hire a candidate or not. It provides us with another opportunity to fully assess the individual's capabilities by asking more focused questions. In this way, it ensures that we have fully investigated the individual's background and credentials. We provide each of our candidates with a written assessment of the report, whether they are hired or not, and ask them to comment on the accuracy of the results. Based on these responses, the report has been assessed at an accuracy of over 90 percent."

Peacock says in closing, "Systems in the workplace will continue to change, but the bottom line is that we need the best people to technically do the job and, most importantly, they must be 'customer focused.' "

Source: Interview with Deborah M. Zinni, July 1995.

Application forms serve several purposes. They provide information that can be used to determine whether an applicant meets the minimum requirements for experience, education, and so forth. They provide a basis for questions the interviewer will ask about the applicant's background. They also offer sources for reference checks. For certain jobs, a short application form such as that shown in Highlights in HRM 1 is appropriate. This example from McDonald's reveals that an application form can be brief while asking for information from an applicant that is highly relevant to job performance. It also provides information regarding the employer's conformity with various laws and regulations. For scientific, professional, and managerial jobs, a more extended form is likely to be used.

Even when applicants come armed with elaborate résumés, it is important that they complete an application form early in the process. Individuals frequently exaggerate or overstate their qualifications on a résumé (see Ethics in HRM for a discussion of this issue). One technique for anticipating problems of misrepresentation is to ask applicants to transcribe specific résumé material onto a standardized application form. The applicant is then asked to sign a statement that the information contained on the form is true and that he or she accepts the employer's right to terminate the candidate's employment if any of the information is subsequently found to be false.[8]

Biographical Information Blanks

One of the oldest methods for predicting job success uses biographical information about job applicants. As early as 1917, the Life Insurance Agency Management Association constructed and validated a biographical information blank (BIB) for life insurance salespersons. It covered such items as hobbies, club memberships, sales experience, and investments. Certain responses to these items were found to be predictive of success on the job. Care must be taken not to ask questions that discriminate on the basis of characteristics like sex or race.

Like application blanks, BIBs reveal information about a person's history that may have shaped his or her behaviour. Both the BIB and the application form can be scored like tests. And because biographical questions rarely have obviously right or wrong answers, BIBs are difficult to fake. The development of a scoring system requires that the items that are valid predictors of job success be identified and that weights be established for different responses to these items. By totalling the scores

HRM highlights

1 MCDONALD'S RESTAURANTS EMPLOYMENT APPLICATION

McDONALD'S RESTAURANTS EMPLOYMENT APPLICATION

PERSONAL INFORMATION

Date: _____
D   M   Y

Name: _____ Phone: (_____) _____
last   first   middle

Present address: _____ How long there? _____
no. & street   city   province   postal code

Position Applied for: _____ Are you presently employed? ☐ Yes ☐ No Date of availability: _____

Have you ever worked for McDonald's before? ☐ Yes ☐ No   If so, where? _____

If you are under 16, please state your age*: _____   Referred by: _____
*Please Note: You may be required to provide proof of age prior to hire.

Have you ever been convicted of a criminal offense related to the position applied for and for which you have not been pardoned? ☐ Yes ☐ No

Are you legally entitled to work in Canada? ☐ Yes ☐ No
(You may be required to provide proof of employment status prior to hire.)

AVAILABILITY

HOURS AVAILABLE	MONDAY	TUESDAY	WEDNESDAY	THURSDAY	FRIDAY	SATURDAY	SUNDAY
FROM							
TO							

EMPLOYMENT BACKGROUND
List your present or last position first

DATE MONTH & YEAR	COMPANY NAME & ADDRESS	TELEPHONE NUMBER INCLUDING AREA CODE	NAME AND POSITION OF SUPERVISOR	YOUR POSITION	SALARY/WAGE START I END	REASON FOR LEAVING
FROM						
TO						
FROM						
TO						
FROM						
TO						

I declare that the information contained in this application is correct to the best of my knowledge and understand that any omission or incorrect information is just cause for the rejection of my application or dismissal in accordance with McDonald's policy. If hired, I understand that I may be transferred to another restaurant because of promotions, training or staffing requirements. I also agree that, at all times, I will follow the rules and regulations of McDonald's restaurants in Canada. I authorize McDonald's, or its agents, to verify the information provided, and to obtain any other information relevant to this application. This information may be obtained by telephone or in writing from educational institutions, my current or former employers, financial institutions, personal information agents and my personal references. This consent is valid during the consideration of my application for employment, and if I am hired, for the duration of my employment.

SIGNATURE: _____ DATE: _____

To the applicant:
Your application will be considered active for 90 days, after which you must submit a new application. The information which you have supplied, and any other information obtained, will be used solely for the assessment of your application for employment. Your application will be kept by the Management Team and, if you are hired, it will become part of your employee file. Your file will be retained in the Manager's office, and may be accessed by the Management Team and Payroll and Human Resources personnel. You may access your file by appointment with a representative of McDonald's. If there are mistakes in your file, you have the right to ask for them to be corrected.

©1994 for the exclusive use of McDonald's Restaurants and its Franchisees

HR-88016 Rev. Oct./94

Printed in Canada on paper made from recycled fibre

> ## ETHICS IN HRM
>
> ### WRITING IT WRONG
>
> Most candidates for white-collar jobs prepare a résumé and submit it to prospective employers. In addition, they also complete the application form, answering questions required by employers for comparison purposes. Some recruitment agencies have noticed that since the recession résumé padding has increased. Applicants are "stretching" the dates of their employment, misleading employers about the nature of the duties, and misrepresenting their salaries. At the time of writing a résumé, adding three months to your previous employment, saying you were a night auditor instead of clerk, and adding $950 to your last salary seem like relatively harmless lies.
>
> What are the facts? Estimates of "creative" résumé writing are that about 30 percent report incorrect dates, 11 percent misrepresent reasons for leaving, and others exaggerate education attainments or omit criminal records. The probability is that about two-thirds of employers check references. Of these, some former employers will give only dates of employment and previous salary ranges.
>
> However, most organizations require you to sign a statement saying that the information you supply is true, and that that if it is not you will be dismissed. Highly publicized cases include a Toronto Stock Exchange manager who was dismissed for lying about a Master's degree, and a Member of Parliament who listed ILB, which normally stands for International Baccalaureate of Law, but which he claimed stood for *Incomplete* Baccalaureate of Law. One heart-wrenching case was that of a person ready to retire who had lied about his age decades earlier in order to get a job. Upon discovery, he was dismissed and lost his pension plan.
>
> Would you pad your résumé?
>
> **Source:** J. Schilder, "Trial by Hire," *Human Resource Professional* 11, no. 2 (March 1994): 21–23.

for each item, it is possible to obtain a composite score on the blank as a whole for each applicant. Studies have shown that an objective scoring of BIB and application forms is one of the most potentially valid methods that can be used to predict job success. This method has been useful in predicting all types of behaviour, including employee theft.[9]

Background Investigations

When the interviewer is satisfied that the applicant is potentially qualified, information about previous employment as well as other information provided by the applicant is investigated. Former employers, university and college officials, credit bureaus, and individuals named as references may be contacted for verification of pertinent information such as length of time on job, type of job, performance evaluation, highest wages, academic degrees earned, possible criminal record, and credit rating. Most of this information is now readily available on existing computer data bases. An Employment Management Association survey found that 93 percent of companies participating in the survey investigate information supplied by job applicants.[10] The most common ruse, according to employers, is to exaggerate one's academic background.

Checking References

Over two-thirds of Canadian employers use reference checks when hiring people for some jobs.[11] Not only are more companies checking references, they are asking for more than the standard three references.[12] Some are asking for as many as fifteen from a variety of people who have interacted with the candidate: superiors, subordinates, peers, and clients. In addition, private companies that check references for a fixed fee are growing. The most common way of soliciting this information is by telephone. References are checked to confirm information provided by the applicant. For example, former employers most commonly confirm employment dates, specific job duties, previous job performance, and reason for leaving. But while references are commonly used to screen and select employees, they have proved successful for predicting employee performance. Written letters of reference are notoriously inflated, and this limits their validity. Generally telephone checks are preferable because they save time and provide for greater candour. The most reliable information usually comes from supervisors, who are in the best position to report on an applicant's work habits and performance. It is often advisable, however, to obtain written verification of information relating to job titles, duties, and pay levels from the former employer's HR office.[13]

The 1982 Canadian Charter of Rights and Freedoms gave individuals greater access to personal information concerning themselves. Managers are often reluctant to place incriminating information in an employee's file for fear that the employee will access that information and misconstrue its intent. Since some information obtained on a reference check may not be positive, most employers prefer using the telephone to check references.

Inadequate reference checking can contribute to high turnover, employee theft, and white-collar crime. By using sources in addition to former employers, organizations can obtain valuable information about an applicant's character and habits. To reduce the risk of negligent hiring and to help employers screen out applicants with false résumés, several Canadian court decisions have recommended that reference checks be conducted. While the American courts have awarded millions of dollars because of slanderous statements made by former employers during reference checks, Canada has had almost no cases involving defamation in employment settings. Most employers, aware that there could be a spillover effect in Canada, are cautious about how reference checks are handled. Employers who provide inaccurate and negative references may face fairly large financial penalties in some wrongful dismissal actions.[14]

Requiring Signed Requests for References

As a legal protection to all concerned, it is important to ask the applicant to fill out forms permitting information to be solicited from former employers and other reference sources. Even with these safeguards, many organizations are reluctant to put into writing an evaluation of a former employee. Firms are wary of being sued by former employees who may discovered that they had been given poor recommendations. As a result of such fears, some employers even hesitate to answer questions and/or verify information about former employees over the phone.

Using Credit Reports

The use of consumer credit reports by employers as a basis for establishing an applicant's eligibility for employment has become more restricted. Positions of trust, such as those that involve the handling of financial instruments in banks and other financial institutions, necessitate the use of credit reports. Applicants must agree in writing to a credit report, and have a right to review its contents. More important, the reason for the credit report must be job-related.

The Polygraph

The polygraph, or lie detector, is a device that measures the changes in breathing, blood pressure, and pulse of the person who is being questioned. It consists of a rubber tube around the chest, a cuff around the arm, and sensors attached to the fingers that record the physiological changes in the examinee as the examiner asks questions that call for an answer of "yes" or "no." Questions typically cover such items as whether a person uses drugs, has stolen from an employer, or has committed a serious undetected crime. In Ontario, the use of lie detector tests for the purpose of employment is prohibited under the Employment Standards Act.[15] Before considering the use of polygraphs, staffing officers should check provincial legislation.

Honesty and Integrity Testing

Alternatives to the polygraph are written honesty and integrity tests. These tests have commonly been used in settings such as retail stores where employees have access to cash or merchandise. Common areas of inquiry include beliefs about frequency and extent of theft in our society, punishment for theft, and perceived ease of theft.[16]

A comprehensive analysis of honesty tests reveals that they are valid for predicting job performance as well as a wide range of disruptive behaviours such as theft, disciplinary problems, and absenteeism.[17] Nevertheless, HRM specialists should use the results from such tests very cautiously and most certainly in conjunction with other sources of information. Again, in Ontario, the use of honesty and integrity testing for the purpose of employment is prohibited under the Employment Standards Act.

Graphology

Graphology, a term that refers to a variety of systems of handwriting analysis, is being used by some employers to make employment decisions. Graphologists obtain a sample of handwriting and then examine such characteristics as the size and slant of letters, amount of pressure applied, and placement of the writing on the page. From their observations they draw inferences about the writer's personality traits, temperament, cognitive abilities, and social traits. Graphology has been used extensively since the 1930s in France, Germany, Switzerland, Israel, and the United Kingdom in making employment decisions.[18] Now handwriting analysis is quietly spreading through corporate North America. Companies such as Ford, General Electric, and Huntington Laboratories of Canada Ltd. have used it for selection.[19]

Organizations using handwriting analysis say they prefer it to typical personality tests because it takes only a few minutes for job candidates to jot down a short essay. By contrast, a battery of personality tests and interviews with psychologists can take several hours and cost thousands of dollars. In addition, the available evidence shows graphology to be a reliable predictor of personality when compared to other psychological tests. However, its predictive validity for job performance and occupational success remains questionable. In the academic community, where formal and rigorous validity studies are conducted, use of graphology for employment decisions has been viewed with considerable scepticism.

objective

Employment Tests

The formal introduction of psychological selection techniques into the Canadian Army in September 1941 represented both a pragmatic response to the exigencies of war and an attempt to make selection processes more democratic.[20] Prior to 1941, entry into officer training was the decision of the commanding officer of a unit and could be attained by proven ability, social rank, or monetary favours. Practical considerations such as efficiency and reduction in selection errors prompted the adoption of new selection procedures to maximize the use of limited "manpower." This decision was at the root of the establishment of selection and assessment centres in Canada. A 1992 survey of North American organizations representing 700,000 employees revealed that 66 percent of the respondents used some form of testing.[21]

The past decade has seen increased interest in employment testing.[22] This is indicative of the fact that employers today are less fearful of lawsuits challenging the soundness of their tests, as well as of a renewed focus on individual competence. Objective standards are making a comeback in both education and employment. Concurrently, methodological changes have made it easier to demonstrate test validity.[23] Too often employers have relied exclusively on the interview to measure or predict skills and abilities that can be measured or predicted more accurately by tests.

Tests have played a more important part in government HR programs where hiring on the basis of merit is a well-grounded principle. The federal government, in particular, has a very strong testing program administered by the Personnel Psychology Centre of the Public Service Commission.

Many organizations utilize professional test consultants to improve their testing programs and to meet human rights requirements. While it is often advisable to use consultants, especially if an organization is considering the use of personality tests, the HR staff should have a basic understanding of the technical aspects of testing and the contributions that tests can make to the HR program.

The Nature of Employment Tests

An employment test is an objective and standardized measure of a sample of behaviour that is used to gauge a person's knowledge, skills, abilities, and other characteristics (KSAOs) in relation to other individuals.[24] The proper sampling of behaviour—whether verbal, manipulative, or some other type—is the responsibility of the test author. It is also the responsibility of the test author to develop tests that meet accepted standards of reliability.[25] Data concerning reliability are ordinarily presented in the manual for the test.

While high reliability is essential, it offers no assurance that the test provides the basis for making valid judgments. It is the responsibility of the HR staff to conduct validation studies before a test is adopted for regular use. Other considerations are cost, time, ease of administration and scoring, and the apparent relevance of the test to the individuals being tested—commonly referred to as *face validity*. While face validity is desirable, it is no substitute for technical validity, described earlier in this chapter. Adopting a test just because it appears relevant is bad practice; many a "good-looking" test has poor validity.

About one-third of Canadian employers use tests in selection decisions.[26] The Public Service Commission uses about 30 selection tests, administered 60,000 times a year.[27] These range from basic skill tests such as typing to the more sophisticated tests required to assess management potential.

Most employers have little inclination to validate tests as well as little understanding of what validity means. Test bias is a particularly serious concern because most employers purchase tests that have been validated in the United States on the basis of that country's demographic composition. Canada is much more multicultural, with a large population of francophones and different proportions of aboriginals, Asians, and Third World immigrants. *Guidelines for Educational and Psychological Testing*, published by the Personnel Psychology Centre of the federal Public Service Commission, outlines testing standards and is helpful to employers wishing to make testing decisions.

Classification of Employment Tests

Employment tests may be classified in different ways. Generally they are viewed as measuring either *aptitude* or *achievement*. **Aptitude tests** refer to measures of a person's capacity to learn or acquire skills. **Achievement tests** refer to measures of what a person knows or can do right now.

Cognitive Ability Tests

Cognitive ability tests measure mental capabilities such as general intelligence, verbal fluency, numerical ability, and reasoning ability. There are a host of written tests that measure cognitive abilities, including the General Aptitude Test Battery (GATB), the Scholastic Aptitude Test (SAT), the Graduate Management Aptitude Test (GMAT), and the Bennett Mechanical Comprehension Test. The issue of validation is important here. The Supreme Court of Canada ruled that Canadian National Railways must cease the use of Bennett Mechanical Comprehension Test because it had an adverse impact on the hiring of women for entry-level blue-collar jobs.[28] Figure 7-3 shows some items that could be used to measure different cognitive abilities.

Although cognitive ability tests can be developed to measure very specialized areas such as reading comprehension spatial relations, many experts believe that the validity of cognitive ability tests simply reflects their connection to general

Aptitude tests
Measures of a person's capacity to learn or acquire skills.

Achievement tests
Measures of what a person knows or can do right now.

FIGURE 7-3 *Sample Measures of Cognitive Ability*

Verbal

1. What is the meaning of the word "surreptitious"?
   a. covert   c. lively
   b. winding   d. sweet

2. How is the noun clause used in the following sentence? "I hope that I can learn this game."
   a. subject   c. direct object
   b. predicate nominative   d. object of the preposition

Quantitative

3. Divide 50 by 0.5 and add 5. What is the result?
   a. 25   c. 95
   b. 30   d. 105

4. What is the value of 144^2?
   a. 12   c. 288
   b. 72   d. 20736

Reasoning

5. _____ is to *boat* as *snow* is to _____ .
   a. Sail, ski   c. Water, ski
   b. Water, winter   d. Engine, water

6. Two women played 5 games of chess. Each woman won the same number of games, yet there were no ties. How can this be?
   a. There was a forfeit.   c. They played different people.
   b. One player cheated.   d. One game is still in progress.

Mechanical

7. If gear A and gear C are both turning counterclockwise, what is happening to gear B?
   a. It is turning counterclockwise.   c. It remains stationary.
   b. It is turning clockwise.   b. The whole system will jam.

A   B   C

Answers: 1. a, 2. c, 3. d, 4. d, 5. c, 6. c, 7. b

---

intelligence. Measures of general intelligence (e.g., IQ) have been shown to be good predictors of performance across a wide variety of jobs.[29]

Personality and Interest Inventories

Whereas cognitive ability tests measure a person's mental capacity, personality tests measure dispositional characteristics such as extroversion, inquisitiveness, and dependability. Interest tests, such as the Kuder Inventory, measure an applicant's preferences for certain activities over others (such as sailing versus poker). The predictive validity of personality and interest inventories historically has been quite low.[30] However, since 1944 Sears has successfully employed an "executive battery" composed of several attitudinal and interest tests to predict managerial success.[31] Beyond the initial hiring decision, personality and interest inventories may be most useful for helping with job placement and career planning.

Physical Ability Tests

In addition to learning about a job candidate's mental capabilities, employers frequently need to assess a person's physical abilities as well. Particularly for demanding and potentially dangerous jobs like those held by firefighters and police officers, physical abilities such as strength and endurance tend to be good predictors not only of performance but of accidents and injuries.[32] The Mississauga Fire Department has a rigorous selection process of which physical testing is one component.[33] Hired candidates must be shown to be physically capable of performing the job, because the department is dealing with life-and-death situations.

Despite their potential value, physical ability tests tend to work to the disadvantage of women and job applicants with disabilities, a tendency that has led to several recent lawsuits. As with other methods for screening potential employees, the use of physical ability tests should be carefully validated based on the necessary requirements of the job.[34]

Job Knowledge Tests

Government agencies and licensing boards usually develop job knowledge tests, a type of achievement test designed to measure a person's level of understanding about a particular job. Most public service examinations, for example, are used to determine whether an applicant possesses the information and understanding that will permit placement on the job without further training.[35] Job knowledge tests should be considered as useful tools for private and public organizations.

Job Sample Tests

Job sample tests, or work sample tests, require the applicant to perform tasks that are actually a part of the work required on the job. Like job knowledge tests, job sample tests are constructed from a carefully developed outline that experts agree includes the major job functions; the tests are thus considered content-valid. They are often used to measure skills for office and clerical jobs.

Job sample tests have also been devised for many diverse jobs: a map-reading test for traffic-control officers, a lathe test for machine operators, a complex coordination test for pilots, an in-basket test for managers, a group discussion test for supervisors, a judgment and decision-making test for administrators, to name a few. The Public Service Commission uses in-basket tests for various positions.[36] Their use in Canada is limited to about 30 percent, due to the high cost of development and administration.[37] Since most companies do not have qualified psychologists on staff, they turn to outside consultants.

In an increasing number of cases, job sample tests are aided by computer simulations, particularly when testing a candidate might prove to be dangerous. This type of test is reported to be cost-effective, reliable, valid, fair, and acceptable to applicants.[38] Also available are tests that do not discriminate against the physically challenged. Among these are audio tests for the blind, and Braille and large-print tests for the partially blind.

four

objective

The Employment Interview

Traditionally the employment interview has had a very important role in the selection process. So much so that it is rare to find an instance where an employee is hired without some sort of interview. Depending upon the type of job, applicants may be interviewed by one person or by several members of the organization. While researchers have raised some doubts about its validity, the interview remains a mainstay of selection because: (1) it is especially practical when there are only a small number of applicants; (2) it serves other purposes such as public relations; and (3) interviewers maintain great faith and confidence in their judgments. Nevertheless, the interview can be plagued by problems of subjectivity and personal bias. In such cases, some interviewers' judgments are more valid than those of others in the evaluation of applicants.[39]

Interviewing Methods

Employment or selection interviews differ according to the methods used to obtain information and to find out an applicant's attitudes and feelings. The most significant difference lies in the amount of structure, or control, that is exercised by the interviewer. In the highly structured interview, the interviewer determines the course that the interview will follow as each question is asked. In the less-structured interview, the applicant plays a larger role in determining the course the discussion will take. The different types of interviews, from the least structured to the most structured, are examined below.

The interview plays a crucial role in the selection process.

Nondirective interview

An interview in which the applicant is allowed the maximum amount of freedom in determining the course of the discussion, while the interviewer carefully refrains from influencing the applicant's remarks.

Nondirective Interview

In the **nondirective interview**, the interviewer carefully refrains from influencing the applicant's remarks. The applicant is allowed the maximum amount of freedom in determining the course of the discussion. The interviewer asks broad, open-ended questions, such as "Tell me more about your experiences on your last job," and permits the applicant to talk freely with a minimum of interruption. Generally the nondirective interviewer listens carefully and does not argue, interrupt, or change the subject abruptly. The interviewer also uses follow-up questions to allow the applicant to elaborate, makes only brief responses, and allows pauses in the conversation; the pausing technique is the most difficult for the beginning interviewer to master.

The greater freedom afforded to the applicant in the nondirective interview is particularly valuable in bringing to the interviewer's attention any information, attitudes, or feelings that may often be concealed by more structured questioning. However, because the applicant determines the course of the interview and no set procedure is followed, little information that comes from these interviews enables interviewers to cross-check agreement with other interviewers. Thus the reliability and validity of the nondirective interview may be expected to be minimal. This method is most likely to be used in interviewing candidates for high-level positions and in counselling.

Structured interview

An interview in which a set of standardized questions, having an established set of answers, is used.

Structured Interview

More attention is being given to the **structured interview** as a result of human rights legislation and a concern for maximizing the validity of selection decisions.[40] Because a structured interview has a set of standardized questions (based on job analysis), and an established set of answers against which applicant responses can be rated, it provides a more consistent basis for evaluating job candidates. For example, staff members of Weyerhauser Company's HR department developed a structured interviewing process with the following characteristics. The program

1. is based exclusively on job duties and requirements critical to job performance;
2. has four types of questions that may be used: situational questions, job knowledge questions, job sample/simulation questions, and worker-requirements questions;
3. Has sample answers to each question determined in advance. Interviewee responses are rated on a five-point scale defined explicitly in advance;
4. has an interview committee so that interviewee responses are evaluated by several raters;
5. consistently follows the same procedures to ensure that each applicant has exactly the same chance as every other applicant; and
6. Is documented for future reference and in case of legal challenge.[41]

A structured interview is more likely to provide the type of information needed for making sound decisions. It also helps to reduce the possibility of legal charges of unfair discrimination. Employers must be aware that the interview is highly vulnerable to legal attack and that more litigation in this area can be expected in the future.

2   THE SITUATION OVERVIEW

QUESTION:

It is the night before your scheduled vacation. You are all packed and ready to go. Just before you get into bed, you receive a phone call from the plant. A problem has arisen that only you can handle. You are asked to come in to take care of things. What would you do in this situation?

RECORD ANSWER:

_____

_____

_____

SCORING GUIDE:

Good: "I would go in to work and make certain that everything is O.K. Then I would go on vacation."
Fair: "There are no problems that *only I* can handle. I would make certain that someone qualified was there to handle things."
Poor: "I would go on vacation."

Most employment interviewers will tend toward either an undirected or a structured format. However, there are other methods that are utilized for special purposes.

Situational interview
An interview in which the applicant is given a hypothetical incident and asked how he or she would respond to it.

Behavioural description interview
An interview in which the applicant is asked questions about what he or she actually did in a given situation.

Situational Interview

One variation of the structured interview is called the **situational interview**.[42] With this approach, an applicant is given a hypothetical incident and asked how he or she would respond to it. The applicant's response is evaluated relative to pre-established benchmark standards. Highlights in HRM 2 shows a sample question from a situational interview used to select analyzer technicians at a chemical plant.

Behavioural Description Interview

Similar to a situational interview, a **behavioural description interview (BDI)** focuses in on real work incidents. However, while a situational interview addresses hypothetical situations, the BDI format asks the job applicant what he or she *actually did* in a given situation. For example, to assess a potential manager's ability to handle a problem employee, an interviewer might ask, "Tell me about the last time you disciplined an employee." Such an approach to interviewing, based on a critical-incidents job analysis, assumes that past performance is the best predictor of future performance. For example, staff members of Rogers Cable Communications Inc. use progressive selection practices based on a behavioural approach. The goal of their plan is to eliminate the guesswork in staffing and reliance on "gut feeling" and take a more scientific and documented process. Rogers is piloting a new approach using a "Targeted Selection Process Model" for its call centre operations. The characteristics of the program are as follows:

1. Focus interviews and selection procedures on job-related information. Dimensions that describe the knowledge, motivations, and behaviours associated with success or failure in a job are targeted. The dimensions are unique to each position.
2. Organize the elements of the selection process into an efficient system. In Targeted Selection, "system" refers to a consistent, step-by-step procedure for collecting information and making hiring decisions. A Dimension Coverage Grid is used to ensure that information is gathered on each dimension, and by the appropriate interviewer.
3. Obtain behavioural information that can be used accurately to predict future behaviour. Using this method, the process of collecting behavioural examples is done using a technique called STAR. To be a good predictor of future behaviour, an example of past behaviour must contain:
4. The Situation or Task the candidate faced.
5. The Action the candidate took (what did the person do?).
6. The Result of the candidate's actions.
7. Access the motivational fit of candidates. Focus on the facets of the target job. Facets are things that people find satisfying or dissatisfying about their jobs or roles.
8. Systematically share information about candidates in an organized data integration session. Each member of the interview process rates each of the dimensions and then, as a group, each dimension is discussed and a consensus rating is applied to each dimension. A hiring decision can now be reached based on a group effort.
9. Make legally credible hiring decisions.

Panel Interview

Another type of interview involves a panel of interviewers who question and observe a single candidate. In a typical **panel interview**, the candidate meets with three to five interviewers who take turns asking questions. After the interview, they pool their observations to reach a consensus about the suitability of the candidate. HRM specialists using this method report that panel interviews provide several significant advantages over traditional one-to-one interviews, including higher validity due to multiple inputs, greater acceptance of the decision, and faster decision time.[43]

Panel interview
An interview in which a board of interviewers question and observe a single candidate.

Computer Interview

As HR professionals use technology more and more to deal with information management, expert systems are similarly being used to assist with the interviewing process. These computerized systems gather preliminary information and enable employers to compare candidates. Typically the system asks candidates 75 to 125 multiple-choice questions tailored to the job, and then compares the applicant's responses to either an ideal profile or to profiles developed on the basis of other candidates' responses. The computer can generate a printed report that contains the applicant's response summary, an itemized list of contradictory responses, a latency response report (time delays for each answer), a summary of potentially problematic responses, and a list of structured interview questions for the job interviewer to ask.[44]

In addition to the benefits of objectivity, some research evidence suggests that applicants may be less likely to engage in "impression management" in computerized interviews than in face-to-face interviews.[45] So far, organizations have used the computer mainly as a complement to, rather than a replacement for, conventional interviews.

Guidelines for Employment Interviewers

Organizations should exercise considerable caution in the selection of employment interviewers. The importance of diversity in the workforce will tend to benefit those candidates who have experience in associating with people from a variety of backgrounds. Given the rapid change occurring in most organizations, the ability to cope with change and to learn are considered desirable traits in candidates.

A training program should be provided on a continuing basis for employment interviewers and at least periodically for managers and supervisors in other departments. Many books on employment interviewing are available as guides. For the HR specialist who desires to explore the topic in depth, a wealth of information is available in books and journals.[46]

There have been several reviews of research studies on the employment interview.[47] Each of these reviews discusses and evaluates numerous studies concerned with such questions as "What traits can be assessed in the interview?" and "How do interviewers reach their decisions?" Highlights in HRM 3 presents some of the major findings of these studies. It shows that information is available that can be used to increase the validity of interviews.

Figure 7-4 summarizes the variables and processes involved in the employment interview. The figure shows that a number of applicant characteristics may influence the perception of the interviewer and influence the hiring decision. In addition, many interviewer and situational factors may also influence the perceptual and decision-making processes. For example, knowing the race and sex of an applicant may shape the expectations, biases, and behaviours of an interviewer, which in turn may affect the interview outcome. Even a limited understanding of the variables shown in Figure 7-4 can help increase the effectiveness of managers and supervisors.

Interviewer training programs should include practice interviews conducted under guidance. Practice interviews may be recorded on videotape and evaluated later in a group training session. Although some variation in technique is only natural, the following list presents ten ground rules for employment interviews that are commonly accepted and supported by research findings. Their apparent simplicity should not lead one to underestimate their importance.

1. *Establish an interview plan.* Examine the purposes of the interview and determine the areas and specific questions to be covered. Review job require-

3 SOME MAJOR FINDINGS FROM RESEARCH STUDIES ON THE INTERVIEW

highlights

1. Structured interviews are more reliable than unstructured interviews.
2. Interviewers are influenced more by unfavourable than by favourable information.
3. Interrater reliability is increased when there is a greater amount of information about the job to be filled.
4. A bias is established early in the interview, and this tends to be followed by either a favourable or an unfavourable decision.
5. Intelligence is the trait most validly estimated by an interview, but the interview information adds nothing to test data.
6. Interviewers can explain why they feel an applicant is likely to be an unsatisfactory employee but not why the applicant may be satisfactory.
7. Factual written data seem to be more important than physical appearance in determining judgments. This increases with interviewing experience.
8. An interviewee is given a more extreme evaluation when preceded by an interviewee of opposing value.
9. Interpersonal skills and motivation are probably best evaluated by the interview.
10. Allowing the applicant time to talk makes rapid first impressions less likely and provides a larger behaviour sample.
11. Nonverbal as well as verbal interactions influence decisions.
12. Experienced interviewers rank applicants in the same order, although they differ in the proportion that they will accept. There is a tendency for experienced interviewers to be more selective than less experienced ones.

ments, application-form data, test scores, and other available information *before* seeing the applicant.

2. *Establish and maintain rapport.* This is accomplished by greeting the applicant pleasantly, by explaining the purpose of the interview, by displaying sincere interest in the applicant, and by listening carefully.

3. *Be an active listener.* Strive to understand, comprehend, and gain insight into what is only suggested or implied. A good listener's mind is alert, and face and posture usually reflect this fact.

4. *Pay attention to nonverbal cues.* An applicant's facial expressions, gestures, body position, and movements often provide clues to that person's attitudes and feelings. Interviewers should be aware of what they themselves are communicating nonverbally.

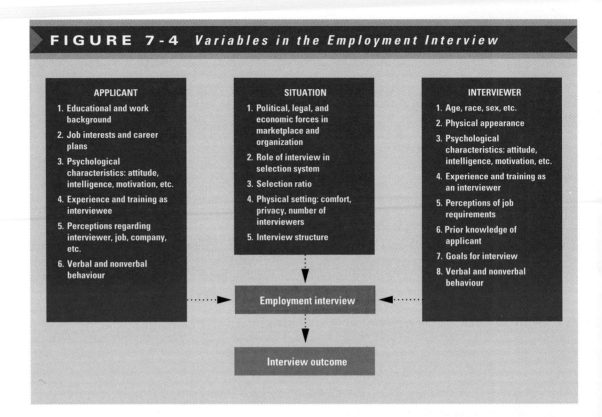

FIGURE 7-4 *Variables in the Employment Interview*

APPLICANT
1. Educational and work background
2. Job interests and career plans
3. Psychological characteristics: attitude, intelligence, motivation, etc.
4. Experience and training as interviewee
5. Perceptions regarding interviewer, job, company, etc.
6. Verbal and nonverbal behaviour

SITUATION
1. Political, legal, and economic forces in marketplace and organization
2. Role of interview in selection system
3. Selection ratio
4. Physical setting: comfort, privacy, number of interviewers
5. Interview structure

INTERVIEWER
1. Age, race, sex, etc.
2. Physical appearance
3. Psychological characteristics: attitude, intelligence, motivation, etc.
4. Experience and training as an interviewer
5. Perceptions of job requirements
6. Prior knowledge of applicant
7. Goals for interview
8. Verbal and nonverbal behaviour

Employment interview

Interview outcome

5. *Provide information as freely and honestly as possible.* Answer the applicant's questions fully and frankly. Present a realistic picture of the job.

6. *Use questions effectively.* To elicit a truthful answer, questions should be phrased as objectively as possible and with no indication of what response is desired.

7. *Separate facts from inferences.* During the interview, record factual information. Later, record your inferences or interpretations of the facts. Compare your inferences with those of other interviewers.

8. *Recognize biases and stereotypes.* One typical bias is for interviewers to consider strangers who have interests, experiences, and backgrounds similar to their own to be more acceptable. *Stereotyping* involves forming generalized opinions of how people of a given gender, race, or ethnic background appear, think, feel, and act. The influence of sex-role stereotyping is central to sex discrimination in employment. Avoid *halo error*, or judging an individual favourably or unfavourably on the basis of one strong point (or weak point) on which you place high value.

9. *Control the course of the interview.* Establish an interview plan and stick to it. Provide the applicant with ample opportunity to talk, but maintain control of the situation in order to reach the interview objectives.

10. *Standardize the questions asked.* To increase reliability and avoid discrimination, ask the same questions of all applicants for a particular job. Keep careful notes, record facts, impressions, and any relevant information, including what was told to the applicant.

Types of Pre-employment Questions to Ask

The entire subject of pre-employment questioning is complex. Federal and provincial requirements sometimes differ in terms of the types of questions that may be asked during an interview. However, most look with disfavour on direct or indirect questions related to race, colour, age, religion, sex, or national origin. Some of the questions that interviewers once felt free to ask can be potentially hazardous. Human rights commissions have severely limited the area of questioning. In general, if a question is job-related, is asked of everyone, and does not discriminate against a certain class of applicants, it is likely to be acceptable to government authorities.

Particular care has to be given to questions asked of female applicants about their family responsibilities. It is inappropriate, for example, to ask, "Do you plan to have children?" "Who will take care of your children while you are at work?" "What is your husband's occupation?" or "Are you engaged?" It is, in fact, inappropriate to ask applicants of either gender questions about matters that have no relevance to job performance. A Saskatchewan employer was found to have discriminated against a woman when, during an interview, he asked her about her marital status, dress, and "personal morality."[48]

Employers have found it advisable to provide interviewers with instructions on how to avoid potentially discriminatory questions in their interviews. The examples of appropriate and inappropriate questions shown in Highlights in HRM 4 may serve as a guideline for application forms as well as for pre-employment interviews. Complete guidelines may be developed from current information available from offices of the Human Rights Commission in most major cities. Once the individual is hired, the information needed but not asked in the interview may be obtained if there is a valid need for it and if it does not lead to discrimination.

Medical Examination

A medical examination is generally given to ensure that the health of applicants is adequate to meet the job requirements. It also provides a baseline against which subsequent medical examinations may be compared and interpreted. The last objective is particularly important in determinations of work-caused disabilities under workers'-compensation law.

In the past, requirements for such physical characteristics as strength, agility, height, and weight were often determined by an employer's unvalidated notion of what should be required. Many such requirements that tend to discriminate against women have been questioned and modified so as to represent typical job demands.

Medical examinations and inquiries about a candidate directed to medical professionals should be conducted only after an offer (preferably written) of employment has been made. The offer can be made conditional on the applicant's ability to

4   APPROPRIATE AND INAPPROPRIATE INTERVIEW QUESTIONS

	APPROPRIATE QUESTIONS	INAPPROPRIATE QUESTIONS
National or ethnic origin	Are you legally entitled to work in Canada?	Where were you born?
Age	Have you reached the minimum or maximum age for work, as defined by the law?	How old are you?
Sex	How would you like to be referred to during the interview?	What are your child-care arrangements?
Marital status	As travel is part of the requirements of our position, would you foresee any problems meeting this obligation?	What does your spouse do for a living? Is there travel involved? Who takes care of the children when you are away?
Disabilities	Do you have any conditions that could affect your ability to do the job?	Do you use drugs or alcohol?
Height and weight	(Ask nothing)	How tall are you? How much do you weigh?
Address	What is your address?	What were your addresses outside Canada?
Religion	Would you be able to work the following schedules?	What are your religious beliefs?
Criminal record	Our job requires that our employees be bonded. Are you bondable?	Have you ever been arrested?
Affiliations	As an engineer are you a member of the engineering society?	What religious associations do you belong to?

perform the essential duties of the job as determined by a job-related medical examination. Any medical inquiries must be directly related to assessing the candidate's abilities to perform the essential duties of the job.[49] This allows the applicant with a disability the opportunity to be considered exclusively on merits during the selection process. Before the introduction of human rights legislation, employers would screen out applicants with disabilities based on medical information requested on application forms or obtained through pre-employment medical examinations. These methods are now deemed discriminatory.

An employer may ask a candidate if she or he has any disability-related needs that would require accommodation to enable performance of the essential duties of the job. The interviewer should be cautioned about probing as to the nature of the disability. Subsequent employment-related decisions may be perceived to be based on this information and thereby characterized as discriminatory. To ensure neutrality, and avoid the possibility of a complaint to the Human Rights Commission, such information should remain exclusively with the examining physician, not in the personnel file.

If the employee has a disability, the employer has a duty to accommodate his or her needs. The accommodation may be accomplished either by changing some of the essential duties of the position or by providing the appropriate equipment. To determine whether an individual can do the essential duties of a particular position, the employer should conduct a physical demands analysis, checklists for which are available through most provincial ministers of labour.[50]

As mentioned above, requirements for physical characteristics such as height were in the past often determined by an employer's notion of what *should be* required. Under human rights legislation, employers are prohibited from imposing their own standards where it has the effect of excluding members of the designated groups, unless it can be shown that the requirements are reasonable and *bona fide*. Such standards are often based on the vital statistics of the average white Anglo-Saxon male. There is little evidence to demonstrate that such characteristics as height and weight constitute *bona fide* occupational requirements.[51]

While there is much publicity about acquired immune deficiency syndrome (AIDS), employers are prohibited from subjecting job applicants to any type of medical testing for the presence of the HIV virus.[52] In addition, the employer is obliged to accommodate the needs of a person with a disability such as AIDS by, for example, redefining work duties and implementing temporary work reassignments. Three occupational situations that justify treating an employee with HIV or AIDS differently from other employees are those in which

1. the individual carries out invasive procedures such as surgery
2. the individual is required to travel to countries where AIDS carriers are denied entry
3. a sudden deterioration of the brain or central nervous system would compromise public safety.

Employers are becoming sensitive to this disease, as reflected in the employee magazine supplement about HIV and AIDS published by Proctor & Gamble Inc.

The supplement, entitled "It's Time for Education, Not Denial," outlines the corporate policy on AIDS, provides information about the disease, and includes interviews with leading experts from Canadian hospitals.[53]

Drug Testing

The Canadian Human Rights Commission and some provincial counterparts have issued policies on employment-related drug testing. Addiction to drugs or alcohol is considered a handicap, and the employer is to be guided by legislation and by practices such as workplace accommodation. The medical examination cannot be conducted until a conditional offer of employment is made in writing, and the examination can determine only the individual's ability to perform the essential duties.

If the employer establishes that drug testing is job-related, the candidate must be informed that job offers are conditional upon successful passing of a drug test, and that this test will be required during the course of employment. The employer then has the right to demand a medical examination. If an employee refuses, he or she can be dismissed. For example, when a Canadian Pacific conductor who had been charged by the police with the cultivation of marijuana (he had received a prior conviction for possession) was asked by his employer to submit to a drug test, he refused to do so. He was terminated as a result, and the decision was upheld by an arbitrator.[54] Toronto-Dominion Bank, Imperial Oil Ltd., and the Federal Transport Department are among the companies that use drug testing.

There is widespread opposition to drug testing in the workplace. The Canadian Civil Liberties Association takes the position that "no person should be required to share urine with a stranger" as a condition of employment.[55] Employee Assistance Programs (EAP) play an important role in helping employees with drug and alcohol problems, and will be discussed in Chapter 14.

Reaching a Selection Decision

objective

While all of the steps in the selection process are important, the most critical step is the decision to accept or reject applicants. Because of the cost of placing new employees on the payroll, the short probationary period in many organizations, and human rights considerations, the final decision must be as sound as possible. Thus it requires systematic consideration of all the relevant information about applicants. It is common to use summary forms and checklists to ensure that all of the pertinent information has been included in the evaluation of applicants.

Summary of Information about Applicants

Fundamentally, an employer is interested in what an applicant *can do* and *will do*. An evaluation of candidates on the basis of assembled information should focus on these two factors, as shown in Figure 7-5.[56] The "can-do" factors include knowledge and skills, as well as the aptitude (potential) for acquiring new knowledge and skills. The "will-do" factors include motivation, interests, and other personality characteristics. Both factors are essential to successful performance on the job. The employee who has the ability (*can do*) but is not motivated to use it (*will not do*) is little better than the employee who lacks the necessary ability.

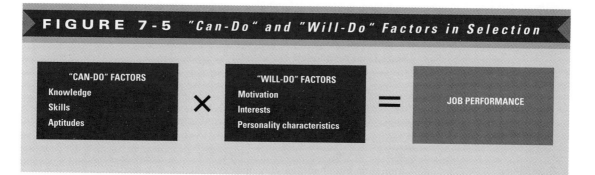

FIGURE 7-5 *"Can-Do" and "Will-Do" Factors in Selection*

It is much easier to measure what individuals "can do" than what they "will do." The "can-do" factors are readily evident from test scores and verified information. What the individual will do can only be inferred. Responses to interview and application-form questions may be used as a basis for obtaining information for making inferences about what an individual will do.

Decision Strategy

The strategy used for making personnel decisions for one category of jobs may differ from that used for another category. The strategy for selecting managerial and executive personnel, to be discussed in Chapter 9, will differ from that used in selecting clerical and technical personnel. While many factors are to be considered in hiring decisions, the following are some of the questions that the HR staff must consider:

1. Should the individuals be hired according to their highest potential or according to the needs of the organization?
2. At what grade or wage level should the individual be started?
3. Should initial selection be concerned primarily with an ideal match of the employee to the job, or should potential for advancement in the organization be considered?
4. To what extent should those who are not qualified but are qualifiable be considered?
5. Should overqualified individuals be considered?
6. What effect will a decision have on meeting employment equity goals and diversity considerations?

In addition to these types of factors, the HR staff must also consider which approach it will use in making hiring decisions. There are two basic approaches to selection: clinical and statistical.

Clinical Approach

In the clinical approach to decision making, those making the selection decision review all the data on applicants. Then, based on their understanding of the job and the individuals who have been successful in that job, they make a decision. Different individuals often arrive at different decisions about an applicant when they use this approach because each evaluator assigns different weights to the applicant's strengths and weaknesses. Furthermore, personal biases and stereotypes are frequently covered up by what appear to be rational bases for acceptance or rejection.

Statistical Approach

In contrast to the clinical approach, the statistical approach to decision making is much more objective. It involves identifying the most valid predictors and weighting them through statistical methods such as multiple regression.[57] Quantified data such as scores or ratings from interviews, tests, and other procedures are then combined according to their weighted value. Individuals with the highest combined scores are selected. A comparison of the clinical approach with the statistical approach in a wide variety of situations has shown that the statistical approach is superior.[58] Although this superiority has been recognized for many decades, the clinical approach continues to be the one most commonly used.

With a strictly statistical approach, a candidate's high score on one predictor (e.g., cognitive ability test) will make up for a low score on another predictor (e.g., the interview). For this reason, this model is a **compensatory model**. However, it is frequently important that applicants achieve some minimum level of proficiency on all selection dimensions. When this is the case, a **multiple cutoff model** can be used in which only those candidates who score above the cutoff on all dimensions are considered. The selection decision is made from that subset of candidates.

A variation of the multiple cutoff is referred to as the **multiple hurdle model**. This decision strategy is sequential in that after candidates go through an initial evaluation stage, the ones who score well are provisionally accepted and are assessed further at each successive stage. The process may continue through several stages before a final decision is made regarding the candidates. This approach is especially useful when either the testing or training procedures are lengthy and expensive.[59]

Each of the statistical approaches requires that a decision be made about where the cutoff lies—that point in the distribution of scores above which a person should be considered and below which the person should be rejected. The score that the applicant must achieve is the cutoff score. Depending upon the labour supply, it may be necessary to lower or raise the cutoff score.

The effects of raising and lowering the cutoff score are illustrated in Figure 7-6. Each dot in the centre of the figure represents the relationship between the test score (or a weighted combination of test scores) and the criterion of success for one individual. In this instance, the test has a fairly high validity, as represented by the elliptical pattern of dots. Note that the high-scoring individuals are concentrated in the "satisfactory" category on job success, whereas the low-scoring individuals are concentrated in the "unsatisfactory" category.

If the cutoff score is set at A, only the individuals represented by areas 1 and 2 will be accepted. Nearly all of them will be successful. If more employees are needed (i.e., an increase in the selection ratio), the cutoff score may be lowered to point B. In this case, a larger number of potential failures will be accepted, as shown in quadrants 2 and 4. Even if the cutoff is lowered to C, the total number of satisfactory individuals selected (represented by the dots in areas 1, 3, and 5) exceeds the total number selected who are unsatisfactory (areas 2, 4, and 6). Thus the test serves to maximize the selection of probable successes and to minimize the selection of probable failures. This is all we can hope for in predicting job success: the probability of

---

Compensatory model

Selection decision model in which a high score in one area cam make up for a low score in another area.

Multiple cutoff model

Selection decision model that requires an applicant to achieve some minimum level of proficiency on all selection dimensions.

Multiple hurdle model

A sequential strategy in which only the applicants with the highest scores at an initial test stage go on to subsequent stages.

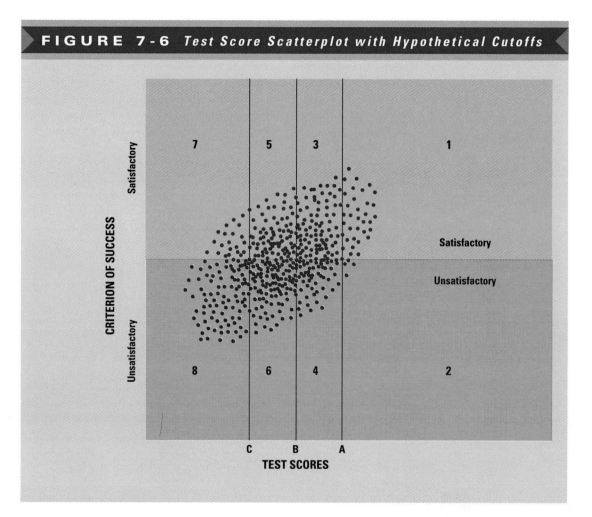

FIGURE 7-6 *Test Score Scatterplot with Hypothetical Cutoffs*

Selection ratio
The number of applicants compared to the number of persons hired.

selecting a greater proportion of individuals who will be successful rather than unsuccessful.

While the most valid predictors should be used with any selection strategy, there is a related factor that contributes to selecting the best-qualified persons. It is selectivity, or having an adequate number of applicants or candidates from which to make a selection. Selectivity is typically expressed in terms of a **selection ratio**, which is the ratio of the number of applicants to be selected to the total number of applicants. A ratio of 0.10, for example, means that 10 percent of the applicants will be selected. A ratio of 0.90 means that 90 percent will be selected. If the selection ratio is low, only the most promising applicants will normally be hired. When the ratio is high, very little selectivity will be possible since even applicants having mediocre ability will have to be hired if the vacancies are to be filled.

It should be noted that how much of a contribution any predictor will make to the improvement of a given selection process is a function not only of the validity of the predictor and the selection ratio, but also of the proportion of persons who are judged successful using current selection procedures.[60]

The Final Decision

After a preliminary selection has been made in the employment department, those applicants who appear to be most promising are then referred to departments with vacancies. There they are interviewed by the managers or supervisors, who usually make the final decision and communicate it to the employment department. Because of the weight that is usually given to their choices, managers and supervisors should be trained so that their role in the selection process does not negate the more scientific efforts of personnel in the HR department.

In large organizations, notifying applicants of the decision and making job offers is generally the responsibility of the HR department. This department should confirm the details of the job, working arrangements, wages, and the like, and specify a deadline by which the applicant must reach a decision. If, at this point, findings from the medical examination are not yet available, an offer is often made contingent upon the applicant's passing the examination.

SUMMARY

one
objective

The selection process should provide as much reliable and valid information as possible about applicants so that their qualifications can be carefully matched with job specifications. The information that is obtained should be clearly job-related or predictive of success on the job and free from potential discrimination. Reliability refers to the consistency of test scores over time and across measures. Validity refers to the accuracy of measurement. Validity can be assessed in terms of whether it is based on a job specification (content validity), whether test scores correlate with performance criteria (predictive validity), and whether the test accurately measures what it purports to measure (construct validity).

two
objective

Interviews are customarily used in conjunction with application forms, biographical information blanks, references, background investigations, medical examinations, cognitive ability tests, job knowledge tests, and work sample tests.

three
objective

While the popularity of tests had declined somewhat since the passage of human rights legislation, in recent years there has been a renewed interest. The value of tests should not be overlooked since they are more objective than the interview and can provide a broader sampling of behaviour. Cognitive ability tests are especially valuable for assessing verbal, quantitative, and reasoning abilities. Physical ability tests are most useful for predicting job performance, accidents, and injuries, particularly for demanding work. Job knowledge and work sample tests are achievement tests that are useful for determining if a candidate can perform the duties of the job without further training.

four
objective

Interviews are an important source of information about job applicants. They can be unstructured, wherein the interviewer is free to pursue whatever approach and sequence of topics might seem appropriate. Alternatively, interviews can be structured, wherein each applicant receives the same set of questions, having pre-established answers. Some interviews are situational and can focus on hypothetical situations or actual behavioural descriptions of previous work experiences. Interviews can be conducted by a single individual, a panel, or via a computer interface. Regardless of the technique chosen, those who conduct interviews should receive special training with respect to interviewing methods and human rights considerations. The training should also make them more aware of the major findings from research studies on the interview and how they can apply these findings.

objective

In the process of making decisions, all "can-do" and "will-do" factors should be assembled and weighted systematically so that the final decision can be based on a composite of the most reliable and valid information. While the clinical approach to decision making is used more than the statistical approach, it lacks the accuracy of statistical approaches. Compensatory models allow a candidate's high score on one predictor make up for a low score on another. However, multiple cut off and multiple hurdle approaches require minimal competency on each selection criteria. Whichever of these approaches is used, the goal is to select a greater proportion of individuals who will be successful on the job.

KEY TERMS

achievement tests

aptitude tests

behavioural description interview

compensatory model

selection

concurrent validity

construct validity

content validity

criterion-related validity

cross-validation

multiple cutoff model

multiple hurdle model

nondirective interview

panel interview

predictive validity

reliability

selection ratio

situational interview

structured interview

validity

validity generalization

1. What is meant by the term *criterion* as it is used in personnel selection? Give some examples of criteria used for jobs with which you are familiar.
2. What are some of the problems that arise in checking references furnished by job applicants? Are there any solutions to these problems?
3. Compare briefly the major types of employment interviews described in this chapter. Which type would you prefer to conduct? Why?
4. What characteristics do job knowledge and job sample tests have that often make them more acceptable to the examinees than other types of tests?
5. In what ways does the clinical approach to selection differ from the statistical approach? How do you account for the fact that one approach is superior to the other?
6. Personality tests, like other tests used in employee selection, have been under attack for several decades. What are some of the reasons applicants find personality tests objectionable? On what basis could their use for selection purposes be justified?

ANSWERS TO QUESTIONS IN FIGURE 7-3

1. a, 2. c, 3. d, 4. d, 5. c, 6. c, 7. b

CASE: The Postsecondary Recruitment Campaign

Historically, the federal Public Service has been Canada's largest and most diverse employer. Its enormous size reflected prosperous times, and it offered a wide variety of programs and services to Canadians.

Times changed, and fiscal restraint became a necessity. The government conducted a review of the way it did business, looking for ways to reduce the size of its workforce and increase its efficiency. In 1995 the Public Service began a restructuring exercise that involved dramatic downsizing. It affected all aspects of government operations, perhaps none more than recruitment, as the number of job opportunities decreased considerably. Young people on the verge of entering the workforce were left wondering just what their chances were of a Public Service career.

But even in a time of reductions, some recruitment must continue in order to ensure that the federal workforce will be composed of individuals who possess the skills the future work environment will demand. Postsecondary recruitment is a prime vehicle for the process of renewal and rejuvenation.

The Public Service Commission (PSC) conducts an annual Post-Secondary Recruitment (PSR) campaign aimed at recruiting and selecting qualified university graduates, with specific academic backgrounds, from across Canada. Current economic constraints and downsizing mean that, for the foreseeable future, recruitment efforts will be strictly targeted and focused on entry-level positions in occupational areas for which government departments anticipate a demand. At present these include lawyers, internal auditors/financial officers, mathematical statisticians, economists, engineers, computer systems analysts, and foreign service officers.

Postsecondary recruitment as conducted by the PSC comprises two components.

1. The PSC recruits qualified university graduates in response to specific needs as identified by government departments.
2. The PSC recruits for its developmental programs, the Management Trainee Program (MTP) and the Accelerated Economist Training Program (AETP).

When the Commission recruits in response to departmental requests, staff in its regional offices receive the completed application forms and assess them to ensure individuals possess the basic job requirements. If this is the case, and if the application is complete and was received by the deadline date, the applicant's name is entered into the computerized national inventory—a "bank" of qualified persons.

The PSC also administers any tests that are necessary. For example, financial officers and internal auditors must write the General Competency Test, Level 2 (GCT2); foreign service officers must write the Foreign Service Knowledge Test (FSKT) and a Written Communication Test. These tests are standardized, and all applicants must undergo them.

The PSC then refers successful candidates to hiring departments, which do the actual assessment of candidates by means of structured interviews. Finally, departments make their selections from among all the qualified individuals.

The PSC also recruits for two developmental programs, the MTP and the AETP. For these, the selection process is more complex.

The MTP is designed to replenish the pool of future Public Service managers by recruiting university graduates with demonstrated management potential and developing them, over the course of five years, to the middle-management level. The program's selection process involves four steps. First, applicants are screened based on their application for employment, their résumé, and a transcript of their marks. Using these documents as a basis, human resourcing specialists at program headquarters measure the person's interest in a Public Service career, as well as his or her written communication skills, organization and planning skills, leadership potential, initiative, analytical ability, and problem-solving ability.

Those who are successful at this first stage are invited to an interview. It lasts about one hour and is designed to assess management potential and a number of qualities, such as verbal communication and interpersonal skills, motivation, and judgment.

The next phase, for those who pass the interview, is a one-day Assessment Centre created especially for the MTP. All candidates undergo a one-day assessment supervised by psychologists, who use recognized methods to measure six management skills: communication, behavioural flexibility, action management, leadership, interpersonal relations, and thinking skills. Simulation exercises, task forces, and structured interviews are among the tools used.

The last phase, final selection, involves compiling the results of the previous three stages and selecting the final roster of successful candidates. These people are then contacted, and the program refers them to participating departments, according to various departmental requirements. Departments choose the individual(s) they want as their trainee(s). A formal letter of offer is sent to the candidate by the program on behalf of the department. When the offer is accepted, the candidate becomes a Management Trainee.

The AETP is a two-year program whose objective is to provide holders of MPAs or Master's degrees in economics or business administration with an opportunity to develop their policy analysis skills and eventually assume economic and public policy responsibilities at the middle-management level in the federal Public Service. Its selection process is similar to that for the MTP.

Sources: Interview with Peter Corner conducted by Deborah M. Zinni in June 1995; and *Communiqué: Perspectives in Staffing*, Public Service Commission, October 1992, September 1993, and November 1993, Ottawa.

Questions

1. Do you think that the selection system used by federal government is valid? Discuss each stage in the process and comment on its effectiveness.
2. In what ways might the selection process be improved?

Résumé Preparation

A résumé is a document that sets forth your knowledge, skills, and abilities (KSA) in two to four pages. This exercise will help you to construct three types of résumés and to determine which is the best one to send to a prospective employer. The three types are the chronological résumé, the functional résumé, and the achievement résumé.

The Chronological Résumé

The chronological résumé requires you to list your educational and work history by time. This format should be used when you are applying for a job that relates directly to your education and experience. For example, if the advertisement asks for a university degree, five years' operational experience, and two years' management experience, your résumé should outline these qualifications in the same order. An example of the chronological-format résumé is presented below.

Name
Address
Phone/fax/e-mail numbers

Education: Highest attainment first
List all awards and honours

Work History: Start with most recent
Group by employer and date, e.g., Northern Industries (1993–present)
Indicate all contract work
List summer employment only if it is recent and/or directly related to the position

Training Courses: List all relevant training courses (e.g., a one-week supervisory course or a two-day conflict management workshop)

Additional Skills: List all software programs you can use.
List all languages in which you are fluent (if you are able only to read in another language, indicate this)

Other: List all volunteer activities, if relevant (e.g., co-chairing a fund-raiser at your school or coaching a junior soccer team are indicative of certain skills or interests)

The Functional Résumé

The functional résumé is useful when you lack experience in an occupation or industry and therefore need to market the generic skills that will enable you to do the job, and learn quickly. The format involves expressing your work, volunteer, and training experience in terms of skills. Books such as *What Colour Is Your Parachute?* and guidance counsellors can help you to identify your skills. An example of the functional résumé format is presented below.

Name
Address
Phone/fax/e-mail

Sales: Sold various products for three years at retail store (part-time)
Door-to-door sales for the local school fund-raiser

Communication: Member of the debating team at school
Prepared brochure for school fund-raiser
Influenced retail customers to increase purchases
Data-base, graphic, and word-processing skills

Work Experience: Prairie Marketing, Data Entry, contract, 1996
The Bay, Sales Associate, part-time, 1992–95
Camp Lac du Nord, Counsellor, summers, 1990, 1991

Languages: English, French, read Spanish

Education: B.A., University of Manitoba

The Achievement Résumé

Some employers prefer to know what you have accomplished, not just where you have spent time. The achievement résumé is similar to the functional résumé, but much more powerful. In it you list your contributions to the organizations in which you have worked or volunteered. Try to restate the items you listed in the functional résumé in terms of achievements/outcomes.

For example:

Sales: Achieved within my division the highest sales figures for three months. Placed in the top quartile for door-to-door sales.

Communication: Won three out of five debating competitions.
Data-base skills rated "excellent" by my supervisor

Résumé Writing Dos and Don'ts

- *Don't* include personal information such as age, country of origin, etc.
- *Don't* use passive voice, as in "was asked to design a brochure."
- *Do* proofread—a typo can kill.
- *Do* include a cover letter highlighting how your skills match the job requirements and/or how you can contribute to the organization.

NOTES AND REFERENCES

1. Frank J. Landy and Laura J. Shankster, "Personnel Selection and Placement," *in Annual Review of Psychology* 45 (Palo Alto, CA: Annual Reviews), 261–296. See also Neal Schmitt and Ivan Robertson, "Personnel Selection," in *Annual Review of Psychology* (Palo Alto, CA: Annual Reviews, 1990). See also Charlene Marmer Solomon, "Testing Is Not at Odds with Diversity Efforts," *Personnel Journal* (March 1993): 100–104.

2. Scott E. Maxwell and Richard D. Arvey, "The Search for Predictors with High Validity and Low Adverse Impact: Compatible or Incompatible Goals?" *Journal of Applied Psychology* 78, no. 3 (June 1993): 433–437. See also James H. Coil III and Charles M. Rice, "Managing Work-Force Diversity in the Nineties: The Impact of the Civil Rights Act of 1991," *Employee Relations Law Journal* 18, no. 4 (Spring 1993): 547–565.

3. Frank J. Landy, "Test Validity Yearbook," *Journal of Business Psychology* 7, no. 2 (1992): 111–257. See also Edwin E. Ghiselli, "The Validity of Aptitude Tests in Personnel Selection," *Personnel Psychology* 26, no. 4 (Winter 1973): 461–477. See also J.E. Hunter and R.H. Hunter, "Validity and Utility of Alternative Predictors of Job Performance," *Psychological Bulletin* 96 (1984): 72–98; and N. Schmitt, R.Z. Gooding, R.A. Noe, and M. Kirsch, "Meta-Analysis of Validity Studies Published between 1964 and 1982 and the Investigation of Study Characteristics," *Personnel Psychology* 37 (1984): 407–422.

4. Society for Industrial and Organizational Psychology, *Principles for the Validation and Use of Personnel Selection Procedures* (College Park, MD: University of Maryland Press, 1987). See also R.L. Schmidt and J.E. Hunter, "The Future of Criterion-Related Validity," *Personnel Psychology* 33 (1980): 41–60.

5. Richard S. Barrett, "Content Validation Form," *Public Personnel Management* 21 (Spring 1992): 41–52. See also C.H. Lawshe, "A Quantitative Approach to Content Validity," *Personnel Psychology* 28 (1975): 563–575; and M.L. Tenopyr, "Content-Construct Confusion," *Personnel Psychology* 30 (1977): 47–54.

6. R.D. Arvey, S.M. Nutting, and T.E. Landon, "Validation Strategies for Physical Ability Testing in Police and Fire Settings," *Public Personnel Management* 21 (1992): 301–312.

7. H.C. Jain, "Human Rights: Issues in Employment," in H.C. Jain and P.C. Wright, eds., *Trends and Challenges in Human Resource Management* (Scarborough: Nelson Canada, 1994), 69.

8. Marlene Brown, "Checking the Facts on a Resume," *Personnel Journal* 72 (January 1993): SS6-SS7. See also T. Lammers, "How to Read between the Lines: Tactics for Evaluating a Resume," *Inc.* (March 1993): 105–107;

and Robert P. Vecchio, "The Problem of Phoney Résumés: How to Spot a Ringer among the Applicants," *Personnel* 61, no. 2 (March-April 1984): 22–27.

9. A.N. Kluger, R.R. Reilly, and C.J. Russell, "Faking Biodata Tests: Are Option-Keyed Instruments More Resistant?" *Journal of Applied Psychology* 76 (December 1991): 889–896. See also T.E. Becker and A.L. Colquitt, "Potential versus Actual Faking of a Biodata Form: An Analysis along Several Dimensions of Item Type," *Personnel Psychology* 45 (Summer 1992): 389–406; and F.A. Mael, "A Conceptual Rationale for the Domain and Attributes of Biodata Items," *Personnel Psychology* 44 (Winter 1991): 763–792.

10. *BNA Policy and Practice Series—Personnel Management* (Washington, DC: Bureau of National Affairs, 1989), 201: 283. See also L. Barani, "Background Investigations: How HR Stays on the Cutting Edge," *HR Focus* 70 (June 1993): 12.

11. S. McShane "Most Employers Use Reference Checks, but Many Fear Defamation Liability," *Canadian HR Reporter*, March 13, 1995, 14.

12. J. Schilder, "Trial by Hire," *Human Resources Professional* 11, no. 2 (March 1994): 21–23.

13. P. Falcone, "Reference Checking: Revitalize a Critical Selection Tool," *HR Focus* 69 (December 1992): 19. See also M.G. Aamondt, D.A. Bryan, and A.J. Whitcomb, "Predicting Performance with Letters of Recommendation," *Public Personnel Management* 22 (Spring 1993): 81–90.

14. McShane, "Most Employers Use Reference Checks," 14.

15. "Workplace Privacy," *Ontario Commissioner's Report, Worklife Report* 9, no. 3 (1994): 8–9.

16. C. Cornell, "The Write Stuff: What Can Recruiters Read between the Lines?" *Human Resource Professional* 7, no. 6 (June 1991): 15–17.

17. T.R. Yan and L.W. Slivinski, *A History of the Assessment Centre Method in the Military*, Staffing Branch, Public Service Commission of Canada, Government of Canada, November 1976, 27–35.

18. P.R. Sackett, L.R. Burris, and C. Callahan, "Integrity Testing for Personnel Selection: An Update," *Personnel Psychology* 42 (Autumn 1989): 491–529. See also C. Gorman, "Honestly, Can We Trust You?" *Time*, January 23, 1989, 44.

19. D.S. Ones, C. Viswesvaran, and F.L. Schmidt, "Comprehensive Meta-analysis of Integrity Test Validities: Findings and Implications for Personnel Selection and Theories of Job Performance," *Journal of Applied Psychology* 78 (August 1993): 679–703. See also Gilbert Fuchsberg, "Attorney General in New York

Urges Integrity Test Ban," *Wall Street Journal*, March 6, 1991.

20. A. Fowler, "An Even-Handed Approach to Graphology," *Personnel Management* 23 (March 1991): 40–43. See also J. Gooding, "By Hand, By Jove," *Across the Board* 28 (December 1991): 43–47; and M.A. Hopper and K.S. Stanford, "A Script for Screening," *Security Management* 36 (May 1992): 72–81.

21. J.W. Thacker and R.J. Cattaneo, *Survey of Personnel Practices in Canadian Organizations: A Summary Report to Respondents*, Faculty of Business Administration, University of Windsor, W92-04, March 1993, 1–29.

22. Eric Rolfe Greenberg, "Workplace Testing: The 1990 AMA Survey, Part 1," *Personnel* (June 1990): 43–51. See also *Resource* (Alexandria, VA: American Society for Personnel Administration, June 1988), 2.

23. Todd J. Maurer and Ralph A. Alexander, "Methods of Improving Employment Test Critical Scores Derived by Judging Test Content: A Review and Critique," *Personnel Psychology*, 45 (Winter 1992): 727–762.

24. For books with comprehensive coverage of testing, including employment testing, see Anne Anastasi, *Psychological Testing*, 5th ed. (New York: Macmillan, 1982); and Lee J. Cronbach, *Essentials of Psychological Testing*, 4th ed. (New York: Harper & Row, 1984).

25. Standards that psychological tests and testing programs should meet are described in *Standards for Educational and Psychological Tests* (Washington, DC: American Psychological Association, 1985). HR managers who need to examine paper-and-pencil tests can obtain specimen sets that include a test manual, a copy of the test, an answer sheet, and a scoring key. The test manual provides the essential information about the construction of the test, its recommended use, and instructions for administering, scoring, and interpreting the test. Test users should not rely entirely on the material furnished by the test author and publisher. Since 1934, a major source of consumer information about commercially available tests—the *Mental Measurements Yearbook* (MMY)—has been available in most libraries. Published periodically, the MMY contains descriptive information plus critical reviews by experts in the various types of tests. The reviews are useful in evaluating a particular test for tryout in employment situations. Other sources of information about tests include *Test Critiques*, a set of volumes containing professional reviews of tests, and *Tests: A Comprehensive Reference for Assessments in Psychology, Education, and Business*. The latter describes more than 3,100 tests published in the English language. Another source, *Principles for the Validation and Use of Personnel Selection Procedures*, published by the Society for Industrial and Organizational Psychology, Inc., is a valuable guide for employers who use tests. Other publications are available that present detailed information on how to avoid discrimination and achieve fairness in testing.

26. H.C. Jain, "Human Rights.

27. L. Coutts, L.W. Slivinski, and K.W. Grant, "Test Bias at a Glance," *Optimum* 14, no. 4 (1983).

28. H.C. Jain, "Human Rights."

29. F.L. Schmidt and J.E. Hunter, "Tacit Knowledge, Practical Intelligence, General Mental Ability, and Job Knowledge," *Current Directions in Psychological Science* 2, no. 1 (1993): 3–13. See also Bruce J. Avolio and David A. Waldman, "An Examination of Age and Cognitive Test Performance across Job Complexity and Occupational Types," *Journal of Applied Psychology* 75 (February 1990): 43–50. See also Linda S. Gottredson, ed., "The g Factor in Employment," *Journal of Vocational Behaviour* 29 (1986): 293–450; Hunter and Hunter, "Validity and Utility," 72–98.

30. Schmitt, Gooding, Noe, and Kirsch, "Meta-Analysis of Validity Studies," 407–422. See also M.R. Barrick and M.K. Mount, "The Big Five Personality Dimensions and Job Performance: A Meta-Analysis," *Personnel Psychology* 44 (1991): 1–26.

31. V.J. Bentz, "The Sears Experience in the Investigation, Description, and Prediction of Executive Behaviour," in J.A. Myers, Jr., ed., *Predicting Managerial Success* (Ann Arbor, MI: Foundation for Research on Human Behaviour, 1968). See also V.J. Bentz, "Executive Selection at Sears: An Update," paper presented at the Fourth Annual Conference of Frontiers of Industrial Psychology, Virginia Polytechnic Institute, Blacksburg, VA, August 1983.

32. J. Hogan, " The Structure of Physical Performance," *Journal of Applied Psychology* 76 (1991): 495–507. See also Richard D. Arvey, Timothy E. Landon, and Steven M. Nutting, "Development of Physical Ability Tests for Police Officers: A Construct Validation Approach," *Journal of Applied Psychology* 77 (December 1992): 996–1009; J. Hogan, "Physical Abilities," in M.D. Dunnette and L.M. Hough, eds., *Handbook of Industrial and Organizational Psychology* (Palo Alto, CA: Consulting Psychologists Press, 1991).

33. "Fire Department Welcomes 22 Rookies," *The Toronto Star*, June 8, 1995, MS 2.

34. Arvey, Nutting, and Landon, "Validation Strategies," 301–312.

35. It is interesting to note that the origins of the civil service system go back to 2200 B.C., when the Chinese emperor examined officials every three years to determine their fitness for continuing in office. In 1115 B.C. candidates for government posts were examined for their proficiency in music, archery, horsemanship, writing, arithmetic, and the rites and ceremonies of public and private life. See Philip H. DuBois, *A History of Psychological Testing* (Boston: Allyn & Bacon, 1970), Chapter 1.

36. *Assessing for Competence: Tests for Personnel Selection* (Ottawa: Public Service Commission of Canada, January 1993), 8–9.

37. Thacker and Cattaneo, 20.

38. Jerry W. Hedge and Mark S. Teachout, "An Interview Approach to Work Sample Criterion Measurement," *Journal of Applied Psychology* 44 (August 1992): 453–461. See also Wayne F. Cascio and Niel F. Phillips, "Performance Testing: A Rose among Thorns?" *Personnel Psychology* 32, no. 4 (Winter 1979): 751–766.

39. Robert L. Dipboye, *Selection Interviews: Process Perspectives* (Cincinnati: South–Western Publishing, 1992).

40. Michael M. Harris, "Reconsidering the Employment Interview: A Review of Recent Literature and Suggestions for Future Research," *Personnel Psychology* 42 (Winter 1989): 691–726. See also Willi H. Wiesner and Steven F. Cronshaw, "A Meta-Analytic Investigation of the Impact of Interview Format and Degree of Structure on the Validity of the Employment Interview," *Journal of Occupational Psychology* 61 (December 1988): 275–290; Robert W. Eder and Gerald R. Ferris, eds., *The Employment Interview—Theory, Research, and Practice* (Newbury Park, CA: Sage Publications, 1989).

41. A.I. Huffert and D.J. Woehr, "A Conceptual Analysis of Interview Structure and the Effects of Structure on the Interview Process," paper presented at the annual meeting of the Society for Industrial Organizational Psychology, Montreal, 1992. See also Patrick M. Wright, Philip A. Lichtenfels, and Elliot D. Pursell, "The Structured Interview: Additional Studies and a Meta-Analysis," *Journal of Occupational Psychology* 62 (September 1989): 191–199; Elliott D. Pursell, Michael A. Campion, and Sarah R. Gaylord, "Structured Interviewing: Avoiding Selection Problems," *Personnel Journal* 59, no. 11 (November 1980): 907–912.

42. T.R. Lin, G.H. Dobbins, and J.L. Fahr, "A Field Study of Race and Age Similarity Effects on Interview Ratings in Conventional and Situational Interviews," *Journal of Applied Psychology* 77, no. 3 (1992): 367–371; see also Ivan T. Robertson, Lynda Gratton, and Usharani Rout, "The Validity of Situational Interviews for Administrative Jobs," *Journal of Organizational Behavior* 11 (January 1990): 69–76. See also Gerald T. Gabris and Steven M. Rock, "Situational Interviews and Job Performance: The Results in One Public Agency," *Public Personnel Management* 20 (Winter 1991): 469–483; Thung-Rung Lin, Gregory H. Dobbins, and Jiing-Lih Fahr, "A Field Study of Race and Age Similarity Effects on Interview Ratings in Conventional and Situational Interviews," *Journal of Applied Psychology* 77 (June 1992): 363–371.

43. Philip L. Roth and James E. Campion, "An Analysis of the Predictive Power of the Panel Interview and Pre-Employment Tests," *Journal of Occupational and Organizational Psychology* 65 (March 1992): 51–60. See also David J. Weston and Dennis L. Warmke, "Dispelling the Myths about Panel Interviews," *Personnel Administrator* 33, no. 5 (May 1988): 109–111.

44. Brooks Mitchell, "Interviewing Face-to-Interface," *Personnel* (January 1990): 23–25.

45. C.L. Martin and D.H. Nagao, "Some Effects of Computerized Interviewing on Job Applicant Responses," *Journal of Applied Psychology* 74 (1989): 72–80.

46. The student who desires to study a comprehensive evaluation of research as it relates to the employment interview may wish to consult Eder and Ferris, *The Employment Interview*. A book designed for executives that contains many helpful suggestions is Auren Uris, *88 Mistakes Interviewers Make and How to Avoid Them* (New York: AMACOM, 1988).

47. E.C. Mayfield, "The Selection Interview—A Reevaluation of Published Research," *Personnel Psychology* 17, no. 3 (Autumn 1964): 239–260; Lynn Ulrich and Don Trumbo, "The Selection Interview since 1949," *Psychological Bulletin* 63, no. 2 (February 1965): 100–116; Orman R. Wright, Jr., "Summary of Research on the Selection Interview since 1964," *Personnel Psychology* 22, no. 4 (Winter 1969): 391–414; Neal Schmitt, "Social and Situational Determinants of Interview Decisions: Implication for the Employment Interview," *Personnel Psychology* 29, no. 1 (Spring 1976): 79–101; Richard D. Arvey and James E. Campion, "The Employment Interview: A Summary and Review of Recent Literature," *Personnel Psychology* 35, no. 2 (Summer 1982): 281–322; and Harris, "Reconsidering the Employment Interview," 691–726.

48. *Hussey v. Merion Management Ltd.*, *1986*, reported in "Human Rights: Issues in Employment" *Human Resources Management in Canada*, Prentice-Hall Canada, January 1989, 50,030.

49. *Ontario Human Rights Commission Discrimination because of Handicap*, Ontario Human Rights Commission, Government of Ontario, May 1991, 5.

50. See, for example, *Ontario Human Rights Commission Policy on Employment-Related Medical Information*, Ontario Human Rights Commission, Government of Ontario, March 1991, 1–2.

51. *Ontario Human Rights Commission Policy on Height and Weight Requirements*, Ontario Human Rights Commission, *Government of Ontario*, 1989, 1.

52. *Ontario Human Rights Commission Policy Statement on HIV/AIDS Related Discrimination*, Ontario Human Rights Commission, Government of Ontario, April 1992, 5.

53. C. Yetman, "AIDS Awareness Promoted in P&G Employee Brochure," *Human Resources Professional* 11, no. 4 (May 1994): 7.

54. C. Hoglund, "Mandatory Drug Testing," *Human Resources Professional* 8, no. 1 (January 1992): 21–22.

55. V. Galt, "Total Ban Sought on Drug Testing by Employers," *The Globe and Mail*, February 22, 1992, A6. See also "Civil Liberties Group Seeks Ban on Drug Testing," *Human Resources Professional* 8, no. 1 (January 1992): 18–22.

56. These two factors are emphasized in a system developed by Robert N. McMurry, *Tested Techniques of Personnel Selection*, rev. ed. (Chicago: Dartnell, n.d.). The system includes a summary sheet for rating the applicant on "can-do" and "will-do" factors and for summarizing the ratings.

57. Multiple regression is a statistical method for evaluating the magnitude of effects of more than one independent variable (e.g., selection predictors) on a dependent variable (e.g., job performance) using principles of correlation and regression. See W.P. Vogt, *Dictionary of Statistics and Methodology* (Newbury Park, CA: Sage Publications, 1993), 146; and F.N. Kerlinger, *Foundations of Behavioral Research*, 3rd ed. (Fort Worth: Holt, Rinehart and Winston, 1986), 527.

58. P.E. Meehl, *Clinical v. Statistical Prediction* (Minneapolis: University of Minnesota Press, 1954); and J. Sawyer, "Measurement and Prediction, Clinical and Statistical," *Psychological Bulletin* 66, no. 3 (September 1966): 178–200.

59. R.R. Reilly and W.R. Manese, "The Validation of a Minicourse for Telephone Company Switching Technicians," *Journal of Applied Psychology* 32 (1979): 83–90.

60. Wayne F. Cascio, *Applied Psychology in Personnel Management*, 4th ed. (Englewood Cliffs, NJ: Prentice-Hall, 1991), 284–287. In addition to Cascio's book, the statistically oriented reader may wish to consult George F. Dreher and Paul R. Sackett, *Perspectives on Employee Staffing and Selection* (Homewood, IL: Richard D. Irwin, 1983).

Part 3

Developing Effectiveness in Human Resources

Part 3 contains three chapters that deal with the training and development of employees. Chapter 8 discusses the process by which an organization plans for its training activities, and it describes the many available nonmanagerial and managerial training programs to improve employees' skills and abilities. Chapter 9 looks at career development and explains how individuals can implement their own career development programs. Chapter 10 provides a comprehensive review of the employee performance appraisal process, offering several suggestions for carrying out a successful employee appraisal interview. Employees perform more effectively when they receive the proper training for their jobs and their work performance is evaluated in an objective and honest matter.

After studying this chapter you should be able to

one
objective
List some of the characteristics of an effective orientation program.

two
objective
Describe the scope of organizational training programs.

three
objective
Identify and describe the five phases of the systems approach to training.

four
objective
Identify the types of training methods used primarily with nonmanagerial personnel.

five
objective
List the different types of training methods for developing managers and supervisors.

six
objective
Describe the special training programs that are currently popular.

Chapter 8

Training

H*R training has become increasingly vital to the success of modern organizations. Rapidly changing technology requires that employees possess the knowledge, skills, and abilities (KSA) needed to cope with new processes and production techniques. The growth of organizations into large, complex operations whose structures are continually changing makes it necessary for managers, as well as employees, to develop the KSA that will enable them to handle new and more demanding assignments.*

There are many forces that determine the types of training required in an organization. Automation and computerization will continue to have a major impact. Economic, social, and political forces likewise have implications for training programs. Committing resources to training also generates respect from potential employees and from other organizations. CEOs across Canada rated Bank of Montreal as the company they respect the most for its management of people, particularly with respect to investment in training. Figure 8-1 lists the top five Canadian leaders in people management.

The most important reason for investing in training is that it does result in performance improvement. Trained employees do more work, make fewer errors, require less supervision, and have higher morale and lower rates of attrition.[1] All of these factors affect an organization's bottom line.

Training is a continuous process, beginning with the orientation of new employees and continuing throughout an employee's tenure with the organization. Its importance is reflected in the money that organizations allocate for training programs. Employers in Canada spend approximately $4 billion on formal training.[2] Training and development dollars are invested in a variety of programs, ranging from new-employee orientation to executive development.

There has been a definite trend toward the creation of career development programs within organizations. We will give special attention to these programs in the next chapter. In this chapter the emphasis will be on the orientation of employees, the scope of training programs, a systems approach to training, training methods, and new programs.

Orientation

Orientation

Formal process of familiarizing new employees with the organization, their job, and the work unit.

The first step in the training process is to get new employees off to a good start. This is generally accomplished through a formal orientation program. **Orientation** is the *formal* process of familiarizing new employees with the organization, their job, and their work unit. Its purpose is to enable new employees to get "in sync" so that they become productive members of the organization.

Benefits of Orientation

objective

In some organizations a formal new-hire orientation program is almost nonexistent or, when it does exist, is performed in a casual manner. Some readers may remember showing up the first day on a new job, being told to work, and receiving no instructions, introductions, or support. This is unfortunate, since there are a number of very practical and cost-effective benefits to be derived from conducting a well-run program. Benefits frequently reported by employers include the following:

1. lower turnover;
2. increased productivity;
3. improved employee morale;

FIGURE 8-1   *Leaders in People Management*[3]

COMPANY	NUMBER OF EMPLOYEES	TRAINING BUDGET (MILLIONS)	TRAINING COST AS % OF REVENUES
1. Bank of Montreal	34,769	55.0	.63
2. IBM Canada	8,633	25.0	.37
3. BCE	50,982	84.5	1.06
4. Dofasco	8,800	20.0	.91
5. Royal Bank	49,208	54.0	.46

Source: W. Lilley, "Banking on Equity," *Report on Business Magazine* (April 1995), 67.

4. lower recruiting and training costs;

5. facilitation of learning; and

6. reduction of the new employee's anxiety.

The more time and effort an organization devotes to making new employees feel welcome, the more likely they are to identify with the organization and become valuable members of it. Unlike training, which emphasizes the *what* and *how*, orientation stresses the *why*. It is designed to develop in employees a particular attitude about the work they will be doing and their role in the organization. It defines the philosophy behind the rules and provides a framework for job-related tasks.

Continuous Process

Since an organization is faced with ever-changing conditions, its plans, policies, and procedures must change with these conditions. Unless current employees are kept up to date with these changes, they may find themselves embarrassingly unaware of activities to which new employees are being oriented. While the discussion that follows focuses primarily on the needs of new employees, it is important that *all* employees be continually reoriented to changing conditions.

Cooperative Endeavour

For a well-integrated orientation program, cooperation between line and staff is essential. The HR department ordinarily is responsible for coordinating orientation activities and for providing new employees with information about conditions of employment, pay, benefits, and other areas not directly under a supervisor's direction. However, the supervisor has the most important role in the orientation program. New employees are interested primarily in what the supervisor says and does and what their new co-workers are like. Before the arrival of a new employee, the supervisor should inform the work group that a new worker is joining the unit. It is also common practice for supervisors or other managerial personnel to recruit co-workers to serve as volunteer "sponsors" for incoming employees. In addition to providing practical help to newcomers, this approach conveys an emphasis on teamwork.

Careful Planning

An orientation program can make an immediate and lasting impression on an employee that can mean the difference between the employee's success and failure on the job. Thus careful planning—with emphasis on program goals, topics to be covered, and methods of organizing and presenting them—is essential. Successful programs emphasize the individual's needs for information, understanding, and a feeling of belonging.

To avoid overlooking items that are important to employees, many organizations devise checklists for use by those responsible for conducting the orientation. Highlights in HRM 1 suggests items to include in an orientation checklist for supervisors. Orientation should focus on matters of immediate concern such as important aspects of the job and organizational behaviour rules (e.g., attendance and safety).

In orientation sessions new employees are often given a packet of materials to read at their leisure. Some of the materials such a packet might include are listed in Highlights in HRM 2. Because statements regarding such matters as tenure, basis for dismissal, and benefits may be viewed by employees and the courts as legally binding on the employer, it is advisable to have the legal department review the packet of materials and write disclaimers to the effect that they do not constitute an employment contract.

Those planning an orientation program should take into account the anxiety employees feel during their first few days on the job. It is natural to experience some anxiety, but if employees are too anxious, training costs, turnover, absenteeism, and even production costs may increase. Early in the orientation program steps should be taken to reduce the anxiety level of new employees. This anxiety reduction can be accomplished by establishing specific times in which the supervisor will be available for questions or coaching. Furthermore, anxiety can be decreased by reassuring newcomers that the performance levels they are observing among their co-workers will be attained, within a predetermined time frame, based on experiences with other newcomers. This reassurance is particularly important for employees with limited work experience who are learning new skills.

Some employers think it does no harm to allow new employees to be oriented by their peers. One danger of failing to ensure that new workers are oriented by their supervisors and not their peers is that unsafe work practices and unacceptable behaviours that conflict with the organization's policies can be perpetuated. The behaviours these employees develop can undermine the organization's policies and procedures.[4]

Follow-up and Evaluation

Supervisors should always consult with their new employees after the first day and frequently throughout the first week on the job. When all of the items on the orientation checklist for the employee have been addressed, both the supervisor and the employee should sign it, and the record should then be placed in the employee's

▶ HIGHLIGHTS IN HRM

highlights

1   SUPERVISORY ORIENTATION CHECKLIST

1. A formal greeting, including introduction to colleagues
2. Explanation of job procedures, duties, and responsibilities
3. Training to be received (when and why)
4. Supervisor and organization expectations regarding attendance and behaviour norms
5. Job standards and production/service levels
6. Performance appraisal criteria, including estimated time frame to achieve peak performance
7. Conditions of employment, including hours of work, pay periods, and overtime requirements
8. Organization and work unit rules, regulations, and policies
9. Safety regulations
10. Those to notify or turn to if problems or questions arise
11. Chain of command for reporting purposes
12. An overall explanation of the organization's operation and purpose
13. Offers of help and encouragement, including a specific time each week (in the early stages of employment) for questions or coaching.

personnel file to document what has been covered. After the employee has been on the job for a month, and again after a year, an HR staff member should follow up to determine how effective the orientation has been. Evaluations can then be conducted through in-depth interviews, questionnaires and surveys, and discussion groups.

objective

The Scope of Training

Many new employees come equipped with most of the KSA needed to start work. Others may require extensive training before they are ready to make much of a contribution to the organization. A majority, however, will require some type of training at one time or another to maintain an effective level of job performance.

Training refers to the acquisition of knowledge, skills, and attitudes that result in improved performance in the current job.[5] The primary purpose of a training program is to help the organization achieve its overall objectives. At the same time, an effective training program should help trainees to satisfy their own personal goals.

The primary reason that organizations train new employees is to bring their KSA up to the level required for satisfactory performance. As they continue on the

HIGHLIGHTS IN HRM

2 ITEMS FOR AN ORIENTATION PACKET

1. Current organization chart
2. Projected organization chart
3. Map of the facility
4. List of key terms unique to the industry, company, and/or job
5. Copy of policy handbook
6. Copy of union contract
7. Copy of specific job goals and descriptions
8. List of holidays
9. List of employee benefits
10. Copies of performance appraisal forms, dates of appraisals, and appraisal procedures
11. Copies of other required forms (e.g., supply requisition and expense reimbursement)
12. List of on-the-job training opportunities
13. Sources of information
14. Detailed outline of emergency and accident-prevention procedures
15. Copy of each important organization publication
16. Telephone numbers and locations of key personnel and operations
17. Copies of insurance plans

Source: Walter D. St. John, "The Complete Employee Orientation Program," *Personnel Journal* (May 1990). Reprinted with permission.

job, additional training provides opportunities for them to acquire new knowledge and skills. As a result of the training, employees may be even more effective on the job and may qualify for jobs at a higher level.

A survey of a large number of organizations reveals that the content of training programs varies widely. Figure 8-2 illustrates the diversity of subjects covered, the percentage or organizations providing different types of training, and the percentage of time allocated to it, based on a survey of 17,000 Canadian firms.

As noted earlier, there are many forces that determine the types of training required in an organization. One study identifies these forces as follows:

1. Increased global and domestic competition is leading to a greater need for competitive strategies, which often include training as an essential element.

FIGURE 8-2 *General Types of Training*[6]		
TYPES OF TRAINING	**% OF ORGANIZATIONS PROVIDING TRAINING**	**PERCENTAGE OF TRAINING TIME**
Orientation	61	20
Computer	57	12
Health and safety	44	11
Managerial	40	11

2. Rapid advances in technology have created an acute need for people with specialized technical skills.

3. Widespread mergers, acquisitions, and divestitures, which realign corporate structures but do not necessarily give people the ability to carry out their new responsibilities, require long-term training plans.

4. A better-educated workforce, which values self-development and personal growth, has brought an enormous desire for learning plus a growing need for new forms of participation at work.

5. The obsolescence of some occupations and the emergence of new occupations resulting from the changing nature of the economy, the shift from manufacturing to service industries, and the impact of research, development, and technology require flexible training policies to prevent increased turnover and lower productivity.[7]

In order to have personnel who have the KSA required for effective organizational performance, training programs are typically organized for two major groups: managerial and supervisory personnel and nonmanagerial personnel. Training for these two major groups and special types of training programs will be discussed after we study the systems approach to training.

objective

The Systems Approach to Training

Since the primary goal of training is to contribute to the organization's overall goals, training programs should be developed with an eye to organizational strategy. Part of the organization's strategy must include recognition of the growing pressure from government and society to attend to the needs of workers who have been displaced by structural shifts in the economy, geographical relocation of jobs, international competition, technological changes, and industry deregulation. Ford Motor Company and General Motors even train their displaced workers who must seek jobs at other organizations.

The problem with some training programs is that one method or gimmick can sometimes become the main focus of the program. The objectives may be hazy or evaluation may be inadequate. Too frequently the popularity of a program as indicated

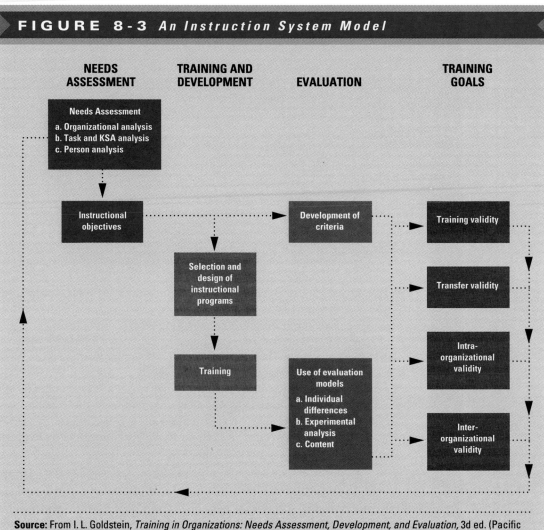

FIGURE 8-3 *An Instruction System Model*

Source: From I. L. Goldstein, *Training in Organizations: Needs Assessment, Development, and Evaluation,* 3d ed. (Pacific Grove, Calif.: Brooks/Cole Publishing, 1986), 21. Copyright 1993 by Wadsworth, Inc. Reprinted by permission of Brooks/Cole Publishing Company.

by the satisfaction of the participants has been used as the sole basis for judging the program's value in meeting the organizational objectives. One recommended solution to these programs is the use of a systems approach to training, which involves a five-step sequence:

1. conduct a needs analysis;
2. formulate instructional objectives;
3. select and design learning experiences to achieve these objectives;
4. devise transfer procedures; and
5. gather information to use in evaluating training programs.

A model that is useful to designers of training programs is presented in Figure 8-3. Note that the model consists of four phases: needs assessment, training and development, evaluation, and meeting training goals.

Needs Analysis Phase

Managers and HR staffs should be alert to indications of what kind of training is needed and where it is needed. The failure of workers to meet production quotas, for example, might signal a need for training. Likewise, an excessive number of rejects or a waste of material might suggest inadequate training. Managers should be careful to approach training needs systematically, however. Three different analyses are recommended for use in the needs assessment phase: organizational analysis, task analysis, and person analysis.

Organizational analysis is an examination of the goals, resources, and environment of the organization to determine where training emphasis should be placed. The resources—technological, financial, and human—that are available to meet objectives also must be considered.

HR policies and organizational climate have an impact on the goals of the training program. External factors such as public policy (as reflected in laws and regulations) also influence where the training emphasis will be placed. For example, training in health and safety is driven largely by laws and court decisions.

Organizations typically collect for use in the analysis data such as information on direct and indirect labour costs, quality of goods or services, absenteeism, turnover, and number of accidents. The availability of potential replacements and the time required to train them are other important factors in organizational analysis. In recent years, organizational analysis has given attention to those factors that determine whether a training program takes place in an environment that allows for behaviour change back on the job.[8] (These factors will be addressed in our discussion of transfer of training later in the chapter.)

Designing a specific training program requires an organization to review the job description that indicates the activities performed in a particular job and the

Organizational analysis
Examination of the goals, resources, and environment of the organization to determine where training emphasis should be placed.

Copyright 1983, Pat Brady. Reprinted with permission.

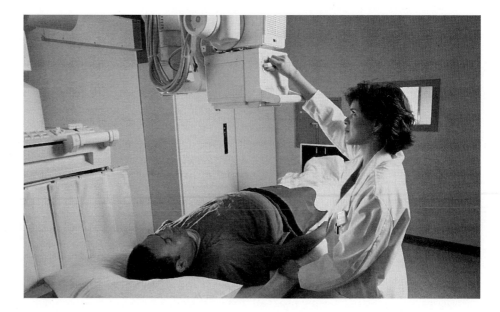

Correctly positioning the X-ray machine above a patient shows just one aspect to a radiologist's job description.

Task analysis
Process of determining the content of a training program based on a study of the tasks or duties involved in the job.

conditions under which they are performed. This review is followed by a **task analysis,** which involves determining the content of the training program based on a study of the tasks or duties involved in the job. Task analysis appears to be shifting from an emphasis on what is currently required to what will be required in the future for an employee to be effective in a particular job.

The first step in task analysis is to list all the tasks or duties included in the job. The second step is to list the steps that the employee performs to complete each task. Once the job is understood thoroughly, the type of performance required (e.g., speech, recall, discrimination, manipulation), along with the skills and knowledge necessary for job performance, can be defined. For example, when performing the task of taking a chest X-ray, a radiologist correctly positions the patient (manipulation), gives special instructions (speech), and checks the proper distance of the X-ray tube from the patient (discrimination).

The types of performance skills and knowledge that trainees need can be determined by observing and questioning skilled jobholders and/or by reviewing job descriptions. This information helps trainers to select program content and choose the most effective training method.

Once the organizational and task analyses have been made, it is necessary to perform a person analysis. **Person analysis** involves determining whether or not task performance is acceptable and studying the characteristics of individuals and groups who will be placed in the training environment. It is important to determine what prospective trainees can and cannot do so that the training program can be designed to emphasize the areas in which they are deficient. By comparing performance standards or expectations to actual performance, analysts can measure the gap and thus determine the specific skills, knowledge, and abilities that need to be acquired. Equally important is identifying those instances in which the employee *can* do the task but *won't*. The ability-versus-motivation dilemma is most easily analyzed by asking a simple question: "Could the employee do the task if his or her life depended

Person analysis
Determination of the specific skills, knowledge, and attitudes required of people on the job.

on it?" If the answer is yes, then the analyst knows that it is not a training problem and that environmental factors such as leadership style and contingencies in the workplace must be examined.

After all the analyses have been made and a picture of the training needs emerges, the desired outcomes of training programs should be stated formally in instructional objectives.

Formulating Instructional Objectives

Instructional objectives involve the acquisition of skills or knowledge or the changing of attitudes. All training focuses on at least three of these areas: the head (knowledge), the heart (attitudes), and the hand (skills). Robert Mager, an internationally known training expert, emphasizes the importance of instructional objectives in offering the following advice:

> Before you prepare for instruction, before you select instructional procedures or subject matter or material, it is important to be able to state clearly just what you intend the results of that instruction to be. A clear statement of instructional objectives will provide a sound basis for choosing methods and materials and for selecting the means for assessing whether the instruction will be successful.[9]

In other words, you must know where you are going before you design programs to get you there.

One type of instructional objective, the *performance-centred objective*, is widely used because it lends itself to an unbiased evaluation of results. For example, the stated objective for one training program might be as follows: "The customer service representative, using standard order-taking procedures, will be able to process ten clients per hour, with surveyed client-satisfaction rates of 95 percent." Performance-centred objectives typically include precise terms such as "to calculate," "to repair," "to adjust," "to construct," "to assemble," and "to classify." Once the performance gaps and objectives have been identified, the next step is to determine the most appropriate methods with which to achieve performance expectations.

Designing the Training Program

Training is extremely costly. Coaching or job aids may provide simpler and cheaper solutions to performance deficiencies. Training-related expenses may force the manager to seek out more cost-effective solutions. The most cost-effective solution can be determined by using a pro forma cost-benefit analysis, described in detail by Wright and Belcourt.[10]

If training is determined to be the most appropriate solution, trainers may go outside the organization to obtain generic programs such as conflict management or computer training. Other program design considerations include the incorporation of adult-learning principles into training program and the implementation of equitable training practices.[11] A major consideration in creating a training environment is choosing a method that will enable the trainee to learn most effectively. The methods commonly used in training personnel at all levels—managerial, supervisory, and nonmanagerial—will be discussed later in the chapter.

Instructional objectives

Formal statements of the desired outcomes of a training program.

Another important factor in the effectiveness of training is the successful transfer to the actual job. There are many steps that might be undertaken to ensure optimum transfer conditions.

Transfer of Training

The success of a training program depends on more than the organization's ability to identify training needs and the care with which it designs the course. If the trainees do not learn what they are supposed to learn, and in a way that is transferable to the job, then the training has not been successful. Indeed, several studies have estimated that only 10 percent of training dollars invested result in actual change on the job.[12]

Transfer of training refers to the implementation in the work environment of the skills acquired during the training program, and the maintenance of these acquired skills over time.[13] To achieve optimum transfer, developers of instructional programs should attend to the basic psychological principles of adult learning. Prescriptions for creating a transfer culture *before*, *during*, and *after* the program are discussed below.

Pretraining

Two preconditions for learning affect the success of those who are to receive training: *readiness* and *motivation*. Trainee readiness refers to both maturity and experience factors in the trainee's background. Prospective trainees should be screened to determine that they have the background knowledge or the skills necessary to absorb what will be presented to them. Recognizing individual differences in readiness is as important in organizational training as it is in any other teaching situation. It is often desirable to group individuals according to their capacity to learn (as determined by test scores) and to provide an alternative type of instruction for those who need it. Providing test results as feedback to participants also increases their motivation to learn.

The receptiveness and readiness of participants in workshops and similar training programs can be increased by having them complete questionnaires asking them why they are attending the workshop and what they want to accomplish. Participants may also be asked to give copies of their completed questionnaires to their supervisors. Highlights in HRM 3 offers an example of a preprogram worksheet. This worksheet actively involves managers in needs identification and helps them to provide a supportive climate when the newly trained employee returns. Support for newly acquired skills can also be increased by assigning a mentor (who has already taken the course and is using the skills) or by sending a group of employees who will assist each other upon return.

The other precondition for learning is that trainees must be properly motivated. That is, for optimum learning to occur trainees must recognize the need for acquiring new information or skills, and they must maintain a desire to learn as training progresses. As one management consultant advises, "It's not enough just to 'tell.' You also have to 'sell' trainees on the material they are supposed to learn if training is to succeed."[14] The manager can assist in this process by identifying gaps in performance and counselling on career development opportunities.

Transfer of training

The implementation in the work environment of the skills acquired during the training program, and the maintenance of those acquired skills over time.

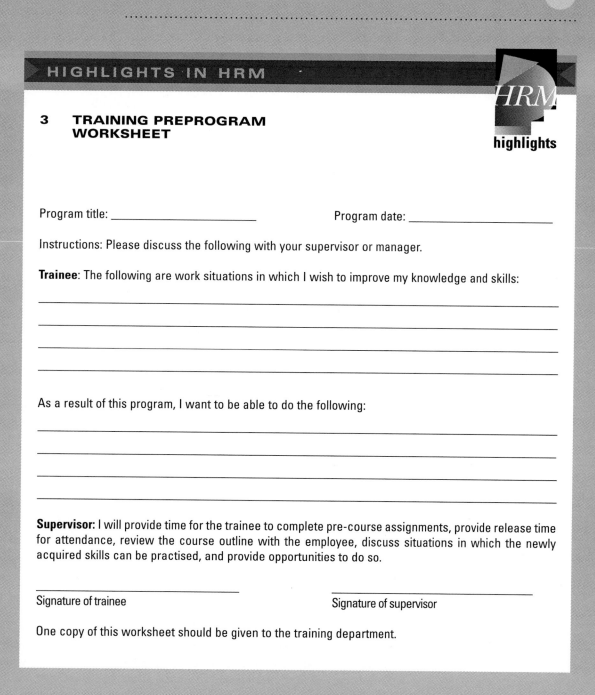

HRM
highlights

3 TRAINING PREPROGRAM WORKSHEET

Program title: _____   Program date: _____

Instructions: Please discuss the following with your supervisor or manager.

Trainee: The following are work situations in which I wish to improve my knowledge and skills:

_____

_____

_____

_____

As a result of this program, I want to be able to do the following:

_____

_____

_____

_____

Supervisor: I will provide time for the trainee to complete pre-course assignments, provide release time for attendance, review the course outline with the employee, discuss situations in which the newly acquired skills can be practised, and provide opportunities to do so.

_____   _____
Signature of trainee   Signature of supervisor

One copy of this worksheet should be given to the training department.

The Training Course

Motivating trainees to want to learn and setting up conditions to facilitate that process are extremely important components in the transfer cycle. A motivating environment can be created by focusing on the trainees rather than on the trainer or training topic. Five strategies that can help are outlined below.

1. *Make presentations meaningful.* One principle of learning is that the material to be learned should be presented in as meaningful a manner as possible. While most workers are motivated by certain generic needs, they differ from one another in the relative importance of these needs at any given time. For example, college graduates often have a high desire for advancement, and they have established specific goals for career progression. Training objectives that are clearly related to employees' individual needs will increase their motivation to succeed in training programs. Unless what is learned in the training situation is applicable to what is required on the job, the training will be of little value. Transfer of training to the job can be facilitated by having conditions in the training program match as closely as possible those on the job. Another approach is to teach trainees how to apply the behaviours they have learned to the specific requirements of the job.

2. *Use positive reinforcement.* Anything that strengthens the trainee's response is called **reinforcement**. It may be in the form of approval from the trainer or the feeling of accomplishment that follows the performance; or it may simply be confirmation that the response was correct. Reinforcement is generally most effective when it occurs immediately after a task has been performed.

In recent years, some industrial organizations have used **behaviour modification,** a technique that operates on the principle that behaviour that is rewarded, or positively reinforced, will be exhibited more frequently in the future, whereas behaviour that is penalized or unrewarded will decrease in frequency.

3. *Provide feedback.* As an employee's training progresses, motivation may be maintained or even increased by providing knowledge of progress or feedback. Progress, as determined by tests and other records, may be plotted on a chart; the plot is commonly referred to as a *learning curve.* Figure 8-4 presents an example of a learning curve that is common in the acquisition of many job skills.

In many learning situations, there are times when progress does not occur. Such periods show up on the curve as a fairly straight horizontal line called a *plateau.* A plateau may be the result of reduced motivation or ineffective methods of task performance. It is a natural phenomenon of learning, and there is usually a spontaneous recovery as Figure 8-4 shows.

4. *Pace learning.* Another factor that determines the effectiveness of training is the distribution of training. Should trainees be given training in five two-hour periods or ten one-hour periods? In most cases, spacing out the training will result in faster learning and longer retention. This is the principle of *distributed learning.* Since the efficiency of the distribution will vary with the type and complexity of the task, trainers should refer to the rapidly growing body of research in this area when they require guidance in designing a specific training situation.[15]

Most tasks and jobs can be broken down into parts that lend themselves to further analyses. Determining the most effective manner for completing each part provides a basis for giving specific instructions. Typing, for example, is made up of several skills that are part of the total process. The typist starts by learning the proper use of each finger; eventually, with practice, the individual finger movements

---

Reinforcement
Anything that strengthens the trainee's response.

Behaviour modification
Technique that operates on the principle that behaviour that is rewarded, or positively reinforced, will be exhibited more frequently in the future, whereas behaviour that is penalized or unrewarded will decrease in frequency.

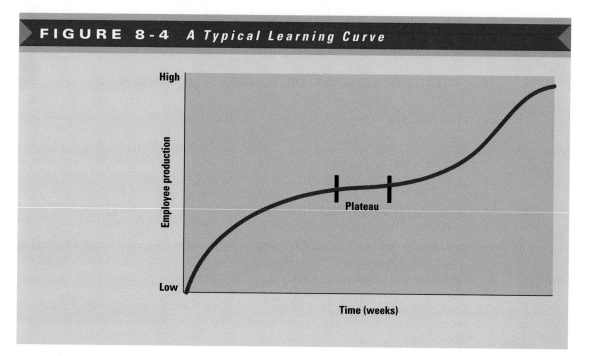

FIGURE 8-4 *A Typical Learning Curve*

become integrated into a total pattern. Practice by moving only the index finger repeatedly on a key is an example of *part learning*. In evaluating whole versus part learning, it is necessary to consider the nature of the task to be learned. If the task *can* be broken down successfully, it probably should be broken down to facilitate learning; otherwise, it probably should be taught as a unit. The material should be arranged such that each experience builds upon preceding ones, and the trainee is able to integrate the experiences into a usable pattern of knowledge and skills.

5. *Provide practice.* Those things we do daily become a part of our repertoire of skills. Trainees should be given frequent opportunities to practise their job tasks in the way that they will ultimately be expected to perform them. The individual who is being taught to operate a machine should have an opportunity to practise on it. Similarly, the supervisor who is being taught how to train should be given supervised practice in training.

An additional element in the success of a training program is the effectiveness of the trainer, discussed in Highlights in HRM 4.

Post Training

Trainees can be trained to manage post-course relapses by setting their own goals (written behaviourial contracts) and by administering their own rewards.[16] Relapse-prevention training produces results because it alerts trainees to the fact that relapse will occur. This type of training involves identifying both the barriers to implementation and the strategies that can be used to overcome these barriers. Job aids or easily referenced instructions can also help.

Once training is completed, the supervisor should ensure that the work environment supports, reinforces, and rewards the trainee for applying new skills and knowledge.

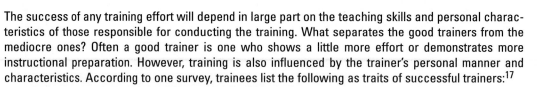

4 CHARACTERISTICS OF SUCCESSFUL TRAINERS

The success of any training effort will depend in large part on the teaching skills and personal characteristics of those responsible for conducting the training. What separates the good trainers from the mediocre ones? Often a good trainer is one who shows a little more effort or demonstrates more instructional preparation. However, training is also influenced by the trainer's personal manner and characteristics. According to one survey, trainees list the following as traits of successful trainers:[17]

1. *Knowledge of subject.* Employees expect trainers to know their job or subject thoroughly.
2. *Adaptability.* Some individuals learn faster or slower than others. Instruction should be therefore matched to the trainee's learning ability.
3. *Sincerity.* Trainees appreciate sincerity in trainers.
4. *Sense of humour.* Learning can be fun. Very often a point can be made with a story or anecdote.
5. *Interest.* Good trainers have a keen interest in the subject they are teaching. This interest is readily conveyed to trainees.
6. *Clear instructions.* Training is accomplished more quickly and retained longer when trainers give clear instructions.
7. *Individual assistance.* When training more than one employee, successful trainers always provide individual assistance.
8. *Enthusiasm.* A dynamic presentation and a vibrant personality show trainees that the trainer enjoys training. Employees tend to respond positively to an enthusiastic climate.[18]

When trainees and students rate instructors, they focus on four critical dimensions: presentation skill, rapport with the learner, structure of the learning experience, and ability to evaluate in a fair and consistent manner. [19]

Evaluation Phase

Training, like any other HRM function, should be evaluated to determine its effectiveness. Unfortunately, few organizations have adequate systems to evaluate the effectiveness of their training programs.

Training can be evaluated in four ways:[20]

1. Reactions—did they like it?
2. Learning—did they learn it?
3. Behaviour—did they use it on the job?
4. Results—did this change measurable organizational outcomes?

While evaluation methods are improving, too many conclusions about training effectiveness are still based on the subjective reactions of trainers and trainees (reactions). It is easy to collect glowing comments from trainees (smile sheets), but this information, however gratifying to the HR staff, may not be very useful to the organization. Training is not provided for its entertainment value. The real issue is whether the training effort will translate to improved behaviour or job performance.

Not only should trainees be tested before and after training, but the same evaluations should also be made of individuals in a control group. The control group contains employees who have not received the training but who match the trainees in such areas as experience, past training, and job level. Some of the criteria used in evaluating the effectiveness of training are increased productivity, greater total sales, decreased costs and waste, and similar evidence of improved performance.

An evaluation should be undertaken to provide data for a specific decision, such as whether or not to adopt or continue a training course or how to improve the course. This latter question was addressed by one police force as it evaluated a training program for police officer recruits. The objectives of this evaluation were (1) to determine the extent to which the training content was job-related, and (2) to identify what changes in training content were needed to improve job relatedness.[21] Planning the evaluation around specific objectives increases the likelihood that findings will produce meaningful changes. Training directors often limit themselves by not being able to prove their effectiveness objectively in terms of the specific benefits of training to the organization and the costs of obtaining those benefits.

According to one study, approximately two-thirds of training managers surveyed reported that they were coming under additional pressure to show that their programs produce "bottom-line" results.[22]

Meeting Training Goals

To help determine the effectiveness of training, the evaluation phase must address the worth of the training program. As the last column of Figure 8-3 showed, a number of goals are possible. The choice of which goal to pursue depends on the information one seeks and the constraints under which one operates. Goldstein describes the four choices as follows:

1. *Training validity.* Whether the trainees learn during training.
2. *Transfer validity.* Whether what has been learned in training translates to enhanced performance in the organization.
3. *Intraorganizational validity.* Whether the performance of a new group of trainees in the organization that developed the training program is consistent with the performance of the original training group in the same organization.
4. *Interorganizational validity.* Whether a training program found effective in one organization can be used successfully in another organization.[23]

The validity of a training system completes the cycle of the training system: needs identification, objective setting, program design, transfer principles, and evaluation. Reality Check illustrates how these principles are practised.

TRAINING AT CIBC

According to Al Flood, Chairman and CEO of the Canadian Imperial Bank of Commerce (CIBC),

> *Learning is now so essential for career success, corporate survival, and national prosperity that it no longer makes sense to relegate it to certain institutions or to particular periods in one's life. Learning is now everybody's business. I define the learning organization as a corporation in which every process, procedure, structure, and every employee is dedicated to constant learning. Learning that advances individual careers as well as the corporation's business goals.*

CIBC is one of the flagship companies committed to success through the continuous improvement of the performance of its employees. Suzanne Jokinen is a key member of the CIBC's Learning Systems Team, which contributes to the achievement of the goals of the organization. Her role is the strategic development of learning programs and products for CIBC Insurance.

To achieve the ultimate goal of being a customer-focused organization, CIBC has established a matrix organization to address the needs of its internal and external clients. Jokinen's team designs, develops, and implements learning plans and products, thus facilitating the learning process within the client group.

Jokinen chairs a Learning Committee composed of vice-presidents of the various divisions. This committee prepares strategic learning plans and recommends programs. The value of this group, Jokinen feels, is that "each VP hears the priorities of the other areas, and sees the big picture." Jokinen's responsibility is to advise the senior team if the requests can be met based on access to resources, budgets, and the demands on the team.

The plan provides input for the designers and developers, who meet with the clients to conduct needs analysis and assess the projects that will lead to the design and development of new programs. The needs analysis includes such questions as What are the business needs and priorities driving this project? What are the performance gaps? What do we want the target group to do? What are they doing/not doing now? What are the knowledge, skill, and attitude components required? In other words: (a) what do they need to know?; (b) what do they need to be able to do?; and (c) how do we want them to feel?

In assessing the project, the team members obtain descriptions of the target population, recommended methodology, key content areas, and resources required. The facilitators will initially deliver the programs and assist the managers in the evaluation process at the end to determine that the learning objectives have been achieved and that there are observable results. Sometimes, the facilitators provide coaching and support to employees who are subject-matter experts and who will thereafter do the training.

The learning consultant is not responsible for the career development of employees. "The responsibility for individual learning plans and further development rests with the employee," Jokinen explains. "The manager's job is to provide support, encouragement, and guidance." Managers and employees work this out, and the consultant is there to ensure that the needs of the organization are met and that individuals are given appropriate tools to make this happen. Jokinen manages her own career development, which makes her a role model in continuous learning.

Source: Interview with Deborah M. Zinni, June 1995.

objective

Training Nonmanagerial Employees

A wide variety of methods are available for training personnel at all levels. Some of the methods have a long history of usage. Newer methods have emerged over the years out of a greater understanding of human behaviour, particularly in the areas of learning, motivation, and interpersonal relationships. More recently, technological advances, especially in electronics, have resulted in training devices that in many instances are more effective and economical than traditional training methods.

On-the-Job Training

On-the-job training (OJT) is one of the most common methods of training nonmanagerial employees. OJT has the advantage of providing "hands-on" experience under normal working conditions and an opportunity for the trainer—a supervisor or senior employee—to build good relationships with new employees.

Although it is used by all types of organizations, OJT is often one of the most poorly implemented training methods. Three common drawbacks are (1) the lack of a well-structured training environment, (2) poor training skills of supervisors, and (3) the absence of well-defined job performance criteria. To overcome these problems, training experts suggest the following:

On-the-job training (OJT)
Method by which employees are given hands-on experience with instructions from their supervisor or other trainer.

1. Develop realistic goals and/or measures for each OJT area.
2. Plan a specific training schedule for each trainee, including setting periods for evaluation and feedback.
3. Help supervisors to establish a nonthreatening atmosphere that is conducive to learning.
4. Conduct periodic evaluations, after training is completed, to prevent regression.[24]

Many successful trainers continue to use a system known as Job Instruction Training (JIT), which was developed by the War Manpower Commission during World War II to acquaint the tens of thousands of newly created industrial supervisors in how to instruct their employees (see Highlights in HRM 5). The JIT card, or an adaptation of it, is used by many small businesses to instruct a new person on the job or a present worker on a new job.[25]

Electronic Performance Support Systems

The need for on-the-job and just-in-time training has led to the development of Electronic Performance Support Systems (EPSS). If you have ever pressed the HELP key on a computer or been guided through a banking procedure at a kiosk, then you have experienced EPSS. A computer-based system improves employee productivity by providing on-the-job access to integrated information, advice, and learning experiences.[26] They are intelligent job aids, which have the advantage of giving information when it is needed, unlike training courses that cram everything into your head at one time. EPSS is highly effective for high-turnover jobs (e.g., bank tellers)[27] and for difficult tasks that are performed infrequently and must be performed perfectly.[28]

> **HIGHLIGHTS IN HRM**

highlights

5   THE JIT CARD

Practical methods to guide you in instructing a new employee on a job, or a present employee on a new job or a new skill

FIRST, here's what *you must* do to *get ready* to teach a job:

1. Decide what the employee must be taught in order to do the job efficiently, safely, economically and intelligently.
2. Have the right tools, equipment, supplies and material ready.
3. Have the work place properly arranged, just as the employee will be expected to keep it.

THEN, you should *instruct* the employee according to the following *four basic steps:*

STEP I—PREPARATION (of the employee)

1. Put the employee at *ease.*
2. Find out what the employee already knows about the job.
3. Get the employee interested and desirous of learning the job.

STEP II—PRESENTATION (of the operations and knowledge)

1. *Tell*, *show*, *illustrate*, and *question* in order to put over the new knowledge and operations.
2. Instruct slowly, clearly, completely and patiently, one point at a time.
3. Check, question and repeat.
4. Make sure the employee really knows.

STEP III—PERFORMANCE TRY-OUT

1. Test the employee by having him or her perform the job.
2. Ask questions beginning with *why*, *how*, *when* or *where*.
3. Observe performance, correct errors, and repeat instructions if necessary.
4. Continue until you *know the employee knows.*

STEP IV—FOLLOW-UP

1. Put the employee "on his or her own."
2. Check frequently to be sure the employee follows instructions.
3. Taper off extra supervision and close follow-up until the employee is qualified to work with normal supervision.

REMEMBER—If the employee hasn't learned, the teacher hasn't taught.

Source: War Manpower Commission, *The Training within Industry Report* (Washington, DC: Bureau of Training, Training within Industry Service, 1945), 195.

Off-the-Job Training

In addition to on-the-job training, it is usually necessary to provide workers with training in settings away from their ordinary workplace. Some methods involve training employees away from their usual workstations but still within the organization's facilities. Other methods involve training employees in locations outside the organization.

Conference or Discussion

A method of individualized instruction frequently used where the training involves primarily the communication of ideas, procedures, and standards is the conference or discussion method. This method allows for considerable flexibility in the amount of employee participation.

Classroom Training

Classroom training enables the maximum number of trainees to be handled by the minimum number of instructors. This method lends itself particularly to training in areas where information and instructions can be presented in lectures, demonstrations, videotapes, and films. Where it is not possible to obtain videotapes, audiotapes can be very valuable. For example, to instruct flight-crew trainees, airlines might play a cockpit tape taken from a doomed aircraft. After listening to the tape, the trainees could discuss the behaviour of the crew during the crisis. By listening to the recorded statements of others and observing their failure to operate as a team, pilot trainees develop an understanding of the need for balancing their sense of self-reliance with an ability to listen to subordinates.[29]

A special type of classroom facility is used in *vestibule training*. Trainees are given instruction in the operation of equipment like that found in operating departments. The emphasis is on instruction rather than production.

Programmed Instruction

One method of instruction uses a book, manual, or computer to present programmed subject matter. *Programmed instruction* breaks down subject-matter content into highly organized, logical sequences that demand continuous responses on the part of the trainee. After being presented with a small segment of information, the trainee is required to answer a question, either by writing it in a response frame or by pushing a button. If the response is correct, the trainee is told so and is presented with the next step (frame) in the material. If the response is incorrect, further explanatory information is given and the trainee is told to try again.

This group of training instructors learns the procedures of an interactive tutorial.

A major advantage of programmed instruction is that it incorporates a number of established learning principles, which we discussed earlier in the chapter. With programmed instruction, training is individualized, trainees are actively involved in the instructional process, and feedback and reinforcement are immediate.

Computer-Based Training

As development of technology proceeds at a rapid pace and the cost of computers continues to decline, high-technology training methods are finding increasing use in industry, academia, and the military.[30]

Computer-based training (CBT) encompasses two distinct techniques: computer-assisted instruction and computer-managed instruction. A **computer-assisted instruction (CAI)** system delivers training material directly through a computer terminal in an interactive format. The memory and storage capabilities of computers make it possible to provide drill and practice, problem solving, simulation, gaming forms of instruction, and certain sophisticated forms of individualized tutorial instruction.

A **computer-managed instruction (CMI)** system is normally used in conjunction with CAI, thereby providing an efficient means of managing the training function. CMI uses a computer to generate and score tests and to determine the level of trainee proficiency. CMI systems can also track the performance of trainees and direct them to appropriate study material to meet their specific needs. With CMI, the computer takes on some of the routine aspects of training, freeing the instructor to spend time on course development or individualized instruction.

CBT is being used more and more to train users of human resources information systems (HRIS). Trainees begin with relatively simple tasks, such as entering a new employee's records in the personnel file, then proceed to more complex procedures as they master each task. The training data are often simulated, but the procedures are real. Some of the advantages of CBT are listed in Highlights in HRM 6.[31]

Simulation Method

Sometimes it is either impractical or unwise to train workers on the actual equipment that is used on the job. An obvious example is the training of personnel to operate aircraft, spacecraft, and other highly technical and expensive equipment. The simulation method emphasizes realism in equipment and its operation at minimum cost and maximum safety. For example, locomotive engineers can receive rigorous training through the use of a locomotive simulator. Employing advanced computer technology, the simulator can realistically depict train-track dynamics, provide taped train sounds and visuals, and duplicate a variety of operations.[32]

Use of Other Training Devices

To teach skills and procedures for many production jobs, certain training devices may be used. For example, devices that look like a portable TV use slides or videotape to

---

Computer-assisted instruction (CAI)

System that delivers instructional material directly through a computer terminal in an interactive format.

Computer-managed instruction (CMI)

System normally used in conjunction with CAI that uses a computer to generate and score tests and to determine the level of training proficiency.

HIGHLIGHTS IN HRM

highlights

6 ADVANTAGES OF COMPUTER-BASED TRAINING

1. Learning is self-paced.
2. Training comes to the employee.
3. All trainees get exactly the same training.
4. New employees do not have to wait for a scheduled training session.
5. Training can focus on specific needs as revealed by built-in tests.
6. Trainees can be referred to on-line help or written material.
7. It is easier to revise a computer program than to change classroom training materials.
8. Recordkeeping is facilitated.
9. The computer program can be linked to video presentations.

Source: Adapted from Ralph E. Ganger, "Computer-Based Training Improves Job Performance," *Personnel Journal* 68, no. 6 (June 1989): 116–123. Reproduced with permission.

illustrate the steps in the manufacture and assembly of electronic and other components. Closed-circuit television and video-recording equipment (such as camcorders) are also standard training devices. Closed-circuit television allows an instructional program to be transmitted to many locations simultaneously. The use of camcorders permits on-the-spot recording and immediate feedback to the trainees.

Two newer training techniques, the *videodisk* and *training by telephone* (or *teletraining*), incorporate positive learning principles while providing flexibility to organizational trainers. Interactive videodisks, an extension of CBT, have an advantage over other programmed learning techniques in that they allow immediate access to any segment of the instructional program. This is especially useful for individualized instruction of trainees with different levels of knowledge and ability. Videodisks are currently used to teach doctors to diagnose illness, to help dairy farmers increase productivity, and to teach CPR trainees in firefighting and other emergency services jobs to revive victims of heart attacks. More recent applications tackle the difficult managerial skills of leadership, supervision, and interpersonal relations.

Among the benefits of teletraining are scheduling flexibility, reduced time and expense of staff travel, increased access to experts, and the ability to reach dispersed groups of trainees in remote locations. Queen's University and Athabaska University offer MBAs via teleconferencing.

Apprenticeship Training

Apprenticeship training

System of training in which a worker entering the skill trades industry is given thorough instruction and experiences, both on and off the job, in the practical and theoretical aspects of the work.

A system of training in which the worker entering industry is given thorough instruction and experience, both on and off the job, in the practical and theoretical aspects of the work in a skilled trade is known as **apprenticeship training**. Apprenticeship programs are based on voluntary cooperation between management and labour, between industry and government, and between the organization and the school system. Although apprenticeship wages are less than those of fully qualified workers, this method does provide training with pay for individuals interested in qualifying for jobs such as machinist, appliance repairer, laboratory technician, and electrician.

Currently the apprenticeship system in Canada covers about 65 occupations in four sectors (construction, motive power, industrial, and service). The federal government plans to spend over $300 million in 1997–98 to create 60,000 apprenticeship positions.[33] In Canada, apprenticeship is not viewed as an acceptable middle-class career goal; even the children of skilled labourers are encouraged to go to university. The result is a shortage of skilled labour, a situation different from that in countries like Germany where apprenticeships are highly regarded.

Cooperative Training, Internships, and Governmental Training

Cooperative training

Training programs that combine practical on-the-job experience with formal educational classes.

Cooperative training programs combine practical on-the-job experience with formal classes. The term *cooperative training* is also used in connection with high-school and college programs that incorporate part- or full-time experiences. In recent years, there has been an increased effort to expand opportunities that combine on-the-job skill training with regular classroom training so that students can pursue either technical work or a college degree program.

Internship programs

Programs jointly sponsored by colleges, universities, and other organizations that offer students the opportunity to gain real-life experience while allowing them to find out how they will perform in work organizations.

Internship programs, jointly sponsored by colleges, universities, and a variety of organizations, offer students the chance to get real-world experience while finding out how they will perform in work organizations. Organizations benefit by getting student-employees with new ideas, energy, and eagerness to accomplish their assignments. Humber College in Toronto and BCIT in Vancouver are just two examples of the many colleges across Canada that allow students to earn credits based on successful job performance and fulfilment of established program requirements.

Government Programs

The federal government and various provincial governments sponsor a multitude of training programs for new and current employees. Frequently these training efforts are aimed at the development of basic job skills for individuals who lack marketable skills. Governments offer labour-market adjustment services, such as entry and re-entry training and job-loss support. These support programs, which extend beyond the $12 billion spent on unemployment insurance, lessen the impact of job loss by providing training, counselling, and information. According to a study conducted by the Canadian Labour Market and Productivity Centre,[34] Canadian governments spent about $4 billion a year on training.[35]

Partnerships

No single employer or government agency can solve the problems of the unemployed citizen or soften the shattering effects of plant closures. Partnerships between governments, employers, unions, and educational institutions have proven to be particularly advantageous in training and finding work for laid-off employees. For example, 1,300 employees of the Firestone Plant in Hamilton, Ontario, benefited from an alliance between the union, the company, and the community. A highly motivated and effective adjustment committee was able to accommodate 95 percent of the laid-off workers through new jobs, retirement, and retraining.

objective

Training Managers and Supervisors

Training and development of managers is a multibillion-dollar business. In a survey of a representative sample of 611 companies, the percentage of companies that reported using this type of training was 93 percent for on-the-job training, 90 percent for external short courses, 80 percent for special projects or task forces, 57 percent for mentoring, 40 percent for job rotation, 31 percent for university residential programs, and 25 percent for executive MBA programs. Significant differences in training practices were found among various industries and between large and small companies.[36] Some of the training methods used for nonmanagerial personnel may also be used to train managers and supervisors.

On-the-Job Experiences

Management skills and abilities cannot be acquired just by listening and observing or by reading about them. They must be acquired through actual practice and experience in which there are opportunities to perform under pressure and to learn from mistakes. On-the-job experiences are used most commonly by organizations to develop executives. Such experiences should be well planned and supervised, and should be meaningful and challenging to the participant. Methods of providing on-the-job experiences include the following:

1. *Coaching* involves a continuing flow of instructions, comments, and suggestions from the superior to the subordinate.
2. *Understudy assignment* grooms an individual to take over the supervisor's job by gaining experience in handling important functions of the job.
3. *Job rotation* provides, through a variety of work experiences, the broadened knowledge and understanding required to manage more effectively.

4. *Lateral transfer* involves horizontal movement through different departments along with upward movement in the organization.

5. *Project and committee assignments* provide an opportunity for the individual to become involved in the study of current organizational problems and in planning and decision-making activities.

6. *Staff meetings* enable participants to become more familiar with problems and events occurring outside their immediate area by exposing them to the ideas and thinking of other managers.

7. *Planned career progressions* (discussed in Chapter 9) utilize all these different methods to provide employees with the training and development necessary to progress through a series of jobs requiring higher and higher levels of knowledge and/or skills.

8. *Interactions with a mentor* (also discussed in Chapter 9) add a personal touch to an informal training process.

Although these methods are used most often to train managers for higher-level positions, they also provide valuable experiences for those who are being groomed for other types of positions in the organization.

Off-the-Job Experiences

While on-the-job experiences constitute the core of management training, certain methods of development away from the job can be used to supplement these experiences. Off-the-job experiences may be provided on either an individual or a group basis and may be taught by means of special programs or seminars. They may include time management, assertiveness training, business-writing skills, strategic planning, employee appraisal, creative thinking, stress management, interpersonal skills, listening skills, and management of change.

Case Study

Particularly useful in classroom learning situations are case studies. These documented examples, which may have been developed from actual experiences within their organizations, can help managers to learn how to gather and interpret facts, to become conscious of the many variables on which a management decision may be based, and, in general, to improve their decision-making skills.

In-Basket Training

A method used to simulate a problem situation is the **in-basket technique**. With this technique, the participants are given several documents, each describing some problem or situation requiring an immediate response. They are thus forced to make decisions under the pressure of time and also to determine what priority to give each problem. In-basket exercises are a common instructional technique used in assessment centres, which are discussed in Chapter 9.

Leaderless Group Discussions

A popular assessment-centre activity is **leaderless group discussions**. With this technique, trainees are gathered in a conference setting to discuss an assigned topic either

---

In-basket technique

Training method in which trainees are given several documents, each describing some problem or situation whose solution requires an immediate decision.

Leaderless group discussions

Assessment-centre activities in which trainees are gathered in a conference setting to discuss an assigned topic either with or without designated group roles.

with or without designated group roles. The participants are given little or no instruction in how to approach the topic, nor are they told what decision to reach. Leaderless group trainees are evaluated on their initiative, leadership skills, and ability to work effectively in a group setting.

Management Games

Training experiences have been brought to life and made more interesting through the development of management games. Players are faced with the task of making a series of decisions affecting a hypothetical organization. The effects that every decision has on each area within the organization can be simulated with a computer that has been programmed for the game. A major advantage of this technique is the high degree of participation that it requires.

Games are now widely used as a training method. Many of them have been designed for general use, and more recently the development of industry-specific games has increased, with the result that there are now simulations for a wide variety of industries.[37] More and more organizations are using simulations of organization dynamics as tools for change. For example, TD Bank uses a simulation called Desert Kings, produced by Eagle's Flight, to encourage more open communication, increase levels of team performance, and increase commitment to both internal and external customer service. Practitioners in the area of management training have come to realize that extensive preparation, planning, and debriefing are needed to realize the potential benefits of this method.

Role Playing

Role playing consists of assuming the attitudes and behaviour—that is, playing the role of others, often a supervisor and a subordinate who are involved in a personnel problem. Role playing can help participants improve their ability to understand and cope with the problems of those they deal with in their daily work. It should also help them to learn how to counsel others by helping them see situations from a different point of view. Role playing is used widely in training health-care personnel to be sensitive to the concerns of patients. It is also used widely in training managers to handle employee issues relating to absenteeism, performance appraisal, and conflict situations.

Laboratory Training

Laboratory training, which typically involves interpersonal interactions in a group setting, has as its primary goal the development of greater sensitivity on the part of its participants, including self-insight and an awareness of group processes. It also provides the opportunity to improve human relations skills by having managers or supervisors better understand themselves and others. This is achieved by encouraging trainees to share their experiences, feelings, emotions, and perceptions with other trainees or fellow employees. The ability to participate constructively in group activities is another benefit of this technique.

One variant of laboratory training is *sensitivity training*. As the term would indicate, this training increases a person's awareness of his or her own behaviour as it is seen by other training participants. Highly popular in the 1970s, sensitivity training came to be viewed as a form of brainwashing because of its often unwarranted intrusion into employees' personal lives. As the popularity of sensitivity training declined,

ETHICS IN HRM

MIND MANIPULATION

A large insurance company hired a consultant to conduct management training for hundreds of supervisors and managers. Unknown to the organization, the consultant was a member of L. Ron Hubbard's Church of Scientology and was teaching management principles developed by Hubbard.

Critics argue that Scientology is not a religion, but a cult. Employees resented being subjected to psychological concepts based on "tones" that catalogue emotions; to the ruthless devotion to ferreting out and firing problem employees; and to "religious scriptures." One Scientology pamphlet maintains that the purpose of the management program is "to instill the ethics, principles, codes and doctrines of the Scientology religion throughout the business world."[38]

Employees in other organizations who have been required to take programs stressing the importance of the individual have argued that these precepts violate their belief that God and family are more important than the individual. Do organizations have the right to manage the motivations, attitudes, and beliefs of their employees?

Source: J. Saunders, "How Scientology's Message Came to Allstate," *Report on Business, The Globe and Mail* (April 24, 1995), B1; R. Sharpe, "Agents of Intimidation," *Report on Business, The Globe and Mail* (March 28, 1995), B8.

a wide variety of "New Age" seminars and self-improvement courses emerged. However, a problem with these programs is that some individuals find that the content of the programs conflicts with their own personal moral, ethical, and religious beliefs. As a result, they resent being forced by their employer to participate. Ethics in HRM above illustrates the harm done by not thoroughly investigating training courses.

Behaviour Modelling

Training programs designed simply to change supervisors' attitudes are no longer as useful as they might have been in the past. Supervisors now must be shown how to put their attitudes to work. One such approach is **behaviour modelling**, or **interaction management**, which emphasizes the need to involve supervisory trainees in handling real-life employee problems and to provide immediate feedback on their own performance. The main purpose of behaviour modelling is to achieve behavioural change. There are four basic steps in behaviour modelling:

1. Managerial trainees view films or videotapes in which a model manager is portrayed dealing with an employee in an effort to improve or maintain the

Behaviour modelling (interaction management)
Approach that emphasizes the involvement of supervisory trainees in handling real-life employee problems and receiving immediate feedback on their performance.

employee's performance. The example shows specifically how to deal with the situation.

2. Trainees participate in extensive practice and rehearsal of the behaviours demonstrated by the models. The greatest percentage of training time is spent in these skill-practice sessions.

3. As the trainee's behaviour increasingly resembles that of the model, the trainer and other trainees provide social reinforcers such as praise, approval, encouragement, and attention. Videotaping behaviour rehearsals provides feedback and reinforcement.

4. Emphasis throughout the training period is placed on transferring the training to the job.[39]

Does behaviour modelling work? Several controlled studies have demonstrated success in changing the behaviour of managers, as well as measurable increases in worker productivity. One study provided objective evidence that behaviour modelling of marketing representatives actually resulted in increased sales.[40]

objective

Special Training Programs

Within any large organization there are likely to be hundreds of jobs, each of which involves a variety of knowledge and skills. Thus training programs will cover a wide range of content reflecting the particular demands of the jobs. In addition to providing training for specific jobs, many employers develop special training programs to meet special needs. Some of the areas that have been the subject of special training programs are literacy, team training, training for diversity, and global training.

Literacy

Surveys have shown that about 30 to 40 percent of the workforce in Canada cannot read simple directions or do the basic mathematics required to add up a restaurant bill or complete a mail-order invoice.[41] These figures have important implications for society at large and for organizations that must assimilate these individuals into the workforce.

In a workplace increasingly dominated by technology, basic mathematics skills have become essential occupational qualifications that have profound implications for product quality, customer service, internal efficiency, and workplace and environmental safety. While there are different possible approaches to the problem, the establishment of in-house basic skills programs has come increasingly into favour.[42] For example, Abitibi-Price has invested approximately $200,000 in literacy projects. Other organizations employing a large immigrant population (e.g., the Château Laurier in Ottawa and Tiger Brand Knitting in Toronto) have discovered that literacy training has the additional benefit of bridging the literacy-level gap among 30 ethnic groups.[43]

Team Training

As organizations rely more on the use of teams to attain organizational goals, the need to enhance team effectiveness has increased. Whether it be an aircrew, a research team, or a manufacturing unit, the contributions of the individual members of the team are not only a function of the KSA of each individual but the interaction of the team members. Teamwork behaviours that differentiate effective teams include effective communication, coordination, mutual performance monitoring, exchange of feedback, and adaptation to varying situational demands. The fact that these behaviours are observable and measurable provides a basis for training team members to function more effectively in the pursuit of their goals.[44]

Training for Diversity

There has been a remarkable increase in diversity training programs in a wide range of organizations in the past few years. Diversity training is based upon an awareness of changing demographics of the national workforce, the challenges of employment equity, the dynamics of stereotyping, and workers' changing values. Diversity training is aimed at teaching such skills as conducting performance appraisals with people from different cultures and teaching male supervisors how to coach female employees toward better career opportunities. As for any proposed program, a thorough needs analysis is the first step. All of the diverse dimensions—race, gender, age, and so on—should be considered in the design of such a program.[45]

Connaught Laboratories has won a host of awards for its diversity training program. About 800 employees participated in a three-hour program that covered such topics as government policies, trends in demographics, terminology, designated groups, and the benefits of a new work environment. Managers attended a one-day workshop on learning to manage diversity.

Organizations that have been successful with diversity training realize that it is a long-term process that requires the highest level of skill. Ineffective training in this area can be very damaging and can create more problems than its solves.

Global Training

The global business environment demands employees who can work effectively across national and cultural boundaries. Training should be devoted to giving employees an overview of cultural differences as they relate to customer service. The extent to which organizations have gone international will determine the emphasis given to special training. Canadian Airlines, for example, went from a domestic airline that offered just a few flights across the Pacific to a full-fledged airline serving approximately two dozen countries.

Another important aspect of global training is the training of executives. The major international corporations have special programs for personnel who are assigned to overseas operations. These individuals, who are referred to as expatriates, require training in several areas in order to perform their assignments successfully. The training program for expatriates will be discussed in detail in Chapter 17.

The Learning Organization

Changes such as increasing globalization, competition, and the explosion of technology have an obvious impact on training. Organizations have to learn faster and better—and continuously. As CIBC acknowledged, learning cannot be limited to a place in time or space. Learning to learn and learning to change must become a conscious process for organizations. The commitment of the learning organization to the process of continuous learning is reflected in a strong vision of the future of the organization; in management support for learning and improvement; in the creation of a climate that encourages the sharing of ideas; in the provision of opportunities for job rotation, cross-functional, and self-directed work teams; and in the use of technology to aid information flow.[46] Training, an integral component of this process, incorporates components of on-the-job training such as mentoring and learning by doing. Employees who learn new skills, knowledge, and abilities are respected and rewarded in multiple ways. Organizations practising these principles have improved productivity, higher customer satisfaction, increased market share, and more efficient and satisfied employees. Continuous learning is a good investment.

SUMMARY

Training begins with orientation and continues throughout an employee's service with an organization. By participating in a formal orientation program, employees acquire the knowledge, skills, and abilities that increase the probabilities of their success with the organization. To make an orientation effective there should be close cooperation between the HR department and other departments in all phases of the program, from initial planning through follow-up and evaluation.

Today we find that organizations cover a broad range of subjects and involve personnel at all levels, from orientation through management development. In addition to providing training needed for effective job performance, employers offer training in such areas as personal growth and wellness.

In order to have effective training programs, the systems approach is recommended. The approach consists of five phases: (1) needs analysis, (2) setting objectives, (3) program design, (4) transfer, and (5) evaluation. The first step includes the assessment of training needs through an analysis of the organization, a task analysis, and a person analysis. This analysis lends to the formulation of instructional objectives and influences the design of the program. Trainees must be prepared and motivated to learn. The efficacy of the training can be increased by applying psychological principles of learning before, during, and after the program. The effectiveness of the program must then be measured. When all five phases are viewed as important, the chances for having a successful training program are greatly increased.

In the training of nonmanagerial personnel, a wide variety of methods are available. On-the-job training is one of the most commonly used methods because it provides the advantage of hands-on experience and an opportunity to build a relationship between supervisor and employee. In addition to on-the-job training, employers have several off-the-job methods that they can use. These include the conference or discussion method, classroom training, programmed instruction, computer-based training, simulation, closed-circuit TV, teletraining, and interactive videodisk. All of these methods can make a contribution to the training effort with relatively little cost because of the number of trainees who can be accommodated.

Apprenticeship training and internships are especially effective because they provide both on- and off-the-job experiences.

The training and development of managers is big business. As with nonmanagerial personnel, a wide variety of training methods are used for developing managers. On-the-job experiences include coaching, understudy assignment, job rotation, lateral transfer, project and committee assignments, and staff meetings. Off-the-job experiences include analysis of case studies, in-basket training, leaderless group discussion, management games, role playing, laboratory training, and behaviour modelling.

Special training programs emerge on the HR scene with great regularity. While there is an infinite number of possible topics, we discuss those that are currently popular—namely, education in basic subjects (reading, writing, grammar, spelling, and mathematics), team training, training for diversity, and global training.

KEY TERMS

apprenticeship training

behaviour modelling (interaction

  management)orientation

behaviour modification

computer-assisted instruction (CAI)

computer-managed instruction (CMI)

cooperative training

in-basket technique

instructional objectives

internship programs

leaderless group discussions

on-the-job training (OJT)

orientation

organizational analysis

person analysis

reinforcement

task analysis

transfer of training

DISCUSSION QUESTIONS

1. Why is employee orientation an important process? What are some benefits of a properly conducted orientation program?
2. A new employee is likely to be anxious the first few days on the job.
    a. What are some possible causes of this anxiety?
    b. How may the anxiety be reduced?

3. What economic, social, and political forces have made employee training even more important than in the past?
4. What analyses should be made to determine the training needs of an organization? List the benefits of doing a needs analysis.
5. Compare computer-assisted instruction with the lecture method in regard to the way they involve the different psychological principles of transfer effectiveness.
6. Suppose that you are the manager of an accounts receivable unit in a large company. You are switching to a new system of billing and recordkeeping and need to train your three supervisors and 28 employees in the new procedures. What training method(s) would you use? Why?
7. Participants in a training course are often asked to evaluate the course by means of a questionnaire. What are the pros and cons of this approach? Are there better ways of evaluating a course?

CASE: Orientation of New Employees at Eyetech

Eyetech opened its first optical store in October 1983. At the forefront of the revolution in the eyeware industry, Eyetech has at each store an on-site computerized and automated optical laboratory that fabricates prescription glasses upon request. Customers can select their frames and watch as their lenses are being made in the laboratory. Each Eyetech store employs about twenty employees who perform a variety of jobs.

Because of the company's rapid growth, Michael Wong was recently promoted to the position of store manager of a new facility. Like all new store managers, Wong will receive a week of managerial training. This training stresses human relations skills and customer services. One training session in particular discusses the importance of first impressions and how initial employees' beliefs and experiences influence their job behaviour. The training instructor emphasizes the importance of establishing a strong employee–supervisor relationship through a well-managed orientation program. The positive work attitudes that Eyetech's strong employee relations program promotes are especially important in light of the optical industry's growing emphasis on service.

Eyetech has a formal employee orientation program. The HR department is responsible for introducing new employees to the company and its benefits, but store managers are required to orient all new employees to store operations and their individual jobs. Supervisors are granted considerable freedom to perform this task.

The new facility is scheduled to open in two weeks. As a new store manager, Wong is concerned about meeting new employees and getting them started on the right foot.

Questions
1. Is Wong's concern with the orientation program a legitimate one?
2. What should be covered during the orientation? How should the orientation be designed?
3. What principles of training system effectiveness should be applied to the orientation process?

Training Lists

As this chapter illustrated, there are many ways to learn knowledge, skills, and abilities. You as individuals have learned many things in formal settings, but you have also learned a lot by reading, observing, and asking questions—activities that correspond to those that occur in on-the-job training.

Make a list of all the training and education you have received since high school. Under the heading "Formal," list those courses and programs you have taken as a student or trainee, ie., learning conducted by an organization. Under the heading "Informal," list all the KSA you have taught yourself by reading, observing, listening to tapes, or watching videos. For example, you may have taught yourself word processing, cooking, or effective-listening skills.

Formal

_____

_____

_____

_____

_____

_____

_____

_____

_____

_____

_____

_____

_____

_____

_____

_____

_____

_____

Informal

_____

_____

_____

_____

_____

_____

_____

_____

_____

_____

_____

_____

_____

_____

_____

_____

_____

_____

_____

_____

_____

_____

_____

_____

Now, refer to the résumé you have prepared, and make any additions necessary.

NOTES AND REFERENCES

1. J. Bowsher, "Making the Call on the CEO," *Training and Development Journal* (May 1990): 65–66.

2. McIntyre, D. *Training and Development: 1993 Policies, Practices, and Expenditures*, Conference Board of Canada report, Toronto, 128–194.

3. W. Lilley, "Banking on Equity," *Report on Business Magazine*, April 1995, 67.

4. For an interesting discussion of the importance of orientation for younger employees, see James W. Sheehy, "New Work Ethic Is Frightening," *Personnel Journal* 69, no. 6 (June 1990): 51–55.

5. M. Belcourt, and P. Wright, *Performance Management through Training and Development*, Nelson Canada Series in Human Resources Management (Series Editor, M. Belcourt) (Scarborough: Nelson Canada, 1995).

6. Canadian Labour Market and Productivity Centre, *National Training Survey 1991*, Executive Summary, Ottawa, 1993.

7. Jill Cassner-Lotto and Associates, *Successful Training Strategies* (San Francisco: Jossey-Bass, 1988), 28–36. See also William Wiggenhorn, "Motorola U: When Training Becomes an Education," *Harvard Business Review* 68, no. 4 (July-August 1990): 71–83, a comprehensive discussion of how Motorola's program widened from emphasis on specific techniques to graduate work in computer-integrated manufacturing. For an account of how four successful companies handle training in today's fast-paced environment, see Linda Thornburg, "Training in a Changing World," *HR Magazine* 37, no.8 (August 1992): 44–47; see also Fred R. Bleakley, "Training Women for Tough Guy's Jobs," *The Wall Street Journal* December 28, 1994, B1.

8. Scott A. Tannenbaum and Gary Yukl, "Training and Development in Work Organizations," in Mark R. Rosenzweig and Lyman W. Porter, eds., *Annual Review of Psychology* (Palo Alto, CA: Annual Reviews, Inc., 1992), 401. See also Craig Eric Schneier, Craig J. Russell, Richard W. Beatty, and Lloyd S. Baird, *Training and Development Sourcebook*, 2nd ed. (Amherst, MA: Human Resource Development Press, 1993). This training classic contains more than 50 articles written by leading professionals in the field.

9. Robert F. Mager, *Preparing Instructional Objectives* (Belmont, CA: David S. Lake, 1984), vi. See also Robert F. Mager, *Making Instruction Work or Skillbloomers* (Belmont, CA.: David S. Lake, 1988), and his *What Every Manager Should Know about Training* (Belmont, CA: Lake Publishing, 1992).

10. P. Wright and M. Belcourt, "Costing Training Activity: A Decision Maker's Dilemma," *Management Decision* 33, no. 2 (February 1995).

11. M. Belcourt and P. Wright, "Equity in Training," Human Resources Division, *Administrative Sciences Association of Canada Conference Proceedings* 15, no. 9, 1995.

12. D.L. Georgenson, "The Problem of Transfer Calls for Partnership," *Training and Development Journal* 36, no. 10 (1982).

13. T.T. Bladwin, and R.J. Magjuka, "Organizational Training and Signals of Importance: Linking Pretraining Perceptions to Intentions to Transfer," *Human Resource Development Quarterly* (Spring 1991): 25–36.

14. Phillip C. Grant, "Employee Motivation: The Key to Training," *Supervisory Management* 34, no. 6 (June 1989). See also Debra J. Cohen, "What Motivates Trainees?" *Training and Development Journal* 44, no. 1 (November 1990): 91–93.

15. *The Journal of Applied Psychology* is an excellent source of research studies of this type. Its articles are indexed in *Psychological Abstracts*.

16. Les Donaldson and Edward E. Scannell, *Human Resource Development: The New Trainers Guide* (Reading, MA: Addison-Wesley, 1983), 142–151.

17. Belcourt and Wright, *Performance Management*.

18. G.P. Latham and C.A. Frayne, "Increasing Job Attendance through Training in Self-Management: A Review of Two Studies," *Journal of Applied Psychology* 74 (1989): 411–416.

19. D.L. Kirkpatrick, *Evaluating Training Programs: The Four Levels* (San Francisco: Berrett-Koehler Publishers, 1995).

20. For other suggestions on successful training, see Carol Haig, "A Line Manager's Guide to Training," *Personnel Journal* 63, no. 10 (October 1984): 42–45; and Leslie A. Bryan, "Making the Manager a Better Trainer," *Supervisory Management* 29, no. 4 (April 1984): 28.

21. J. Kevin Ford and Steven P. Wroten, "Introducing New Methods for Conducting Training Evaluation and for Linking Training Evaluation to Program Redesign," *Personnel Psychology* 37, no. 4 (Winter 1984): 651–665. See also Paul R. Erickson, "Evaluating Training Results," *Training and Development Journal* 44, no. 1 (January 1990): 57–59.

22. A.P. Carnevale and E.R. Schulz, "Evaluation Practices," *Training and Development* 44 (1990): S23–S29. See also Anthony R. Montebello and Maureen Haga, "To Justify Training Test, Test Again," *Personnel Journal* 73, no. 1 (January 1994): 83–87; Jack E. Smith and Sharon Merchant, "Using Competency Exams for Evaluating Training," *Training and Development Journal* 44, no. 8 (August 1990): 65f.

23. Irwin L. Goldstein, *Training in Organizations: Needs Assessment, Development, and Evaluation*, 3rd ed. (Monterey, CA: Brooks/Cole, 1993), 23.

24. Robert F. Sullivan and Donald C. Miklas, "On-the-Job Training That Works," *Training and Development Journal* 39, no. 5 (May 1985): 118–121.

25. See also Marcia Ann Pulich, "The Basics of On-the-Job Training and Development," *Supervisory Management* 29, no. 2 (January 1984): 7–11; William J. Rothwell and H.C. Kazanas, "Planned OJT Is Production OJT," *Training and Development Journal* 44, no. 10 (October 1990): 53–56. For a comprehensive discussion of training in small business, see Sarah Vickerstaff, "The Training Needs of Small Firms, *Human Resource Management Journal* 2, no.3 (Spring 1992): 1–15.

26. B. Raybould, "Solving Human Performance Problems with Computers: A Case Study: Building an Electronic Performance Support System," *Performance and Instruction* (November-December, 1990): 4–14.

27. B. Gebber, "Help! The Rise of Performance Support Systems," *Training Magazine* 28, no. 12 (December 1991): 23–29.

28. K. Ruyle, "Developing Intelligent Job Aids," *Technical and Skills Training* (February/March 1991): 9–14.

29. Judith Valente and Bridget O'Brian, "Airline Cockpits Are No Place to Solo," *The Wall Street Journal,* August 2, 1989, B1.

30. Tannenbaum and Yukl, "Training and Development," 408.

31. Ralph E. Ganger, "Computer Based Training Improves Job Performance," *Personnel Journal* 68, no. 6 (June 1989): 116–123. See also Carolyn Spitz, "Multimedia Training at Hewlett-Packard," *Training and Development* 46, no. 6 (June 1992): 39–41; Ralph Ganger, "Computer Based Training Works," *Personnel Journal* 69, no. 9 (September 1990): 85–91.

32. Walter W. Wager, A. Stuart Polkinghorne, and Roger Powley, "Simulation: Selection and Development," *Performance Improvement Quarterly* 5, no. 2 (1992): 47–64.

33. P. Menyasz, "Job Creation, Training: Priorities for HR Minister," *Canadian HR Reporter*, November 1993.

34. Canadian Labour Market Productivity Centre, *National Training Survey*, Ottawa, 1991.

35. See Belcourt and Wright, *Performance Management*, Chapter 3, for a detailed description of the roles and programs of the three levels of government.

36. Tannenbaum and Yukl, "Training and Development," 427.

37. Ibid., 407–408. For information on some of the available games, see George C. Thornton III and Jeannette N. Cleveland, "Developing Managerial Talent through Simulation," *American Psychologist* 45, no. 2 (February 1990): 190–199.

38. R. Sharpe, "Agents of Intimidation," *The Globe and Mail*, March 28, 1995, B8.

39. Phillip J. Decker, "The Effects of Rehearsal Group Size and Video Feedback in Behaviour Modelling Training," *Personnel Psychology* 36, no. 4 (Winter 1983): 763–773. While four basic steps in behaviour modelling are normally discussed, some authors note a fifth step—the use of retention aids. See also William M. Fox, "Getting the Most from Behaviour Modelling," *National Productivity Review* 7 (Summer 1988): 238–45.

40. Stephen Wehrenberg and Robert Kuhnle, "How Training through Behaviour Modelling Works," *Personnel Journal* 59, no. 7 (July 1980): 576–580; Herbert H. Meyer and Michael S. Raich, "An Objective Evaluation of a Behaviour Modelling Training Program," *Personnel Psychology* 36, no. 4 (Winter 1983): 755–761.

41. G. Geis, *As Training Moves toward the Next Decade* (Toronto: Ontario Training Corporation, 1991).

42. Richard G. Zalman, "The Basics of In-House Skill Training," *HR Magazine* 36, no. 2 (February 1991): 74–78. For a detailed account of the programs of two companies, see Patricia L. May, Sinclair E. Hugh, and Edward A. Quesada, "Back to Basics," *Personnel Journal* 69, no. 10 (October 1990): 62–71. See also Patrick J. O'Connor, "Getting Down to Basics," *Training and Development* 47, no. 7 (July 1993): 62–64; Edward E. Gordon, Judith A. Ponticel, and Ronald R. Morgan, *Closing the Literacy Gap in American Business: A Guide for Trainers and Human Resource Specialists* (New York: Quorum Books, 1991).

43. "Case Studies in Literacy," *Canadian Business Review* 18, no. 1 (Spring 1991).

44. Tannenbaum and Yukl, "Training and Development," 430–432. See also D. Keith Denton, "Multiskilled Teams Replace Old Systems," *HR Magazine* 37, no. 9 (September 1992): 48–50; R. Glenn Ray, Jeff Hines, and Dave Wilcox, "Training Internal Facilitators," *Training and Development* 48, no. 11 (November 1994): 45–48; and Paul Froiland, "Who's Getting Trained?" *Training* 30, no. 10 (October 1993): 53–60. A special section in this article is devoted to "The teaming of America."

45. Ann Perkins Delatte and Larry Baytos, "Guidelines for Successful Diversity Training," *Training* 30, no. 1 (January 1993): 55–60. See also Joyce E. Santora, "Kinney Shoe Steps into Diversity," *Personnel Journal* 70, no. 9 (September 1991): 72ff.

46. J. Kremer-Bennet and M.J. O'Brien, "The Building Blocks of the Learning Organization," *Training* 31, no. 6 (June 1994): 41–49.

Chapter 9

Career Development

T*he functions of human resources management that we have discussed so far have a fairly long history. Beginning in the 1960s, more and more employers recognized the need of employees for satisfying careers and thus established programs that would enable employees to attain their personal goals within the organization. By the 1980s, the emphasis had changed: organizational career development was seen as a tool for addressing business needs in a vastly changed corporate environment. In the 1990s, the focus is on a balance between the two. Organizational career development is now viewed as a strategic process in which maximizing an individual's career potential is a way of enhancing the success of the organization as a whole.[1]*

Increased competition for promotion, constant innovation in technology, pressures for equal employment opportunities, corporate right-sizing and restructuring, globalization of the North American economy, and employees' desire to get the most out of their careers are all major forces pushing organizations to offer career development programs. The desire of employers to make better use of their employees' knowledge and skills and to retain those who are valuable to the organization are also important considerations. In this chapter, we will examine career development as an HRM function and provide some suggestions that readers may consider in regard to their own career development. In addition, the Career Counsel feature at the end of each chapter provides the student with a comprehensive career planning package.

Phases of a Career Development Program

Organizations have traditionally engaged in human resources planning and development. As we noted in Chapter 4, this activity involves charting the moves of large numbers of employees through various positions in an organization and identifying future staffing needs. Career development programs, with their greater emphasis on the individual, introduce a personalized aspect to the process.

A common approach to establishing a career development program is to integrate it with the existing HR functions and structures in the organization. Integrating the HR program with the career development program reinforces both programs. Figure 9-1 illustrates how HR structures relate to some of the essential aspects of the career development process. For example, in planning careers, employees need organizational information—information that strategic planning, forecasting, succession planning, and skills inventories can provide. Similarly, as they obtain information about themselves and use it in career planning, employees need to know how management views their performance and the career paths within the organization.[2]

objective

Determining Individual and Organizational Needs

A career development program should be viewed as a dynamic process that attempts to meet the needs of managers, their subordinates, and the organization. Individual employees are responsible for initiating their own career planning. It is up to them to identify their knowledge, skills, abilities, interests, and values, and to seek out information about career options so that they can set goals and develop career plans. Managers should encourage subordinates to take responsibility for their own careers, offering continuing assistance in the form of feedback on individual performance,

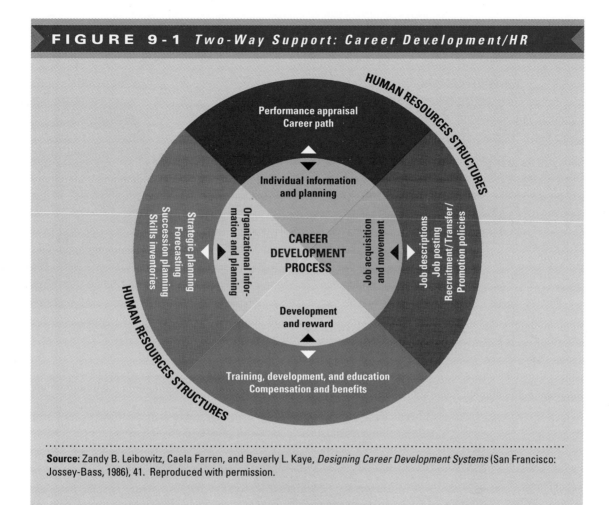

FIGURE 9-1 *Two-Way Support: Career Development/HR*

HUMAN RESOURCES STRUCTURES

Performance appraisal
Career path

Individual information
and planning

Strategic planning
Forecasting
Succession planning
Skills inventories

Organizational infor-
mation and planning

**CAREER
DEVELOPMENT
PROCESS**

Job acquisition
and movement

Job descriptions
Job posting
Recruitment/Transfer/
Promotion policies

Development
and reward

Training, development, and education
Compensation and benefits

HUMAN RESOURCES STRUCTURES

Source: Zandy B. Leibowitz, Caela Farren, and Beverly L. Kaye, *Designing Career Development Systems* (San Francisco: Jossey-Bass, 1986), 41. Reproduced with permission.

information about the organization, job information, and information about career opportunities that might be of interest. The organization is responsible for supplying information about its mission, policies, and plans, as well as for providing support for employee self-assessment, training, and development. Significant career growth can occur when individual initiative combines with organizational opportunity. Career development programs benefit managers by giving them increased skill in managing their own careers, greater retention of valued employees, increased understanding of the organization, and enhanced reputations as people-developers. As with other HR programs, the inauguration of a career development program should be based on the organization's needs as well.

Assessment of needs should take a variety of forms (surveys, informal group discussions, interviews, etc.) and should involve personnel from different groups, such as new employees, managers, plateaued employees, designated groups, and technical and professional employees. Identifying the needs and problems of these groups provides the starting point for the organization's career development efforts. As shown in Figure 9-2, organizational needs should be linked with individual career

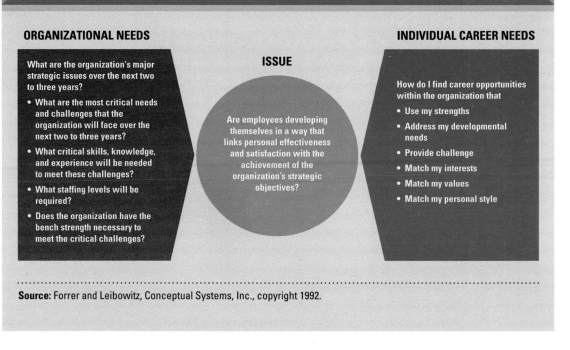

FIGURE 9-2 *Linking Organizational and Individual Needs*

ORGANIZATIONAL NEEDS

- What are the organization's major strategic issues over the next two to three years?
- What are the most critical needs and challenges that the organization will face over the next two to three years?
- What critical skills, knowledge, and experience will be needed to meet these challenges?
- What staffing levels will be required?
- Does the organization have the bench strength necessary to meet the critical challenges?

ISSUE

Are employees developing themselves in a way that links personal effectiveness and satisfaction with the achievement of the organization's strategic objectives?

INDIVIDUAL CAREER NEEDS

How do I find career opportunities within the organization that

- Use my strengths
- Address my developmental needs
- Provide challenge
- Match my interests
- Match my values
- Match my personal style

Source: Forrer and Leibowitz, Conceptual Systems, Inc., copyright 1992.

needs in a way that joins personal effectiveness and satisfaction of employees with the achievement of the organization's strategic objectives.

objective

Creating Favourable Conditions

While a career development program requires many special processes and techniques, which we will describe later, some basic conditions must be present if it is to be successful. These conditions create a favourable climate for the program.

Management Support

If career development is to succeed, it must receive the complete support of top management. Ideally, senior line managers and HR department managers should work together to design and implement a career development system. The system should reflect the goals and culture of the organization, and the HR philosophy should be woven throughout. An HR philosophy can provide employees with a clear set of expectations and directions for their own career development. For a program to be effective, managerial personnel at all levels must be trained in the fundamentals of job design, performance appraisal, career planning, and counselling.

Goal Setting

Before individuals can engage in meaningful career planning, they must not only have an awareness of the organization's philosophy, but they must also have a clear understanding of the organization's more immediate goals. Otherwise they may plan for personal change and growth without knowing if or how their own goals match those of the organization. For example, if the technology of a business is changing and new skills are needed, will the organization retrain to meet this need or else hire new talent? Is there growth, stability, or decline in the number of employees needed? How will turnover affect this need? Clearly, an organizational plan that answers these kinds of questions is essential to individual career planning.

Changes in HRM Policies

To ensure that its career development program will be effective, an organization may need to alter its current HRM policies. For example, a policy of lifelong job rotation can counteract obsolescence and maintain employee flexibility. Another policy that can aid development involves job transfers and promotions.

A **transfer** is the placement of an employee in another job for which the duties, responsibilities, status, and remuneration are approximately equal to those of the previous job. A transfer may require the employee to change work group, workplace, work shift, or organizational unit, or even to move to another geographic area. Transfers make it possible for an organization to place its employees in jobs where there is a greater need for their services and where they can acquire new knowledge and skills. A downward transfer, or demotion, moves an individual into a lower-level job; although it can provide developmental opportunities, such a move is ordinarily considered unfavourable, especially by the individual who is demoted.

A promotion is a change of assignment to a job at a higher level in the organization. The new job normally provides an increase in pay and status and demands more skill or carries more responsibility. Promotions enable an organization to utilize the skills and abilities of its personnel more effectively, and the opportunity to gain a promotion serves as an incentive for good performance. The two principal criteria for determining promotions are *merit* and *seniority*. Often the problem is to determine how much consideration to give to each factor.

Transfers and promotions require the individual to adjust to new job demands and usually to a different work environment. A transfer that involves moving to a new location within Canada or abroad places greater demands on employees, because it requires them to adapt not only to a new work environment but also to new living conditions. Those with families have the added responsibility of helping family members adjust to the new living arrangements. Even though some employers provide all types of **relocation services**—including moving, help in selling a home, cultural orientation, and language training—there is always some loss of productive time. Pretransfer training, whether in regard to job skills or lifestyle, has been suggested as one of the most effective ways to reduce lost productivity.

Many organizations now provide **outplacement services** to help terminated employees find a job somewhere else. These services can be used to enhance a productive employee's career, as well as to terminate an employee who is unproductive. If an organization cannot meet its career development responsibilities to its productive workers, HR policy should assist them in finding more suitable career opportunities elsewhere.

Publicizing the Program

The career development program should be publicized throughout the organization. The objectives and opportunities can be communicated in several ways, including the following:

Transfer
Placement of an individual in another job for which the duties, responsibilities, status, and remuneration are approximately equal to those of the previous job.

Relocation services
Services provided to an employee who is transferred to a new location, which include help in moving, selling of a home, cultural orientation, and language training.

Outplacement services
Services provided by organizations to help terminated employees get a new job.

1. Publication in newsletters
2. Inclusion in employee manuals
3. Publication in a special career guide or as part of career planning workshops
4. Inclusion in videotaped or live presentations
5. Inclusion in computer-assisted programs

At the very least, a manual that spells out the basic job families, career progression possibilities, and related requirements should be given to each manager and made available to every employee.

objective

Inventorying Job Opportunities

While career development usually involves many different types of training experiences (as discussed in the preceding chapter), the most important of these experiences occur on the job. It is here that the individual is exposed to a wide variety of situations, and it is here that contributions are made to the organization.

Job Competencies

It is important for an organization to study its jobs carefully to identify and assign weights to the knowledge and skills that each one requires. This can be achieved with job analysis and evaluation systems such as those used in compensation programs. The system used at Sears measures three basic competencies for each job: *know-how*, *problem solving*, and *accountability*. Know-how is broken down into three types of job knowledge: technical, managerial, and human relations. Problem solving and accountability also have several dimensions. Scores for each of these three major competencies are assigned to each job, and a total value is computed for each job. For any planned job transfer, the amount of increase (or decrease) the next job represents in each of the skill areas, as well as in the total point values, can be computed. This information is then used to make certain that a transfer to a different job is a move that requires growth on the part of the employee.

Sears designs career development paths to provide the following experiences: (1) an increase in at least one skill area on each new assignment, (2) an increase of at least 10 percent in total points on each new assignment, and (3) assignments in several different functional areas.[3]

Job Progression

Once the skill demands of jobs are identified and weighted according to their importance, it is then possible to plan **job progression**. A new employee with no experience is typically assigned to a "starting job." After a period of time in that job, the employee can be promoted to one that requires more knowledge and/or skill. While most organizations concentrate on developing job progression for managerial, professional, and technical jobs, progression can be developed for all categories of jobs. These job progressions then can serve as a basis for developing **career paths**—the lines of advancement within an organization—for individuals.

Figure 9-3 illustrates a typical line of advancement in the human resources department of a large multinational corporation. It is apparent that one must be prepared to move geographically in order to advance very far in HRM. This would also be true of other career fields within the organization.

Job progression
The different jobs that a new employee experiences, ranging from a starting job to successive jobs that require more knowledge and/or skill. (10)

Career paths
Lines of advancement within an organization in an occupational field.

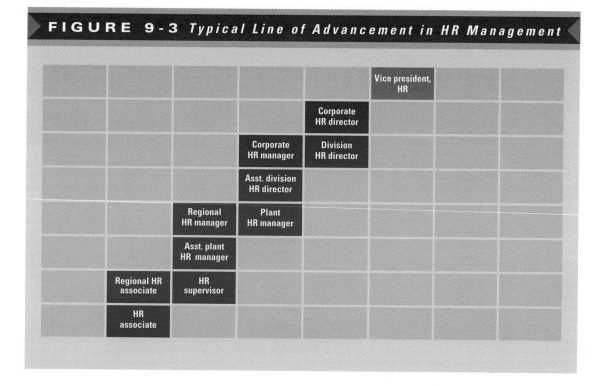

FIGURE 9-3 *Typical Line of Advancement in HR Management*

Dual Career Paths

Not too long ago, moving upward in an organization meant that an employee would eventually become a manager and perform those functions that are typically associated with a managerial position. This was the only way to recognize the worth of an individual to the organization and to compensate the outstanding scientist, technical specialist, or professional person. It became apparent that there must be another way to compensate such individuals without elevating them to a management position. The solution was to develop dual career paths or tracks that provide for progression in special areas such as finance, marketing, and engineering with compensation that is comparable to that received by managers at different levels.[4] Many organizations have developed dual career paths in order to keep employees with valuable knowledge and skills performing important tasks that are as important to the organization as those performed by managers. Figure 9-4 shows the dual career path available to information system specialists once they have attained a level 3 position.

Training Needs

There are likely to be points in one's career path where training beyond that received on the job is essential. Such points should be identified and appropriate training made available to prevent progress from being impaired by a lack of knowledge or skills. Because the training needs of individual employees differ, these needs must be monitored closely.

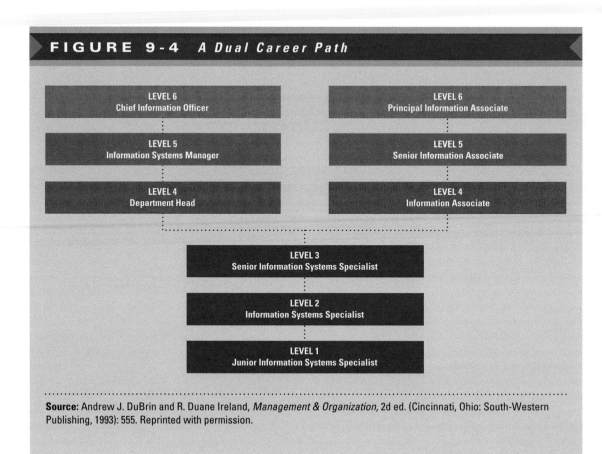

FIGURE 9-4 *A Dual Career Path*

Source: Andrew J. DuBrin and R. Duane Ireland, *Management & Organization,* 2d ed. (Cincinnati, Ohio: South-Western Publishing, 1993): 555. Reprinted with permission.

Gauging Employee Potential

Probably the most important objective of any career development program is to provide the tools and techniques that will enable employees to gauge their potential for success in a career path. This objective may be achieved in various ways, all of which naturally involve the active participation of the employees themselves. Informal counselling by HR staff and supervisors is used widely. Many organizations give their employees information on educational assistance, employment equity programs and policies, salary administration, and job requirements. Career planning workbooks and workshops are also popular means of helping employees identify their potential and the strength of their interests.

Career Planning Workbooks
Several organizations have put together workbooks to guide their employees individually through systematic self-assessment of values, interests, abilities, goals, and personal development plans. Ontario Hydro uses assessment tools such as the Barbara Moses Career Planning Workbooks, the Holland Self-Directed Search, and the Strong Campbell Interest Inventory. A computer-based program called Discover contains a self-assessment component that provides information on occupations,

skill requirements, and educational institutions. Employees can also make use of a reference library that contains books on careers and job-search strategies.

Some organizations prefer to use workbooks written for the general public. Popular ones include *Where Do I Go from Here with My Life?* by John Crystal and Richard N. Bolles—a workbook follow-up to Bolles's *What Colour Is Your Parachute?* Andrew H. Souerwine's *Career Strategies: Planning for Personal Growth* and John Holland's *Self-Directed Search* are also used frequently.[5] These same books are recommended to students seeking assistance in planning their careers.

Career Planning Workshops

Workshops offer experiences similar to those provided by workbooks. However, they have the advantage of giving employees an opportunity to compare and discuss their attitudes, concerns, and plans with others in similar situations. Some workshops focus on current job performance and development plans. Others deal with broader life and career plans and values.

As mentioned earlier, employees should be encouraged to assume responsibility for their own careers. A career workshop can help them do that. It can also help them learn how to make career decisions, set career goals, create career options, seek career planning information, and at the same time build confidence and self-esteem.[6]

Career Counselling

Career counselling involves talking with employees about their current job activities and performance, personal and career interests and goals, personal skills, and suitable career development objectives. While some organizations make counselling a part of the annual performance appraisal, career counselling is usually voluntary.

Many organizations have designated career counsellors who are available to employees on a full-time basis. When an active counsellor is not on staff, the manager may assume the role of counsellor. Resource centres may be established as another means of providing employees with information. The Public Service Commission has a Career Resource Centre (CRC) that assists employees who are making career transitions. The goal of CRC is to promote a self-directed approach to career planning by providing surplus employees with career-related information and tools. The CRC reference library contains extensive material on change management, résumé writing, job-search and interview techniques, career planning and management, stress management, self-assessment, and financial management. This material can be accessed through books, videos, and interactive computer programs.[7]

As employees approach retirement, they may be encouraged to participate in preretirement programs, which often include counselling along with other helping activities. Career counselling may be provided by the HR staff, superiors, specialized staff counsellors, or outside professionals. Preretirement programs will be discussed in Chapter 13.

Career counselling

Process of discussing with employees their current job activities and performance, their personal job and career goals, their personal skills, and suitable career development objectives.

Career Development Programs for a Diverse Workforce

Organizations differ widely in the types of career development programs they offer. Some organizations provide for all levels of employees formal programs that cover a broad array of topics. Others have offerings limited to career counselling incorporated into annual performance reviews. The more extensive career development programs also frequently include programs geared to special groups, such as management development programs or programs for women, minorities, or dual-career couples. Let us examine some of these special programs more closely.

Management Development Programs

objective

Contemporary organizations must have competent managers who can cope with the growing complexity of the problems affecting their operations. A formal management development program helps to ensure that developmental experiences both on and off the job are coordinated and in line with the individual's and the organization's needs.

Inventorying Management Requirements and Talent

An important part of a management development program is an inventory of managerial positions. The inventory directs attention to the developmental needs of employees both in their present jobs and in managerial jobs to which they may be promoted. An equally important part of the program is identifying employees who may be groomed as replacements for managers who are reassigned, retire, or otherwise vacate a position. Replacement charts, discussed in Chapter 4, provide the information needed to fill vacancies in key positions.

The Role of Managers

Identifying and developing talent in individuals is a role that all managers should take seriously. As they conduct formal appraisals, they should be concerned with their subordinates' potential for managerial jobs and should encourage their growth in that direction. In addition to immediate superiors, there should be others in the organization who have the power to evaluate, nominate, and sponsor employees who show promise. Companies that emphasize developing human assets as well as turning a profit typically have the talent they need and some to spare. Companies such as Xerox, Procter & Gamble, and General Motors have inadvertently become "academy" companies that provide a source of talented managers for organizations that lack good management development programs of their own. Companies that invest heavily in training and development programs are often bitterly disappointed when their trained talent leaves, an issue discussed in Ethics in HRM.

Use of Assessment Centres

Assessment centre

Process by which individuals are evaluated as they participate in a series of situations that resemble what they might be called upon to handle on the job.

Pioneered in the mid-1950s by Dr. Douglas Bray and his associates at AT&T, corporate-operated assessment centres are considered one of the most effective methods for evaluating personnel. An **assessment centre** is a process (not a place) by which individuals are evaluated as they participate in a series of situations that resemble what they might be called upon to handle on the job. The the assessment centre can enhance an organization's ability not only to select employees who will perform successfully in management positions but also to promote the development of skills employees need for their current position. These centres may use in-basket exercises, role playing, and other approaches to employee development that we discussed in Chapter 8.

The schedule of the various activities undertaken by one manager in a provincial government department is given in Highlights in HRM 1. Participation in these

ETHICS IN HRM

WHOSE CAREER IS IT?

Organizations like Procter & Gamble and IBM invest a great deal of time and money in developing their professional sales staff and management personnel. Similarly, the federal government offers up to six months of language training, tuition-paid university courses, and skills training of several weeks duration to new university recruits within their first two years on the job.

Other organizations refuse to invest in the long-term development of their employees; they cite statistics suggesting that over one-third of university recruits will quit within the first year, and argue, moreover, that other corporations will raid these highly trained personnel.

Do employees who have undertaken extensive development programs at the employer's expense have an obligation to remain with the employer so that the company can realize a return on its investment?

activities provides samples of behaviour that are representative of what is required for advancement. At the end of the assessment-centre period, the assessors' observations are combined and integrated to develop an overall picture of the strengths and needs of the participants. A report is normally submitted to top management, and feedback is given to the participants.

Increasing attention is being given to the validity of assessment-centre procedures. As with employment tests, the assessments provided must be valid. Before the assessment centre is run, the characteristics or dimensions to be studied should be determined through job analyses. The exercises used in the centre should reflect the job for which the person is being evaluated (i.e., the exercises should have content validity). While the assessment-centre methodology lends itself readily to content validation, predictive validity has also been observed in many instances. A strong positive relationship is found between assessments and future performance on the job.[8]

The Public Service Commission has undertaken the challenge of identifying and selecting the best leadership and management talent through assessment centres developed and operated by the Personnel Psychology Centre (PPC), a division within the Public Service Commission. The PPC helps managers identify highly competent individuals who will be able to develop and implement federal government policies and programs. The PPC is an internationally recognized leader in personnel assessment.

While assessment centres have proved quite valuable in identifying managerial talent and in helping with the development of individuals, it should be noted that the method tends to favour those who are strong in interpersonal skills and have the

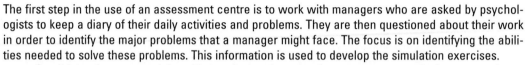

HIGHLIGHTS IN HRM

1 THE PERSONNEL PSYCHOLOGY ASSESSMENT CENTRE

The first step in the use of an assessment centre is to work with managers who are asked by psychologists to keep a diary of their daily activities and problems. They are then questioned about their work in order to identify the major problems that a manager might face. The focus is on identifying the abilities needed to solve these problems. This information is used to develop the simulation exercises.

Candidates for managerial positions, playing the role of a manager, are asked to respond to a series of letters, memos, variance reports, etc. They then present, in oral and written forms, the approach they would use to solve the problem. These approaches include the establishment of priorities, plans, solutions, and decisions.

The selection board, composed of the hiring manager, at least one outside manager, and a staffing officer, is trained to understand the simulation and the various effective approaches. The candidates are evaluated on how well they get their ideas across, and on how well they plan, monitor, and control programs.

Everyone involved strongly identifies with the realistic nature of the simulation. Candidates get so involved in the simulation that they forget it is a test, and managers feel they can actually visualize these people at work. Even unsuccessful candidates claim that they learn about themselves in the process.

Source: The Personnel Psychology Centre, Public Service Commission, Government of Canada, Ottawa.

ability to influence others. Some individuals find it difficult to perform at their best in a situation that for them is as threatening as taking a test. The manner in which assessment-centre personnel conduct the exercises and provide feedback to the participants will play a major role in determining how individuals react to the experience.

Management positions are the usual targets of assessment centres. However, adaptations of the assessment-centre method can be used for nonmanagerial positions, such as those in sales. One adaptation involves playing videotaped scenarios for applicants, then using a multiple-choice test to find out how they would respond to the situations depicted.

Determining Individual Development Needs

Because the requirements of each management position and the qualifications of the person performing it are different, no two managers will have identical developmental needs. For one individual, self-development may consist of developing the ability to write reports, give talks, or lead conferences. For another, it may require learning to communicate and relate more effectively with others in the organization. Periodic performance appraisals can provide a basis for determining each manager's progress. Conferences in which these appraisals are discussed are an essential part of self-improvement efforts.

In helping individuals plan their careers, it is important for organizations to recognize that younger managers today seek meaningful training assignments that are interesting and involve challenge, responsibility, and a "piece of the action." Younger managers today also have a greater concern for the contribution that their work in the organization will make to society. Unfortunately, they are frequently given responsibilities they view as rudimentary, boring, and composed of too many "make-work" activities. Some organizations are attempting to retain young managers with high potential by offering a **fast-track program** that enables them to advance more rapidly than those with less potential. A fast-track program may allow for a relatively rapid progression—lateral transfers or promotions—through a number of managerial positions requiring exposure to different organizational functions, as well as providing opportunities to make meaningful decisions.

Mentoring

When one talks with men and women about their employment experiences, it is common to hear them mention individuals at work who influenced them. They frequently refer to immediate superiors who were especially helpful as career developers. But they also mention others at higher levels in the organization who provided guidance and support to them in the development of their careers. These executives and managers who coach, advise, and encourage employees of lesser rank are called **mentors**.

Informal mentoring goes on daily within every type of organization. Generally the mentor initiates the relationship, but sometimes an employee will approach a potential mentor for advice. Most mentoring relationships develop over time on an informal basis. However, in the 1980s there was a rapid growth of formal mentoring plans that call for the assignment of a mentor to those employees considered for upward movement in the organization. Under a good mentor, learning focuses on goals, opportunities, expectations, standards, and assistance in fulfilling one's potential.[9]

The University of Calgary adopted a low-cost approach to mentoring.[10] After a study revealed that women professors were vastly outnumbered by their male colleagues, and moving more slowly through the ranks, the Academic Women's Association developed a matching program. All new female appointees are offered the chance to be assigned a mentor, a woman who has already reached full professorship. The mentor makes the first contact; after that, most are consulted regularly about a wide range of career issues. The program is mutually beneficial in that mentors recommend their protégés for service in task forces, while the protégés, who tend to be more computer literate, assist their mentors with computer-related tasks.

Analysis of a large number of research studies revealed that the **mentoring functions** can be divided into two broad categories: *career functions* and *psychosocial functions*. The functions are listed in Figure 9-5. Career functions are those aspects of the relationship that enhance career advancement; psychosocial functions are those aspects that enhance the protégé's sense of competence, identity, and effectiveness

---

Fast-track program

Program that encourages young managers with high potential to remain with an organization by enabling them to advance more rapidly than those with less potential.

Mentors

Executives who coach, advise, and encourage individuals of lesser rank.

Mentoring functions

Functions concerned with the career advancement and psychological aspects of the person being mentored.

FIGURE 9-5 *Mentoring Functions*

CAREER FUNCTIONS	PSYCHOSOCIAL FUNCTIONS
Sponshorship	Role modelling
Exposure and visibility	Acceptance and confirmation
Coaching	Counselling
Protection	Friendship
Challenging assignments	

Source: Kathy E. Kram, *Mentoring at Work*, University of Press America, Lanham, Md., 1988. Reprinted with permission.

---

in a professional role. Both kinds of functions are viewed as critical to management development.[11]

Organizations with formal mentoring programs include Imperial Oil, Ontario Public Service, and the Bank of Montreal.[12] The Bank of Montreal is in the early stages of its mentoring program. To ensure its survival, those being mentored select their mentors. Each mentor is assigned a male and female protégé to ensure equality in the process.[13]

An alternative form of mentoring is provided by professional associations. For example, WISE (Women in Science and Engineering) or business womens' associations (which can be found in many large cities) offer opportunities for women to learn from more experienced colleagues.

Another new form of mentoring, sponsored by the MS Foundation for Women, provides an opportunity for girls aged 9 to 15 to spend a day on the job with mothers or friends. The program is designed to give girls more attention and to provide them with role career models. Many of the larger companies have participated in this program. It is hoped that through such programs girls will think more broadly in their career planning.[14]

Problems associated with mergers and the rise of the cross-cultural corporation could be ameliorated by assigning mentors to improve communication and ensure the continuity of the organizational culture. Not only have formal mentoring programs been valuable for management development, but more organizations are turning to them to help a diverse workforce move more quickly throughout the organization.

Career Development for Women

In Chapter 3, we discussed some of the current trends in the employment of women in jobs that until recently were held predominantly by men. Included among these jobs are management-level positions. Organizations are continually concerned—as a result of human rights legislation and employment equity requirements and because of the need for strong leadership—with increasing the proportion of women they employ as managers.

Professional women today assume higher-level positions in many organizations

Eliminating Barriers to Advancement

Women in management have been disadvantaged by not their exclusion from the so-called *old boy network*, an informal network of interpersonal relationships that has traditionally provided a means for senior (male) members of the organization to pass along news of advancement opportunities and other career tips to junior (male) members. Women have typically been outside the network, lacking role models to serve as mentors.

To combat the difficulty they experience in advancing to management positions, women in several organizations have developed their own *women's networks*. At the Bank of Montreal, a women's network that any female employee may join serves as a system for encouraging and fostering women's career development and for sharing information, experiences, and insights. Corporate officers are invited to regularly scheduled network meetings to discuss such matters as planning, development, and company performance. Network members view these sessions as an opportunity to let corporate officers know of women who are interested in and capable of furthering their own careers.

The advancement of women in management has been hindered by a series of sex-role stereotypes that have shaped the destiny of women and working women in particular. Fortunately, there is substantial evidence that stereotyped attitudes toward women are changing. As women pursue career goals assertively and attitudes continue to change, the climate for women in management will be even more favourable. The attitudes of younger male managers tend to be more progressive than those of older male managers. As the younger men move into positions of greater responsibility and power, their organizations should be more receptive to the advancement of women managers.

A 1993 report by Statistics Canada suggests that opportunities for women, especially those in high-paying occupations, have been increasing dramatically.[15] According to 1991 census data, the number of women in the ten highest-paying occupations surged by 53 percent in the five-year period between 1985 and 1990. During the same period, the total number of men in these occupations moved ahead by only 1 percent. The highest-paying occupations for women were judges and magistrates, physicians and surgeons, dentists, lawyers and notaries, and general managers. While these data suggest there that has been progress, there is much left to do break the "glass ceiling"—that invisible barrier of attitudes, prejudices, and "old boy" networks that blocks the progress of women who seek important positions in an organization.[16]

Preparing Women for Management

As noted above, opportunities for women to move into management positions are definitely improving. In addition to breaking down the barriers to advancement, the development of women managers demands a better understanding of women's needs and the requirements of the management world.

Business today needs all the leadership, talent, quality, competence, productivity, innovation, and creativity possible, for it faces more effective worldwide competition. Companies committed to equal opportunities for women and men will undoubtedly keep the best talent available. A list of actions organizations can take to maximize the human resource of women are presented in Highlights in HRM 2.[17]

Many employers now offer special training to women who are on a management career path. They may use their own staff or outside firms to conduct this training. Opportunities are also available for women to participate in seminars and workshops that provide instruction and experiences in a wide variety of management topics.

In the past several years, the number of women enrolled in college and university degree programs in management has increased significantly. At the same time, more women trained in management have joined management-department faculties at business schools, thus creating an environment that fosters the development of women as professionals capable of assuming higher-level positions in work organizations.

In addition to formal training opportunities, women today are provided with a wealth of information and guidance in books and magazines. Business sections in bookstores are stocked with numerous books written especially for women who want a better idea of the career opportunities available to them. Many books are devoted to the pursuit of careers in specific fields.[18]

Popular magazines that contain many articles about women and jobs include *Working Woman*, *New Woman*, *Savvy*, and *Enterprising Women*. These magazines are also recommended reading for men who want a better understanding of the problems that women face in the world of work.

Accommodating Families

One of the major problems women have faced is that of having both a managerial career and a family. Women managers whose children are at an age at which they require close parental attention often experience conflict between their responsibility to the children and their duty to the employer. If the conflict becomes too painful, they may decide to forego their careers, at least temporarily, and leave their jobs.

In recent years, many employers, including Apple Canada, Royal Bank, Bell Canada, and Warner-Lambert Canada, have inaugurated programs that are mutually

HRM

highlights

2 MAXIMIZING THE HUMAN RESOURCES OF FEMALE MANAGERS

1. Ensure that women receive frequent and specific feedback on their job performance. Women need and want candid reviews of their work. Clearly articulated suggestions for improvement, standards for work performance, and plans for career advancement will make women feel more involved in their jobs and help make them better employees.
2. Accept women as valued members of the management team. Include them in every kind of communication. Listen to their needs and concerns, and encourage their contributions.
3. Give talented women the same opportunities given to talented men to grow, develop, and contribute to company profitability. Give them the responsibility to direct major projects and plan and implement systems and programs. Expect them to travel and relocate, and to make the same commitment to the company as men aspiring to leadership positions.
4. Give women the same level of counseling on professional career advancement opportunities as that given to men.
5. Identify women as potential managers early in their employment and facilitate their advancement through training and other developmental activities.
6. Assist women in strengthening their assertion skills. Reinforce strategic career planning to encourage women's commitment to their careers and long-term career plans.
7. Accelerate the development of qualified women through fast-track programs. Either formally or informally, this method will provide women with the exposure, knowledge, and positioning for career advancement.
8. Provide opportunities for women to develop mentoring or sponsoring relationships with employees. Women do not often have equal or easy access (compared to their male colleagues) to senior employees. The overall goal should be to provide advice, counsel, and support to promising female employees from knowledgeable, senior-level men and women.
9. Encourage company co-ed management support systems and networks. Sharing experiences and information with other men and women who are managers provides invaluable support to peers. These activities provide the opportunity for women to meet and learn from men and women in more advanced stages of their careers—a helpful way of identifying potential mentors or role models.
10. Examine the feasibility of increasing participation of women in company-sponsored planning retreats, use of company facilities, social functions, and so forth. With notable exceptions, men are still generally more comfortable with other men, and as a result, women miss many of the career and business opportunities that arise during social functions. In addition, women may not have access to information about the company's informal political and social systems. Encourage male managers to include women when socializing with other business associates.

Source: Rose Mary Wentling, "Women in Middle Management: Their Career Development and Aspirations," *Business Horizons* 35, no. 1 (January-February 1992): 47-54. Reproduced with permission.

advantageous to the career-oriented woman and the employer.[19] These programs, which include alternative career paths, extended leave, flextime, job sharing, and telecommuting, provide new ways to balance career and family. The number of employers moving to protect their investment in top-flight women is still small, but more of them are defining a separate track for women managers.[20]

In a provocative article that appeared in the *Harvard Business Review*, Felice Schwartz, founder and president of Catalyst, offers justification for two separate groups—"career-primary" women and "career and family" women. She advises helping women in the latter group to be productive but not necessarily upwardly mobile.[21] Many women, as well as men, criticize Schwartz's approach for perpetuating the inequities of a double standard and for pitting women against women—those with children against those without. On the other side, there are those who believe that this approach at least gives women choices.

Career Development for Visible Minorities

Many organizations have specific career planning programs for minority employees, often mandated as part of the organization's employment equity commitments. These programs are intended to equip employees with career planning skills and development opportunities that will help them compete effectively for advancement.

We observed in Chapter 6 that many employers make a special effort to recruit minorities. Once individuals from minority groups are on the job, it is important for employers to provide opportunities for them to move ahead in the organization as they improve their job skills and abilities.

Advancement of Visible Minorities to Management Positions

While figures from Canada's 1991 census show increases, ranging from 6.3 percent to 9.1 percent, in the employment of visible minorities in Canada from 1986 to 1991, little information is available on how well they fare in rising up the corporate ladder.[22] Many organizations are taking the position that their employees should reflect the communities in which they function. The Bank of Montreal, for example, upon discovering that visible minorities were more highly represented in professional positions than in management jobs, made improvements to the candidate selection and career planning processes.[23] The Bank of Montreal requires their managers to develop diversity plans that include quantitative and qualitative goals. The performance of the managers is monitored against these plans.[24] "Each One Teach One" is a program administered by Frontier College in Ontario, which provides black women with successful role models and mentor relationships.

While minority managers do play a part in creating a better climate for groups that are discriminated against in advancement opportunities, top management and the HR department have the primary responsibility to create conditions in the organization that are conducive to the recognition and rewarding of performance based on objective, nondiscriminatory criteria.

Dual-Career Couples

As noted in Chapter 2, the employment of both members of a couple has become a way of life in North America, a trend encouraged by economic necessity and social forces. Statistics Canada notes that 63.5 percent of all working people are in **dual-**

A flexible working schedule allows this half of a dual-career couple to work at home.

Dual-career partnerships
Partnerships in which both members follow their own careers and actively support each other's career development.

career partnerships in which both members follow their own careers and actively support each other's career development.[25] Another study reported that one-fifth of dual-earner couples worked 90 hours or more between them.[26]

As with most lifestyles, the dual-career arrangement has its positive and negative sides. A significant number of organizations, concerned with the problems facing dual-career couples, are offering assistance to them, most frequently in the form of flexible working schedules. Other arrangements include leave policies that allow either parent to stay home with a newborn, policies that allow work to be performed at home, day care on organization premises, and job sharing.

The difficulties that dual-career couples face include the need for child care, time constraints, emotional stress, and, above all, the threat of relocation. Many large organizations now offer some kind of job-finding assistance for spouses of employees who are relocated, including payment of fees charged by employment agencies, job counselling firms, and executive-search firms. Organizations are also developing networking relationships with other employers to find jobs for the spouses of their relocating employees. These networks can provide a way to "share the wealth and talent" in a community while simultaneously assisting in the recruitment efforts of the participating organizations.

The relocating of dual-career couples to foreign facilities is a major issue confronting international employers. Fewer employees are willing to relocate unless some form of assistance is offered to their spouses. Many employers have developed effective methods for integrating the various allowances typically paid for overseas assignments when husband and wife work for the same employer. Far more complex are the problems that arise when couples work for two different employers.[27] These problems associated with overseas assignments of dual-career couples will be examined in greater detail in Chapter 17.

objective

Personal Career Development

We have observed that there are numerous ways for an employer to contribute to an individual employee's career development and at the same time meet the organization's HR needs. The organization can certainly be a positive force in the development process, but the primary responsibility for personal career growth still rests with the individual. One's career may begin before and often continue after a period of employment with an organization. To help employees achieve their career objectives, HRM professionals should have an understanding of the stages one goes through in developing a career and the actions one should take to be successful.

Stages of Career Development

Knowledge, skills, abilities, and attitudes as well as career aspirations change as one matures. While the work that individuals in different occupations perform can vary significantly, the challenges and frustrations that they face at the same stage in their careers are remarkably similar. A model describing these stages is shown in Figure 9-6. The stages are (1) preparation for work, (2) organizational entry, (3) early career, (4) mid-career, and (5) late career. The typical age range and the major tasks associated with each stage are also presented in the figure. Career issues within each age group are presented in Reality Check.

The first stage—preparation for work—encompasses the period prior to entering an organization, often extending until age 25. It is a period in which individuals must acquire the knowledge, abilities, and skills they will need to compete in the marketplace. In this stage, careful planning based on sound information should be the focus. The second stage, typically extending from ages 18 to 25, is devoted to soliciting job offers and selecting an appropriate job. During this period, one may also be involved in preparing for work. The next three stages entail fitting into a chosen occupation and organization, modifying goals, making choices, remaining productive, and, finally, preparing for retirement. In the remainder of the chapter, we will examine some of the activities of primary concern to the student, who is likely to be in the early stages. Retirement planning will be discussed in Chapter 13.

Developing Personal Skills

In planning a career, one should not attend only to acquiring specific job knowledge and skills. Job know-how is clearly essential, but there are other skills one must develop to be successful as an employee. To succeed as a manager or supervisor, one must achieve a still higher level of proficiency in such major areas as communication, time management, organization of work, interpersonal relationships, and the broad area of leadership.

Hundreds of self-help books have been written on these topics, and a myriad of opportunities to participate in workshops are available, often under the sponsorship of one's employer.[28] One should not overlook sources of valuable information such as articles in general-interest magazines and professional journals. For example, the pointers on the basic skills of successful career management listed in Highlights in HRM 3 are taken from a *Personnel Journal* article in which the eight skills are discussed.

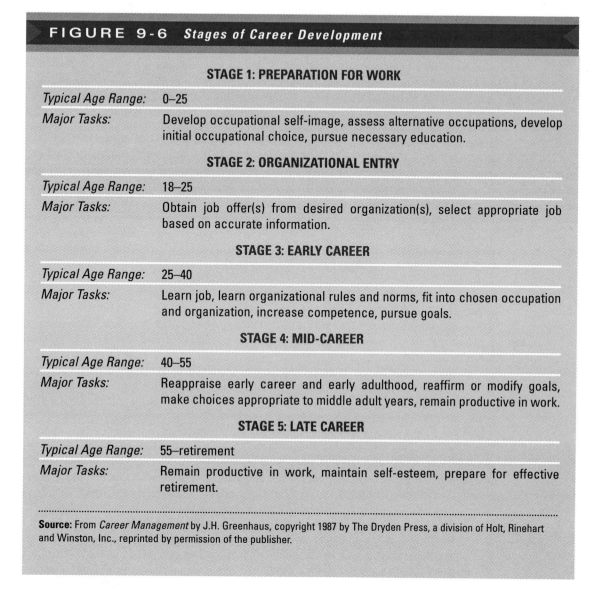

FIGURE 9-6 *Stages of Career Development*

STAGE 1: PREPARATION FOR WORK

Typical Age Range:	0–25
Major Tasks:	Develop occupational self-image, assess alternative occupations, develop initial occupational choice, pursue necessary education.

STAGE 2: ORGANIZATIONAL ENTRY

Typical Age Range:	18–25
Major Tasks:	Obtain job offer(s) from desired organization(s), select appropriate job based on accurate information.

STAGE 3: EARLY CAREER

Typical Age Range:	25–40
Major Tasks:	Learn job, learn organizational rules and norms, fit into chosen occupation and organization, increase competence, pursue goals.

STAGE 4: MID-CAREER

Typical Age Range:	40–55
Major Tasks:	Reappraise early career and early adulthood, reaffirm or modify goals, make choices appropriate to middle adult years, remain productive in work.

STAGE 5: LATE CAREER

Typical Age Range:	55–retirement
Major Tasks:	Remain productive in work, maintain self-esteem, prepare for effective retirement.

Source: From *Career Management* by J.H. Greenhaus, copyright 1987 by The Dryden Press, a division of Holt, Rinehart and Winston, Inc., reprinted by permission of the publisher.

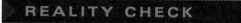

REALITY CHECK

We asked ten people, at various stages in their career development, what their career meant to them and what they were doing about their careers. Here are their responses:

STAGE 1: PREPARATION FOR WORK (0–18)

Brooker, Grade 4: Career is a job. A job means money. To have a good job, you need a good education. You have to be good in maths and be good in business.

Suzanne, Grade 10: Career is more than a job. It has to be something I would really enjoy. I would like to be a doctor; therefore, I am taking courses in science and mathematics. I am also taking other courses in case I don't realize my dreams. I am also checking out universities to find out about their requirements.

STAGE 2: ORGANIZATIONAL ENTRY (18–25)

Marc, second-year university: Career means a lot of things. It's a combination of stability and security along with happiness and control. With control comes freedom. During the summer I am taking an internship with an international marketing firm that caters to sports and event marketing. With my sociology degree and my internship experience, I hope to continue in event marketing by taking a program at one of the local colleges.

Christine, job seeker: Career means being able to find a job that I am qualified for and that I will be happy doing. I am trying to find a job as an esthetician so I am taking courses related to that field. In the meantime, I am applying for positions as a receptionist and clerk. I really don't want to work in those jobs, but I will take any position so that I can get working and be independent.

STAGE 3: EARLY CAREER (25–40)

Sylvie, executive assistant: Career is the balance between your job and your personal life. I've sought a career that complements my lifestyle, provides a challenge for me, and financial compensation for services rendered.

Marie, entrepreneur: Career is something that fulfils me intellectually, rewards me appropriately, and provides a social network with others in my field of expertise. I ensure that I join associations and align myself with others in my field so that I have a sounding board for my ideas. I am pursuing higher levels of education so I can achieve higher levels in my field.

STAGE 4: MID-CAREER (40–55)

Joe, senior sales consultant: Career means being successful at what I do and being happy with the choices I have made for myself. I have recently moved from a technical position to sales, so I am adjusting to a new role. I am learning to acquire the necessary skills to become successful in sales. I am reading as much as I can about proven sales techniques, and I try to spend as much time as I can with people in my organization that have been successful.

Lou, contractor/engineer: A career is something that goes beyond just doing a job. It means being able to build on information and experience and to use it as you go through each career opportunity. I try to work within my career parameters, and I surround myself with others who are able to provide the support I need in my field. I network by being active in community events and by keeping in touch with engineers I went to school with. This allows us to share information and keep current.

STAGE 5: LATE CAREER (55–RETIREMENT)

Art, consultant to International Finance Corporation (private-sector investment arm of the World Bank): Most people think a career involves selecting one thing and staying with it—that's not me. I go with the opportunity I see at the time. It has to be something different, exciting, and challenging.

Carolyn, retired high-school principal: Career is an extension of my lifestyle—wanting to do something productive for others as well as for me. Once I retired, I started a consulting business, working on projects such as focus groups on Canada's immigration policy and leading management seminars.

▶ HIGHLIGHTS IN HRM

HRM
highlights

**3   BASIC SKILLS OF SUCCESSFUL
    CAREER MANAGEMENT**

1. Develop a positive attitude.
2. Take responsibility for your own career.
3. Establish goals.
4. Be aware of success factors.
5. Present yourself in a positive manner.
6. Be in the right place at the right time.
7. Establish a relationship with a mentor or guide.
8. Adopt the mindset of your superiors.

Source: Lewis Newman, "Career Management: Start with Goals," *Personnel Journal* 68, no. 4 (April 1989): 91–92.
Reproduced with permission.

Choosing a Career

When asked about career choice, Peter Drucker said, "The probability that the first job choice you make is the right one for you is roughly one in a million. If you decide your first choice is the right one, chances are that you are just plain lazy."[29] The implications of this statement are that one must often do a lot of searching and changing to find a career path that is psychologically and financially satisfying.

Use of Available Resources

A variety of resources are available to aid in the process of choosing a satisfying career. Counsellors at colleges and universities, as well as those in private practice, are equipped to assist individuals in evaluating their aptitudes, abilities, interests, and values as they relate to career selection. There is a broad interest among business schools in a formal instructional program in career planning and development, and other units in the institutions, such as placement offices and continuing education centres, offer some type of career planning assistance.

Accuracy of Self-Evaluation

Successful career development depends in part on an individual's ability to conduct an accurate self-evaluation. In making a self-evaluation, one needs to consider those factors that are personally significant. The most important internal factors are one's academic aptitude and achievement, occupational aptitudes and skills, social skills, communication skills, leadership abilities, interests, and values. The latter should include consideration of salary level, status, opportunities for advancement, and growth on the job. External factors that should be assessed include family values and expectations, economic conditions, employment trends, job-market information, and perceived effect of physical or psychological disabilities on success.[30]

Significance of Interest Inventories

Psychologists who specialize in career counselling typically administer a battery of tests such as those mentioned in Chapter 7. The Strong Vocational Interest Blank (SVIB), developed in the 1920s by E.K. Strong, Jr., was among the first of the interest tests.[31] Somewhat later, G. Frederic Kuder developed inventories to measure degree of interest in mechanical, clerical, scientific, and persuasive activities, among others. Both the Strong and the Kuder interest inventories have been used widely in vocational counselling.

Strong found that there are substantial differences in interests that vary from occupation to occupation, and that a person's interest pattern, especially after age 21, tends to become quite stable. By taking his test, now known as *The Strong-Campbell Interest Inventory (SCII)*, one can learn the degree to which his or her interests correspond with those of successful people in a wide range of occupations. Those results that are profiled on the basis of computer scoring also reveal one's personality type, using Holland's categories. According to Holland, most people can be categorized using the following six personality types:

1. Realistic
2. Investigative
3. Artistic
4. Social
5. Enterprising
6. Conventional

These categories characterize not only a type of personality, but also the type of working environment that a person would find most congenial. In the actual application of Holland's theory, combinations of the six types are examined. For example, a person may be classified as realistic-investigative-enterprising (RIE). Jobs in the RIE category include mechanical engineer, watch repairer, lineperson, and air-traffic controller.[32] To facilitate searching for occupations that match one's category, such as RIE, Holland has devised a series of tables that correlate the Holland categories with jobs in the *Dictionary of Occupational Titles (DOT)* and the *National Occupation Classification (NOC)* described in Chapter 4.

Another inventory that measures *both* interests and skills is the *Campbell Interest and Skill Survey (CISS)*.[33] The CISS can be used not only to assist employees in exploring career paths and options but also to help organizations develop their employees or else reassign them as a consequence of major organizational changes. In completing the inventory, individuals report their level of interest and skill using a six-point response scale on 200 interest items and 120 skill items. *CISS* item responses are translated into seven orientations—influencing, organizing, helping, creating, analyzing, producing, and adventuring—and further categorized into 29 basic scales, such as leadership, supervision, and counselling, to identify occupations that reflect today's workplace.

Highlights in HRM 4 shows a sample profile for one individual. Note that at the top of the profile the range of scores is from 30 to 70, with 50 in the mid-range. Corresponding verbal descriptions of scores range from very low to very high. Also note that on the profile two types of scores are profiled: *interest* (a solid diamond ◆) and *skill* (an open diamond ◇). The interest score ◆ shows how much the individual likes the specified activities; the skill score ◇ shows how confident the individual feels about performing these activities.

There are four noteworthy patterns of combinations of the interest and skill scores:

Pursue	Interests high, skills high
Develop	Interests high, skills lower
Explore	Interests lower, skills high
Avoid	Interests low, skills low

For the individual whose scores are profiled in Highlights in HRM 4, one would interpret the scores on the seven orientation scales (as shown in the right-hand column of the profile) as follows:

Influencing	Pursue
Organizing	Indeterminate
Helping	Pursue
Creating	Avoid
Analyzing	Avoid
Producing	Indeterminate
Adventuring	Develop

On the basis of such profiles, individuals can see how their interests and skills compare with those of a sample of people happily employed in a wide range of occupations. Completed answer sheets can be mailed to a scoring centre, or software is available and may be obtained for in-house scoring.

Evaluation of Long-Term Employment Opportunities

In making a career choice, one should attempt to determine the probable long-term opportunities in the occupational fields one is considering. While even the experts can err in their predictions, one should give at least some attention to the opinions that are available. Many libraries have publications that provide details about jobs and career fields. In recent years, a considerable amount of computer software has been developed to facilitate access to information about career fields and to enable individuals to match their abilities, aptitudes, interests, and experiences with the requirements of occupational areas.

Choosing an Employer

Once an individual has made a career choice, even if only tentatively, the next major step is deciding where to work. The choice of employer may be based primarily on

HIGHLIGHTS IN HRM

4 CAMPBELL INTEREST AND SKILL SURVEY: INDIVIDUAL PROFILE

highlights

SAMPLE   **ORIENTATIONS AND BASIC SCALES**   DATE SCORED 10/20/92

Orientations and Basic Scales	Interest ◆	Skill ◇	Interest/Skill Pattern
Influencing	**61**	**60**	Pursue
Leadership	65	64	Pursue
Law/Politics	48	57	Explore
Public Speaking	63	59	Pursue
Sales	46	58	Explore
Advertising/Marketing	47	42	
Organizing	**46**	**37**	
Supervision	68	58	Pursue
Financial Services	35	31	Avoid
Office Practices	44	42	Avoid
Helping	**60**	**68**	Pursue
Adult Development	62	58	Pursue
Counseling	58	68	Pursue
Child Development	56	43	Develop
Religious Activities	70	60	Pursue
Medical Practice	52	56	Explore
Creating	**23**	**37**	Avoid
Art/Design	19	32	Avoid
Performing Arts	41	39	Avoid
Writing	32	36	Avoid
International Activities	50	64	Explore
Fashion	35	48	
Culinary Arts	48	43	
Analyzing	**33**	**33**	Avoid
Mathematics	34	33	Avoid
Science	31	36	Avoid
Producing	**37**	**46**	
Mechanical Crafts	33	35	Avoid
Woodworking	32	39	Avoid
Farming/Forestry	46	44	
Plants/Gardens	51	51	
Animal Care	50	49	

Scale range indicators: Very Low 30 35, Low 40 45, Mid-Range 50 55, High 60, Very High 65 70

Adventuring	59	54						Develop
Athletics/Physical Fitness	58	47						Develop
Military/Law Enforcement	63	66						Pursue
Risks/Adventure	46	52						

location, immediate availability of a position, starting salary, and other basic considerations. However, the college graduate who has prepared for a professional or managerial career is likely to have more sophisticated concerns. According to Douglas Hall, people frequently choose an organization on the basis of its climate and how it appears to fit their needs:

> *People with high needs for achievement may choose aggressive, achievement-oriented organizations. Power-oriented people may choose influential, prestigious, power-oriented organizations. Affiliative people may choose warm, friendly, supportive organizations. We know that people whose needs fit with the climate of an organization are rewarded more and are more satisfied than those who fit in less well, so it is natural to reason that fit would also be a factor in one's choice of an organization.*

Hall suggests further that because the relevant theory and measurement technology are available, the prediction of organizational choice is a promising area for researchers.[34]

The "Plateauing Trap"

Judith Bardwick was the first to label the plateauing phenomenon.[35] A **career plateau** is a situation in which for either organizational or personal reasons the probability of moving up the career ladder is low. According to Bardwick, only 1 percent of the labour force will *not* plateau in their working lives. There are three types of plateaus: structural, content, and life. A *structural plateau* marks the end of promotions; one will now have to leave the organization to find new opportunities and challenges. A *content plateau* occurs when a person has learned a job too well and is bored with day-to-day activities. According to Susan Brooks, a *life plateau* is more profound and may feel like a midlife crisis.[36] People who experience life plateaus often have allowed work or some other major factor to become the most significant aspect of their lives, and they experience a loss of identity and self-esteem when there is no longer success in that area.

Organizations can help individuals cope with plateaus by providing opportunities for lateral growth where opportunities for advancement do not exist. Employers

Career plateau
Situation in which for either organizational or personal reasons the probability of moving up the career ladder is low.

such as CIBC are using an approach that encourages career self-management. Abitibi-Price offers lateral rotation to its employees on a case-by-case basis.[37] Jobs are loosely defined so that the workers can take on more responsibility and challenge. IBM Canada has developed elaborate horizontal career paths as an alternative to the traditional upward route through management. According to one expert, "It is a process for helping people learn more about what gives them satisfaction within the company, as well as what kinds of opportunities will make them happiest if they go elsewhere."[38] The corporate ladder is beginning to look like a spiral staircase.

While employers are recognizing the importance of helping employees with their plateauing experiences, each employee must assume responsibility for his or her professional self-development and make constructive use of time and opportunities. Gone are the days when one could expect continuing employment with any employer.[39] Indeed, the average person can expect to take on several different jobs over a working lifetime. According to Rob Notman of the outplacement firm Murray Axsmith Associates, the average lifespan of a job today is five years.[40] Cradle-to-grave employment is now as rare as job hopping once was.

Becoming an Entrepreneur

No discussion of careers in the 1990s would be complete if the opportunities to be an entrepreneur were not mentioned. Similarly, the individual who is planning a career is not doing a thorough job if the possibilities for being an entrepreneur are overlooked. Being an **entrepreneur**—one who starts, organizes, manages, and assumes responsibility for a business or other enterprise—offers a personal challenge that many individuals prefer over being an employee. Small businesses are typically run by entrepreneurs who accept the personal financial risks that go with owning a business but who also benefit directly from the success of the business.[41]

Small businesses are actually big employers and play a vital role in the Canadian economy. Over 97 percent of all businesses employ fewer than 50 people.[42] (In Canada, firms with less than 50 employees are considered small, while firms with 50–4999 employees are classified as medium-sized.) Small firms employ 36 percent of the Canadian workforce, which makes small business the source of one-third of wage and salary jobs in this country.

Individuals who are interested in starting a small business can obtain assistance from the Federal Business Development Bank, which advises and assists thousands of small businesses in Canada. The potential small-business owner should obtain as much information as possible not only from the Federal Business Development Bank but also from libraries and organizations and from individuals who are knowledgeable about the type of business being considered.

Of particular note is the increasing number of women entrepreneurs in Canada. According to Revenue Canada data, women made up 40 percent of business proprietors in 1992.[43] Over the past decade, the number of self-employed women has nearly doubled, while for men the increase was less than one-third. Possible reasons for this increase are given in Highlights in HRM 5.

Since the details of organizing a business are beyond the scope of this book, Figure 9-7 is presented to provide an overview of the basic steps for starting a new business.[44]

Entrepreneur
One who starts, organizes, manages, and assumes responsibility for a business or other enterprise.

highlights

5   WOMEN AND SELF-EMPLOYMENT

Increasing numbers of women are choosing self-employment as a career option. Mona Bandeen, Director, Women's Entrepreneurship Program at the University of Toronto, cites five reasons for this increase:

1. Women have a long tradition of being entrepreneurs. Early in Canada's history, men worked the land, clearing it for development, while women worked the farms to yield crops and served as midwives or in other medical capacities.
2. More and more women are receiving or have received business education and training. Although women in their 30s are acting in senior roles in corporations, they have yet to reach the CEO level.
3. The increase in the number of single-parent families means that women must be more aggressive as they seek out ways to meet financial needs.
4. Layoffs resulting from mergers and acquisitions have compelled many women to consider other employment options.
5. The Woman Entrepreneur of the Year Awards and similar events are spotlighting women's achievements.

   Businesses run by women tend to survive longer than those run by men (although they also tend not to earn as much money).

Sources: Discussion with Mona Bandeen, University of Toronto, June 1995; M. Belcourt, H. Lee-Gosselin, and R. Burke, *The Glass Box* (Ottawa: Canadian Advisory Council on the Status of Women, 1991).

Keeping a Career in Perspective

For most people, work is a primary factor in the overall quality of their lives. It provides a setting for satisfying practically the whole range of human needs and is thus of considerable value to an individual. Nevertheless, it is advisable to keep one's career in perspective so that other important areas of life are not neglected.

Off-the-Job Interests

Satisfaction with one's life is a product of many forces. Some of the more important ingredients are physical health, emotional well-being, harmonious interpersonal relationships, freedom from too much stress, and achievement of one's goals. While a career can provide some of the satisfaction that one needs, most people find it

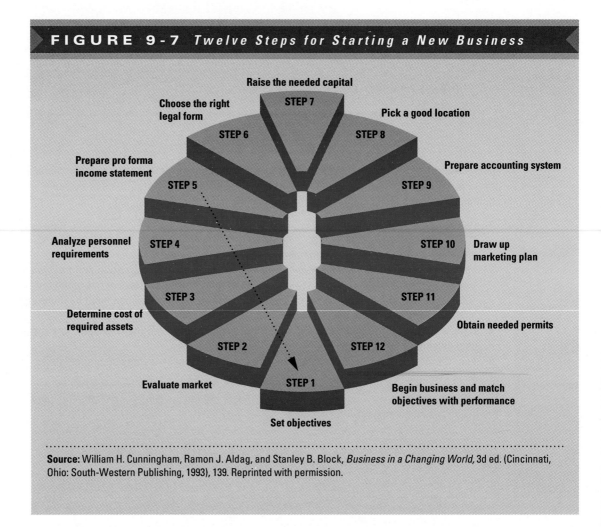

FIGURE 9-7 *Twelve Steps for Starting a New Business*

Raise the needed capital — STEP 7

Choose the right legal form — STEP 6

Pick a good location — STEP 8

Prepare pro forma income statement — STEP 5

Prepare accounting system — STEP 9

Analyze personnel requirements — STEP 4

Draw up marketing plan — STEP 10

Determine cost of required assets — STEP 3

STEP 11

Evaluate market — STEP 2

Obtain needed permits

STEP 12

Begin business and match objectives with performance

STEP 1 — Set objectives

Source: William H. Cunningham, Ramon J. Aldag, and Stanley B. Block, *Business in a Changing World*, 3d ed. (Cincinnati, Ohio: South-Western Publishing, 1993), 139. Reprinted with permission.

necessary to turn to interests and activities outside their career. Off-the-job activities not only provide a respite from daily work responsibilities but also offer satisfaction in areas unrelated to work.

Marital and/or Family Life

The career development plans of an individual as well as an organization must take into account the needs of spouses and children. As we have said, the one event that often poses the greatest threat to family needs is relocation. Conflict between a desire to advance in one's career and a strong desire to stay in one place and put down family roots often borders on the disastrous. Many employers now provide complete assistance in this area, including relocation counselling, in an effort to reduce the severity of the pain that can accompany relocations.

While relocation may be the most serious threat to employees with families, there are also other sources of conflict between career and family. Some of the work-related sources of conflict are numbers of hours worked per week, frequency of overtime, and the presence and irregularity of shift work. In addition, ambiguity and/or conflict within the employee's work role, low level of leader support, and disappointments due to unfulfilled expectations affect one's life away from the job. Some of the family-related sources of conflict include having to spend an unusually large amount of time with the family and its concerns, spouse employment patterns, and dissimilarity in a couple's career orientations. Greenhaus and Beutell, who have examined research studies that identify the sources of work conflict, point out the need for refined measuring devices that can be used to study work–family relations more accurately. They emphasize that public policy decisions should rest on a solid foundation of accumulated knowledge.[45]

Planning for Retirement

While retirement appears to be a long way off for the individual who is still in the early stages of a career, it is never too early to make plans for it. In order to enjoy retirement, one should prepare for it by giving careful attention to health, finances, family, and interpersonal relationships throughout one's adult life. While most of the larger organizations have preretirement programs, most of the participants are close to actual retirement. Thus it is each individual's responsibility to plan earlier in order to have time to set the stage for a healthy and satisfying retirement as free as possible from worries–especially those that could have been avoided or minimized earlier in life. While employer-sponsored preretirement programs are usually considered very helpful by the participants, as we will see in Chapter 13, they are not a substitute for continual personal concern for oneself.

Maintaining a Balance

Those who are "married" to their jobs to the extent that they fail to provide the attention and caring essential to marriage and family relationships can be said to lack an appreciation for the balance needed for a satisfying life. One should always be aware that "to be a success in the business world takes hard work, long hours, persistent effort, and constant attention. To be a success in marriage takes hard work, long hours, persistent effort, and constant attention. ... The problem is giving each its due and not shortchanging the other."[46]

SUMMARY

one
objective

A career development program is a dynamic process that should integrate individual employee needs with those of the organization. It is the responsibility of the employee to identify his or her own KSA, as well as interests and values, and to seek out information about career options. The organization should provide information not only about its mission, policies, and plans but also about what it will provide in the way of training and development for the employee.

two
objective

In order to be successful, a career development program must receive the support of top management. The program should reflect the goals and the culture of the organization, and managerial personnel at all levels must be trained in the fundamentals of job design, performance appraisal, career planning, and counselling.

Employees should have an awareness of the organization's philosophy and its goals, otherwise they will not know how their goals match those of the organization. HRM policies, especially those concerning rotation, transfers, and promotions, should be consistent with the goals. The objectives and opportunities of the career development program should be publicized throughout the organization.

objective

Job opportunities may be identified by studying jobs and determining the knowledge and skills each one requires. Once that is accomplished, it is possible to plan job progression, which can then serve as a basis for developing career paths. Once career paths are developed and employees are identified on the career ladders, it is possible to inventory the jobs and determine where individuals with the required skills and knowledge are needed or will be needed.

objective

Identifying and developing managerial talent is a responsibility of all managers. In addition to immediate superiors, there should be others in the organization who can nominate and sponsor employees who show promise. Many organizations use assessment centres to identify managerial talent and recommend developmental experiences that will enable each individual to reach her or his full potential. Mentoring has been found to be valuable for providing guidance and support to potential managers.

objective

The first step in facilitating the career development of women and minorities is to eliminate barriers to advancement. Establishing women's networks, providing special training for women, accepting women as valued members of the organization, and providing women with mentors have been found to be effective ways to facilitate a woman's career development.

objective

While a diversified workforce is composed of many different groups, an important segment is minority groups. Also requiring the attention of management are dual-career couples who often need to have flexible working schedules.

objective

In choosing a career, one should use all available resources. Consideration should be given to internal factors such as academic aptitude and achievement, occupational aptitudes and skills, communication skills, leadership abilities, and interests and values. External factors such as economic conditions, employment trends, and job-market information must also be considered. In choosing a career, it is desirable to make use of interest and skill inventories. Long-term employment opportunities in an occupational field should be assessed by utilizing various publications, including those published by the government.

KEY TERMS

assessment centre

career counselling

career paths

career plateau

dual-career partnerships

entrepreneurtransfer

fast-track program

job progression

mentors

mentoring functions

outplacement services

relocation services

DISCUSSION QUESTIONS

1. What are the reasons for the trend toward increased emphasis on career development programs?

2. A major bank maintains for its retired executives a special suite of offices at its headquarters. Two of the bank's former chief executives use their offices regularly.
   a. Of what value is this arrangement to the corporation? To the individuals?
   b. How might retired executives in any organization assist in the career development of current employees?

3. What contributions can a career development program make to an organization that is forced to downsize its operations?

4. One recruiter has said, "Next to talent, the second most important factor in career success is taking the time and effort to develop visibility." What are some ways of developing visibility?

5. Over 50 percent of all MBAs leave their first employer within five years. While the change may mean career growth for the individuals, it represents a loss to the employers. What are some of the probable reasons an MBA would leave his or her first employer?

6. What are some of the barriers that have limited women's advancement opportunities in many organizations?

7. List the advantages and disadvantages of being an entrepreneur.

8. In your opinion, what personal characteristics are employers looking for in individuals whom they are considering for long-term employment and probable advancement in the organization? To what extent can one develop these characteristics?

CASE: Preparing a Career
Development Plan

Susan Scott was a telephone operator at the headquarters of a large corporation. A high-school graduate, she had no particular skills. Nevertheless, Scott wanted very much to improve her economic position. Recognizing her educational limitations, she began taking accounting courses on a random basis as part of an evening adult education program. Unfortunately, she did not have any particular plan for career development.

Scott also took advantage of the corporation's job bidding system by applying for openings that were posted, even though in many instances she did not meet the specifications listed for them. After being rejected several times, she became discouraged. Her depressed spirits were observed by Elizabeth Burroughs, one of the department managers in the corporation. Burroughs invited Scott to come to her office for a talk about the problems she was having. Scott took full advantage of the opportunity to express her frustrations and disappointments. As she unburdened herself, it became apparent that, besides lacking special skills and career objectives, during interviews she tended to apologize for having "only a high-school education." This made it difficult for the interviewers to select her over other candidates who were putting their best foot forward. Burroughs suggested that perhaps Scott might try taking a more positive approach during her interviews. For example, she could stress her self-improvement efforts at night school and the fact that she was a dependable and cooperative person who was willing to work hard to succeed in the job for which she was applying.

Following Burroughs' advice, Susan selected a job for which she felt she was qualified. She made a very forceful and positive presentation during her interview, stressing the favourable qualities that she possessed. As a result of this approach, she was selected for the job of invoice clerk. While this job did not pay much more than that of telephone operator, it did offer an avenue for possible advancement into the accounting field, where the accounting courses she was taking would be of value.

Questions

1. What are some of the possible reasons Scott did not seek or receive advice from her immediate supervisor?
2. After reviewing the chapter, suggest all possible ways in which Scott can prepare herself for career advancement.

Assessing Values

An important component of a career plan is an awareness of your career interests. This chapter has suggested many strategies you can use to determine your interests, from reading career planning workbooks to visiting career counsellors who are qualified to administer interest and skill inventories. You can also request self-scoring interest tests from the Guidance Centre of the Ontario Institute for Studies in Education, 70 Gordon Baker Road, Toronto, Ontario M2H 3R7.

Although any of the above tests will guide you in your choice of a career, the choices will be very generic (e.g., teacher, lawyer, or technician). A further step in career planning is to identify your *values*, so that you can determine how you can achieve satisfaction in an occupation. For example, there are many ways to "be" a teacher. If you value security, then you might want to teach in a school or university system where there is tenure; if you value monetary rewards, you might prefer to develop training materials from which you could receive royalties; if you want status, you might wish to lead executives in skills acquisition or head the Ministry of Education; an interest in caring for others might lead you to be a personal classroom assistant for a handicapped child; a desire for independence would be translated into freelance tutoring or training. As you can see, while all these jobs involve "teaching," an individual's value system is satisfied in a different way in each.

Perform the following steps in order to identify values that are important to you.

Step 1: Each of the squares below represents a value. Cut out each so that you are left with fifteen separate squares.

Recognition	Money	Interesting Work
Security	Helping others	Power
Responsibility	Opporturnity to achieve	
Creativity	Independence Frame	
Respect	Intellectually challenging work	
Use talents	Independence	

Step 2: Divide the squares into three groups or piles, not necessarily equal in size. One group should consist of those "value squares" that are most important to you; the next group should consist of those values that are least important, while the middle group should represent values that fall somewhere in the middle.

Step 3: Within each group, rank each value square from most to least important. You should now have a ranking of numbers from 1 to 15 representing your value system. Consult this value system if (or when) you have established an occupational choice. Your values will help you determine exactly which job within that occupational category will give you the most satisfaction.

NOTES AND REFERENCES

1. Thomas G. Gutteridge, Zandy B. Leibowitz, and Jane E. Shore, *Organizational Career Development* (San Francisco: Jossey-Bass, 1993), xvii–xix, 1–3. See also Beverly Kaye and Zandy Leibowitz, "Career Development—Don't Let It Fizzle," *HR Magazine* 39, no. 9 (September 1994): 78–83.

2. Zandy B. Leibowitz, Caela Farren, and Beverly L. Kaye, *Designing Career Development Systems* (San Francisco: Jossey-Bass, 1986): 40–42. See also Paul Herriot, *The Career Management Challenge—Balancing Individual and Organizational Needs* (Thousand Oaks, CA: Sage Publications, 1992).

3. K.J. Nilan, S. Walls, S.L. Davis, and M.E. Lund, "Creating Hierarchical Career Progression," *Personnel Administrator* 32, no. 6 (June 1987): 168–183; and R.J. Sahl, "Succession Planning: A Blueprint for Your Company's Future," *Personnel Administrator* 32, no. 9 (September 1987): 101–108.

4. Milan Moravec and Beverly McKee, "Designing Dual Career Paths and Compensation," *Personnel* 67, no. 8 (August 1990): 5. See also Robert Tucker, Milan Moravec, and Ken Ideus, "Designing a Dual-Track Career System," *Training and Development*, 46 no. 6 (June 1992): 55–58.

5. For other sources of career information and advice on how to select a professional career counsellor, see Berkeley Rice, "Why Am I in This Job?" *Psychology Today*, January 1985, 54–59. For a book that provides guidance as well as an opportunity for self-analysis, see Julie Griffin Levitt, *Your Career—How to Make It Happen*, 2nd ed. (Cincinnati, OH: South-Western, 1990).

6. Jean R. Haskell, "Getting Employees to Take Charge of Their Careers," *Training and Development* 47 no. 2 (February 1993): 51–54. See also Harry Levinson, *Career Mastery* (San Francisco: Barrett-Koehler Publishers, 1992).

7. Discussion with Peter Cormer, Public Service Commission, June 1995.

8. Denis A. Joiner, "Exploring the Accuracy and Value of Self-Assessments," *Training and Development Journal* 43, no. 5 (1989): 88. See also Dennis A. Joiner, "Demystifying Assessment Center Exercises," *Fire Chief* (September 1990): 51–53. A classic book on assessment centres is G.C. Thornton III and W.C. Byham, *Assessment Centers and Managerial Performance* (New York: Academic Press, 1982).

9. George S. Odiorne, "Mentoring: An American Management Innovation," *Personnel Administrator* 1 30, no. 5 (May 1985): 63–70.

10. L. Krueger, "Mentor Program Gets Good Marks at University," *The Globe and Mail*, June 2, 1995, A16.

11. Kathy E. Kram, *Mentoring at Work: Developmental Relationships in Organizational Life* (Glenview, IL: Scott, Foresman, 1985), 22–24. See also Belle Rose Ragins and Terri A. Scandura, "Gender Differences in Expected Outcomes of Mentoring Relationships," *Academy of Management Journal* 37, no. 4 (August 1994): 957–971; James A. Wilson and Nancy S. Elman, "Organization Benefits of Mentoring," *The Executive* IV, no. 4 (November 1990): 88–94.

12. L. Goodson, "The Mentor Model," *Human Resources Professional* 8, No. 3 (March 1992): 19–22.

13. Discussion with Joanne Totta, Bank of Montreal, June 1995.

14. Lori Bongiorno, "Big Ideas for Little Girls," *Business Week*, May 3, 1993, 38–39; Sue Shellenberger, "Women Mentors Hope to Make Lasting Impact," *Wall Street Journal*, April 28, 1993, B1. See also Stephenie Overman, "Business Gives Students a Hand," *HR Magazine* 38, no. 4 (April 1993): 46–50.

15. A. Freeman "More High Wage Jobs Going to Women," *The Globe and Mail*, April 14, 1993, A1.

16. Dan R. Dalton and Idelene F. Kesner, "Cracks in the Glass: The Silent Competence of Women," *Business Horizons* 36, no. 2 (March-April 1993): 6–11. See also Peggy Stuart, "What Does the Glass Ceiling Cost You?" *Personnel Journal* 71, no. 11 (November 1992): 70–80, Charlene Marmer Solomon, "Careers under Glass," *Personnel Journal* 69, no. 4 (April 1990): 96–105; and Rochelle Sharpe, "The Waiting Game: Women Make Strides but Men Stay Firmly in Top Company Jobs," *The Wall Street Journal*, March 29, 1994, A1.

17. See also Michelle Neely Martinez, "The High Potential Woman," *HR Magazine* 36, no. 6 (June 1991): 46–51.

18. The interested reader should find the following books very informative: Helen Gurley Brown, *Having It All* (New York: Simon and Schuster, 1982); and Johanna Hunsaker and Phillip Hunsaker, *Strategies and Skills for Managerial Women* (Cincinnati, OH: South-Western, 1991).

19. T. McCallum "The Old Seven to Three," *Human Resources Professional* 12, no. 4 (June 1995): 12–14.

20. Elizabeth Ehrlich, "The Mommy Track," *Business Week*, March 20, 1989, 126–134; and Ehrlich, "Is the Mommy Track a Blessing or Betrayal?" *Business Week*, May 15, 1989, 98–99.

21. Felice Schwartz, "Management Women and the New Facts of Life," *Harvard Business Review* 89, no. 1 (January-February 1989): 65–82. See also Hal Lancaster, "A Big Six Firm Decides Detours Won't Derail a Career," *The Wall Street Journal*, December 20, 1994, B1.

22. "Employment Equity in the Federal Sector: A Progress Report," *Worklife Report* 9, no. 3 (1994): 1–2.

23. M. Neely, "Equality Effort Sharpens Bank's Edge," *HR Magazine* 40, no. 1 (January 1995): 38–43.

24. "Towards Equity—1993 Merit Awards," *Human Resources Development*, Employment Equity Branch, Government of Canada, June 1994, 5.

25. Statistics Canada, *Perspectives on Labour and Income* (Ottawa: Ministry of Supply and Services, 1995), Report 75-001.

26. M. Gibb-Clark, "Jobs Keeping Couples Apart," *The Globe and Mail*, June 2, 1995, A1.

27. Ibid.

28. A selection of self-help publications on a variety of topics may be found in any bookstore. College and university bookstores typically have a very wide selection in their trade or general books department. A recent popular book that presents a principle-centred approach to time management is Stephen R. Corey, A. Roger Merrill, and Rebecca R. Merrill, *First Things First* (New York: Simon and Schuster, 1994).

29. Mary Harrington Hall, "A Conversation with Peter Drucker," *Psychology Today*, March 1968, 22.

30. Lila B. Stair, *Careers in Business: Selecting and Planning Your Career Path* (Homewood, IL: Richard D. Irwin, 1980), 8. See also Walter Kiechel III, "A Manager's Career in the New Economy," *Fortune*, April 4, 1994, 68–72; Sander I. Marcus and Jotham G. Friedland, "14 Steps on a New Career Path," *HR Magazine* 38, no. 3, (March 1993): 55–56; and Stephanie Overman, "Weighing Career Anchors," *HR Magazine* 38, no. 3 (March 1993): 56–58.

31. E.K. Strong, Jr., of Stanford University, was active in the measurement of interests from the early 1920s to the time of his death in 1963. Since then, his work has been carried on by the staff of the Measurement Research Center, University of Minnesota. *The Strong-Campbell Interest Inventory (SCII)* is distributed by Consulting Psychologists Press, Inc., P.O. Box 60070, Palo Alto, CA 94306, to qualified persons under an exclusive licence from the publisher, Stanford University Press.

32. John I. Holland, *Making Vocational Choices: A Theory of Careers*, 2nd ed. (Englewood Cliffs, NJ: Prentice-Hall, 1984).

33. *The Campbell Interest and Skill Survey* (copyright 1992) is published and distributed by NCS Assessments, P.O. Box 1416, Minneapolis, MN 55440.

34. Douglas T. Hall, *Careers in Organizations* (Santa Monica, CA: Goodyear Publishing, 1976), 36. See also Douglas T. Hall and Associates, *Career Development in Organizations* (San Francisco: Jossey-Bass, 1986).

35. Judith Bardwick, *The Plateauing Trap* (New York: AMACOM, 1986).

36. Susan Sonnsesyn Brooks, "Moving Up Is Not the Only Option," *HR Magazine* 39, no. 3 (March 1994): 79–82.

37. J. Schilder, "The New Darwinian Workplace," *Human Resources Professional* 11, no. 6 (August 1994): 9–11. J. Sisto "Onward and ... Oops! What Happens When the Corporate Ladder Runs Out?" *Canadian Business*, July 1990, 70–71.

38. Brooks, "Moving Up."

39. William Bridges, *Job Shift* (Reading, MA: Addison-Wesley, 1994).

40. G. Powers, "Job Hopping the Smart Way," *The Globe and Mail*, April 1, 1995, B19.

41. William H. Cunningham, Ramon J. Aldag, and Stanley B. Block, *Business in a Changing World*, 3rd ed. (Cincinnati, OH: South-Western, 1993): 130–131. See also Bruce Nussbaum, Alice Cuneo, Barbara Carlson, and Gary McWilliams, "Corporate Refugees," *Business Week*, April 12, 1993, 58–65; Ronald Henkoff, "Winning the New Career Game," *Fortune* July 12, 1993, 46–49; John Naisbitt and Patricia Aburdene, *Megatrends 2000* (New York: William Morrow, 1990), 300–302, 311–313.

42. P. Thompson, *Small Business and Job Creation in Canada—1991* (WIllowdale, ON: Canadian Federation of Independent Business, March 1995).

43. *Small Business: An Equal Opportunity Employer. A Review of Women Entrepreneurs in Canada*, Canadian Federation of Independent Business, December 1994. See also D. Cefaloni, "More Women Doing It For Themselves," *Halifax Chronicle Herald*, December 8, 1994, C12.

44. Cunningham, Aldag, and Block, *Business in a Changing World*, Chapter 6. See also Gary Brenner, Joel Ewan, and Henry Custer, *The Complete Handbook for the Entrepreneur* (Englewood Cliffs, NJ: Prentice-Hall, 1990). This book was written by an attorney, a bank officer, and a CPA.

45. Jeffrey H. Greenhaus and Nicholas J. Beutell, "Sources of Conflict between Work and Family Roles," *Academy of Management Review* 10, no. 1 (January 1985): 76–88. See also Sue Shellenbarger, "How Some Companies Help Their Employees Get a Life," *The Wall Street Journal*, November 16, 1994, B1.

46. Richard W. Ogden, *How to Succeed in Business and Marriage* (New York: AMACOM, 1978), 2.

Chapter 10

Appraising and Improving Performance

In the preceding chapters, we discussed the programs that an organization uses to procure and develop a productive workforce. In this chapter, we turn to performance appraisal programs, which are among the most helpful tools an organization can use to maintain and enhance its productivity. Of course, performance appraisals take place in every organization whether there is a formal program or not. Managers are constantly observing the way their employees carry out their assignments and thereby forming impressions about the relative worth of these employees to the organization. Most organizations, however, do seem to use a formal program. In a study of 208 organizations, 85 percent reported having such a program and another 6 percent were planning to implement one within the next twelve months—a clear indication that performance appraisal is a potentially valuable activity.[1]

The success or failure of a performance appraisal program depends on the philosophy underlying it and the attitudes and skills of those responsible for its administration. Many different methods can be used to gather information about employee performance. However, gathering information is only the first step in the appraisal process. The information must then be evaluated in the context of organizational needs and communicated to employees so that it will result in high levels of performance.

objective

Performance Appraisal Programs

Formal programs for performance appraisal and merit ratings are by no means new to organizations. Formal programs for performance appraisal programs have been used in both the public and private sectors for decades. Advocates see these HR programs as among the most logical means to appraise, develop, and thus effectively utilize the knowledge and abilities of employees. However, a growing number of observers point out that performance appraisals frequently fall short of their potential.[2]

Recent interest in total quality management (TQM), for example, has caused numerous organizations to rethink their approach to performance appraisal. The late W. Edward Deming, a pioneer in TQM, identified performance appraisal as one of seven deadly diseases of management. While most managers still recognize the benefits of performance appraisal, TQM challenges some long-standing assumptions about how it should be conducted. PCL Constructors Inc. and Kraft General Foods Canada, for example, have modified their appraisal systems to better acknowledge *quality of performance* (in addition to quantity), *teamwork* (in addition to individual accomplishment), and *process improvements* (in addition to performance outcomes).[3] Each of these issues is discussed at greater length throughout the chapter.

Purposes of Performance Appraisal

A performance appraisal program can serve many purposes that benefit both the organization and the employee whose performance is being appraised. A large insurance company has the following objectives for its performance appraisal program. They are similar to the objectives of other organizations.

1. To give employees the opportunity to discuss performance and performance standards regularly with their supervisor
2. To provide the supervisor with a means of identifying the strengths and weaknesses of an employee's performance

3. To provide a format enabling the supervisor to recommend a specific program designed to help an employee improve performance

4. To provide a basis for salary recommendations[4]

Figure 10-1 shows the most common uses of performance appraisals. In general, these can be classified as either administrative or developmental.

FIGURE 10-1 *Uses of Performance Appraisal*

RANKING	RATING*
1. Salary administration	5.85
2. Performance feedback	5.67
3. Identification of individual strengths and weaknesses	5.41
4. Documentation of personnel decisions	5.15
5. Recognition of individual performance	5.02
6. Determination of promotion	4.80
7. Identification of poor performance	4.96
8. Assistance in goal identification	4.90
9. Decision in retention or termination	4.75
10. Evaluation of goal achievement	4.72
11. Meeting legal requirements	4.58
12. Determination of transfers and assignments	3.66
13. Decision on layoffs	3.51
14. Identification of individual training needs	3.42
15. Determination of organizational training needs	2.74
16. Personnel planning	2.72
17. Reinforcement of authority structure	2.65
18. Identification of organizational development needs	2.63
19. Establishment of criteria for validation research	2.30
20. Evaluation of personnel systems	2.04

*Ratings are on a seven-point scale.

Source: Adapted from Jeanette N. Cleveland, Kevin R. Murphy, and Richard E. Williams, "Multiple Uses of Performance Appraisal: Prevalence and Correlates," *Journal of Applied Psychology* 74 (1989): 130–135. Copyright 1989 by the American Psychological Association. Adapted by permission.

Administrative Purposes

From the standpoint of administration, appraisal programs provide input that can be used for the entire range of HRM activities. For example, research has shown that performance appraisals are used most widely as a basis for compensation decisions.[5] The practice of "pay-for-performance" is found in all types of organizations. Performance appraisal is also directly related to a number of other major HR functions, such as promotion, transfer, and layoff decisions. Performance appraisal data may also be used in HR planning to determine the relative worth of jobs under a job evaluation program, and as criteria for validating selection tests. Performance appraisals also provide a "paper trail" for documenting HRM actions that may result in legal action. Employers must maintain accurate, objective records of employee performance in order to defend themselves against possible charges of discrimination in connection with such HRM actions as promotion, salary determination, and termination. Finally, it is important to recognize that the success of the entire HR program depends on knowing how the performance of employees compares with the goals established for them. This knowledge is best derived from a carefully planned and administered HR appraisal program. Appraisal systems have the capability to influence employee behaviour, thereby leading directly to improved organizational performance.

Developmental Purposes

From the standpoint of individual development, appraisal provides the feedback essential for discussing strengths and weaknesses as well as improving performance. Regardless of the employee's level of performance, the appraisal process provides an opportunity to identify issues for discussion, eliminate any potential problems, and set new goals for achieving high performance. Newer approaches to performance appraisal emphasize training as well as development and growth plans for employees. A developmental approach to appraisal recognizes that the purpose of a manager is to improve job behaviour, not simply to evaluate past performance. Having a sound basis for improving performance is one of the major benefits of an appraisal program.

Why Appraisal Programs Sometimes Fail

In actual practice, and for a number of reasons, formal performance appraisal programs sometimes yield disappointing results. Figure 10-2 shows that the primary culprits include lack of top-management information and support, unclear performance standards, rater bias, too many forms to complete, and use of the program for conflicting purposes. For example, if an appraisal program is used to provide a written appraisal for salary action and at the same time to motivate employees to improve their work, the administrative and developmental purposes may be in conflict. As a result, the appraisal interview may become a discussion about salary in which the manager seeks to justify the action taken. In such cases, the discussion might have little influence on the employee's future job performance.

As with all HR functions, if the support of top management is lacking, the appraisal program will not be successful. The Reality Check that follows describes how one CEO actively supports the performance appraisal program. Even the best-conceived program will not work in an environment where appraisers are not encouraged by their superiors to take the program seriously. To underscore the impor-

FIGURE 10-2 *Top Ten Reasons Performance Appraisals Can Fail*

1. Manager lacks information concerning an employee's actual performance.

2. Standards by which to evaluate an employee's performance are unclear.

3. Manager does not take the appraisal seriously.

4. Manager is not prepared for the appraisal review with the employees.

5. Manager is not honest/sincere during the evaluation.

6. Manager lacks appraisal skills.

7. Employee does not receive ongoing performance feedback.

8. Insufficient resources are provided to reward performance.

9. There is ineffective discussion of employee development.

10. Managers uses unclear/ambigous language in the evaluation process.

Source: Adapted with permission from Clinton O. Longnecker and Denise R. McGinnis, "Appraising People: Pitfalls and Solutions," Journal of Systems Management (December 1992): 12-16; and Clinton O. Longnecker and Stephen J. Goff, "Why Performance Appraisals Still Fail," Journal of Compensation and Benefits 6, no. 3 (November/December 1990): 36-41. Copyright 1992 and 1990 by Warren, Gorham & Lamont, Park Square Building, 31 St. James Avenue, Boston, MA 02116-4112. 1-800-950-1216. All rights reserved.

tance of this responsibility, top management should announce that effectiveness in appraising subordinates is a standard by which the appraisers themselves will be evaluated.

Other possible reasons for the failure of performance appraisal programs to yield the desired results include the following:

1. Managers feel that little or no benefit will be derived from the time and energy spent in the process.

2. Managers dislike the face-to-face confrontation involved in appraisal interviews.

3. Managers are not sufficiently adept at providing appraisal feedback.

4. The judgmental role of appraisal conflicts with the helping role of developing employees.

Performance appraisal at many organizations is a once-a-year activity in which the appraisal interview becomes a source of friction for both managers and employees. An important principle of performance appraisal is that continual feedback and employee coaching must be a positive daily activity.[6] The annual or semiannual performance review should simply be a logical extension of the day-to-day supervision process.

One of the main concerns of employees is the fairness of the performance appraisal system, since the process is central to so many HRM decisions. Employees who believe the system is unfair may consider the appraisal interview a waste of time

A MANAGER'S PERSPECTIVE ON PERFORMANCE APPRAISAL

TransLogic Limited, Mississauga, Ontario is a leading supplier of computerized material transport systems in Canada, with installations worldwide. Paul Collings is the president, with additional responsibility for international business development. His goal is to motivate his staff to perform their functions professionally and successfully.

"In my opinion the technical aspects of a performance appraisal system should be tailored to suit each particular circumstance. The system has to be dynamic so that it meets the needs of our changing and diverse operations," states Collings. "There must be some structure in place such as filling out the appropriate paperwork, timing, follow up, and so forth, but it must also be flexible enough to deal with the different groups of employees that work within our organization, and deal with `people as people.'

"For instance, in order to tie the results of our sales staff to the overall business plan, we knew we had to deviate from our standard performance appraisal system and adopt a unique program geared to measure the direct results of our sales staff. Using the standard format that we had used for so many years had not addressed the particular competencies that mattered most to value-added selling, such as sourcing new clients, selecting the right client to match the profile of our organization, or the ability to read situations that would help to close sales. The system we have devised is geared to measure the direct, day-to-day results that we expect of our sales staff. In fact, the paperwork that we have to complete is a summary of little talks we have had along the way. The real issue surrounding performance is how we deal with it on a daily basis. When employees achieve a milestone, we let them know how proud we are, just the same as letting them know when an area requires improvement. We work together with employees to ensure that they have full support as a means of achieving results. It doesn't do an employee any good to let things slide—you need to deal with issues as they occur. Because we deal with performance on a daily basis, it cuts down on the annual anxieties sometimes felt because there are no surprises. All issues, positive or otherwise, are dealt with as they occur."

Collings approaches employee issues in a positive fashion. "I believe the basic premise is that employees want to do a good job, accomplish goals, be as successful as they can, and be acknowledged for their results. They also want to know when improvement is needed so they can get their performance back on track. When employees are successful on the job, there is a spinoff effect in their personal lives. Sometimes, though, personal issues can affect performance. When a person is not happy at work or at home, it can become a vicious circle. Therefore, we may need to be a little more understanding at times and accept less than acceptable performance to help a person work through issues in the short term. In the long term, the job still needs to get done. If employees are having personal problems, I expect them to be open with me so that we can work together to resolve these situations."

Collings adds in closing, "I try to show our employees that objectives are common, and we can improve outcomes when we work together to develop increased performance levels."

Source: Interview with Deborah M. Zinni, August 1995.

The appraisal process should take place in an environment where both parties feel free to talk.

and leave the interview with feelings of anxiety or frustration. Also, they may view compliance with the appraisal system as perfunctory and thus play only a passive role during the interview process. By addressing these employee concerns during the planning stage of the appraisal process, the organization will help the appraisal program to succeed in reaching its goals.

Finally, organizational politics can introduce a bias even in fairly administered employee appraisals.[7] For example, managers may inflate evaluations because they desire higher salaries for their employees or because higher subordinate ratings make them look good as managers. Alternatively, managers may want to get rid of troublesome employees, passing them off to another department by inflating their ratings.

Developing an Effective Appraisal Program

objective

The HR department ordinarily has the primary responsibility for overseeing and coordinating the appraisal program. Managers from the operating departments must also be actively involved, particularly in helping to establish the objectives for the program. Furthermore, employees are more likely to accept and be satisfied with the performance appraisal program when they have the chance to participate in its development. Their concerns about fairness and accuracy in determining raises, promotions, and the like tend to be alleviated somewhat when they have been involved at the planning stage and have helped develop the performance standards themselves.

Establishing Performance Standards

Before any appraisal is conducted, the standards by which performance is to be evaluated should be clearly defined and communicated to the employee. As discussed in

Chapter 5, these standards should be based on job-related requirements derived from job analysis and reflected in the job descriptions and job specifications. When performance standards are properly established, they help translate organizational goals and objectives into job requirements that convey acceptable and unacceptable levels of performance to employees.[8]

In establishing performance standards, there are four basic considerations: strategic relevance, criterion deficiency, criterion contamination, and reliability.

Strategic Relevance

Strategic relevance refers to the extent to which standards relate to the strategic objectives of the organization. For example, if a TQM program has established a standard that "95 percent of all customer complaints are to be resolved in one day," then it is relevant for the customer service representatives to use such a standard for their evaluations. Companies such as 3M and Rubbermaid have strategic objectives that 25 to 30 percent of their sales are to be generated from products developed within the past five years. These objectives are translated into performance standards for their employees.[9] The Edmonton Telephone (ED TEL) program provides a link between what people do and what the company wants to do.[10] This process involves six steps: (1) strategic analysis, (2) process (what people do) definition, (3) measures development, (4) performance data collection, (5) gap analysis, and (6) ongoing management. There is a strong awareness of the relationship between strategy and measurement.

Criterion Deficiency

A second consideration in establishing performance standards is the extent to which the standards capture the entire range of an employee's responsibilities. When performance standards focus on a single criterion (e.g., sales revenues) to the exclusion of other important but less quantifiable performance dimensions (e.g., customer service), then the appraisal system is said to suffer from criterion deficiency.

Criterion Contamination

Just as performance criteria can be deficient, they can also be contaminated. There are factors outside an employee's control that can influence his or her performance. A comparison of performance of production workers, for example, should not be contaminated by the fact that some have newer machines than others. A comparison of the performance of travelling salespersons should not be contaminated by the fact that territories differ in terms of sales potential.

Reliability

As discussed in Chapter 7, reliability refers to the stability or consistency of a standard, or the extent to which individuals tend to maintain a certain level of performance over time. In ratings, reliability may be measured by correlating two sets of ratings made by a single rater or by two different raters.[11] For example, two managers may rate the same individual and estimate his or her suitability for a promotion. Their ratings could be compared to determine interrater reliability.

Performance standards will permit managers to specify and communicate precise information to employees regarding quality and quantity of output. Therefore, when performance standards are written, they should be defined in quantifiable and measurable terms. For example, "ability and willingness to handle customer orders" is not as good a performance standard as "all customer orders will be filled in four hours, with a 98 percent accuracy rate." When standards are expressed in specific, measurable terms, comparing the employee's performance against the standard results in a more justifiable appraisal.

Complying with the Law

Since performance appraisals are used as one basis for HRM actions, they must meet certain legal requirements. The legality of any performance appraisal system is measured against criteria of reliability, fairness, and validity. *Reliability* refers to whether performance is measured consistently among the employee participants. *Fairness* refers to the extent to which the system avoids bias caused by any factors unrelated to performance. *Validity* refers to the extent to which the system is job-related and accurate. Under the Charter of Rights and Freedom, and other federal and provincial human rights requirements, appraisal systems must be, above all, valid. Worker performance must be evaluated on the basis of job requirements to ensure legal compliance.

Although currently there is little litigation pertaining to performance appraisals systems in Canada, the spillover effect of litigation in the United States has prompted organizations to try to eliminate vagueness in descriptions of traits such as attitude, cooperation, dependability, initiative, and leadership. For example, the trait "dependability" can be made much less vague if it is spelled out in terms of employee tardiness and/or unexcused absences. In general, reducing room for subjective judgments will improve the entire appraisal process.

Employers might face legal challenges to their appraisal systems when appraisals indicate acceptable or above-average performance but employees are later passed over for promotion, disciplined for poor performance, discharged, or laid off from the organization. In these cases, the performance appraisals can undermine the legitimacy of the subsequent personnel decision. Therefore, performance appraisals should meet the following guidelines:

- Performance ratings must be job-related, with performance standards developed through job analysis.
- Employees must be given a written copy of their job standards in advance of appraisals.
- Managers who conduct the appraisal must be able to observe the behaviour they are rating. This implies having a measurable standard with which to compare employee behaviour.
- Supervisors should be trained to use the appraisal form correctly. They should be instructed in how to apply appraisal standards when making judgments.
- Appraisals should be discussed openly with employees and counselling or corrective guidance offered to help poor performers improve their performance.
- An appeals procedure should be established to enable employees to express disagreement with the appraisal.[12]

Employers must ensure that managers and supervisors document appraisals and reasons for subsequent HRM actions. This information may prove decisive should an employee take legal action. An employer's credibility is strengthened when it can support performance appraisal ratings by documenting instances of poor performance.[13]

objective

Deciding Who Should Appraise Performance

Just as there are multiple standards by which to evaluate performance, there are also multiple candidates for appraising performance. Given the complexity of today's jobs, it is often unrealistic to presume that one person can fully observe and evaluate an employee's performance. Companies such as Canadian Tire have begun to use multiple-rater approaches to performance evaluation. As shown in Figure 10-3, these raters may include supervisors, peers, team members, self, subordinates, and customers, each of whom may be more or less useful for the administrative and developmental purposes we discussed earlier.

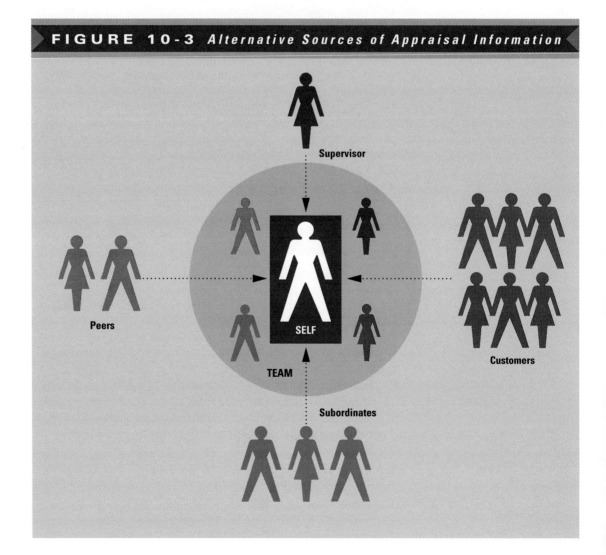

FIGURE 10-3 *Alternative Sources of Appraisal Information*

> ## ETHICS IN HRM
>
> ### SUPERVISING OR SPYING?
>
> Cameras monitor much of our everyday living, often without our knowledge. Surveillance systems may monitor you as you leave the lobby of your apartment building, as you enter the underground garage parking lot, as you drive on the highway to work, as you purchase a coffee at the variety store, and even at some workplaces.
>
> Employees who work as customer service representatives, handling 60 to 80 calls a day, may have their conversations monitored by supervisors or trainers to ensure that the information they give is accurate and that service standards are maintained. At one firm that handles the mail of private companies and donations for charities, employees work under very rigid evaluation systems. Employees must make 8500 keystrokes an hour; failure to achieve this norm is noted electronically. (Distractions are minimized by covering the windows, forbidding conversation unrelated to business, and facing all desks in the same direction.) Eight TV cameras are capable of zooming in on any desk in case any employee is displaying material unrelated to work.
>
> Even babysitters are being targeted for electronic monitoring. Cameras hidden in books watch the children and the nanny while anxious parents are at work. Parents insist that this surveillance enables them to ensure the safety and emotional security of their children; babysitters are outraged at the lack of trust and the invasion of their privacy.
>
> Would you work differently if your performance was continually monitored? Is it ethical for employers to do this?
>
> **Sources:** M. Gooderham, "Rise in Video Technology Lets Everyone Be a Spy," *The Globe and Mail*, June 7, 1995, A1; A.M. Stewart, "For a Nervous Breakdown, Please Press 1," *The Globe and Mail*, June 1, 1994, A25; and R. Fulford, "Tolerating Electronic Sweatshops," *The Globe and Mail*, December 14, 1994, C1.

Manager and/or supervisor appraisal
Performance appraisal done by an employee's manager and often reviewed by a manager one level above the superior.

Manager/Supervisor Appraisal

Manager and/or supervisor appraisal has been the traditional method of evaluating a subordinate's performance. In most instances, managers or supervisors are in the best position to perform this function, although it may not always be possible for them to do so. Managers often complain that they do not have the time to fully observe the performance of employees. The result is a less-than-objective appraisal. These managers must then rely on performance records or on the observations of others to complete the appraisal. For example, CIBC Insurance uses individuals as telephone monitors to gauge the quality of conversation between a service-centre representative and a customer. At CIBC, employees are aware they are being monitored, for developmental purposes only. Some issues about monitoring are raised in Ethics in HRM.

When a supervisor appraises employees independently, provision is often made for a review of the appraisals by the supervisor's superior. Having appraisals reviewed by a supervisor's superior reduces the chance of superficial or biased evaluations. Reviews by superiors generally are more objective and provide a broader perspective of employee performance than do appraisals by immediate supervisors.

Self-Appraisal

Sometimes employees are asked to evaluate themselves on a self-appraisal form.[14] Self-appraisals are beneficial when managers seek to increase employees' involvement in the review process. A **self-appraisal** system requires an employee to complete the appraisal form prior to the performance interview. At a minimum, this gets the employee thinking about his or her strengths and weaknesses and may lead to discussions about barriers to effective performance. During the performance interview, the manager and the employee discuss job performance and agree on a final appraisal. This approach also works well when the manager and the employee jointly establish future performance goals or employee development plans. Critics of self-appraisal argue that self-raters are more lenient than managers in their assessments and tend to present themselves in a highly favourable light.[15] For this reason, self-appraisals may be best for developmental purposes rather than for administrative decisions. Used in conjunction with other methods, self-appraisals can be a valuable source of appraisal information.

Subordinate Appraisal

Subordinate appraisal has been used in companies such as Xerox and IBM to give managers feedback on how their subordinates view them.[16] Subordinates are in a good position to evaluate their managers since they are in frequent contact with their superiors and occupy a unique position from which to observe many performance-related behaviours. Those performance dimensions judged most appropriate for subordinate appraisals include leadership, oral communication, delegation of authority, coordination of team efforts, and interest in subordinates. However, dimensions related to managers' specific job tasks, such as planning and organizing, budgeting, creativity, and analytical ability, are not usually seen as appropriate for subordinate appraisal.

Since subordinate appraisals give employees power over their bosses, the managers themselves may be hesitant to endorse such a system, particularly when it might be used as a basis for compensation decisions. However, when the information is used for developmental purposes, managers tend to be more open to the idea.[17] Nevertheless, to avoid potential problems, subordinate appraisals should be submitted anonymously and combined across several individual raters.

Peer Appraisal

Individuals of equal rank who work together are increasingly asked to evaluate each other. A **peer appraisal** provides information that differs to some degree from ratings by a superior, since peers often see different dimensions of performance. Peers can readily identify leadership and interpersonal skills along with other strengths and weaknesses of their co-workers. A superior asked to rate a patrol officer on a dimension such as "dealing with the public" may not have had much opportunity to observe it. Fellow officers, on the other hand, have the opportunity to observe this behaviour regularly.

Self-appraisal
Performance appraisal done by the employee being evaluated, generally on an appraisal form completed by the employee prior to the performance interview.

Subordinate appraisal
Performance appraisal of a superior by an employee, which is more appropriate for developmental than administrative purposes.

Peer appraisal
Performance appraisal done by one's colleagues, generally on forms that are compiled into a single profile for use in the performance interview conducted by the employee's manager.

One advantage of peer appraisals is the belief that they furnish more accurate and valid information than appraisals by superiors. The supervisor often sees employees putting their best foot forward, while those who work with their fellow employees on a regular basis may be presented with a more realistic picture. With peer appraisals, co-workers complete an evaluation on the employee. The forms are then usually compiled into a single profile, which is given to the supervisor for use in the final appraisal.[18]

Despite the evidence that peer appraisals are possibly the most accurate method of judging employee behaviour, a number of factors have prevented them from being used more frequently.[19] Following are the most common criticisms of peer appraisal:

1. Peer ratings are simply a popularity contest.
2. Managers are reluctant to give up control over the appraisal process.
3. Those receiving low ratings might retaliate against their peers.
4. Peers rely on stereotypes in ratings.

When peers are in competition with one another, as is the case with sales associates, peer appraisals may not be advisable for administrative decisions such as salary or bonuses. Employers using peer appraisals must also be sure to safeguard confidentiality in handling the review forms. Any breach of confidentiality can create interpersonal rivalries or hurt feelings and provoke hostility among fellow employees.

Team Appraisal

Team appraisal

Performance appraisal, based on TQM concepts, that recognizes team accomplishment rather than individual performance.

An extension of the peer appraisal is the **team appraisal**. While peers are on equal standing with one another, they may not work closely together. In a team setting, it may be nearly impossible to separate out an individual's contribution. Advocates of team appraisal argue that, in such cases, individual appraisal can be dysfunctional since it detracts from the critical issues of the team. To address this issue, organizations such as General Foods and Digital have begun developing team appraisals to evaluate the performance of the team as a whole.[20]

A company's interest in team appraisals is frequently driven by its commitment to TQM principles and practices. At its root, TQM is a control system that involves setting standards (based on customer requirements), measuring performance against those standards, and identifying opportunities for continuous improvement. In this regard, TQM and performance appraisal are perfectly complementary. However, a basic tenet of TQM is that performance is best understood at the level of the system as a whole, whereas performance appraisal traditionally has focused on individual performance. Team appraisals represent one way to break down barriers between individuals and encourage their collective effort.[21] Frequently the system is complemented by use of team incentives or group variable pay (see Chapter 12).

Customer Appraisal

Customer appraisal

Performance appraisal that, like team appraisal, is based on TQM concepts and seeks evaluation from both external and internal customers.

Also driven by TQM concerns, an increasing number of organizations use internal and external **customer appraisal** as a source of performance appraisal information. External customers' evaluations, of course, have been used for some time to appraise restaurant personnel. However, companies such as Sun Life of Canada have begun utilizing external customers as well. Within Honda's Acura division, a system has been developed that combines customer appraisals and team appraisal. Its Precision Team Program asks customers to rate a dealership on its overall service. This

The customers are being asked to evaluate the overall service of the car dealership

evaluation incorporates salespeople, customer service, and the parts department. Dealerships that score well in all three departments receive both group and individual rewards.[22]

In contrast to external customers, internal customers include anyone inside the organization who depends upon an employee's work output. For example, managers who rely on the HR department for selection and training services would be candidates for conducting internal customer evaluations. For both developmental and administrative reasons, internal customers can provide extremely useful feedback about the value added by an employee or team of employees.[23] The $3-billion Taurus/Sable program at Ford Motor represents a classic example of how internal customers were used to re-engineer manufacturing processes in order to improve performance.[24]

Training Appraisers

A weakness of many performance appraisal programs is that managers and supervisors are not adequately trained for the appraisal task and provide little meaningful feedback to subordinates. Because they lack precise standards for appraising subordinates' performance and have not developed the necessary observational and feedback skills, their appraisals often become nondirective and meaningless. Some ways in which training appraisers can improve the performance appraisal process are discussed below.

Establishing an Appraisal Plan

Training programs are most effective when they follow a systematic process that begins with an explanation of the objectives of the performance appraisal system.[25] It is important for the rater to know the purpose for which the appraisal is to be used. For example, using the appraisal for compensation decisions rather than development purposes may affect how the rater evaluates the employee, and it may change the rater's opinion of how the appraisal form should be completed. The mechanics of the rating system should also be explained, including how frequently the appraisals are to be conducted, who will conduct them, and what the standards of performance are. In addition, appraisal training should alert raters to the weaknesses and problems of appraisal systems so they can be avoided.

Eliminating Rater Error

Appraisal training should focus on eliminating the subjective errors made by managers in the rating process. Gary Latham and Kenneth Wexley stress the importance of performance appraisal training by noting that:

> Observer bias in performance appraisals can be largely attributed to well-known rating errors ... that occur in a systematic manner when an individual observes and evaluates another. In order to minimize the occurrence of rating

error and costly litigation battles, organizations, regardless of the appraisal instrument they use, are well advised to expose people who evaluate employees to a training program to minimize rating errors.[26]

With any rating method, certain types of errors can arise that should be considered. The "halo error" discussed in Chapter 7 is also common with respect to rating scales, especially those that do not include carefully developed descriptions of the employee behaviours being rated.[27] Provision for comments on the rating form tends to reduce halo error.

Some types of rating errors are *distributional* errors in that they involve a group of ratings given across various employees. For example, raters who are reluctant to assign either extremely high or extremely low ratings commit the **error of central tendency**. In this case, all employees are rated about average. To such raters it is a good idea to explain that, among large numbers of employees, one should expect to find significant differences in behaviour, productivity, and other characteristics.

In contrast to central tendency errors, it is also common for some raters to give unusually high or low ratings. For example, a manager may erroneously assert, "All my employees are excellent" or "None of my people are good enough." These beliefs give rise to what is called **leniency or strictness error**. One way to reduce this error is to clearly define the characteristics or dimensions of performance, and to provide meaningful descriptions of behaviour, known as *anchors*, on the scale. Another approach is to require ratings to conform to a *forced distribution*. Managers appraising employees under a forced-distribution system would be required to place a certain percentage of employees into various performance categories. For example, it may be required that 10 percent of ratings be poor (or excellent). This is similar to the requirement in some schools that instructors grade on a curve. However, while a forced distribution may solve leniency and strictness error, it may create other errors in the accuracy of ratings—particularly if most employees are performing above standard.

Some rating errors are *temporal* in that the performance review is biased either favourably or unfavourably, depending on the way performance information is selected, evaluated, and organized by the rater over time.[28] For example, when the appraisal is based largely on the employee's recent behaviour, good or bad, the rater has committed the **recency error**. Managers who give higher ratings because they believe an employee is "showing improvement" may unwittingly be committing recency error. Without work-record documentation for the entire appraisal period, the rater is forced to recall recent employee behaviour to establish the rating. The recency error can be minimized by having the rater routinely document employee accomplishments and failures throughout the whole appraisal period. Rater training also will help reduce this error.

Contrast error occurs when an employee's evaluation is biased either upward or downward because of comparison with the performance of another employee who was evaluated just previously. For example, an average employee may appear especially productive when compared with a poor performer. However, that same employee may appear unproductive when compared with a star performer. Contrast errors are most likely when raters are required to rank employees in order from the best to the poorest. Employees are evaluated against one another, usually on the basis of some organizational standard or guideline. For example, they may be compared on the basis of their ability to meet production standards or their "overall" ability to

---

Error of central tendency
Performance rating error in which all employees are rated above average.

Leniency or strictness error
Performance-rating error in which the appraiser tends to give employees either unusually high or unusually low ratings.

Recency error
Performance-rating error in which the appraisal is based largely on the employee's most recent behaviour rather than on behaviour throughout the appraisal period.

Contrast error
Performance-rating error in which an employee's evaluation is biased either upward or downward because of comparison with another employee who was evaluated just previously.

perform their job. As with other types of rating error, contrast error can be reduced through training that focuses on using objective standards and behavioural anchors to appraise performance.

Similar-to-me error occurs when appraisers inflate the evaluations of people with whom they have something in common. For example, if both the manager and the employee are from small towns, the manager may unwittingly have a more favourable impression of the employee. The effects of a similar-to-me error can be powerful, and when the similarity is based on race, religion, gender, or some other protected category, it may result in discrimination.

Furthermore, raters should be aware of any stereotypes they may hold toward particular groups—e.g., male/female, Caucasian/visible minorities—because the observation and interpretation of performance can be clouded by these stereotypes. Results from a study examining how individual differences in stereotypes of women affect performance ratings suggested that women evaluated by raters who have traditional stereotypes of women are at a disadvantage in obtaining merit pay increases and promotions.[29] This problem will be aggravated when employees are appraised on the basis of poorly defined performance standards and subjective performance traits.

Formal training programs can reduce the subjective errors commonly made during the rating process. This training can pay off, particularly when participants have the opportunity to (1) observe other managers making errors, (2) actively participate in discovering their own errors, and (3) practise job-related tasks to reduce the errors they tend to make.[30]

Providing Feedback

Finally, a training program for raters should provide some general points to consider for planning and conducting the feedback interview. This interview not only provides employees with knowledge of results of their evaluation, but it allows the manager and employee to discuss current problems and set future goals. Training in specific skills should cover at least three basic areas: (1) communicating effectively, (2) diagnosing the root causes of performance problems, and (3) setting goals and objectives.[31] A checklist can be used to assist supervisors in preparing for the appraisal interview. The sample checklist shown in Highlights in HRM 1 reflects the growing tendency of organizations to have employees assess their own performance prior to the appraisal interview. The performance appraisal interview will be discussed in detail later in the chapter.

objective

Performance Appraisal Methods

Since the early years of their use, methods of evaluating personnel have evolved considerably. Old systems have been replaced by new methods that represent technical improvements and legal requirements and are more consistent with the purposes of appraisal. In the discussion that follows, we will examine in some detail those methods that have found widespread use, and we will briefly touch on other methods that are used less frequently. Performance appraisal methods can be broadly classified as measuring traits, behaviours, or results. Trait approaches continue to be the more popular systems despite their inherent subjectivity. Behavioural approaches provide more action-oriented information to employees and therefore may be best

HIGHLIGHTS IN HRM

HRM
highlights

1   SUPERVISOR'S CHECKLIST FOR THE PERFORMANCE APPRAISAL

Scheduling

1. Schedule the review and notify the employee ten days or two weeks in advance.
2. Ask the employee to prepare for the session by reviewing his or her performance, job objectives, and development goals.
3. Clearly state that this will be the formal annual performance appraisal.

Preparing for the Review

1. Review the performance documentation collected throughout the year. Concentrate on work patterns that have developed.
2. Be prepared to give specific examples of above- or below-average performance.
3. When performance falls short of expectations, determine what changes need to be made. If performance meets or exceeds expectations, discuss this and plan how to reinforce it.
4. After the appraisal is written, set it aside for a few days and then review it again.
5. Follow whatever steps are required by your organization's performance appraisal system.

Conducting the Review

1. Select a location that is comfortable and free of distractions. The location should encourage a frank and candid conversation.
2. Discuss each item in the appraisal one at a time, considering both strengths and shortcomings.
3. Be specific and descriptive, not general or judgmental. Report rather than evaluate occurrences.
4. Discuss your differences and resolve them. Solicit agreement with the evaluation.
5. Jointly discuss and design plans for taking corrective action for growth and development.
6. Maintain a professional and supportive approach to the appraisal discussion.

Source: Adapted from "The Performance-Management Process, Part 1 and 2," *Straight Talk* (AT&T) 1, nos. 8 and 9 (December 1987).

for development. The results-oriented approach is gaining popularity because it focuses on the measurable contributions that employees make to the organization.

Trait Methods

Trait approaches to performance appraisal are designed to measure the extent to which an employee possesses certain characteristics—such as dependability, creativity, initiative, and leadership—that are viewed as important for the job in particular and the organization in general. The fact that trait methods are the most popular method is due in large part to the ease with which they are developed. However, if not designed carefully on the basis of job analysis, trait appraisals can be notoriously biased and subjective.

Graphic Rating Scales

Graphic rating scale method

A trait approach to performance appraisal whereby each employee is rated according to a scale of characteristics.

In the **graphic rating scale method**, each trait or characteristic to be rated is represented by a scale on which a rater indicates the degree to which an employee possesses that trait or characteristic. An example of this type of scale is shown in Highlights in HRM 2. There are many variations of the graphic rating scale. The differences are to be found in (1) the characteristics or dimensions on which individuals are rated, (2) the degree to which the performance dimension is defined for the rater, and (3) how clearly the points on the scale are defined. In Highlights in HRM 2, the dimensions are defined briefly and some attempt is made to define the points on the scale. Subjectivity bias is reduced somewhat when the dimensions on the scale and the scale points are defined as precisely as possible. This can be achieved by training raters and by including descriptive appraisal guidelines in a performance appraisal reference book developed by the organization.

Finally, the rating form should provide sufficient space for comments on the behaviour associated with each scale. These comments improve the accuracy of the appraisal since they require the rater to think in terms of observable employee behaviours while providing specific examples to discuss with the employee during the appraisal interview.

Mixed Standard Scales

Mixed standard scale method

A trait approach to performance appraisal similar to other scale methods but based on comparison with (better than, equal to, or worse than) a standard.

The **mixed standard scale method** is a modification of the basic rating scale method. Rather than being required to evaluate traits according to a single scale, the rater is given three specific descriptions of each trait. These descriptions reflect three levels of performance: superior, average, and inferior. After the three descriptions for each trait are written, they are randomly sequenced to form the mixed standard scale.[32] As shown in Highlights in HRM 3, supervisors evaluate employees by indicating whether their performance is better than, equal to, or worse than the standard for each behaviour.

Forced-Choice Method

Forced-choice method

A trait approach to performance appraisal that requires the rater to choose from statements designed to distinguish between successful and unsuccessful performance.

The **forced-choice method** requires the rater to choose from statements, often appearing in pairs, that appear equally favourable or equally unfavourable and are designed to distinguish between successful and unsuccessful performance. The rater selects one statement from the pair without knowing which statement correctly describes successful job behaviour. For example, forced-choice pairs might include the following:

1a. Works hard
1b. Works quickly

2a. Is responsive to customers
2b. Shows initiative

HIGHLIGHTS IN HRM

HRM
highlights

2   GRAPHIC RATING SCALE WITH PROVISION FOR COMMENTS

Appraise employee's performance in PRESENT ASSIGNMENT. Check (✔) most appropriate square. Appraisers are *urged to freely use* the "Remarks" sections for significant comments descriptive of the individual.

1. KNOWLEDGE OF WORK: Understanding of all phases of his/her work and related matters	Needs instruction or guidance	Has required knowledge of own and related work	Has exceptional knowledge of own and related work
	☐ ☐ ☐ ☑ ☐		
	Remarks: *Is particularly good on gas engines.*		

2. INITIATIVE: Ability to originate or develop ideas and to get things started	Lacks imagination	Meets necessary requirements	Unusually resourceful
	☐ ☑ ☐ ☐ ☐		
	Remarks: *Has good ideas when asked for an opinion, but otherwise will not offer them. Somewhat lacking in self-confidence.*		

3. APPLICATION: Attention and application to his/her work	Wastes time Needs close supervision	Steady and willing worker	Exceptionally industrious
	☐ ☐ ☑ ☐ ☐		
	Remarks: *Accepts new jobs when assigned.*		

4. QUALITY OF WORK: Thoroughness, neatness, and accuracy of work	Needs improvement	Regularly meets recognized standards	Consistently maintains highest quality
	☐ ☐ ☐ ☐ ☑		
	Remarks: *The work he turns out is always of the highest possible quality.*		

5. VOLUME OF WORK: Quantity of acceptable work	Should be increased	Regularly meets recognized standards	Unusually high output
	☐ ☐ ☑ ☐ ☐		
	Remarks: *Would be higher if he did not spend so much time checking and rechecking his work.*		

HIGHLIGHTS IN HRM

3 **EXAMPLE OF MIXED STANDARD SCALE**

HRM
highlights

DIRECTIONS: Please indicate whether the individual's performance is above (+), equal to (0), or lower (−) than each of the following standards.

1. _____ Employee uses good judgment when addressing problems and provides workable alternatives; however, at times does not take actions to prevent problems. *(medium PROBLEM SOLVING)*

2. _____ Employee lacks supervisory skills; frequently handles employees poorly and is at times argumentative. *(low LEADERSHIP)*

3. _____ Employee is extremely cooperative; can be expected to take the lead in developing cooperation among employees; completes job tasks with a positive attitude. *(high COOPERATION)*

4. _____ Employee has effective supervision skills; encourages productivity, quality, and employee development. *(medium LEADERSHIP)*

5. _____ Employee normally displays an argumentative or defensive attitude toward fellow employees and job assignments. *(low COOPERATION)*

6. _____ Employee is generally agreeable but becomes argumentative at times when given job assignments; cooperates with other employees as expected. *(medium COOPERATION)*

7. _____ Employee is not good at solving problems; uses poor judgment and does not anticipate potential difficulties. *(low PROBLEM SOLVING)*

8. _____ Employee anticipates potential problems and provides creative, proactive alternative solutions; has good attention to follow-up. *(high PROBLEM SOLVING)*

9. _____ Employee displays skilled direction; effectively coordinates unit activities; is generally a dynamic leader and motivates employees to high performance. *(high LEADERSHIP)*

3a. Produces poor quality
3b. Lacks good work habits

The forced-choice method is not without limitations, the primary one being the cost of establishing and maintaining its validity. The fact that it has been a source of frustration to many raters has sometimes caused the method to be eliminated from appraisal programs. In addition, it cannot be used as effectively as some of the other methods to help achieve the commonly held objective of using appraisals as a tool for developing employees by such means as the appraisal interview.

Essay method

A trait approach to performance appraisal that requires the rater to compose a statement describing employee behaviour.

Essay Method

Unlike rating scales, which provide a structured form of appraisal, the **essay method** requires the appraiser to compose a statement that best describes the employee being appraised. The appraiser is usually instructed to describe the employee's strengths and weaknesses and to make recommendations for his or her development. Often the essay method is combined with other rating methods. Essays may provide additional descriptive information on performance that is not obtained with, for example, a structured rating scale.

The essay method provides an excellent opportunity to point out the unique characteristics of the employee being appraised. This aspect of the method is heightened when a supervisor is instructed to describe specific points about the employee's promotability, special talents, skills, strengths, and weaknesses. A major limitation of the essay method is that composing an essay that attempts to cover all of an employee's essential characteristics is a very time-consuming task (though when combined with other methods, this method does not require a lengthy statement). Another disadvantage of the essay method is that the quality of the performance appraisal may be influenced by the supervisor's writing skills and composition style. Good writers may simply be able to produce more favourable appraisals. A final drawback of this appraisal method is that it tends to be subjective and may not focus on relevant aspects of job performance.

Behavioural Methods

As mentioned above, one of the potential drawbacks of a trait-oriented performance appraisal is that traits tend to be vague and subjective. We discussed earlier that one way to improve a rating scale is to have descriptions of behaviour along a scale, or continuum. These descriptions permit the rater to readily identify the point where a particular employee falls on the scale. Behavioural methods have been developed to describe specifically which actions should (or should not) be exhibited on the job. They are frequently more useful for providing employees with developmental feedback.

Critical incident

Unusual event that denotes superior or inferior employee performance in some part of the job.

Critical Incidents Method

The critical incident method, described in Chapter 5 in connection with job analysis, is also used as a method of appraisal. Recall that a **critical incident** occurs when employee behaviour results in unusual success or unusual failure on some part of the job. A favourable critical incident is illustrated by the janitor who observed that a file cabinet containing classified documents had been left unlocked at the close of business. The janitor called the security officer, who took the necessary action to correct the problem. An unfavourable incident is illustrated by the mail clerk who failed to deliver a Priority Post package immediately, instead putting it in with regular mail to be routed two hours later. One advantage of the critical incident method is that it covers the entire appraisal period (and therefore may guard against recency error). And because the behavioural incidents are specific, they can facilitate employee feedback and development. However, unless both favourable and unfavourable incidents are discussed, employees who are appraised may have negative feelings about this method. Some employees have been known to refer to it as the "little black book" approach. Perhaps its greatest contribution is in developing job specifications and in constructing the types of appraisal procedures discussed below.

Behavioural Checklist Method

One of the oldest appraisal techniques is the behavioural checklist method. It consists of having the rater check those statements on a list that the rater believes are characteristic of the employee's performance or behaviour. A checklist developed for computer salespersons might include a number of statements like the following:

- Is able to explain equipment clearly
- Keeps abreast of new developments in technology
- Tends to be a steady worker
- Reacts quickly to customer needs
- Processes orders correctly

Behaviourally Anchored Rating Scale (BARS)

A **behaviourally anchored rating scale (BARS)** consists of a series of five to ten vertical scales—one for each important dimension of performance identified through job analysis. These dimensions are anchored by behaviours identified through a critical incidents job analysis. The critical incidents are placed along the scale and are assigned point values according to the opinions of experts. A BARS for the job of firefighter is shown in Highlights in HRM 4. Note that this particular scale is for the dimension described as "Firefighting Strategy: Knowledge of Fire Characteristics."

A BARS is typically developed by a committee that includes both subordinates and managers.[33] The committee's task is to identify all the relevant characteristics or dimensions of the job. Behavioural anchors in the form of statements are then established for each of the job dimensions. Several participants are asked to review the anchor statements and indicate which job dimension each anchor illustrates. The only anchors retained are those which at least 70 percent of the group agree belong with a particular dimension. Finally, anchors are attached to their job dimensions and placed on the appropriate scales according to values that the group assigns to them.

At present there is no strong evidence that a BARS reduces *all* of the rating errors mentioned previously.[34] However, some studies have shown that scales of this type can yield more accurate ratings.[35] One major advantage of a BARS is that personnel outside of the HR department participate with HR staff in its development. Employee participation can lead to greater acceptance of the performance appraisal process and of the performance measures that it uses.

The procedures followed in developing a BARS also result in scales that have a high degree of content validity. The main disadvantage of a BARS is that it requires considerable time and effort to develop. In addition, because the scales are specific to particular jobs, a scale designed for one job may not apply to another.

Behaviour Observation Scale (BOS)

A **behaviour observation scale (BOS)** is similar to BARS in that they are both based on critical incidents. However, Highlights in HRM 5 shows that, rather than requiring the evaluator to choose the most representative behavioural anchor, BOS is designed to measure how *frequently* each of the behaviours has been observed.

The value of BOS is that this approach allows the appraiser to play the role of observer rather than judge.[36] In this way, he or she may more easily provide constructive feedback to the employee. Users of the system frequently prefer BOS over BARS

Behaviourally anchored rating scale (BARS)

A behavioural approach to performance appraisal that consists of a series of vertical scales, one for each important dimension of job performance.

Behaviour observation scale (BOS)

A behavioural approach to performance appraisal that measures the frequency of observed behaviour.

HIGHLIGHTS IN HRM

4   EXAMPLE OF BARS FOR MUNICIPAL FIRE COMPANIES

FIREFIGHTING STRATEGY: Knowledge of Fire Characteristics. This area of performance concerns the ability of a firefighter to use his or her knowledge of fire characteristics to develop the best strategy for fighting a fire. It involves the following activities: Observe fire and smoke conditions and locate source of fire. Size up fire and identify appropriate extinguishing techniques and ventilation procedures. Consult preplan reports. Apply knowledge of heat and fluid mechanics to anticipate fire behaviour. Identify and screen or saturate potential exposures using direct or fog streams or water curtains. Identify and remove or protect flammable or hazardous materials.

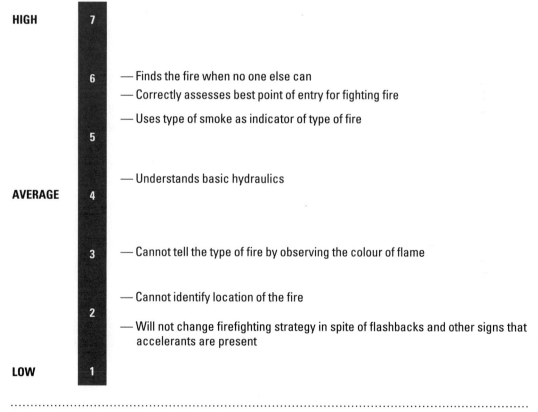

Source: Adapted from Landy, Jacobs, and Associates. Reprinted with permission.

HIGHLIGHTS IN HRM

5   **SAMPLE ITEMS FROM BEHAVIOUR OBSERVATION SCALES**

highlights

INSTRUCTIONS: Please consider the Sales Representative's behaviour on the job in the past rating period. Read each statement carefully, then circle the number that indicates the extent to which the employee has demonstrated this *effective* or *ineffective* behaviour.

For each behaviour observed, use the following scale:

5 represents almost always 95–100% of the time
4 represents frequently   85–94% of the time
3 represents sometimes   75–84% of the time
2 represents seldom   65–74% of the time
1 represents almost never   0–64% of the time

SALES PRODUCTIVITY	ALMOST NEVER				ALMOST ALWAYS
1. Reviews individual productivity results with manager	1	2	3	4	5
2. Suggests to peers ways of building sales	1	2	3	4	5
3. Formulates specific objectives for each contact	1	2	3	4	5
4. Focuses on product rather than customer problem	1	2	3	4	5
5. Keep account plans updated	1	2	3	4	5
6. Keeps customer waiting for service	1	2	3	4	5
7. Anticipates and prepares for customer concerns	1	2	3	4	5
8. Follows up on customer leads	1	2	3	4	5

Management by objectives (MBO)
Philosophy of management that rates performance on the basis of employee achievement of goals set by mutual agreement of employee and manager.

or trait scales because it (1) maintains objectivity, (2) distinguishes good from poor performers, (3) provides feedback, and (4) identifies training needs.[37]

Results Method: Management by Objectives

Management by objectives (MBO) is a philosophy of management first proposed by Peter Drucker in 1954.[38] MBO seeks to judge the performance of employees on the basis of their success in achieving the objectives they established through consultation with their superiors. Performance-improvement efforts under MBO focus on the goals to be achieved by employees rather than on the activities they perform or the traits they exhibit in connection with their assigned duties.

MBO is a system involving a cycle (see Figure 10-4) that begins with setting the organization's common goals and objectives and ultimately returns to that step. The system acts as a goal-setting process whereby objectives are established for the organ-ization (step 1), departments (step 2), and individual managers and employees (step 3).

As Figure 10-4 illustrates, a significant feature of the cycle is the establishment of specific goals by the employee, but those goals are based on a broad statement of employee responsibilities prepared by the supervisor. Employee-established goals are discussed with the supervisor and jointly reviewed and modified until both parties are satisfied with them (step 4). The goal statements are accompanied by a detailed account of the actions the employee proposes to take in order to reach the goals. During periodic reviews, as objective data are made available, the progress that the employee is making toward the goals is then assessed (step 5). Goals may be changed at this time as new or additional data are received. At the conclusion of a period of time (usually six months or one year), the employee makes a self-appraisal of what she or he has accomplished, substantiating the self-appraisal with factual data wher-ever possible. The "interview" is an examination of the employee's self-appraisal by the supervisor and the employee together (step 6). The final step (step 7) is review-ing the connection between individual and organizational performance.

Requirements for a Successful MBO Program

If they are to succeed, MBO programs should meet several requirements. First, objec-tives set at each level of the organization should be quantifiable and measurable for both the long and short term. Second, the expected results must be under the employee's control, and goals (e.g., profit, cost of product made, sales per product, quality control) must be consistent for each level (top executive, manager, and employee). Third, managers and employees must establish specific times when goals are to be reviewed and evaluated. Finally, each employee goal statement must be accompanied by a description of how that goal will be accomplished. Highlights in HRM 6 presents the goal-setting worksheet used by Universal Service Corporation. Note that this worksheet contains sections for the setting of goals and the evaluation of goal achievement.

George Odiorne states that the success of an MBO program depends heavily on a behavioural change on the part of both the supervisor and the subordinate.[39] Both individuals must be willing to *mutually* establish goals and measurable standards for employee performance. Furthermore, MBO must be viewed as part of a system of managing, not as merely an addition to the manager's job. Managers who adopt MBO as a system of managing must be willing to delegate responsibility for reaching goals to their subordinates.

A major advantage of MBO is that it requires the setting of employee-estab-lished goals. Goal setting has been shown to improve employee performance, thereby leading to increased productivity.[40] Measurable increases in job performance typi-cally range from 10 to 25 percent, and in some cases they have been even higher.[41] Goal setting works because it allows employees to focus their efforts on important job tasks and makes them accountable for completing these tasks. Furthermore, goal setting establishes an automatic feedback system, since employees can regularly

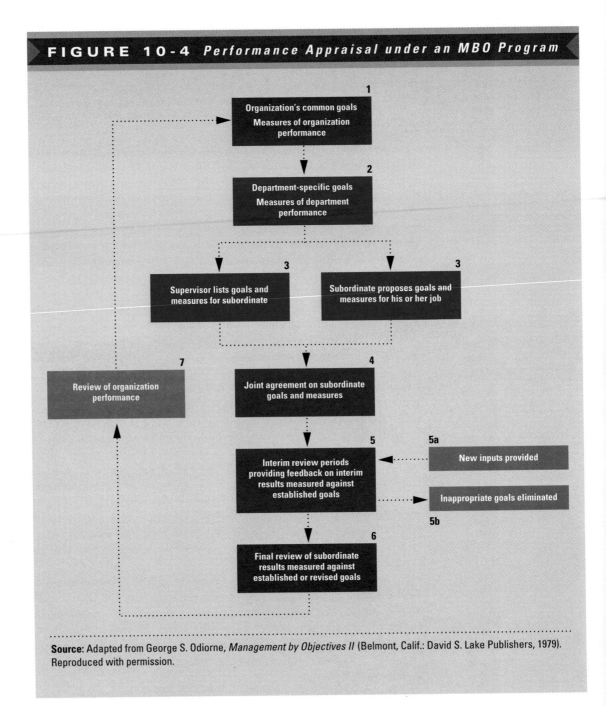

FIGURE 10-4 *Performance Appraisal under an MBO Program*

Source: Adapted from George S. Odiorne, *Management by Objectives II* (Belmont, Calif.: David S. Lake Publishers, 1979). Reproduced with permission.

evaluate their performance against their goals. Goal setting has been of benefit to groups as diverse as clerical personnel, scientists, maintenance employees, computer analysts, and engineers.

HIGHLIGHTS IN HRM

HRM highlights

6   EXAMPLE OF A GOAL-SETTING WORKSHEET

UNIVERSAL SERVICE CORPORATION

Employee's Rating Record

Name _____   Date _____

Job Title _____   Department _____

Appraised by _____   Date Started _____

Summary of Appraisal

Development Needs

Major Responsibilities and Period Goals	**Evaluation of Attainment of Goals**
Responsibility	
Goal	
Responsibility	
Goal	
Responsibility	
Goal	

Criticisms of MBO

The MBO system is not without its critics. One researcher contends that MBO is a lengthy and costly appraisal system that has only a moderate impact on organizational success.[42] Another criticism of MBO is that since performance data are designed to measure results, they may be affected by factors that are out of an individual's control; this raises the issue of *criterion contamination* discussed earlier in this chapter.

MBO systems may inadvertently encourage employees to "look good" on a short-term basis, while ignoring the long-term ramifications. Line supervisors, for example, may let their equipment suffer to reduce maintenance costs. If the MBO program focuses on a narrow set of results criteria to the exclusion of other important process issues, the system may suffer from *criterion deficiency* and may unintentionally foster the attitude that "what gets measured gets done." In fact, in any job involving interaction with others, it is not enough to meet certain production or sales objectives. Factors such as cooperation, adaptability, initiative, and concern for human relations may also be important to job success. If these factors are important job standards, they should be added to the appraisal review. Thus, to be realistic, both the results *and* the method used to achieve them should be considered.

Which Performance Appraisal Method to Use?

The choice of method should be based largely on the purpose of the appraisal. Figure 10-5 lists some of the strengths and weaknesses of trait, behaviour, and results approaches to appraisal. Note that the simplest and least expensive techniques often yield the least accurate information. However, research has not always supported a clear choice among appraisal methods. For example, results from a study comparing the relative advantages of BARS versus an overall rating scale in terms of dispersion, test/retest reliability, halo effect, and criterion-related validity showed that the BARS was not superior to the overall rating scale in the properties examined.[43] In addition, another recent study showed that an MBO-based system was no better than a graphic rating system for motivating performance.[44] However, evidence suggests that a BOS system may lead to higher satisfaction than a system based on graphic ratings.[45] While researchers and HR managers generally believe that the more sophisticated and more time-consuming methods offer more useful information, this may not always be the case. Managers must make cost-benefit decisions about which methods to use.

Appraisal Interviews

The appraisal interview is perhaps the most important part of the entire performance appraisal process. The appraisal interview gives a manager the opportunity to discuss a subordinate's performance record and to explore areas of possible improvement and growth. It also provides an opportunity to identify the subordinate's attitudes and feelings more thoroughly and thus to improve communication.

Unfortunately, the interviewer can become overburdened by attempting to discuss too much, such as the employee's past performance and future development goals. Dividing the appraisal interview into two sessions, one for the performance

FIGURE 10-5   *Summary of Various Appraisal Methods*

	ADVANTAGES	DISADVANTAGES
Trait Methods	1. Are inexpensive to develop 2. Use meaningful dimensions 3. Are easy to use	1. Have high potential for rating errors 2. Are not useful for employee counseling 3. Are not useful for allocating rewards 4. Are not useful for promotion decisions
Behavioral Methods	1. Use specific performance dimensions 2. Are acceptable to employees and superiors 3. Are useful for providing feedback 4. Are fair for reward and promotion decisions	1. Can be time-consuming to develop/use 2. Can be costly to develop 3. Have some potential for rating error
Results Method	1. Has less subjectivity bias 2. Is acceptable to employees and superiors 3. Links individual performance to organizational performance 4. Encourages mutual goal setting 5. Is good for reward and promotion decisions	1. Is time-consuming to develop/use 2. May encourage short-term perspective 3. May use contaminated criteria 4. May use deficient criteria

review and the other for the employee's growth plans, can alleviate time pressures. Moreover, by separating the interview into two sessions, the interviewer can give each session the proper attention it deserves. It can be difficult for a supervisor to perform the role of both evaluator and counsellor in the same review period. Dividing the sessions may also improve communication between the parties, thereby reducing stress and defensiveness.

The format for the appraisal interview will be determined in large part by the purpose of the interview, the type of appraisal system used, and the organization of the interview form. Most appraisal interviews attempt to give feedback to employees on how well they are performing their jobs and on planning for their future development. Interviews should be scheduled far enough in advance to allow the interviewee, as well as the interviewer, to prepare for the discussion. Usually ten days to two weeks is a sufficient amount of lead time.

Three Types of Appraisal Interviews

The individual who has probably studied different approaches to performance appraisal interviews most thoroughly is Norman R.F. Maier. In his classic book *The Appraisal Interview*, he analyzes the cause-and-effect relationships in three types of appraisal interviews: tell-and-sell, tell-and-listen, and problem solving.[46]

- *Tell-and-sell interview.* The skills required in the tell-and-sell interview include the ability to persuade an employee to change in a prescribed manner. This may require the development of new behaviours on the part of the employee and skilful use of motivational incentives on the part of the appraiser/supervisor.
- *Tell-and-listen interview.* In the tell-and-listen interview, the skills required during the first part of the interview include the ability to communicate the strong and weak points of an employee's job performance. During the second part of the interview, the employee's feelings about the appraisal are thoroughly explored. The supervisor is still in the role of appraiser, but the method requires listening to disagreement and coping with defensive behaviour without attempting to refute any statements. The tell-and-listen method assumes that the opportunity to release frustrated feelings will help to reduce or remove those feelings.
- *Problem-solving interview.* The skills associated with the problem-solving interview are consistent with the nondirective procedures of the tell-and-listen method in that listening, accepting, and responding to feelings are essential. However, the problem-solving method goes beyond an interest in the employee's feelings. It seeks to stimulate growth and development in the employee by discussing the problems, needs, innovations, satisfactions, and dissatisfactions the employee has encountered on the job since the last appraisal interview. Maier recommends this method, since the objective of appraisal is normally to stimulate growth and development in the employee.

Managers should not assume that only one type of appraisal interview is appropriate for every review session. Rather, they should be able to use one or more of the interview types, depending on the topic being discussed or on the behaviour of the employee being appraised. The interview should be seen as requiring a flexible approach.[47]

Conducting the Appraisal Interview

While there are probably no hard-and-fast rules for how to conduct an appraisal interview, there are some guidelines that may increase the employee's acceptance of the feedback, satisfaction with the interview, and intention to improve in the future. Many of the principles of effective interviewing discussed in Chapter 7 apply to performance appraisal interviews as well. Below are some other guidelines that should also be considered.

- *Ask for a self-assessment.* As noted earlier in the chapter, it is useful to have employees evaluate their own performance prior to the appraisal interview. Even if this information is not used formally, the self-appraisal starts the employee thinking about his or her accomplishments. Self-appraisal also ensures that the employee knows against what criteria he or she is being evaluated, thus eliminating any potential surprises. When the employee has evaluated his or her own performance, the interview can be used to discuss those areas where the manager and the employee have reached different conclusions.

- *Invite participation.* The core purpose of a performance appraisal interview is to initiate a dialogue that will help an employee improve her or his performance. To the extent that an employee is an active participant in that discussion, the more likely it is that the root causes and obstacles to performance will be uncovered, and the more likely it is that constructive ideas for improvement will be raised. In addition, research evidence suggests that participation is strongly related to an employee's satisfaction with the appraisal feedback as well as her or his intention to improve performance.[48] As a rule of thumb, supervisors should spend only about 30 to 35 percent of the time talking during the interview. The rest of the time they should be listening to employees respond to questions.

- *Express appreciation.* Praise is a powerful motivator, and in an appraisal interview, particularly, employees are seeking out positive feedback. It is frequently beneficial to start the appraisal interview by expressing appreciation for what the employee has done well. In this way, he or she may be less defensive and more likely to talk about aspects of the job that are not going so well. However, try to avoid obvious use of the "sandwich technique," in which positive statements are followed by negative ones, which are then followed by positive statements. This approach may not work for several reasons. Praise often alerts the employee that criticism will be coming. Positive comments following the criticism then suggest to the employee that no more negative comments will come for a while. If managers follow an appraisal form, the problem of the sandwich technique will oftentimes be avoided. Furthermore, if employees receive feedback about their performance on a regular basis, there will be no need for this appraisal technique to be used.

- *Minimize criticism.* Employees who have a good relationship with their managers may be able to handle criticism better than those who do not. However, even the most stoic employees can absorb only so much criticism before they start to get defensive. If an employee has many areas in need of improvement, managers should focus on those few objective issues that are most problematic or most important to the job.[49]

- *Change the behaviour, not the person.* Managers frequently try to play psychologist, to "figure out" why an employee has acted a certain way. However, when dealing with a problem area, in particular, remember that it is not the person who is bad, but the actions they have exhibited on the job. Avoid suggestions about personal traits to change; instead suggest more acceptable ways of performing. For example, instead of focusing on a person's "unreliability," a manager might focus on the fact that the employee "has been late to work seven times this month." It is difficult for employees to change who they are; it is usually much easier for them to change how they act.

- *Focus on solving problems.* In addressing performance issues, it is frequently tempting to get into the "blame game" in which both manager and employee enter into a potentially endless discussion of why a situation has arisen. Frequently, solving problems requires an analysis of the causes, but ultimately the appraisal interview should be directed at devising a solution to the problem.

- *Be supportive*. One of the better techniques for engaging an employee in the problem-solving process is for the manager to ask, "What can I do to help?" Employees frequently attribute performance problems to either real or perceived obstacles (such as bureaucratic procedures or inadequate resources). By being open and supportive, the manager conveys to the employee that he or she will try to eliminate external roadblocks and work with the employee to achieve higher standards.
- *Establish goals*. Since a major purpose of the appraisal interview is to make plans for improvement, it is important to focus the interviewee's attention on the future rather than the past. In setting goals with an employee, the manager should observe the following points:

  1. Emphasize strengths on which the employee can build rather than weaknesses to overcome.
  2. Concentrate on opportunities for growth that exist within the framework of the employee's present position.
  3. Limit plans for growth to a few important items that can be accomplished within a reasonable period of time.
  4. Establish specific action plans that spell out how each goal will be achieved. These action plans may also include a list of contacts, resources, and timetables for follow-up.

- *Follow up day to day*. Ideally, performance feedback should be an ongoing part of a manager's job.[50] Feedback is most useful when it is immediate and specific to a particular situation. Unfortunately, both managers and employees are frequently happy to finish the interview and file away the appraisal form. A better approach is to have informal talks periodically to follow up on the issues raised in the appraisal interview. This practice may also allow the manager to play more of a coaching role than a judging role.

Improving Performance

In many instances, the appraisal interview will provide the basis for noting deficiencies in employee performance and for making plans for improvement. Unless these deficiencies are brought to the employee's attention, they are likely to continue until they become quite serious. Sometimes underperformers may not understand exactly what is expected of them. However, once their responsibilities are clarified, they are in a position to take the corrective action needed to improve their perform-ance.

Identifying Sources of Ineffective Performance

An employee's performance might not meet the standards for various reasons. First, each individual has a unique pattern of strengths and weaknesses that play a part in shaping job performance. In addition, other factors—such as the work environment, the external environment (including home and community), and personal problems—have an impact on job performance. To provide a better understanding of possible sources of ineffective performance related to these environments, we have devised the comprehensive list shown in Figure 10-6.

A diagnosis of poor employee performance should focus on three interactive elements: skill, effort, and external conditions. For example, if an employee's perfor-

FIGURE 10-6   *Sources of Ineffective Performance*

ORGANIZATION POLICIES AND PRACTICES

- Ineffective placement
- Insufficient job training
- Ineffectual employment practices
- Permissiveness with enforcing policies or job standards
- Heavy-handed management
- Lack of attention to employee needs or concerns
- Inadequate communication within organization
- Unclear reporting relationships

PERSONAL PROBLEMS

- Marital problems
- Financial worries
- Emotional disorders (including depression, guilt, anxiety, fear)
- Conflict between work demands and family demands
- Physical limitations, including disabilities
- Low work ethic
- Other family problems
- Lack of effort
- Immaturity

JOB CONCERNS

- Unclear or constantly changing work requirements
- Boredom with job
- Lack of job growth or advancement opportunities
- Management–employee conflict
- Problems with fellow employees
- Unsafe working conditions
- Unavailable or inadequate equipment or materials
- Inability to perform the job
- Excessive workload
- Lack of job skills

EXTERNAL FACTORS

- Industry decline or extreme competition
- Legal constraints
- Conflict between ethical standards and job demands
- Union–management conflict

mance is not up to standards, the cause could be a skill problem (knowledge, abilities, technical competencies), an effort problem (motivation to get the job done), and/or some problem in the external conditions of work (poor economic conditions, supply shortages, difficult sales territories).[51] Any one of these problem areas could cause performance to suffer.

Managing Ineffective Performance

Once the sources of performance problems are known, a course of action can be planned. This action might involve training the employee in those areas that would increase the knowledge and/or skills he or she needs for effective performance. A transfer to another job or department might give an employee a chance to become a more effective member of the organization. In other instances, greater attention may have to be focused on ways to motivate the individual.[52]

If ineffective performance persists, it may be necessary to transfer the employee, take disciplinary action, or discharge the person from the organization. Whatever action is taken to cope with ineffective performance, it should be done with objectivity, fairness, and a recognition of the feelings of the individual involved.

SUMMARY

objective

Performance appraisal programs serve many purposes, but in general those purposes can be divided into two categories: administrative and developmental. Administrative purposes include decisions about who will be promoted, transferred, or laid off. They can also include compensation decisions and the like. Developmental purposes are related to improving and enhancing an individual's capabilities. They include identifying a person's strengths and weaknesses, eliminating external performance obstacles, establishing training needs, and so on. The combination of administrative and developmental purposes of performance appraisal reflect, in a specific way, human resources management's larger role of integrating the individual with the organization. In many organizations, performance appraisals are seen as a necessary evil. Managers frequently avoid conducting appraisals because managers dislike playing the role of judge. Further, if managers are not adequately trained, subjectivity and organizational politics can distort the reviews. This situation tends to be self-defeating in that such managers frequently do not develop good feedback skills and are often not prepared to conduct an appraisal. As a consequence, the appraisal is done begrudgingly once a year and then forgotten.

objective

The success of an organization depends largely on the performance of its human resources. To determine the contributions of each individual, it is necessary to have a formal appraisal program with clearly stated objectives. Carefully defined performance standards that are reliable, strategically relevant, and free from either criterion deficiency or contamination are essential foundations for evaluation. Appraisal systems must also comply with the law. The concerns about validity that apply to selection tests should also apply to appraisals. For example, ratings must be job-related, employees must understand their performance standards in advance, appraisers must be able to observe job performance, appraisers must be trained, feedback must be given, and an appeals procedure must be established.

objective

Using multiple raters is frequently a good idea because different individuals see different facets of an employee's performance. The supervisor, for example, has legitimate authority over an employee and is in a good position to discern whether he or she is contributing to the goals of the organization. Peers and team members, on the other hand, often have an unfiltered view of an employee's work activity, particularly as it relates to such issues as cooperation and dependability. Subordinates often provide good information about whether an employee is facilitating their work, and customers (both internal and external) can convey the extent to which an employee adds value and meets their requirements. Self-appraisal is useful, if for no other reason than that it encourages employees to think about their strengths, weaknesses, and future goals. Regardless of the source of appraisal information, appraisers should be thoroughly trained in the particular methods they will use to evaluate their subordinates. Participation in developing rating scales, such as a BARS, automatically provides such training.

objective

There are several methods that can be used for performance appraisal. These include trait approaches (such as graphic rating scales, mixed standard scales, forced-choice forms, and essays), behavioural methods (such as critical incidents ratings, checklists, BARS, and BOS), and results methods (MBO). The choice of method depends on the purpose of the appraisal. Trait appraisals are simple to develop and complete, but they have problems with respect to subjectivity and are not useful for feedback. Behavioural methods provide more specific information for giving feedback, but they can be time-consuming and costly to develop. Results appraisals are more objective and can link individual performance to the organization as a whole, but they may encourage a short-term perspective (e.g., annual goals) and may not include subtle yet important aspects of performance.

objective

The degree to which the performance appraisal program benefits the organization and its members is directly related to the quality of the appraisal interviews that are conducted. Interviewing skills are best developed through instruction and supervised practice. Although there are various approaches to the interview, research suggests that employee participation and goal setting lead to higher satisfaction and improved performance. Discussing problems, showing support, minimizing criticism, and rewarding effective performance are also beneficial practices. In the interview, deficiencies in employee performance can be discussed and plans for improvement can be made.

KEY TERMS

behaviour observation scale (BOS)

behaviourally anchored

contrast error

critical incident

customer appraisal

error of central tendency

essay method

forced-choice method

graphic rating scale method

leniency or strictness error

management by objectives (MBO)

manager and or supervisor appraisal

mixed standard scale method

peer appraisal

rating scale (BARS)

recency error

self-appraisal

similar-to-me error

subordinate appraisal

team appraisal

> ## DISCUSSION QUESTIONS

1. What are the major purposes of performance appraisal? In what ways might these purposes be contradictory?
2. Describe the relationships among performance appraisal and selection, compensation management, and training and development.
3. How can performance appraisals be adjusted to include the principles underlying total quality management (TQM)?
4. Describe the characteristics of the ideal appraisal system.
5. What performance standards could be used to evaluate the performance of people working in the following jobs?
    a.   Sales representative
    b.   TV repairer
    c.   Director of nursing in a hospital
    d.   HR manager
    e.   Air-traffic controller
6. Discuss the guidelines that performance appraisals should meet in order to be legally defensible.
7. What are the pros and cons of trait, behaviour, and results appraisals?
8. In many organizations, evaluators submit ratings to their immediate superiors for review before discussing them with the individual employees they have rated. What are the advantages of this procedure?
9. Three types of appraisal interviews are described in this chapter.
    a.   What different skills are required for each type of appraisal interview? What reactions can one expect from using these different skills?
    b.   How can one develop the skills needed for the problem-solving type of interview?
    c.   Which method do you feel is the least desirable? Why?
10. Discuss how you would diagnose poor performance. List several factors to consider.

CASE: Setting Performance Standards at General Telephone

Raymond Gosselin, a new college graduate with a degree in human resources, was recently hired by General Telephone in central Canada. His job assignment was to work as a college and university recruiter, filling entry-level supervisory positions and staff assignments in accounting, finance, data processing, and marketing. He was in charge of a recruiting schedule that included twelve colleges and universities.

Over the past two years, the company had made a concerted effort to develop a comprehensive and effective university and college recruiting program. It was decided that part of this effort should be devoted to creating a positive and continuing relationship with the placement offices, as well as with certain professors who would be in a position to refer students for job openings. Establishing this relationship with the schools, which was viewed as critical for identifying and selecting high-potential employees, was Gosselin's responsibility, as important as filling the positions for General Telephone.

Daniel Turner, manager of the company's HR department, established yearly performance standards for each of his subordinates. Company guidelines indicated that, where possible, observable and measurable performance standards should be set. When Gosselin completed his first three months with GT, he and Turner agreed to set his performance standards for the upcoming recruitment period, although both acknowledged that setting measurable standards might be somewhat difficult because of the subjective nature of college/university recruiting. The job description stated only that the person who held the position should develop and maintain rapport with the colleges and universities, that openings should be filled in a timely manner, and that graduates selected for company interviews should be of high quality. (GT's annual HR planning schedule, listing the types and numbers of college/university graduates needed by each department and operating area, was completed by December of each year, and managers requesting new graduates also stated on the employment requisition form the date by which the positions were to be filled.)

Now Turner asked Gosselin to come up with four to six observable and measurable performance standards that would capture the duties and responsibilities of the college/university recruiter's job.

Source: Based on an actual case known to the authors; employee names are fictitious.

Questions

1. Develop four to six observable and measurable performance standards suitable to Gosselin's position as college and university recruiter.
2. Discuss any obstacles that might make this task difficult.

Performance Feedback

People who work in large organizations often receive feedback on performance or traits related to the job requirements. However, students and employees working in small organizations may never have experienced any kind of feedback. The purpose of this career planning exercise is to solicit feedback that will help you in your career.

The first step is to develop a list of competencies or characteristics that you feel you need in order to succeed. You can consult the "dream job" requirements that you developed in an earlier Career Counsel (see Chapter 5) or review the skills that you developed for your résumé (see Career Counsel, Chapter 7).

The next step is to develop a performance appraisal form that will help your raters to evaluate you objectively. Review the various forms prescribed in this chapter and insert your competencies or characteristics in the one you have chosen.

Now, choose people who have had an opportunity to observe your work performance. These raters may include students or co-workers on project teams or supervisors at work, summer jobs, volunteer jobs, etc. You might even solicit feedback from people you have supervised, coached, or managed in any capacity. When choosing your raters, ensure that they have knowledge of your work performance, that you respect their views, that their feedback will be sincere and helpful, and that your privacy will be respected. You, in turn, must be willing to listen to and be open to feedback. Ask your raters to rate you on the form you have prepared; where possible, ask them to provide critical incidents.

(If you do not wish to have such a formal evaluation, you could simply ask your raters such questions as "What do you see as my strengths/weaknesses? How can I capitalize on my strengths? How can I correct my deficiencies?")

Develop an action plan to close the gaps between your rated performance and your desired performance.

NOTES AND REFERENCES

1. *1994/95 Annual Salary Survey: General Employment Practices Report* (Toronto: KPMG, 1994), 57.
2. Michael A. Verespej, "Performance Reviews Get Mixed Reviews," *Industry Week*, August 20, 1990, 49–54.
3. P.G. Green, "Total Quality Management in the Construction Industry: A Cultural Challenge," *Engineering Management Journal* 5, no. 2 (June 1993): 21–27. See also T.C. Keiser and D.A. Smith, "Customer Driven Strategies: Moving from Talk to Action," *Planning Review* 21, no. 5 (September/October 1993): 25–32.
4. *Your Guide to Performance Appraisal*, The Travelers, rev. September 1978, 2.
5. Jeanette N. Cleveland, Kevin R. Murphy, and Richard E. Williams, "Multiple Uses of Performance Appraisal: Prevalence and Correlates," *Journal of Applied Psychology* 74 (1989): 130–135. See also David A. Waldman and Ron S. Kent, "Improve Performance by Appraisal," *HR Magazine* 35, no. 7 (July 1990): 66–69.
6. Dave Day, "Performance Management Year-Round," *Personnel* 66, no. 8 (August 1989): 43–45.
7. Gerald R. Ferris and Thomas R. King, "Politics in Human Resources Decisions: A Walk on the Dark Side," *Organizational Dynamics* 20 (Autumn 1991): 59–71.
8. Stephanie Overman, "Best Appraisals Measure Goals, Not Traits," *Resource* 8, no. 2 (February 1989): 16.
9. Ashok K. Gupta and Arvind Singhal, "Managing Human Resources for Innovation and Creativity," *Research Technology Management* (May-June 1993): 41–48.
10. P. Sharman, "How to Implement Performance Measurement in Your Organization," CMA *Magazine*, May 1995, 33–37.
11. S.W.J. Kozlowski and K. Hattrup, "A Disagreement about Within-Group Agreement: Disentangling Issues of Consistency versus Consensus," *Journal of Applied Psychology* 77 (1992): 161–167.
12. For a review of performance appraisal court cases, see David C. Martin and Kathryn M. Bartol, "The Legal Ramifications of Performance Appraisal: An Update," *Employee Relations* 17 (Autumn 1991): 257–286. See also Robert W. Goddard, "Is Your Appraisal System Headed for Court?" *Personnel Journal* 68, no. 1 (January 1989): 114–118.
13. David I. Rosen, "Appraisals Can Make—Or Break—Your Court Case," *Personnel Journal* (November 1992): 113–118.
14. Loriann Robertson, Steven Torkel, Audrey Korsgaard, and Doug Klein, "Self-Appraisal and Perceptions of the Appraisal Discussion: A Field Experiment," *Journal of Organizational Behavior* 14 (March 1993): 129–142. See also John W. Lawrie, "Your Performance: Appraise It

Yourself," *Personnel* 66, no. 1 (January 1989): 21–23; and Len Sandler, "Two-Sided Performance Reviews," *Personnel Journal* 69, no. 1 (January 1990): 75–78.
15. Paul E. Levy, "Self-Appraisal and Attributions: A Test of a Model," *Journal of Management* 19 (Spring 1993): 51–62. See also Saul Fox and Yossi Dinur, "Validity of Self-Assessment: A Field Evaluation," *Personnel Psychology* 41, no. 3 (Autumn 1988): 582.
16. Mark R. Edwards, "Assessment: A Joint Effort Leads to Accurate Appraisals," *Personnel Journal* (June 1990): 122–128. Robert McGarvey and Scott Smith, "When Workers Rate the Boss," *Training* 30 (March 1993): 31–34; Tom Redman and Ed Snape, "Upward and Onward: Can Staff Appraise Their Managers?" *Personnel Review* 21 (1992): 32–46.
17. Glenn M. McEvoy, "Evaluating the Boss," *Personnel Administrator* 33, no. 9 (September 1988): 115–120. See also Paul Nevels, "Why Employees Are Being Asked to Rate Their Supervisors," *Supervisory Management* 34, no. 12 (December 1989): 5–11.
18. Edwards, "Assessment." See also Mark R. Edwards, "An Alternative to Traditional Appraisal Systems," *Supervisory Management* 35 (June 1990): 3; and Mark R. Edwards, "Joint-Appraisal Efforts," *Personnel Journal* 69, no. 6 (June 1990): 122–128.
19. Glenn M. McEvoy and Paul F. Buller, "User Acceptance of Peer Appraisals in an Industrial Setting," *Personnel Psychology* 40, no. 4 (Winter 1987): 785–797.
20. Kenneth P. Carson, Robert L. Cardy, and Gregory H. Dobbins, "Upgrade the Employee Evaluation Process," *HR Magazine* (November 1992): 88–92; Richard Blackburn and Benson Rosen, "Total Quality and Human Resources Management: Lessons Learned from Baldrige Award-Winning Companies," *Academy of Management Executive* 7, no. 3 (1993): 49–66; Carol A. Norman and Robert A. Zawacki, "Team Appraisals— Team Approach," *Personnel Journal* (September 1991): 101–104; Marilyn Moats Kennedy, "Where Teams Drop the Ball," *Across the Board* (September 1993): 9–10; and Joshua Hyatt, "Surviving on Chaos," *Inc.* (May 1990): 60–71.
21. David E. Bowen and E.E. Lawler III, "Total Quality-Oriented Human Resource Management," *Organizational Dynamics* 21 (1992): 29–41. Also see Nancy K. Austin, "Updating the Performance Review," *Working Woman* 17, no. 11 (November 1992): 32–35.
22. Margaret Kaeter, "Driving toward Sales and Satisfaction," *Training* (August 1990): 19–22.
23. J.M. Juran, *Juran on Quality by Design* (New York: Free Press, 1992).
24. For a more complete description of the Taurus program, see James Brian Quinn, "Ford: Team Taurus," in Henry Mintzberg and James Brian Quinn, eds., *The Strategy

Process, Concepts, Context, Cases (Englewood Cliffs, NJ: Prentice-Hall, 1991), 481–504.

25. Robert H. Buckham, "Appraisal Training: Not Just for Managers," *Training and Development Journal* 44, no. 6 (June 1990): 18, 21. See also Stephen B. Wehrenberg, "Train Supervisors to Measure and Evaluate Performance," *Training* 67, no. 2 (February 1988): 77–79.

26. Gary P. Latham and Kenneth N. Wexley, *Increasing Productivity through Performance Appraisal* (Reading, MA: Addison-Wesley, 1981), 116.

27. William K. Balzer and Lorne M. Sulsky, "Halo and Performance Appraisal: A Critical Examination," *Journal of Applied Psychology* 77, no. 6 (December 1992): 975–985; Keven Murphy, Robert A. Jako, and Rebecca L. Anhalt, "Nature and Consequences of Halo Error: A Critical Analysis," *Journal of Applied Psychology* 78, no. 2 (April 1993): 218–225; Kevin R. Murphy and William K. Balzer, "Rater Errors and Rating Accuracy," *Journal of Applied Psychology* 74, no. 4 (August 1989): 619–624.

28. Robert A. Gacalone, "Image Control: The Strategies of Impression Management," *Personnel* 66, no. 5 (May 1989): 52–55.

29. Gregory H. Dobbins, Robert L. Cardy, and Donald M. Truxillo, "The Effects of Purpose of Appraisal and Individual Differences in Stereotypes of Women on Sex Differences in Performance Ratings: A Laboratory and Field Study," *Journal of Applied Psychology* 73, no. 3 (August 1988): 551–558.

30. Kenneth N. Wexley and Gary P. Latham, *Developing and Training Human Resources in Organizations* (Glenview, IL: Scott, Foresman, 1981).

31. Buckham, "Appraisal Training," 18, 21.

32. Philip G. Benson, M. Ronald Buckley, and Sid Hall, "The Impact of Rating Scale Format on Rater Accuracy: An Evaluation of the Mixed Standard Scale," *Journal of Management* 14, no. 3 (September 1988): 415–423.

33. Margaret E. Griffin, "Personnel Research in Testing, Selection, and Performance Appraisal," *Public Personnel Management* 18, no. 2 (Summer 1989): 130.

34. Brendan D. Bannister, Angelo J. Kinicki, Angelo S. Dinisi, and Peter Hom, "A New Method for the Statistical Control of Rating Error in Performance Ratings," *Educational and Psychological Measurement* 47, no. 3 (Autumn 1987): 583–596.

35. For a comprehensive review of the research on BARS, see Chapter 6 in H. John Bernardin and Richard W. Beatty, *Performance Appraisal: Assessing Human Behaviour at Work* (Boston: Kent, 1984). Also see Kevin R. Murphy and Jeanette N. Cleveland, *Performance Appraisal* (Boston: Allyn and Bacon, 1991).

36. Latham and Wexley, *Increasing Productivity*, 55–64.

37. U. Wiersma and G. Latham, "The Practicality of Behavioral Observation Scales, Behavioral Expectation Scales, and Trait Scales," *Personnel Psychology* 39 (1986): 619–628.

38. Peter F. Drucker, *The Practice of Management* (New York: Harper and Brothers, 1954).

39. George S. Odiorne, *Management by Objectives* (New York: Pitman, 1965), 77–79.

40. E. Locke and G. Latham, *A Theory of Goal Setting and Task Performance* (Englewood Cliffs, NJ: Prentice-Hall, 1990).

41. Robert D. Pritchard, Philip L. Roth, Steven D. Jones, Patricia J. Galgay, and Margaret D. Watson, "Designing a Goal-Setting System to Enhance Performance: A Practical Guide," *Organizational Dynamics* 17, no. 1 (Summer 1988): 70. See also Albert Schrader and Taylor G. Seward, "MBO Makes Dollar Sense," *Personnel Journal* 68, no. 7 (July 1989): 32–37.

42. Dennis Daley, "Performance Appraisal and Organizational Success: Public Employee Perceptions in an MBO-Based Appraisal System," *Review of Public Personnel Administration* 9, no. 1 (Fall 1988): 17–27. See also David Halpern and Stephen Osfsky, "A Dissenting View of MBO," *Public Personnel Management* 19, no. 3 (Fall 1990): 321–330.

43. Luis R. Gomez-Mejia, "Evaluating Employee Performance: Does the Appraisal Instrument Make a Difference?" *Journal of Organizational Behavior Management* 9, no. 2 (Fall 1988): 155–172.

44. Dennis M. Daley, "Great Expectations, or a Tale of Two Systems: Employee Attitudes toward Graphic Rating Scales and MBO-Based Performance Appraisal," *Public Administration Quarterly* 15, no. 2 (Summer 1991): 188–209.

45. Aharon Tziner and Gary P. Latham, "The Effects of Appraisal Instrument, Feedback and Goal-Setting on Worker Satisfaction and Commitment," *Journal of Organizational Behavior* 10, no. 2 (April 1989): 145–153.

46. Norman R.F. Maier, *The Appraisal Interview* (New York: John Wiley and Sons, 1958); and Maier, *The Appraisal Interview—Three Basic Approaches* (San Diego: University Associates, 1976).

47. Howard J. Klein and Scott A. Snell, "The Impact of Interview Process and Context on Performance Appraisal Interview Effectiveness," *Journal of Managerial Issues* 6, no. 2 (Summer 1994): 160–175. See also Howard J. Klein, Scott A. Snell, and Kenneth N. Wexley, "Systems Model of the Performance Appraisal Interview Process," *Industrial Relations* 26, no. 3 (Fall 1987): 267–279; and James McAlister, "Appraisal Do's and Don'ts," *Supervisory Management* 38, no. 4 (April 1993): 12.

48. W. Giles and K. Mossholder, "Employee Reactions to Contextual and Session Components of Performance Appraisal," *Journal of Applied Psychology* 75 (1990): 371–377. See also Klein and Snell, "Impact of Interview Process"; Theodore J. Krein, "Performance Reviews That Rate an 'A'," *Personnel* 67, no. 5 (May

1990): 38–40; and Sandler, "Two-Sided Performance Reviews."

49. Andrew S. Grove, "Criticism: Giving It Effectively," *Working Woman* 18, no. 6 (June 1993): 20–73.

50. George S. Odiorne, "The Trend toward the Quarterly Performance Review," *Business Horizons 33*, no. 4 (July/August 1990): 38–41.

51. Scott A. Snell and Kenneth N. Wexley, "Performance Diagnosis: Identifying the Causes of Poor Performance," *Personnel Administrator* 30, no. 4 (April 1985): 117–127.

52. Dorri Jacobs, "Coaching to Reverse Poor Performance," *Supervisory Management* 10, no. 2 (July 1989): 21–28.

Part 4

Implementing Compensation and Security

The four chapters in Part 4 focus on employee compensation and security issues. Chapter 11 deals with evaluating organizational jobs and establishing monetary rates for these jobs based on both internal and external influences. Also discussed in this chapter are the legal requirements of compensation management. Chapter 12 looks at incentive payment plans for nonmanagerial, managerial, and executive employees. Chapter 13 completes the discussion of compensation administration by reviewing the myriad of benefit programs offered by organizations to their employees. Included here is a relevant discussion of employee benefit costs and various cost containment programs. Chapter 14 is concerned with issues pertaining to employee safety and health. It contains discussions related to employee workplace stress, alcoholism, and substance abuse. When managers pay attention to the compensation and security needs of employees, they provide a framework that contributes to both employee job satisfaction and organizational success.

After studying this chapter, you should be able to

one
objective

Explain employer concerns in developing the compensation program.

two
objective

Identify the various factors that influence the setting of wages.

three
objective

Discuss the mechanics of each of the major job evaluation systems.

four
objective

Explain the purpose of a wage survey.

five
objective

Define the wage curve, pay grades, and rate ranges as parts of the compensation structure.

six
objective

Identify the major provisions of the legislation affecting compensation.

seven
objective

Discuss the current issues of equal pay for work of equal value, pay compression, and two-tier wage structures.

Chapter 11

Managing Compensation

A n extensive review of the literature indicates that important work-related variables leading to job satisfaction include challenging work, interesting job assignments, equitable rewards, competent supervision, and rewarding careers.[1] In Chapter 2, we emphasized that employees currently in the workforce are more concerned than were their predecessors with the quality of their work life and with the psychological rewards to be derived from their employment. It is doubtful, however, whether many of them would continue working were it not for the money they earn. Employees desire compensation systems that they perceive as being fair and commensurate with their skills and expectations. Pay, therefore, is a major consideration in HRM because it provides employees with a tangible reward for their services, as well as a source of recognition and livelihood. Employee compensation includes all forms of pay and rewards received by employees for the performance of their jobs. Direct compensation encompasses employee wages and salaries, incentives, bonuses, and commissions. Indirect compensation comprises the many benefits supplied by employers, and nonfinancial compensation includes employee recognition programs, rewarding jobs, and flexible work hours to accommodate personal needs.

Both HR professionals and scholars agree that the way compensation is allocated among employees sends a message about what management believes is important and the types of activities it encourages. Furthermore, for an employer, the payroll constitutes a sizable operating cost. In manufacturing firms, compensation is seldom as low as 20 percent of total expenditures, and in service enterprises it often exceeds 80 percent.[2] A sound compensation program, therefore, is essential so that pay can serve to motivate employee production sufficiently to keep labour costs at an acceptable level. This chapter will be concerned with the management of a compensation program, job evaluation systems, and pay structures for determining compensation payments. Included will be a discussion of legislation that affects wage and salary rates. Chapter 12 will review financial incentive plans for employees. Employee benefits that are part of the total compensation package are then discussed in Chapter 13.

objective

The Compensation Program

A significant interaction occurs between compensation management and the other functions of the HR program. For example, in the recruitment of new employees, the rate of pay for jobs can increase or limit the supply of applicants. Many fast-food restaurants, traditionally low-wage employers, have needed to raise their starting wages to attract a sufficient number of job applicants to meet staffing requirements. If rates of pay are high, creating a large applicant pool, then organizations may choose to raise their selection standards and hire better-qualified employees. This in turn can reduce employer training costs. When employees perform at exceptional levels, their performance appraisals may justify an increased pay rate. For these reasons and others, an organization should develop a formal HR program to manage employee compensation. This program should establish its intended objectives, the policies for determining compensation payments, and the methods by which the payments will be disbursed. The program should also include communicating to employees information concerning wages and benefits.

Compensation Objectives and Policies

Compensation objectives should facilitate the effective utilization and management of an organization's human resources, while also contributing to the overall objectives of the organization. A compensation program, therefore, must be tailored to the needs of an organization and its employees.[3]

In Reality Check, Morty Moorthy, an award-winning compensation expert, describes how Ontario Hydro's compensation program was developed in tandem with the company's organizational goals.

It is not uncommon for organizations to establish very specific goals for their compensation program.[4] Formalized compensation goals serve as guidelines for managers to ensure that wage and benefit policies achieve their intended purpose. The more common goals of compensation policy include:

1. To reward employees' past performance
2. To remain competitive in the labour market
3. To maintain salary equity among employees
4. To motivate employees' future performance
5. To maintain the budget
6. To attract new employees
7. To reduce unnecessary turnover

To achieve these goals, policies must be established to guide management in its decision making. Formal statements of compensation policies typically include the following:

1. The rate of pay within the organization and whether it is to be above, below, or at the prevailing community rate
2. The ability of the pay program to gain employee acceptance while motivating employees to perform to the best of their abilities
3. The pay level at which employees may be recruited and the pay differential between new and more senior employees
4. The intervals at which pay raises are to be granted and the extent to which merit and/or seniority will influence the raises
5. The pay levels needed to facilitate the achievement of a sound financial position in relation to the products or services offered

The Pay-for-Performance Standard

Pay-for-performance standard
Standard by which managers tie compensation to employee effort and performance.

To raise productivity and lower labour costs in today's competitive economic environment, organizations are increasingly setting compensation objectives based on a **pay-for-performance standard**.[5] It is agreed that managers must tie at least some reward to employee effort and performance. Without this standard, motivation to perform with greater effort will be low, resulting in higher wage costs to the organization.[6]

The term "pay-for-performance" refers to a wide range of compensation options, including merit pay, cash bonuses, incentive pay, and various gainsharing plans. (Gainsharing plans are discussed in Chapter 12.) Each of these compensation systems seeks to differentiate between the pay of average and outstanding performers. When Star Data Systems Inc. of Markham, Ontario, implemented its

COMPENSATION STRATEGIES AT ONTARIO HYDRO

Compensation trends are changing as enlightened companies prepare to meet the new challenges of becoming more profitable and efficient.

Ontario Hydro's director of corporate compensation and benefits, Morty Moorthy, uses his vision to help the organization achieve its goals. Moorthy received the 1995 ACA (American Compensation Association) Keystone Award, a first for a Canadian. This achievement is is indicative of the level of expertise and leadership he brings to Ontario Hydro. In an interview, he discussed the development of compensation strategies at the company.

"We knew that we are in for a major transformation of our culture. We were a crown agency behaving like a public utility, heavily unionized and with a strong sense of entitlement. When Maurice Stong became chairman, he immediately saw that things had to change if Hydro were to remain a contender in the market of the future. The focus was moving from construction to maintenance of our infrastructures and efficient operations of our electrical system. The heavy demands on capital are no longer required. Additionally, technology is changing rapidly and the customer base is shifting due to greater global competition. With all these things in mind, a task force was assembled and a paradigm shift in compensation was seen as one of the agents of change to make Hydro more competitive.

"In devising our new executive compensation strategies at the corporate level, we had to look at the gaps between where we were and where we wanted to be. For instance, our 'entitlement mindset' needed to change. Compensation needed to reinforce short- and long-term results. In the past, when one group of employees received something, the other group felt it would automatically receive the same. Additionally, we were looking for a more appropriate mix of base and variable/risk pay relative to the combination of high base and some merit pay, and a more team-oriented organization than in the past. We looked at what pay was supposed to accomplish, and we determined that it was to influence and reward results and behaviours. We saw the answer as a combination of base pay related to competencies and a more flexible salary administration system using broadbanding to facilitate movement through the ranges based on competencies and capabilities, and a performance pay program for executives tied primarily to corporate results. This system provides flexibility for everyone. If the organization succeeds, so does the employee. Merit pay was trying to do too many things, and we had to make fundamental changes.

"To integrate competencies we looked at a variety of models and consultants. Ultimately, we decided to work with Hay/McBer for the most part. They had a large international data base, provided research-oriented advice, and were known to us as we were already using their job evaluation system. To make things happen, you have to involve your staff," states Moorthy. "We started the development of our strategies with the business unit leaders. Using behavioural interviewing techniques, these leaders were asked about the kinds of things that they were looking for in their people as a means to developing competencies for their business. Key performers' behaviours were used as competency benchmarks. What we learned was that the needs of each business were different, and today we have different competency requirements for each business unit, ranging from about five to eight competencies, with some commonality across the businesses. Strategic thinking, for example, is very important for most of the executives in most of our business units. Depending on the opportunities for the individual, a different level of strategic thinking will be required. This involvement generated the commitment we needed from our managers.

"Competencies had to be translated into pay. Using three zones—developmental, maturity, and expert—the manager would assess the competency of an individual against a standard for the job. Conceptually, new executives being brought into a position would be assessed as developmental; as they grew they would move toward the mature zone, and eventually, if warranted, could be assessed against the standards of the expert zone. An approximation of these zones is then reflected within each of the broad pay bands, and judgments are made concerning base pay.

"Results are what drive the other component of compensation rewards, and these results must tie back to the strategic plan. We ensure that our results are measured in terms of what our stakeholders expect as reflected in our corporate mission. For example, with our customers, we measure customer satisfaction; shareholders look at the net income; our employees tie back to productivity and employee safety; and with the public we look at nuclear safety, internal energy savings, and greenhouse gas emissions. Each stakeholder is looking for a different result, and we set this up in our business plan as a strategy so that the system is complete. For example, to ensure that the measures were appropriate for corporate satisfaction, we surveyed 10,000 customers and asked them to assess a number of attributes, including perception, quality, pricing, etc. A baseline score of where we wanted to be in five years was created, and we have established interim targets with which to measure against. If we want to be in the Stanley Cup, we have to set ambitious but realistic targets. However, sometimes one set of measures can be achieved, but another cannot. If corporate targets are met, employees can expect to receive a target of 10 percent in performance pay to be distributed among its business units. If the corporate targets are not met, then the 10 percent will not be distributed. If a business unit does well and meets its objectives, then a reduced performance payment will be granted to that unit. Our employees had to take a 5 percent cut in base salary before this program started. In this way, we moved away from base salary and toward a variable rate.

"The effect of these changes has been to really focus executives on results. Quarterly reports are sent to managers so that they can see how we are doing and, in turn, they advise their staff. The next task is to bring this concept down to the next level of the organization to make this plan a reality for them and have all our employees share in our successes."

Source: Interview with Deborah M. Zinni, July 1995.

compensation program, its objectives in doing so were "to fairly and equitably manage salaries, to establish compensation practices that are fairly and consistently applied internally and to ensure compliance with legislative requirements."[7] Interestingly, productivity studies show that employees will increase their output by 15 to 35 percent when an organization installs a pay-for-performance program.[8]

Unfortunately, designing a sound pay-for-performance system is not easy. Considerations must be given to how employee performance will be measured, the monies to be allocated for compensation increases, which employees to cover, the payout method, and the periods when payments will be made. A critical issue concerns the size of the monetary increase and its perceived value to employees. The Canadian Compensation Association reports that annual salary budgets for nonmanagement employees decreased from 5.8 percent in 1988 to 2.1 percent in 1994.[9] These percentages only slightly exceed yearly increases in the cost of living. While differences exist as to how large a wage or salary increase must be before it is perceived as meaningful, a pay-for-performance program will lack its full potential when pay increases only approximate rises in the cost of living.

The Motivating Value of Compensation

Pay constitutes a quantitative measure of an employee's relative worth. For most employees, pay has a direct bearing not only on their standard of living but also on the status and recognition they may be able to achieve both on and off the job. Since pay represents a reward received in exchange for an employee's contributions, it is essential, according to the equity theory, that the pay be equitable in terms of those contributions. It is essential also that an employee's pay be equitable in terms of what other employees are receiving for their contributions.[10]

Pay Equity

Pay equity
An employee's perception that compensation received is equal to the value of the work performed.

Equity can be defined as anything of value earned through the investment of something of value. Marc Wallace and Charles Fay report that "fairness is achieved when the return on equity is equivalent to the investment made."[11] For employees, **pay equity** is achieved when the compensation received is equal to the value of the work performed.

E.A. Savinelli, founder and chairman/CEO of Aquatec Chemical International Inc., realizes that the perception of internal pay equity is important to employee performance. According to Savinelli:

> Internal equity is especially important in an organization where teamwork is critical to success. In our type of operation, which focuses on high-tech services to customers that require a cross-section of skills and talents and interdisciplinary teamwork, coworkers need confidence in themselves and their colleagues. An important part of creating an environment in which teamwork is effective is a pay policy that reflects the true value of work to the overall organization, and helps all members of the team respect one another's contribution and role.[12]

Not only must pay be equitable, it must also be perceived as such by employees. Research clearly demonstrates that employees' perceptions of pay equity, or inequity, can have dramatic effects on their motivation for both work behaviour and productivity. Managers must therefore develop pay practices that are both internally and externally equitable. Employees must believe that wage rates for jobs within the organization approximate the job's worth to the organization. Also, the employer's wage rates must correspond closely to prevailing market rates for the employee's occupation.

Pay Expectancy

The expectancy theory of motivation predicts that one's level of motivation depends on the attractiveness of the reward sought. The theory therefore holds that employees should exert greater work effort if they have reason to expect that it will result in a reward that is valued.[13] To motivate this effort, the value of any monetary reward should be attractive. Employees also must believe that good performance is valued by their employer and will result in their receiving the expected reward.

Figure 11-1 illustrates the relationship between pay-for-performance and the expectancy theory of motivation. The model predicts that high effort will lead to high performance (expectancy), and that high performance in turn will lead to monetary rewards that are appreciated (valued). Since we previously stated that pay-for-performance leads to a feeling of pay satisfaction, this feeling should reinforce one's high level of effort.

Thus, employee perceptions of compensation can be an important factor in determining the motivational value of compensation. Furthermore, the effective communication of pay information, together with an organizational environment that elicits employee trust in management, can contribute to employees having more accurate perceptions of their pay. The perceptions employees develop concerning their pay are influenced by the accuracy of their knowledge and understanding of the compensation program.

Pay Secrecy

Employee misperceptions concerning the equity of their pay and its relationship to performance can be created by secrecy about the pay that others receive. There is reason to believe that secrecy can generate distrust in the compensation system, reduce employee motivation, and inhibit organizational effectiveness. Yet pay secrecy seems to be an accepted practice in many organizations in both the private and the public sector.

Managers may justify secrecy on the grounds that most employees prefer to have their own pay kept secret. Probably one of the reasons for pay secrecy that managers may be unwilling to admit is that it gives them greater freedom in compensation management, since pay decisions are not disclosed and there is no need to justify or defend them. Employees who are not supposed to know what others are being paid have no objective base for pursuing grievances about their own pay. Secrecy also serves to cover up inequities existing within the pay structure. Furthermore, secrecy surrounding compensation decisions may lead employees to believe that there is no direct relationship between pay and performance.

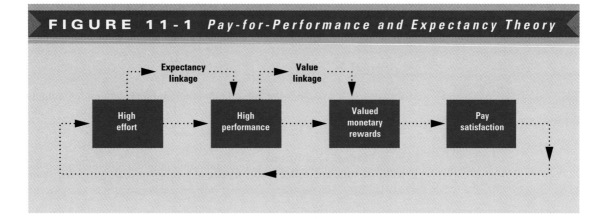

FIGURE 11-1 *Pay-for-Performance and Expectancy Theory*

Expectancy linkage — Value linkage

High effort → High performance → Valued monetary rewards → Pay satisfaction

The Bases for Compensation

Work performed in most private, public, and not-for-profit organizations has traditionally been compensated on an hourly basis. It is referred to as **hourly or day work**, in contrast to **piecework**, in which employees are paid according to the number of units they produce. Hourly work, however, is far more prevalent than piecework as a basis for compensating employees.

Employees compensated on an hourly basis are classified as *hourly employees*, or wage earners. Those whose compensation is computed on the basis of weekly, biweekly, or monthly pay periods are classified as *salaried employees*. Hourly employees are normally paid only for the time they work. Salaried employees, by contrast, are generally paid the same for each pay period, even though they occasionally may work more or fewer hours than the regular number of hours in a period.

In each province, employment practices are regulated by employment standards Acts. Each province's Act contains a provision that requires an employer to reimburse an employee at the specified rate after he or she works the minimum required hours. This rate is usually 1.5 times the employee's base hourly rate of pay. A number of employers offer overtime pay that is more generous than that stipulated in the Act. Some Acts provide for time off in lieu of overtime; thus four hours of overtime paid at 1.5 would be the equivalent of six hours pay, or time off in lieu of payment. Supervisory and management personnel are not normally paid overtime; an issue that is discussed in Ethics in HRM. Each of the employment standards Acts contains a list of persons who are exempt from the overtime provision.

Due to the vast numbers of American companies operating in Canada, the terms *exempt* and *nonexempt* are often heard, although they have no relevance in Canadian legislation. These terms are used specifically to denote *supervisory* and *nonsupervisory*; only nonexempt workers, therefore, are entitled to overtime.

objective

Components of the Wage Mix

A combination of *external* and *internal* factors can influence, directly or indirectly, the rates at which employees are paid. Through their interaction these factors constitute the wage mix, as shown in Figure 11-2. For example, the area wage rate for administrative assistants might be $8.50 per hour. However, one employer may elect to pay its administrative assistants $10.25 per hour because of their excellent perform-ance. The influence of government legislation on the wage mix will be discussed later in the chapter.

External Factors

The major external factors that influence wage rates include labour market conditions, area wage rates, cost of living, legal requirements, and (if the employer is unionized) collective bargaining.

Labour Market Conditions
The labour market reflects the forces of supply and demand for qualified labour within an area. These forces help to influence the wage rates required to recruit or

ETHICS IN HRM

WHO'S THE BOSS?

Elaine Chu works at a local fast-food restaurant to earn enough money to support herself while she attends university part-time. Her job title is night manager, and she works the 4 p.m. to 11 p.m. shift. During this shift, she is the only one on duty, and does much of the food preparation, serving, and clean-up. Most nights, customers arrive after the movies (around 11 p.m.), and Chu is expected to work into the next shift until the crowd disperses. She receives no overtime pay for these extra hours of work because employers are not required to pay overtime rates for managers.

Has Chu's employer misused the title "manager" in order to circumvent its obligations with respect to overtime pay? To be deemed a true manager, an individual should have staff reporting to him or her, should have responsibility for a major aspect of the business, and should provide counselling to more junior staff through performance appraisal. Is Chu a manager? Should she be paid overtime?

FIGURE 11-2 *Factors Affecting the Wage Mix*

EXTERNAL FACTORS

- Conditions of the labor market
- Area wage rates
- Cost of living
- Collective bargaining
- Legal requirements

WAGE MIX

INTERNAL FACTORS

- Compensation policy of organization
- Worth of job
- Employee's relative worth
- Employer's ability to pay

retain competent employees. It must be recognized, however, that counterforces can reduce the full impact of supply and demand on the labour market. The economic power of unions, for example, may prevent employers from lowering wage rates even when unemployment is high among union members. Government regulations also may prevent an employer from paying at a market rate less than an established minimum.

Area Wage Rates
A formal wage structure should provide rates that are in line with those being paid by other employers for comparable jobs within the area. Data pertaining to area wage rates may be obtained from local wage surveys. For example, the Board of Trade for Toronto, the Professional Engineering Association of Ontario, and the Weston Personnel Association conduct surveys on behalf of their members. Most of these surveys are inexpensive and therefore accessible to many employers, regardless of size. Robert Half International Inc. publishes a Canadian salary survey annually and distributes it to organizations throughout Canada. Highlights in HRM 1 shows the 1994–95 salaries paid for various accounting jobs; a table of geographic variances is also provided.

Data from area wage surveys can be used to prevent the rates for certain jobs from drifting too far above or below those of other employers in the region. When rates rise above existing area levels, an employer's labour costs may become excessive. Conversely, if they drop too far below area levels, it may be difficult to recruit and retain competent personnel. Wage-survey data must also take into account indirect wages paid in the form of benefits.

Cost of Living
Because of inflation, compensation rates have had to be adjusted upward periodically to help employees maintain their purchasing power. This can be achieved through **escalator clauses** found in various collective agreements. These clauses provide for quarterly cost-of-living adjustments (COLA) in wages based on changes in the **consumer price index (CPI)**. The CPI is a measure of the average change in prices over time in a fixed "market basket" of goods and services.[14] The most common adjustments are 1 cent per hour for each 0.3- or 0.4-point change in the CPI.

The CPI is largely used to set wages. The index is based on prices of food, clothing, shelter, and fuels; transportation fares; charges for medical services; and prices of other goods and services that people buy for day-to-day living. Statistics Canada collects price information on a monthly basis and calculates the CPI for Canada as a whole as well as for various Canadian cities. Separate indexes are also published by size of city and by region of the country. Employers in a number of communities base their compensation decisions on changes in the CPI.

Changes in the CPI can have important effects on pay rates. Granting wage increases solely on the basis of the CPI helps to compress pay rates within a pay structure, thereby creating inequities among those who receive the wage increase. Inequities also result from the fact that adjustments are made on a cent-per-hour rather than a percentage basis. For example, a cost-of-living adjustment of 50 cents represents a 10 percent increase for an employee earning $5 per hour, but only a 5 percent increase for one earning $10 per hour. Unless adjustments are made periodically in employee base rates, the desired differential between higher- and lower-

Escalator clauses
Clauses in collective agreements that provide for quarterly cost-of-living adjustments in wages, basing the adjustments upon changes in the consumer price index.

Consumer price index (CPI)
Measure of the average change in prices over time in a fixed "market basket" of goods and services.

paying jobs will gradually be reduced. The incentive to accept more demanding jobs will also be reduced.

Collective Bargaining

One of the primary functions of a labour union, as will be emphasized in Chapter 15, is to bargain collectively over conditions of employment, the most important of which is compensation. The union's goal in each new agreement is to achieve increases in **real wages**—wage increases larger than the increase in the CPI—thereby improving the purchasing power and standard of living of its members. This goal includes gaining wage settlements that equal, if not exceed, the pattern established by other unions within the area.

The agreements negotiated by unions tend to establish rate patterns within the labour market. As a result, wages are generally higher in areas where organized labour is strong. To recruit and retain competent personnel, nonunion employers must either meet or exceed these rates. The "union scale" also becomes the prevailing rate that all employers must pay for work performed under government contract. The impact of collective bargaining therefore extends beyond that segment of the labour force that is unionized.

Internal Factors

The internal factors that influence wage rates are the employer's compensation policy, the worth of a job, an employee's relative worth in meeting job requirements, and an employer's ability to pay.

Employer's Compensation Policy

Highlights in HRM 2 illustrates the compensation objectives of two organizations, CIBC Insurance and Hewlett-Packard. The pay objective of Hewlett-Packard is to be an industry pay leader, while CIBC Insurance seeks to be wage-competitive. Both employers strive to promote a compensation policy that is fair and competitive.

CIBC Insurance and Hewlett-Packard, like other employers, will establish numerous compensation objectives that affect the pay employees receive. As a minimum, both large and small employers should set pay policies reflecting (1) the internal wage relationship among jobs and skill levels, (2) the external competition or an employer's pay position relative to what competitors are paying, (3) a policy of rewarding employee performance, and (4) administrative decisions concerning elements of the pay system such as overtime premiums, payment periods, and short-term or long-term incentives.[15]

Worth of a Job

Organizations without a formal compensation program generally base the worth of jobs on the subjective opinions of people familiar with the jobs.[16] In such instances, pay rates may be influenced heavily by the labour market or, in the case of unionized employers, by collective bargaining. Organizations with formal compensation programs, however, are more likely to rely on a system of job evaluation to aid in rate determination. Even when rates are subject to collective bargaining, job evaluation can assist the organization in maintaining some degree of control over its wage structure.

Real wages
Wage increases larger than rises in the consumer price index; that is, the real earning power of wages.

HIGHLIGHTS IN HRM

1 WAGE SURVEY DATA FROM ROBERT HALF INTERNATIONAL'S *1995 SALARY GUIDE*

HOW TO USE THIS SURVEY

The salary figures given in the tables reflect national averages. Taking into account geographic variances, we have created an adjustment formula. Make the following changes for salaries of less than $60,000 per year:

- Use the percentage on the following table of "Geographic Variances" to increase (decrease) the salary.
- If the job opening is located in a city with a population of more than one million, increase the salary by 5%.

Positions paying more than $60,000 per year show few regional variations.

GEOGRAPHIC VARIANCES

West Coast

Vancouver	+2%
British Columbia	0%

Prairies

Alberta Petroleum	+1%
Alberta Non-Petroleum	−2%
Saskatchewan	−4%
Manitoba	+4%

Ontario

Northwestern	−7%
Northern	−6%
Southwestern	−1%
Metro Toronto	+2%
Eastern	−1%

Quebec

Montreal	−2%
Quebec	−4%

Atlantic

Newfoundland	−10%
Nova Scotia	−8%
Prince Edward Island	−9%
New Brunswick	−8%

SAMPLE OF SURVEY

CFO, TREASURERS

Company $Volume (in Millions)	1994	1995	% Change
50 – 100	$72,000 – $91,000	$72,000 – $91,000	0.0%
100 – 250	$80,000 – $105,000	$80,000 – $105,000	0.0%
250+	$100,000 – $171,000	$100,000 – $172,000	0.4%
0			
0			

(This category assumes that there is a controller who reports to the CFO.)

CONTROLLER — Corporate

Company (Division) $Volume (in Millions)	1994	1995	% Change
0 – 50	$50,000 – $75,000	$50,000 – $75,000	0.0%
50 – 100	$60,000 – $75,000	$60,000 – $76,000	0.7%
100 – 250	$70,000 – $95,000	$70,000 – $95,000	0.0%
250+	$80,000 – $150,000	$80,000 – $150,000	0.0%

CONTROLLER — ASSISTANT/ DIVISIONAL/ PLANT, & ASSISTANT TREASURERS

Company (Division) $Volume (in Millions)	1994	1995	% Change
0 – 10	$40,000 – $54,000	$41,000 – $54,000	1.1%
10 – 50	$46,000 – $62,000	$46,000 – $62,000	0.0%
50 – 100	$52,000 – $70,000	$52,000 – $71,000	0.8%
100 – 250	$60,000 – $77,500	$61,000 – $78,000	1.1%
250+	$70,000 – $103,000	$70,000 – $103,000	0.0%

TAX MANAGERS — Corporate

Company (Division) $ Volume (in Millions)	1994	1995	% Change
50 – 250	$65,000 – $102,000	$65,000 – $102,000	0.0%
250+	$95,000 – $140,500	$95,000 – $140,500	0.0%

PUBLIC ACCOUNTANTS
Large Firms*

Experience/Title	1994	1995	% Change
to 1 year	$24,000 – $27,000	$24,000 – $28,000	2.0%
1 – 3 years	$27,500 – $37,500	$27,500 – $38,000	0.8%
Senior	$36,000 – $49,000	$36,000 – $49,000	0.0%
Supervisor	$40,000 – $60,000	$40,000 – $61,000	1.0%
Manager	$55,000 – $75,000	$55,000 – $75,000	0.0%

*Large firms = $250+ million in sales

Source: 1995 *Salary Guide*, Robert Half International, 1994.

2 COMPENSATION OBJECTIVES AT CIBC INSURANCE AND HEWLETT-PACKARD

CIBC INSURANCE
- Align with objectives and key performance measures
- Encourage teamwork and positive relations
- Provide rewards for excellent performance
- Ensure strong link between pay and performance
- Be market-competitive
- Attract, retain, and motivate high-calibre employees
- Ensure fair treatment

HEWLETT-PACKARD
- Help H-P continue to attract creative and enthusiastic people who contribute to its success
- Pay employees at top end of pay scale
- Reflect sustained relative contribution of unit, division, and H-P
- Be open and understandable
- Ensure fair treatment
- Be innovative, competitive, and equitable

Sources: Personal correspondence with Gail Cohen, CIBC Insurance, July 1995; and G.T. Milkovich and J.M. Newman, *Compensation*, 4th ed. (Homewood, IL: Irwin, 1993). Used with permission.

The use of job evaluation is widespread in both the public and the private sector. The City of Mississauga uses job evaluation in establishing wage structures, as do Star Data Systems Inc. The jobs covered most frequently by job evaluation comprise clerical, technical, and various blue-collar groups, whereas those jobs covered least frequently are managerial and top-executive positions.

Employee's Relative Worth

It is common practice in some industries, notably construction, for unions to negotiate a single rate for jobs in a particular occupation. This egalitarian practice is based on the argument that employees who possess the same qualifications should receive the same rate of pay. Furthermore, the itinerant nature of work in the construction industry usually prevents the accumulation of employment seniority on which pay differentials might be based.

"A raise just isn't feasible at this time, Osgood, but we're going to give you the 'wave.'"

Copyright 1994. Reprinted courtesy of Bunny Hoest and *Parade Magazine.*

In industrial and office jobs, differences in employee performance can be recognized and rewarded through promotion and with various incentive systems. (The incentive systems used most often will be discussed in the next chapter.) Superior performance can also be rewarded by granting merit raises on the basis of steps within a rate range established for a job class. If merit raises are to have their intended value, however, they must be determined by an effective performance appraisal system that differentiates between those employees who deserve the raises and those who do not.[17] This system, moreover, must provide a visible and credible relationship between performance and any raises received. Unfortunately, too many so-called merit systems provide for raises to be granted automatically. As a result, employees tend to be rewarded more for merely being present than for being productive on the job.

Employer's Ability to Pay

In the public sector, the amount of pay and benefits employees can receive is limited by the funds budgeted for this purpose and by the willingness of taxpayers to provide them. In the private sector, pay levels are limited by profits and other financial resources available to employers. Thus an organization's ability to pay is determined in part by the productivity of its employees. This productivity is a result not only of employee performance, but also of the amount of capital the organization has invested in labour-saving equipment. Increases in capital investment reduce the number of employees required to perform the work and increase an employer's ability to provide higher pay for those it employs.

Economic conditions and competition faced by employers can also significantly affect the rates they are able to pay. Competition and recessions can force prices down and reduce the income from which compensation payments are derived. In such situations, employers have little choice but to reduce wages and/or lay off employees, or, even worse, to go out of business. Employers and workers in the trucking and airline industries, for example, can attest to the competitive effects of deregulation and its influence on wage levels and job security. Likewise, companies such as Ford and Goodyear have had their ability to pay large wage increases severely limited by growing competition from the international market.

Job Evaluation Systems

objective

Job evaluation
Systematic process of determining the relative worth of jobs in order to establish which jobs should be paid more than others within an organization.

As we discussed earlier, one important component of the wage mix is the worth of the job. Organizations formally determine the value of jobs through the process of job evaluation. **Job evaluation** is the systematic process of determining the relative worth of jobs in order to establish which jobs should be paid more than others within the organization. Job evaluation helps to establish internal equity between various jobs. The relative worth of a job may be determined by comparing it with others within the organization or by comparing it with a scale that has been constructed for this purpose. Each method of comparison, furthermore, may be made on the basis of the jobs as a whole or on the basis of the parts that constitute the jobs.

Four methods of comparison are shown in Figure 11-3. They provide the basis for the principal systems of job evaluation. We will begin by discussing the simpler, nonquantitative approaches and conclude by reviewing the more popular, quantitative systems. Regardless of the methodology used, it is important to remember that all job evaluation methods require varying degrees of managerial judgment.[18]

Job Ranking System

Job ranking system
Simplest and oldest system of job evaluation by which jobs are arrayed on the basis of their relative worth.

The simplest and oldest system of job evaluation is the **job ranking system**, which arrays jobs on the basis of their relative worth. One technique used to rank jobs consists of having the raters arrange cards listing the duties and responsibilities of each job in order of the importance of the jobs. Job ranking can be done by a single individual who is knowledgeable about all jobs or by a committee composed of management and employee representatives.

FIGURE 11-3 *Different Job Evaluation Systems*

BASIS FOR COMPARISON	SCOPE OF COMPARISON	
	JOB AS A WHOLE (NONQUANTITATIVE)	JOB PARTS OR FACTORS (QUANTITATIVE)
Job vs. Job	Job ranking system	Factor comparison system
Job vs. scale	Job classification system	Point system

Another common approach to job ranking is the *paired-comparison method.* Raters compare each job with all other jobs by means of a paired-comparison ranking table that lists the jobs in both rows and columns, as shown in Figure 11-4. To use the table, raters compare a job from a row with the jobs from each of the columns. If the row job is ranked higher than a column job, an X is placed in the appropriate cell. After all the jobs have been compared, raters total the Xs for row jobs. The total number of Xs for a row job will establish its worth relative to other jobs.[19] Differences in rankings should then be reconciled into a single rating for all jobs. After jobs are evaluated, wage rates can be assigned to them through use of the salary survey discussed later in the chapter.

The basic weakness of the job ranking system is that it does not provide a very refined measure of each job's worth. Since the comparisons are normally made on the basis of the job as a whole, it is quite easy for one or more of the factors of a job to bias the ranking given to a job, particularly if the job is complex. This drawback can be partially eliminated by having the raters—prior to the evaluation process—agree on one or two important factors with which to evaluate jobs and on the weights to be assigned these factors. Another disadvantage of the job ranking system is that the final ranking of jobs merely indicates the relative importance of the jobs, not the differences in the degree of importance that may exist between jobs. A final

FIGURE 11-4   *Paired-Comparison Job Ranking Table*

Row Jobs \ Column Jobs	Senior Administrative Secretary	Data-Entry Operator	Data Processing Director	File Clerk	Systems Analyst	Programmer	Total
Senior Administrative Secretary	—	X		X		X	3
Data-Entry Operator		—		X			1
Data Processing Director	X	X	—	X	X	X	5
File Clerk				—			0
Systems Analyst	X	X		X	—	X	4
Programmer		X		X		—	2

Directions: Place an X in cell where the value of a row job is higher than that of a column job.

limitation of the job ranking method is that it can be used only with a small number of jobs, probably no more than fifteen. Its simplicity, however, makes it ideal for use by smaller employers.

Job Classification System

In the **job classification system**, jobs are classified and grouped according to a series of predetermined grades. Successive grades require increasing amounts of job responsibility, skill, knowledge, ability, or other factors selected to compare jobs. For example, Grade GS-1 from the U.S. federal government grade descriptions reads as follows:

> GS-1 includes those classes of positions the duties of which are to perform, under immediate supervision, with little or no latitude for the exercise of independent judgment (A) the simplest routine work in office, business, or fiscal operations; or (B) elementary work of a subordinate technical character in a professional, scientific, or technical field.

The descriptions of each of the job classes constitute the scale against which the specifications for the various jobs are compared. Managers then evaluate jobs by comparing job descriptions with the different wage grades in order to "slot" the job into the appropriate grade. While this system has the advantage of simplicity, it is less precise than the point and factor comparison systems (discussed in the next sections) because the job is evaluated as a whole. The federal public service job classification system is probably the best-known system of this type. The job classification system is used by federal and provincial governments in Canada.[20]

Point System

The **point system** is a quantitative job evaluation procedure that determines a job's relative value by calculating the total points assigned to it. It has been successfully used by high-visibility organizations such as Honeywell Limited and by many public and private organizations, both large and small. Although point systems are rather complicated to establish, once in place they are relatively simple to understand and use. The principal advantage of the point system is that it provides a more refined basis for making judgments than either the ranking or classification systems and thereby can produce results that are more valid and less easy to manipulate.

The point system permits jobs to be evaluated quantitatively on the basis of factors or elements—commonly called *compensable factors*—that constitute the job. The skills, efforts, responsibilities, and working conditions that a job usually entails are the more common major compensable factors that serve to rank one job as more or less important than another.[21] The number of compensable factors an organization uses depends on the nature of the organization and the jobs to be evaluated. Once selected, compensable factors will be assigned weights according to their relative importance to the organization. For example, if responsibility is considered extremely important to the organization, it could be assigned a weight of 40 percent. Next, each factor will be divided into a number of degrees. Degrees represent different levels of difficulty associated with each factor.

The point system requires the use of a *point manual*. The point manual is, in effect, a handbook that contains a description of the compensable factors and the

3   POINT VALUES FOR JOB FACTORS OF THE AMERICAN ASSOCIATION OF INDUSTRIAL MANAGEMENT

highlights

FACTORS	1ST DEGREE	2ND DEGREE	3RD DEGREE	4TH DEGREE	5TH DEGREE
Skill					
1. Job knowledge	14	28	42	56	70
2. Experience	22	44	66	88	110
3. Initiative and ingenuity	14	28	42	56	70
Effort					
4. Physical demand	10	20	30	40	50
5. Mental or visual demand	5	10	15	20	25
Responsibility					
6. Equipment or process	5	10	15	20	25
7. Material or product	5	10	15	20	25
8. Safety of others	5	10	15	20	25
9. Work of others	5	10	15	20	25
Job Conditions					
10. Working conditions	10	20	30	40	50
11. Hazards	5	10	15	20	25

Source: Developed by the National Metal Trades Association. Reproduced with permission of the American Association of Industrial Management, Springfield, Mass.

degrees to which these factors may exist within the jobs. A manual also will indicate—usually by means of a table (see Highlights in HRM 3)—the number of points allocated to each factor and to each of the degrees into which these factors are divided. The point value assigned to a job represents the sum of the numerical degree values of each compensable factor that the job possesses.

Developing a Point Manual

A variety of point manuals have been developed by organizations, trade associations, and management consultants. An organization that seeks to use one of these

4 DESCRIPTION OF JOB KNOWLEDGE FACTOR AND DEGREES OF THE AMERICAN ASSOCIATION OF INDUSTRIAL MANAGEMENT

highlights

1. Job Knowledge

This factor measures the knowledge or equivalent training required to perform the position duties.

1st Degree Use of reading and writing, adding and subtracting of whole numbers; following of instructions; use of fixed gauges, direct reading instruments, and similar devices where interpretation is not required.

2nd Degree Use of addition, subtraction, multiplication, and division of numbers including decimals and fractions; simple use of formulas, charts, tables, drawings, specifications, schedules, wiring diagrams; use of adjustable measuring instruments; checking of reports, forms, records, and comparable data where interpretation is required.

3rd Degree Use of mathematics together with the use of complicated drawings, specifications, charts, tables; various types of precision measuring instruments. Equivalent to one to three years' applied trades training in a particular or specialized occupation.

4th Degree Use of advanced trades mathematics, together with the use of complicated drawings, specifications, charts, tables, handbook formulas; all varieties of precision measuring instruments. Equivalent to complete accredited apprenticeship in a recognized trade, craft or occupation; or equivalent to a two-year technical college education.

5th Degree Use of higher mathematics involved in the application of engineering principles and their performance of related practical operations, together with a comprehensive knowledge of the theories and practices of mechanical, electrical, chemical, civil, or like engineering field. Equivalent to complete four years of technical college or university education.

Source: Developed by the National Metal Trades Association. Reproduced with permission of the American Association of Industrial Management, Springfield, Mass.

existing manuals should make certain that the manual is suited to its particular jobs and conditions of operation. If necessary, the organization should modify the manual or develop its own to suit its needs.

The job factors that are illustrated in Highlights in HRM 3 represent those covered by the American Association of Industrial Management point manual. Each of the factors listed in this manual has been divided into five degrees. The number of degrees into which the factors in a manual are to be divided, however, can be greater or smaller than this number, depending on the relative weight assigned to each factor and the ease with which the individual degrees can be defined or distinguished.[22]

After the job factors in the point manual have been divided into degrees, a statement must be prepared defining each of these degrees, as well as each factor as a whole. The definitions should be concise and yet distinguish the factors and each of their degrees. Highlights in HRM 4 on page 396 represents another portion of the point manual used by the American Association of Industrial Management to describe each of the degrees for the job knowledge factor. These descriptions enable those conducting a job evaluation to determine the degree to which the factors exist in each job being evaluated.

The final step in developing a point manual is to determine the number of points to be assigned to each factor and to each degree within these factors. Although the total number of points is arbitrary, 500 points is often the maximum.

Using the Point Manual

Job evaluation under the point system is accomplished by comparing the job descriptions and job specifications, factor by factor, against the various factor-degree descriptions contained in the manual. Each factor within the job being evaluated is then assigned the number of points specified in the manual. When the points for each factor have been determined from the manual, the total point value for the job as a whole can be calculated. The relative worth of the job is then determined from the total points that have been assigned to that job.[23]

Factor Comparison System

The **factor comparison system**, like the point system, permits the job evaluation process to be accomplished on a factor-by-factor basis. It differs from the point system, however, in that the compensable factors of the jobs to be evaluated are compared against the compensable factors of *key jobs* within the organization that serve as the job evaluation scale. Thus, instead of beginning with an established point scale, the factor comparison system requires a scale to be developed as part of the job evaluation process.[24]

Developing a Factor Comparison Scale

There are four basic steps in developing and using a factor comparison scale: (1) selecting and ranking key jobs, (2) allocating wage rates for key jobs across compensable factors, (3) setting up the factor comparison scale, and (4) evaluating nonkey jobs.

Step 1. Select and rank key jobs on the basis of compensable factors. Key jobs can be defined as those jobs that are important for wage-setting purposes and are widely known in the labour market. Key jobs have the following characteristics:

1. They are important to employees and the organization.
2. They vary in terms of job requirements.
3. They have relatively stable job content.
4. They are used in salary surveys for wage determination.

Factor comparison system

Job evaluation system that permits the evaluation process to be accomplished on a factor-by-factor basis by developing a factor comparison scale.

Key jobs are normally ranked against five factors—skill, mental effort, physical effort, responsibility, and working conditions. It is normal for the ranking of each key job to be different because of the different requirements of jobs. The ranking of three key jobs is shown in Figure 11-5, although usually fifteen to twenty key jobs will constitute a factor comparison scale.

Step 2. Next, determine the proportion of the current wage being paid on a key job to each of the factors composing the job. Thus the proportion of a key job's wage rate allocated to the skill factor will depend on the importance of skill in comparison with mental effort, physical effort, responsibility, and working conditions. It is important that the factor rankings in step 1 be consistent with the wage-apportionment rankings in step 2. Figure 11-6 illustrates how the rate for three key jobs has been allocated according to the relative importance of the basic factors that make up these jobs.

Step 3. After the wages for each key job have been apportioned across the factors, the data are displayed on a factor comparison scale, which is shown in Figure 11-7. The location of the key jobs on the scale and the compensable factors for these jobs provide the benchmarks against which other jobs are evaluated.

Step 4. We are now ready to compare the nonkey jobs against the key jobs in Figure 11-7. As an example of how the scale is used, let's assume that the job of screw machine operator is to be evaluated through the use of the factor comparison scale. By comparing the skill factor for screw machine operator with the skill factors of the key jobs on the table, it is decided that the skill demands of the job places it about halfway between those of storekeeper and punch press operator. The job is therefore placed at the $5.55 point on the scale. The same procedure is used to place the job at the appropriate point on the scale for the remaining factors.

Using the Factor Comparison Scale

The evaluated worth of the jobs added to the scale is computed by adding up the money values for each factor as determined by where the job has been placed on the scale for each factor. Thus the evaluated worth of the screw machine operator at $9.72 would be determined by totalling the monetary value for each factor as follows:

FIGURE 11-5   *Ranking Key Jobs by Compensable Factors*

JOB	SKILL	MENTAL EFFORT	PHYSICAL EFFORT	RESPON- SIBILITY	WORKING CONDITIONS
Machinist planner	1	1	3	1	
Punch press operator	2	2	1	3	2
Storekeeper	3	3	2	2	1

FIGURE 11-5 *Wages Apportionment for Each Factor*

JOB	TOTAL	SKILL	MENTAL EFFORT	PHYSICAL EFFORT	RESPON- SIBILITY	WORKING CONDITIONS
Machinist planner	$13.00	$6.50 (1)	$3.50 (1)	$0.50 (3)	$1.60 (1)	$0.90 (3)
Punch press operator	11.30	6.20 (2)	1.60 (2)	1.00 (1)	0.80 (3)	1.70 (2)
Storekeeper	9.85	4.90 (3)	1.30 (3)	0.70 (2)	1.20 (2)	1.75 (1)

Skill	$5.55
Mental effort	1.35
Physical effort	0.82
Responsibility	0.60
Working conditions	1.40
	$9.72

Job Evaluation for Management Positions

Because management positions are more difficult to evaluate and involve certain demands not found in jobs at the lower levels, some organizations do not attempt to include them in their job evaluation programs. Those employers that do evaluate these positions, however, may extend their regular system of evaluation to include such positions, or they may develop a separate evaluation system for management positions.

Hay profile method
Job evaluation technique using three factors—knowledge, mental activity, and accountability—to evaluate executive and managerial positions.

Several systems have been developed especially for the evaluation of executive, managerial, and professional positions. One of the better known is the **Hay profile method**, developed by Edward N. Hay. The three broad factors that constitute the evaluation in the "profile" include knowledge (or know-how), mental activity (or problem solving), and accountability.[25] The Hay method uses only three factors because it is assumed that these factors represent the most important aspects of all executive and managerial positions. The profile for each position is developed by determining the percentage value to be assigned to each of the three factors. Jobs are then ranked on the basis of each factor, and point values that make up the profile are assigned to each job on the basis of the percentage-value level at which the job is ranked. Highlights in HRM 5 illustrates how one company used this system to achieve its compensation objectives.

The Compensation Structure

Job evaluation systems provide for internal equity and serve as the basis for wage-rate determination. They do not in themselves determine the wage rate. The evaluated worth of each job in terms of its rank, class, points, or monetary worth must be

FIGURE 11-7 *Factor Comparison Scale*

HOURLY RATE	SKILL	MENTAL EFFORT	PHYSICAL EFFORT	RESPON-SIBILITY	WORKING CONDITIONS
6.50	• Machinist planner				
6.25					
6.00	• Punch press operator				
5.75					
5.50	• *Skrew mach. operator*				
5.25					
5.00	• Storekeeper				
4.75					
4.50					
4.25					
4.00					
3.75					
3.50		• Machinist planner			
3.25					
3.00					
2.75					
2.50					
2.25					
2.00					
1.75					• Storekeeper • Punch press operator
1.50		• Punch press operator		• Machinist planner	• *Skrew mach. operator*
1.25		• *Skrew mach. operator*			
1.00		• Storekeeper		• Storekeeper	• Machinist planner
0.75			• Punch press operator	• Punch press operator	
0.50			• *Skrew mach operator* • Storekeeper • Machinist planner	• *Skrew mac., operator*	

Note: If this scale contained the fifteen to twenty key jobs that typically constitute a factor comparison scale, the gaps between jobs on the scale would be reduced substiantially.

highlights

5   PROVEN METHODS IN JOB EVALUATION

Star Data Systems Inc. of Markham, Ontario, currently employs approximately 220 employees. The company is is a growing presence in its market. To facilitate Star Data's growth, the director of human resources implemented a job evaluation program as a means of "paying people fairly and equitably, complying with pay equity legislation, and being able to attract high-calibre candidates."

Following proven models, all employees were required to complete job questionnaires in order to develop their job descriptions. The process involved having the employees answer questions that related to the compensable factors chosen for the job evaluation process. Of the 92 descriptions prepared, 47 were deemed benchmark positions and 45 were deemed nonbenchmark positions. Examples of benchmark positions within Star Data included marketing coordinator, network support technicians, assistant controller, and shipper/receiver. Among the nonbenchmark positions were exchange reporter, product specialist, and technical sales analyst.

To ensure fairness and equity in the evaluation process, Star Data formed a job evaluation committee comprising employees from various levels within the organization. An outside consultant was hired to train committee members to evaluate positions in an unbiased manner. Using a point-factor method, job evaluation was used to determine the relative value placed on all positions within the organization. The focus for evaluating the positions was based on the requirements of the job, and was measured against four compensable factors, namely, *skill*, which includes the subfactors of knowledge and experience; *working conditions,* which involves consideration of work environment factors; *responsibility*, which focuses on interpersonal skills/contact/communications, complexity/ judgment/problem solving, scope of responsibility, and impact of results; and *effort*. All of these compensable factors, along with their subfactors, were tailor-made to fit Star Data's business needs.

Weightings were determined for each of the compensable factors in the evaluation process based on the value of the particular factor to the organization, the value placed on the factors by other companies in the industry, requirements of pay equity legislation, and input from the consulting group. Since working conditions/effort were not deemed to be a deterrent for completing the work, only a 5 percent weight was assigned to that factor; in contrast, skill received a 40 percent weighting.

Having completed their evaluation of the positions, the committee assigned a point total to each position, allowing a hierarchy to be developed. Based on the point totals, the positions were divided into groups to form twelve salary grades. Using the benchmark positions that are found in each salary grade, salary and pay information was collected from competitors and other organizations to arrive, via salary surveys, at an average market salary as the midpoint. This methodology ensured that the plan was competitive with the external marketplace.

Star Data, with a new salary grade format, was in a position to analyze internal salaries against the new ranges and to review any pay equity issues. All employees in the organization knew their own salary ranges, their position within the range, and whether salary adjustments would be necessary.

In the future, Star Data will ensure that the system is maintained in a bias-free manner, that the salary administration program remains competitive with the external marketplace, and that salaries are administered fairly and consistently. The company plans to remain competitive by participating in annual surveys and by making necessary salary and range adjustments as conditions warrant. The ultimate responsibility rests with the managers to provide constructive and timely performance reviews and salary increases that are tied directly to performance.

Source: Discussion with Tracy Callahan, Director of Human Resources, Star Data Systems Inc., July 1995.

converted into an hourly, daily, weekly, or monthly wage rate. The compensation tool used to help set wages is the wage and salary survey.

Wage and Salary Surveys

four
objective

Wage and salary survey
Survey of the wages paid to employees of other employers in the surveying organization's relevant labour market.

The **wage and salary survey** is a survey of the wages paid by employers in an organization's relevant labour market—local, regional, or national, depending on the job. The labour market is frequently defined as that area from which employers obtain certain types of workers. The labour market for office personnel would be local, whereas the labour market for engineers would be national. It is the wage and salary survey that permits an organization to maintain external equity, that is, to pay its employees wages equivalent to the wages similar employees earn in other establishments. Although surveys are primarily conducted to gather competitive wage data, they can also collect information on employee benefits or organizational pay practices (e.g., overtime rates or shift differentials).

Collecting Survey Data

While many organizations conduct their own wage and salary surveys, a variety of salary surveys are available throughout Canada, either through professional associations or through professional consulting firms. Companies such as KPMG, Wyatt Company, Robert Half International Inc., Hewitt Associates, and Hay Management Consultants conduct annual surveys, as do professional associations such as ITAC. Towers Perrin's overseas compensation survey reports on payment practices in twenty countries.

While all of these third-party surveys provide certain benefits to their users, they also have various limitations. Two problems with all published surveys are that (1) they are not always compatible with the user's jobs, and (2) the user cannot specify what specific data to collect. To overcome these problems, organizations may collect their own compensation data.

Employer-Initiated Surveys

Employers wishing to conduct their own wage and salary survey must first select the jobs to be used in the survey and identify the organizations with whom they actually compete for employees.[26] Since it is not feasible to survey all the jobs in an organization, normally only key jobs are used. The survey of key jobs will usually be sent to ten or fifteen organizations that represent a valid sample of other employers likely to compete for the employees of the surveying organization. A diversity of organizations should be selected—large and small, public and private, new and established, and union and nonunion—since each classification of employer is likely to pay different wage rates for surveyed jobs.

After the key jobs and the employers to be surveyed have been identified, the surveying organization must decide what information to gather on wages, benefit types, and pay policies. For example, when requesting pay data, it is important to specify whether hourly, daily, or weekly pay figures are needed. In addition, those conducting surveys must state if the wage data are needed for new hires or for senior employees. Precisely defining the compensation data needed will greatly increase the accuracy of the information received and the number of purposes for which it can be used. Once the survey data are tabulated, the compensation structure can be completed.

The Wage Curve

objective

Wage curve

Curve in a scattergram representing the relationship between relative worth of jobs and wage rates.

The relationship between the relative worth of jobs and their wage rates can be represented by means of a **wage curve**. This curve may indicate the rates currently paid for jobs within an organization, the new rates resulting from job evaluation, or the rates for similar jobs currently being paid by other organizations within the labour market. A curve may be constructed graphically by preparing a scattergram consisting of a series of dots that represent the current wage rates. As shown in Figure 11-8, a freehand curve is then drawn through the cluster of dots in such a manner as to leave approximately an equal number of dots above and below the curve. The wage curve can be relatively straight or curved. This curve can then be used to determine the relationship between the value of a job and its wage rate at any given point on the line.

Pay Grades

Pay grades

Groups of jobs within a particular class that are paid the same rate or rate range.

From an administrative standpoint, it is generally preferable to group jobs into **pay grades** and to pay all jobs within a particular grade the same rate or rate range. When

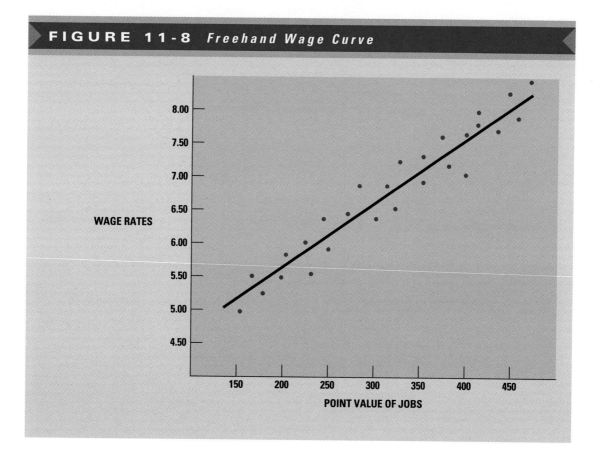

FIGURE 11-8   *Freehand Wage Curve*

the classification system of job evaluation is used, jobs are grouped into grades as part of the evaluation process. When the point and factor comparison systems are used, however, pay grades must be established at selected intervals that represent either the point or the evaluated monetary value of these jobs. The graph in Figure 11-9 illustrates a series of pay grades designated along the horizontal axis at 50-point intervals.

The grades within a wage structure may vary in number. The number is determined by such factors as the slope of the wage curve, the number and distribution of the jobs within the structure, and the organization's wage administration and promotion policies. The number utilized should be sufficient to permit difficulty levels to be distinguished, but not so great as to make the distinction between two adjoining grades insignificant.

Rate Ranges

Although a single rate may be created for each pay grade, as shown in Figure 11-9, it is more common to provide a range of rates for each pay grade. The rate ranges may

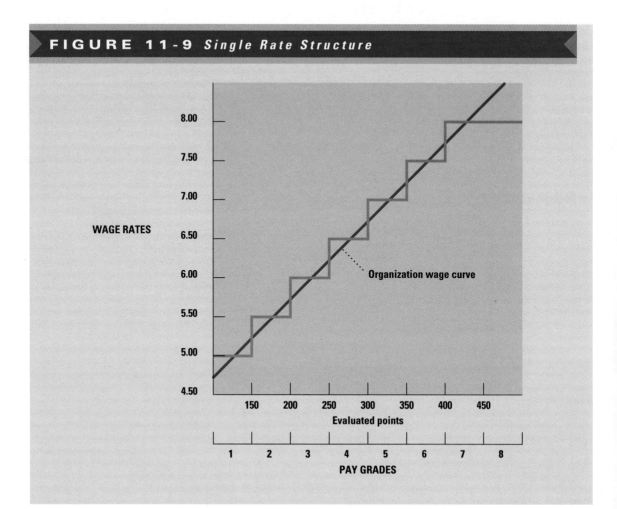

FIGURE 11-9 *Single Rate Structure*

be the same for each grade or proportionately greater for each successive grade, as shown in Figure 11-10. Rate ranges constructed on the latter basis provide a greater incentive for employees to accept a promotion to a job in a higher grade.

Rate ranges generally are divided into a series of steps that permit employees to receive increases up to the maximum rate for the range on the basis of merit or seniority or a combination of the two. Most salary structures provide for the ranges of adjoining pay grades to overlap. The purpose of the overlap is to permit an employee with experience to earn as much as or more than a person with less experience in a higher job classification.

Classification of Jobs

The final step in setting up a wage structure is to determine the appropriate pay grade into which each job should be placed on the basis of its evaluated worth. Traditionally, this worth is determined on the basis of job requirements without

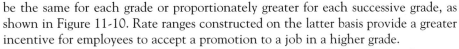

FIGURE 11-10   *Wage Structure with Increasing Rate Ranges*

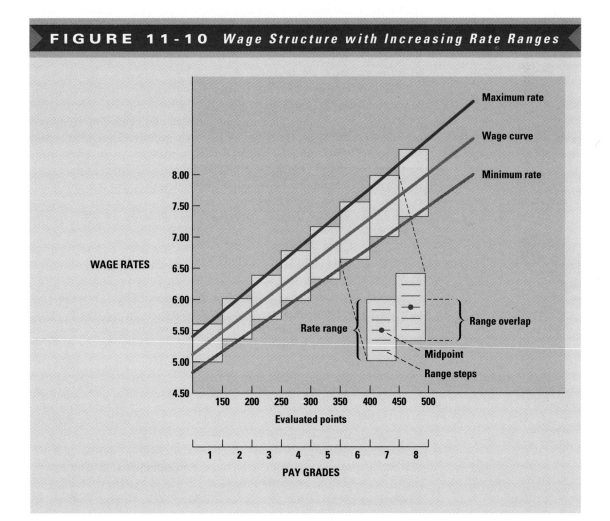

regard to the performance of the person in that job. Under this system, the performance of those who exceed the requirements of a job may be acknowledged by merit increases within the grade range or by promotion to a job in a higher pay grade.

Unfortunately, such a system often fails to reward employees for the skills or knowledge they possess or to encourage them to learn new job-related skills. It tends to consider employees as jobholders rather than as individuals. To correct these weaknesses, organizations such as General Mills, NorTel, Sherwin-Williams, and London Life have introduced **skill-based pay** plans.[27] Also referred to as multiskill-based, knowledge-based, or pay-for-knowledge plans, these programs compensate employees for the skills and knowledge they possess rather than for the jobs they hold in a designated job category.

Although the types of skill-based plans are sometimes thought to be interchangeable, there are important differences between them. Organizations using skill-based pay systems compensate employees for the number of different skills they learn and can apply to different jobs in the organization. Skill-based pay plans are frequently used where employees are part of autonomous work groups or employee teams. As one research study noted, skill-based pay reinforces employee-involvement practices. It increases employee flexibility, which broadens employee perspectives on the overall production or service-delivery system. Rewards for learning multiple jobs may also facilitate job rotation and cross-training, which are essential to self-managing team designs.[28]

Skill-based pay plans are particularly attractive to organizations looking for greater job-staffing flexibility. Unfortunately, these plans may bring some long-term difficulties. Some plans limit the amount of compensation employees can earn, regardless of the new skills or knowledge they acquire. Thus, after achieving the top wage, employees may be reluctant to continue their educational training. Furthermore, employees can become discouraged when they acquire new abilities but find that there are no higher-rated jobs to which they can transfer. Finally, unless all employees have the opportunity to increase their pay through the attainment of new skills, employees who are not given this opportunity may feel disgruntled.

Skill-based pay

Pay based on how many skills employees have or how many jobs they can perform.

objective

Governmental Regulation of Compensation

Compensation management, like the other areas of HRM, is subject to federal and provincial legislation. An employment standards Act in each of the provinces establishes minimum requirements with respect to wages, hours of work, and overtime. Provincial as well as federal minimum requirements can be obtained by contacting the appropriate federal or provincial office.

Canada Labour Code

Part III of the Canada Labour Code and the Canada Labour Standards Regulations sets minimum labour standards for all employees and employers in works or undertakings that fall within federal jurisdiction, including interprovincial highway and rail transportation, pipelines, telephone and television, air transport, fishing and banking. Federal crown corporations are covered by the Code, but federal public service employees are not. Employees working under these classifications are subject to a 40-hour workweek. Managerial and professional employees are not covered by the hours-of-work provisions and may be required in excess of those hours. Constant revisions are made to these standards; HR managers must keep abreast of these changes to ensure compliance in the workplace.

Employment Standards Acts

Each of the provinces and territories is legislated under an employment standards Act that establishes minimum standards with a view to protecting employees and employers in certain employment situations. Collective agreements may override the provisions of the Acts as long as employees are not being provided with less than what the Acts have stipulated and it is to the benefit of the employee. Employers who operate in more than one province must become fully informed of the different requirements that exist in each province.

Each province's Act contains a provision that stipulates that an overtime rate of 1.5 times the base rate must be paid for all hours worked in excess of the set minimum prescribed in the province. For example, if an employee works 45 hours in a province that legislates the minimum workweek as 40 hours, then the extra five hours would qualify the individual for overtime at 1.5 times his or her base rate. Particular groups, including lawyers, doctors, engineers, and managers, are exempt from overtime requirements.

Child Labour Provisions

In all provinces, legislation has been passed to prevent the abuse of children in work situations. For instance, in Ontario, where some of the strictest laws are enforced, persons under the age of 16 cannot work during school hours unless they have completed secondary schooling or its equivalent. The province has also legislated the following age restrictions:

Minimum Age	Operation
16	logging operation or mining
15	factory or construction work
14	any industry
18	underground or surface mines

Persons under 16 may not be employed in workplaces to which the public has access from 9 p.m. to 6 a.m.

Other Legislation

Employment equity is legislated under federal legislation for all federally regulated companies and for those companies not covered under the Canada Labour Code that have dealings with federally legislated companies. Pay equity is covered provincially where applicable. As we discussed in Chapter 3, employment equity and pay equity legislation is designed to ensure that fair employment practices are applied to all members of designated groups.

objective

Significant Compensation Issues

As with other HR activities, compensation management operates in a dynamic environment. For example, as managers strive to reward employees in a fair manner, they must consider controls over labour costs, legal issues regarding male and female wage payments, and internal pay equity concerns. Each of these concerns is highlighted in three important compensation issues: equal pay for work of comparable value, wage-rate compression, and two-tier wage systems.

Equal Pay for Work of Comparable Value

Comparable value
The concept that male and female jobs that are dissimilar, but equal in terms of value or worth to the employer, should be paid the same.

One of the most important gender issues in compensation is equal pay for work of **comparable value**. The issue stems from the fact that jobs performed predominantly by women are paid less than those performed by men. This practice results in what critics term *systemic discrimination*, whereby women receive less pay for jobs that may be different from but comparable in value to those performed by men. The issue of comparable value goes beyond providing equal pay for jobs that involve the same duties for women as for men. It is not concerned with whether a female secretary should receive the same pay as a male secretary. Rather, the argument for equal pay for work of comparable value is that jobs held by women are not compensated the same as those held by men, even though both job types may contribute equally to organizational success.[29]

Problem of Measuring Comparability

Advocates of comparable value argue that the difference in wage rates for predominantly male and female occupations rests in the undervaluing of traditional female occupations. To remedy this situation, they propose that wages should be equal for jobs that are "somehow" equivalent in total value or compensation to the organization. Unfortunately, there is no consensus on a comparable worth standard by which to evaluate jobs, nor is there agreement on the ability of present job evaluation techniques to remedy the problem.[30] Indeed, organizations may dodge the comparable value issue by using one job evaluation system for clerical and secretarial jobs and another system for other jobs. Furthermore, the advocates of comparable value argue that current job evaluation techniques simply serve to continue the differences in pay between the sexes. However, others believe that job evaluation systems can be designed to measure different types of jobs, in the same way that apples and oranges can be compared, as illustrated in Figure 11-11.

The argument over comparable value is likely to remain an important HR issue for many years to come. Unanswered questions such as the following will serve to keep the issue alive:

1. If comparable value is adopted, who will determine the value of jobs, and by what means?
2. How much would comparable value cost employers?
3. Would comparable value reduce the wage gap between men and women caused by labour market supply-and-demand forces?
4. Would comparable value reduce the number of employment opportunities for women?

> **FIGURE 11-11** *How Can You Compare Apples and Oranges?*

	Weight	
150.0 grams	Weight	150.0 grams
87	Calories	73
21.7 grams	Carbohydrates	18.3 grams
0.3 grams	Protein	1.5 grams
1.5 grams	Fibre	1.8 grams
140 IU	Vitamin A	300 IU

Source: M. Belcourt, "Human Resource Management," in *Introduction to Canadian Business and Management*, edited by J. Pleniussen (Toronto: McGraw-Hill Ryerson and Captus Press, 1994), 410.

Finally, organizations implementing comparable value policies have raised women's wages. In one public-sector study of the impact of comparable value on men's and women's earnings, the researcher concluded that when comparable value is implemented through special wage increases, public-sector wages move ahead of local prevailing wage standards and the male/female pay differentials are greatly reduced.[31] The compensation gap between men and women will not disappear overnight, but the persistence of comparable value advocates will help to shrink it.

Wage-Rate Compression

Wage-rate compression
Compression of differentials between job classes, particularly the differential between hourly workers and their managers.

Earlier, when we discussed the compensation structure, it was noted that the primary purpose of the pay differentials between the wage classes is to provide an incentive for employees to prepare for and accept more demanding jobs. Unfortunately, this incentive is being significantly reduced by **wage-rate compression**—the reduction of differences between job classes. Wage-rate compression is largely an internal pay equity concern. The problem occurs when employees perceive that there is too narrow a difference between their compensation and that of colleagues in lower-rated jobs.

HR professionals acknowledge that wage-rate compression is a widespread organizational problem affecting diverse occupational groups: white-collar and blue-collar workers, technical and professional employees, and managerial personnel. It can cause low employee morale, leading to issues of reduced employee performance, higher absenteeism and turnover, and even delinquent behaviour such as employee theft.

There is no single cause of wage-rate compression.[32] For example, it can occur when unions negotiate across-the-board increases for hourly employees but managerial personnel are not granted corresponding wage differentials. Such increases can result in part from COLAs provided for in labour agreements. Other inequities have resulted from the scarcity of applicants in computers, engineering, and other professional and technical fields. Job applicants in these fields frequently have been offered starting salaries not far below those paid to employees with considerable experience and seniority. Wage-rate compression often occurs when organizations grant pay adjustments for lower-rated jobs without providing commensurate adjustments for occupations at the top of the job hierarchy.

Identifying wage-rate compression and its causes is far simpler than implementing organizational policies to alleviate its effect. Organizations wishing to minimize the problem may incorporate the following ideas into their pay policies:

Two-tier wage system

Wage system whereby newly hired employees performing the same jobs as senior employees receive lower rates of pay.

1. Give larger compensation increases to employees with greater seniority.
2. Emphasize pay-for-performance and reward merit-worthy employees.
3. Limit the hiring of new applicants seeking exorbitant salaries.
4. Design the pay structure to allow a wide spread between hourly and supervisory jobs or between new hires and senior employees.
5. Provide equity adjustments for selected employees hardest hit by pay compression.

Two-Tier Wage Systems

Many organizations affected by deregulation, foreign competition, and aggressive nonunionized competitors implement two-tier wage systems as a means of lowering their labour costs. A **two-tier wage system** is a compensation plan that pays newly hired employees less than present employees performing the same or similar jobs. With some two-tier wage systems, new employees may receive reduced benefit packages. Examples of companies using two-tiered wage systems are Miracle Food Mart of Canada and New Dominion Stores.

A two-tier wage system can give rise to perceptions of unfairness when new hires and senior employees perform the same job but receive different wages. Feelings of inequity can, in turn, lead to low levels of job commitment, work attendance problems, reduced productivity, and employee resentment.

Whether two-tier wage systems will continue as a method of labour cost control seems uncertain. Recent reports show that employers are phasing out these programs because of high employee turnover and morale problems.[33] Thus the gap in employee wages caused by these pay plans will likely decline. If this trend contin-

Under a two-tier wage system, a new employee will have to work perhaps ten years before earning the same wages as this senior airline mechanic.

ues, employers are likely to implement other cost-cutting pay strategies such as incentive pay plans, the subject of Chapter 12.

SUMMARY

Establishing compensation programs requires both large and small organizations to consider specific goals—employee retention, compensation distribution, and adherence to a budget, for instance. Compensation must reward employees for past efforts (pay-for-performance) while serving to motivate employees' future performance. Internal and external equity of the pay program affects employees' concepts of fairness. Organizations must balance each of these concerns while still remaining competitive. The ability to attract qualified employees while controlling labour costs are major factors in allowing organizations to remain viable in domestic or international markets.

The basis on which compensation payments are determined, and the way they are administered, can significantly affect employee productivity and the achievement of organizational goals. External factors influencing wage rates include labour market conditions, area wage rates, cost of living, legal requirements, and the outcomes of collective bargaining. Internal influences include the employer's compensation policy, the worth of the job, performance of the employee, and the employer's ability to pay.

Organizations use one of four basic job evaluation techniques to determine the relative worth of jobs. The job ranking system arranges jobs in numerical order on the basis of the importance of the job's duties and responsibilities to the organization. The job classification system slots jobs into pre-established grades. Higher-rated grades require greater amounts of job responsibility. The point system of job evaluation uses a point scheme based upon the compensable job factors of skill, effort, responsibility, and working conditions. The more compensable factors a job possesses, the more points are assigned to it. Jobs with higher accumulated points are considered more valuable to the organization. The factor comparison system evaluates jobs on a factor-by-factor basis against key jobs in the organization.

Wage surveys determine the external equity of jobs. Data obtained from surveys will facilitate establishing the organization's wage policy while ensuring that the employer does not pay more, or less, than needed for jobs in the relevant labour market.

The wage structure is composed of the wage curve, pay grades, and rate ranges. The wage curve depicts graphically the pay rates assigned to jobs within each pay grade. Pay grades represent the grouping of similar jobs on the basis of their relative worth. Each pay grade includes a rate range. Rate ranges have a midpoint and minimum and maximum pay rates for all jobs in the pay grade.

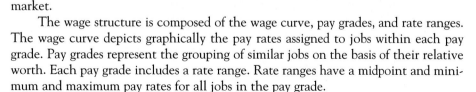

Compensation is regulated by federal and provincial governments through the Canada Labour Code, employment standards Acts, child labour provisions, and employment equity/pay equity legislation.

The concept of comparable value seeks to overcome the fact that jobs held by women are compensated at a lower rate than those performed by men. This happens

objective

even though both types of jobs may contribute equally to organizational productivity. Wage-rate compression largely affects managerial and senior employees as the pay given to new employees or the wage increases gained through union agreements erode the pay differences between these groups. Employers wishing to lower labour costs may establish two-tier systems, in which separate pay schedules are used to compensate junior and senior employees who perform the same job.

KEY TERMS

comparable value	pay-for-performance standard
consumer price index (CPI)	pay grades
escalator clauses	piecework
factor comparison system	point system
Hay profile method	real wages
hourly or day work	skill-based pay
job classification system	two-tier wage system
job evaluation	wage and salary survey
job ranking system	wage curve
pay equity	wage-rate compression

DISCUSSION QUESTIONS

1. What are the disadvantages of pay secrecy? Despite its disadvantages, why do some managers prefer pay secrecy?
2. Since employees may differ in terms of their job performance, would it not be more feasible to determine the wage rate for each employee on the basis of his or her relative worth to the organization?
3. What are some of the criticisms being raised concerning COLA and the CPI on which COLA is based?
4. During collective bargaining, unions have sometimes responded to a company claim of inability to pay with the statement that the union should not be expected to subsidize inefficient management. Does this response have any merit?

5. Describe the basic steps in conducting a wage and salary survey. What are some factors to consider?

6. One of the objections to granting wage increases on a percentage basis is that the lowest-paid employees, who are having the most trouble making ends meet, get the smallest increase, while the highest-paid employees get the largest increase. Is this objection a valid one?

7. What are some of the problems that emerge when an organization attempts to develop a pay system based on equal pay for work of comparable value?

CASE: Pay Decisions at Performance Sports

Katie Perkins' career objective while attending Durham College was to obtain a degree in small-business management and, upon graduation, to start her own business. Her ultimate desire was to combine her love of sports and her strong interest in marketing by establishing a mail-order golf equipment business aimed specifically at beginning golfers.

In February 1991, after extensive development of a strategic business plan and a loan in the amount of $75,000 from the Federal Business Development Bank, Performance Sports was open for business. A marketing plan that stressed fast delivery, error-free customer service, and large discount pricing contributed to the company's rapid growth. At present, Performance Sports employs sixteen people: eight customer service representatives earning between $9.75 and $11.25 per hour; four shipping and receiving associates paid between $8.50 and $9.50 per hour; two clerical employees, each earning $8.75 per hour; an assistant manager earning $12.10 per hour; and a general manager who receives a wage of $13.25 per hour. Both the manager and assistant manager are former customer service representatives.

Perkins intends to create a new managerial position—purchasing agent—to handle the complex duties of purchasing golf equipment from the company's numerous equipment manufacturers. Also, the mail-order catalogue from Performance Sports will be expanded to handle a complete line of tennis equipment. Since the position of purchasing agent is new, Perkins isn't sure how much to pay this person. She wants to employ an experienced individual who has between five and eight years of experience in sports-equipment purchasing.

While attending an equipment manufacturers' convention in Montreal, Perkins learns that a competitor—Ottawa Valley Sports—pays its customer service representatives on a pay-for-performance basis. Intrigued, Perkins asks her assistant manager, George Balkin, to research the pros and cons of this payment strategy. Her request has become a priority since only last week two customer service representatives expressed dissatisfaction with their hourly wage. Both complained that they felt underpaid relative to the large amount of sales revenue each generates for the company.

Questions

1. What factors should Perkins consider when setting the wage for the purchasing agent position? What resources are available for her to consult when establishing this wage?
2. Suggest advantages and disadvantages of a pay-for-performance policy for Performance Sports.
3. Suggest a new payment plan for the customer service representatives.

Compensation in Your Career

Exercises that you completed in previous chapters should have led you to identify one or more occupations you wish to pursue as a career. The purpose of this exercise is to learn what compensation you might receive should you pursue this career. To determine the salaries in your chosen field for an entry-level or junior person, an employee with several years' experience, and a senior professional, consult some of the following sources:

- *Community colleges and universities.* Speak to the placement officer and ask what students are receiving as job offers from companies in the field that interests you.
- *Advertisements.* Read newspapers and trade magazines, and check bulletin boards in the organizations in which you work. If the salary range is not given, phone the company and ask for this information.
- *Working professionals.* Through friends or colleagues, identify people who are already working in your field. Ask their permission to contact these working professionals, and then talk to them, explaining your career interest.
- *Professional associations.* Most occupations are represented by a union or professional association that can provide you with compensation information. Ask the relevant organization if it conducts, uses, or publishes compensation surveys.
- *Consultants.* Compensation surveys are conducted by professional consulting firms such as KPMG, Wyatt Company, Robert Half International Inc., Hewitt Associates, and Hay Management Consultants. Phone these companies to find out if they publish these surveys and if they are willing to provide you with a copy for a nominal fee.

NOTES AND REFERENCES

1. Robert Kreitner and Angelo Kinicki, *Organizational Behavior*, 3rd ed. (Homewood, IL: BPI/Irwin, 1995), Chapter 15.

2. Howard W. Risher, "Strategic Salary Planning," *Compensation and Benefits Review* 25, no. 1 (January-February 1993): 46–50. See also Milton L. Rock and Lance A. Berger, *The Compensation Handbook*, 3rd ed. (New York: McGraw-Hill, 1991).

3. Luis R. Gomez-Mejia and David B. Balkin, *Compensation, Organizational Strategy, and Firm Performance* (Cincinnati: South-Western Publishing, 1992), Chapter 2. See also Peter V. Leblanc, "Pay for Work: Reviving an Old Idea for the New Customer Focus," *Compensation and Benefits Review* 26, no. 4 (July-August 1994): 5–14; Caroline L. Weber and Sara L. Rymes, "Effects of Compensation Strategy on Job Pay Decisions," *Academy of Management Journal* 34, no. 1 (March 1991): 86–109.

4. Edward E. Lawler III, *Strategic Pay: Aligning Organizational Strategies and Pay Systems* (San Francisco: Jossey-Bass, 1990).

5. Jay R. Schuster and Patricia K. Zingheim, *Linking Employee and Organizational Performance* (Lexington, MA: Lexington Books, 1992). See also Peter R. Eyes, "Realignment Ties Pay to Performance," *Personnel Journal* 72, no. 1 (January 1993): 74–77; James P. Guthrie and Edward P. Cunningham, "Pay for Performance for Hourly Workers: The Quaker Oats Alternative," *Compensation and Benefits Review* 24, no. 2 (March-April 1992): 18–23.

6. Arturo R. Thomann, "Flex-Base Addresses Pay Problems," *Personnel Journal* 71, no. 2 (February 1992): 51–55.

7. Discussion with Tracy Callahan, Director of Human Resources, Star Data Systems Inc., July 1995.

8. George Milkovich and Carolyn Milkovich, "Strengthening the Pay-Performance Relationship: The Research," *Compensation and Benefits Review* 24, no. 6 (November-December 1992): 53. See also Edward E. Lawler III, "Pay-for-Performance: A Strategic Analysis," in Luis R. Gomez-Mejia, ed., *Compensation Benefits* (Washington, DC: American Society for Personnel Administration/Bureau of National Affairs, 1989), 3–16.

9. Canadian Compensation Association, *1994–1995 Salary Budget Survey*, August 1994, 1–55.

10. R. Bradley Hill, "A Two-Component Approach to Compensation," *Personnel Journal* 72, no. 5 (May 1993): 154.

11. Marc J. Wallace, Jr., and Charles H. Fay, *Compensation Theory and Practice*, 2nd ed. (Boston: PWS-Kent, 1988): 14.

12. Mary A. Hopkinson, "After the Merger: Paying for Keeps," *Personnel Journal* 70, no. 8 (August 1991): 29–31. See also Anne M. Saunier and Elizabeth J. Hawk, "Realizing the Potential of Teams through Team-Based Rewards," *Compensation and Benefits Review* 26, no. 4 (July-August 1994): 24–33.

13. Jeffrey A. Bradt, "Pay for Impact," *Personnel Journal* 10, no. 6 (May 1991): 76.

14. *CPI Detailed Report March 1993* (U.S. Department of Labor, Bureau of Labor Statistics, March 1993), 96.

15. George T. Milkovich and Jerry M. Newman, *Compensation*, 4th ed. (Homewood, IL: Irwin, 1993), 10–12.

16. Robert J. Greene, "Determinants of Occupational Worth," *Personnel Administrator* 34, no. 8 (August 1989): 78–82.

17. Laurent Dufetel, "Job Evaluation: Still at the Frontier," *Compensation and Benefits Review* 23, no. 4 (July-August 1991): 53–67.

18. Sandra M. Emerson, "Job Evaluation: A Barrier to Excellence?" *Compensation and Benefits Review* 23, no. 1 (January-February 1991): 39–51.

19. Frederick S. Hills, *Compensation Decision Making*, 2nd ed. (Chicago: Dryden Press, 1994).

20. *Modernizing Federal Classification: An Opportunity for Excellence* (Washington, DC: National Academy of Public Administration, 1991).

21. Howard W. Risher, "Job Evaluation: Validity and Reliability," *Compensation and Benefits Review* 21, no. 1 (January-February 1989): 32–33.

22. Kermit Davis, Jr., and William Sauser, Jr., "Effects of Alternative Weighting Methods in a Policy-Capturing Approach to Job Evaluation," *Personnel Psychology* 44, no. 1 (Spring 1991): 85–127. See also Leonard R. Burgess, *Compensation Administration*, 2nd ed. (Columbus, OH: Merrill, 1989): 166.

23. Kermit R. Davis, Jr., and William I. Sauer, Jr., "A Comparison of Factor Weighting Methods in Job Evaluation: Implications for Compensation Systems," *Public Personnel Management* 22, no. 1 (Spring 1993): 91–103.

24. For an expanded discussion of both the point system and the factor comparison system, see Milkovich and Newman, *Compensation*, Chapter 4.

25. Richard I. Henderson, *Compensation Management*, 6th ed. (Reston, VA: Reston Publishing, 1993).

26. Robert J. Sahl, "Job-Content Salary Surveys: Survey Design and Selection Features," *Compensation and Benefits Review* 23, no. 3 (May-June 1991): 14–21.

27. Gerald E. Ledford, Jr., "Three Case Studies on Skill-Based Pay: An Overview," *Compensation and Benefits Review* 23, no. 2 (March-April 1991): 11–23. See also Richard L. Bunning, "Models for Skill-Based Pay

Plans," *HR Magazine* 37, no. 2 (February 1992): 62–64; Fred Luthans and Marilyn L. Fox, "Update on Skill-Based Pay," *Personnel* 66, no. 3 (March 1989): 26–31.

28. Edward E. Lawler III, Gerald E. Ledford, Jr., and Lei Chang, "Who Uses Skill-Based Pay and Why?" *Compensation and Benefits Review* 25, no. 2 (March-April 1993): 22–26. See also Dale Fever, "Paying for Knowledge," *Training* 24, no. 5 (May 1987): 58.

29. Mary V. Moore and Yohannan T. Abraham, "Comparable Worth: Is It a Moot Issue?" *Public Personnel Management* 21, no. 4 (Winter 1992): 455–68.

30. Richard W. Scholl and Elizabeth Cooper, "The Use of Job Evaluation to Eliminate Gender Based Pay Differentials," *Public Personnel Management* 20, no. 1 (Spring 1991): 1–17.

31. Greg Hundley, "The Effects of Comparable Worth in the Public Sector on Public/Private Occupational Relative Wages," *Journal of Human Resources* 28, no. 2 (Spring 1993): 319–340. See also Elaine Sorensen, "Effect of Comparable Worth Policies on Earnings," *Industrial Relations* 26, no. 3 (Fall 1987): 227–239.

32. Thomas J. Bergmann, Marilyn A. Bergmann, Desiree Roff, and Vida Scarpello, "Salary Compression: Causes and Solutions," *Compensation and Benefits Review* 23, no. 6 (November-December 1991): 7–16.

33. Edward J. Wasilewski, Jr., "Collective Bargaining in 1992: Contract Talks and Other Activity," *Monthly Labor Review* 115, no. 1 (January 1992): 14.

Chapter 12

Incentive Compensation

I*n the previous chapter, we emphasized that the worth of a job is a significant factor in determining the pay rate for that job. However, pay based solely on this measure may fail to motivate employees to perform to their full capacity. Unmotivated employees are likely to meet only minimum performance standards.*

Recognizing this fact, organizations such as W.K. Buckley Ltd., Delta Mountain Inn, and Pillsbury Canada offer some form of incentive to workers.[1] These organizations are attempting to get more motivational mileage out of employee compensation by tying it more clearly to employee performance. Managers at Magma Copper Company note that incentive linked with output "causes workers to more fully apply their skills and knowledge to their jobs while encouraging them to work together as a team." Marshall Campbell, vice-president of human resources, remarked, "If we increase production of ore extraction, and tie output to employee compensation, we operate with lower costs and that makes us more competitive in the national and international marketplace."[2]

In their attempt to raise productivity, managers are focusing on the many variables that help to determine the effectiveness of pay as a motivator. Financial incentive plans are being developed—on the basis of knowledge acquired by researchers and HR practitioners—to meet the needs of both employees and employers more satisfactorily.[3]

In this chapter, we will discuss incentive plans in terms of the objectives they hope to achieve and the various factors that may affect their success. We will also attempt to identify the plans that are most effective in motivating different categories of employees to achieve these objectives. For discussion purposes, incentive plans have been grouped into two broad categories, individual incentive plans and group incentive plans, as shown in Figure 12-1.

Reasons and Requirements for Incentive Plans

objective

Reasons for Adopting an Incentive Plan

A clear trend in compensation management is the growth of incentive plans, also called variable pay programs, for employees below the executive level. Incentive plans emphasize a shared focus on organizational success by broadening the opportu-

---

FIGURE 12-1   *Types of Incentive Plans*

INDIVIDUAL		GROUP
Hourly:	*Sales Personnel:*	*Hourly and Managerial:*
Piecework	Sales incentive plans	Scanlon Plan
Bonuses	*Professional:*	Rucker Plan
Standard hour plan	Maturity curves	Improshare
Managerial:	Executive:	Profit sharing
Merit raises	Bonuses	
	Stock options	

nities for incentives to nontraditional groups while operating outside the merit (base pay) increase system.[4] Incentive plans create an operating environment that champions a philosophy of shared commitment through the belief that every individual contributes to organizational success.

Over the years, organizations have implemented incentive plans for a variety of reasons: high labour costs, competitive product markets, slow technological advances, and high potential for production bottlenecks.[5] While these reasons are still cited, contemporary arguments for incentive plans focus on pay-for-performance and improved organizational productivity.[6] By linking compensation to employee effort, organizations believe that employees will improve their job performance. Incentives are designed to encourage employees to put out more effort to complete their job tasks—effort they might not be motivated to expend under hourly and/or seniority-based compensation systems. Financial incentives are therefore offered to improve or maintain high levels of productivity and quality, which in turn improves the market for Canadian goods and services in a global economy. Figure 12-2 summarizes the major advantages of incentive pay programs as noted by researchers and HR professionals.

Do incentive plans work? Various studies have demonstrated a measurable relationship between incentive plans and improved organizational performance. In a survey of organizations with more than 500 employees, conducted by the New York Stock Exchange, 70 percent of organizations with gainsharing programs stated that those programs improved productivity.[7] In the area of manufacturing, productivity will often improve by as much as 20 percent after the adoption of incentive plans.[8] Improvements, however, are not limited to goods-producing industries. Service organizations, not-for-profit, and government agencies also show productivity gains when incentives are linked to organizational goals. For example, after beginning an incentive pay program, Sun Life of Canada reduced unit costs of various business service (the per unit cost of processing claims) while at the same time improving customer service. Similarly, Taco Bell Corporation reduced food costs and improved customer service scores after it began an employee bonus program in 1991.[9]

FIGURE 12-2 *Advantages of Incentive Pay Programs*

- Incentives focus employee efforts on specific performance targets. They provide real motivation that produces important employee and organizational gains.
- Incentive payouts are variable costs linked to the achievement of results. Base salaries are fixed costs largely unrelated to output.
- Incentive compensation is directly related to operating performance. If performance objectives (quantity and/or quality) are met, incentives are paid. If objectives are not achieved, incentives are withheld.
- Incentives foster teamwork and unit cohesiveness when payments to individuals are based on team results.
- Incentives are a way to distribute success among those responsible for producing that success.

1 MAKING IT WORK: A LOOK AT GROUP INCENTIVES

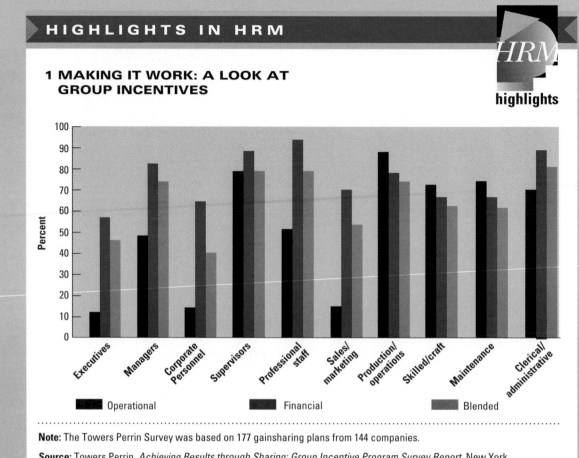

Note: The Towers Perrin Survey was based on 177 gainsharing plans from 144 companies.

Source: Towers Perrin, *Achieving Results through Sharing: Group Incentive Program Survey Report,* New York, April 1990, 10. Reprinted with permission.

According to a Towers Perrin survey of *Fortune* 1000 companies, there has been an increase in the use of group incentives, and participation in gainsharing is increasing since its inception 40 years ago.[10] Highlights in HRM 1 shows the results of a Towers Perrin national survey that measured the differences in participation by plan type.

However, for two main reasons, incentive plans have not always led to organizational improvement. First, incentive plans sometimes fail to satisfy employee needs. Second, management may have failed to give adequate attention to the design and implementation of the plan.[11] Furthermore, the success of an incentive plan will depend on the environment that exists within an organization. A plan is more likely to work in an organization where morale is high, employees believe they are being treated fairly, and there is harmony between employees and management.

Requirements for a Successful Incentive Plan

For an incentive plan to succeed, employees must have some desire for the plan. This desire can be influenced in part by how successful management is in introducing the plan and convincing employees of its benefits. Encouraging employees to participate in administering the plan is likely to increase their willingness to accept it.

Employees must be able to see a clear connection between the incentive payments they receive and their job performance. This connection is more visible if there are objective quality or quantity standards by which they can judge their performance. Commitment by employees to meet these standards is also essential for incentive plans to succeed. This requires mutual trust and understanding between employees and their supervisors, which can be achieved only through open, two-way channels of communication. Management should never allow incentive payments to be seen as an entitlement.[12] Instead, these payments should be viewed as a reward that must be earned through effort. This perception can be strengthened if the incentive money is distributed to employees in a separate cheque.

Setting Performance Measures

Measurement is key to the success of incentive plans because it communicates the importance of established organizational goals. What gets measured and rewarded gets attention. For example, if the organization desires to be a leader in quality, then performance indexes may focus on customer satisfaction, timeliness, or being error-free. If being a low-priced producer is the goal, then the emphasis should be on cost reduction or increased productivity with lower acceptable levels of quality. While a variety of performance options are available, most focus on quality, cost control, or productivity.

One authority on incentive plans notes that the failure of most incentive plans can be traced to the choice of performance measures.[13] Therefore measures that are quantitative, simple, and structured to show a clear relationship to improved performance are best. Overly quantitative, complex measures are to be avoided. Also, when selecting a performance measure, it is necessary to evaluate the extent to which the employees involved can actually influence the measurement. Finally, employers must guard against "ratcheting-up" performance goals by continually trying to exceed previous results. This eventually leads to employee frustration and employee perception that the standards are unattainable. The result will be a mistrust of management and a backlash against the entire incentive program.

Administering Incentive Plans

While incentive plans based on productivity can reduce direct labour costs, to achieve their full benefit they must be carefully thought out, implemented, and maintained. A cardinal rule is that thorough planning must be combined with a "proceed with caution" approach. Compensation managers repeatedly stress the following three points related to the effective administration of incentive plans:

1. Incentive systems are effective only when managers are willing to grant incentives based on differences in individual performance. Allowing

TOTAL COMPENSATION AT EATON'S

The T. Eaton Company Limited has been a household name in Canada for decades. Committed to excellence achieved through their leading-edge human resources practices, they continue to develop strategies that bring all the company's people management processes together, to work interdependently with one another.

Glenn Quarrington, vice-president of human resources, is committed to bringing "a total compensation" value system, which includes cash and noncash, to Eaton's. As part of his mandate, he oversees the development of incentive compensation plans through the Motivation and Rewards Department.

"In support of our corporate vision for the future, we had to develop ways to motivate people to behave and perform in new ways. Human resources strategies and systems had to be aligned more with the business needs than they had in the past. As a basis for this alignment, we needed to consider the key performance drivers or measures of success for the business. How could we improve customer service? How could we increase sales productivity? We also had to consider whether to focus on the individual, to be team based, or to do a combination of the two. Also important, we needed to be able to attract, motivate, and retain key performers. Having the right people, in the right job, at the right time was only part of the equation. Results could only be achieved through the addition of appropriate motivational factors. Therefore, we had to determine what were the right reward systems to help produce results.

"Recognizing that we needed the views and feelings of our people toward various design options, a large sample of employees complete a questionnaire about monetary and nonmonetary rewards. You do not want to make assumptions about what might motivate people, you need to ask them," adds Quarrington. Employees were asked if money was a motivator, what the ideal way to earn bonuses was—through teams, individually, or in combination—and how much was enough. The results of the questionnaire reflected very reasonable responses. From it an effective model was developed because of their input.

"In terms of base pay, our old system used a step progression formula based on time on the job, with no relationship to performance. We needed to move from an 'entitlement' mindset to one where pay was based on performance. We changed the salary structure to a range with a minimum and a job rate (considered the maximum for most) and then another category above for high potential. People who invest in their own self-development, have advanced skills and competencies, and are promotable can move into the high-potential end of the range. To be credible, entry to the high- potential range must be very rigidly controlled. The philosophy around this section of the range is pay-for-knowledge and advancement potential.

"For example, for sales associates, in addition to their salary structure, quarterly bonuses could be earned based on individual and team measures. All elements of the pay had to be tied to performance, including adjustments to base pay. Most employees were enthusiastic that they could earn additional bonuses based on measured performance results. The higher the level of the position in the organization, the higher the stake—the reward. Our sales associates have no base pay at risk and have the opportunity to earn incremental bonuses. More senior staff may have an element of base pay at risk (as part of their bonus structure) if performance challenges are not achieved.

"If you look at our associates only, today we have almost 17,000 people involved in the program. Individual performance is assessed largely on behavioural observations made by their supervisors. Sales productivity, customer service, team work, and product knowledge are some of the elements assessed by the supervisors every 90 days. Sales productivity and customer service are the most heavily weighted performance items. If the scores are in a certain range they can earn bonuses starting at 1 percent of base and increasing from there. As well as the supervisor's views, supplemental assessments are made through our service excellence programs, which include customer comments, shopping reports, and commendations. Therefore, teamwork must exist in order to maximize the team's overall performance. If the team hits or exceeds its target, then everyone receives additional bonus percentages.

"Our vision states that 'we must create a climate for success.' Recognition, or nonmonetary rewards, is also important. We encourage our managers to look for opportunities to recognize success and to develop programs that will work best for their staff. This may include a range of options such as acknowledging their staff member in national newsletters or locally through the presentation of a pin in front of their peers. Our role in Human Resources is to work together with the managers to develop recognition programs and ideas. It's their job to deliver the message directly to their employees. Through our questionnaire, the employees gave us a lot of good ideas to work with. A catalogue is being developed so managers can select awards they want to use for their programs. Also, we encourage the managers to recognize and reward outstanding performance in their stores.

"As part of our move toward total compensation, we include the benefits program. Employees want to be responsible for themselves and we must address the needs of our diversified workforce and range of lifestyles. All of our employees, based on a prescribed calculation, are provided with a spending account where they can purchase the amount and kind of coverage they feel is necessary. The only obligatory base benefit is long-term disability. All others may be purchased from the spending account. If the account is not spent, it can be taken as income.

"As a caution when embarking on a total remuneration and performance pay strategy, there is a lot of development and employee input required to make the pay strategy work. It is absolutely essential that the employees be part of the strategy. When you say that you will pay for performance on a quarterly basis, you must be able to deliver that cheque in a short period of time to be meaningful. Giving that cheque six months later will only deflate your program. When an employee's name is put in the newsletter, it needs to be spelled correctly. The processes must be in place to avoid these types of pitfalls. To get motivational value, ensure that performance targets are given well before the measurement period starts. Administratively, there is usually an added financial burden to get this type of program running, as well as systems and infrastructure changes. However, if properly designed, there is an expected payback in a short period of time because (1) payment is contingent on performance— in traditional programs, payment was made whether or not results were achieved; and (2) you can convert otherwise fixed salary costs to variable costs. When presenting the strategy to your decision makers, make sure you provide them with a business plan to support what you are trying to achieve. This will provide the business link and partnership you require as a human resources professional."

Source: Interview with Glen Quarrington, August 1995.

incentive payments to become pay guarantees defeats the motivational intent of the incentive. The primary purpose of an incentive compensation plan is not to pay off under almost all circumstances, but rather to motivate performance. Thus, if the plan is to succeed, poor performance must go unrewarded.

2. Annual salary budgets must be large enough to reward and reinforce exceptional performance. When compensation budgets are set to ensure that pay increases do not exceed certain limits (often established as a percentage of payroll or sales), these constraints may prohibit rewarding outstanding individual or group performance.

3. The overhead costs associated with plan implementation and administration must be determined. These may include the cost of establishing performance standards and the added cost of recordkeeping. The time consumed in communicating the plan to employees, answering questions, and resolving any complaints about it must also be included in these costs.

Incentives for Nonmanagement Employees

objective

Many factors influence the design of incentive plans for nonmanagement employees. For example, incentive plans for this group are designed with consideration for the type of work these employees do and the technology they use. Also, when employees work in teams, a team incentive plan may be preferred since individual effort may not be distinguishable from team effort.[14] Organizations may also use team incentives in cases where some employees are likely to try to maximize their output at the expense of their co-workers. One report stated that team incentives may reduce rivalry and promote cooperation and concern for the unit's overall performance.[15] In addition, in highly competitive industries such as foods and retailing, low profit margins will affect the availability of monies for incentive payouts. All these considerations suggest that tradition and philosophy, as well as economics and technology, help to govern the design of nonmanagement incentive systems. The various gainsharing plans discussed later in the chapter are typically offered to both nonmanagement and management employees.

Incentives for Hourly Employees

Incentive payments for hourly employees may be determined by the number of units produced, by the achievement of specific performance goals, or by productivity improvements in the organization as a whole. In the majority of incentive plans, incentive payments serve to supplement the employee's basic wage.

Piecework

One of the oldest incentive plans is based on piecework. Under **straight piecework**, employees receive a certain rate for each unit produced. Their compensation is determined by the number of units they produce during a pay period. Under a **differential piece rate**, employees whose production exceeds the standard receive a higher rate for *all* of their work than the rate paid to those who do not exceed the standard.

Straight piecework
Incentive plan under which employees receive a certain rate for each unit produced.

Differential piece rate
Compensation rate under which employees whose production exceeds the standard amount of output receive a higher rate for all of their work than the rate paid to those who do not exceed the standard amount.

Employers include piecework in their compensation strategy for several reasons. The wage payment for each employee is simple to compute, and the plan permits an organization to predict its labour costs with considerable accuracy, since these costs are the same for each unit of output. The piecework system is more likely to succeed when units of output can be measured readily, when the quality of the product is less critical, when the job is fairly standardized, and when a constant flow of work can be maintained.

Under the piecework system, employees normally are not paid for the time they are idle unless the idleness is due to conditions for which the organization is responsible, such as delays in work flow, defective materials, inoperative equipment, or power failures. When the delay is not the fault of employees, they are paid for the time they are idle.

Computing the piece rate. Although time standards establish the time required to perform a given amount of work, they do not by themselves determine what the incentive rate should be. The incentive rates must be based on hourly wage rates that would otherwise be paid for the type of work being performed. Say, for example, the standard time for producing one unit of work in a job paying $6.50 per hour was set at twelve minutes. The piece rate would be $1.30 per unit, computed as follows:

$$\frac{60 \text{ (minutes per hour)}}{12 \text{ (standard time per unit)}} = 5 \text{ units per hour}$$

$$\frac{\$6.50 \text{ (hourly rate)}}{5 \text{ (units per hour)}} = \$1.30 \text{ per unit}$$

Limited use of piecework. In spite of its incentive value, the use of piecework is limited. One reason for this is that production standards on which piecework must

Piecework incentive programs have been used for many years in the garment industry.

be based can be difficult to develop for many types of jobs. In some instances, the cost of determining and maintaining this standard may exceed the benefits gained from the system. Jobs in which individual contributions are difficult to distinguish or measure, or in which the work is mechanized to the point that the employee exercises very little control over output, also may be unsuited to piecework. The same is true of jobs in which employees are learning the work or in which high standards of quality are paramount.

One of the most significant weaknesses of piecework, as well as of other incentive plans based on individual effort, is that it may not always be an effective motivator. If employees believe that an increase in their output will provoke disapproval from fellow workers, they may avoid exerting maximum effort because their desire for peer approval outweighs their desire for more money.[16] Over a period of time, the standards on which piece rates are based tend to loosen, either because of peer pressure to relax the standards or because employees discover ways to do the work in less than standard time. In either case, employees are not required to exert as much effort to receive the same amount of incentive pay, so the incentive value is reduced.[17]

Negative reaction to piecework. Despite the opportunity to earn additional pay, employees, especially those belonging to unions, have negative attitudes toward piecework plans. Some union leaders have feared that management will use piecework or similar systems to try to speed up production, getting more work from employees for the same amount of money. Another fear is that the system may induce employees to compete against one another, thereby taking jobs away from workers who are shown to be less productive. There is also the belief that the system will cause some employees to lose their jobs as productivity increases or will cause craft standards of workmanship to suffer.

Individual Bonuses

Bonus

Incentive payment that is supplemental to the base wage.

A **bonus** is an incentive payment that is supplemental to the basic wage. It has the advantage of providing employees with more pay for exerting greater effort, while at the same time they still have the security of a basic wage. A bonus payment may be based on the number of units that an individual produces, as in the case of piecework. For example, at the basic wage rate of $7 an hour plus a bonus of 15 cents per unit, an employee who produces 100 units during an eight-hour period is paid $71, computed as follows:

$$\text{(Hours} \times \text{wage rate)} + \text{(number of units} \times \text{unit rate)} = \text{Wages}$$
$$(\quad 8 \quad \times \quad \$7) + (\quad 100 \quad \times \quad 15¢) = \$71$$

Bonuses may also be determined on the basis of cost reduction, quality improvement, or performance criteria established by the organization.

Team Bonuses

Team bonuses, as Highlights in HRM 2 illustrates, are most desirable to use when the contributions of individual employees either are difficult to distinguish or depend on group cooperation.[18] Thus, as production has become more automated, as teamwork and coordination among workers have become more important, and as the contributions of those engaged indirectly in production work have increased, team bonuses have grown more popular. Most team bonus plans developed in recent years base

2 COMPUTING THE TEAM BONUS AT BF GOODRICH

The BF Goodrich Terre Haute plant links team performance and rewards with plant goals. The Performance Lets Us Share (PLUS) program encourages higher levels of team performance through employee involvement. The PLUS program works in the following ways:

- Base levels of performance are set for specific measurement areas—quality, productivity, cost, and customer service. Base levels are reviewed annually, and they are affected by historical performance and improvements.
- Separate financial pools are used to reward gains in each measurement area.
- Savings generated are shared by the organization and employees. The percentage employees receive depends on the pool, but it ranges from 10 to 50 percent of the gain. The more important an item, and the more control employees have over the item, the higher the percentage.
- Employees receive 50 percent of savings distributed in monthly bonus checks paid separately from the employee's regular paycheck. Each employee's amount is a percentage of the employee's earnings for hours worked during the month.
- The employees' remaining share of 50 percent is placed in a monthly accumulating reserve account. Where monthly performance falls below the baseline, the employees' share of the loss is deducted from the reserve account. Year-end excesses are paid to employees; losses are absorbed by the company.

Source: Adapted, by permission of publisher, from Robert L. Masternak and Timothy L. Ross, "A Bonus Plan or Employee Involvement?" *Compensation and Benefits Review* 24, no. 1 (January-February 1992): 46–54. American Management Association. All rights reserved.

incentive payments on such factors as improvements in efficiency, product quality, or reductions in labour costs. Organizations can use team bonus plans to support group planning and problem solving, thereby building a "team culture."

Team bonuses, unlike incentive plans based solely on output, can broaden the scope of the contributions that employees are motivated to make. For example, if labour costs represent 30 percent of an organization's sales dollars and the organization is willing to pay a bonus to employees, then whenever employee labour costs represent less than 30 percent of sales dollars, those savings are put into a bonus pool for employees. Information on the status of the pool is reported to employees on a weekly or monthly basis, explaining why a bonus was or was not earned. The team bonus may be distributed to employees equally, in proportion to their base pay, or on the basis of their relative contribution to the team.

Standard Hour Plan

Another common incentive technique is the **standard hour plan**, which sets incentive rates based on a predetermined "standard time" for completing a job. If employees finish the work in less than the expected time, their pay is still based on the standard time for the job multiplied by their hourly rate. For example, if the standard time to install an engine in a half-ton truck is five hours and the mechanic completes the job in four and a half hours, the payment would be the mechanic's hourly rate times five hours. Standard hour plans are particularly suited to long-cycle operations or those jobs or tasks that are nonrepetitive and require a variety of skills.[19]

The Wood Products Southern Division of Potlatch Corporation has successfully used a standard hour plan for the production of numerous wood products. The incentive payment is based on the standard hours calculated to produce and package 1000 feet (300 m) of wood panelling. If employees can produce the panelling in less time than the standard, incentives are paid on the basis of the percentage improvement. Thus, with a 1000-hour standard and completion of the wood panelling in 900 hours, a 10 percent incentive is paid. Each employee's base hourly wage is increased by 10 percent and then multiplied by the hours worked.

While standard hour plans can motivate employees to produce more, employers must ensure that equipment maintenance and product quality does not suffer as employees strive to do their work faster to earn additional income.

Incentives for Management Employees

Merit raises constitute one of the financial incentive systems used most commonly for managerial employees. Most recent studies of pay practices indicate that as many as 90 percent of large public- and private-sector organizations have merit pay programs for one or more of their employee groups.[20] Incentive pay may also be provided through different types of bonuses. Like those for hourly employees, these bonuses may be based on a variety of criteria involving either individual or group performance. As stated earlier, managerial employees are also usually included in the different types of gainsharing plans. Although they may not technically manage employees, sales employees and professional employees will also be discussed in this section.

Merit Raises

Merit raises can serve to motivate managerial, sales, and professional employees if they perceive the raises to be related to the performance required to earn them. Furthermore, theories of motivation, in addition to behavioural science research, provide justification for merit pay plans as well as other pay-for-performance programs.[21] For employees to see the link between pay and performance, however, their performance must be evaluated in light of objective criteria. If this evaluation also includes the use of subjective judgment by their superiors, employees must have confidence in the validity of this judgment. Most important, any increases granted on the basis of merit should be distinguishable from employees' regular pay and from any cost-of-living or other general increases. When merit increases are based on pay-for-performance, merit pay should be withheld if performance is seen to decline.[22]

objective

Problems with Merit Raises

Merit raises may not always achieve their intended purpose. Unlike a bonus, a merit raise may be perpetuated year after year even when performance declines. When this happens, employees come to expect the increase and see it as being unrelated to their performance. Furthermore, employees in some organizations are opposed to merit raises because, among other reasons, they do not really trust management. What are referred to as merit raises often turn out to be increases based on seniority or favouritism, or raises to accommodate increases in cost of living or in area wage rates.[23] Even when merit raises are determined by performance, the employee's gains may be offset by inflation and higher income taxes. Compensation specialists also recognize the following problems with merit pay plans:

1. Money available for merit increases may be inadequate to satisfactorily raise employees' base pay.
2. Managers may have no guidance in how to define and measure performance; there may be vagueness regarding merit award criteria.
3. Employees may not believe that their compensation is tied to effort and performance; they may be unable to differentiate between merit pay and other types of pay increases.
4. Employees may believe that organizational politics plays a significant factor in merit pay decisions, despite the presence of a formal merit pay system.
5. There may be a lack of honesty and cooperation between management and employees.
6. It has been shown that "overall" merit pay plans do not motivate higher levels of employee performance.[24]

Probably one of the major weaknesses of merit raises lies in the performance appraisal system on which the increases are based. Even with an effective system, performance may be difficult to measure. Furthermore, any deficiencies in the performance appraisal program (these were discussed in Chapter 10) can impair the operation of a merit pay plan. Moreover, the performance appraisal objectives of employees and their superiors are often at odds. Employees typically want to maximize their pay increases, whereas superiors may seek to reward employees in an equitable manner on the basis of their performance. In some instances, employee pressures for pay increases actually may have a harmful effect on their performance appraisal.

Merit guidelines

Guidelines for awarding merit raises that are tied to performance objectives.

While there are no easy solutions to these problems, organizations using a true merit pay plan often base the percentage pay raise on **merit guidelines** tied to performance appraisals. For example, Figure 12-3 illustrates a guideline chart for awarding merit raises. The percentages may change each year, depending on various internal or external concerns such as profit levels or national economic conditions as indicated by changes in the consumer price index. Under the illustrated merit plan, to prevent all employees from being rated outstanding or above average, managers may be required to distribute the performance rating according to some pre-established formula (e.g., only 10 percent can be rated outstanding).

....

FIGURE 12-3 *Merit Guideline Chart*

GRADE 0

EXAMPLE

Salary Ranges:

Minimum		Midpoint		Maximum
$20,000	22,500	25,000	27,500	30,000
	Q1	Q2	Q3	Q4

Merit Matrix Guidelines:

Performance Ratings	Salary Range Placements				
	Minimum to Q1	Q1 to Midpoint	Midpoint to Q3	Q3 to Maximum	Over Maximum
Consistently Exceeds Requirements	4.0–5.0%	3.0–4.0%	2.0–3.0%	2.0–3.0%	0%
Successfully Meets Requirements	3.0–4.0%	2.0–3.0%	2.0–3.0%	1.0–2.0%	0%
Occasionally Meets Requirements	0–2.0%	0–2.0%	0%	0%	0%
Fails to Meet Requirements	0%	0%	0%	0%	0%

Source: *1995 Salary Ranges and Merit Matrix Guidelines,* Star Data Systems Inc., Markham, Ontario, 1995.

Additionally, when setting merit percentage guidelines, organizations should consider individual performance along with such factors as training, experience, and current earnings.

Lump-Sum Merit Pay

Lump-sum merit program
Program under which employees receive a year-end merit payment, which is not added to their base pay.

To make merit increases more flexible and visible, organizations such as Boeing, Timex, and Westinghouse have implemented a **lump-sum merit program**. Under this type of plan, employees receive a single lump-sum increase at the time of their review, an increase that is not added to their base salary. Unless management takes further steps to compensate employees, their base salary is essentially frozen until they receive a promotion.[25]

Lump-sum merit programs offer several advantages. For employers, this innovative approach provides financial control by maintaining annual salary expenses. Merit increases granted on a lump-sum basis do not contribute to escalating base salary levels. In addition, organizations can contain employee benefit costs, since the levels of benefits are normally calculated from current salary levels. For employees, receiving a single lump-sum merit payment can provide a clear link between pay and performance. For example, a 6 percent merit increase granted to an employee earning $25,000 a year translates into a weekly increase of $28.84—a figure that looks small compared with a lump-sum payment of $1500.

Organizations using a lump-sum merit program will want to adjust base salaries upward after a certain period of time. This can be done yearly or after several years. These adjustments should keep pace with the rising cost of living and increases in the general market wage.

objective

Incentives for Sales Employees

The enthusiasm and drive required in most types of sales work demand that sales employees be highly motivated. This fact, as well as the competitive nature of selling, explains why financial incentives for salespeople are widely used. These incentive plans must provide a source of motivation that will elicit cooperation and trust. Motivation is particularly important for employees away from the office who cannot be supervised closely and who, as a result, must exercise a high degree of self-discipline.

Unique Needs of Sales Incentive Plans

Incentive systems for salespeople are complicated by the wide differences in the types of sales jobs. These range from department store clerks who ring up customer purchases to industrial salespersons at Congoleum Corporation in Winnipeg, Manitoba. Cash bonuses are paid to salespeople for the number of square feet of product sold. Salespersons' performance may be measured by the dollar volume of their sales and by their ability to establish new accounts. Other measures are the ability to promote new products or services and to provide various forms of customer service and assistance that do not produce immediate sales revenues. Sales associates at the Gap in the Toronto Eaton Centre are awarded unique items such as Gap watches (which cannot be bought and are only for contests) for the most units sold per transaction (multiple sales).

Performance standards for sales employees are difficult to develop, however, because their performance is often affected by external factors beyond their control.[26] Economic and seasonal fluctuations, sales competition, changes in demand, and the nature of the sales territory can all affect an individual's sales record. Sales volume alone therefore may not be an accurate indicator of the effort salespeople have expended.

In developing incentive plans for salespeople, managers are also confronted with the problem of how to reward extra sales effort and at the same time compensate for activities that do not contribute directly or immediately to sales. Furthermore, sales employees must be able to enjoy some degree of income stability.

Types of Sales Incentive Plans

Compensation plans for sales employees may consist of a straight salary plan, a straight commission plan, or a combination salary and commission plan.[27] **A straight salary plan** permits salespeople to be paid for performing various duties not reflected immediately in their sales volume. It enables them to devote more time to providing

Straight salary plan
Compensation plan that permits salespeople to be paid for performing various duties that are not reflected immediately in their sales volume.

services and building up the goodwill of customers without jeopardizing their income. The principal limitation of the straight salary plan is that it may not motivate salespeople to exert sufficient effort in maximizing their sales volume.

Straight commission plan

Compensation plan based upon a percentage of sales.

On the other hand, the **straight commission plan**, based on a percentage of sales, provides maximum incentive and is easy to compute and understand. For example, the hot dog vendor at the SkyDome in Toronto receives 15 percent for every hot dog he sells. Organizations that pay a straight commission based on total volume may use the following simple formulas:

$$\text{Total cash compensation} = 2\% \times \text{total volume}$$

or

$$\text{Total cash compensation} = 2\% \times \text{total volume up to quota}$$
$$+ \ 4\% \times \text{volume over quota}$$

However, the straight commission plan has the following disadvantages:

1. Emphasis is on sales volume rather than on profits (except in those rare cases where the commission rate is a percentage of the profit on the sale).
2. Territories tend to be milked rather than worked.
3. Customer service after the sale is likely to be neglected.
4. Earnings tend to fluctuate widely between good and poor periods of business, and turnover of trained sales employees tends to increase in poor periods.
5. Salespeople are tempted to grant price concessions.
6. Salespeople are tempted to overload their wholesale customers with inventory.

Combined salary and commission plan

Compensation plan that includes a straight salary and a commission.

When a **combined salary and commission plan** is used, the percentage of cash compensation paid out in commissions (i.e., incentives) is called *leverage*. Leverage is usually expressed as a ratio of base salary to commission. For example, a salesperson working under a 70/30 combination plan would receive total cash compensation paid out as 70 percent base salary and 30 percent commission. The amount of leverage will be determined after considering the constraining factors affecting perform-ance (discussed earlier) and the sales objectives of the organization. The following advantages indicate why the combination salary and commission plan is so widely used:

1. The right kind of incentive compensation, if linked to salary in the right proportion, has most of the advantages of both the straight salary and the straight commission forms of compensation.
2. A salary-plus-incentive compensation plan offers greater design flexibility and can therefore be more readily set up to help maximize company profits.
3. The plan can develop the most favourable ratio of selling expense to sales.
4. The field sales force can be motivated to achieve specific company marketing objectives in addition to sales volume.

Incentives for Professional Employees

Like other salaried workers, professional employees—engineers, scientists, and lawyers, for example—may be motivated through bonuses and merit increases. In

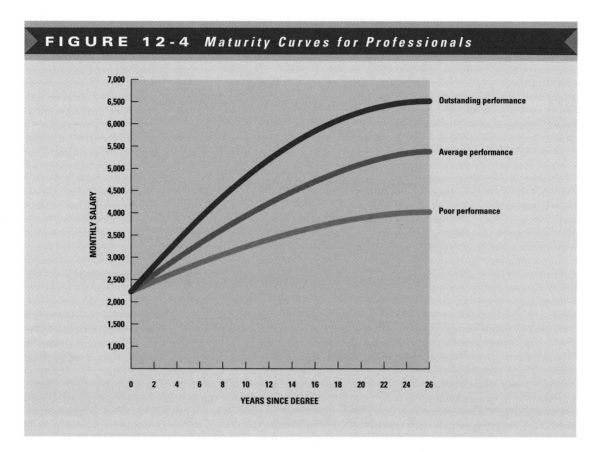

FIGURE 12-4 *Maturity Curves for Professionals*

some organizations, unfortunately, professional employees cannot advance beyond a certain point in the salary structure unless they are willing to take an administrative assignment. When they are promoted, their professional talents are no longer utilized fully. In the process, the organization may lose a good professional employee and gain a poor administrator. To avoid this situation, some organizations have extended the salary range for professional positions to equal or nearly equal that for administrative positions. The extension of this range provides a double-track wage system, as illustrated in Chapter 9, whereby professionals who do not aspire to become administrators still have an opportunity to earn comparable salaries.

Career curves (maturity curves)
Experience or performance bases for providing salary increases for professional employees.

Organizations also use **career curves** or **maturity curves** as a basis for providing salary increases to professional employees. Curves such as the ones shown in Figure 12-4 provide for the annual salary rate to be based on experience and performance. Separate curves are established to reflect different levels of performance and to provide for annual increases. The curves representing higher levels of performance tend to rise to a higher level and at a faster rate than the curves representing lower performance levels.

Professional employees can receive compensation beyond base pay. For example, scientists and engineers employed by high-tech firms are included in performance-based incentive programs such as profit sharing or stock ownership. These plans encourage greater levels of individual performance. Cash bonuses can be awarded to those who complete projects on or before deadline dates. Payments may also be given to individuals elected to professional societies, granted patents, or meeting professional licensing standards.[28]

Incentives for Executive Employees

A major function of incentive plans for executives is to motivate them to develop and use their abilities and contribute their energies to the fullest extent possible. Incentive plans should also facilitate the recruitment and retention of competent executive employees. This can be accomplished with plans that will enable them to accumulate a financial estate and to shelter a portion of their compensation from current income taxes.

Components of Executive Compensation

Organizations commonly have more than one compensation strategy for executives in order to meet various organizational goals and executive needs. For example, chief executive officers (CEOs) may have their compensation packages heavily weighted toward long-term incentives, because CEOs should be more concerned about the long-term impact of their decisions than the short-term implications. Group vice-presidents, on the other hand, may receive more short-term incentives since their decisions affect operations on a six- to twelve-month basis. Regardless of the mix, executive compensation plans consist of four basic components: (1) base salary, (2) short-term incentives or bonuses, (3) long-term incentives or stock plans, and (4) perquisites.[29] Another important element in compensation strategy is the compensation mix to be paid to managers and executives who accept overseas assignments.

Bases for Executive Salaries
The levels of competitive salaries in the job market exert perhaps the greatest influence on executive base salaries. An organization's compensation committee—which normally comprises members of the board of directors—will order a salary survey to find out what executives earn in comparable enterprises.[30] Comparisons may be based on organization size, sales volume, or industry grouping. By analyzing the survey data, the committee can determine the equity of the compensation package outside the organization.[31]

Job evaluation allows the organization to establish internal equity between top managers and executives. For executives, the Hay profile method (see Chapter 11) is probably the most widely used method of job evaluation. Finally, base pay is influenced by the performance of the executive. Most organizations evaluate their executives according to a set of predetermined goals or objectives.

Bases for Executive Short-Term Incentives
Incentive bonuses for executives should be based on the contribution the individual makes to the organization. A variety of formulas have been developed for this purpose. Incentive bonuses may be based on a percentage of a company's total profits or a percentage of profits in excess of a specific return on stockholders' invest-

ments. In other instances, the payments may be tied to an annual profit plan whereby the amount is determined by the extent to which an agreed-upon profit level is exceeded. Payments may also be based on performance ratings or on the achievement of specific objectives established with the agreement of executives and the board of directors. Objectives influencing the creation of shareholder value include sales, operating margin, cost of capital, and service and quality measures.[32]

Top corporate executives have the opportunity to earn large sums of money. Frequently, a significant part of their total compensation comes from incentive bonuses. When long-term compensation is added to annual base salary increases and bonuses, the total compensation of some executives may well reach into the millions of dollars. Highlights in HRM 3 shows the compensation received in 1994 by the 25 highest-paid executives in Canada. These top executives were paid the most money that year—including salary, bonuses, long-term incentives, severance pay and all other kinds of compensation (excluding stock options)—by companies listed on the TSE 300 last year.

Pros and cons of executive bonuses. Are top executives worth the salaries and bonuses they receive? The answer may depend largely on whom you ask.[33] Corporate compensation committees justify big bonuses as a way to reward superior perform-ance. Other reasons for defending high levels of compensation include the following:

1. Executives are responsible for large amounts of capital.
2. Business competition is pressure-filled and demanding.
3. Good executive talent is in great demand.
4. Effective executives create shareholder value.

Some observers justify high compensation as a "fact of business life" reflecting market compensation trends.[34]

Nevertheless, others have strongly criticized the practice of awarding high salaries and bonuses to senior executives.[35] Some critics attack the size of incentive bonuses and the often vague criteria on which bonuses are based. Others point out that some executives receive record bonuses while their organizations are in finan-cial trouble and employees are asked to make wage and benefits concessions. Large bonuses can also serve to raise prices, ultimately leading to inflation and higher unemployment. Even when people are not shareholders in a company, they are curi-ous and sometimes outraged at executive salaries, as shown in Ethics in HRM.

Another criticism of some executive incentive plans is that the time period for which executive performance is measured is often too short and the rewards are too large. This encourages executives to focus on short-term items such as quarterly earn-ings growth and to neglect longer-term items such as research and development and market share.[36] In the long run, therefore, stockholders may not receive a return equal to what they might have earned from other investments, and they might look for a better investment with a different organization.

Form of bonus payment. A bonus payment may take the form of cash or stock. Also, the timing of the payment may vary. Payment can be immediate (which is frequently the case), deferred for a short term, or deferred until retirement.

Most organizations pay their short-term incentive bonuses in cash (in the form of a supplemental cheque), in keeping with their pay-for-performance strategy. By

HIGHLIGHTS IN HRM

HRM highlights

3 THE 25 HIGHEST-PAID EXECUTIVES IN CANADA (1994)

PAY RANK	NAME/TITLE/COMPANY	SALARY	BONUS	OTHER COMP.	VALUE OF LONG-TERM INCENTIVES	ALL OTHER	TOTAL
1	FRANK STRONACH, Chairman, Magna International Inc.	$ 200,000	$7,312,000			$6,319,000	$13,831,000
2	ROBERT HALL, Executive VP, Thomson Corp.	1,190,000	4,375,000		7,560,000	6,300	13,131,300
3	JACK EDWARDS, Former CEO, Malsham Group, Molson Cos. Ltd.	513,750	0	0	0	6,028,800*	6,542,550
4	JAMES HANKINSON, Former Pres. & CEO, Canadian Pacific Ltd.	511,090	233,889	43,759	518,688	2,644,710*	3,952,136
5	GERRY SCHWARTZ, CEO, Onex Corp.	650,000	3,000,000	0	0	0	3,650,000
6	IAN DELANEY, Chairman and CEO, Sherritt Inc.	270,000	0	40,000	0	3,336,541	3,646,541
7	DEREK COMTHWAITE, Former CEO Molson Cos. Ltd.	667,500	0	150,247	100,000	2,702,500*	3,620,247
8	DOM D'ALESSANDRO, Pres. & CEO, Laurentian Bank of Canada	87,500	0	0	0	3,393,752	3,481,252
9	JOHN DODDRIDGE, Vice Chairman & CEO, Magna International Inc.	710,000	2,330,504	345,344	0	2,272	3,388,120
10	RICHARD HALLISEY, Vice-Chairman, First Marathon Inc.	0	3,344,000	0	0	0	3,344,000
11	BRIAN HANNAN, Former CEO, Methanex Corp.	459,418	0	0	0	2,438,886*	2,898,304
12	DAVID JOLLEY, Former Co-CEO, Torstar Corp.	232,419	0	38,401	0	2,532,969*	2,803,789
13	LAWRENCE BLOOMBERG, Pres. & CEO, First Marathon Inc.	0	2,742,000	0	0	0	2,742,000

#							
14	JEAN MONTY, President & CEO, Northern Telecom Ltd.	952,000	1,190,000	268,618	0	279,518	2,690,136
15	ALLAN TAYLOR, Chairman & CEO, Royal Bank of Canada	950,000	950,000	160,433	562,307	28,422	2,651,162
16	CONRAD BLACK, Chairman & CEO, Hollinger Inc.	1,179,880	943,904	403,453	0	0	2,527,237
17	DONALD WALKER, President & COO	100,000	2,222,300	0	0	92,300	2,414,600
18	RICHARD CURRIE, President, Loblaw Cos. Ltd., George Weston Ltd.	1,400,000	1,000,000	0	0	0	2,400,000
19	DAVID RADLER, President & COO, Hollinger Inc.	1,161,728	813,210	361,618	0	0	2,336,556
20	NIGEL HARRISON, Executive VP and CFO, Thomson Corp.	826,000	1,190,000	121,006	0	6,300	2,143,306
21	MICHAEL BROWN, President, Thomson Corp.	1,918,000	0	108,381	0	6,300	2,032,681
22	PURDY CRAWFORD, Chairman & CEO, Imasco Ltd.	731,253	500,025	11,783	487,500	300,015	2,030,576
23	EDWARD MCDONNELL, President, Seagram Spirits, Seagram Co. Ltd.	700,020	1,188,027	49,961	0	54,289	1,992,297
24	DONALD JACKSON, Former Pres. & CEO, Laidlaw Inc.	75,000	0	0	0	1,900,000*	1,975,000
25	RICHARD HARRINGTON, Exec. Vice-President, Thomson Corp.	875,000	1,025,937	26,950	0	6,300	1,934,187

Note: An asterisk (*) indicates that the executive received a severance package.

Source: Rick Haliechuk, "Bosses' Big Pay Cushions Fall," *The Toronto Star*, June 18, 1995, A1, D1, D3

> ETHICS IN HRM

PAY-OFF TIME

Frank Stronach, chairman of Magna International Inc., earned nearly $14 million in 1994. Shareholders, and the public, were uncharacteristically quiet in their response to this amount, because Stronach had engineered a spectacular turnaround and profits for his company. However, the critics were less kind to the CEOs of companies such as Canadian Pacific and Molson whose corporate results were less than spectacular, but who received very generous compensation. The argument for paying bonuses to CEOs of money-losing companies?—"if he hadn't been there, it would have been a lot worse," says Dunbar, a consultant with Ernst and Young.

Towers Perrin, an organization that specializes in compensation, sees a trend toward tying executive compensation directly to key business strategies, including results. However, corporate fortunes are often beyond the control of any one individual, and are more likely determined by outside factors, including global economic conditions, new players, and changing technologies. A second issue concerns the magnitude of the rewards. Is any effort—particularly when it cannot be attributed to the work of only one individual—worth $14 million?

Source: "Big Bonuses Enrich Top Bosses' Pay," *The Toronto Star*, June 18, 1995, D1, D3.

providing a reward soon after the performance, and thus linking it to the effort on which it is based, they can use cash bonuses as a significant motivator. Cash payment also best serves those executives who must satisfy immediate financial needs. If the money is not needed right away, the executive can invest it elsewhere and receive a greater return than would otherwise be earned in a deferred plan.

Use of deferred bonuses. A deferred bonus can be used to provide the sole source of retirement benefits or to supplement a regular pension plan. If they are in a lower tax bracket when the deferred benefits are ultimately received—which is not always the case—executives can realize income tax savings. In addition, interest on the deferred amount can allow it to appreciate without being taxed until it is received. However, deferred income funds also become a part of the company's indebtedness, a part or all of which might be lost should the company become insolvent. If these funds do not appreciate with inflation, participants also stand to suffer a loss from inflation.

Bases for Executive Long-Term Incentives
Short-term incentive bonuses are criticized for causing top executives to focus on quarterly profit goals to the detriment of long-term survival and growth objectives.

Emhart Corporation faced this problem when deciding whether to update and expand a profitable facility that manufactured industrial hardware. At one time, Emhart would have opted not to expand, since the executives making this decision received their incentive bonuses primarily on the basis of profit growth. Expansion of the hardware plant would not increase short-term profit growth and thus would cut into their bonuses. But Emhart revamped its compensation plan, deciding to link executive bonuses with the long-term price of stock. Consequently, according to Emhart chairman T. Mitchell Ford, the company authorized the expansion. "The plan lets us manage with a long-term view of the business," said Sherman B. Carpenter, vice-president of administration.[37]

Other companies, like Emhart, have adopted compensation strategies that tie executive pay to long-term performance measures. Each of these organizations recognizes that, while incentive payments for executives may be based on the achievement of specific goals relating to their positions, the plans must also take into account the performance of the organization as a whole. Important to stockholders are such performance results as growth in earnings per share, return on stockholders' equity, and, ultimately, stock price appreciation. A variety of incentive plans, therefore, have been developed to tie rewards to these performance results, particularly over the long term.

Stock options are the primary long-term incentive offered to executives. The basic principle behind stock options is that executives should have a stake in the business so that they have the same perspective as the owners (i.e., stockholders).[38] The major long-term incentives fall into three broad categories:

Perquisites
Special benefits given to executives—often referred to as perks.

1. Stock price appreciation grants
2. Restricted stock and restricted cash grants
3. Performance-based grants

Each of these broad categories includes various stock grants or cash incentives for the payment of executive performance. (See Figure 12-5 for definitions of the different grant types.) Often, as one observer notes, organizations combine stock options with tandem stock appreciation rights plus performance-based grants to balance market performance and internal, strategic performance.[39] The granting of stock options contributes substantially to executives' million-dollar compensation packages, as Highlights in HRM 3 demonstrates.

Executive Perquisites

In addition to incentive programs, executive employees are often given special benefits and perquisites. **Perquisites**, or "perks," are a means of demonstrating the executives' importance to the organization while giving them an incentive to improve their performance. Furthermore, perks serve as a status symbol both inside and outside the organization. Perquisites can also provide a tax saving to executives, since some are not taxed as income. Some of the more common perquisites include

A club membership is a common executive perk.

FIGURE 12-5 *Types of Long-Term Incentive Plans*

STOCK PRICE APPRECIATION PLANS

Stock options	Rights granted to executives to purchase shares of their organization's stock at an established price for a fixed period of time. Stock price is usually set at market value at the time the option is granted.
Stock appreciation rights (SARs)	Cash or stock award determined by increase in stock price during any time chosen by the executive in the option period; does not require executive financing.
Stock purchase	Opportunities for executives to purchase shares of their organization's stock valued at full market or a discount price, often with the organization providing financial assistance.
Phantom stock	Grant of units equal in value to the fair market value or book value of a share of stock; on a specified date the executive will be paid the appreciation in the value of the units up to that time.

RESTRICTED STOCK/CASH PLANS

Restricted stock	Grant of stock or stock units at a reduced price with the condition that the stock not be transferred or sold (by risk of forfeiture) before a specified employment date.
Restricted cash	Grant of fixed-dollar amounts subject to transfer or forfeiture restrictions before a specified employment date.

PERFORMANCE-BASED PLANS

Performance units	Grants analogous to annual bonuses except that the measurement period exceeds one year. The value of the grant can be expressed as a flat dollar amount or converted to a number of "units" of equivalent aggregate value.
Performance shares	Grants of actual stock or phantom units. Value is contingent both on predetermined performance objectives over a specified period of time and the stock market.
Formula-value grants	Rights to receive units or the gain in value of units determined by a formula (such as book value or an earnings multiplier) rather than changes in market price.
Dividend units	Rights to receive an amount equal to the dividends paid on a specified number of shares; typically granted in conjunction with other grant types, such as performance shares.

assigned chauffeurs, club memberships, special vacation policies, executive physical exams, use of an executive dining room, car phones, liability insurance, and financial counselling.[40]

. . . .

Compensation in a Global Environment

With the growth of multinational organizations, HR managers have had to develop compensation packages for managers and executives involved in overseas assignments.[41] While those assigned to foreign positions may still participate in the traditional pay practices of their organizations—merit raises, bonuses, and stock options—they may also receive compensation payments unique to a position overseas.[42] For example, managers and executives asked to go abroad are sometimes given a financial incentive to accept these assignments, to compensate them for any reluctance to relocate.[43] Furthermore, they may be provided with supplemental living allowances to compensate for the additional living expenses. In addition, they are often provided with financial assistance covering such items as moving costs, storage payments, and children's educational expenses.[44] Because of the importance of compensation to international HRM, we will elaborate on this topic in Chapter 17.

Challenges for Executive Compensation

Executive compensation is today a highly publicized topic.[45] The large compensation packages given to senior managers and top-level executives have resulted in cries for performance accountability and openness. For example, to justify the $2.1 million paid Joseph E. Antonini, chief executive officer of K mart, the compensation committee of the board of directors hired an independent consultant to offer an "outside perspective" on the compensation received.[46] Compensation professionals note several challenges facing executive compensation:[47]

1. Performance measurement techniques must be refined to reflect individual contributions. The measurement and rewarding of executive performance will require creative compensation approaches.
2. Organizations will need to comply with increased government regulation of executive compensation. Whereas in the United States salaries are monitored under the Securities and Exchange Commission (SEC), in Canada executive compensation disclosure regulations vary by province. For example, the Ontario Securities Commission requires the disclosure of executive compensation, including base pay, bonuses, and long-term incentives.
3. Organizations will need to continually fend off general attacks on high executive compensation while gaining the acceptance of innovative variable pay strategies.
4. Executive compensation practices will need to support global value-creating strategies with well-considered incentive pay programs. Hard questions to be answered include: "What exactly are the implications of global competitiveness and the corresponding strategies required to improve Canadian corporations' effectiveness?" and "How do these new strategies affect organizations and their compensation systems?"[48]

Gainsharing Incentive Plans

The emphasis on total quality management has led many organizations to implement a variety of gainsharing plans.[49] **Gainsharing plans** enable employees to share in the benefits of improved efficiency realized by the organization or major units within it. Many of these plans cover managers and executives as well as hourly workers. The plans encourage teamwork among all employees and reward them for their total contribution to the organization. Such features are particularly desirable when working conditions make individual performance difficult, if not impossible, to measure.

The basic principle of gainsharing, according to some authorities on productivity and incentives, is to establish effective structures and processes of employee involvement and a fair means of rewarding system-wide performance improvement.[50] At its root, gainsharing is an organizational program designed to increase productivity (or decrease labour costs) and share the monetary gains with employees.[51]

Inherent in gainsharing is the idea that involved employees will improve productivity through more effective use of labour, capital, and raw materials, and will share the financial gains according to a formula that reflects improved productivity and profitability. The more common gainsharing plans include profit-sharing plans, the Scanlon and Rucker plans, Improshare, and employee stock ownership plans (ESOPs). Highlights in HRM 4 shows the usage of different gainsharing plans according to one study of 1639 organizations.

Profit-Sharing Plans

objective

Probably no incentive plan has been the subject of more widespread interest, attention, and misunderstanding than profit sharing. **Profit sharing** is any procedure by which an employer pays, or makes available to all regular employees, special current or deferred sums based on the organization's profits. As defined here, profit sharing represents cash payments made to eligible employees at designated time periods, as distinct from profit sharing in the form of contributions to employee pension funds.[52]

Profit-sharing plans are intended to give employees the opportunity to increase their earnings by contributing to the growth of their organization's profits. These contributions may be directed toward improving product quality, reducing operating costs, improving work methods, and building goodwill rather than just increasing rates of production. Profit sharing can help to stimulate employees to think and feel more like partners in the enterprise and thus to concern themselves with the welfare of the organization as a whole. Its purpose, therefore, is to motivate a total commitment from employees rather than simply to have them contribute in specific areas.

A popular example of a highly successful profit-sharing plan is the one in use at Lincoln Electric Company, a manufacturer of arc welding equipment and supplies. This plan was started in 1934 by J.F. Lincoln, president of the company. Each year, the company distributes a large percentage of its profits to employees in accordance with their salary level and merit ratings. In recent years, the annual bonus has ranged from a low of 55 percent to a high of 115 percent of annual wages. In addition, Lincoln's program includes a piecework plan with cash awards for employee suggestions, a guarantee of employment for 30 hours of the 40-hour workweek, and an employee stock purchase plan.

The success of Lincoln Electric's incentive system depends on a high level of contribution by each employee. The performance evaluations employees receive twice a year are based on four factors—dependability, quality, output, and ideas and

HIGHLIGHTS IN HRM

HRM highlights

4 TYPES OF GAINSHARING PROGRAMS ACROSS SIC GROUPS

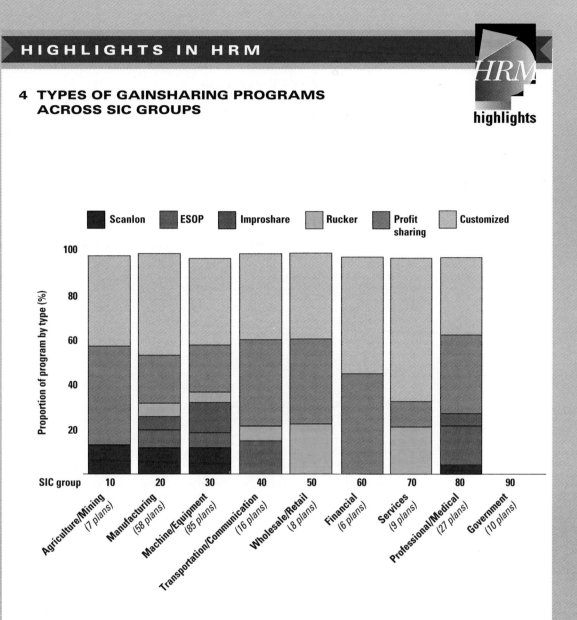

* This national study of gainsharing programs was based on returns from 1,639 HR managers, directors, and vice presidents.

Source: Steven E. Markham, K. Dow Scott, And Beverly L. Little, "National Gainsharing Study: The Importance of Industry Differences," *Compensation and Benefits Review* 24, no. 1 (January-February 1992): 34–45. Reprinted with permission of the publisher, American Management Association, New York.

cooperation. There is a high degree of respect among employees and management for Lincoln's organizational goals and for the profit-sharing program.[53]

Variations in Profit-Sharing Plans

Profit-sharing plans differ in the proportion of profits shared with employees and in the distribution and form of payment. The amount shared with employees may range from 5 to 50 percent of the net profit. In most plans, however, about 20 to 25 percent of the net profit is shared. Profit distributions may be made to all employees on an equal basis, or they may be based on regular salaries or some formula that takes into account seniority and/or merit. The payments may be disbursed in cash, deferred, or made on the basis of combining the two forms of payment.

Requirements for Successful Profit-Sharing Plans

Most authorities in the field agree that to have a successful profit-sharing program, an organization must first have a sound HR program, good labour relations, and the trust and confidence of its employees. Profit sharing thus is a refinement of a good HR program and a supplement to an adequate wage scale rather than a substitute for either one. As with all incentive plans, it is the underlying philosophy of management, rather than the mechanics of the plan, that may determine its success. Particularly important to the success of a profit-sharing plan are the provisions that enable employees to participate in decisions affecting their jobs and their performance.

Weaknesses of Profit-Sharing Plans

In spite of their potential advantages, profit-sharing plans are also prone to certain weaknesses. The profits shared with employees may be the result of inventory speculation, climatic factors, economic conditions, national emergencies, or other factors over which employees have no control. Conversely, losses may occur during years when employee contributions have been at a maximum. The fact that profit-sharing payments are made only once a year or deferred until retirement may reduce their motivational value. If a plan fails to pay off for several years in a row, this can have an adverse effect on productivity and employee morale.

Three Unique Bonus Plans

objective

To provide employees with bonuses that encourage maximum effort and cooperation but are not tied to profit fluctuation, three unique plans have been developed. Two plans, which bear the names of their originators, Joe Scanlon and Alan W. Rucker, are similar in their philosophy. Both plans emphasize participative management. Both encourage cost reduction by sharing with employees any savings resulting from these reductions. The formulas on which the bonuses are based, however, are somewhat different. The third plan, Improshare, is a gainsharing program based on the number of finished goods that employee work teams complete in an established period.

The Scanlon Plan

Scanlon Plan
Bonus incentive plan using employee and management committees to gain cost-reduction improvements.

The philosophy behind the **Scanlon Plan** is that employees should offer ideas and suggestions to improve productivity and, in turn, be rewarded for their constructive efforts. The plan requires good management, leadership, trust, and respect between employees and managers, and a workforce dedicated to responsible decision making. When correctly implemented, the Scanlon Plan can result in improved efficiency and profitability for the organization and steady employment and high compensation for employees.

According to Scanlon's proponents, effective employee participation, which includes the use of committees on which employees are represented, is the most significant feature of the Scanlon Plan.[54] This gives employees the opportunity to communicate their ideas and opinions and to exercise some degree of influence over decisions affecting their work and their welfare within the organization. Employees have an opportunity to become managers of their time and energy, equipment usage, the quality and quantity of their production, and other factors relating to their work. They accept changes in production methods more readily and volunteer new ideas. The Scanlon Plan encourages greater teamwork and sharing of knowledge at the lower levels. It demands more efficient management and better planning as workers try to reduce overtime and to work smarter rather than harder or faster.

The primary mechanisms for employee participation in the Scanlon Plan are the shop committees established in each department. (See Figure 12-6 for an

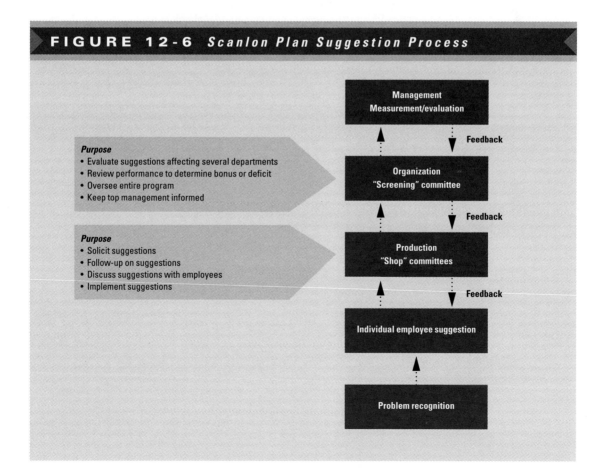

FIGURE 12-6 *Scanlon Plan Suggestion Process*

illustration of the Scanlon Plan suggestion process.) These committees consider production problems and make suggestions for improvement within their respective departments to an organization-wide screening committee. The function of the screening committee is to oversee the operation of the plan, to act on suggestions received from the shop committees, and to review the data on which monthly bonuses are to be based. The screening committee is also responsible for consulting with and advising top management, which retains decision-making authority. Both the shop committees and the screening committee are composed of equal numbers of employees and managers.

Financial incentives under the Scanlon Plan are ordinarily offered to all employees (a significant feature of the plan) on the basis of an established formula. This formula is based on increases in employee productivity as determined by a norm that has been established for labour costs. The norm, which is subject to review, reflects the relationship between labour costs and the sales value of production (SVOP). The SVOP includes sales revenue and the value of goods in inventory. Figure 12-7 illustrates how the two figures are used to determine the Scanlon Plan incentive bonus.

The plan also provides for the establishment of a reserve fund into which 25 percent of any earned bonus is paid to cover deficits during the months when labour costs exceed the norm. After the reserve portion has been deducted, the remainder of the bonus is distributed, with 25 percent going to the organization and 75 percent to the employees. At the end of the year, any surplus that has been accumulated in the reserve fund is distributed to employees according to the same formula.

FIGURE 12-7 *Determining the Scanlon Plan Incentive Bonus*

1994 ANNUAL BASE YEAR FIGURES

Sales value of production (SVOP)	=	$15,000,000			
Total wage bill	=	$ 4,750,000			
$\dfrac{\text{Total wage bill}}{\text{SVOP}}$ (Norm)	=	$\dfrac{4,750,000}{15,000,000}$	=	0.316	= 31.6%

CURRENT PRODUCTION MONTH

SVOP	$ 1,600,000
Allowable wage bill	.316 x $1,600,000 = $ 505,600
Monthly wage bill	$ 450,000
Labour cost savings	$ 55,600
Scanlon Plan bonus available for distribution	$ 55,600

Source: Adapted from George T. Milkovich and Jerry M. Newman, *Compensation* (Homewood, Ill.: Irwin, 1993), 366. Used with permission.

The Scanlon Plan (and variations of it) has become a fundamental way of managing, if not a way of life, in organizations such as Neelon Casting in Sudbury, Ontario. The Xaloy Corporation, a major manufacturer of bimetallic cylinders, uses a modified Scanlon program based on the following four principles:

Identity	Employee involvement is linked to the company's mission and purpose statement.
Competence	A high level of competence is expected from employees.
Participation	A suggestion process taps into employee ideas.
Equity	Organizational success is based upon a partnership forged among employees, customers, and investors.[55]

The Rucker Plan

Rucker Plan

Bonus incentive plan based on the relationship over time between the total earnings of hourly employees and the production value created by the employees.

The share of production plan (SOP), or **Rucker Plan**, normally covers just production workers but may be expanded to cover all employees. As with the Scanlon Plan, committees are formed to elicit and evaluate employee suggestions. The Rucker Plan, however, uses a far less elaborate participatory structure. As one authority noted, "It commonly represents a type of program that is used as an alternative to the Scanlon Plan in firms attempting to move from a traditional style of management toward a higher level of employee involvement."[56]

The financial incentive of the Rucker Plan is based on the relationship over time between the total earnings of hourly employees and the production value that employees create. The bonus is based on any improvement in this relationship that employees are able to realize. Thus, for every 1 percent increase in production value that is achieved, workers receive a bonus of 1 percent of their total payroll costs.[57]

Lessons from the Scanlon and Rucker Plans

Perhaps the most important lesson to be learned from the Scanlon and Rucker plans is that any management expecting to gain the cooperation of its employees in improving efficiency must permit them to become involved psychologically as well as financially in the organization. If employees are to contribute maximum effort, they must have a feeling of involvement and identification with their organization, which does not come out of the traditional manager–subordinate relationship. Consequently, it is important for organizations to realize that while employee cooperation is essential to the successful administration of the Scanlon and Rucker plans, the plans themselves do not necessarily stimulate this cooperation.

The attitude of management is of paramount importance to the success of either plan. For example, in organizations where managers show little confidence and trust in their employees, the plans tend to fail. Managers further note that Scanlon and Rucker plans are successful only when the following are true:

- Bonus formulas are clearly understood and can be reviewed by employees.
- Management is highly committed to making the plan succeed.
- Adequate training is given to both employees and supervisors.
- Adequate potential exists for employee rewards.

Like any other incentive plan, the Scanlon and Rucker plans are no better than the organizational environment in which they are used.

Improshare
Gainsharing program under which bonuses are based upon the overall productivity of the work team.

Improshare

Improshare—improved productivity through sharing—is a gainsharing program developed by Mitchell Fain, an industrial engineer with experience in traditional individual incentive systems. Whereas individual production bonuses are typically based on how much an employee produces above some standard amount, Improshare bonuses are based on the overall productivity of the work team. Improshare output is measured by the number of finished products that a work team produces in a given period. Both production (direct) employees and nonproduction (indirect) employees are included in the determination of the bonus.[58] Since a cooperative environment benefits all, Improshare promotes increased interaction and support between employees and management.

The bonus is based not on dollar savings, as in the Scanlon and Rucker plans, but on productivity gains that result from reducing the time it takes to produce a finished product. Bonuses are determined monthly by calculating the difference between standard hours (Improshare hours) and actual hours, and dividing the result by actual hours. The employees and the company each receive payment for 50 percent of the improvement. Companies such as Hinderliter Energy Equipment Corporation pay the bonus as a separate cheque to emphasize that it is extra income.

Stock Ownership

Stock ownership plans for employees have existed in some organizations for many years. These programs are sometimes implemented as part of an employee benefit plan. However, organizations that offer stock ownership programs to employees do so with the belief that there is some incentive value to the systems. By allowing employees to purchase stock, the organization hopes they will increase their productivity and thus cause the stock price to rise.

Not uncommon are plans for purchasing stock on an installment basis through payroll deductions and without the payment of brokerage fees. Over the years, the stock of some of the larger companies such as Sears, Canadian Tire, Warner Communications, and Ralston Purina has proved to be a good investment for their employees. Furthermore, stock ownership programs have become a popular way to salvage a failing organization, thereby saving employee jobs.

Employee Stock Ownership Plans (ESOPs)

Employee Stock Ownership Plan (ESOP)
Stock plans in which an organization contributes shares of its stock to an established trust for the purpose of stock purchases by its employees.

An **Employee Stock Ownership Plan (ESOP)** is a defined contribution employee benefit plan that allows employees to become stockholders at their workplaces. The goal of these plans is to encourage more competition, innovation, and harmonious work practices. ESOPs have grown significantly during the past ten years, adding 600 to 800 plans annually that covered a total of 500,000 to 1 million employees.[59] Recently, ESOPS were the mechanism used by the United Steelworkers of America to buy out Algoma and by the Transport Communications International Union to buy out Canadian Pacific Express and Transport Limited.[60] ESOPs have also been used to save jobs and prevent plant closures resulting from hostile takeover bids. Companies have used these plans to generate funds and have purchased with these funds company stock that was otherwise available to outside raiders.[61]

Employee stock ownership plans take two primary forms: a stock bonus plan and a leveraged plan. With a stock bonus plan, each year the organization gives stock to the ESOP or gives cash to the ESOP to buy outstanding stock. The ESOP holds the stock for employees, who are routinely informed of the value of their accounts. Stock allocations can be based on employee wages or seniority. When employees leave the organization or retire, they can sell their stock back to the organization, or they can sell it on the open market if it is traded publicly. Leveraged ESOPs work in much the same way as do stock bonus plans, except that the ESOP borrows money from a bank or other financial institution to purchase stock. The organization then makes annual tax-deductible payments to the ESOP, which in turn repays the lending institution. Organizations may also use the stock placed in an ESOP trust as collateral for a bank loan. As the loan is repaid, the stock used as collateral is allocated to employee accounts. Payments of both the principal and interest can be deducted from the organization's income tax liability.

Federal support for ESOPs is available through the Labour Sponsored Venture Capital Fund (LSVC). Employees investing in LSVCs are eligible to receive a 20 percent federal tax credit on their investment, to a maximum of $1000 in any one year. Various provinces have introduced their own ESOPs that offer similar tax incentives. There is no federal legislation in Canada that deals exclusively with employee share ownership; legislation governing Deferred Profit Sharing Plans (DSPSs) and employee stock options is used as a guide.

Advantages of ESOPs

Encouraged by favourable federal income tax provisions, employers utilize ESOPs as a means of providing retirement benefits for their employees. Favourable tax incentives permit a portion of earnings to be excluded from taxation if that portion is assigned to employees in the form of shares of stock. Employers can therefore provide retirement benefits for their employees at relatively low cost, because stock contributions are in effect subsidized by the federal government. ESOPs can also increase employees' pride of ownership in the organization, providing an incentive for them to increase productivity and help the organization prosper and grow. Enthusiastic promoters of ESOPs go so far as to claim that these plans will make organizations more competitive in world markets. The plans, they maintain, will increase productivity, improve employee–management relations, and promote economic justice.[62]

Problems with ESOPs

Generally, ESOPs are more likely to serve their intended purposes in publicly held companies than in closely held ones. A major problem with the closely held company is its potential inability to buy back the stock of employees when they retire. Unfortunately, these employees do not have the alternative of disposing of their stock on the open market. Requiring organizations to establish a sinking fund to be used exclusively for repurchasing stock could eliminate this problem.

A growing problem with ESOPs is that as more retirement income comes from these plans, the more dependent a pensioner becomes on the price of company stock. Future retirees are vulnerable to stock market fluctuations as well as to management mistakes. Finally, although studies show that productivity improves when ESOPs are implemented, these gains are not guaranteed. ESOPs help little unless managers are willing to involve employees in organizational decision making. Unfortunately, ESOPs are sometimes set up in ways that restrict employee decision making and expose the ESOP to risk, though providing investors with large potential gains.

North American and international research indicates that ESOPs are most successful when a union is present, employees are allowed to share in corporate growth, and labour management goals are developed jointly. When these conditions are present, productivity and profits improve and cooperation and involvement increase.[63]

SUMMARY

one
objective

The success of an incentive pay plan depends on the organizational climate in which it must operate, employee confidence in it, and its suitability to employee and organizational needs. Employees must view their incentive pay as being equitable and related to their performance. Performance measures should be quantifiable, easily understood, and bear a demonstrated relationship to organizational performance.

two
objective

Piecework plans pay employees a given rate for each unit satisfactorily completed. Employers implement these plans when output is easily measured and when the production process is fairly standardized. Bonuses are incentive payments above base wages paid on either an individual or team basis. A bonus is offered to encourage employees to exert greater effort. Standard hour plans establish a standard time for job completion. An incentive is paid for finishing the job in less than the pre-established time. These plans are popular for jobs with a fixed time for completion.

three
objective

Merit raises will not serve to motivate employees when they are seen as entitlements, which occurs when these raises are given yearly without regard to changes in employee performance. Merit raises are not motivational when they are given because of seniority or favouritism or when merit budgets fail to sufficiently reward employee performance. To be motivational, merit raises must be such that employees see a clear relationship between pay and performance; in addition, the salary increase must be large enough to compensate for inflation and higher income taxes.

four
objective

Salespersons may be compensated in the form of a straight salary, a combination of salary and commission, or a commission only. A straight salary allows employees to focus on tasks other than sales, such as service and customer goodwill. A straight commission plan causes employees to emphasize sales goals. A combination of salary and commission provides the advantages of both the straight salary and the straight commission form of payments.

five
objective

Executive bonuses are tied to agreed-upon criteria of organizational performance. Performance objectives might include profit levels; return on capital or operating indexes covering sales, market share, service, and quality measures; or operating margins. A bonus can be received as either cash or stock, and the timing of the payment may vary. Immediate, short-term, and long-term (deferred until retirement) are typical payout periods. Executive compensation will normally also include different types of stock plans as well as other desirable perquisites.

six
objective

Profit-sharing plans pay to employees sums of money based on the organization's profits. Cash payments are made to eligible employees at specified times, normally yearly. The primary purpose of profit sharing is to provide employees with additional income through their participation in organizational achievement. Employee commitment to improved productivity, quality, and customer service will contribute to organizational success and, in turn, to their compensation. Profit-sharing plans may not achieve their stated gains when employee performance is unrelated to organizational success or failure. This may occur because of economic conditions, other competition, or environmental circumstances. Profit-sharing plans can have a negative effect on employee morale when plans fail to reward employees consistently.

seven
objective

The Scanlon, Rucker, and Improshare gainsharing plans pay to employees bonuses that are unrelated to profit levels. Each of these plans attempts to maximize employee performance and cooperation by encouraging employees to offer suggestions for improving organizational performance. The Scanlon Plan pays employees a bonus based on saved labour cost measured against the organization's sales value of production. The bonus under the Rucker Plan is based on any improvement in the relationship between the total earnings of hourly employees and the value of production that employees create. The Improshare bonus is paid when employees increase production output above a given target level.

KEY TERMS

bonus	perquisites
career curves (maturity curves)	profit sharing
combined salary and commission plan	Rucker Pla
differential piece rate	Scanlon Plan
Employee Stock Ownership Plan (ESOP)	standard hour plan
gainsharing plans	straight commission plan
Improshare	straight salary plan
lump-sum merit program	straight piecework
merit guidelines	

DISCUSSION QUESTIONS

1. A company that paid its production employees entirely on a piece-rate system pointed with pride to the fact that it permitted its employees "to go into business for themselves." To what extent do you feel this claim is true or untrue?

2. The standard time for producing one unit of a product is four minutes. What would the piece rate per unit be if the rate for this particular type of work was $6 an hour?

3. Suggest ways in which the motivating value of merit raises might be increased.

4. What are the reasons for using different payment methods for sales employees?

5. What are some of the primary objectives of financial incentive plans for managers, and how do these plans differ from those for nonmanagement employees?

6. What are some of the advantages and disadvantages for employees of a deferred, as opposed to a cash, bonus plan?

7. What are the reasons for the success of the Scanlon and Rucker plans?

8. What are some of the reasons for the rapid growth of ESOPs? Cite some of the potential problems concerning their use.

CASE: Incentive Pay: Success at Viking Freight

Federal deregulation of the trucking industry created a fiercely competitive market force among freight companies. Trucking firms learned that superior employee performance and productivity was a main factor in maintaining a competitive edge. At Viking Freight Systems Inc., one key to developing an effective workforce was to compensate employees for superior performance through an incentive pay program measured against the achievement of corporate objectives. Under the Viking Performance Earnings Plan (VPEP), hourly employees can earn a maximum of 7.5 percent of their gross pay for a four-week accounting period, supervisors can earn up to 11.2 percent, salespeople 12.5 percent, department managers 15 percent, and terminal managers as much as 20 percent when company objectives are met.

At each of Viking's 47 freight terminals, employees are divided into distinct groups that share common goals and performance criteria. VPEP objectives are set for groups such as truck drivers, claims administrators, salespersons, and maintenance employees. A customized VPEP is therefore established for each group at each terminal. Measurable performance standards are set by Viking's executive committee and the performance engineering group to sustain or improve key quality or cost-related areas. Individual performance and market conditions are considered when objectives are set. In order to obtain maximum incentive payout, objectives are established that require employees to stretch their performance. Incentive payouts are based entirely upon the company's operating ratio. This ratio is defined as operating expenses divided by revenues before interest and taxes. If Viking's operating ratio for the four-week period isn't less than 95 percent, then no payouts are made, regardless of performance levels.

Terminal performance data are gathered weekly and distributed to individual groups each Monday. Data are presented in easy-to-read bar charts showing particular performance objectives. Employees can quickly identify areas needing improvement. Additionally, regular employee meetings are held, allowing employees to share ideas about how to improve their terminal's performance.

Terry Stambaugh, vice-president of human resources, identifies seven factors as contributing to the plan's success:

1. All employees are included in the plan, generating company-wide cooperation and support.
2. Objectives reflect the company's critical performance areas, are controllable by employees, and are easily measured.
3. The incentive program is tied to the company's bottom line; payments aren't made unless the company is profitable.
4. Communication is at the base of everything.
5. Payments are kept separate from base wages for greater visibility.
6. Employees are listened to.
7. The program is regularly reviewed and is revised as necessary to ensure that it continues to meet company objectives.

Source: Adapted from Terry Stambaugh, "An Incentive Pay Success Story," *Personnel Journal* 74, No. 4 (April 1992): 48–54.

Questions
1. Suggest different objectives by which terminal performance could be measured.
2. Discuss ways to keep employees motivated under an incentive pay plan such as Viking's.
3. Recommend other methods that Viking Freight could use to improve employee performance.

Assessing Your Incentives

What motivates you in your career—money or having your contribution recognized in front of your peers? Determining the type of incentive program that will motivate you is an important part of your career search. Complete the following questionnaire to determine what motivates you in your career.

INCENTIVE SURVEY

Instructions: Rank your responses to the following questions. Assign a value of 4 points for the response that is most important or most true for you, down to 1 point for the response that is least important or least true.

1. For me, the most important reward for my work efforts is
   a.____ Receiving a large cash bonus
   b.____ Being named top person in my field at a public ceremony
   c.____ Being complimented by senior executives on a performance appraisal form
   d.____ Receiving merit increases on my paycheque

2. My morale would suffer if I accomplished a lot and
   a.____ My boss and other senior executives never mentioned it
   b.____ My peers and others in the industry were unaware of my accomplishments
   c.____ I received no merit increase
   d.____ I did not win the big prize of a cruise with the other achievers

3. The kind of reward that brings out the best in me is
   a.____ A corporate plaque listing my achievement, hung in the main lobby
   b.____ A private dinner with the CEO
   c.____ Winning the top cash prize in a sales competition
   d.____ Knowing my efforts will increase my chances for a promotion

4. I would work overtime for
   a.____ The chance to work on an interesting project
   b.____ Overtime pay
   c.____ Public appreciation from my boss
   d.____ The chance to receive some corporate goods and services

5. I would quit my job and accept a new position for the chance to
   a.____ Earn big commissions
   b.____ Become a leader in my field
   c.____ Learn something new

d.____ Be nominated as the most productive person and receive a huge cash award

SCORING
Place the values you assigned to the responses in each question in the spaces provided on the scoring key. (Note that the letters are not always in the same place for each question.) Add up the values in each of the incentive columns to obtain a total score.

Scoring Key

Questions	E-Public	E-Private	I-Public	I-Private
1.	a ____	d ____	b ____	c ____
2.	d ____	c ____	b ____	a ____
3.	d ____	d ____	a ____	b ____
4.	d ____	b ____	c ____	a ____
5.	d ____	a ____	b ____	c ____

TOTAL SCORE

Interpreting the Scoring Key
The incentive survey measures the degree to which you are motivated by extrinsic (E) rewards or intrinsic (I) rewards. Examples of extrinsic rewards are money (bonuses, commissions, or merit pay), trips, cars, and televisions. Examples of intrinsic rewards are recognition, praise, and personal satisfaction. Therefore, high scores in columns 1 and 2 indicate that your incentives tend to be extrinsic, while high scores in columns 3 and 4 indicate that you are motivated by intrinsic factors.

The survey also reveals whether your rewards should be given publicly or whether a private incentive is adequate. So, look at the differences between E-Public and E-Private to determine the extent to which you want others to notice your efforts or accomplishments.

When identifying a career or accepting a job offer, use this scale to determine if there will be the kind of incentives that motivate you.

NOTES AND REFERENCES

1. J. Meehan, "Keeping Bad Taste in the Family," *Business Quarterly* 59, no. 3 (Spring 1995). See also L. Jaquette "Employee Incentives Pay Off for Hoteliers," *Hotel and Motel Management* 207, no. 17 (October 5, 1992): 3, 6; Louise Kin Ross, "Sharing the Pain Rather than the Gain: Can Profit Sharing Plans Motivate Staff to Achieve Corporate Goals When Pay-Outs Are Shrinking?" *Canadian HR Reporter* 6, no. 10 (May 28, 1993): 8–9.

2. Personal interview with one of the authors, Tucson, Arizona, August 27, 1993.

3. Richard L. Bunning, "Rewarding a Job Well Done," *Personnel Administrator* 34, no. 1 (January 1989): 60–63.

4. Steven E. Gross and Jeffrey P. Bacher, "The New Variable Pay Programs: How Some Succeed, Why Some Don't," *Compensation and Benefits Review* 25, no. 1 (January-February 1993): 51.

5. Susan Reynolds Baine, "Incentives for the Masses: A Variable Pay Program," *Compensation and Benefits Review* 22, no. 6 (November-December 1990): 50–58.

6. Robert L. Masternak and Timothy L. Ross, "Gainsharing: A Bonus Plan or Employee Involvement?" *Compensation and Benefits Review* 24, no. 1 (January-February 1992): 46–54.

7. David Beck, "Implementing a Gainsharing Plan: What Companies Need to Know," *Compensation and Benefits Review* 24, no. 1 (January-February 1992): 23.

8. Gary W. Florkowski, "Analyzing Group Incentive Plans," *HR Magazine* 35, no. 1 (January 1990): 36–38.

9. Terry Stambaugh, "An Incentive Pay Success Story," *Personnel Journal* 71, no. 4 (April 1992): 48–54; and Shari Caudron, "Variable-Pay Program Increases Taco Bell's Profits," *Personnel Journal* 72, no. 6 (June 1993): 64G.

10. *Achieving Results through Sharing: Group Incentive Program Survey Report*, Towers Perrin, April 1990.

11. Jay R. Schuster and Patricia K. Zingheim, "The New Variable Pay: Key Design Issues," *Compensation and Benefits Review* 25, no. 2 (March-April 1993): 27–34.

12. Baine, "Incentives for the Masses," 57.

13. Beck, "Implementing a Gainsharing Plan," 26.

14. Theresa M. Welbourne and Luis R. Gomez-Mejia, "Team Incentives in the Workplace," in Milton L. Rock and Lance A. Berger, *The Compensation Handbook*, 3rd ed. (New York: McGraw-Hill, 1991), 237–247.

15. Robert D. Pritchard, Philip L. Roth, Patricia Galgay Roth, Margaret D. Watson, and Steven D. Jones, "Incentive Systems: Success by Design," *Personnel* 66, no. 5 (May 1989), 63–68.

16. George T. Milkovich and Jerry M. Newman, *Compensation*, 4th ed. (Homewood, IL: Irwin, 1993), 352–354.

17. Thomas B. Wilson, "Is It Time to Eliminate the Piece Rate Incentive System?" *Compensation and Benefits Review* 24, no. 2 (March-April 1992): 43–49.

18. David W. Belcher and Thomas J. Atchinson, *Compensation Administration*, 2nd ed. (Englewood Cliffs, NJ: Prentice-Hall, 1987): 285. See also James E. Nickel and Sandra O'Neal, "Small Group Incentives: Gain Sharing in the Microcosm," *Compensation and Benefits Review* 22, no. 2 (March-April 1990): 22–29.

19. Milkovich and Newman, *Compensation*, 360.

20. Jerry M. Newman and Daniel J. Fisher, "Strategic Impact Merit Pay," *Compensation and Benefits Review* 24, no. 4 (July-August 1992): 38. See also Dale A. Arahood, *How to Design and Install Management Incentive Compensation* (Nashville, TN: Incentive Compensation Publications, 1993).

21. Jeffrey A. Bradt, "Pay for Impact," *Personnel Journal* 70, no. 5 (May 1991): 76–79.

22. Barry L. Wisdom, "Before Implementing a Merit System ... Know the Environment and Situations That Demand Caution," *Personnel Administrator* 34, no. 10 (October 1989): 46–49.

23. Glenn Bassett, "Merit Pay Increases Are a Mistake," *Compensation and Benefits Review* 26, no. 2 (March-April 1994): 20–25. See also Lena B. Prewitt, J. Donald Phillips, and Khalad Yasin, "Merit Pay in Academia: Perceptions from the School of Business," *Public Personnel Management* 20, no. 4 (Winter 1991): 409–416.

24. J. Edward Kellough and Haoran Lu, "The Paradox of Merit Pay in the Public Sector: Persistence of a Problematic Procedure," *Public Personnel Administration* 13, no. 2 (Spring 1993): 45–61. See also Herbert G. Heneman and I. Phillip Young, "Assessment of a Merit Pay Program for School District Administrators," *Public Personnel Management* 20, no. 1 (Spring 1991): 35–46.

25. R. Bradley Hill, "A Two-Component Approach to Compensation," *Personnel Journal* 72, no. 5 (May 1993): 154–161.

26. John K. Moynahan, *The Sales Compensation Handbook* (New York: AMACOM, 1991).

27. To promote higher sales efforts, organizations may also offer special cash incentives and noncash incentives such as merchandise, travel awards, and status and recognition awards. One study showed that the majority of responding organizations use noncash incentives in addition to their standard compensation plan. See Alfred J. Candrilli, "Success through a Quality-Based Sales Incentive Program," *Compensation and Benefits Review* 22, no. 5 (September-October 1990): 54–59; and Jerry McAdams, "Rewarding Sales and Marketing Performance," *Personnel* 64, no. 10 (October 1987): 8–16.

28. George T. Milkovich, "Compensation Systems in High Technology Companies," in David B. Balkin and Luis R. Gomez-Mejia, eds., *New Perspectives on Compensation* (Englewood Cliffs, NJ: Prentice-Hall, 1987), 247–281.

29. John D. McMillan, "Executive Pay a New Way," *HR Magazine* 37, no. 6 (June 1992): 46–48.

30. Lawrence M. Baytos, "Board Compensation Committees: Collaboration or Confrontation?" *Compensation and Benefits Review* 23, no. 3 (May-June 1991): 33–38.

31. William L. White, "Managing the Board Review of Executive Pay," *Compensation and Benefits Review* 24, no. 6 (November-December 1992): 35.

32. William L. White and Raymond W. Fife, "New Challenges for Executive Compensation in the 1990's," *Compensation and Benefits Review* 25, no. 1 (January-February 1993): 27–35.

33. Charles F. Schultz and N. Elizabeth Fried, "Fending Off Unreasonable Compensation Attacks," *HR Magazine* 37, no. 6 (June 1992): 49–54.

34. Nandini Rajagopalah and John E. Prescott, "Determinants of Top Management Compensation: Explaining the Impact of Economic, Behavioral, and Strategic Constructs and the Moderating Effects of Industry," *Journal of Management* 16, no. 3 (1990): 515–538.

35. Graef S. Crystal, "Why CEO Compensation Is So High," *California Management Review* 34, no. 1 (Fall 1991): 9.

36. "It's Not How Much You Pay CEOs, But How," *The Wall Street Journal*, May 17, 1990, A16.

37. Jeffrey M. Kanter and Matthew P. Ward, "Long Term Incentives for Managers, Part 4: Performance Plans," *Compensation and Benefits Review* 22, no. 1 (January-February 1990): 36–49.

38. Frederick W. Cook, "How Much Stock Should Management Own?" *Compensation and Benefits Review* 22, no. 5 (September-October 1990): 20–28. See also John D. England, "Don't Be Afraid of Phantom Stock," *Compensation and Benefits Review* 24, no. 5 (September-October 1992): 39–46.

39. Ira T. Kay, "Beyond Stock Options: Emerging Practices in Executive Incentive Programs," *Compensation and Benefits Review* 23, no. 6 (November-December 1991): 18–29.

40. "Labour Letter," *The Wall Street Journal*, September 22, 1992, A1.

41. Douglas J. Carey and Paul D. Howes, "Developing a Global Pay Program," Journal of International *Compensation and Benefits* (July 1992).

42. Ranae M. Hyer, "Executive Compensation in the International Arena: Back to the Basics," *Compensation and Benefits Review* 25, no. 2 (March-April 1993): 49–54.

43. Luis R. Gomez-Mejia and Theresa Welbourne, "Compensation Strategies in a Global Context," *Human Resource Planning* 14, no. 1 (1991): 29–41.

44. Lin P. Crandall and Mark I. Phelps, "Pay for a Global Work Force," *Personnel Journal* 70, no. 2 (February 1991): 28–33.

45. Andrew E. Serwer, "Payday! Payday!" *Fortune*, June 14, 1993, 102–111. See also Mark D. Fefer, "Your CEO Will Get Paid," *Fortune*, October 3, 1994, 18.

46. "Executive Pay: The Party Ain't Over Yet," *Business Week*, April 26, 1993, 56–64.

47. Peter Chingos, "Executive Compensation in the 1990s: The Challenges Ahead," *Compensation and Benefits Review* 22, no. 6 (November-December 1990): 20–30.

48. White, "Managing the Board Review," 27.

49. John G. Belcher, Jr., *Gainsharing: The New Path to Profits and Productivity* (Houston, TX: Gulf Publishing Company, 1991). See also Robert J. Doyle and Paul I. Doyle, *Gainmanagement: A System for Building Teamwork, Productivity and Profitability throughout Your Organization* (New York: AMACOM, 1992).

50. Denis Collins, Larry Hatcher, and Timothy L. Ross, "The Decision to Implement Gainsharing: The Role of Work Climate, Expected Outcomes, and Union Status," *Personnel Psychology* 46, no. 1 (Spring 1993): 79.

51. Steven E. Markham, K. Dow Scott, and Beverly L. Little, "National Gainsharing Study: The Importance of Industry Differences," *Compensation and Benefits Review* 24, no. 1 (January-February 1992): 34.

52. Thomas H. Patten and Mark G. Damico, "Survey Details Profit-Sharing Plans: Is Revealing Allocation Formulas a Performance Incentive?" *National Productivity Review* 12, no. 3 (Summer 1993): 383–394.

53. Harry C. Handlin, "The Company Built upon the Golden Rule: Lincoln Electric," *Journal of Organizational Behavior* 12, no. 1 (January 1992): 151–163.

54. Steven E. Markham, K. Dow Scott, and Walter G. Cox, Jr., "The Evolutionary Development of a Scanlon Plan," *Compensation and Benefits Review* 24, no. 2 (March-April 1992): 50–56.

55. Ibid., 51.

56. Edward Ost, "Gain Sharing's Potential," *Personnel Administrator* 34, no. 7 (July 1989): 94.

57. The Rucker Plan uses a somewhat more complex formula to determine employee bonuses. For a detailed example of the Rucker bonus, see Milkovich and Newman, *Compensation*, 366.

58. The standard of Improshare's measurement system is the base productivity factor (BPF), which is the ratio of standard direct labour hours produced to total actual hours worked in a base period. The productivity of subsequent periods is then measured by enlarging standard direct labour hours earned by the BPF ratio to establish Improshare hours (IH). The IH is then compared with actual hours worked in the same period. If earned hours exceed actual hours, 50 percent of the gain is divided by actual hours worked in order to establish a bonus percentage for all employees in the plan.

59. Ronald Farella and Barry M. Subhow, "ESOPs Fables," *PA CPA Journal* 60, no. 4 (Spring 1990): 42–45.

60. "Employee Share-Ownership Plans (ESOPs)—Workplace Innovations: Dialogue on Changes in the Workplace" *Collective Bargaining Review* (December 1994), 103–107. Published by the Bureau of Labour Information, Human Resources Development Canada.

61. "How to Keep Raiders at Bay—On the Cheap," *Business Week*, January 29, 1990, 59.

62. William Smith, Harold Lazarus, and Harold Murray Kalkstein, "Employee Stock Ownership Plans: Motivation and Morale Issues," *Compensation and Benefits Review* 22, no. 5 (September-October 1990): 37–47.

63. "Employee Share Ownership Plans (ESOPs)," *Collective Bargaining Review*.

Chapter 13

Employee Benefits

In the previous chapter, we discussed the different types of incentive compensation plans that organizations use to motivate employees. As we noted, some of those plans provide for deferred payment of compensation, thereby serving as a source of retirement income. Because this deferment reduces the incentive value of these compensation plans, some companies classify profit sharing, stock ownership, and similar deferred incentive plans as employee benefits plans. Whether or not they offer these particular plans, virtually all employers provide a variety of benefits to supplement the cash wages or salaries paid to their employees. These benefits, some of which are required by law, must be considered a part of their total compensation.

In this chapter, we examine the characteristics of employee benefits programs. We will study the types of benefits required by law, the major discretionary benefits that employers offer, the employee services provided, and the retirement programs in use.

Employee Benefits Programs

objective

Employee benefits constitute an indirect form of compensation that is intended to improve the quality of work life for employees. In return, employers generally expect employees to be loyal to the organization and to be productive. Since employees have come to expect an increasing number of benefits, the motivational value of these benefits depends on how the benefits program is designed and communicated. Once viewed as a gift from the employer, benefits are now considered rights to which all employees are entitled, and they have become one of the fastest-growing areas of employment law and litigation. Many employers now have a professionally staffed division in the HR department to develop and manage a wide variety of benefits and services.

Growth of Employee Benefits

Not until the 1920s were employee benefits offered by more than just a few employers. Because these benefits were supplemental to the paycheque and were of minor value, they were referred to initially as *fringe benefits*. From this rather meagre beginning, benefits programs have expanded in terms of both the types of benefits offered and their cost.

Initially employee benefits were introduced to promote and reward employee loyalty and to discourage unionization. The Great Depression in the 1930s slowed the demand for benefits. However, during the Second World War, controls on wages stimulated the growth of benefits. Unions successfully bargained for pensions, life insurance plans, and medical insurance.[1] Another factor in the growth of employee benefits was the exemption from personal income tax on benefits paid for by the employer.

Requirements for a Sound Benefits Program

Too often a particular benefit is provided because other employers are doing it, because someone in authority believes it is a good idea, or because there is union pressure. However, the contributions that benefits make to the HR program depend on how much attention is paid to certain basic considerations.

Health benefits must be compatible with the needs of an organization's employees.

Establishing Specific Objectives

Like any other component of the HR program, an employee benefits program should be based on specific objectives. The objectives an organization establishes will depend on many factors, including the size of the firm; its location, degree of unionization, and profitability; and industry patterns. Most important, these aims must be compatible with the philosophy and policies of the organization. The chief objectives of most benefits programs are to improve employee satisfaction, to meet employee health and security requirements, to attract and motivate employees, to reduce turnover, to keep the union out, and to maintain a favourable competitive position. Further, these objectives must be considered within the framework of cost containment—a major issue in today's programs.[2]

Unless an organization has a flexible benefits plan (to be discussed later), a uniform package of benefits should be developed. This involves careful consideration of the various benefits that can be offered, the relative preference shown for each benefit by management and the employees, the estimated cost of each benefit, and the total amount of money available for the entire benefits package.

Allowing for Employee Input

Before a new benefit is introduced, the need for it should first be determined through consultation with employees. Many organizations establish committees composed of managers and employees to administer, interpret, and oversee their benefits policies. Opinion surveys are also used to obtain employee input. Having employees participate in designing benefits programs helps to ensure that management is moving in the direction of satisfying employee wants. Quaker Oats and Nike ask employees to help them improve benefits plans. The companies then ask teams to design a new benefits package that offers more choices without raising costs.[3]

Modifying Employee Benefits

To serve their intended purpose, employee benefits programs must reflect the changes that are continually occurring within our society. Particularly significant are changes in the composition and lifestyles of the workforce. These changes make it necessary to develop new types of benefits to meet shifting needs.[4] For example, as we indicated in Chapter 2, the number of women in the workforce is continuing to grow. Which benefits are most valuable to them (and to men) will be determined largely by whether they have dependent children and whether they have a spouse who has benefit coverage.

Many benefits plans create an environment of disincentives for the young and single, limiting the organization's ability to attract and retain such employees. For example, while many employers provide extra compensation (in the form of dependant coverage) to workers with families, the principle of equal pay for equal work suggests that all employees doing the same job should receive the same total compensation, regardless of family status. Similarly, the employer's contribution to the pension plan for a 30-year-old employee is approximately one-fourth the contribution for a 50-year-old employee for the same amount of pension commencing at age 65. This difference in funds spent on older workers in effect discriminates against the younger worker, although legally it is not regarded as discriminatory.[5] These examples illustrate the need for benefits programs that take into account the differing needs of a variety of workers in order to attract a highly capable workforce.

Providing for Flexibility

Flexible benefits plans (cafeteria plans)

Benefit plans that enable individual employees to choose the benefits that are best suited to their particular needs.

To accommodate the individual needs of employees, there is a trend toward **flexible benefits plans**, also known as **cafeteria plans**. These plans enable individual employees to choose the benefits that are best suited to their particular needs. They also prevent certain benefits from being wasted on employees who have no need for them. Typically employees are offered a basic or core benefits package of life and health insurance, sick leave, and vacation, plus a specified number of credits they may use to "buy" whatever other benefits they need.

Benefits programs must be flexible enough to accommodate the constant flow of new legislation that affects them. A number of benefits-consulting firms are available to help managers keep up with changes in all phases of the programs they oversee. There is also an abundance of computer software for processing employee benefits records that incorporates the latest legislative and regulatory changes.

Communicating Employee Benefits Information

The true measure of a successful benefits program is the degree of trust, understanding, and appreciation it earns from the employees. Employers should carefully communicate information about complicated insurance and pension plans so that there will be no misunderstanding about what the plans will and will not provide.

While the communication of employee benefits information is important, there is no legislation that mandates the distribution of this information. Various provincial pension benefits Acts and federal laws regulating pension benefits state that employers operating a pension plan must provide specified information to employees. However, there are differences between provinces in terms of what must be communicated. The sponsor of a Registered Pension Plan (RPP) has six months after the end of the plan's fiscal year to provide active plan members with a statement of their pension benefits. (Quebec regulations require annual pension statements for retired and deferred vested members.) Included in the pension statement are the employee's name, date of birth, and date of hire as well as pension plan membership date, vesting date, and normal retirement date. Most provinces also require the names of the employee's spouse and pension plan beneficiary.[6]

A widely used method of communication is in-house publications, including employee benefits handbooks and organization newsletters. To ensure that employees are familiar with the benefits program, managers should be allowed sufficient time in new-hire orientation and other training classes to present information regarding benefits and to answer questions.

The most common means by which employers communicate with employees the status of their benefits is the personalized computer-generated statement of benefits, as exemplified in Highlights in HRM 1.

A number of organizations are offering a Benefits Information Line that allows employers to provide employees with instant access to a wide variety of benefits and HR information from any touch-tone telephone. For example, 13,000 employees at NorTel who had recently enrolled in the company's flexible benefit plan used an Interactive Voice Response System to select their benefits. This software then fed the information to the Human Resources Information System (HRIS), thus eliminating time-consuming paperwork and freeing up staff to answer more complex benefits questions.[7] Some employers summarize benefit information on a paycheque stub as a reminder to employees of their total compensation.

Computerized data also enable management to keep accurate records of the cost of each benefit. As the field of benefits becomes increasingly complex, and the sophistication of employees in financial planning increases, the need to hire and train benefits experts also grows. For those interested in specializing in this field, a good career move would be to become a Certified Employee Benefit Specialist (CEBS). In cooperation with the Wharton School at the University of Pennsylvania, Dalhousie University in Halifax sponsors a college-level program leading to the (CEBS) designation.[8] The ten-course program includes total compensation, health benefits, and strategic human resources management.[9]

objective *two*

Concerns of Management

Managing an employee benefits program requires close attention to the many forces that must be kept in balance if the program is to succeed. Management must consider union demands, the benefits other employers are offering, tax consequences, rising costs, and legal ramifications. We will briefly examine the last two concerns.

Rising Costs

According to a 1994 KPMG study of 234 companies representing 28 industry leaders, the costs of employee benefits in that year averaged 44.2 percent of payroll, as shown in Figure 13-1.[10] The average distribution of these benefits was $17,635 per employee per year. Costs of benefits were higher in the municipal governments at 54.6 percent, followed by hospitals and other health-care services at 50.2 percent.

Since many benefits represent a fixed rather than a variable cost, management must decide whether or not it can afford this cost under less favourable economic conditions. If an organization is forced to discontinue a benefit, the negative effects

highlights

1   A STATEMENT OF BENEFITS

YORK UNIVERSITY PENSION PLAN
ANNUAL PENSION STATEMENT
JANUARY 1, 1992

The benefits shown in this statement are based on the following information in our pension records.

S.I.N.

CREDITED SERVICE TO DATE; 05

BENEFICIARY

STATEMENT OF YOUR POSITION

The funds in your account with the York University Pension Plan have accumulated since the date you joined the pension plan. The University matches your required contributions to the Pension Plan and in addition, makes payments as required to provide for all plan obligations.

ACCOUNT	Value Jan 1/91	1991 Contributions	Credited Interest	Value Jan 1/92
Money Purchase	$33,158	$8,149	$6,572	$47,879
Additional Voluntary	$0	$0	$0	$0
Special Transferred	$16,740	$0	$2,989	$19,729

YOUR RETIREMENT BENEFITS

The income you received upon retirement will be provided by the York University Pension Plan, Old Age Security and The Canada Pension Plan.

Also your personal savings must not be overlooked, as all sources of income will complement each other to provide financial security during retirement.

The estimated benefits listed below have been calculated based on the assumption that your income will continue at its present level to your normal retirement date, and other factors affecting your personal situation will remain unchanged. All pensions are calculated on your life only.

Your benefits under the Canada Pension Plan have been calculated on the basis that your past and future contributions will qualify you fully for each of the items included. Old Age Security has been included assuming that you will meet residency requirements and be eligible for the benefits.

ESTIMATED RETIREMENT BENEFITS AT JULY 1, 2012		
BENEFITS FROM THE YORK UNIVERSITY PENSION PLAN		
Money Purchase Component Pension		$33,312
Minimum Guaranteed Pension	$34,102	
Supplementary Pension		$790
Voluntary Contribution Pension		$0
Special Transferred Contribution Pension		$3,887
TOTAL PENSION FROM YORK UNIVERSITY		$37,989
GOVERNMENT BENEFITS		
Canada Pension Plan		$8,050
Old Age Security		$4,489
Total Government Benefits		$12,539
TOTAL ESTIMATED BENEFITS		$50,528

of cutting it may outweigh any positive effects that may have accrued from providing it.

To minimize negative effects and avoid unnecessary expense, many employers enlist the cooperation of employees in evaluating the importance of particular benefits. Increasingly, employers are requiring employees to pay part of the costs of certain benefits. At all times, benefit plan administrators are expected to select vendors of benefit services who have the most to offer for the cost.

The escalating cost of health-care benefits is a concern to employers, who must strike an appropriate balance between offering quality benefits and keeping costs under control. The shift in benefit planning from entitlement to self-responsibility is discussed in Reality Check.

Legal Concerns

Benefits can become a source of union grievances, employee complaints, and even legal actions. Food services, parking, and similar facilities can become a magnet for complaints. An extreme example may be lawsuits by employees over injuries incurred in organization-sponsored recreational activities during or following organizational social functions where alcohol is served.

three
objective

Employee Benefits Required by Law

Legally required employee benefits constitute 11.2 percent of the benefits package that employers provide.[11] These benefits include employer contributions to

FIGURE 13-1   *Cost of Employee Benefits as a % of Gross Annual Payroll*

	Overall	Public Sector	Education	Government—Federal including Crown Corporations	Government—Provincial	Government—Municipal	Hospitals and Other Health Care Services	Private Sector	Automotive	Banks and Trust Companies	Broadcasting, Communications, Publishing and Printing	Construction Products	Electronics	Energy, Oil and Gas
Statutory Holiday Pay	2.7	3.2	0.1	3.6	0.1	2.6	3.0	1.5	1.5	1.1	0.5	1.6	2.0	4.9
Vacation Pay	5.6	6.7	0.7	6.6	1.0	17.5	6.7	3.2	2.0	1.4	5.1	3.4	3.8	5.6
Incentive of Production Bonus	0.4	0.0	0.0	0.0	0.0	0.0	0.0	1.1	0.0	0.5	0.6	0.2	3.8	2.3
Bereavement, Jury Duty, Military Duty	0.1	0.1	0.0	0.1	0.1	0.1	0.1	0.2	0.0	0.0	1.0	0.0	0.7	0.2
Rest Periods, Coffee Breaks, etc.	2.3	3.2	0.0	3.9	0.0	0.2	0.1	0.7	0.0	0.2	3.4	0.9	1.1	0.0
Self-insured STD	2.0	2.5	0.0	2.9	0.0	1.4	0.7	0.8	0.0	0.4	2.7	0.2	0.6	1.1
Maternity Benefits (salary continuance)	0.0	0.0	0.0	0.1	0.1	0.3	0.3	0.0	0.0	0.0	0.0	0.0	0.0	0.0
Other	2.3	2.1	0.0	2.1	0.0	2.6	15.1	2.7	0.0	4.1	4.9	1.9	1.2	0.3
Pay For Time Not Worked	**15.4**	**18.0**	**0.8**	**19.2**	**1.3**	**24.5**	**26.1**	**10.1**	**3.5**	**7.7**	**18.3**	**8.2**	**13.3**	**14.4**
Unemployment Insurance	5.3	5.3	5.6	5.1	5.9	5.9	5.4	5.2	8.0	5.7	3.8	6.2	5.1	4.4
CPP/QPP	3.2	3.3	3.4	3.2	3.6	3.3	3.4	3.1	2.8	3.4	2.2	3.7	3.3	2.7
Workers' Compensation	0.8	0.7	0.4	0.7	0.8	1.2	1.8	1.1	1.5	0.1	0.7	2.3	0.9	1.7
Provincial Health Insurance	1.9	1.9	1.6	2.0	1.2	1.4	1.9	1.8	2.5	2.1	1.5	0.9	1.8	1.3
Statutory Benefits	**11.2**	**11.2**	**11.0**	**11.1**	**11.5**	**11.8**	**12.4**	**11.2**	**14.8**	**11.4**	**8.2**	**13.1**	**11.0**	**10.0**
Group Life	0.5	0.5	0.4	0.5	0.4	0.6	0.3	0.4	0.3	0.3	0.2	0.6	0.3	0.4
Survivor Benefits	0.0	0.0	0.0	0.0	0.0	0.0	0.0	0.0	0.0	0.0	0.0	0.0	0.0	0.0
Group Accident	0.0	0.0	0.0	0.0	0.1	0.0	0.0	0.0	0.1	0.1	0.0	0.1	0.0	0.0
Business Travel Accident	0.0	0.0	0.0	0.0	0.0	0.0	0.0	0.0	0.0	0.0	0.0	0.0	0.0	0.0
Hospital and Health Care	0.8	0.7	0.8	0.6	0.8	1.2	1.0	1.0	1.1	1.2	0.5	1.8	1.0	1.2
Dental Care	1.0	1.0	1.7	0.9	1.4	1.6	0.8	1.0	1.7	0.8	1.4	0.8	1.0	1.4
Maternity Benefits	0.0	0.0	0.1	0.0	0.1	0.0	0.3	0.0	0.0	0.0	0.0	0.0	0.0	0.0
Short-term Disability	0.6	0.4	0.0	0.1	2.5	2.1	0.5	1.0	0.4	0.0	3.0	1.6	0.7	1.1
Long-term Disability	0.8	0.9	0.9	0.9	1.3	1.1	0.0	0.6	0.3	0.8	0.3	0.8	0.4	0.6
Pension Plan	11.5	14.0	10.2	14.7	11.1	11.6	6.9	6.3	2.1	7.0	8.2	4.2	4.5	3.1
Savings or Thrift Plan	0.4	0.1	0.0	0.0	1.1	0.0	0.1	0.8	0.7	0.0	0.0	0.5	0.8	8.2
Share Purchase Plan	0.3	0.0	0.0	0.0	0.0	0.0	0.0	0.9	0.0	0.7	0.6	0.0	0.9	0.1
Employer-Sponsored Benefits	**15.9**	**17.6**	**14.1**	**17.7**	**18.8**	**18.2**	**10.9**	**12.3**	**6.8**	**11.0**	**14.2**	**10.3**	**9.6**	**16.3**
Bonuses	0.2	0.0	0.0	0.0	0.0	0.0	0.0	0.7	4.0	0.2	0.2	0.9	1.2	2.0
Profit Sharing Plan	0.1	0.0	0.0	0.0	0.0	0.0	0.0	0.2	0.0	0.0	0.0	1.1	0.6	0.0
Termination Severance Pay	1.4	1.6	0.0	1.9	0.0	0.1	0.8	0.9	1.3	1.2	0.4	1.4	1.0	1.1
Additional Compensation	**1.7**	**1.6**	**0.0**	**1.9**	**0.0**	**0.1**	**0.8**	**1.8**	**5.3**	**1.4**	**0.6**	**3.4**	**2.9**	**3.1**
TOTAL	**44.2**	**48.4**	**25.9**	**49.9**	**31.6**	**54.6**	**50.2**	**35.4**	**30.4**	**31.5**	**41.3**	**35.0**	**36.8**	**43.9**

N.B. Due to the effect of rounding to one decimal point, there may be minor variances in the addition of certain columns.

Source: "Cost of Individual Employee Benefits Expressed as a Percentage of Gross Annual Payout," *Nineteenth Survey of Employee Benefit Costs in Canada* (Toronto:KPMG, 1994), Table 9.

FIGURE 13-1 *(cont.d)*

Engineering and Construction	Finance	Food, Beverage and Tobacco	Forest Products and Packaging	Hospitality, Tourism and Recreation	Insurance	Manufacturing—General	Manufacturing—Industrial Equipment	Non-Profit Organizations	Pharmaceuticals, Chemicals and Allied Products	Professional Firms	Real Estate Development	Retail Trade	Service Organizations	Transportation	Utilities	WholeSale Trade
3.0	0.3	2.4	0.6	1.5	0.6	2.4	1.5	2.2	1.7	0.0	0.6	2.5	0.2	2.8	3.0	1.7
5.8	0.3	3.4	2.6	3.5	1.6	4.1	3.7	4.1	0.5	0.8	2.2	6.6	1.4	4.2	5.0	3.5
0.4	3.6	0.6	0.0	2.7	2.2	1.3	0.8	0.1	3.4	1.1	1.2	0.4	2.7	1.4	0.2	1.3
0.0	0.0	0.1	0.0	0.0	0.0	0.1	0.0	0.0	0.0	0.0	0.0	0.1	0.0	0.1	0.1	0.0
0.0	0.0	0.0	0.1	0.0	0.0	0.1	0.3	0.3	0.1	0.0	0.0	0.0	0.0	0.0	0.1	0.7
1.5	0.0	0.4	0.2	0.0	0.7	0.2	0.5	1.1	0.1	0.4	0.0	0.0	0.0	0.1	0.5	0.2
0.0	0.1	0.0	0.0	0.0	0.0	0.0	0.0	0.1	0.0	0.3	0.0	0.0	0.0	0.0	0.0	0.0
1.3	0.2	0.9	0.0	1.2	0.7	0.8	3.6	3.6	0.9	0.1	6.0	0.0	1.8	3.3	3.0	6.1
12.0	**4.5**	**7.8**	**3.6**	**8.9**	**5.9**	**9.0**	**10.4**	**13.9**	**6.7**	**2.6**	**10.0**	**9.6**	**6.1**	**11.9**	**11.8**	**13.6**
5.1	4.5	5.3	4.7	5.1	5.9	5.8	5.4	4.6	5.3	5.8	5.8	6.2	5.6	6.4	4.9	5.6
2.9	2.7	3.2	3.1	2.6	3.7	3.5	3.3	2.7	3.1	3.6	3.6	4.0	3.4	4.1	2.9	3.6
0.7	0.1	3.0	2.7	1.7	0.1	2.8	2.3	0.8	1.8	0.1	3.7	0.5	2.6	2.9	0.7	1.4
2.4	1.8	1.8	1.6	1.7	2.0	2.9	1.7	1.4	2.8	1.6	1.7	1.9	2.1	1.2	0.8	1.8
11.0	**9.1**	**13.4**	**12.1**	**11.1**	**11.8**	**14.9**	**12.8**	**9.5**	**12.9**	**11.1**	**14.8**	**12.6**	**13.6**	**14.7**	**9.3**	**12.4**
0.4	0.4	0.7	0.6	0.1	0.7	0.4	0.5	0.5	0.9	0.9	0.4	0.9	0.4	0.3	0.6	0.8
0.0	0.0	0.0	0.0	0.0	0.0	0.0	0.0	0.0	0.0	0.0	0.0	0.0	0.0	0.0	0.0	0.0
0.0	0.0	0.1	0.1	0.0	0.1	0.0	0.0	0.0	0.0	0.0	0.1	0.1	0.1	0.0	0.0	0.0
0.0	0.0	0.0	0.0	0.0	0.0	0.0	0.0	0.0	0.0	0.0	0.0	0.0	0.0	0.0	0.0	0.0
0.6	1.1	1.2	0.7	1.0	1.7	0.9	1.1	1.6	0.8	0.4	1.0	1.4	1.1	1.0	0.7	0.8
0.7	1.3	1.5	1.0	0.5	1.1	1.0	1.0	1.1	0.8	0.9	1.0	2.4	1.1	0.9	1.0	0.8
0.0	0.1	0.0	0.0	0.0	0.0	0.0	0.0	0.1	0.0	0.3	0.0	0.0	0.0	0.0	0.0	0.0
1.0	0.0	0.8	2.1	0.0	0.6	1.6	0.8	0.8	0.1	0.4	0.2	2.1	0.6	0.7	0.5	0.4
0.4	0.6	0.8	1.4	0.2	0.7	0.4	0.6	0.6	0.4	0.4	0.7	0.6	0.7	0.4	0.3	0.4
2.6	5.7	8.5	9.2	0.9	8.0	6.1	5.6	5.1	5.6	2.7	1.4	0.4	3.7	1.0	8.6	2.6
4.1	1.2	0.4	0.0	0.2	0.0	0.4	0.3	0.4	2.6	0.0	0.0	0.0	0.1	0.1	0.6	0.9
0.3	0.0	1.8	5.4	0.0	0.6	0.0	0.0	0.1	0.0	0.0	0.0	0.0	0.1	0.1	0.0	0.0
10.1	**10.5**	**15.8**	**20.4**	**3.0**	**13.6**	**10.9**	**10.0**	**10.3**	**11.2**	**6.0**	**4.7**	**7.9**	**7.6**	**4.6**	**13.4**	**6.9**
0.4	4.2	0.4	0.0	1.0	0.5	1.1	1.3	0.2	2.9	1.1	0.2	0.4	2.4	0.6	0.0	0.7
0.1	0.3	1.8	0.0	0.0	0.7	0.0	0.4	0.0	0.4	0.0	0.7	0.0	0.5	0.6	0.0	0.3
0.7	0.5	0.1	0.8	0.2	2.4	0.2	1.6	0.6	1.6	0.1	0.2	0.1	1.0	0.1	0.1	0.5
1.3	**5.0**	**2.4**	**0.8**	**1.2**	**3.6**	**1.3**	**3.3**	**0.9**	**5.0**	**1.2**	**1.1**	**0.4**	**3.9**	**1.4**	**0.2**	**1.5**
34.5	**29.0**	**39.3**	**36.9**	**24.3**	**34.9**	**36.0**	**36.6**	**34.6**	**35.9**	**20.9**	**30.6**	**30.5**	**31.3**	**32.5**	**34.6**	**34.5**

BENEFIT PLANNING: FROM ENTITLEMENT TO SELF-RESPONSIBILITY

The advent of the 90s has brought about rapid upheavals in the area of benefits. Never before have we experienced such large increases in the cost of providing benefits as senior executives in companies throughout Canada try to change the "entitlement mindset" so prevalent in employees. Human resource professionals and senior executives can no longer make decisions regarding benefit plans without the assistance of benefits consultants. We have met with Daphne Woolf, Principal of William H. Mercer Limited, to discuss what is happening today and where we are going.

Woolf specializes in the design and implementation of flexible benefit plans, strategic planning as it relates to compensation and benefits, and workplace health promotion program design and monitoring. She provides companies with extensive experience in evaluating funding, administration, and utilization for the purpose of identifying ways to contain benefit plan costs. A visionary in her own right, she leads the National and Central Region Task Forces on Flexible Benefits for Mercer.

"First of all, we need to look at the drivers of change. We see four things happening. Our demographics are changing as people age; we have double-income families and the workplace is becoming increasingly diverse; benefits are being taxed to greater extents; and human rights legislation is changing with respect to who should be covered. Due to the high costs of providing benefit coverage, we are seeing a shift in responsibility from the provinces to third parties and individuals. The provinces are covering less, and this trend will continue to grow. The final, most important, underlying issue is increased sensitivity to the magnitude of these trends and the resulting benefit cost impacts.

"The entitlement mindset stems from the fact that, fifteen years ago, benefits were considered fringe. Now they are viewed as part of total compensation, which is a change in mentality. Employers are starting to move away from this entitlement mindset to self-responsibility. Employees are not used to making their own health-care decisions, and it is a challenge for employers to educate their employees sufficiently and sway them to a different way of thinking. As the population ages, employees' need for benefits are increasing; at the same time the quality of their benefits must decrease in response to the high costs. Based on some of our studies, what we are seeing for the first time is that employees are making employment decisions based on benefits. Employers look at dealing with these benefit trends by revisiting their philosophy and benefits objectives. For example, does an employer pay for smoking cessation, include high deductibles, offer choice, or provide coverage for dependants?

"We are seeing an increase in flexible benefit plans. Our belief is that in five years the majority of plans will be flexible, and an employer who waits may be disadvantaged. Employers are better off as flex leaders than flex followers. You want to create your own plan, not have to base your program design on what someone else has done. Now you can `anti-select' the benefit costs of the spouses' plan, allowing your employee to `cash-out' or allocate flex credits to stock plans or an RRSP. In the future, however, employees and their dependants may not opt out of your plan, and this would potentially increase your costs. So going flex sooner than later, if it's in keeping with corporate objectives, makes sense for many employers who have employees with spouses who work elsewhere. It is going to be a much tougher sell in the future if employees don't learn what the costs are today—they'll still be thinking entitlement when they get older and their provincial Medicare does not cover as much.

"Managers have to start watching the cost of illness and absenteeism and realize the lost production costs of paying for time off. These costs add to the overall cost of benefits and should be tied to compensation so that employees can appreciate those benefits.

"We are also moving toward 'managed care.' We have to look at providing the same level of health care at the same cost. That means putting caps on dispensing fees where drugs are concerned and getting second opinions to ensure that unnecessary procedures are not being administered.

"Americans have moved to a two-tiered system, and Canada is not far behind. While this is not currently a problem, it will be soon. For instance, if a patient wants a second opinion for something serious such as cancer, he or she may have to wait to see another specialist. In a two-tiered system, the patient can pay to have a second opinion immediately. This would not be reimbursed by the provincial health plan. We are beginning to see the collapse of provincial Medicare as we now know it.

"There is an increase in health promotion. We are talking about wellness programs, which may focus on stress reduction, fitness in the workplace, and smoking cessation programs. Employers are seeing the value in keeping employees healthy and productive, that is, preventing the claims costs. In one of my presentations, 'Taking the Fluff' Out of Health Promotion, I specifically outline the advantages of introducing health promotion programs to target cost pressures within the organization. Employers can yield a favourable return on investment if they ensure the right steps are taken to implement health promotion to secure effective cost containment. We are also diverging from traditional medicine to naturopathy and other paramedic services.

In essence, employers are revisiting the extension of benefits to part-timers, retirees, and dependants. There is a movement toward providing incentive-based benefits, that is, using benefits to reward performance, and with this, bringing things back to the overall compensation strategy. Employee expectations have become unrealistic mainly because they have not been educated. Once informed, we find that employees become a valuable resource. They need to understand the numbers. Employee focus groups are fast becoming the way to heed the transition from entitlement mindset to self-responsibility.

"In closing, the trends are moving somewhere in the middle between the American health-care system and Canada's. As we near the year 2000, flexible benefit plans will be the plan of choice so that educating the employee will be paramount if we are to move from an entitlement mindset to self-responsibility. Your plan should be devised considering an overall philosophy with particular attention to the strategic plan of your organization. Benefits can no longer be taken for granted as the costs of providing this commodity are at a premium. What constitutes benefits must be expanded beyond your basic dental, life insurance, and drug plans. Benefits strategies cannot be short term, but rather must be long range, and in this regard benefit consultants can provide value-added advice. Selecting the right consultant to work with you is just as important as determining your overall benefits philosophy. This philosophy is key to the design of your program as it sets the stage for what your benefit plan will entail."

Source: Interview by Deborah M. Zinni with Daphne Woolf, Principal at William M. Mercer Ltd., July 1995.

Canada/Quebec pension plans, unemployment insurance, workers' compensation insurance, and, in some provinces, provincial medicare.

Canada and Quebec Pension Plans (CPP/QPP)

The Canada and Quebec pension plans came into effect January 1, 1966. Since 1974, all pensions have been adjusted annually to reflect increases in the consumer price index. These plans cover almost all Canadian employees between the ages of 18 and 65. (Certain migratory and casual workers who work and earn less than the specified amount may be excluded.) To receive a retirement benefit, an individual must apply to the Human Resource Centre at least six months in advance of retirement.

Although similar in concept, CPP and QPP differ in terms of the benefit levels paid to participants. Both plans require the employer to match the amount of contributions made by the employee. The revenues generated by these contributions are used to pay three major types of benefits—namely, retirement pensions, disability benefits, and survivors' benefits. Governments do not subsidize these plans; all contributions come from employers and employees. Self-employed individuals can also contribute to the plan.

To qualify for retirement pensions, contributors may elect to start receiving retirement benefits any time after age 60. If they work beyond the normal retirement age of 65, they may defer receiving benefits until as late as age 70. For those who elect to begin receiving their pension before they reach age 65, the amount of pension calculated by the normal formula is reduced by 0.5 percent for each month prior to age 65. For those who start receiving benefits after age 65, entitlements are increased by 0.5 percent for each month after age 65.

The amount of pension paid is equal to 25 percent of the person's average pensionable earnings, adjusted upward in relation to the average final three-year Year's Maximum Pensionable Earnings (YMPE). Adjustments may be made for those persons who have periods of low earnings. To receive the maximum allowable retirement benefit, an individual would have to have earnings at or above YMPE for the whole contributory period of employment.

A disability payment is paid, on application, to a contributor who has incurred a long-term disability that is severe enough to prevent the person from being self-supporting. Contributions must have been made for at least two years out of the preceding three, or for five years out of the preceding ten. The amount of pension is a total of two components: a basic flat-rate benefit and an earnings-related benefit, which is 75 percent of the imputed retirement pension based on contributions made to date. The basic pension is payable until death, attainment of age 65, or recovery, whichever occurs first. A flat-rate benefit is also payable to each dependent child of a disabled contributor; this benefit ceases when the child reaches age 18 (or 25 if still in school).

Survivors' benefits represent a form of life insurance paid to surviving family members who meet the eligibility requirements. A lump-sum death benefit—which is related to the value of the contributor's earnings, to a maximum of 10 percent of the YMPE at the date of the contributor's death—is payable to the contributor's estate immediately on approval of the executor's or estate administrator's application for benefits. A monthly pension is payable to the surviving spouse based on the

ETHICS IN HRM

WHO CAN BE LEGALLY DESIGNATED AS A BENEFICIARY?

What constitutes a family? This is the underlying concern surrounding the issue of same-sex benefits. Originally, pension and life insurance plans allowed the employee to designate his or her beneficiary. The designation of the beneficiary was regulated, and was intended to help the wife and family of the working man. Eventually, common-law spouses became eligible to collect survivor benefits. Now, the Canadian Union of Public Employees (CUPE) has been fighting in court to extend this right to same-sex couples; if CUPE succeeds in its legal battle it will set a precedent for private pension plans across Canada.

A gay couple from British Columbia recently lost their fight to receive supplementary benefits under Old Age Security. The courts argued that the plan was intended to help older women (widows) living in poverty. Is this discrimination? All employees make the same contributions to the plan. Do they have the right to designate their beneficiary? Could single parents, for example, designate their own parents or children, or even friends?

contributor's earnings and contributions under the plan. The amount varies depending on the age of the spouse at the time of death. In addition to the above, a set amount is payable monthly for each dependent child.

On termination of a marriage or common-law relationship, pension credits earned by one or both spouses during the years of the relationship may be divided equally between them on the dissolution of that marriage or relationship, subject to certain qualifications and conditions existing when application is made. Spouses in an ongoing relationship can apply to share their CPP retirement pension benefits.

A critical issue before the courts concerns who can be legally designated as a beneficiary (see Ethics in HRM). Canada has international agreements with several countries to protect the acquired social security rights of persons who have worked and lived in both countries, and who meet the minimum qualifications for benefits from either countries. A contributor's rights to benefits under CPP or QPP are not affected or impaired in any way by a change of employment or residence in Canada. All Canadian workers have "universal portability"—the right to claim benefit credits wherever they are employed in Canada.

Unemployment Insurance (UI)

Unemployment insurance (UI) benefits were introduced in 1942 to offer income protection to employees who were between jobs. These benefits are payable to claimants who have been unemployed and who are actively seeking employment.

When a person becomes unemployed, he or she must immediately submit an application for UI benefits with a local Human Resource Centre.

The amount of benefit paid is determined by the number of weeks of employment in the past year and the regional unemployment rate. The weekly benefit is currently based on 55 percent of the claimant's average insured earnings for the last twenty insured weeks in the qualifying period. Individuals are entitled to unemployment insurance after they have contributed enough for a qualifying period and after a waiting period. The waiting period may differ depending on each individual's situation. Additionally, employees who resign from their positions or who are terminated for cause may become ineligible for benefits unless they can prove there was no reasonable alternative to leaving their job.

Additional benefits may be extended for situations involving illness, injury, or quarantine, or for maternity, parental, or adoption leave. If an organization does not offer sick-leave benefits, then the employee may have to apply to UI for sick benefits. The benefit amount, which is calculated on the same basis as the regular benefit, varies across jurisdictions. Sickness or disability benefits are available for up to fifteen weeks. A combination of maternity, parental, or adoptive benefits may be available up to a cumulative maximum of thirty weeks.

Employees and employers both contribute to the UI fund. A UI premium reduction is available to employers who cover their employees under an approved wage-loss plan. The amount of the reduction depends on the supplement being given to the employee, and therefore will differ from company to company. Work-sharing programs have recently come into existence as a means of reducing the overall burden on UI. Under work sharing, an organization may reduce the workweek of all employees in a particular group instead of laying them off. The company pays for the time worked, and the employee draws UI for the rest of the workweek.

Supplemental Unemployment Benefits (SUBs)

Supplemental unemployment benefits (SUBs)
An employer-sponsored plan that enables an employee who is laid off to draw, in addition to state unemployment compensation, weekly benefits that are paid from a fund created for this purpose.

Supplemental unemployment benefits (SUBs) were first introduced in Canada in the 1950s as the result of collective bargaining. These employer-financed plans enable an employee who is laid off to draw, in addition to UI benefits, additional weekly benefits that are paid from a fund created for this purpose. Companies such as Ford Canada and General Motors of Canada offer SUBs.

In recent years, many SUB plans have been liberalized to permit employees to receive weekly benefits if the length of their workweek is reduced or a lump-sum payment if their employment is terminated permanently. The amount of benefits is determined by length of service and wage rate. Employer liability under the plan is limited to the amount of money accumulated within the fund from employer contributions based on the total hours of work performed by employees.

To be eligible, SUBs must be approved by the Unemployment Insurance Commission (UIC). Under a SUB plan, employees who are off work due to layoff, illness, or maternity are given income benefits in addition to UI benefits. These plans maintain income levels that are much closer to the working level than those offered by UI.

Workers' Compensation Insurance

**Workers'
compensation
insurance**
Insurance provided to
workers to defray the
loss of income and cost
of treatment due to
work-related injuries
or illness.

Workers' compensation insurance is based on the theory that compensation for work-related accidents and illnesses should be considered one of the costs of doing business and should ultimately be passed on to the consumer. Individual employees should not be required to bear the cost of their treatment or loss of income; nor should they be subjected to complicated, delaying, and expensive legal procedures.

Workers' compensation is a form of insurance that was created by an Act of Parliament to help workers who are injured on the job return to the workplace. Various boards within each of the provinces and territories are empowered by the relevant provincial legislation to amend and collect assessments (i.e., insurance premiums) to determine the right to compensation and to pay the amount due to the injured worker. This system of collective liability is compulsory. Employers in various industrial sectors are assessed at a percentage rate of their payroll on the basis of the accidents' costs of their classification and number of employees. For example, a high-risk industry like mining would have higher assessment rates than would a knowledge-based sector.

Workers' compensation is based on the following principals: (1) employers share collective liability while recognizing various degrees of risk in the amount of contribution paid (some provinces punish employers who do not maintain safe and healthy work environments by levying additional fines); (2) injured workers are compensated regardless of the financial status of the employer, and this compensation is based on loss of earnings; and (3) it is a no-fault, nonadversarial system and thus offers no recourse to the courts.

Benefits are paid out of an employer-financed fund and include medical expenses stemming from work-related injuries, survivors' benefits (including burial expenses and pensions), and wage-loss payments for temporary total or partial disability. Permanent disability benefits may be disbursed as a lump-sum payment or as a permanent disability pension with rehabilitation services. The amount paid depends on the employee's earnings and provincial legislation.

Employees cannot be required either to make contributions toward a workers' compensation fund or to waive their rights to receive compensation benefits. Payments made to claimants are effectively nontaxable. Premiums paid for by the employer may be deducted as expenses and are not deemed a taxable benefit for employees.

Workers' comp costs have skyrocketed to the point where they are affecting hiring decisions in some companies. For instance, in Ontario, which is considered the hardest-hit province, employers could be looking at as much as a 50 percent rate hike to cover the full costs of the Workers' Compensation Board. In 1993, Ontario employers paid an average levy of 3 percent of payroll, while in 1995, the Ontario board faced a $12-billion unfunded liability. Injured workers in Ontario receive 90 percent of pretax income, as compared with a maximum of 70 percent for private plans and 60 for unemployment insurance. It is anticipated that Ontario will follow other provinces in reducing its workers' comp payout.

Steps that the HR department can take to control workers' comp costs include the following:

1. Perform an audit to assess high-risk areas within a workplace.

2. Prevent injuries by ensuring proper ergonomic design of the workplace, effective assessment of job candidates, and worker training.

3. Provide to injured employees quality medical care from physicians with experience and preferably with training in occupational health.

4. Reduce litigation by ensuring effective communication between the employer and the injured worker.

5. Manage the care of an injured worker from time of injury until return to work. Keep a partially recovered employee at the worksite.[12]

6. Should a claim arise, ensure that all the information and queries are immediately brought to the attention of the adjudicator at the comp board.

To this point, the discussion has focused on what is important to the employer and the insurance carrier. Managers, HR staff, and safety personnel should recognize that a workplace injury presents several problems to the injured worker—medical, financial, insurance, and employment security, and possibly legal problems. Injured employees are likely to feel isolated, and complain when they receive insufficient information about their rights and obligations. Co-workers and supervisors often fail to understand that many disabilities, such as back pain, do not show. There is also a tendency to "blame the victim." This can range from simple accusations of malingering, laziness, or dishonesty to suggestions of a mental disorder. An important step in developing a smoothly functioning system for comp cases is for managers and professionals to consider the perspective of the injured worker and to provide the information and assistance needed in a positive, supportive manner.[13]

Provincial Hospital and Medical Services

Medicare came into existence in 1968.[14] Under a system of subsidy payments from the federal to provincial governments, each province has jurisdiction over hospital and medical services. The services offered differ from one province to the next. In order to qualify for subsidy payments, provinces must meet minimum standards of service and administration as stated under the Canada Health Act (1984).

Most provinces fund health-care costs from general tax revenue and federal cost sharing. Ontario, Quebec, and Newfoundland also levy a payroll tax, while other provinces such as Alberta and British Columbia charge premiums that are payable by the resident or an agent, usually the employer (subsidies for low-income residents are provided).

Persons who have been resident in a Canadian province for three months are eligible to receive health-care benefits. Applications must be made and approval given before coverage becomes effective. Benefits include services provided by physicians, surgeons, or other qualified health professionals, along with hospital services such as standard ward accommodation and meals, laboratory and diagnostic procedures, and hospital-administered drugs. A number of employers offer third-party benefit coverage, which entitles their employees to additional benefits such as semi-private or private accommodation, prescription drugs, private nursing, ambulance services, out-of-country medical expenses that exceed provincial limits, vision and dental care, and paramedic services. Depending on the employer, all or just a portion of the services may be covered.

Most provinces provide coverage for nonresident Canadians; the rates applied are based on that province's fee schedule. Coverage outside Canada varies, with each province offering different maximums for reimbursement of hospital charges. Canadians who travel outside Canada should have additional insurance to cover medical expenses that may exceed Canadian limits.

The cost of providing health care has escalated to the point where major reform in Canada's health-care system is becoming inevitable. For instance, in metro Toronto the number of people over the age of 85 is expected to double in the next ten years, imposing a tremendous burden on the health-care system.[15] Some observers anticipate the emergence of two-tiered medical systems under which patients with private health insurance would be able to jump waiting lists; doctors would be allowed to make arrangements with U.S. insurance carriers to sell "excess capacity," including some surgical procedures and the use of high-tech diagnostic tools such as CAT scans; and private companies would be allowed to offer a full range of supplementary health insurance.[16]

Leaves without Pay

Most employers grant leaves of absence to employees who request them for personal reasons. These leaves are usually taken without pay, but also without loss of seniority or benefits. An unpaid leave may be granted for a variety of reasons, including extended illness, illness in the family, pregnancy, the birth or adoption of a child, educational or political activities, and social service activities.

Supporters of leaves without pay anticipate that they will especially help today's "sandwich generation"—baby boomers born from 1946 to 1964—as they enter middle age and rear children while simultaneously caring for aging parents.[17] Temporary-help firms expect to profit by providing workers to fill in for permanent employees who take time off to care for relatives. The temp agencies are prepared to provide temporary managers and executives as well as clerical help.[18]

Discretionary Major Employee Benefits

Employee benefits may be categorized in different ways. In Figure 13-1, we saw the categories of benefits that have been used by the KPMG benefits surveys in Canada since 1953. In the discussion that follows, we will use a somewhat different but compatible grouping of benefits to highlight the important issues and trends related to managing an employee benefits program.

Health-Care Benefits

The benefits that receive the most attention from employers today, due to sharply rising costs and employee concern, are health-care benefits. In the past, health insurance plans covered only medical, surgical, and hospital expenses. Today, employers are under pressure to include prescription drugs as well as dental, optical, and mental health-care benefits in the package they offer their workers.

Escalating Costs
According to KPMG's 1994 benefits survey, employer-sponsored benefits that include group life and survivor benefits, dental care, hospital and health care, pension plans, and so forth average the largest proportion of payroll costs at

15.9 percent. Increases in health-care premiums are estimated to be as high as 12 percent, well above the approximate 2 percent rate of inflation. The main reason for the increase is that the cost of medical care has risen more than twice the increase in CPI for all items.

The growth in health-care costs is attributed to a number of factors, including the greater need for health care by an aging population, the costs associated with technological advances in medicine, the growing costs of health-care labour, and the overuse of costly health-care services.

Cost Containment

The approaches used to contain the costs of health-care benefits include reductions in coverage, increased deductibles or co-payments, and increased coordination of benefits to make sure the same expense is not paid by more than one insurance reimbursement. Other cost-containment efforts involve alternatives to traditional medical care: the use of health maintenance organizations and preferred providers, incentives for outpatient surgery and testing, and mandatory second opinions for surgical procedures. Employee assistance programs and wellness programs may also allow an organization to cut the costs of its health-care benefits. Highlights in HRM 2 focuses on a team approach to cost reduction.

Health maintenance organizations (HMOs) are unknown in Canada but widespread in the United States. (With the anticipated restructuring of Canada's provincial medicare system, it is anticipated that HMOs will be studied as a means to reduce health-care costs.) HMOs are organizations of physicians and other health-care professionals that provide a wide range of services to subscribers and their dependants on a prepaid basis. Although HMO premiums were once higher than those offered by traditional plans, the latter's premiums have increased so much that HMOs are now being used to contain the costs of employee health care. Because they must provide all covered services for a fixed dollar amount, HMOs generally emphasize preventive care and early intervention.

Preferred provider organizations have also helped to contain costs. The **preferred provider organization (PPO)** is a hospital or group of physicians who establish an organization that guarantees lower costs to the employer. The employer reciprocates by steering workers to the PPO. In an effort to exert more control over medical costs, many insurance companies in the United States have become active in organizing PPOs. The push by employees and the federal government for improved health care will cause many employers to seek out an active program for purposes of cost containment.[19]

Other Health Benefits

Dental-care insurance as an employee benefit has grown very rapidly in the past two decades. Dental plans are designed to help pay for dental-care costs and to encourage employees to receive regular dental attention. Like medical plans, dental care may be reimbursed by insurance companies. Typically, the insurance pays a portion of the charges and the subscriber pays the remainder.

Optical-care reimbursement is another, relatively new benefit that many employers are offering. Coverage can include visual examinations and a percentage of the costs of lenses and frames.

Health maintenance organizations (HMOs)

Organizations of physicians and health-care professionals that provide a wide range of services to subscribers and dependants on a prepaid basis.

Preferred provider organization (PPO)

A hospital or group of physicians who establish an organization that guarantees lower health-care costs to the employer.

2 A TEAM APPROACH TO BENEFITS ADMINISTRATION

The University of New Brunswick in Fredericton has long done what so many other organizations are only starting to do—it has used its employees to assist it in devising strategies to combat increases in benefit costs. In 1974, a Fringe Benefits Review Committee was established. According to Jim O'Sullivan, the university's vice-president of finance and administration, the committee was organized in "an effort to repair relations with angry faculty representatives after the university's board of governors was perceived to have unilaterally eliminated an existing benefit."

The committee, which comprises management as well as unionized and nonunionized employees, has the task of reviewing the university's group life, health, and long-term disability (LTD) plans. Although the board of governors still holds the final decision-making authority, the committee alone is responsible for making benefits recommendations and working out the details; its efforts have resulted in a $3.8-million benefits surplus.

For the past twenty years, the employees have shared the costs of the university's group insurance plan, thus allowing the university to maintain effective cost control and to plan redesigns. Because the plan costs are shared, employees are aware that increasing benefits will mean higher contributions for both sides. To keep LTD claims down, employees have allowed the university to follow up directly with workers on disability claims to help them return to work faster. UNB leads the way with the lowest claims among other universities with similar workforces. While for many other organizations the price tag for health-care, drug, and dental benefits has grown annually, UNB has managed to hold benefit costs below the general rate of inflation. O'Sullivan attributes the savings to the cost-sharing partnership.

As in many other organizations, the employee assistance program is fully paid for by the employer. However, because the development of this program was discussed with the committee, employees played a major role in selling this plan. O'Sullivan believes that the plan is cost-effective in the long term. "Failure to seek treatment for personal problems," he notes, "would eventually affect job performance and lead to higher costs for health and LTD insurance."

The university has been self-insuring benefits, with a pay-as-you-go philosophy, since the 1970s. Commercial insurance is purchased only to provide protection against catastrophic losses. For example, the LTD plan is self-insured for the first ten years of any claim, after which commercial insurance coverage comes into effect.

Employer and employee representative groups each have control over their half share of surplus funds. Consideration has been given to contribution holidays or to implementing new benefits, but both sides, concerned that the good times could come to an end, have decided to act conservatively. The surplus funds are invested by the university's endowment fund investment managers; investment income is used to improve employees' benefits.

"I do believe we have developed a realistic balance between the operation of a responsive and competitive benefits package and the need to maintain effective cost controls," states O'Sullivan. "In this way, we have not only helped meet our overall financial objectives, but have created positive spin-offs for labour–management relations generally."

Source: Discussion with Jim O'Sullivan, vice-president of finance and administration, University of New Brunswick, July 1995.

objective

Pay for Time Not Worked

The "pay for time not worked" category of benefits includes statutory holiday pay, vacation pay, incentive or production bonuses, bereavement, jury duty, military duty, rest periods, coffee breaks, self-insured STD, maternity benefits (salary continuance). As Figure 13-1 showed, these benefits account for the second largest portion of payroll costs, at 15.4 percent.

Vacations with Pay

It is generally agreed that vacations are essential to the well-being of an employee. Eligibility for vacations varies by industry, locale, and organization size. To qualify for longer vacations of three, four, or five weeks, one may expect to work for seven, fifteen, and twenty years, respectively.

As shown in Figure 13-2, European professional and managerial personnel tend to receive more vacation time than do their Canadian, U.S., and Japanese counterparts. Although most countries have government mandates for employers to guarantee vacation time to workers, the United States and United Kingdom do not.

Paid Holidays

Both hourly and salaried workers can expect to be paid for statutory holidays as designated in each province. The standard statutory holidays are New Year's Day, Good Friday, Canada Day (Memorial Day in Newfoundland), Labour Day, and Christmas Day. Other holidays that are recognized by various provinces are Victoria Day,

---

FIGURE 13-2   *Vacation Day: A Global Look*

COUNTRY	LEGAL MINIMUM	TYPICAL PRACTICE	PUBLIC HOLIDAYS
Brazil	22	22	11
Canada	10	20	11
France	25	25–30	13
Germany	18	30–33	13
Hong Kong	7	20–30	17
Japan	19	20	14
Mexico	14	15–20	19
Sweden	30	30–32	10
United Kingdom	0	25–30	9
United States	0	20	10

Source: William M. Mercer, Inc. Reprinted with permission. Data are for professional and managerial personnel.

Thanksgiving Day, and Remembrance Day. Additionally, each province may designate special holidays important to that province only. Many employers give workers an additional one to three personal days off.

Sick Leave

There are several ways in which employees may be compensated during periods when they are unable to work because of illness or injury. Most public employees, as well as many in private firms, particularly in white-collar jobs, receive a set number of sick-leave days each year to cover such absences. Where permitted, sick leave that employees do not use can be accumulated to cover prolonged absences. Accumulated vacation leave may sometimes be used as a source of income when sick-leave benefits have been exhausted. Group insurance that provides income protection during a long-term disability is also becoming more common. As discussed earlier in the chapter, income lost during absences resulting from job-related injuries may be reimbursed, at least partially, through workers' compensation insurance.

Severance Pay

A one-time payment is sometimes given to employees who are being terminated. Known as severance pay, it may cover only a few days' wages or wages for several months, usually depending on the employee's length of service. Employers that are downsizing often use severance pay as a means of lessening the negative effects of unexpected termination on employees.

Life Insurance

One of the oldest and most popular employee benefits is group term life insurance, which provides death benefits to beneficiaries and may also provide accidental death and dismemberment benefits. It is nearly universal in Canada, with over $58 billion worth of group life insurance and $101 billion of individual insurance in force in 1993.[20]

Retirement Programs

Retirement is an important part of life and requires sufficient and careful preparation. In convincing job applicants that theirs is a good organization to work for, employers usually emphasize the retirement benefits that can be expected after a certain number of years of employment. As we observed earlier in the chapter, each employee is typically given an annual personalized statement of benefits that contains information about projected retirement income from pensions and employee investment plans.

Retirement Policies

Widespread downsizing in Canadian organizations has forced a number of individuals to consider early retirement. An estimated 60 percent of men and 70 percent women now leave the workforce before age 65.[21] Although the usual retirement age in Canada is 65, an individual may retire at 55 and begin drawing a reduced pension from CPP/QPP as well as funds from other sources such as RRSPs. Alternatively, some individuals can work until age 71, at which time they must retire. As we have seen, there is a growing trend for individuals in their golden years to take on part-time employment as a means to supplement their income.

To avoid layoffs and to reduce salary and benefit costs, employers often encourage early retirement. Encouragement comes in the form of increased pension benefits or cash bonuses, sometimes referred to as the **silver handshake**. Companies such as IBM Canada have given generously to enhance the early retirement of individuals. Ontario Hydro presented its employees with opportunities to retire under an early retirement allowance, a voluntary separation allowance, a special retirement program, or a voluntary retirement program; the incentive proposals were successful enough that most employees with 25 years of service opted for the special retirement program.[22] Employers can offset the costs of retirement incentives by paying lower compensation to replacements and/or by reducing their workforce.

The major factors affecting the decision to retire early are the individual's personal financial condition and health and the extent to which he or she receives satisfaction from the work. Attractive pension benefits, possibilities of future layoffs, and inability to meet the demands of their jobs are also among the reasons workers choose to retire early.

Preretirement Programs

While most people eagerly anticipate retirement, many are bitterly disappointed once they reach this stage of life. Employers may offer preretirement planning programs to help make employees aware of the kinds of adjustments they may need to make when they retire. These adjustments may include learning to live on a reduced, fixed income and having to cope with the problems of lost prestige, family problems, and idleness that retirement may create.

Preretirement programs typically include seminars and workshops that include lectures, videos, and printed materials. Topics covered include pension plans, health insurance coverage, retirement benefits and provincial health care, personal financial planning, and lifestyle adjustments.

A number of corporations offer preretirement programs. At Consumers Gas, employees aged 50 to 53 can attend, with their spouses, a three-day group seminar that covers six subject areas: positive outlook, leisure time, health, home, financial planning, and estate planning. Other organizations believe that retirement planning should be more individually focused. CIBC, which deals with over 40,000 employees in as many as 1800 different locations, provides for its employees with such training tools as tapes, books, video disks, and computer programs. Retirement Counsel of Canada suggests that 1 percent of a company's pension should cover the cost of a complete retirement planning program.[23]

Evidence shows that some organizations are considering offering retirement seminars as young as 35. For instance, at Siemens Canada, young employees age 35 and up are offered the same financial sessions as their employees 55 and over.

To help older workers get used to the idea of retirement, some organizations experiment with retirement rehearsal. Polaroid, for example, offers employees an opportunity to try out retirement through an unpaid three-month leave program. The company also offers a program that permits employees to cut their hours gradually before retirement. Employees are paid only for hours worked, but they receive full medical insurance and prorated pension credits. Most experts agree that preretirement planning is a much-needed, cost-effective employee benefit.[24]

Silver handshake
An early-retirement incentive in the form of increased pension benefits or a cash bonus.

Pension Plans

Originally, pensions were based on a *reward philosophy*, which viewed pensions primarily as a way to retain personnel by rewarding them for staying with the organization until they retired. Those employees who quit or who were terminated before retirement were not considered deserving of such rewards. Because of the vesting requirements negotiated into most union contracts and more recently required by law, pensions are now based on an *earnings philosophy*. This philosophy regards a pension as deferred income that employees accumulate during their working lives and that belongs to them after a specified number of years of service, whether or not they remain with the employer until retirement.

Since the passage of the CPP/QPP legislation in 1966, pension plans have been used to supplement the floor of protection provided by government-sponsored security programs. The majority of private pension plans and a significant number of public plans integrate their benefits with CPP/QPP benefits.

The decision whether or not to offer a pension plan is up to the employer. Due to the high costs of these plans, companies are opting for the most economical means to provide employees with this benefit. As of 1994, almost 40 percent of Canadian employees were covered by employer pension plans. There has been a decrease in the percentage of men with pension plans because of corporate downsizings and fewer unionized manufacturing jobs. However, because so many more women are working today, the share of women with their own coverage has increased greatly.[25]

Types of Pension Plans

There are two major ways to categorize pension plans: (1) according to contributions made by the employer, and (2) according to the amount of pension benefits to be paid. In a **contributory plan**, contributions to a pension plan are made jointly by employees and employers. In a **noncontributory plan**, the contributions are made

Contributory plan
A pension plan in which contributions are made jointly by employees and employers.

Noncontributory plan
A pension plan in which contributions are made solely by the employer.

A fulfilling life after retirement requires careful planning.

solely by the employer. Most of the plans existing in privately held organizations are contributory.

When pension plans are classified by the amount of pension benefits to be paid, there are two basic types: the defined-benefit plan and the defined-contribution plan. Under a **defined-benefit plan**, the amount an employee is to receive upon retirement is specifically set forth. This amount is usually based on the employee's years of service, average earnings during a specific period of time, and age at time of retirement. While a variety of formulas exist for determining pension benefits, the one used most often is based on the employee's average earnings (usually over a three- to five-year period immediately preceding retirement) multiplied by the number of years of service with the organization. A deduction is then made for each year the retiree is under age 65. As noted earlier, pension benefits are usually integrated with CPP/QPP.

A **defined-contribution plan** establishes the basis on which an employer will contribute to the pension fund. The contributions may be made through profit sharing, matches of employee contributions, employer-sponsored RRSP plans, and various other means. The amount of benefits employees receive on retirement is determined by the funds accumulated in their account at the time of retirement and what retirement benefits (usually an annuity) these funds will purchase. These plans do not offer the benefit-security predictability of a defined-benefit plan. However, even under defined-benefit plans, retirees may not receive the benefits promised them if the plan is not adequately funded.

The use of traditional defined-benefit plans, with their fixed payouts, is in decline. Defined-benefit plans are less popular with employers because they cost more and because they require compliance with complicated government rules.[26] Some experts, however, believe that employers may consider returning to defined-benefit plans, which allow for flexibility in plan design by opening paths for the advancement of younger employees while enabling older workers to retire.[27]

Registered Retirement Savings Plans (RRSPs) have experienced tremendous growth in recent years because the funds in these plans are allowed to accumulate tax-free until they are withdrawn. RRSPs are subject to regulations concerning annual contribution limits and preretirement withdrawals. Some employers offer a group RRSP to help employees plan for their future. The advantages of a group RRSP over an individual RRSP include payroll deduction and mass-purchasing power. Highlights in HRM 3 shows how employees can increase their retirement savings under a group RRSP.

Federal Regulation of Pension Plans

Registered Pension Plans (RPPs) are subject to federal and provincial regulations. Canada's Income Tax Act prescribes limits and standards that affect the amount of contributions that can be deducted from income as well as the conditions of taxability of benefit payments. (It is estimated that the government loses about $5 billion dollars a year in taxes because it does not tax private pension plans.) Laws regulating pension benefits, which exist in both federal and most provincial jurisdictions, control the terms and operation of plans. Actuarial assumptions on which the funding is based must be certified by an actuary at specified intervals. Of special concern to the individual employee is the matter of vesting.

Defined-benefit plan

A pension plan in which the amount an employee is to receive upon retirement is specifically set forth.

Defined-contribution plan

A pension plan that establishes the basis on which an employer will contribute to the pension fund.

3 MAXIMIZING EMPLOYEE SAVINGS WITH A GROUP RRSP

HRM
highlights

GETTING THE MOST FROM SAVING

The following tables demonstrate how employees can maximize their savings with an RRSP established by their employer. Table 1 assumes that the employee is in a 25% marginal tax bracket, saves $1000 each year, and earns 8% within the RRSP. Table 2 assumes the same interest rate but a 45% tax bracket.

The "After-Tax RRSP Account" figure assumes a lump-sum withdrawal and payment of taxes at the tax bracket rate. The "Ratio" figure shows how valuable the tax-deferral process is, especially over long periods of time and for employees in the higher tax bracket.

Table 1

	Regular Savings Account A	Pre-Tax RRSP Account	After-Tax RRSP Account B	Ratio of B to A
Out-of-Pocket Savings	1,000	$1,000		
Income Tax	250	0		
Net Savings	750	1,000		
Interest on Savings	60	80		
Tax on Interest	15	0		
Net Investment after Year 1	795	1,080	810	102%
Net Investment after Year 20	29,245	49,423	37,067	127%
Net Investment after Year 40	123,036	279,781	209,836	171%

Table 2

	Regular Savings Account A	Pre-Tax RRSP Account	After-Tax RRSP Account B	Ratio of B to A
Out-of-Pocket Savings	1,000	1,000		
Income Tax	450	0		
Net Savings	550	1,000		
Interest on Savings	44	80		
Tax on Interest	20	0		
Net Investment after Year 1	574	1,080	594	103%
Net Investment after Year 20	17,826	49,423	27,183	152%
Net Investment after Year 40	60,002	279,781	153,880	256%

Source: Robert G. Camp, senior vice-president, Sedgwick Noble Lowndes.

Vesting
A guarantee of accrued benefits to participants at retirement age, regardless of their employment status at that time.

Vesting is a guarantee of accrued benefits to participants at retirement age, regardless of their employment status at that time. Vested benefits that have been earned by an employee cannot be revoked by an employer. Employees with two years of service in an organization are considered, in terms of their pension plans, fully vested and locked-in. Prior to 1987, employees' pension funds were fully vested and locked-in if they reached age 45 having put in ten years of service. The locked-in provision means that the individual does not have access to these funds until retirement, thereby ensuring that they will have pension money available at that time.

There are increasing concerns regarding the pensions of women. A report conducted by the Canadian Advisory Council on the Status of Women concluded that many women aged 45 to 54 have inadequate RRSP or private pension plans, largely because they did not enter the workforce until their children were raised. Only 35 percent of working women are covered by private pension plans; 45 percent of working women aged 45 to 54 contribute to RRSPs (the average annual contribution is $2300).[28]

Pension Portability

A traditional weakness in most traditional pension plans is that they lacked the portability to enable employees who change employment to maintain equity in a single pension. Unions sought to address this problem by encouraging multiple-employer plans that covered the employees of two or more unrelated organizations in accordance with a collective bargaining agreement. Such plans are governed by employer and union representatives who constitute the plan's board of trustees. Multiple-employer plans tend to be found in industries where the typical company has too few employees to justify an individual plan. They are also found more frequently in industries where there is seasonal or irregular employment. Manufacturing industries where these plans exist include apparel, printing, furniture, leather, and metalworking. They are also used in such nonmanufacturing industries as mining, construction, transport, entertainment, and private higher education.

Employees who leave an organization can leave their locked-in funds in their current pension plan or transfer the funds into either a locked-in RRSP or their new employer's pension plan (if one exists).

Pension Funds

Pension funds may be administered through either a trusted or an insured plan. In a trusted pension plan, pension contributions are placed in a trust fund. The investment and administration of the fund are handled by trustees appointed by the employer or, if the employees are unionized, by either the employer or the union. Contributions to an insured pension plan are used to purchase insurance annuities. The responsibility for administering these funds rests with the insurance company providing the annuities.

Private and public pension funds constitute the largest pool of investment capital in the world, with over $4 trillion in assets. Still, one cannot be complacent about the future. Government benefits such as CPP/QPP and Old Age Security will be stretched thin as baby boomers age, and some private pensions may be vulnerable to poorly performing investments. It should also be noted that the pension funds of some organizations are not adequate to cover their obligations.[29] Such deficiencies present legal and ethical problems that must be addressed.

Current pension fund difficulties have been caused in part by the fact that the wages on which pension benefits are based today drastically exceed the wages on which pension fund contributions were based in earlier years. Furthermore, those drawing pensions are living beyond the life expectancies on which their pension benefits were calculated.

While fund managers are supposed to invest funds where the return will be most profitable, employees often demand a greater voice in determining where pension funds will be invested. There is also a movement to have more pension funds diverted to investments that employees consider "socially desirable," such as health centres, child-care centres, and hospitals in areas where members live. Any policy of investing in socially desirable projects must give consideration to the laws regulating pension benefits, which requires that fiduciaries (fund managers) act solely in the interest of the participants and beneficiaries for the exclusive purpose of providing benefits.

objective

Employee Services

Employee services provided by employers are generally not included in the benefit cost data compiled by KPMG in its benefit surveys. However, services, like other benefits, also represent a cost to the employer. The utility that employees and employers derive from services, however, can far exceed their cost. In recent years, new types of services are being offered to make life at work more rewarding and to enhance the well-being of employees.

Employee Assistance Programs

Employee assistance program (EAP)
Service provided by employers to help workers cope with a wide variety of problems that interfere with the way they perform their jobs.

To help workers cope with a wide variety of problems that interfere with the way they perform their jobs, organizations have developed employee assistance programs. An **employee assistance program (EAP)** typically provides diagnosis, counselling, and referral for advice or treatment when necessary for problems related to alcohol or drug abuse, emotional difficulties, and financial or family difficulties. (EAPs will be discussed in detail in Chapter 14.) The main intent is to help employees solve their personal problems or at least to prevent problems from turning into crises that affect their ability to work productively. To handle crises, many EAPs offer 24-hour hotlines.[30]

Counselling Services

An important part of an EAP is the counselling services it provides to employees. While most organizations expect managers to counsel subordinates, some employees may have problems that require the services of professional counsellors. Most organizations refer such individuals to outside counselling services such as family counselling services, marriage counsellors, and mental health clinics. Some organizations have on staff a clinical psychologist, counsellor, or comparable specialist to whom employees may be referred.

Educational Assistance Plans

One of the benefits most frequently mentioned in literature for employees is the educational assistance plan. The primary purpose of this plan is to help employees keep up to date with advances in their fields and to help them get ahead in the organization. Usually the employer covers the costs of tuition and fees, while the employee is required to pay for books, meals, transportation, and other expenses.

Child Care

The increased employment of women with dependent children has created an unprecedented demand for child-care arrangements. In the past, working parents had to make their own arrangements with sitters or with nursery schools for preschool children. Today benefits may include financial assistance, alternative work schedules, family leave, and work-site child-care centres. On-site or near-site child centres are the most visible, prestigious, and desired solution.[31]

Canada's first work-site day-care centre was built in 1964 at Toronto's Riverdale Hospital. Currently, in Canada there are 91 work-site centres, with a capacity of 3950 spaces.[32] Demand for work-site day care is expected to grow as more women enter the labour force. Sunnybrook Creche at Sunnybrook Hospital and Hydrokids at Ontario Hydro are two Toronto-based day cares. Organizations that do not offer day care may assist employees by providing expenses (Ford Motor Company of Canada) or a referral service (Bank of Montreal).

Child care is "the new benefit of the 1990s," according to one company president. "It is a critical need that companies that can afford it will meet because it is the right thing to do. Even companies that have limited means may be forced to support child care from a competitive standpoint, to attract, retain, and motivate personnel."[33]

Elder care
Care provided to an elderly relative by an individual who remains active in the workforce.

Elder Care

Responsibility for the care of aging parents and other relatives is another fact of life for increasing numbers of employees. The term **elder care**, as used in the context of employment, refers to the care provided to an elderly relative by an individual who remains active in the workforce. The majority of caregivers are women.

Many experts believe the worries and distractions caused by elder care can be more damaging to productivity than child-care problems. It is estimated that by the year 2000 77 percent of all employees will have elder-care responsibilities.[34] Only 43 percent of 1026 employers surveyed by Hewitt Associates offer elder-care benefits, as compared with 74 percent that offer some kind of child-care assistance.[35] Interest in and demand for elder-care programs will increase dramatically when baby boomers enter their early 50s, and find themselves simultaneously managing organizations and taking on elder-care responsibilities.[36] The Royal Bank offers an elder-care service, stating that family-friendly policies make good business sense in the attraction and retention of employees.

Other Services

The variety of benefits and services that employers offer today could not have been imagined a few years ago. Some are fairly standard, and we will cover them briefly. Some are unique and obviously grew out of specific concerns, needs, and interests. Among the more unique benefits are free baseball tickets for families and friends, summer staff parties on cruise boats, and subsidized haircuts for MPs. These examples represent only a few of the possibilities for benefits that go beyond those typically offered.[37]

Food Services

Vending machines represent the most prevalent form of food service program (87 percent of organizations), with cafeterias second (57 percent), according to a survey of organizational subscribers to *Personnel Journal.* Coffee trucks and lunch wagons rank third (15 percent).[38] The food is often offered at a subsidized or reduced rate.

Most employers contract with an outside firm. The HR department manages the program in 43 percent of the organizations; in 32 percent of the organizations, it has the responsibility for one or more decisions in this area.[39] By offering food services on the premises, organizations can reduce expenses associated with the business lunch and at the same time increase productivity by conducting business over lunch.

Legal Services

One of the fastest-growing employee benefits is the prepaid legal service plan. There are two general types: access plans and comprehensive plans. Access plans provide free telephone or office consultation, document review, and discounts on legal fees for more complex matters. Comprehensive plans cover other services such as representation in divorce cases, real-estate transactions, and civil and criminal trials.

Financial Planning

One of the newer benefits is financial planning. As yet offered primarily to executives and middle-level managers, it is likely to become available to more employees through flexible benefits programs. Such programs cover investments, tax planning and management, estate planning, and related topics.

Housing and Moving Expenses

The days of "company houses" are now past, except in mining or logging operations, construction projects in remote areas, and the armed forces. However, a variety of housing services are usually provided in nearly all organizations that move employees from one office or plant to another in connection with a transfer or plant relocation. These services may include helping employees find living quarters, paying for travel and moving expenses, and protecting transferred employees from loss when selling their homes.

Transportation Assistance

Daily transportation to and from work is often a major concern of employees. The result may be considerable time and energy devoted to organizing car pools and scrambling for parking spaces. Employer-organized van pooling is common among private and public organizations with operations in metropolitan areas. Many employers report that tardiness and absenteeism are reduced by van pooling. Proctor and Redfern Limited, a company located in Don Mills, Ontario, assists employees who have to walk from a distant bus stop. Caldwell Partners and Polo Ralph Lauren Canada cover taxi expenses for employees who work late.

Purchasing Assistance

Organizations may use various methods to assist their employees in purchasing merchandise more conveniently and at a discount. Retailers often offer their employees a discount on purchases made at the store. Most firms sell their own products at a discount to their employees, and in some instances they procure certain items from other manufacturers that they then offer to employees at a discount.

Credit Unions

Credit unions exist in many organizations to serve the financial needs of employees. They offer a variety of deposits as well as other banking services and make loans to their members. Although the employer may provide office space and a payroll deduction service, credit unions are operated by the employees under federal and provincial legislation.

Recreational and Social Services

Many organizations offer some type of sports program in which personnel may participate on a voluntary basis. Bowling, softball, golf, baseball, curling, squash, and tennis are quite often included in an intramural program. In addition to intramurals, many organizations have teams that represent them in competitions with other local organizations. Memberships or discount on membership fees at health clubs and fitness centres are also popular offerings.

Many social functions are organized for employees and their families. Employees should have a major part in planning if these functions are to be successful. However, the employer should retain control of all events associated with the organization because of possible legal liability. Accidents occurring while an employee is driving to or from an employer-sponsored event that the employee was encouraged to attend could trigger liability for an employer.[40] Employees should sign releases to minimize the liability of the employer.

Awards

Awards are often used to recognize productivity, special contributions, and service to an organization. Typically they are presented by top management at special meetings, banquets, and other functions where the honoured employees will receive wide recognition. While cash awards are usually given for cost-saving suggestions from employees, a noncash gift is often a more appropriate way to recognize special achievement. For example, travel has emerged as an important part of many sales incentive programs. An all-expense-paid trip for two to Paris is likely to be a unique and more memorable experience than a cash gift.[41]

Canada Post employees have the opportunity to win national recognition as most outstanding employee. The Golden Postmark Award, which is given at an awards dinner, honours employees from across Canada for outstanding achievements both on the job and in their respective communities.[42]

SUMMARY

Since the 1930s, benefit programs have expanded in terms of types of benefits offered and their costs, so that today's employees receive a sizable portion of their compensation in the form of benefits. Initially employers offered benefits to discourage unionization, but as the unions became stronger they were able to obtain additional benefits. Employers found that they could retain their employees by providing benefits. Now benefits are an established and integral part of the total compensation package. In order to have a sound benefits program there are certain basic considerations. It is essential that a program be based on specific objectives that are compatible with organizational philosophy and policies as well as affordable. Through committees and surveys, a benefits package can be developed to meet employees' needs. Through the use of flexible benefit plans, employees are able to choose those benefits that best meet their individual needs. An important factor in how employees view the program is the full communication of benefits information through meetings, printed material, and annual personalized statements of benefits.

According to a 1994 study, the costs of employee benefits in that year averaged 44.2 percent of payroll or $17,635 per employee. Since many of the benefits represent a fixed cost, management must pay close attention when assuming more benefit expense. Increasingly, employers are requiring employees to pay part of the costs of certain benefits. Employers also shop for benefit services that are competitively priced.

Nearly a quarter of the benefits package that employers provide is legally required. These benefits include retirement benefits, unemployment insurance, and workers' compensation insurance.

The cost of health-care programs has become a major concern in the area of employee benefits. Several approaches are used to contain health-care costs, including reduction in coverage, increased coordination of benefits, and increased deductible or co-payments. Employee assistance programs and wellness programs may also contribute to cutting the costs of health-care benefits.

Included in the category of benefits that involve payments for time not worked are vacations with pay, paid holidays, sick leave, and severance pay. The government mandates that the employer guarantee vacation time to workers. The typical practice in Canada is to give twenty days' vacation leave and eleven holidays. In addition to vacation time, most employees, particularly in white-collar jobs, receive a set number of sick-leave days. A one-time payment of severance pay may be given to employees who are being terminated.

Normal retirement age is 65, although in some provinces employees can work until age 71. Employees have the option to retire as early as age 55 in return for reduced pension benefits. Many employers provide incentives for early retirement in the form of increased pension benefits or cash bonuses. Some organizations provide preretirement programs that may include seminars, workshops, and informational materials.

Whether or not to offer a pension plan is the employers' prerogative. However, once a plan is established it is then subject to federal and provincial regulations to ensure that benefits will be available when an employee retires. While there are two types of plans available—defined benefit and defined contribution—most employers now opt for the latter. The amount an employee receives upon retirement is based on years of service, average earnings, and age at time of retirement. Pension benefits are typically integrated with CPP/QPP benefits. The use of individual and group RRSPs is growing. Pension funds may be administered through either a trusted or an insurance plan.

objective

The types of service benefits that employers typically provide include employee assistance programs, counselling services, educational assistance plans, child care, and elder care. Other benefits are food services, legal services, financial planning, housing and moving, transportation assistance, purchase assistance, credit unions, social and recreational services, and awards.

KEY TERMS

contributory plan

defined-benefit plan

defined-contribution plan

elder care

employee assistance program (EAP)

flexible benefits plans (cafeteria plans)

health maintenance organizations
   (HMOs)

noncontributory plan

preferred provider organization (PPO)

silver handshake

supplemental unemployment benefits
   (SUBs)

vesting

workers' compensation insurance

DISCUSSION QUESTIONS

1. Many organizations are concerned about the rising cost of employee benefits and question their value to the organization and to the employees.
   a. In your opinion, what benefits are of greatest value to employees? To the organization? Why?
   b. What can management do to increase the value to the organization of the benefits provided to employees?
2. Employee benefits were found to cost over $17,000 a year per employee in organizations surveyed by KPMG.

    a.   What would you think of a plan that called for removing all benefits, except those required by law, and giving the employees this amount in cash as part of wages?

    b.   Discuss the advantages and disadvantages of such a plan.

3.   What are some of the reasons for the greater attention organizations are devoting to the communication of benefits information to employees?

4.   Some organizations offer their employees a choice of certain benefits in a flexible benefits plan. What are the advantages and disadvantages of this type of plan to the employee? To the employer?

5.   What effect is further government intrusion in the area of employee benefits likely to have on benefits programs?

6.   How can the HR program affect employee health?

7.   Employers used to prescribe a mandatory retirement age—usually 65 years. What are the advantages and disadvantages of a mandatory retirement age?

8.   What factors may affect an individual's decision to retire at a particular time, and what factors may affect his or her ability to adjust to retirement?

CASE: Keeping the Corporate Connection

Various community organizations recruit retirees as volunteers and promote and coordinate volunteer activities, but company-sponsored programs have proven to be uniquely productive. There was a time when retirees were completely separated from their former employers except for a monthly pension cheque. But this is no longer the case. A company-sponsored retiree volunteer program provides a valuable link between a retiree and the company that benefits the community in which both reside. A company knows its retirees, how to reach them, and something about what they can do. It also provides the retiree with a comfortable environment—familiar faces and past shared experiences, an esprit de corps, and extension of the workplace that is so important to many retirees. Community organizations do not have this advantage.

An outstanding example of company/retiree partnership is the highly successful Honeywell Retiree Volunteer Project (HRVP), the first formally organized corporate retiree volunteer program. Honeywell initiated this program in 1979 as part of an effort to expand its role with nonprofit community service agencies. Since then, HRVP has placed more than 1600 retirees in responsible volunteer positions at more than 335 volunteer and nonprofit agencies. It is estimated that in 1990 these active seniors contributed more than 350,000 hours to the community. At a nominal $6 an hour, this would be about $2.1 million in-kind contributions.

Although the program has top Honeywell support, it is managed entirely by the retirees themselves, who even share the management responsibilities. Each retiree manager contributes one or two days a week to the project—recruiting volunteers, talking with the various community nonprofit agencies, and managing the day-to-day routine of the project. In addition, each day manager is responsible for certain ongoing projects and interest areas and for referring matters concerning other special projects to the responsible day manager. When a special project becomes too large to be handled as part of the daily routine, a project manager is appointed to oversee its activities and growth. The status of these projects is reviewed at monthly staff meetings.

Every attempt is made to involve retirees in community work that is rewarding, interesting, and challenging. An important step in this process is HRVP's one-on-one interview of each new prospective retiree volunteer to determine individual interest, ability, desire, and motivation. These are then matched, as closely as possible, to a nonprofit agency's needs according to their job descriptions. The prospective volunteer is then interviewed by the agency so that both parties can determine if a match can be made. As a result of this careful interviewing and matching, the turnover rate of HRVP's volunteers after placement is only 6 percent.

Most volunteers work on their own terms, ranging from half a day a week to as much as five days a week. Honeywell retirees are engaged in a variety of community activities: youth and adult educational programs, technical services, rehabilitation services, health services, and recreation and civic organizational projects. These diverse activities meet the needs of the retirees and also of the company and the community. According to Elmer Frykman, HRVP's first manager, "The volunteers like the work because they keep up with their skills and feel useful, and because they maintain the camaraderie established during their working years."

Source: Bernard L. Mooney, manager, promotional projects, Honeywell Retiree Volunteer Project, July 14, 1994. Prepared especially for this text and reproduced with permission.

Questions
1. How does a volunteer program like this one benefit the company?
2. In what ways can an HR department assist the staff that manages the program?
3. Why would some retirees choose to serve as volunteers rather than seek employment in the community?

Flexible Benefits

Does the company for which you would like to work or where you are currently employed offer a flexible approach to benefits? This exercise will help you determine how you would like to spend the approximately 42 percent of your salary that is designated for benefits, including legally required benefits.

Assume that you live in Ontario and have accepted a job that pays $60,000, based on a 40-hour workweek. This salary means you will have about $25,200 in benefits accruing. Included in this amount are mandatory benefits totalling $9686. This leaves you with just over $15,514 with which to purchase your choice of such benefits as dental care or club membership. You can mix and match the different benefits offered under Benefit Selections. You can select income in lieu of benefits provided they do not contravene the Employment Standards Act minimum vacation and statutory vacation requirements. You must be aware of the Revenue Canada rules that apply when making a choice. Because group benefits are purchased as a group, you will not be able to purchase the same value of benefit outside this group arrangement.

BENEFIT SELECTIONS

Benefit	Options		Total Value
SHORTENED WORK DAY @ 28.85 per hour	# of Hours = ___ # of Days = ___	$28.85 =	
SHORTENED WORK WEEK @ 230.80 per day	# of Days = ___	$230.80 =	
STATUTORY HOLIDAYS @ 230.80 per day	Select up to Ten Days Min. and 14 Days Max. List of choices and dates: _____ _____ _____ _____		
	10 days legally required	$230.80 =	2308.00
	Total # of days excessive of legal min. ___	$230.80 =	
VACATION WEEKS @ 1154 per week	Select up to two weeks min.		
	2 Weeks legally required		2308.00
	Extra weeks requested	$1154.00	

MEDICAL COVERAGE:	Select One Option:		
	Plan A: No Coverage	@ $ 0 per year =	
	Plan B: Weak Coverage (Individual)	@ $ 400 per year =	
	Plan C: Weak Coverage (Family)	@ $ 800 per year =	
	Plan D: Strong Coverage (Individual)	@ $ 650 per year =	
	Plan E: Strong Coverage (Family)	@ $1600 per year =	

DENTAL COVERAGE	Select One Option:		
	Plan A: No Coverage	@ $ 0 per year =	
	Plan B: Weak Coverage (Individual)	@ $ 200 per year =	
	Plan C: Strong Coverage (Family)	@ $ 600 per year =	

DISABILITY INSURANCE	Select One Option:		
	Plan A: No Coverage	@ $ 0 per year =	
	Plan B: Weak (Short term only)	@ $ 600 per year =	
	Plan C: Strong (Short and Long Term)	@ $1200 per year =	

LIFE INSURANCE	Select One Option:		
	Plan A: No Coverage	@ $0 per year =	
	Plan B: Weak Coverage (2 × salary)	@ $ 400 per year =	
	Plan C: Strong Coverage (4 × salary)	@ $ 800 per year =	

PENSION	Select One Option:		
	Plan A: No Coverage	@ $ 0 per year =	
	Plan B: Weak Contribution (3% Salary)	@ $1800 per year =	
	Plan C: Strong Contribution (8% Salary)	@ $4800 per year =	

EDUCATIONAL REIMBURSEMENT	Select One Option:		
	Plan A: No Reimbursement	@ $ 0 per year =	
	Plan B: Weak Reimbursement (50%)	@ $1000 per year =	
	Plan C: Strong Reimbursement (100%)	@ $5000 per year =	

CHILD/ELDER CARE	Select One Option:		
	Plan A: No Care	@ $ 0 per year =	
	Plan B: Half Day Care	@ $2000 per year =	
	Plan C: Full Day Care	@ $4000 per year =	

PERKS A	Select One Option:		
	Plan A: No Perks	@ $ 0 per year =	
	Plan B: 10 Box Tickets to Sports or Theatre, Opera or Symphony	@ $ 250 per year =	
	Plan C: Sports, Social or Recreational	@ $1500 per year =	

PERSONAL SERVICES	Select One Option:		
	Plan A: No Services	@ $ 0 per year =	
	Plan B: Financial Planning	@ $ 500 per year =	
	Plan C: Financial Planning, Legal Assistance	@ $1500 per year =	

BONUS	$10,000 less Employment Standards Minimum Vacations and Statutory Vacations	=	

SUBTOTAL

LEGALLY
REQUIRED
CONTRIBUTIONS CPP $1702
               UIC $3051
               WORKERS COMPENSATION $ 200
               HEALTH INSURANCE $ 117

               Total Mandatory Benefits $5070
               Including Vacation Requirements $4616

TOTAL BENEFITS $25,200

....

Source: Adapted from G. Kroeck & S. Fraser, "Choose Your Benefits." *Practical Experiences in Human Resources Management.* Toronto: The Dryden Press, Harcourt Brace & Co., 1994.

NOTES AND REFERENCES

1. D.L. McPherson and J.T. Wallance, "Design and Administration of Employee Benefit Plans," *Human Resources Management in Canada* (Scarborough, ON: Prentice-Hall, 1992) 45.

2. William E. Wymer, George Faulkner, and Joseph A. Parent, "Achieving Benefit Program Objectives," *HR Magazine* 37, no. 3 (March 1992): 55–62. See also Charles R. Sundermeyer, "Employee Benefit Planning for Small Businesses," *Benefits Quarterly* 9, no. 4 (Fourth Quarter 1993): 78–84; and Lesley Alderman, "Smart Ways to Maximize Your Company Benefits," *Money* 24, no. 11 (November 1994): 183–196.

3. Marlene L. Morgenstern, "Compensation and Benefits Challenges for the 1990s: The Board Speaks Out," *Compensation and Benefits Review* 25, no. 1 (January-February 1993): 22–26. See also Joyce E. Santora, "Employee Team Designs Flexible Benefits Program," *Personnel Journal* 73, no. 4 (April 1994): 30–39; and "The Changing Role of Flexible Benefit Plans," *HR Focus* 71, no. 3 (March 1994): 16.

4. William J. Wiatrowski, "Family-Related Benefits in the Workplace," *Monthly Labor Review* 13, no. 3 (March 1990): 28–33. See also Lisa Jenner, "Issues and Options for Childless Employees," *HR Focus* 71, no. 3 (March 1994): 22–23; Joy E. Hitchcock, "Southwest Airlines Renovates Benefits System," *HR Magazine* 37, no. 7 (July 1992): 54–56; and Jennifer J. Laabs, "Unmarried ... with Benefits," *Personnel Journal* 70, no. 12 (December 1991): 62–70.

5. William E. Wymer, George Faulkner, and Joseph A. Parente, "Achieving Benefit Program Objectives," *HR Magazine* 37, no. 3 (March 1992): 55–62. See also David E. Bowen and Christopher A. Wadley, "Designing a Strategic Benefits Program," *Compensation and Benefits Review* 21, no. 5 (September-October 1989): 44–56; and John S. Rybka, "Outsourcing Employee Benefits: How to Tell if It's Right for Your Organization," *Employee Benefits Journal* 18, no. 4 (December 1993): 2–8.

6. M. Patterson, "Making a Statement: Are You Ready to Turn an Obligation into an Opportunity?" *Benefits Canada,* February 1995, 19–21.

7. C. Nolan, "Plugged In: Delivering the Benefits Message Goes Interactive," *Benefits Canada*, June 1995, 38–45.

8. For over 40 years, benefit professionals have relied on the International Foundation of Employee Benefit Plans for education and information about employee benefits. Total membership consists of 35,000 individuals who represent more than 7400 trust funds, corporations, professional firms, and public employee funds throughout Canada, the United States, and overseas. The headquarters address is P.O. Box 69, Brookfield,

WI 53008-0069. One of their many publications is a valuable reference book: *Employee Benefit Plans: A Glossary of Terms*, 8th ed. (Brookfield, WI: International Foundation of Employee Benefit Plans, 1993).

9. A. O'Neil, "Retooling the Brain Trust," *Benefits Canada*, September 1994, 45.

10. "Cost of Individual Employee Benefits Expressed as a Percentage of Gross Annual Payroll," *Nineteenth Survey of Employee Benefits Costs in Canada* (Toronto: KPMG, 1994), Tables 9 and 10.

11. Ibid., Table 9.

12. Robert J. McCunney and Cheryl Barbanel, "Auditing Workers' Compensation Claims Targets Expensive Injuries, Job Tasks," *Occupational Health and Safety* 32, no. 10 (October 1993): 75–84; Geoffrey Leavenworth, "Setting Standards for Workers' Comp," *Business & Health* 12, no. 10 (October 1994): 49–54.

13. Karen Roberts and Sandra E. Gleason, "What Employees Want from Workers' Comp," *HR Magazine* 36, no. 12 (December 1991): 49–52.

14. Michael Bliss, "2-Tiered Medicare Is More Canadian Than It May Seem," *The Toronto Star*, April 21, 1995, A23.

15. Elaine Carey, "Rise in Over-80's Potential Health Disaster," *The Toronto Star*, May 12, 1995, A1.

16. Lisa Priest, "Patients to Pay if MDs Have Way," *The Toronto Star*, June 8, 1995, A1, A36.

17. William H. Carlile, "Family-Leave Law to Usher in New Era," *Arizona Republic*, July 31, 1993, 1; Michelle N. Martinex, "FMLA: Headache or Opportunity?" *HR Magazine* 39, no. 2 (February 1994): 42–45.

18. Rhonda Richards, "Family Leave Means Work for Temps," *USA Today*, February 11, 1993, B1.

19. Linda Thornburg, "What to Do Now about Health-Care Costs," *HR Magazine* 39, no. 1 (January 1994): 44–47; Shari Caudron, "Health-Care Reform: Act Now or Pay Later," *Personnel Journal* 73, no. 3 (March 1994): 57–67.

20. *Canadian Life and Health Insurance Facts* (Toronto: Canadian Life and Health Insurance Association Inc., 1994), 40.

21. Margot Gibb-Clark, "Delayed Retirement May Be a Hard Sell," *The Globe and Mail*, B6.

22. Doug Burn, "Wheel of Fortune: How Much Should an Organization Gamble on Early Retirement Planning?" *Human Resources Professional* 11, no. 4 (May 1994): 13–17.

23. David McCabe, "Retiring the Side: Approaches to Manage Retirement Planning Range from the Conservative to the Revolutionary," *Human Resources Professional* 11, no. 4 (May 1994): 9–11. See also Burn, "Wheel of Fortune."

24. Catherine D. Fyock, "Crafting Secure Retirements," *HR Magazine* 35, no. 7 (July 1990): 30–33; Samuel Greengard, "HR Teaches the Retirement Game," *Personnel Journal* 73, no. 11 (November 1994): 38–44.

25. Data provided by the Employee Benefit Research Institute in Washington, DC. See also Aaron Bernstein, "In Search of the Vanishing Nest Egg," *Business Week*, July 30, 1990, 46; and Mary Howland, "Pension Options for Small Firms, *Nation's Business*, March 1994, 25–27.

26. Larry Light, "The Power of the Pension Funds," *Business Week*, November 6, 1989, 154–158.

27. Donald J. Segal and Howard J. Small, "Are Defined Benefit Pension Plans about to Come Out of Retirement?" *Compensation and Benefits Review* (May-June 1993): 22–26.

28. David Vienneau, "Women's Pensions Lagging: Report," *The Toronto Star*, April 18, 1995, A1, A12.

29. Ellen E. Schultz, "Underfunded Pension Plan? Don't Panic Yet," *The Wall Street Journal*, December 3, 1993, C1.

30. Eileen G. Settineri, "Effectively Measuring the Costs of EAPs," *HR Magazine* 36, no. 4 (April 1991): 53–56. See also Ellen E. Schultz, "If You Use Firm's Counsellors, Remember Your Secrets Could Be Used Against You," *The Wall Street Journal*, May 26, 1994, C1.

31. Elanna Yalow, "Corporate Child Care Helps Recruit and Retain Workers," *Personnel Journal* 69, no. 6 (June 1990): 48–55; Jennifer Haupt, "Employee Action Prompts Management to Respond to Work-and-Family Needs," *Personnel Journal* 72, no. 2 (February 1993): 96–107.

32. *Work-Related Day Care in Canada: A Study for the Federal Task Force on Child Care*, Rothman Beach Associates, 1985; *Workplace Innovations Overview*, 1994, Bureau of Labour Information, 1994, 53; *The Task Force on the Advancement of Women in the Bank*, Bank of Montreal, November 1991, 24.

33. Karen Woodford, "Child Care Soars at America West," *Personnel Journal* 69, no. 2 (December 1990): 46–47; Yalow, "Corporate Child Care." See also Haupt, "Employee Action Prompts Management"; Charlene M. Solomon, "Work/Family's Failing Grade: Why Today's Initiatives Aren't Enough," *Personnel Journal* 73, no. 5 (May 1994): 72–87.

34. "Eldercare: The Next Wave in Work and Family Programs," *Canadian HR Reporter* 6, no. 13 (July 16, 1993): 8, 9, 15.

35. Sue Shellenbarger, "Employers Try New Ways to Help with Child Care," *The Wall Street Journal*, May 19, 1993, B1.

36. Sue Shellenbarger, "The Aging of America Is Making Elder Care a Big Workplace Issue," *The Wall Street Journal*, February 16, 1994, A1; see also Shellenbarger, "With Elder Care Comes a Professional and Personal Crisis," *The Wall Street Journal*, November 9, 1994, B1.

37. Robert Levering and Milton Moskowitz, *The 100 Best Companies to Work for in America* (New York: Doubleday, 1993), 107.

38. Ibid., 181.

39. Morton E. Grossman and Margaret Magnus, "Order Up Food Services," *Personnel Journal* 68, no. 3 (March 1989): 70–72.

40. "Employer Liable for Actions of Drunk Employee," *The California Labor Letter* V, no. 1 (January 1994): 3.

41. William H. Wagel, "Make Their Day—the Noncash Way," *Personnel* 67, no. 5 (May 1990): 41–44.

42. "Canada Post Employees Earn National Recognition," *The Mississauga News*, May 17, 1995, C7.

objective **one**

Summarize the common elements of federal and provincial occupational health and safety legislation.

objective **two**

Describe what management can do to create a safe work environment.

objective **three**

Cite the measures that should be taken to control and eliminate health hazards.

objective **four**

Describe the organizational services and programs for building better health.

objective **five**

Explain the role of employee assistance programs in HRM.

objective **six**

Describe the employer's role in the management of stress.

Chapter 14

Occupational Health and Safety

In the preceding chapters, we examined the various compensation and benefit programs that are designed to meet the needs of employees for economic security. Their needs for physical and emotional security demand equal attention. Employers are required by law to provide working conditions that do not impair the health or safety of their employees. Therefore, employers must ensure a work environment that protects employees from physical hazards, unhealthy conditions, and unsafe acts of other personnel. Through effective health and safety programs, the physical and emotional well-being, as well as the economic security, of employees may be preserved and even enhanced.

While the laws safeguarding employees' physical and emotional well-being are certainly an incentive, many employers are motivated to provide desirable working conditions by virtue of their sensitivity to human needs and rights. The more cost-oriented employer recognizes the importance of avoiding accidents and illnesses wherever possible. Costs associated with sick leave, disability payments, replacement of employees who are injured or killed, and workers' compensation far exceed the costs of maintaining a safety and health program. Accidents and illnesses attributable to the workplace may also have pronounced effects on employee morale and on the goodwill that the organization enjoys in the community and in the business world.

In today's litigious environment, an organization must be able to document how diligently its management makes an attempt at, and succeeds in, protecting employees on the job. The HR department is generally responsible for coordinating efforts and communicating crucial information on health and safety issues as well as maintaining records needed for documentation.[1]

After discussing the legal requirements for health and safety, we shall focus in the rest of this chapter on the creation of a safe and healthy work environment and on the management of stress.

Legal Requirements for Health and Safety

objective

Occupational health and safety is regulated by the federal, provincial, and territorial governments. While statutes and standards differ slightly from jurisdiction to jurisdiction, there have been attempts to harmonize the various acts and regulations. Health and safety legislation has had an impact on workplace injuries and illnesses. The number of workplace accidents in Canada declined from 554,793 in 1985 to 423,184 in 1993, despite an increase of about two million workers during the same period.[2]

An occupational injury is any cut, fracture, sprain, or amputation resulting from a workplace accident or from an exposure involving an accident in the work environment. An occupational illness is any abnormal condition or disorder, other than one resulting from an occupational injury, caused by exposure to environmental factors associated with employment. It includes acute and chronic illnesses or diseases that may be caused by inhalation, absorption, ingestion, or direct contact. In terms of parts of the body affected by accidents, injuries to the back occur most frequently, followed by leg, arm, and finger injuries as shown in Figure 14-1.[3]

It is more difficult to make simple comparisons of occupational illnesses reported today and those reported in the early 1980s. It is important to note, however, that of 125,118 or 30 percent of the national cases of occupational illnesses recognized or diagnosed in 1993, disorders associated with repetitive strain injury

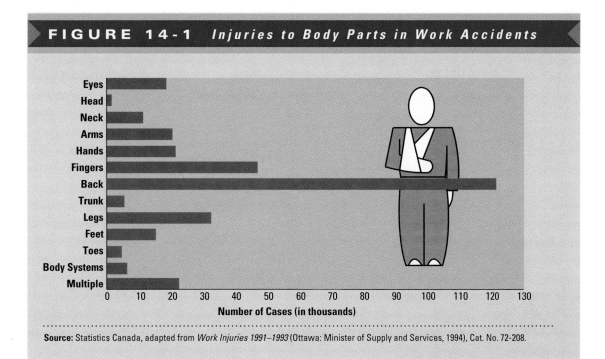

FIGURE 14-1 *Injuries to Body Parts in Work Accidents*

Number of Cases (in thousands)

Source: Statistics Canada, adapted from *Work Injuries 1991–1993* (Ottawa: Minister of Supply and Services, 1994), Cat. No. 72-208.

were the most common illness with 6283 cases, followed by poisoning (582) and chemical burns (443).[4]

Acts and Regulations

All HR managers should become familiar with the occupational health and safety legislation governing the jurisdiction under which their organization operates. The various Acts and government departments that enforce the legislation are listed in Figure 14-2.

Duties and Responsibilities

The fundamental duty of every employer is to take every reasonable precaution to ensure employee safety. The motivating forces behind workplace legislation were effectively articulated in the landmark case *Cory v. Wholesale Travel Group:*

> *Regulatory legislation is essential to the operation of our complex industrial society; it plays a legitimate and vital role in protecting those who are most vulnerable and least able to protect themselves. The extent and importance of that role has increased continuously since the onset of the Industrial Revolution. Before effective workplace legislation was enacted, labourers— including children—worked unconscionably long hours in dangerous and unhealthy surroundings that evoke visions of Dante's inferno. It was regulatory legislation with its enforcement provisions which brought to an end the shameful situations that existed in mines, factories and workshops in the nineteenth*

FIGURE 14-2 *Occupational Health and Safety in Canada*

JURISDICTION	LEGISLATION	ENFORCEMENT
Canada	Canada Labour Code, Regulations	Labour Canada
Alberta	Occupational Health and Safety Act	Department of Labour
British Columbia	Regulations under Workers' Compensation Act	Workers' Compensation Board
Manitoba	Workplace Safety and Health Act	Department of Environment and Workplace Health and Safety
New Brunswick	Occupational Health and Safety	Occupational Health and Safety Commission
Newfoundland	Occupational Health and Safety Act	Department of Labour
Nova Scotia	Occupational Health and Safety Act	Department of Labour
Ontario	Occupational Health and Safety Act	Ministry of Labour
Prince Edward Island	Occupational Health and Safety Act	Department of Fisheries and Labour
Quebec	Act respecting Occupational Health and Safety	Commission de la Santé et de la Sécurité du Travail
Saskatchewan	Occupational Health and Safety Act	Department of Labour
Northwest Territories	Safety Act	Commissioner NWT
Yukon Territory	Occupational Health and Safety Act	Commissioner of the Yukon Territories; administered by the Workers' Compensation Board

century. The differential treatment of regulatory offences is justified by their common goal of protecting the vulnerable.

Duties of Employers

In addition to providing a hazard-free workplace and complying with the applicable statutes and regulations, employers must inform their employees about safety and health requirements. Employers are also required to keep certain records, to compile an annual summary of work-related injuries and illnesses, and to ensure that supervisors are familiar with the work and its associated hazards (the supervisor, in turn, must ensure that workers are aware of those hazards).

Organizations with large numbers of employees may have a full-time health and safety officer. The health and safety manager at the Peel Board of Education is profiled in Reality Check.

In all jurisdictions, employers are required to report to the Workers' Compensation Board accidents that cause injuries and diseases. Accidents resulting in death or critical injuries must be reported immediately; the accident must then be investigated and a written report submitted.

Finally, employers must provide safety training and be prepared to discipline employees for failing to comply with safety rules. The poster in Highlights in HRM 1 outlines what must be done in case of an accident.

Duties of Workers

Employees are required to comply with all applicable Acts and regulations, to report hazardous conditions or defective equipment, and to follow all employer safety and health rules and regulations, including those prescribing the use of protective equipment.

Workers have many rights that pertain to requesting and receiving information about safety and health conditions. They also have the right to refuse unsafe work without fear or reprisal. (Some professionals such as police, firefighters, teachers, and health-care workers have only a limited right of refusal in the sense that their work is inherently dangerous.) An employee who suspects hazardous work conditions can report this concern to his or her supervisor, triggering an investigation by the supervisor and a worker representative. See Highlights in HRM 2 for an example of the work-refusal process.

A work-refusal investigation can result in either the employee's return to work or his or her continued refusal. In the latter case, the appropriate ministry is notified and an investigator is dispatched to the job site to provide a written decision. If a replacement worker is used, he or she must be notified of the previous employee's refusal to work.

Duties of Supervisors

A *supervisor* is generally defined as a person (with or without a title) who has charge of a workplace and authority over a worker. Occupational health and safety Acts require supervisors to advise employees of potential workplace hazards; ensure that workers use or wear safety equipment, devices, or clothing; provide written instructions where applicable; and take every reasonable precaution to guarantee the safety of workers.

HEALTH AND SAFETY AT THE PEEL BOARD OF EDUCATION

Mary Smith, manager of health and safety for the Peel Board of Education, is dedicated to making the work environment safer and healthier. In the early 1970s, Smith managed crews of workers on demolition sites in Ontario and saw first-hand the effects of ignorance of safety legislation. There were numerous tragic accidents. At that time, laws covering occupational health and safety were enforced at the municipal level. Smith went on to become the first woman construction inspector for the Ontario Ministry of Labour. In the early 1980s, she transferred to the Industrial Safety division before moving on to the Ministry of Environment, where she served as a laboratory safety officer. In 1986, the Peel Board of Education hired her to design and implement a health and safety program.

For the past nine years, Smith has worked hard to build a model program for the Peel Board. A team of five ensures the safety of 10,000 employees. What makes her team unique, she feels, is that two of the members are worker representatives. This gives the program more credibility. Additionally, she and the safety officer are not members of the joint health and safety committees, although they do serve as a resource to the two committees. According to Smith, this arrangement "keeps us at arm's length, bringing neutrality to the process. Our role is to support and be consultants to the system at all levels."

The health and safety team at the Peel Board conducts inspections of 182 locations, responds to worker concerns, reviews accident reports, follows up on site supervisor investigations, and interacts with various labour ministry inspectors. The team also concentrates on maintaining up-to-date chemical inventories as well as arranging for chemical disposal. Environmental legislation must also be scrupulously followed; Smith and her associates keep current by reading environmental health and safety journals, conducting literature searches, and watching developments in case law.

Smith describes the process involved in dealing with such issues as air quality, workplace violence, and ergonomics. "Many times there is a breakdown in communications and we need to find solutions. Employees just want to know you are listening, taking their concerns seriously, and trying to find solutions to their concerns. For example, if there is an air-quality concern that is brought to our attention we will work with the site manager or principal to help that person take the initial steps to investigate the situation. This may involve discussion with the worker and building occupants and having the plant maintenance staff ensure that the mechanical ventilation systems are functioning well. If all else fails, we involve an outside consultant. We set the mechanisms in place, but the supervisors actually take care of the issues."

A growing concern in the schools is workplace violence. The Peel Board is developing policies and procedures to address this concern. "Reviewing our statistics we saw a growing trend in our workers' compensation claims," Smith explains, "and we knew it was time to put some additional measures in place." Twenty-five percent of lost time accidents for one worker group were primarily the result of violent incidents. Education and training for affected staff will include modules on health and safety rights and responsibilities, back care, and nonviolent intervention and restraint.

"In reviewing the Peel Board successes, I must mention the development of the computerized Workplace Hazardous Material Information System (WHMIS), Vital Signs, that addresses both the legislated WHMIS training requirements and more importantly literacy in the workplace." Working in conjunction with the Peel Board Community Education Department, Smith and the health and safety officer contributed to the development of this program as technical consultants. The program won the 1992 OSH Award of Excellence. The honour is awarded annually at the OSH Conference sponsored by the Southam Corporation for, among other categories, the most innovative health and safety product or service. "Additionally, our train the trainer programs have been successful in WHMIS as well as in asbestos management. In such a large workforce the health and safety department would require an enormous influx of additional staff in order to deliver safety training. The economics of a publicly funded institution demanded a different solution. Supervisors responsible for worker safety were trained to train in safety areas. The down side is that it is difficult to ensure a consistent message; the upside is the acceptance of responsibility for health and safety by the supervisor."

Government intervention can have a major impact on how health and safety is administered in each province. Smith believes strongly that government must take ultimate responsibility for setting health and safety regulations that will protect workers and for ensuring that employers comply with those regulations. Labour and management must work together and demand equal status as stakeholders in this process.

Source: Interview with Deborah M. Zinni, June 1995.

Duties of Joint Health and Safety Committees

Most jurisdictions require the formation of health and safety committees operated jointly by union and management representatives. This arrangement is intended to create a nonadversarial climate in which labour and management work together to create a safe and healthy workplace. In Ontario, at least one management committee member and one worker representative must be certified. The certification program provides training in such subjects as safety laws, sanitation, general safety, rights and duties, and indoor air quality. Preliminary research indicates that joint health and safety committees can lower the number of occupational injuries and diseases.[5]

Penalties for Employer Noncompliance

Penalties for violations of occupational health and safety regulations vary across provinces and territories. The Ontario Health and Safety Act provides for fines up to $500,000, and offenders can be sent to jail. For example, ESM Metallurgical Products Inc., based in Ontario, was fined $150,000, after two workers died of asphyxiation. The company, which manufactures chemicals used in the iron and steel industry, failed to ensure that a confined space was tested before workers entered it.[6] Toronto Hydro was fined $200,000 in October 1994 when one of its employees was killed when an underground transformer exploded while the employee was trying to run a switch to the ground. The company pleaded guilty and agreed to train health and safety committee members and supervisors.[7] Under specified circumstances, the law provides for appeal by employers or employees.[8]

Workers' Compensation

Under workers' compensation, the injured workers can receive benefits in the form of a cash payout (if the disability is permanent) or wage-loss payments (if the worker can no longer earn the same amount of money). Unlimited medical aid is also

1 JOB SAFETY AND HEALTH PROTECTION POSTER

 Saskatchewan
Workers'
Compensation
Board

notice to workers injured at work

If necessary, receive professional treatment.

Advise your health care practitioner to report to the Board.

Complete and submit a Worker's Initial Report of Injury to the Board.

Please complete the entire form as all questions are important. If there is anything you don't understand, phone the Board for assistance. Complete and sign the form in ink. Send or bring your form to the Board as quickly as possible.

Report your injury to your employer.

Your employer will then submit an Employer's Initial Report of Injury to the Board.

Following these guidelines will enable us to provide you with timely service.

For more information:
The Workers' Compensation Board
200-1881 Scarth Street
Regina, Saskatchewan, S4P 4L1
Phone: (306) 787-4370
Toll Free 1-800-667-7590
Fax: (306) 787-7582

Recycled Paper

HIGHLIGHTS IN HRM

highlights

2   AN EMPLOYEE'S RIGHT TO REFUSE

The right of an employee to refuse to do work that he or she has reasonable cause to believe would be dangerous was an issue that emerged in the case of an asthmatic railway conductor. On one particular Via Rail run from Montreal to Toronto, the smoking section was filled up. At Kingston, the halfway point, the conductor informed a Via Rail manager that the smoke-filled coaches put him at risk of having an asthma attack. The manager accepted the conductor's refusal to work and assigned another conductor to the smoking coaches. In Toronto, a government safety officer inspected the coaches after discussing the problem with the conductor and others. However, by the time of the inspection, the smoke had dissipated—the passengers had gone and the doors were open. The officer concluded that there was no evidence that a dangerous condition had previously existed. Timing was clearly the problematic factor in this investigation of the conductor's refusal to work.

Source: "Reasonable Cause and the Rights to Refuse," *Worklife* (February 1993), 14–15.

Industrial disease
A disease resulting from exposure relating to a particular process, trade, or occupation in industry.

provided, along with vocational rehabilitation, which includes physical, social, and psychological services. The goal is to return the employee to his or her job (or some modification thereof) as soon as possible.

Compensation has become a complex issue. The definitions of accidents and injuries have recently been expanded to include industrial diseases and stress. An **industrial disease** is a disease resulting from exposure to a substance relating to a particular process, trade, or occupation within industry. Cause and effect can be difficult to determine. Consider, for example, the case of a mine worker who has contracted a lung disease, but who also smokes heavily.

Equally problematic is compensation for stress. Stress-related disabilities are normally divided into three groups: physical injuries leading to mental disabilities (e.g., clinical depression after a serious accident); mental stress resulting in a physical disability (ulcers or migraines); and mental stress resulting in a mental condition (anxiety over workload or downsizing leading to depression). Most claims, it should be point out, result from accidents and injuries.

The emphasis in workers' compensation has been shifting from assessments and payments to the creation of a safety-conscious environment intended to reduce the number of work-related accidents, disabilities, and diseases. Conjointly, employers within certain industrial sectors are working to establish rules and training programs to further the cause of accident prevention.

objective

Creating a Safe Work Environment

We have seen that employers are required by law to provide safe working conditions for their employees. To achieve this objective, the majority of employers have a formal safety program, for which the HR department or the industrial relations department is typically responsible. While the success of a safety program depends largely on managers and supervisors of operating departments, the HR department typically coordinates the safety communication and training programs, maintains required safety records, and works closely with managers and supervisors in a cooperative effort to make the program a success. In some organizations, joint health and safety committees are responsible for these tasks.

Safety Motivation and Knowledge

Probably the most important role of a safety program is motivating managers, supervisors, and subordinates to be aware of safety considerations. If managers and supervisors fail to demonstrate this awareness, their subordinates can hardly be expected to do so. Unfortunately, most managers and supervisors wear their "safety hat" far less often than their "production, quality control, and methods improvement hats." Just as important as safety motivation are a knowledge of safety and an understanding of where to place safety efforts. Training can help personnel on all levels understand the organization's policy on safety, its safety procedures, and its system of establishing accountability.[9] Under occupational health and safety legislation, managers are required to educate employees about hazardous substances and handling procedures.

Safety Awareness Programs

Most organizations have a safety awareness program that entails the use of several different media. Safety lectures, commercially produced films, specially developed videocassettes to meet the specific needs of an organization, and other media such as pamphlets are useful for teaching and motivating employees to follow safe work procedures. A page from one of these pamphlets is shown in Highlights in HRM 3. Posters have been found very effective because they can be displayed in strategic locations where workers will be sure to see them. For example, a shipyard found that placing posters at the work site helped reduce accidents by making employees more conscious of the hazards of using scaffolds.[10]

Safety awareness efforts are usually coordinated by a safety director whose primary function is to enlist the interest and cooperation of all personnel. However, the safety director depends a great deal on managerial and supervisory personnel for the success of the program. It is essential that these personnel set safety goals and provide subordinates with feedback concerning their department's performance in meeting these goals.

Communication Role of the Supervisor

One of a supervisor's major responsibilities is to communicate to an employee the need to work safely. Beginning with new employee orientation, safety should be emphasized continually. Proper work procedures, the use of protective clothing and devices, and potential hazards should be explained thoroughly. Furthermore, employees' understanding of all these considerations should be verified during training

> ## HIGHLIGHTS IN HRM

3 PAGE FROM A SAFETY AWARENESS PAMPHLET

Ask your supervisor which of the following personal protective equipment is requires for the equipment, operation or process you work with.

Head Protection
- ❏ Wear a safety hard hat and add other head protection as needed, such as a face shield, goggles or hood.
- ❏ Make sure your hard hat fits securely.
- ❏ Check the hat for gouges and cracks. Look for straps or sweatbands that are frayed or broken.
- ❏ Clean the shell of your hard hat to remove oil, grease and chemicals.

Eye Protection
- ❏ Wear industry-rated eye protection.
- ❏ Get medical help as soon as possible if your eye is injured.
- ❏ Contact lenses alone won't protect your eyes. ❏Add safety goggles or safety glasses.
- ❏ Don't wear contact lenses if you're exposed to chemicals, vapors, splashes, radiant or intensive heat, or suspended particles.

Source: National Safety Council. Reproduced with permission.

sessions, and employees should be encouraged to take some initiative in maintaining a concern for safety.[11] Since training alone does not ensure continual adherence to safe work practices, supervisors must observe employees at work and reinforce safe practices. Where unsafe acts are detected, supervisors should take immediate action to find the cause. Supervisors should also foster a team spirit of safety among the work group.

Safety Training Programs

The safety training programs found in many organizations include first aid, defensive driving, accident-prevention techniques, handling of hazardous equipment, and emergency procedures. These programs emphasize the use of emergency first-aid equipment and personal safety equipment. The most common types of personal safety equipment are safety glasses and goggles, face protectors, safety shoes, hard hats, hair protectors, and safety belts. There are also a variety of devices used in many jobs to protect hearing and respiration. Furthermore, many organizations provide training in off-the-job safety—at home, on the highway, etc.—as well as in first aid. Injuries and fatalities away from the job occur much more frequently than those on the job and are reflected in employer costs for insurance premiums, wage continuation, and interrupted production.

The Industrial Accident and Prevention Association (IAPA) offers six diploma programs for workers, supervisors, managers, health and safety professionals, joint health and safety committee members, and health and safety representatives. Course topics include health and safety legislation, hazard identification, and workplace inspection.

Safety Incentives

For safety training programs to reach their objectives, special attention must be given to the incentives that managers and supervisors use to motivate safe behaviour in their subordinates. The goal of each safety incentive program is to reduce accidents and make the workplace safer. Too often, however, an incentive program is based more on penalties and punishments than on rewards. Two researchers recently looked at 24 studies where positive reinforcement and feedback were used to reinforce safe behaviour. In all of the studies, they found these incentives successful in improving safety conditions or reducing accidents. The incentives included praise, public recognition, cash awards, and certificates that could be exchanged for company products. Each study emphasized the use of feedback.[12]

Safety Campaigns

In addition to organizing the regular safety training programs, safety directors often plan special safety campaigns. These campaigns typically emphasize competition among departments or plants, with the department or plant having the best safety record receiving some type of award or trophy. In some organizations, cash bonuses are given to employees who have outstanding safety records. However, some organizations have cautioned that this competition leads to the concealment of accidents.

Workplace Hazardous Materials Information Systems

Believing that workers have the right to know about potential workplace hazards, industry, labour, and government joined forces to develop a common information system for labelling hazardous substances. The Workplace Hazardous Materials Information Systems (WHMIS) is based on three elements:

Material Safety Data Sheet (MSDS)

Document that contains vital information about a hazardous substance.

1. *Labels.* Labels are designed to alert the worker that the container holds a potentially hazardous substance. The two types of labels (supplier labels and workplace labels) must contain specified and regulated information, including product identifiers and data on safe handling and material safety. WHMIS class symbols and subclass designations are shown in Figure 14-3.

2. ***Material Safety Data Sheet (MSDS).*** The MSDS identifies the product and its potentially hazardous ingredients, and suggests procedures for safe handling of the product. The MSDS information must be comprehensive, current, and available in English and French. See Figure 14-4 for a sample MSDS.

3. *Training.* Workers must be trained to check for labels and to follow specific procedures for handling spills. Training workers is part of the due diligence required of employers; it also becomes an important factor in the event of a lawsuit. The Peel Board of Eduction in Ontario has developed a computer-based program to train workers in WHMIS, allowing illiterate workers to respond to audio commands by touching the screen, thus giving the right response.

Enforcement of Safety Rules

Specific rules and regulations concerning safety are communicated through supervisors, bulletin-board notices, employee handbooks, and signs attached to equipment. Safety rules are also emphasized in regular safety meetings, at new employee orientations, and in manuals of standard operating procedures. Such rules typically refer to the following types of employee behaviours:

- Using proper safety devices
- Using proper work procedures
- Following good housekeeping practices
- Complying with accident-and-injury reporting procedures
- Wearing required safety clothing and equipment
- Avoiding carelessness or horseplay

Penalties for violation of safety rules are usually stated in the employee handbook. In a large percentage of organizations, the penalties imposed on violators are the same as those imposed for violations of other rules. They include an oral or written warning for the first violation, suspension or disciplinary layoff for repeated violations, and, as a last resort, dismissal. However, for serious violations—such as smoking around volatile substances—even the first offence may be cause for termination.

Accident Investigations and Records

Every accident, even those considered minor, should be investigated by the supervisor and a member of the safety committee. Such an investigation may determine the factors contributing to the accident and may reveal what corrections are needed to prevent it from happening again. Correction may require rearranging workstations,

FIGURE 14-3   *WHMIS Class Symbols and Subclass Designations*

The subclass designations are shown below the Class designation.

CLASS & SUBCLASS DESIGNATIONS

COMPRESSED GAS

FLAMMABLE AND
COMBUSTIBLE MATERIAL
   Flammable Gas
   Flammable Liquid
   Flammable Solid
   Flammable Aerosol
   Reactive Flammable Material

OXIDIZING MATERIAL

POISONOUS AND
INFECTIOUS MATERIAL
   Materials Causing
   Immediate and
   Serious Toxic Effects

Materials Causing
other Toxic Effects

Biohazardous
Infectious
Material

CORROSIVE MATERIAL

DANGEROUS REACTIVE
MATERIAL

Source: Industrial Accident Prevention Association, *Solvents in the Workplace*, Toronto, March 1990, Cat. No. B01230.

FIGURE 14-4 *Material Safety Data Sheet*

Form #CH3 **MATERIAL SAFETY DATA SHEET**   name of product:

SECTION I—HAZARDOUS INGREDIENTS

Chemical Identity	Concentration	CAS Number	PIN Number	LD_{50} Species and Route	LC_{50} Species and Route

SECTION II—PREPARATION INFORMATION

Prepared by (Group, Department, Etc.)	Phone Number	Date of Preparation

SECTION III—PRODUCT INFORMATION

Product Identifier

Manufacturer's Name		Supplier's Name	
Street Address		Street Address	
City	Province	City	Province
Postal Code	Emergency Tel. No.	Postal Code	Emergency Tel. No.

Product Use

SECTION IV—PHYSICAL DATA

Physical State	Odour and Appearance		Odour Threshold
Specific Gravity (water = 1)	Co-efficient of Water/Oil Distribution		Vapour Pressure
Boiling Point (°C)	Freezing Point (°C)	pH	Vapour Density (Air = 1)
Evaporation Rate (BuAc = 1)	Percent Volatile (by volume)		

FIGURE 14-4 *(cont.d)*

Form #CH3   **MATERIAL SAFETY DATA SHEET**   name of product:

SECTION V- FIRE OR EXPLOSION HAZARD

Conditions of Flammability

Means of Extinction

Explosion Data
Sensitivity to Mechanical Impact   Sensitivity to Static Discharge

Flashpoint (°C) and Method	Upper Flammable Limit %	Lower Flammable Limit %
Autoignition Temperature (°C)	Hazardous Combustion Products	

SECTION VI- REACTIVITY DATA

Stability

Incompatible Materials

Conditions of Reactivity

Hazardous Decomposition Products

SECTION VII- TOXICOLOGICAL PROPERTIES

Route of Entry
☐ Skin Contact   ☐ Skin Absorption   ☐ Eye Contact   ☐ Inhalation   ☐ Ingestion

Effects of Acute Exposure to Product

Effects of Chronic Exposure to Product

Exposure Limits	Irritancy of Product	Synergistic Products
Evidence of Carcinogenicity, Reproductive Toxicity, Teratogenicity or Mutagenicity?		Sensitization to Product

> **FIGURE 14-4** *(cont.d)*

Form #CH3 **MATERIAL SAFETY DATA SHEET** name of product:

SECTION VIII- PREVENTIVE MEASURES

Personal Protective Equipment

Gloves (specify)	Respiratory (specify)
Eye (specify)	Footwear (specify)

Other Equipment (specify)

Engineering Controls (e.g. ventilation, enclosed process, specify)

Leak and Spill Procedure

Waste Disposal

Handling Procedures and Equipment

Storage Requirements

Special Shipping Information

SECTION IX- FIRST AID MEASURES

Inhalation

Ingestion

Eye Contact

Skin Contact

Additional Information	Sources Used

BURY THE RECORD

A supervisor was instructing a group of new recruits in the cleaning of metal parts in an assembly plant. He was attempting to demonstrate the cleaning technique to two employees at one workstation, while at another workstation another new employee was trying to clean the parts himself. The cleaning liquid was highly toxic. The employee felt restricted by his safety gloves and so removed them. His eyes started to water, and instinctively he rubbed his eyes with his solution-soaked hands. The pain was overwhelming, and no water was immediately available with which he could rinse his eyes. The employee suffered some temporary vision loss.

Who is to blame? The worker who started to clean without receiving full instructions and without using the issued gloves? The supervisor who could have forbidden the worker to start work until the safety aspects were explained? Or the company that failed to post warning signs about the hazardous nature of the cleaning solvent and have available an eye-washing facility?

Because workplace accidents increase workers' compensation premiums and the number of inspections, the company had an interest in not reporting the accident. Furthermore, because the company had instituted a reward program that provided incentives to employees for accident-free days, even the employees did not want to report the accident. Thus the supervisor and the employees agreed to "bury the record." What are the consequences of this decision?

installing safety guards or controls, or, more often, giving employees additional safety training and reassessing their motivation for safety. However, reporting and investigating accidents can make an organization subject to more inspections, higher insurance premiums, and possible lawsuits (see Ethics in HRM).

objective

Creating a Healthy Work Environment

Occupational health and safety legislation, as its name suggests, is clearly designed to protect the health as well as the safety of employees. However, because of the dramatic impact of workplace accidents, managers and employees alike may pay more attention to these kinds of immediate safety concerns than to job conditions that endanger their health. It is essential, therefore, that health hazards be identified and controlled. Attention should also be given to nonwork-related illnesses and injuries and their impact on the organization and its members. Special health programs may also be developed to provide assistance to employees with health problems. Pressure from the federal government and unions, as well as increased public awareness of environmental issues, has given employers a strong incentive to provide the safest and healthiest work environment possible.

Health Hazards and Issues

At one time, health hazards were associated primarily with jobs found in industrial processing operations. In recent years, however, hazards in jobs outside the plant, such as in offices, health-care facilities, and airports, have been recognized and preventive measures taken. Substituting materials, altering processes, enclosing or isolating a process, issuing protective equipment, and improving ventilation are some of the common preventions. General conditions of health with respect to sanitation, housekeeping, cleanliness, ventilation, water supply, pest control, and food handling are also important to monitor.

Proliferating Chemicals

It is estimated that there are currently in use more than 65,000 different chemicals with which humans may come into contact. As of 1993, cases of poisoning and chemical burns due to toxic agents were outnumbered only by disorders associated with repeated trauma to the wrists and arms.[13] Of increasing concern are the reproductive health hazards faced by employees.

No toxicity data are available for about 80 percent of those chemicals that are used commercially.[14] Many of these chemicals are harmful, and may lurk in the body for years with no outward symptoms until the disease they cause is well established. Cancer, for example, may develop 20 to 40 years after the original exposure to a carcinogen. This time-bomb effect can embroil government, industry, labour, and ultimately the public in controversy over how to care for victims of past exposure and how to develop preventive controls. Specialists in HRM inevitably must participate in helping to solve many specific problems that arise as a result of this controversy.

Indoor Air Quality

As a consequence of the energy crisis of the 1970s, commercial and some residential construction techniques were changed to increase energy efficiency of heating, ventilating, and air-conditioning systems. Such practices as sealing windows, reducing outside air, and in general "buttoning up" buildings have resulted in the "sick building" phenomenon, with its attendant employee complaints of headaches, dizziness, disorientation, fatigue, and eye, ear, and throat irritation.[15] One-third of the adult workforce, according to Statistics Canada, has been affected in terms of health by exposure to indoor hazards such as poor air quality. In Ontario, local public health units and various ministry inspectors investigated over 2000 air-quality complaints over a twelve-year period.[16] About three-quarters of Canadian and U.S. companies are monitoring indoor air quality, checking for contaminants.[17]

There are four basic requirements for overcoming sick-building syndrome: (1) eliminate tobacco smoke, (2) provide adequate ventilation, (3) maintain the ventilating system, and (4) remove sources of pollution. Figure 14-5 shows the common sources of pollutants in the typical office building. Study the figure carefully in order to have a better understanding of the sources of irritants that can affect the well-being and job performance of the building occupants.[18] It should be noted that carpeting made from synthetic fibres is a major source of problems.[19]

Tobacco smoke. Probably the most heated workplace health issue of the 1990s is smoking. Nonsmokers—fuelled by studies linking "passive smoking" (inhaling other

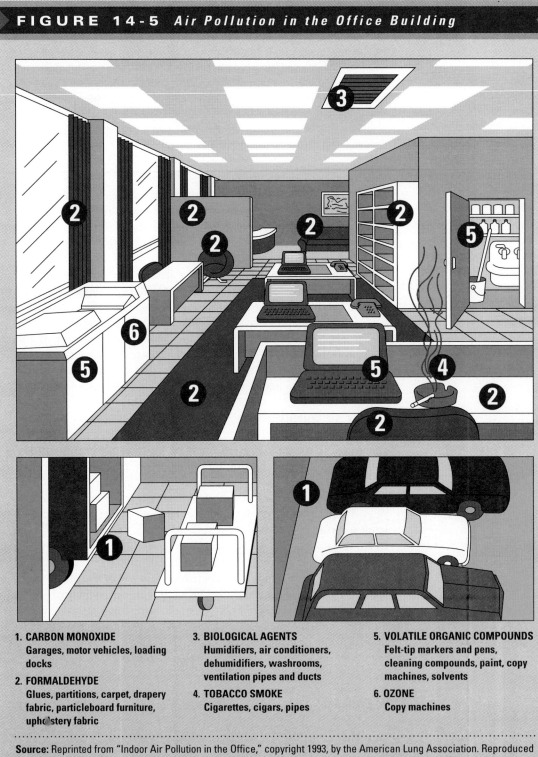

FIGURE 14-5 *Air Pollution in the Office Building*

1. **CARBON MONOXIDE**
   Garages, motor vehicles, loading docks

2. **FORMALDEHYDE**
   Glues, partitions, carpet, drapery fabric, particleboard furniture, upholstery fabric

3. **BIOLOGICAL AGENTS**
   Humidifiers, air conditioners, dehumidifiers, washrooms, ventilation pipes and ducts

4. **TOBACCO SMOKE**
   Cigarettes, cigars, pipes

5. **VOLATILE ORGANIC COMPOUNDS**
   Felt-tip markers and pens, cleaning compounds, paint, copy machines, solvents

6. **OZONE**
   Copy machines

Source: Reprinted from "Indoor Air Pollution in the Office," copyright 1993, by the American Lung Association. Reproduced with permission.

people's smoke) with disease and death, and irritated by smoke getting in their eyes, noses, throats, and clothes—have been extremely vocal in demanding a smoke-free environment.

The number of organizations restricting smoking in the workplace has risen dramatically, driven by legislation in most provinces. Banning smoking releases employers from worries about future lawsuits or being forced into installing ventilation for smokers.[20] Virtually all of the larger organizations and many of the smaller ones have instituted smoking policies. Yamaha Motor Canada and Nestlé Canada have smoke-free policies.[21]

Efforts to help employees quit smoking are being promoted by many employers. The two most popular steps taken are to distribute "quit-smoking" literature and to sponsor employee wellness programs that encourage workers to stop smoking.

Because of documented higher health-care costs for smokers, some employers are charging smokers more for health insurance or are reducing their benefits. Many employers, however, prefer positive reinforcement through wellness programs to encourage their employees to stop smoking.[22] (See Highlights in HRM 4 for an outline of Hallmark's program.)

Video Display Terminals

The expanding use of computers and video display terminals (VDTs) in the workplace has generated intense debate over the possible hazards to which VDT users may be exposed. Many fears about VDT use have been shown to be unfounded, but serious health complaints remain an issue, drawing attention to the need for more information, education, and positive action. Problems that HR managers have to confront in this area fall into four major groups:[23]

1. *Visual difficulties.* VDT operators frequently complain of blurred vision, sore eyes, burning and itching eyes, and glare.

Managers must balance the benefits of computers with the health of employees.

4 HALLMARKERS PREPARE FOR SMOKE-FREE WORKPLACE

Kicking the smoking habit has become a priority for many Hallmarkers. In March, about 40 Hallmarkers began attending smoking cessation classes. Another session gets under way next month.

The classes, offered by Hallmark through St. Luke's Hospital, are designed to help smokers adopt healthy lifestyle habits and become non-smokers. Classes focus on breaking the smoking habit, mastering smoking urges, and developing strategies and support systems for maintaining a smoke-free commitment. They also include counselling in nutrition, stress management and weight control.

The cost of the class is $100. Hallmark pays $50 of the fee when you enrol. You may use payroll deductions. If you complete the program and do not smoke for a year, the company will reimburse the $50 you paid.

The classes are being offered as part of our company commitment to health and wellness. They are a resource that Hallmark smokers can use to prepare for the implementation of a smoke-free workplace in Hallmark facilities.

"We want to assist Hallmarkers in making this change," says Jack Gabriel, director of Employee Relations. "The decision was made to go smoke-free because of Hallmarkers' concern about their health and well-being."

Source: Hallmark Cards, Inc. Reproduced with permission.

2. *Radiation hazards.* Cataract formation and reproductive problems, including miscarriages and birth defects, have been attributed to VDT use. The risks of exposure to VDT radiation have yet to be determined.

3. *Muscular aches and pains.* Pains in the back, neck, and shoulders are common complaints of VDT operators.

4. *Job stress.* Eye strain, postural problems, noise, insufficient training, excessive workloads, and monotonous work are complaints reported by three-quarters of VDT users.[24]

To capitalize on the benefits of VDTs while safeguarding employee health, organizations are advised to consider several strategies. These include educating employees in the proper use of VDTs, involving employees in system design, encouraging open-door communication with management so that concerns may be voiced and solutions found; using rest periods and job rotation; using ergonomically designed equipment; and ensuring that workstations have appropriate lighting.

Repetitive-Strain Injury (RSI)

Data processors, butchers, grocery-store cashiers, office workers at computer terminals, dental hygienists, hair stylists, and others whose jobs require repetitive motion of the fingers, hands, or arms are reporting injuries in growing percentages. In Ontario, RSI complaints have increased 25 percent from 1990 to 1993. It has been reported that 50 percent of cashiers, 40 percent of data-entry workers, and 31 percent of Bell operators have some form of RSI.[25]

According to Paul Forder, co-chairperson for Ontario's Workplace Health and Safety Agency, "Musculoskeletical injuries are at epidemic proportions."[26] Known as *cumulative trauma disorders (CTDs)* in the United States, and **repetitive-strain injuries**(RSIs) in Canada, these injuries involve tendons that become inflamed from repeated stresses and strains. One of the more common conditions is *carpal tunnel syndrome*, which is characterized by tingling or numbness in the fingers occurring when a tunnel of bones and ligaments in the wrist narrows and pinches nerves that reach the fingers and base of the thumb. To prevent *repetitive-motion injuries*, mini-breaks involving exercises, properly designed workstations, the changing of positions, and improvement in tool design have been found helpful. These kinds of injuries often go away if they are caught early. If they are not, they may require months or years of treatment or even surgical correction.

Unfortunately, many physicians do not see a connection between employees' symptoms and their work environments, and they tell patients that the problem is psychosomatic. Such reports lead employers to believe that workers are malingering. Gradually, however, more physicians are realizing that work is the source of these disorders.[27] While managers are not expected to play the role of doctor, they should be alert to injuries that occur among employees who perform similar tasks under similar conditions, and they should assume a proactive role in reducing these injuries.

Contagious Diseases

Communicable diseases, such as herpes simplex (cold sores), influenza, athlete's foot, and AIDS (acquired immune deficiency syndrome) are covered not in occupational health and safety legislation, but in public health legislation. In recent years, few workplace issues have received as much attention as AIDS. Many legal and medical questions have arisen that have made it imperative for employers to provide answers to everyone concerned.

Employers subject to public health and human rights laws under which AIDS victims are likely to be considered disabled are required to hire or retain an AIDS victim who is qualified to perform the essential functions of his or her job. These laws require employers to give reasonable accommodation to the person through job restructuring, modified work schedules, and less rigid physical requirements.[28]

While there is still no evidence that AIDS can be spread through casual contact in the typical workplace, one of the major problems employers face is the concern that many people have about contracting it. Employers have found it important to have programs to educate managers about the transmission of AIDS and to educate the entire workforce about AIDS through newsletters, posters, and seminars.[29]

Because of the controversial nature of AIDS, employers have found that managers and HR personnel must be carefully briefed on all aspects of the issue so they may act in the best interests of all concerned. HR journals, as well as health

Repetitive-strain injuries (RSIs)

Injuries involving tendons of the fingers, hands, and arms that become inflamed from repeated stresses and strains.

journals, have published numerous articles in the past several years that can be useful in developing reading files for the HR staff and for managerial and supervisory personnel.

objective

Building Better Health

Along with improving working conditions that are hazardous to employee health, many employers provide health services and have programs that encourage employees to improve their health habits. It is recognized that better health not only benefits the individual, but also pays off for the organization in the form of reduced absenteeism, increased efficiency, better morale, and other savings. An increased understanding of the close relationship between physical/emotional health and job performance has made broad health-building programs attractive to employers as well as to employees.

Health Services

The type of health services employers provide is primarily related to the size of the organization and the importance of such services. Small organizations have only limited facilities, such as those needed to handle first-aid cases, while very large firms offer complete medical diagnostic, treatment, and emergency surgical services. Since employers are required to provide medical services after an injury, they usually have nursing personnel on full-time duty and physicians on call. Medium-sized and larger organizations have one or more physicians on duty as regular employees.

We noted in Chapter 7 that some employers give medical examinations to prospective employees after a job offer has been received. The examination should include a medical history with special reference to previous hazardous exposures. Exposure to hazards whose effects may be cumulative, such as noise, lead, and radiation, are especially relevant. For jobs involving unusual physical demands, the applicant's muscular development, flexibility, agility, range of motion, and cardiac and respiratory functions should be evaluated. Many organizations also give periodic examinations on either a required or a voluntary basis. Such examinations are useful in determining the effects of potential hazards in the workplace, as well as detecting any health problems to which an employee's particular lifestyle or health habits may contribute.

Wellness Programs

Many organizations have developed programs that emphasize regular exercise, proper nutrition, weight control, and avoidance of substances harmful to health. For example, the employee health management program at Xerox includes cardiovascular fitness through aerobic exercises such as jogging, skipping rope, and racquet sports. The company gives its employees a *Fitbook* that provides instructions and illustrations relating to a variety of exercises. The book also includes chapters on the hazards of smoking and the effects of alcohol and drug abuse, facts on nutrition and weight control, and guidelines for managing stress and learning to relax.[30] Smaller organizations may distribute booklets available from services specializing in employee-communication materials.

An initiative in wellness took place in 1975 when Labatt Breweries of Canada began implementing fitness and health programs in its London, Ontario, facility. A centre was established that offered employees aerobic classes, weight training, and cardiovascular equipment, and such specialized programs as back care, smoking cessation, and self-defence. There is no cost to employees who utilize the centre. A fitness coordinator is on hand to conduct fitness appraisals and design programs for interested employees. Over the past 20 years the Labatt Fitness and Wellness Centre has provided employees with the latest fitness equipment and programs and has doubled its membership.[31]

Research shows that companies with occupational medicine departments are less likely than those without such departments to adopt health-related innovations. This may occur because health management programs are based on a disease prevention, health promotion plan rather than on the traditional medical model.[32]

Focus on Nutrition

There is mounting evidence to support the link between certain nutritional deficiencies and various physiological and psychological disorders, including alcoholism, depression, nervousness, low energy level, perceptual inaccuracy, and lack of reasonability. In fact, a person's mental and emotional states are affected by the foods he or she consumes, hence the wisdom of such sayings as "You are what you eat" and "What you eat today you walk and talk tomorrow." Proponents suggest that the potential return on a minimal investment in a sound nutritional plan is great, in terms of both dollars and morale, because human behaviour might be more easily and quickly modified by dietary changes than by more sophisticated organizational modification techniques.[33]

Many employers provide their employees the opportunity to participate in special programs. These programs provide training in proper *diet* and *exercise*, primarily walking. The late Nathan Pritikin and his colleagues developed a plan, known as the "2100 Program," that has been successful in helping people overcome degenerative diseases. The basis for the diet is given in Pritikin's books, which are now considered classics.[34]

objective

Employee Assistance Programs

A broad view of health includes the emotional as well as the physical aspects of one's life. While emotional problems, personal crises, alcoholism, and drug abuse are considered to be personal matters, they become organizational problems when they affect behaviour at work and interfere with job performance.

Some larger employers offer an employee assistance program (EAP). Typically, such a program refers employees in need of assistance to in-house counsellors or outside professionals. Supervisors are often given training and policy guidance in the type of help they can offer their subordinates. In contracting with professional counsellors outside the organization, the HR department needs to give special attention to their credentials, liability and confidentiality, cost, accountability, and service capabilities.

Personal Crises

The most prevalent problems among employees are personal crises involving marital, family, financial, or legal matters. Such problems often come to a supervisor's attention. In most instances, the supervisor can usually provide the best help simply by being understanding and supportive and by helping the individual find the type of assistance he or she needs. In many cases, in-house counselling or referral to an outside professional is recommended. In recent years, crisis hotlines have been set up in many communities to provide counselling by telephone for those too distraught to wait for an appointment with a counsellor.

Emotional Problems

While personal crises are typically fraught with emotion, most of them are resolved in a reasonable period of time and the troubled individual's equilibrium is restored. There will, however, be a small percentage of employees—roughly 3 percent on average—who have emotional problems serious enough to require professional treatment. Whether such individuals will be able to perform their jobs must be determined on an individual basis. In reviewing such cases, the organization should pay particular attention to workplace safety factors, since there is general agreement that emotional disturbances are primary or secondary factors in a large proportion of industrial accidents.

Managers should also be aware that the behaviour of some individuals is adversely affected by substances in the workplace that apparently do not affect others, or at least not as severely. Such individuals are, in fact, allergic to these substances. They may simply need to be reassigned to a different work environment rather than sent to a physician. Physicians who work in this area, called **clinical ecology**, report numerous cases of individuals whose behaviour on and off the job is affected by petrochemicals, moulds, cleaning substances, cosmetics and toiletries, plastics, tobacco smoke—in fact, virtually anything that can be found in the environment.

Those who are allergic to such items may exhibit behavioural symptoms, ranging from severe depression to extreme hyperactivity, that interfere with job performance. Remove the substance, or get the individuals away from the substance, and the symptoms disappear. Dr. Theron Randolph, an allergist, was among the first to write about the importance of environmental chemicals, in addition to foods, as the cause of many physical and emotional illnesses.[35]

Alcoholism

Business and industry lose billions of dollars each year because of alcoholism. According to a 1992 Conference Board of Canada report, the total social cost of alcohol abuse in Ontario alone was $4.3 billion.[36] Alcoholism affects workers in every occupational category—blue-collar, white-collar, and managerial.[37]

In confronting the problem, employers must recognize that alcoholism is a disease that follows a rather predictable course. Thus, they can take specific actions to deal with employees who show symptoms of the disease at particular stages of its progression. Alcoholism typically begins with social drinking getting out of control. As the disease progresses, the alcoholic loses control over how much to drink and eventually cannot keep from drinking, even at inappropriate times. The person uses denial to avoid facing the problems created by the abuse of alcohol and often blames others for these problems. One counsellor states that the first step in helping the alcoholic is to awaken the person to the reality of his or her situation.[38]

To identify alcoholism as early as possible, it is essential that supervisors monitor the performance of all personnel regularly and systematically. A supervisor should

Clinical ecology
Study of an individual's reactions to substances in the work environment, such as inhaled chemicals and fumes, that adversely affect the behaviour of some workers.

carefully document evidence of declining performance on the job and then confront the employee with unequivocal proof that work performance is suffering. The employee should be assured that help will be made available without penalty. Since the evaluations are made solely in terms of lagging job performance, a supervisor can avoid any mention of alcoholism and allow such employees to seek aid as they would for any other problem. Disciplinary action may be taken against employees who refuse to take advantage of such assistance or whose performance does not improve with repeated warnings. Between 70 and 80 percent of the employees accept the offer to get help and resolve their problems. It is important for employers to recognize, however, that in discharge cases brought by alcoholic employees, arbitrators look at on-the-job alcoholism as a sickness, not as a disciplinary matter.

EAPs typically provide assistance to the alcoholic employee. Rehabilitation is generally conducted by referral agencies. A large percentage of medical insurance now covers part of the treatment costs for alcoholism, making it possible to receive treatment at reasonable costs.

objective

The Management of Stress

Many jobs require employees to adjust to conditions that place unusual demands on them. In time these demands create stresses that can affect the health of employees as well as their productivity and satisfaction. Fortunately, increasing attention is being given to ways of identifying and preventing undue stress on the job. Even greater attention must be given to identifying and removing sources of stress to protect the well-being of employees and to reduce the costs to organizations. The costs of stress in health insurance claims, disability claims, and lost productivity alone are great. Looking to the mid-1990s and beyond, there is a need for greater emphasis on ways to reduce stress in the workplace.[39]

What Is Stress?

Stress is any demand on the individual that requires coping behaviour. Stress comes from two basic sources: physical activity and mental or emotional activity. The physical reaction of the body to both sources is the same. According to the late Hans Selye, a Canadian physician, human beings thrive on stress because "stress is the spice of life."[40] Selye uses two separate terms to distinguish between positive and negative life consequences of stress for the individual, even though reactions to the two forms of stress are the same biochemically. **Eustress** is positive stress that accompanies achievement and exhilaration. Eustress is the stress of meeting challenges such as those found in a managerial, technical, or public-contact job. Selye regards eustress as a beneficial force that helps us to forge ahead against obstacles. He is of the opinion that what is harmful is **distress**. Stress becomes distress when we begin to sense a loss of our feelings of security and adequacy. Helplessness, desperation, and disappointment turn stress into distress.

The stress reaction is a coordinated chemical mobilization of the entire body to meet the requirements of fight-or-flight in a situation perceived to be stressful. The sympathetic nervous system activates the secretion of hormones from the endocrine glands, which places the body on a "war footing." This response, commonly referred

Stress
Any adjustive demand, caused by physical, mental, or emotional factors, that requires coping behaviour.

Eustress
Positive stress that accompanies achievement and exhilaration. (48)

Distress
Harmful stress characterized by a loss of feelings of security and adequacy. (48)

Alarm reaction
Response to stress that involves an elevated heart rate, increased respiration, elevated levels of adrenaline in the blood, and increased blood pressure.

to as the **alarm reaction**, involves an elevated heart rate, increased respiration, elevated levels of adrenaline in the blood, and increased blood pressure. It persists until one's estimate of the relative threat to well-being has been re-evaluated. While the alarm reaction may have made life safer for our ancestors who were confronted daily with physical peril, it lacks value for most of the invisible enemies typical of contemporary life.

If distress persists long enough, it can result in fatigue, exhaustion, and even physical and/or emotional breakdown. When Selye first published his experimental findings, many medical practitioners failed to recognize the role of stress in a wide range of illnesses for which there is no specific cause. Some research has suggested a link between stress and heart disease. A recent study is the first to show a connection between chronic stress and hypertension (high blood pressure). High blood pressure, the most common cause of strokes, contributes to heart disease.[41]

A more common symptom is depression. The Canadian Mental Health Association reports that approximately 5 percent of the workforce experiences depression and that stress is a contributing factor. In 1994, the costs of depression, in terms of lost productivity, was more than $300 million.[42] Drowsiness, frequent absences, difficulty making decisions, and hostile behaviour are all symptoms of depression; workplace impact includes decreased productivity and reduced efficiency. (See Highlights in HRM 5 for a comprehensive list of the symptoms of depression.) It has been estimated that mental illness (including depression) accounts for about 60 percent of absences from work.[43]

Job-Related Stress

Although the body experiences a certain degree of stress (either eustress or distress) in all situations, here we are primarily concerned with stress as it relates to the work setting. It is in this setting that management can use some preventive approaches.

A surgeon finds a quiet spot to relieve his stress.

HIGHLIGHTS IN HRM

5   DEPRESSION IN THE WORKPLACE

RECOGNIZING DEPRESSION

When a depressed mood persists for a few weeks, deepens, and eventually starts interfering with work and other aspects of everyday life, it has likely become an illness—or a clinical depression. In the workplace, a person with depression will exhibit many of the following signs:

Personal Changes

- irritability, hostility
- hopelessness, despair
- slowness of speech
- chronic fatigue
- withdrawal from or extreme dependency on others
- alcohol or drug abuse

Workplace Changes

- difficulty in making decisions
- decreased productivity
- inability to concentrate
- decline in dependability
- unusual increase in errors in work
- being prone to accidents
- frequent tardiness, increased "sick" days
- lack of enthusiasm for work

Someone who has been experiencing many of these signs for a few weeks or more should seek help immediately.

Source: Canadian Mental Health Association, National Office, 2160 Yonge St., Toronto M4S 2Z3 (416) 484-7750.

Sources of Job-Related Stress

Disagreements with supervisors or fellow employees are a common cause of distress. A myriad of other events may also prove distressful. One individual, for example, remembers the time when he was made to rewrite a letter thirteen times. "I couldn't walk off the job," he recalls, "so I went to the men's room and hit the wall so hard my co-workers came in to see what was wrong." Feeling trapped in a job for which a person is ill-suited can be equally distressing. An airline attendant said that she was sick of "smiling when I don't want to smile" and "making excuses for the airline to furious passengers," but she did not consider herself qualified for other jobs with similar pay and benefits.

Many minor irritations can also be sources of distress. Lack of privacy in offices, unappealing music, excessive noise, and other conditions can be distressful to one person or another. There are even more serious conditions related to the management of personnel. Potentially distressful factors include having little to say about how a job is performed, overspecialization, lack of communication on the job, and lack of recognition for a job well done.

Burnout

More severe stage of distress, manifesting itself in depression, frustration, and loss of productivity.

Burnout is the most severe stage of distress. Career burnout generally occurs when a person begins questioning his or her own personal values. Quite simply, one no longer feels that what he or she is doing is important. Depression, frustration, and a loss of productivity are all symptoms of burnout. Burnout is due primarily to a lack of personal fulfilment in the job or a lack of positive feedback about performance.[44]

Employer Responsibility for Job-Related Distress

The issue of stress on the job has received considerable publicity in the various media. As a result, employees have begun to recognize that stress may have caused them psychological harm. Employers that once gave minimal attention to stress on the job are now required to take positive steps to identify specific sources of organizational stressors and to take corrective action.

In the past decade, the number of mental-stress workers' compensation claims have mushroomed because of (1) the growing number of employees in service jobs in which the work is more mental than manual, (2) the repetitive nature of tasks, and (3) the trend toward seeking compensation for mental as well as physical injuries.

Awareness of the legal implications of workplace stressors will help managers to initiate programs. In 1994, the Prince Edward Island Supreme Court ruled that stress in the workplace should fall under the heading of "accident" and be covered by workers' compensation.[45] The decision was triggered by the case of a lab technician who missed several months of work due to a reactive depression, which was attributed to lengthy exposure to stress and tension at work. Under the Workers' Compensation Board's previous rulings, emotional conditions must result from a traumatic workplace event that is both excessive and unusual; the Court, however, felt that a broader interpretation of the Act was needed.

Citing landmark cases that have provided compensation for psychological injuries resulting from emotional stress, several experts recommend the following five-step program:

1. Formulate a preventive legal strategy through analysis and forecasting of trends that indicate the direction of new legislation.
2. Develop a stress diagnostic system to increase awareness and sensitivity to employee concerns.
3. Involve top-level management in developing priorities and procedures for correcting problem areas.
4. Evaluate current programs by determining if stress-related problems still remain.

5. Document what has been done to correct situations that result in stress, and be prepared to take further corrective action.[46]

BC Tel has created a software program to help its 14,000 employees to manage stress.[47] The program includes a stress quiz, with questions about physical, behavioural, and emotional symptoms, and presents various coping strategies relating to diet, exercise, and assertiveness training. Professional help may be recommended. The service is confidential.

Training managers to recognize the symptoms of stress, to refer employees who may need professional help, and to implement programs for monitoring and treating problems is an important responsibility of the HR department. It is generally agreed that stress-management programs usually result in a net savings rather than a cost.

Stress-Management Programs

Many employers have developed stress-management programs to teach employees how to minimize the negative effects of job-related stress. A typical program might include relaxation techniques, coping skills, listening skills, methods of dealing with difficult people, time management, and assertion. All of these techniques are designed to break the pattern of tension that accompanies stress situations and to help participants achieve greater control of their lives. Organizational techniques, such as clarifying the employee's work role, redesigning and enriching jobs, correcting physical factors in the environment, and effectively handling interpersonal factors, should not be overlooked in the process of teaching employees how to handle stress. A review of research on work-site stress-management programs reveals that organizational stressors have not received the attention they should. There has been too much emphasis on helping individuals adjust to undesirable working conditions rather than on changing the conditions themselves.[48]

Even though the number and severity of organizational stressors can be reduced, everyone encounters situations that may be described as distressful. Those in good physical health are generally better able to cope with the stressors they encounter.

Employees should be made aware that some of the popular rituals that are supposed to relieve stress, such as the "coffee break," may be counterproductive if they lead to overconsumption of beverages containing caffeine. Many individuals develop anxiety symptoms from overdoses of caffeine. Their condition, which is often misdiagnosed as a psychological ailment, may well affect their behaviour and their productivity on the job. Instead of coffee breaks, many organizations are encouraging their employees to take exercise breaks.

While sabbatical leaves have been a long-standing tradition in colleges and universities, it is only recently that companies have introduced them in the form of personal-growth leaves. Bell Canada has found such leaves helpful to their professionals who work long and stressful hours. High-tech firms such as Apple Computer and Tandem Computer are among firms that have introduced personal-growth leaves. The expected payoffs to the firm are increased employee productivity and retention.[49]

Before concluding this discussion, we should observe that stress that is harmful to some employees may be healthy for others. Most executives learn to handle distress effectively and find that it actually stimulates better performance. Highlights in HRM 6 describes the very active life of Michael Cowpland, who is able to cope

HIGHLIGHTS IN HRM

highlights

6   PERSONAL POWER

Michael Cowpland, in his early 50s, is the president of Corel, a software giant. He has founded and managed two high-tech success stories: Mitel in the 1970s, Corel in the 1980s. His net worth is around $200 million, and he is expanding rapidly into the CD-ROM market. He is known for his hands-on management style, becoming involved in every decision and having few middle managers. Virtually everyone in his company reports to him. He has no secretary, and answers and returns his own calls.

Cowpland regularly works 80-hour weeks. He reads 50 industry magazines in one week (he is beyond speed-reading and into hyper-reading, he says). He plays tennis five times weekly, squash three times, and watches a wall of sixteen televisions all at the same time. He handles stress well.

According to one stress researcher, the only factor that has any significant impact on a person's ability to withstand work pressure is "personal power"—having control over your time, resources, important information, work load, etc. It is not the volume of work or work demands that makes people sick; it is the extent to which they can control it. Michael Cowpland is an example of a man who controls his work environment.

Sources: "Racquet Scientist," *Canadian Business*, June 1995; P. Froiland, "What Cures Job Stress?" *Training*, December 1993, 32–36.

with amounts of stress that would render most people dysfunctional. However, there will always be those who are unable to handle stress and need assistance in learning to cope with it. The increased interest of young and old alike in developing habits that will enable them to lead happier and more productive lives will undoubtedly be beneficial to them as individuals, to the organizations where they work, and to a society whose members are becoming more and more interdependent.

SUMMARY

Occupational health and safety Acts were designed to assure so far as possible healthful and safe working conditions to every working person. In general, the Acts extend to all employers and employees. Both employers and employees have certain responsibilities and rights. Employers are not only required to provide a hazard-free work environment but must keep employees informed and provide protective equipment. Under the "right to know" regulations, employers are required to keep employees informed of hazardous substances and what to do about them. Employees, in turn, are required to report hazardous conditions and follow all employer health and safety regulations.

In order to provide safe working conditions for their employees, employers typically establish a formal program that, in a large percentage of organizations, is under the direction of the HR manager. The program may have many facets, including providing safety knowledge and motivating employees to use it, making employees aware of the need for safety, and rewarding them for safe behaviour. Such incentives as praise, public recognition, and awards are used to involve employees in the safety program. Maintenance of required records from accident investigations provides a basis for information that can be used to create a safer work environment.

Job conditions that are dangerous to the health of employees are now receiving much greater attention than in the past. There is special concern about toxic chemicals that proliferate at a rapid rate and may lurk in the body for years without presenting outward symptoms. Health hazards other than those found in industrial processing operations—e.g., indoor air pollution, video display terminals, and cumulative trauma disorders—present special problems that must be addressed. Tobacco smoke is no longer tolerated in the work environment. While there is no evidence that AIDS can be spread through casual contact in the workplace, employers have come to recognize the importance of introducing programs that educate managers and employees about AIDS and assist those who are afflicted.

Along with providing safer and healthier work environments, employers may establish programs that encourage employees to improve their health habits. Many of the larger employers have opened primary care clinics for employees and their dependants in order to provide better health-care service and to reduce costs. Wellness programs that emphasize exercise, nutrition, weight control, and avoidance of harmful substances serve employees at all organizational levels.

Virtually all of the larger organizations and many of the smaller ones have found that an employee assistance program is beneficial to all concerned. While emotional problems, personal crises, alcoholism, and drug abuse are often viewed as personal matters, it is apparent that they affect behaviour at work and interfere with job performance. An employee assistance program typically provides professional assistance from in-house counsellors or outside professionals where it is needed. In contracting with professional persons outside the organization, the HR department should give special attention to their credentials.

An important dimension to health and safety is stress that comes from physical activity and mental or emotional activity. While stress is an integral part of being alive, when it turns into distress it becomes harmful. We have seen that there are many sources of stress that are job-related. Recognizing the need for reducing stress, many employers have developed stress-management programs to help their employees acquire techniques for coping with stress. In addition, organizations need to take action to redesign and enrich jobs, to clarify the employee's work role, to correct physical problems in the environment, and to take other actions that will help reduce stress on the job.

KEY TERMS

alarm reaction

burnout

clinical ecology

distress

eustress

industrial disease

Material Safety Data Sheet (MSDS)

repetitive-straint injuries (RSIs)

stress

DISCUSSION QUESTIONS

1. What effects have occupational health and safety Acts and regulations had on employer and employee behaviour?
2. What steps should be taken by management to increase motivation for safety?
3. Many occupational health hazards that once existed no longer do. However, industry has to remain vigilant to the possibility of new hazards.
   a. What are some of the occupational health hazards that were once common but are seldom found today? What factors contributed to their elimination?
   b. What are some possible present and future hazards that did not exist in the past?
   c. What role should periodic medical examinations play in the detection and elimination of occupational hazards?
4. What value would periodic consultations with a professional counsellor have for an executive? Who should pay for this service?
5. We observed that the field of clinical ecology relates directly to work situations.
   a. Have you noticed any chemicals that appear to affect how you feel or your behaviour?
   b. On what jobs are these chemicals likely to be found?
   c. How can specialists in HRM use this information?
6. Identify the sources of stress in an organization.

a. In what ways do they affect the individual employee? The organization?

b. What can managers and supervisors do to make the workplace less stressful?

CASE: Safety Issues at Metro University

More than 40,000 students study at Metro University's two campuses. The 200-hectare campus houses all faculties, in addition to several residences. Downing College, a liberal arts college, has its own campus. But, in fact, the world is Metro's campus, because its employees conduct research and do field studies in locations around the globe.

Approximately 1000 professors teach and conduct reasearch at Metro. An additional 10,000 employees work in such areas as administration and maintenance. Metro's *Health and Safety Policy* states: "Metro University is committed to the prevention of illness and injury through the provision and maintenance of healthy and safe conditions on its premises. The University endeavours to provide a hazard-free environment and minimize risks by adherence to all relevant legislation, and where appropriate, through development and implementation of additional internal standards, programs, and procedures. Metro University requires that health and safety be a primary objective in every area of operation and that all persons utilizing university premises comply with procedures, regulations and standards relating to health and safety."

Health and safety issues at Metro are not just the typical concerns found in a white-collar environment. The Faculty of Science, for example, handles chemicals not normally found in most office environments. Unexpected reactions to chemical spills are just one hazard. There can also be a malfunctioning of equipment, such as a fume hood that does not draw toxins. Research on animals exposes employees to rabies, bites, and even allergies. One researcher who worked with grasshoppers on a daily basis developed an allergy to them.

As part of their training, students in the behavioural sciences and physical education draw blood and do medical testing on themselves, which exposes them to blood-borne pathogens. Students and staff are at risk of physical injury even when walking from the outlying parking lots to the building during the winter. As the following chart indicates, Metro deals with a wide variety of medical claims. Repetitive-motion injuries are increasing because, like most organizations, the purchase of ergonomically designed furnishings and equipment has been a low priority.

Metro University Claims by Medical Code

Type	Number
Ache/pain	40
Allergic condition/reaction	7
Burn or scald	3
Contusion/crush, bruise, or swelling	15
Cut, laceration/puncture	16
Dermatitis	1
Fracture	5

Hearing loss/impairment	1
Occupational illness	10
Repetitive-motion injury	14
Scratches, abrasions	3
Sprains, strains	30

Researchers and professors tend to be very dedicated to their work, which may cause them to persist with a project while injured or to view safety measures as an impediment to the completion of that project. Furthermore, safety issues relating to new discoveries in various fields of research are not always immediately apparent.

Questions

1. Choose one faculty or department, such as the Faculty of Science or the physical education department, and list all the health and safety concerns of students and staff.
2. Develop for Metro a safety awareness program that takes into account faculty members who work off-site and students who commute to campus.

Job Stress Assessment

Stress is a natural part of any career journey. The goal of a stress-management program is not to eliminate stress, but to recognize when stress is intolerably high, and to manage its consequences. The exercise below is designed to help you measure the amount of stress you are experiencing at work. Then, a number of strategies are suggested for the management of this stress.

Part A: Identifying Work-Related Stress Levels

Being in competition with associates for important promotion	100
Being fired	95
Breakup of partnership by dissolution	90
Death of partner or associate	85
Promotion of an insider over your head	80
Promotion of an outsider over your head	75
Demotion	75
Handing in your resignation	70
Being transferred to another town or country	65
Having to refinance business	65
Merger of your firm with larger organization	60
New immediate superior	60
Starting work with new firm	60
Lawsuit against your firm	60
Finding close colleague is trying to stab you in the back	55
Personal public recognition (in press, by professional association)	50
Decrease in income	50
Having to fire close colleague	50
Change in character/status of important client (hence need for your firm to change the business)	50
Serious personality change in associate	50
Lack of appreciation by superiors of your efforts	45
Resignation of secretary/assistant	45
Loss of important customer	45
Sale of equity in company to staff	45
Promotion	45
Lack of gratitude by colleague for favours	40
New secretary/assistant starting	40
Continuing corporate bank overdraft	40
Change in type of work	40
Strike against your firm	35
Relocation of your office or plant	35

Covering up mistake of colleague	30
Public criticism which is damaging to the firm	30
Having to fire competent staff	30
Increase in income	25
Being criticized by superior	25
Failure to meet contract deadline more than once a month	20
Increase in cost of materials	20
Securing important contract	20
Postal or other public-service disruption	20
Vacation (self or close staff)	15
Minor sickness (self or close staff)	15
Failure of supplier to meet your deadline	15
Complaint by client (but not backed up by action)	15
Disagreement with associates	10
Attendance in one week at more than three meetings involving three or more people	10
Car breakdown or similar inconvenience	10
Reading important financial or political news	___
TOTAL	___

Part B: Strategies for Managing Stress
The average and normal stress level for optimum performance is around 300. Some people can tolerate a much higher level. However, most people will experience some of the following symptoms at higher levels: upset stomach, headache, increased smoking and drinking, muscular tension, the desire to be left alone, insomnia, tightness in the chest, depression, irritability, low self-esteem, and a proneness to frequent forgetfulness, errors, and poor performance.

If you are experiencing these symptoms, and feel they are a result of high stress levels, then you should consider:

- Relaxation exercises
- Stress-reduction seminars
- Employee assistance programs
- Physical fitness programs
- Biofeedback techniques

Source: Olga I. Crocker, *Experiential Exercises in Canadian Personnel Administration* (Toronto: Methuen, 1986), 508.

NOTES AND REFERENCES

1. Matthew P. Weinstock, "Rewarding Safety," *Occupational Hazards* 56, no. 3 (March 1994): 73–76; Christopher J. Bachler, "Workers Take Leave of Job Stress," *Personnel Journal* 74, no. 1 (January 1995): 38–44. See also Cecily A. Waterman and Karen H. Peteros, "Health Safety Concerns Knock on HR Doors," *HR Magazine* 37, no. 7 (July 1992): 89–91; and Daniel R. Ilgen, "Health Issues at Work: Opportunities for Industrial/Organizational Psychology," *American Psychologist* 45, no. 2 (February 1990): 273–283.

2. Canada Safety Council, *Fatality for 1985, International Accident Facts*, 1995, 76; Statistics Canada, *Work Injuries 1983–1985* and *Work Injuries 1991–1993* (Ottawa: Ministry of Supply and Services, 1987 and 1994, Cat. No. 72-208).

3. Statistics Canada, *Work Injuries 1991–1993* (Ottawa: Ministry of Supply and Services, 1994), Cat. No. 72-208.

4. T. Van Alpen, "New Epidemic in the Workplace? RSI Pains, Strains and Computers," *The Toronto Star*, April 17, 1995, B1, B3.

5. G.K. Bryce and P. Manga, "The Effectiveness of Health and Safety Committees," *Industrial Relations* 40, no. 2 (1985): 257–283.

6. "Company Fined $150,000 after Deaths," *The Globe and Mail*, May 3, 1995, A12.

7. "Utility Fined," *The Globe and Mail*, October 15, 1994, B2.

8. U.S. Department of Labor, Occupational Safety and Health Administration, *All about OSHA*, rev. ed. (Washington, DC: U.S. Government Printing Office, 1992), 24–27.

9. Dan Petersen, *Safety Management—A Human Approach*, 2nd ed. (Rivervale, NJ: Aloray, 1988), 33–36.

10. Kaija Leena Saarela, "A Poster Campaign for Improving Safety on Shipyard Scaffolds," *Journal of Safety Research* 20 (1989): 177–185. See also Charles D. Spielberger and Robert G. Frank, "Injury Control: A Promising Field for Psychologists," *American Psychologist* 47, no. 8 (August 1992): 1029–1030.

11. John A. Jenkins, "Self-Directed Work Force Promotes Safety," *HR Magazine* 35, no. 2 (February 1990): 177–185. See also Robert F. Scherer, James D. Brodzinski, and Elaine A. Crable, "The Human Factor," *HR Magazine* 38, no. 4 (April 1993): 92–97.

12. R. Bruce McAffee and Ashley R. Winn, "The Use of Incentives/Feedback to Enhance Work Place Safety: A Critique of the Literature," *Journal of Safety Research* 20 (1989): 7–19. See also Thomas R. Krause, John H. Hidley, and Stanley J. Hodson, "Broad-Based Changes in Behavior Key to Improving Safety Culture," *Occupational Health and Safety* 59, no. 7 (July 1990): 31–37, 50; and Mathew P. Weinstock, "Rewarding Safety," *Occupational Hazards* 56, no. 3 (March 1994): 73–76.

13. Van Alphen, "New Epidemic in the Workplace?"

14. Tina Adler, "Experts Urge Control of Aerospace Toxics," *APA Monitor* (American Psychological Association, May 1989): 1. For coverage of other health issues, see David H. Wegman and Lawrence J. Fine, "Occupational Health in the 1990s," *Annual Review of Public Health* (Palo Alto, CA: Annual Reviews, May 1990).

15. Zack Mansdorf, "Indoor Air Quality: A Modern-Day Dilemma," *Occupational Hazards* 55, no. 3 (March 1993): 11–14. *Accident Facts—1994 Edition* (Chicago: National Safety Council, 1994), 42.

16. G.S. Rajhans, "Indoor Air Quality." Presented at The American Society of Heating Refrigeration, and Air Conditioning Engineers/Society of Occupational Environment Health. Toronto, April 12–15, 1989.

17. "Take a Deep Breath and Say 'I love my job'" *Canadian Business*, June 1995, 21.

18. *Indoor Air Pollution in the Office* (New York: American Lung Association, 1993).

19. Debra Lynn Dadd, *The Nontoxic Home & Office* (Los Angeles, CA: Tarcher, 1992), Chapters 10–13. See also John Bower, *The Healthy House* (New York: Carol Publishing, 1991).

20. Jeffrey S. Harris, "Clearing the Air," *HR Magazine* 38, no. 2 (February 1993): 72–79; and Jennifer J. Laabs, "Companies Kick the Smoking Habit," *Personnel Journal* 73, no. 1 (January 1994): 38–48.

21. L. Goodson, "Pricing the Puff," *Human Resources Professional* 11, no. 1 (January-February 1994): 17–18.

22. Ron Winslow, "Some Firms Put a Price on Smoking," *The Wall Street Journal*, March 6, 1990, B1; Junda Woo, "Employers Fume over New Legislation Barring Discrimination against Smokers," *The Wall Street Journal*, June 4, 1993, B1; and Laabs, "Companies Kick the Smoking Habit.".

23. J.A. Savage, "Are Computer Terminals Zapping Workers' Health?" *Business and Society Review*, no. 84 (Winter 1993): 41–43.

24. *BNA Policy and Practice Series—Personnel Management* (Washington, DC: Bureau of National Affairs, 1988), 274:164.

25. Van Alphen, "New Epidemic in the Workplace?"

26. L. Priest and T. Van Alphen, "Silent Crippler an 'Epidemic' in Workplace," *The Toronto Star*, April 15, 1995, A1.

27. Howard M. Sandler, "Are We Ready to Regulate Cumulative Trauma Disorders?" *Occupational Hazards* 55, no. 6 (June 1993): 51–53. See also Marilyn Joyce and Ulrika Wallersteiner, *Ergonomics—Humanizing the Automated Office* (Cincinnati: South-Western, 1989), 85.

28. Linda C. Kramer, "Legal and Ethical Issues Affect Conduct Toward AIDS Sufferers," *Occupational Health and Safety* 59, no. 1 (January 1990): 49–50, 57.

29. I. MacAllister Booth, "Corporations That Confront the Scourge of AIDS," *Business & Society Review* no. 85 (Spring 1993): 21–23.

30. Shari Caudron, "Are Health Incentives Disincentives?" *Personnel Journal* 71, no. 8 (August 1992): 34–40.

31. Discussion with Cathy Andrigo, Labatt Fitness and Wellness Coordinator, Labatt Breweries of Canada, August 1995.

32. Richard A. Wolfe and Donald F. Parker, "Employee Health Management: Challenges and Opportunities," *The Academy of Management Executive* VIII, no. 2 (May 1994): 22–31.

33. John A. McDougall, *The McDougall Program—12 Days to Dynamic Health* (New York: Penguin Books, Plume Edition, 1991), Part 1. See also Jonathan Dahl, "The Business Traveler's Menu: Fat, Fat, Fat," *The Wall Street Journal*, September 8, 1994, B1; Allan Halcrow, "For Your Information: A Nutritious Plan for Improved Productivity," *Personnel Journal* 64, no. 8 (August 1985): 17; Linus Pauling, *How to Live Longer and Feel Better* (New York: W.H. Freeman, 1986). This book by the two-time Nobel laureate (Chemistry and Peace) contains sound advice on good nutrition and health maintenance.

34. The "2100 Program" is described in Robert Pritikin, *The New Pritikin Program* (New York: Simon & Schuster, 1990). See also two classics: Nathan Pritikin with Patrick M. McGrady, Jr., *The Pritikin Program for Diet and Exercise* (New York: Grosset & Dunlap, 1979); and Nathan Pritikin, *The Pritikin Promise: 28 Days to a Longer, Healthier Life* (New York: Simon & Schuster, 1983). For an interesting biography of Nathan Pritikin, see Tom Monte with Ilene Pritikin, *Pritikin: The Man Who Healed America's Heart* (Emmaus, PA: Rodale Press, 1988).

35. The following books are classics in the field of environmental allergies: Theron G. Randolph, *Human Ecology and Susceptibility to the Chemical Environment* (Springfield, IL: Charles C. Thomas, 1962); and Theron G. Randolph and Ralph W. Moss, *An Alternative Approach to Allergies* (New York: Lippincott & Crowell, 1980). See also David Rousseau, W.J. Rea, MD, and Jean Enwright, *Your Home, Your Health, and Well-Being* (Berkeley, CA: Ten Speed Press, 1990); Carolyn P. Gorman, *Less-Toxic Living*, 6th ed. (Dallas, TX: Environmental Health Centre, 1993). This latter publication may be obtained from the American Environmental Health Foundation, Inc., 8345 Walnut Hill Lane, Suite 225, Dallas, TX 75231-4262. The AEHF is a nonprofit organization designed to further the practice of environmental medicine and dedicated to the study and treatment of adverse environmental effects on the individual.

36. Shahid Alvi, "Corporate Response to Substance Abuse in the Workplace" (Ottawa: Conference Board of Canada), 1, Report No. 87–92.

37. Jim Castelli, "Addiction," *HR Magazine* 35, no. 4 (April 1990): 55–58. See also Alan R. Sell and Richard G. Newman, "Alcohol Abuse in the Workplace: A Management Dilemma," *Business Horizons* 35, no. 6 (November/December 1992): 64–71.

38. Delores A. Rumpel, "Motivating Alcoholic Workers to Seek Help," *Management Review* 78, no. 7 (July 1989): 37–39. See also Dianna L. Stone and Debra A. Kotch, "Individuals' Attitudes toward Organizational Drug Testing Policies and Practices," *Journal of Applied Psychology* 74, no. 3 (June 1989): 518–521; Joseph G. Rosse, Deborah F. Crown, and Howard D. Feldman, "Alternative Solutions to the Workplace Drug Problem: Results of a Survey of Personnel Managers," *Journal of Employment Counseling* 27, no. 2 (June 1990): 60–75.

39. Mark O. Hatfield, "Stress and the American Worker," *American Psychologist* 45, no. 10 (October 1990): 1162–1164. See also Timothy Newton, Joycelyn Handy, and Stephen Fineman, *Managing Stress* (Thousand Oaks, CA: Sage Publications, 1995); Charlene Marmer Solomon, "Working Smarter: How HR Can Help," *Personnel Journal* 72, no. 6 (June 1993): 54–64; James Campbell Quick, Lawrence R. Murphy, and Joseph J. Hurrell, Jr., *Stress and Well-Being at Work: Assessment and Intervention for Occupational Mental Health* (Washington, DC: American Psychological Association, 1992); John M. Ivancevich, Michael T. Matteson, Sara M. Freedman, and James F. Phillips, "Work-Site Stress Management Interventions," *American Psychologist* 45, no. 2 (February 1990): 252–261.

40. Hans Selye, *Stress without Distress* (Philadelphia: Lippincott, 1974; Signet Books Reprint, 1975), 83. This book, and others by Dr. Selye, are considered classics in the field of stress management.

41. *USA Today*, April 11, 1990, 1A.

42. "Costs of Depression," *Human Resources Professional* 12, no. 3 (June 1995): 15.

43. G. Goldberg and P. Klaas, "Identification and Management of Depression in the Workplace" *Occupational Health in Ontario* 13, no. 2 (1992): 16–32.

44. Cynthia L. Cordes and Thomas W. Dougherty, "A Review and Integration of Research on Job Burnout," *The Academy of Management Review* 18, no. 4 (October 1993): 621–656.

45. "Stress Claimable for Compensation," *The Gazette* (Montreal), November 27, 1994, A7.

46. John M. Ivancevich, Michael T. Matteson, and Edward P. Richards III, "Who's Liable for Stress on the Job?" *Harvard Business Review* 85, no. 2 (March-April 1985): 60–72.

47. D. Smith. "BC Tel dials in Computer Program to Help Stressed-Out Employees" *Vancouver Sun*, December 13, 1994, D1.

48. Ivancevich, et al., "Work-Site Stress Management," 258.

49. "Sabbaticals Being Tried for Stressed Employees," *The Arizona Republic*, May 3, 1993, E6.

Part 5

Strengthening Employee-Management Relations

The two chapters in Part 5 discuss employee representation by labour unions. Chapter 15 focuses on issues involved in the unionization of employees, including the legal statutes governing this very specific area of HR maanagement. Included in Chapter 15 is a discussion of the structures and functions of unions, and challenges currently facing them. Chapter 16 explores the relationship between labour and management once employees elect to unionize and a collective agreement is negotiated between the two parties. The administration of this collective agreement, including mechanisms for resolving grievances, is reviewed. An understanding of labour relations and its processes will improve the supervisory skills of managers in both union and nonunion enterprises.

After studying this chapter, you should be able to

one
objective

Identify and explain the principal legislation that provides the framework for labour relations.

two
objective

Cite the reasons why employees join unions.

three
objective

Describe the process by which unions organize employees and gain recognition as their bargaining agent.

four
objective

Describe the overall structure of the labour movement and the functions labour unions perform at the national and local levels.

five
objective

Describe the differences between private-sector and public-sector labour relations.

six
objective

Discuss some of the effects that changing conditions are having on labour organizations.

Chapter 15

The Dynamics of Labour Relations

Mention the word "union" and most people will have some opinion, positive or negative, regarding labour organizations. To some, the word evokes images of labour–management unrest—grievances, strikes, picketing, boycotts. To others, the word represents industrial democracy, fairness, opportunity, equal representation. Many think of unions as simply creating an adversarial relationship between employees and managers.

Regardless of attitudes toward them, since the mid-1800s unions have been an important force shaping organizational practices, legislation, and political thought in Canada. Today unions remain of interest because of their influence on organizational productivity, competitiveness, the development of labour law, and HR policies and practices. Like business organizations themselves, unions are undergoing changes in both operation and philosophy. Labour–management cooperative programs, company buyouts by unions, and labour's increased interest in global trade are illustrative of labour's new role in society.

In spite of the long history of unions, the intricacies of labour relations are unfamiliar to many individuals. Therefore, this chapter describes government regulation of labour relations, the labour relations process, the reasons why workers join labour organizations, the structure and leadership of labour unions, and contemporary challenges to labour organizations.

Unions and other labour organizations can affect significantly the ability of managers to direct and control the various functions of HRM. For example, union seniority provisions in the labour contract may influence who is selected for job promotions or training programs. Pay rates may be determined through union negotiations, or unions may impose restrictions on management's employee appraisal methods. Therefore, it is essential that managers understand how unions operate and be thoroughly familiar with the growing body of law governing labour relations. Labour relations is a highly specialized function of HRM to which managers must give appropriate consideration.

Government Regulation of Labour Relations

objective

Unions have a long history in North America, and the regulations governing labour relations have evolved from labour's historical developments. Initially, employers strongly opposed union growth, using court injunctions (e.g., court orders forbidding various union activities, such as picketing and strikes) and devices such as the "yellow-dog contract." A yellow-dog contract was an employer's anti-union tactic by which employees bound themselves not to join a union while working for the employer's organization. Using strikebreakers, blacklisting employees (e.g., circulating the names of union supporters to other employers), and discriminating against those who favoured unionization were other defensive manoeuvres of employers.

Today the laws governing labour relations seek to create an environment where both unions and employers can discharge their respective rights and responsibilities. Knowledge of labour relations laws will facilitate the understanding of how union–management relations operate in Canada.

Labour Relations Legislation

The first labour relations legislation, the Trades Unions Act, was passed by the federal Parliament in 1872. This Act exempted unions from charges of criminal conspiracy, allowed them to pursue goals of collective bargaining without persecution, and gave them the ability to strike. Between 1872 and 1900, legislation to settle industrial disputes was enacted in a number of provinces, including Quebec, Ontario, British Columbia, and Nova Scotia. Although these Acts are no longer in effect, they did mark Canada's early recognition of the rights of unions.

A multiplicity of laws at the federal and provincial levels currently regulates labour relations. There are specific laws, or Acts, for different sectors, industries, and workers. It is a highly decentralized system. For example, federal jurisdiction governs interprovincial transportation and communications, while provincial legislation governs manufacturing and mining. However, 90 percent of the workforce is governed by provincial legislation. It is beyond the scope of this chapter to cover the labour legislation in each province, but much of provincial legislation is modelled after the federal War Labour Order, more popularly known as P.C. 1003, which was approved in 1944 and translated into a federal statute in 1948.

Industrial Relations Disputes and Investigation Act (IRDI)

This Act specified the rights of workers to join unions, allowed unions to be certified as bargaining agents by a labour relations board, required management to recognize a certified union as the exclusive bargaining agent for a group of employees, required both unions and management to negotiate in good faith, outlined unfair labour practices by both unions and management, and created a two-stage compulsory conciliation process that was mandatory before strikes or lockouts became legal.[1]

The federal government has since incorporated these rights into a more comprehensive piece of legislation known as the Canada Labour Code. The Canada Labour Relations Board (LRB) was also established to administer and enforce the code. Similarly, each province has a labour relations board, whose members are appointed by the government and who administer labour law. (The exception is Quebec, which has a labour court and commissioners). The LRB is generally autonomous from the federal government and is composed of representatives from labour and management. The duties of the LRB include, but are not limited to:

- Administrating the statutory procedures for the acquisition, transfer, and termination of bargaining rights
- Hearing complaints related to unfair labour practices
- Determining if bargaining was done in good faith
- Remedying violations of collective bargaining legislation.[2]

The Labour Relations Process

Labour relations process

Logical sequence of four events: (1) workers desire collective representation, (2) union begins its organizing drive, (3) collective negotiations lead to a contract, and (4) the contract is administered.

Individually, employees may be able to exercise relatively little power in their relations with employers. The treatment and benefits they receive depend in large part on how their employers view their worth to the organization. Of course, if employees believe they are not being treated fairly, they have the option of quitting. However, another way to correct the situation is to organize and bargain with the employer collectively. When employees pursue this direction, the labour relations process begins. As Figure 15-1 illustrates, the **labour relations process** consists of a logical sequence of four events: (1) workers desire collective representation, (2) union begins its organizing campaign, (3) collective negotiations lead to a contract,

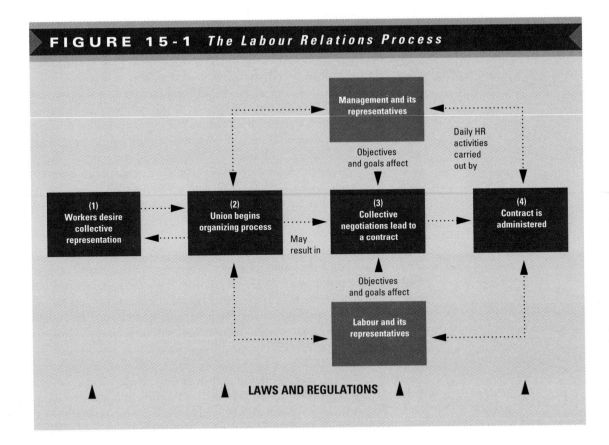

FIGURE 15-1 *The Labour Relations Process*

and (4) the contract is administered. Laws and administrative rulings influence each of the separate events by granting special privileges to, or imposing defined constraints on, workers, managers, and union officials.[3] Rules may vary by province, and information specific to each province is available through provincial labour relations boards.

objective

Why Employees Unionize

The majority of research on why employees unionize comes from the study of blue-collar employees in the private sector. These studies generally conclude that employees unionize as a result of economic need, because of a general dissatisfaction with managerial practices, and/or as a way to fulfil social and status needs. In short, employees see unionism as a way to achieve results they cannot achieve acting individually.

It should be pointed out that some employees join unions because of the union-shop provisions of the collective agreement. Where permitted, a **union shop** requires employees to join as a condition of employment. Even when compelled to join, however, many employees accept the concept of unionism once they become involved in the union as a member.

Union shop
Provision of the collective agreement that requires employees to join the union as a condition of employment.

Economic Needs

Whether or not a union can become the bargaining agent for a group of employees will be influenced by the employees' degree of dissatisfaction, if any, with their employment conditions. It will depend also on whether the employees perceive the union as likely to be effective in improving these conditions.[4] Dissatisfaction with wages, benefits, and working conditions appears to provide the strongest reason to join a union. This point is continually supported by research studies that find that both union members and nonmembers have their highest expectations of union performance regarding the "bread and butter" issues of collective bargaining.[5] It is these traditional issues of wages and benefits on which unions are built. Research indicates that unions are effective in achieving this economic goal. One research study has estimated that unionized employees in Canada receive approximately 15 percent more in wages than nonunionized workers who possess similar attributes and work in similar jobs.[6]

Dissatisfaction with Management

Employees may seek unionization when they perceive that managerial practices regarding promotion, transfer, shift assignment, or other job-related policies are administered in an unfair or biased manner. Employees cite favouritism shown by managers as a major reason for joining unions. This is particularly true when the favouritism concerns the HR areas of discipline, promotion, and wage increases.

The failure of employers to give employees an opportunity to participate in decisions affecting their welfare may also encourage union membership. It is widely believed that one reason managers begin employee involvement programs and seek to empower their employees is to avoid collective action by employees. In a highly publicized organizing effort by the United Auto Workers at one Nissan plant, the union lost the election because workers were satisfied with the voice in decision making that Nissan's participatory style of management gave them. Nissan's director of HR noted, "We pride ourselves in being a company that functions in a participatory way. The vote was a statement of support for the strongly participatory management at Nissan."[7]

Social and Status Concerns

Employees whose needs for status and recognition are being frustrated may join unions as a means of satisfying these needs. Through their union, they have an opportunity to fraternize with other employees who have similar desires, interests, problems, and gripes. Joining the union also enables them to put leadership talents to use.

The limited studies conducted on employee unionization in the public sector generally find public employees unionizing for reasons similar to those of their private-sector counterparts. For example, higher wages and benefits, job security, and protection against arbitrary and unfair management treatment are primary motives for unionization among public-sector employees. However, other issues such as professional development and participation in decision making are perceived as important. In the final analysis, the extent to which employees perceive that the benefits of joining a union outweigh the costs associated with membership is likely to be the deciding factor.[8]

Gender, Race, and Ethnic Issues in Unionization

While managers have always been interested in discovering why employees unionize, recent interest and research have focused on those groups of workers who show the greatest propensity to unionize. For example, an important finding of one study showed that white-collar women, representing over half of the female nonunion workforce, are more favourably disposed toward voting for a union than are their male counterparts. The Corporation and Labour Unions Returns Act (CALURA) reported that female membership in Canadian labour unions grew nearly eight times faster than male membership in the 1980s. The proportion of female union members rose from 16.6 percent in 1965 to 37.2 percent in 1987. Nearly 60 percent of these women work in service industries such as health and education.[9] Women's prounion sentiments may reflect their belief that a union can improve their wages and enable them to participate more favourably in workplace decisions.[10] Some feminist trade unionists have been working diligently to convince union leaders and members that a new agenda is needed to ensure the equality of women and men in the workplace. The balancing of constituent demands is illustrated in Reality Check.

As increasing numbers of visible minorities enter the labour force, unions have had to respond to concerns about discrimination in employment. In 1981, the Ontario Federation of Labour launched an advertising campaign to increase public awareness that "racism hurts everyone." Subsequently, it organized seminars across the province to sensitize union members to the issues of systemic racial discrimination. Larger unions such as the Canadian Auto Workers have made issues of fair treatment part of their negotiations.[11]

Organizing Campaigns

objective

Once employees desire to unionize, a formal organizing campaign may be started either by a union organizer or by employees acting on their own behalf. Contrary to popular belief, most organizing campaigns are begun by employees rather than by union organizers. Large national unions like the Canadian Auto Workers, the United Brotherhood of Carpenters, the United Steelworkers, and the Teamsters, however, have formal organizing departments whose purpose is to identify organizing opportunities and launch organizing campaigns.

Since such campaigns can be expensive, union leaders carefully evaluate their chances of success and the possible benefits to be gained from their efforts. Important in this evaluation is the employer's vulnerability to unionization.[12] Union leaders also consider the effect that allowing an employer to remain nonunion may have on the strength of their union within the area. A nonunion employer can impair a union's efforts to standardize employment conditions within an industry or geographic area, as well as weaken the union's bargaining power with employers it has unionized.

Organizing Steps

Gary Fane, organizing director, Canadian Auto Workers (CAW), notes that the typical organizing campaign follows a series of progressive steps that can lead to employee representation. The organizing process normally includes the following steps:

1. Employee/union contact
2. Initial organizational meeting

> ▶ **REALITY CHECK** ◀   *RC* ◀

THE CANADIAN AUTO WORKERS

Buzz Hargrove, president of the Canadian Auto Workers, oversees the operations of Canada's largest private-sector union. The CAW was established in 1985 after breaking away from its American affiliate, the United Auto Workers. Membership has since increased from 118,000 to 208,000 through mergers with twenty other unions, including Mine Mill Workers, the Canadian Brotherhood of Railway Transportation, and General Workers. In an interview, Hargrove explained the CAW structure:

"Our union is a centrally directed organization. The CAW council meets three times a year with our national workplace representatives to openly discuss issues and establish policies that affect our members. The policy issues include social, collective bargaining, economic, or international issues. Whatever could possibly affect our workers is discussed. This is referred to as an 'accountability session.' We are the only union that discusses matters with our local leadership on a national basis so frequently. Working collectively as a team brings the issues to the forefront of all our representatives' minds, and makes us a more solid force to better represent our members. The real strength in our union is this ability we have to bring local leadership together with the national leadership to collectively debate issues that affect our membership.

"Every three years, we hold a conference to discuss collective bargaining and political education issues. At this conference we develop our collective bargaining objectives—such as wages, pensions, benefits, work hours, job creation, equality, and diversity—for the next three years. Through our strong representation of women, we have been able to better understand their issues and represent them more fairly than we had in the past. We also hold our constitutional convention every three years, where elections of union officers takes place.

"The strength of our structure is built around the auto industry. When we win concessions through these negotiations, there is a spin-off effect felt throughout the entire union. We often help other workers who are represented in other unions win rights because we instil confidence in all workers that certain issues can be won.

"Our members join unions for different reasons. Some members want their earnings levels to increase. Others feel that earning respect for their years of service is important. For others, [union membership] may be centred on equality issues, or affordable housing, or child-care arrangements. However, the majority of our members are realistic about what they can expect in their own set of negotiations.

"I am personally concerned that we have lost some of our political base over the past few years. Our members are not listening to social issues such as employment equity or same-sex spousal coverage, or issues like gun control. On a national basis, we supported gun control, but a number of our members did not agree, and we have been debating the issue for a long time.

"The future of the CAW is to increase the size of our union by signing on new members and more union mergers. There are a lot of smaller unions that do not have the resources to represent their membership appropriately; by pooling resources, they will be better represented. We also can't keep increasing our member dues. [Our members] have been faced with large tax increases and they just can't make any more financial sacrifices. The manufacturing sector will remain an important target, since we believe that it will continue to grow over the next few decades. The service sector will be another target. Key to these strategies will be the rebuilding of our political base in Canada and finding means to bring our members around to the concepts of equity and diversity."

Source: Interview with Deborah M. Zinni, August 1995.

3. Formation of in-house organizing committee
4. Application to labour relations board
5. Issuance of certificate by labour relations board
6. Election of bargaining committee and contract negotiations.

Step 1. The first step begins when employees and union officials make contact to explore the possibility of unionization. During these discussions, employees will investigate the advantages of labour representation, and union officials will begin to gather information on employee needs, problems, and grievances. Labour organizers will also seek specific information about the employer's financial health, supervisory styles, and organizational policies and practices. To win employee support, labour organizers must build a case against the employer and for the union.

Step 2. As an organizing campaign gathers momentum, the organizer will schedule an initial union meeting to attract more supporters. The organizer will use the information gathered in step 1 to address employee needs and explain how the union can secure these goals. Two additional purposes of organizational meetings are (1) to identify employees who can help the organizer direct the campaign, and (2) to establish communication chains that reach all employees.

Step 3. The third important step in the organizing drive is to form an in-house organizing committee composed of employees willing to provide leadership to the campaign. The committee's role is to interest other employees in joining the union and in supporting its campaign. An important task of the committee is to have employees sign an **authorization card** (see Highlights in HRM 1) indicating their willingness to be represented by a labour union in collective bargaining with their employer. The number of signed authorization cards demonstrates the potential strength of the labour union. Legislation across Canada states that unions must have a majority of employees as members in a bargaining unit before they can apply for certification election. However, most jurisdictions now interpret this to mean that at least 50 percent of those voting constitute a majority. In other words, those who do not cast ballots are not assumed to be voting against the certification of the union. The union membership card, once signed, is confidential and only the labour board has access to the cards.

Step 4. Application is made to the appropriate labour relations board. In Canada, a majority of unions are certified without a vote if the labour relations board finds that the union does has the support of the majority of the employees, based on the number of signed cards.

Step 5. The labour relations board reviews the application, and a certificate is issued (see Highlights in HRM 2). This certificate allows the union to represent the employees as a recognized union under provincial labour relations legislation.

Step 6. Once the certification is issued, the bargaining committee is elected by secret ballot. A national representative works with the bargaining committee to negotiate a collective agreement with the company. The committee is often assisted by specialists in benefits and health and safety.

Employer Tactics

Employers must not interfere with the labour relations process of certification. They are prohibited by law from dismissing, disciplining, or threatening employees for exercising their rights to form a union. Employers cannot promise better conditions,

---

Authorization card

A statement signed by an employee authorizing a union to act as a representative of the employee for purposes of collective bargaining.

HIGHLIGHTS IN HRM

HRM
highlights

1   **CANADIAN AUTO WORKERS UNION AUTHORIZATION CARD**

CAW ⬥ TCA CANADA

OFFICIAL APPLICATION FOR MEMBERSHIP

NATIONAL AUTOMOBILE, AEROSPACE, TRANSPORTATION AND GENERAL WORKERS UNION OF CANADA (CAW-CANADA)

National Headquarters: 205 Placer Court, North York, Willowdale, Ont. M2H 3H9

I hereby apply for and accept membership in, and authorize the C.A.W.-Canada, its agents or representatives, to act for me as my exclusive representative in collective bargaining, in respect to all the terms and conditions of my employment and to enter into contract with my employer covering all such matters.

X Date .... 19 ....   **X** ....

Signature of Applicant

Application for membership received by ....

Signature of Recipient

X Date .... 19 ....

Form 0-301-94   63

(OVER)

VOID

May we mail letters to your home?   YES ☐   NO ☐

LAST NAME PRINT

FIRST NAME

ADDRESS .... APT. # ....

CITY .... PROV. ....

POSTAL CODE .... PHONE # (.....) ....   SHIFT   DAYS ☐   AFTERNOONS ☐   MIDNIGHTS ☐

Employed by .... Employee No. ....
(NAME OF FIRM)

CLASSIFICATION .... SALARY OR HOURLY RATE ....

HOW LONG EMPLOYED (Approx.) .... DEPT. NO. ....

VOID

Source: CAW-Canada

2 CERTIFICATION NOTICE

**ALBERTA
LABOUR
RELATIONS
BOARD
NOTICE TO EMPLOYER
AND EMPLOYEES**

On (Application date) the (Applicant name) applied under the Labour Relations Code to become the certified bargaining agent for a unit of employees of (Respondent name) comprising:

(Bargaining unit applied for)

The Board will hear submissions from affected parties and decide on this application at a hearing, to be held:

DATE OF HEARING: (hearing date)
TIME: (hearing start time)
LOCATION: (hearing room)
                                    (hearing address)
                                    (hearing city province)

If the Board finds that the application meets the Code's requirements, it will conduct a secret ballot representation vote. The ballot will ask employees if they want the applicant trade union to represent them in collective bargaining with the employer.

Employees with objections to this application must file them with the Board in writing, providing full particulars to support their position. The objections must be received by the Board at least one full business day before the hearing. If they are not received within that time frame, the Board may proceed without considering the objections and make its decision on the material before it.

Should the affected employees wish, they may have an agent or lawyer represent them at the hearing. People filing objections, or their spokesperson, must attend the hearing to give evidence and argument to support their position. If no one objects to the application, the Board may cancel the hearing.

If you have any questions regarding this matter please contact (LRO responsible) or any other Board Officer at 427-8547 in Edmonton or 297-2338 in Calgary, or toll free to the Edmonton Office at 1-800-463-ALRB (2572).

If any person has any questions relating to this matter, please contact:

Director of Settlement   Labour Relations Board
Labour Relations Board   #308, 1212 – 31 Avenue N.E.
#503, 10808 – 99 Avenue   Deerfoot Junction, Tower 3
Edmonton, Alberta T5K 0G5   Calgary, Alberta T2E 7S8
Tel: 427-8547   Tel: 297-2338

1-800-463-ALRB (2572)

such as increased vacation days, if the employees vote for no union or choose one union over another. They cannot unilaterally change wages and working conditions during certification proceedings or during collective bargaining. Like unions, they must bargain in good faith, meaning that they must demonstrate a commitment to bargain seriously and fairly. In addition, they cannot participate in the formation, selection, or support of unions representing employees.

None of these prohibitions prevents an employer from making the case that the employees have a right not to join a union or that they can deal directly with the employer on any issue. When Wal-Mart consolidated its entry into Canada by buying 122 nonunionized Woolco stores, the company was widely viewed as anti-union. However, Wal-Mart spokespersons insist that they are not anti-union, but rather "pro-associate" (the Wal-Mart term for the retail sales clerk). During a 1995 organizing drive by the United Food and Commercial Workers Union, Wal-Mart's management stated that they believed strongly in their people, would take care of them, and were ready to listen and discuss any issue.[13]

Attempts by employers to influence employees are scrutinized closely by both officials of the organizing unions and the labour relations board. In one case, an employer interfered with the organizing process, and the union was automatically recognized by the labour board, with only 5 percent of the employees having signed the authorization cards.[14]

Union Tactics

Unions also have a duty to act in accordance with labour legislation. Unions are prohibited from interfering with the formation of an employer's organization. They cannot intimidate or coerce employees to become or remain members of a union. Nor can they force employers to dismiss, discipline, or discriminate against nonunion employees. They must provide fair representation for all employees in the **bargaining unit**, whether in collective bargaining or in grievance procedure cases. Unions cannot engage in activities such as strikes before the expiration of the union contract.

Any of the prohibited activities listed above for both employers and unions are considered **unfair labour practices (ULPs)**. Charges of ULPs are registered with the labour relations board, whose duty is to enforce the Industrial Relations Disputes and Investigations Act (IRDI). Over 1200 charges of unfair labour practices against employers were levied in 1992–93 under federal legislation, as compared with 313 charges against unions in the same period.[15]

How Employees Become Unionized

The procedures for union certification vary across Canadian jurisdictions. As mention earlier, the common practice is for unions to present documentation to the appropriate labour relations board for certification. The labour relations board must certify a union in order for it to act as a bargaining unit for a group of employees. The union must demonstrate that it has obtained the minimum level of membership support required by the labour relations board in order to acquire certification. The union normally provides evidence by submitting signed authorization cards and proof that initiation dues or fees have been paid.[16] Recognition of a union may be obtained through voluntary recognition, regular certification, or a prehearing vote.

Bargaining unit
Group of two or more employees who share common employment interests and conditions and may reasonably be grouped together with additional employees who have common employment interests and conditions for purposes of collective bargaining,

Unfair labour practices (ULPs)
Specific employer and union illegal practices that operate to deny employees their rights and benefits under federal and provincial labour laws.

Voluntary Recognition

All employers, except those in the province of Quebec, may voluntarily recognize and accept a union. This rarely happens, except in the construction industry where there is a great reliance on union hiring halls.

Regular Certification

The regular certification process begins with the union submitting the required minimum membership evidence to the labour relations board. Generally, if an applicant union can demonstrate that it has sufficient support in the proposed bargaining unit, labour boards may grant certification on that basis. (However, with changes in government, labour relations legislation is often reformed. Therefore, requirements for granting certification may change.) The labour relations board may order a representative vote if a sizable minority of workers have indicated either support or opposition to the unionization. Then a formal election is held.

Prehearing Votes

If there is evidence of irregularities, such as unfair labour practices taking place during the organizing drive, a prehearing vote may be taken. The purpose of this vote is to establish the level of support among the workers. In jurisdictions where the prehearing vote is allowed, the labour relations board will conduct the vote and seal the ballots pending the outcome of the investigation. If the labour relations board determines that the employees support the union, then it will certify the union. Failure to reach the required proportional support could result in decertification of the union.

Decertification

All legislation allows for decertification of unions under certain conditions. If the majority of employees indicate that they do not want to be represented by the union or that they want to be represented by another union, or if the union has failed to bargain, an application for decertification can be made to the labour relations board. If a collective agreement has been reached with the employer, this application can be made only at specified times, such as a few months before the agreement expires. The application for decertification can be initiated by either employees or the employer if the union fails to bargain.

Contract Negotiation

Once a bargaining unit has been certified by the labour relations board, the employer and the union are legally obliged to bargain in good faith over the terms and conditions of a collective agreement. Normally the terms of a collective agreement apply for a minimum of one year and a maximum of three years. As the contract expiry date approaches, either party must notify the other of its intention to bargain for a renewal collective agreement or contract negotiation.

Impact of Unionization on HRM

The unionization of employees can affect HRM in several ways. Perhaps most significant is the effect it can have on the prerogatives exercised by management in making decisions about employees. Furthermore, unionization restricts the freedom of management to formulate HR policy unilaterally and can challenge the authority of supervisors.

Challenges to Management Prerogatives

Unions typically attempt to achieve greater participation in management decisions that affect their members. Specifically, these decisions may involve such issues as the subcontracting of work, productivity standards, and job content. Employers quite naturally seek to claim many of these decisions as their exclusive **management prerogatives**—decisions over which management claims exclusive rights. However, these prerogatives are subject to challenge and erosion by the union, whether at the bargaining table, through the grievance procedure, or through strikes.

Bilateral Formulation of HR Policies

Some HR policies, such as those covering wages, work hours, work rules, and benefits, must be consistent with the terms of the collective agreement. When formulating these policies, management should consult with the union to gain the union's acceptance of them as well as its cooperation in administering them. Because unions are on the lookout for inconsistencies in the treatment of employees, a more centralized coordination in the enforcement of HR policies may be required. Such coordination provides a greater role for the HR staff.

Possible Dilution of Supervisory Authority

The focal point of the union's impact is at the operating level, where supervisors administer the terms of the collective agreement. These terms can determine what corrective action is to be taken in directing and in disciplining employees. When disciplining employees, supervisors must be certain they can demonstrate just cause for their actions, because these actions can be challenged by the union and the supervisor called as defendant during a grievance hearing. If the challenge is upheld, the supervisor's effectiveness in coping with subsequent disciplinary problems may be impaired.

objective

Structures, Functions, and Leadership of Labour Unions

Unions that represent skilled craft workers, such as carpenters or masons, are called **craft unions**. Craft unions include the International Brotherhood of Electric Workers, the United Brotherhood of Carpenters and Joiners of America, and the United Association of Journeymen and Apprentices of the Plumbing and Pipefitting Industry. Unions that represent unskilled and semiskilled workers employed along industry lines are known as **industrial unions**. The Canadian Union of Postal Workers is an industrial union, as are the United Steelworkers of America, the Office and Professional Employees International Union, and the Ontario Secondary School Teachers' Federation. While the distinction between craft and industrial unions still exists, technological changes and competition among unions for members have helped to reduce it. Today skilled and unskilled workers, white-collar and blue-collar workers, and professional groups are being represented by both types of union.

Management prerogatives
Decisions regarding organizational operations over which management claims exclusive rights.

Craft unions
Unions that represent skilled craft workers.

Industrial unions
Unions that represent all workers—skilled, semiskilled, unskilled—employed along industry lines.

Teachers are examples of white-collar professionals in unions.

Employee associations
Labour organizations that represent various groups of professional and white-collar employees in labour–management relations, but that have not been certified by a labour relations board.

Besides unions, there are also **employee associations** representing various groups of professional and white-collar employees. Examples of employee associations include the Federation of Quebec Nurses and the Alberta Teachers' Association. In competing with unions, these associations, for all purposes, may function as unions and become just as aggressive as unions in representing members.

Regardless of their type, labour organizations are diverse organizations, each with their own method of governance and objectives. Furthermore, they have their own structures that serve to bind them together. For example, when describing labour organizations, most researchers divide them into three levels: (1) central labour congresses, (2) international and national unions, and (3) local unions belonging to a parent national or international union. Each level has its own purpose for existence as well as its own operating policies and procedures.

Structure and Functions of the Canadian Labour Congress

The Canadian Labour Congress (CLC) is a central federation of unions that, as Figure 15-2 illustrates, is similar in structure to the American Federation of Labor and Congress of Industrial Organizations (AFL-CIO). The two organizations operate independently, although many local unions are members of both organizations.

The CLC represents most of the unions in Canada. Its total membership in 1993 was reported at 2.4 million, or 59.7 percent of unionized employees.[17] Due to its size and resources, the CLC is considered the most influential labour federation in Canada. It is primarily a service organization representing over 90 international and national unions that finance the CLC through dues, based on membership size. Like the AFL-CIO, the CLC attempts to influence legislation and promote programs that are of interest to labour. It does this by lobbying, resolving jurisdictional disputes, maintaining ethical stands, providing education and training to its

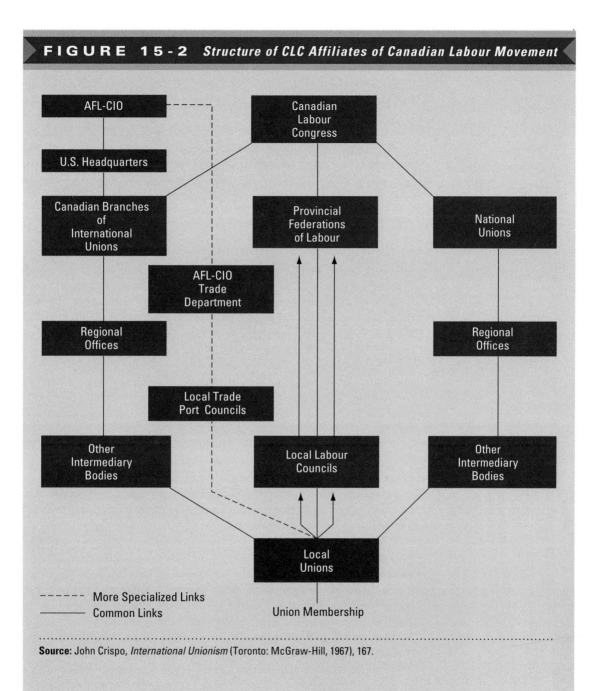

FIGURE 15-2 *Structure of CLC Affiliates of Canadian Labour Movement*

Source: John Crispo, *International Unionism* (Toronto: McGraw-Hill, 1967), 167.

members, conducting research, and representing Canadian interests within the international labour movement.

Every year, the CLC presents a memorandum to the federal government. Often critical of government policy (e.g., the CLC opposed both the FTA and NAFTA), this memorandum outlines the labour movement objectives that the CLC thinks the government should pursue. The CLC reacts to changes in economic conditions such as the unemployment rate by issuing press releases. As knowledge and service workers are being targeted for certification, the CLC is playing an increasingly important jurisdictional role in refereeing disputes between unions competing for the same workers. The CLC does not have any formal authority over its members and must align its members in common causes by consensus and moral suasion.

Structure and Functions of International and National Unions

International unions tend to be affiliates of American unions, with headquarters in the United States. The large membership base provides a good deal of financial leverage to local unions engaged in strike action. For example, the merger of three international unions—the United Steelworkers of America, the United Auto Workers, and the International Association of Machinists—into the largest industrial union in North America resulted in a strike fund of $1 billion.[18]

Both international and national unions are made up of local unions. The objectives of these unions are to help organize local unions, to provide strike support, and to assist local unions with negotiations, grievance procedures, and the like. These unions also represent membership interest with internal and external constituents. By ensuring that all employers pay similar wages to their unionized workers, they serve the additional role of removing higher wages as a competitive disadvantage.[19]

In Canada, most of the decision-making authority in national unions is vested in the local union or at the bargaining unit level. This is often referred to as "bottom-up unionism." Many international unions, particularly craft unions, are more likely to retain a greater degree of control over the affairs of the local union. This is often referred to as "top-down unionism."

The officers of both types of union typically include a president, a secretary-treasurer, and several vice-presidents, all officially elected. These officers make up the executive board, which is the top policy-making body. A typical national structure is depicted in Figure 15-3. Other positions at the national level include lawyer, economist, statistician, and public relations officer. An economics director gathers, analyzes, and disseminates economic and other information of value in collective bargaining. Many national unions also have an education director whose job is to provide training for local union officers and stewards.

International and national unions often have social and political objectives outside their traditional goal of representing member interests. This is a contentious issue, as discussed in Ethics in HRM.

Structure and Functions of Local Unions

Employees of any organization can form their own union, with no affiliation to a national or international union. In this case, the local is the union. However, most

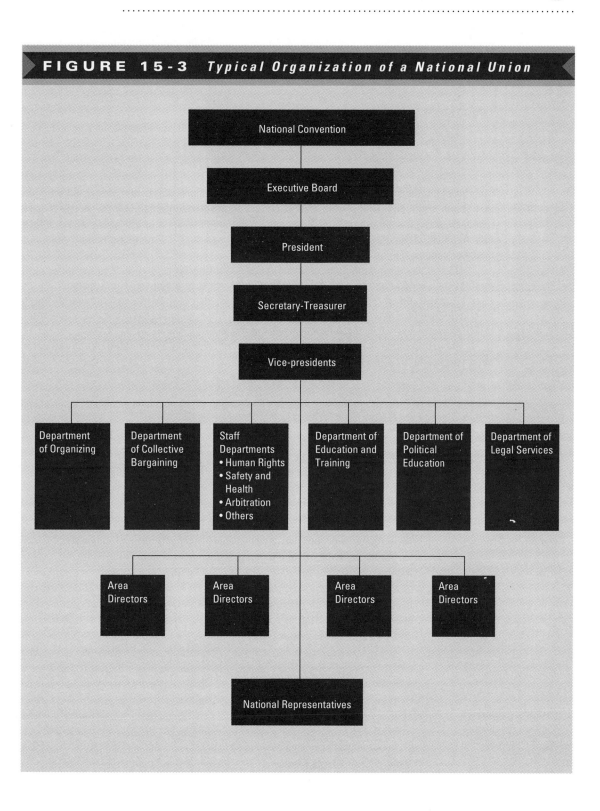

FIGURE 15-3 *Typical Organization of a National Union*

> ▶ **ETHICS IN HRM**
>
> ### UNION DUES
>
> Members of unions and associations pay dues to support union activities. Most of this money is used to finance traditional union activities such as contract negotiation, labour market and economic research, and grievance handling. However, sometimes the union, particularly at the international or national level, dedicates some of these funds to causes such as opposing human rights violations in China or supporting gun control in Canada.
>
> Union members challenged, under the Canadian Charter of Rights, their obligation to contribute through their union dues to political causes with which they disagree. The Supreme Court of Canada ruled (1) that trade unions are not in violation of the Charter if they use union dues for purposes other than collective bargaining in the narrow sense, and (2) that unionized workers who object to the use of their dues have to try to get the money back themselves.
>
> Should union dues be allocated for purposes other than those related directly to contract negotiation and collective bargaining?
>
> **Sources:** P.E. Larson, "Fighting for Labour," *Canadian Business Review* 13, no. 4 (Winter 1986): 8–12; and P. Poiter, "Court Dashes Labour's Hope of More Rights," *The Globe and Mail*, June 28, 1991, A5.

local unions are members of national/international unions or the CLC, which make available to them financial resources and advice. There are an estimated 13,000 locals in Canada.

Each dues-paying member has one vote and can participate in the election of the officials. Smaller unions typically have a president, a secretary-treasurer, and an executive board. Larger locals have a business agent, and a negotiating committee and/or a grievance committee.

The officers of a local union are usually responsible for negotiating the local collective agreement, for ensuring the agreement is adhered to, and for investigating and processing member grievances. Most important, they assist in preventing the members of the local union from being treated by their employers in ways that run counter to management-established HR policies.[20] They also keep members informed through meetings and newsletters.

Role of the Shop Steward
Regardless of size, all locals have at least one **shop steward** who is usually elected by the employees of each department in the organization. The shop steward's job is to

Shop steward
Employee who as a nonpaid union official represents the interests of members in their relations with management.

protect the rights of workers and represent their interests in relations with immediate supervisors and other members of management. Since stewards are full-time employees of the organization, they tend to spend considerable time, after working hours, investigating and handling member problems. When stewards represent members during grievance meetings on organization time, their wages are paid by the local union, or by the company if provided for in the collective agreement.

As described by Al Nash, the union steward is a person caught between conflicting interests and groups:

> The steward's role as grievance handler and maid-of-all-work for the union thrusts him/her into a number of roles. He/she represents the workers in the internal and external government of the union and in negotiating with management. He/she is an agent of the union leadership within the workplace and, to some extent, a quasi-agent of management in enforcing the collective bargaining agreement and company rules. His/her role-set, then, consists of members of his/her own constituency, some of whom may be non-union members, members of immediate management, and higher union officials with whom he/she must deal.[21]

It is evident from the preceding definition that if stewards perform their tasks effectively, they serve as important links between union members and their employer. Their attitudes and actions can have an important bearing on union–management cooperation and on the efficiency and morale of the employees they represent.[22]

Role of the Business Agent

Negotiating and administering the labour agreement and working to resolve problems arising in connection with it are major responsibilities of the **business agent**. In performing these duties, business agents must be all things to all persons within their unions. They frequently are required to assume the role of counsellor in helping union members with both personal and job-related problems. They are also expected to dispose satisfactorily of the members' grievances that cannot be settled by the union stewards. Administering the daily affairs of the local union is another significant part of the business agent's job.

Business agent
Normally a paid labour official responsible for negotiating and administering the labour agreement and working to resolve union members' problems.

Union Leadership Approaches and Philosophies

To evaluate the role of union leaders accurately, one must understand the nature of their backgrounds and ambitions and recognize the political nature of the offices they occupy. The national leaders of many unions have been able to develop political alliances that enable them to defeat opposition candidates and to perpetuate themselves in office.[23] Tenure for the leaders of a local union, however, is less secure. In the local union, it is quite common for officers to run for re-election at least every two years. If they are to remain in office, they must be able to convince a majority of the members that they are serving them effectively.

Although it is true that union leaders occupy positions of power within their organizations, rank-and-file members can and often do exercise a very strong influence over these leaders, particularly with respect to the negotiation and administration of the collective agreement. It is important for managers to understand that union officials are elected to office and, like any political officials, must be responsive to the views of their constituency. The union leader who ignores the demands of union members may risk (1) being voted out of office, (2) having members vote the union out as their bargaining agent, (3) having members refuse to ratify the collective agreement, or (4) having members engage in wildcat strikes or work stoppages.

To be effective leaders, labour officials must also pay constant attention to the general goals and philosophies of the labour movement. **Business unionism** is the general label given to the goals of many labour organizations: increased pay and benefits, job security, and improved working conditions. Furthermore, union leaders also know that unions must address the broader social, economic, and legislative issues of concern to members. For example, the Canadian Auto Workers continually lobbies for legislation favourable to the auto industry. The CLC has been an active promoter of women's issues and policies promoting job creation over deficit reduction. Finally, as part of Canada's adjustment to increased global competition, union leaders are forced to concentrate on more intangible quality-of-work-life issues while attempting to make their employing industries more competitive.

Business unionism
Term applied to the goals of labour organizations, which collectively bargain for improvements in wages, hours, job security, and working conditions.

objective

Labour Relations in the Public Sector

Collective bargaining among federal, provincial, and municipal government employees, and among employees in parapublic agencies (private agencies or branches of the government acting as extensions of government programs), has increased dramatically since the 1960s. Over 75 percent of all public employees belong to a union.[24] The three largest unions in Canada represent public-sector employees. The Canadian Union of Public Employees (CUPE) is the largest union in Canada, representing 412,200 members. The second largest union, with 307,600 members, is the National Union of Provincial Government Employees (NUPGE), which represents employees at the provincial level. The largest union representing employees at the federal level is the Public Service Alliance of Canada (PSAC), with 171,100 members. The PSAC is made up of seventeen different unions representing various groups such as the Professional Institute of the Public Service of Canada (PIPS), the Economists, Sociologists and Statisticians Associations (ESSA), and the Air Traffic Controllers.[25] Growth in these unions is threatened by increased cost-cutting efforts of governments at all levels, resulting in employee reductions.

While public- and private-sector collective bargaining have many features in common, a number of factors differentiate the two sectors. In this section, we will highlight several of the major differences between public-sector and private-sector industrial relations and discuss how these differences affect HRM. Three areas will be explored: (1) legislation governing collective bargaining

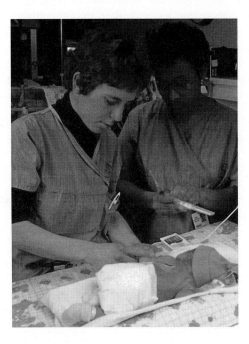

Nurses often have different interests when negotiating their labour agreements

in the public sector, (2) the political nature of the labour–management relationship, and (3) public-sector strikes.

Public-Sector Legislation

The Public Service Staff Relations Act (PSSRA), passed by Parliament in 1967, grants to federal civil servants bargaining rights, including the right to strike and the right to bargain for wages, hours, and working conditions. The PSSRA created the Public Service Staff Relations Board, which, like the labour relations boards governing the private sector, has responsibility for certification of unions as bargaining agents and for conflict resolution. Differences between the labour relations boards and the PSSRB are discussed later in the chapter.

At the provincial level, labour legislation applies to both the public and private sectors. For example, the Quebec Labour Code, the Saskatchewan Trade Union Act, and the British Columbia Industrial Relations Act apply to both sectors. Other jurisdictions may operate under more than one piece of legislation; in Ontario, for example, seven different statutes are operative. Some statutes cover more than one sector; in jurisdictions like New Brunswick, for example, statutes cover hospitals, schools, and public utilities. See Figure 15-4 for a list of provincial public-sector labour legislation.

Political Nature of the Labour–Management Relationship

Government employees are not able to negotiate with their employers on the same basis as their counterparts in private organizations. It is doubtful that they will ever be able to do so because of inherent differences between the public and private sectors.

One of the significant differences is that labour relations in the private sector has an economic foundation, whereas in government its foundation tends to be political. Since private employers must stay in business in order to sell their goods or services, their employees are not likely to make demands that could bankrupt them. A strike in the private sector is a test of the employer's economic staying power, and usually the employer's customers have alternative sources of supply. Governments, on the other hand, must stay in business because alternative services are usually not available.

Another difference between the labour–management relationship in the public and private sectors is the source of management authority. In a private organization, the authority flows downward from the board of directors and, ultimately, from the shareholders. In the public sector, however, authority flows upward from the public at large to their elected representatives and to the appointed or elected managers. Therefore public employees can exert influence not only as union members but also as pressure groups and voting citizens.[26]

Strikes in the Public Sector

Strikes by government employees create a problem for lawmakers and for the general public. Because the services that government employees provide, such as police work and firefighting, are often considered essential to the well-being of the public, public

FIGURE 15-4 *Public-Sector Labour Legislation*

JURISDICTION	HOSPITALS	TEACHERS	CIVIL SERVICE	GOVERNMENT ENTERPRISE
Federal	Public Service Staff Relations Act	Public Service Staff Relations Act	Public Service Staff Relations Act	Canada Labour Code
British Columbia	Labour Relations Code	Labour Relations Code	Public Service Labour Relations Act	Labour Relations Code
Alberta	Labour Relations Code	Labour Relations Code	Public Service Employee Relations Act	Labour Relations Code
Saskatchewan	Trade Union Act	Education Act	Trade Union Act	Trade Union Act
Manitoba	Labour Relations Act	Public Schools Act	Labour Relations Act; Civil Service Act	Labour Relations Act
Ontario	Labour Relations Act; Hospital Labour Disputes Arbitration Act	School Boards and Teachers Collective Negotiations Act	Crown Employees Collective Bargaining Act	Crown Employees Collective Bargaining Act; Labour Relations Act
Quebec	Labour Code; Public Service Act	Labour Code; Public Service Act	Labour Code; Public Service Act; Civil Service Act	Labour Code; Public Service Act; Civil Service Act
New Brunswick	Public Service Labour Relations Act	Public Service Labour Relations Act	Public Service Labour Relations Act	Public Service Labour Relations Act
Nova Scotia	Trade Union Act	Teachers' Collective Bargaining Act	Civil Service Collective Bargaining Act	Trade Union Act
PEI	Labour Act	School Act	Civil Service Act	Civil Service Act
Newfoundland	Public Service Collective Bargaining Act	Nfld. Teachers Collective Bargaining Act	Public Service Collective Bargaining Act	Public Service Collective Bargaining Act

JURISDICTION	PRIVATE SECTOR	MUNICIPAL	POLICE	FIREFIGHTERS
Federal	Canada Labour Code	Canada Labour Code	None for the RCMP	Public Service Staff Relations Act
British Columbia	Labour Relations Code	Labour Relations Code	Labour Relations Code	Labour Relations Code
Alberta	Labour Relations Code	Labour Relations Code	Police Officers Collective Bargaining Act	Labour Relations Code
Saskatchewan	Trade Union Act	Trade Union Act	Police Act	Fire Dept. Platoon Act
Manitoba	Labour Relations Act	Labour Relations Act	Labour Relations Act; Police Act; City of Winnipeg Act	Labour Relations Act; Fire Dept. Arbitration Act
Ontario	Labour Relations Act	Labour Relations Act	Police Services Act; Ontario Provincial Police Public Service Act	Fire Department's Act
Quebec	Labour Code	Labour Code	Labour Code, Div. II; Civil Service Act; Police Force Sûreté du Québec	Labour Code, Div. II
New Brunswick	Industrial Relations Act	Industrial Relations Act	Industrial Relations Act; Police Act	Industrial Relations Act
Nova Scotia	Trade Union Act	Trade Union Act	Trade Union Act	Trade Union Act
PEI	Labour Act	Labour Act	Labour Act; Police Act	Labour Act
Newfoundland	Labour Relations Act	Labour Relations Act	Labour Relations Act; Royal Newfoundland Constabulary Act	Labour Relations Act; St. John's Fire Dept. Act

Source: P. Barnade, "Labour Legislation and Public Policy Reference Tables" (Kingston: IRC Press, Queen's University, 1989).

policy is opposed to such strikes. However, various provincial legislatures have granted public employees the right to strike. Where striking is permitted, the right is limited to specific groups of employees—those performing nonessential services—and the strike cannot endanger the public's health, safety, or welfare. Public-sector unions contend, however, that by denying them the same right to strike as employees in the private sector, their power during collective bargaining is greatly reduced.

One test of the unions' right to strike occurred when the federal government, under provisions in the PSSRA, attempted to designate all air traffic controllers as essential, even though the parties had previously agreed that all commercial flights would be cancelled in the event of a strike by controllers. The dispute went all the way to the Supreme Court, which ruled in favour of the government and, furthermore, gave the government the authority to determine the necessary level of service. The federal government ultimately declared that 100 percent of the bargaining unit were essential employees.

Public employees who perform essential services do in fact strike. Teachers, sanitation employees, police, transit employees, firefighters, and postal employees have all engaged in strike action. To avoid a potentially critical situation, various arbitration methods are used for resolving collective bargaining deadlocks in the public sector. One is **compulsory binding arbitration** for employees such as police officers, firefighters, and others in jobs where strikes cannot be tolerated. Another method is **final-offer arbitration**, under which the arbitrator must select one or the other of the final offers submitted by the disputing parties. With this method, the arbitrator's award is more likely to go to the party whose final bargaining offer has moved the closest to a reasonable settlement. The government can also enact back-to-work legislation, an option being used with increasing frequency.

Compulsory binding arbitration
Binding method of resolving collective bargaining deadlocks by a neutral third party.

Final-offer arbitration
Method of resolving collective bargaining deadlocks whereby the arbitrator has no power to compromise but must select one or another of the final offers submitted by the two parties.

objective

Contemporary Challenges to Labour Organizations

Among the changes that pose challenges to labour organizations today are foreign competition and technological advances, a decline in labour's public image, the unionization of white-collar employees, and innovative work practices that have the potential to change employer–employee relations.

Foreign Competition and Technological Change

The importation of steel, consumer electronics, automobiles, clothing, textiles, and shoes from foreign countries creates a loss of jobs for workers who produce these products.[27] Furthermore, foreign subsidiaries of Canadian-owned corporations such as NorTel have been accused by labour unions of exporting the jobs of Canadian workers. As a result, unions are demanding more government protection against imports. Such protection has spurred lively parliamentary debate between those who argue that protective trade barriers create higher prices for consumers and those who seek to protect jobs from low-cost overseas producers. Canadian unions were highly opposed to passage of the North American Free Trade Agreement (NAFTA), claiming that Canadian jobs would be lost to low-wage employees in Mexico and to the hostile labour environment that exists in many U.S. states that have enacted "right to work" statutes that weaken union security provisions in the collective agreement.

Coupled with the threat of foreign competition is the challenge to labour brought about by rapid technological advances.[28] Improvements in computer technology and highly automated operating systems have lowered the demand for certain types of employees. Decline in membership in the auto, steel, rubber, and transportation unions illustrates this fact. Technological advances have also diminished the effectiveness of strikes because highly automated organizations are capable of maintaining satisfactory levels of operation with minimum staffing levels during work stoppages.

Decline in Public Image of Labour

Organized labour has suffered a decline in its public image.[29] For example, critics of labour cite wage increases gained by labour unions as a factor that not only contributes to inflation but also helps to drive products out of the foreign and domestic markets. Moreover, public resentment of strikes by public-sector unions has affected the image of all labour unions.[30]

At present, the labour movement is working toward creating a more favourable image of unions. The CAW, for example, has participated in many community events such as building a child-care centre for shift workers, developing more than 1000 affordable-housing units, leading United Way campaigns, contributing to food banks, women's shelters, and undertaking various projects in the Windsor area.[31]

However the public may feel about unions, union membership in Canada has increased slowly from 26.6 percent of the workforce in 1971 to 29.5 percent in 1993.[32] In fact, the actual number of union members is at an all-time high. The situation is very different in the United States, where the combination of a growing labour force and decreasing union membership dropped organized labour's share of the civilian workforce to a new modern-era low of 15.8 percent in 1993.[33] Union membership in the two countries is compared in Figure 15-5.

Efforts to Unionize White-Collar Employees

In past years, white-collar employees tended to identify themselves with owners or managers as a group enjoying certain privileges (e.g., not having to punch a time clock) and socioeconomic status that blue-collar workers did not possess. Improvements in working conditions, for which union members had to make sacrifices, generally were extended to the white-collar group without any need for collective action on their part. The high turnover rate of employees in clerical jobs also increased the difficulty of organizing them. For these reasons, and because union drives to organize white-collar employees were not attuned psychologically to their needs and thinking, white-collar employees have been slow to unionize. In recent years, however, growth in the size of private organizations has tended to depersonalize the work of white-collar groups and to isolate them from management. The lack of job security during layoffs, together with growing difficulties in attempting to resolve grievances, has helped to push white-collar workers toward unionization. Even disgruntled law students are becoming members of the Canadian Union of Public Employees.[34]

In response to these changes, unions are stepping up their efforts to organize white-collar workers. Some unions are targeting the financial sectors, including banking and insurance. Other unions are recruiting employees of small businesses

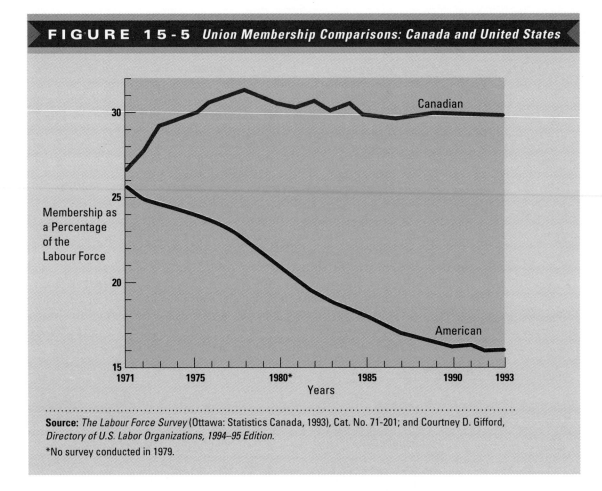

FIGURE 15-5 *Union Membership Comparisons: Canada and United States*

Source: *The Labour Force Survey* (Ottawa: Statistics Canada, 1993), Cat. No. 71-201; and Courtney D. Gifford, *Directory of U.S. Labor Organizations, 1994–95 Edition.*
*No survey conducted in 1979.

and employees in the so-called pink-collar ghetto, a term describing low-paying clerical and sales positions traditionally held by women. Unions are also capitalizing on new health and safety issues in white-collar jobs, such as the effects of working at video display terminals or working with potentially hazardous substances.

Innovative Workplace Practices

Organizations have been undergoing experiments in workplace restructuring that affect how work is organized and allocated.

The "autonomic-type" workplace, where employees are given a high degree of autonomy, and where performance is monitored and either rewarded or disciplined, may change union–management relationships.[35] Workplace structures that are emerging under this type of workplace include semi-autonomous work teams that determine work allocation, pace, skill upgrades, and the like. This kind of structure changes the role of the supervisor by reducing the need for rules, regulations, and close supervision. Pay in these environments is sometimes contingent upon performance, and profit sharing and gainsharing are increasing. Highlights in HRM 3 shows the percentage of innovative workplace practices in 1994.

HIGHLIGHTS IN HRM

3 PERCENTAGE OF INNOVATIVE WORKPLACE PRACTICES IN 1994

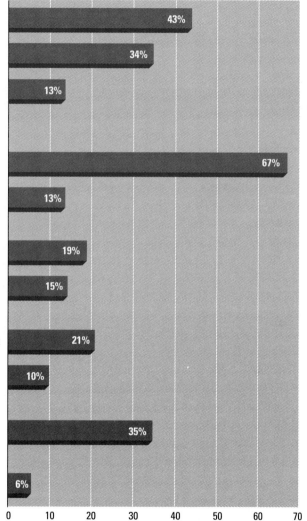

Organization of Work:
- Jobs: changes, consolidation, evaluation, flexibility — 43%
- Restructuring/reorganization/ job security/alternatives — 34%
- Work schedule/job sharing/ workweek/leave — 13%

Information, Consultation and Employee Involvement:
- Use of committee within the organization — 67%
- Teams and mutual assistance — 13%

Financial Innovations:
- Variable pay including bonus — 19%
- Gain and profit-sharing — 15%

Labour Relations:
- Bargaining process or content — 21%
- Harassment / Employment Equity — 10%

Training and Development:
- Training, skills upgrade, skills mix change — 35%

Technology:
- Technological change — 6%

Source: Based on 114 bargaining units reporting innovative practices (from a total of 407 settlements reported in the Collective Bargaining Review) Negotech, Workplace Information Labour Branch, Human Resources Development Canada, 1994.

Critics argue that innovative workplace practices undermine union power by co-opting employees and aligning employee interests with management interests.[36] However, one survey reported that workplace reorganization has had mainly neutral effects on the local unions. Some unions reported more input into decision making and less militant members.[37] One example of an innovative approach to the workplace that has yielded impressive results is the one created by unions and management at the highly automated Shell Canada plant in Sarnia, Ontario, where multiskilled workers are responsible for planning, scheduling, hiring, and training, and are compensated according to knowledge and skill. The result is higher output, low absenteeism, fewer grievances, and excellent product quality. The plant is seen as a model of a new approach to working life.[38]

SUMMARY

one objective

Labour relations legislation in Canada recognizes employee rights to form and join unions, and prohibits unfair labour practices on the part of both unions and employers. Provincial labour relations laws are administered and enforced by labour relations boards.

two objective

Studies show that workers unionize for different economic, psychological, and social reasons. While some employees may join unions because they are required to do so, most belong to unions because they are convinced that unions help them to improve their wages, benefits, and various working conditions. Employee unionization is largely caused by dissatisfaction with managerial practices and procedures.

three objective

A formal union organizing campaign will be used to solicit employee support for the union. In most jurisdictions, if more than 50 percent of those voting in the election vote for the union, the union will file an application with the labour relations board for approval of the union as the certified bargaining agent. The labour relations board has the option to call for a vote if it feels that there were irregularities in the application process.

four objective

The Canadian labour movement is composed of three basic units: (1) National labour federations such as the Canadian Labour Congress, a federation to which national and international unions can elect to belong; (2) international and national unions; and (3) local unions chartered by the various national and international labour organizations. National and international unions and their locals perform for members various functions that include negotiating the contract, handling grievances, training union officials, offering social functions, and providing legal and political activity.

five objective

Legislation governing labour relations in the public sector differs from private-sector legislation. A large number of public employees, especially those designated as providing essential services, are denied the right to strike. Another difference is that collective bargaining in the private sector has an economic base, whereas in the public sector the base is often political. Additionally, in the private sector, authority flows downward along clear lines of responsibility; in the public sector, authority flows upward and is much more diffuse in establishing clear authority.

objective

Challenges facing union leaders today include the effects of technology and international competition, the decline in labour's public image, the unionization of white-collar employees, and changing relations resulting from innovating work practices.

KEY TERMS

authorization card

bargaining unit

business agent

business unionism

compulsory binding arbitration

craft unions

employee associations

final-offer arbitration

industrial unions

labour relations process

management prerogatives

shop steward

unfair labour practices (ULPs)

union shop

DISCUSSION QUESTIONS

1. How is the management of an organization's human resources likely to be affected by the unionization of its employees?
2. Contrast the arguments concerning union membership that are likely to be presented by a union with those presented by an employer.
3. What are the functions of (i) the national or international union and (ii) the local union?
4. Which unfair labour practices apply to both unions and employers?
5. What arguments would public-sector managers put forth in opposition to unionization?
6. What are some of the actions being taken by unions to cope with the contemporary challenges they face?

....

CASE: # The Unfair Labour Practice Charge Against Northern Industries

Bob Thomas was discharged after nineteen years as a plant maintenance engineer with Northern Industries. During that time, he had received average and sometimes below-average annual performance appraisals. Thomas was known as something of a complainer and troublemaker, and he was highly critical of management. Prior to his termination, his attendance record for the previous five years had been very poor. However, Northern Industries had never enforced its attendance policy, and Thomas had never been disciplined for his attendance problems. In fact, until recently, Northern Industries management had been rather laid-back in its dealings with employees.

Northern Industries produces general component parts for the communications industry—an industry beset since 1989 by intense competitive pressures. To meet this competitive challenge, Jean Lipski, HR director, held a series of meetings with managers in which she instructed them to tighten up their supervisory relationship with employees. They were told to enforce HR policies strictly and to begin disciplinary action against employees who did not conform to company policy. These changes did not sit well with employees, particularly Bob Thomas. Upon hearing of the new management approach, Thomas became irate and announced, "They can't get away with this. I wrote the book around here." Secretly, Thomas believed his past conduct was catching up with him, and he became concerned about protecting his job.

One night after work, Thomas called a union organizer of the Brotherhood of Machine Engineers and asked that a union drive begin at Northern. Within a week employees began handing out flyers announcing a union meeting. When Lipski heard of the organizing campaign and Thomas's leadership in it, she decided to terminate his employment. Thomas's termination paper read: "Discharged for poor work performance and unsatisfactory attendance." Thomas was called into Lipski's office and told of the discharge. After leaving her office, Thomas called the union organizer, and they both went to the regional office of the labour relations board to file an unfair labour practice charge on Thomas's behalf. The ULP alleged that he was fired for his support of the union and the organizing drive.

Questions
1. What, if any, violation of the law did Northern Industries commit?
2. What arguments will Jean Lipski and Bob Thomas use to support their cases?

Conflict Management Styles

Managing conflict between employees and managers, bosses and subordinates, and co-workers is an important career skill. The following conflict management questionnaire will provide you with some feedback on how you handle conflict.

Indicate how often you do the following when you differ with someone.

WHEN I DIFFER WITH SOMEONE:

	Usually	Sometimes	Seldom
1. I explore our differences, not backing down, but not imposing my view either.	☐	☐	☐
2. I disagree openly, then invite more discussion about our differences.	☐	☐	☐
3. I look for a mutually satisfactory solution.	☐	☐	☐
4. Rather than let the other person make a decision without my input, I make sure I am heard and also that I hear the other out.	☐	☐	☐
5. I agree to a middle ground rather than look for a completely satisfying solution.	☐	☐	☐
6. I admit I am half wrong rather than explore our differences.	☐	☐	☐
7. I have a reputation for meeting a person halfway.	☐	☐	☐
8. I expect to get out about half of what I really want to say.	☐	☐	☐
9. I give in totally rather than to try to change another's opinion.	☐	☐	☐
10. I put aside any controversial aspects of an issue.	☐	☐	☐
11. I agree early on, rather than argue about a point.	☐	☐	☐
12. I give in as soon as the other party gets emotional about an issue.	☐	☐	☐
13. I try to win the other person over.	☐	☐	☐
14. I work to come out victorious, no matter what.	☐	☐	☐
15. I never back away from a good argument.	☐	☐	☐
16. I would rather win than end up compromising.	☐	☐	☐

Scoring Key and Interpretation

Total your choices as follows: Give yourself 5 points for "Usually," 3 points for "Sometimes," and 1 point for "seldom." Then total them for each set of statements, grouped as follows:

Set A: items 13–16   Set C: items 5–8
Set B: items 9–12   Set D: items 1–4

Treat each set separately. A score of 17 or above on any set is considered high; scores of 12 to 16 are moderately high; scores of 8 to 11 are moderately low; and scores of 7 or less are considered low.

Sets A, B, C, and D represent different conflict-resolution strategies:

A = Forcing/domination. I win, you lose.
B = Accommodation. I lose, you win.
C = Compromise. Both win some, lose some.
D = Collaboration. I win, you win.

Everyone has a basic or underlying conflict-handling style. Your scores on this exercise indicate the strategies you rely upon most.

Source: Reprinted with permission of Macmillan Publishing Co. From *Supervision: Managerial Skills for a New Era* by Thomas J. Von de Embse. Copyright © 1987 by Macmillan Publishing Co.

....

NOTES AND REFERENCES

1. C. Heron, *The Canadian Labour Movement: A Short History* (Toronto: James Lorimer & Company, 1989).
2. J.C. Anderson, M. Gunderson, and A. Ponak, *Union Management Relations in Canada,* 2nd ed. (Don Mills, ON: Addison-Wesley, 1989).
3. Readers interested in reading more about the labour relations process can consult J. Godard, *Industrial Relations: The Economy and Society* (Toronto: McGraw-Hill Ryerson, 1994); and Anderson, Gunderson, and Ponak, *Union Management Relations in Canada.*
4. Masoud Hemmasi and Lee A. Graf, "Determinants of Faculty Voting Behaviour in Union Representation Elections: A Multivariate Model," *Journal of Management* 19, no. 1 (Spring 1993): 13–32.
5. John A. Fossum, *Labor Relations: Development, Structure, Process,* 6th ed. (Homewood, IL: Irwin, 1995), 3.
6. R. Swidinsky and M. Kupferschmidt, "Longitudinal Estimates of the Union Effects on Wages, Wage Dispersion and Pension Fringe Benefits," *Relations Industrielles* 46 (1991): 720–749.
7. Stephenie Overman, "Nissan Sees Union's Loss as Management Style's Win," *Resource* 8, no. 10 (September 1989): 1.
8. Hugh D. Hindman and Charles G. Smith, "Correlates of Union Membership and Joining Intentions in a Unit of Federal Employees," *Journal of Labor Research* 14, no. 4 (Fall 1993): 441.
9. "Union Membership Patterns: The CALURA Report," *Worklife* 7, no. 2 (1989): 2–3.
10. Lisa A. Schur and Douglas L. Kruse, "Gender Differences in Attitudes toward Unions," *Industrial and Labor Relations Review* 46, no. 1 (October 1992): 89–102.
11. Heron, *The Canadian Labour Movement,* 157–159.
12. For a discussion of union organizers, see Thomas F. Reed, "Profiles of Union Organizers from Manufacturing and Service Unions," *Journal of Labor Research* 11, no. 1 (Winter 1990): 73–80.
13. J. Heinz, "Union Attempts to Organize Wal-Mart Stores in Ontario," *The Globe and Mail,* June 3, 1995, B3.
14. Discussion with CAW business representative, July 1995.
15. *20th Annual Report,* Canada Labour Relations Board, Labour Canada, 1992–93.
16. Canada Labour Relations Board regulations and Ontario Labour Relations Act.
17. *Union Membership in Canada 1993,* Government of Canada, Ottawa, 1993, 1, 10, 11.
18. T.V. Alphen, "Unions Eye Blockbuster Merger Plan," *The Toronto Star,* July 28, 1995, A3.
19. Godard, *Industrial Relations,* 228.
20. E. Kevin Kelloway and Julian Barling, "Members' Participation in Local Union Activities: Measurement, Prediction, and Replication," *Journal of Applied Psychology* 78, no. 2 (April 1993): 262–278.
21. The research of Al Nash on union stewards is considered a major work on these important labour officials. He is frequently cited when the function and power of union stewards is discussed. See Al Nash, *The Union Steward: Duties, Rights, and Status,* Key Issues Series no. 22 (Ithaca, NY: ILR Press, 1983), 11–12.
22. Researchers have discussed the erosion of shop steward power in contract administration. The loss of power has been attributed to bureaucratization and centralization of labour relations activity within both unions and management hierarchies. While no one doubts the influence—positive or negative—that stewards can have on labour–management relations, the shifting power of the steward is important in deciding labour–management controversies. See Patricia A. Simpson, "A Preliminary Investigation of Determinants of Local Union Steward Power," *Labor Studies Journal* 18, no. 2 (Summer 1993): 51–67.
23. J. Lawrence French, "The Power and Pay of International Union Officials," *Journal of Labor Research* 13, no. 2 (Spring 1992): 157–171.
24. *Union Membership in Canada 1993,* 7, Table 4.
25. A.W.J. Craig and N. Solomon, *The System of Industrial Relations in Canada* (Scarborough, ON: Prentice-Hall Canada, 1993), 260.
26. Harry C. Katz and Thomas A. Kochan, *An Introduction to Collective Bargaining and Industrial Relations* (New York: McGraw-Hill, 1992), 372–373.
27. Mark Partridge, "Technology, International Competitiveness, and Union Behaviour," *Journal of Labor Research* 14, no. 2 (Spring 1993): 131–145.
28. Yonatan Reshef, "Employees, Unions, and Technological Changes: A Research Agenda," *Journal of Labor Research* 14, no. 2 (Spring 1993): 111–127.
29. Diane E. Schmidt, "Public Opinion and Media Coverage of Labour Unions," *Journal of Labor Research* 14, no. 2 (Spring 1993): 151–163.
30. D. Girard, "Changing Face of the Labour Movement," *The Toronto Star,* August 8, 1995, A11.
31. Discussion with Susan Spratt, communications national representative, CAW, August 1995.
32. *The Labour Force Survey* (Ottawa: Statistics Canada, 1993), Cat. No. 71-201.
33. C. McDonald, "U.S. Union Membership in Future Decades: A Trade Unionist's Perspective," *Industrial Relations* 31, no. 1 (Winter): 1992. See also M.H. Leroy, "State of the Unions: Assessment of Elite American Labor Leaders," *Journal of Labor Research* 13, no. 4 (Fall 1992): 371–377.

34. S. Fine, "Beleaguered Law Students Join Trade Union," *The Globe and Mail*, April 19, 1995, A1.

35. Godard *Industrial Relations*, 132.

36. G. Betcherman, K. McMullen, N. Leckie, and C. Caron, *The Canadian Workplace in Transition* (Kingston, ON: IRC Press, Queen's University, 1994).

37. "Ontario Workplace Reorganization Survey," unpublished background paper for the Human Resources Management Project, Ekos Research Associates, Ottawa, 1993b.

38. H. Jain, "Worker Participation in Canada," *Economic and Industrial Democracy* II (1990): 279–290.

objective one

Discuss the bargaining process and the bargaining goals and strategies of a union and an employer.

objective two

Describe the forms of bargaining power that a union and an employer may utilize to enforce their bargaining demands.

objective three

Cite the principal methods by which bargaining deadlocks may be resolved.

objective four

Give examples of current collective bargaining trends.

objective five

Identify the major provisions of a collective agreement and describe the issue of management rights.

objective six

Describe a typical union grievance procedure.

objective seven

Explain the basis for arbitration awards.

Chapter 16

Collective Bargaining and Contract Administration

A *major function of labour organizations is to bargain collectively over conditions of employment for those in the bargaining unit. According to labour law, once the union wins negotiating rights for bargaining unit members, it must represent everyone in the unit equally, regardless of whether employees subsequently join the union or elect to remain nonmembers. The collective agreement that ultimately is negotiated establishes the wages, hours, employee benefits, job security, and other conditions under which represented employees agree to work.*

This chapter is important to managers since it discusses the process by which an agreement is reached between labour and management. It is concerned also with the changes that have occurred in the bargaining relationship as it evolves from an adversarial relationship to a more cooperative one. Even under cooperative conditions, however, collective bargaining requires that negotiators possess special skills and knowledge if they are to represent their parties successfully. Negotiators for a union must be able to produce a labour agreement that members will find acceptable. An employer's negotiators, on the other hand, must come up with an agreement that will allow the employer to remain competitive. The agreement must be one that can be administered with a minimum of conflict and that facilitates HRM.

objective

The Bargaining Process

Those unfamiliar with contract negotiations often view the process as an emotional conflict between labour and management, complete with marathon sessions, fist pounding, and smoke-filled rooms. In reality, negotiating a labour agreement entails long hours of extensive preparation combined with diplomatic manoeuvring and the development of bargaining strategies.[1] Furthermore, negotiation is only one part of the **collective bargaining process**. Collective bargaining also may include the use of economic pressures in the form of strikes and boycotts by a union. Lockouts, plant closures, and the replacement of strikers are similar pressures used by an employer. In addition, either or both parties may seek support from the general public or from the courts as a means of pressuring the opposing side.

> **Collective bargaining process**
> Process of negotiating a collective agreement, including the use of economic pressures by both parties.

Good-Faith Bargaining

Once a union has been recognized as the representative for employees, an employer is obligated to negotiate in good faith with the union's representative over conditions of employment. Good faith requires the employer's negotiators to meet with their union counterparts at a reasonable time and place to discuss these conditions. It requires also that the proposals submitted by each party be realistic (i.e. that neither party deliberately distorts information or misleads the other party). Additionally, neither party can engage in **surface bargaining**—going through the motions with no intention of making meaningful concessions.[2]

> **Surface bargaining**
> Occurs when either party goes through the motions of bargaining with no intention of making meaningful concessions.

Furthermore, management cannot override the bargaining process by making an offer directly to the employees. This practice, called Boulwarism, was named after Lemuel Boulware, vice-president of General Electric, who used this strategy in the 1950s. Figure 16-1 illustrates several prevalent examples of bad-faith employer bargaining.

FIGURE 16-1   *Example of Bad-Faith Employer Bargaining*

- Using delaying tactics such as frequent postponements of bargaining sessions
- Withdrawing concessions previously granted
- Insisting that the union stop striking before resuming negotiations
- Unilaterally changing bargaining topics
- Negotiating with individual employees other than bargaining unit representatives
- Engaging in mere surface bargaining rather than honest negotiations
- Refusing to meet with duly appointed or elected union representatives

Preparing for Negotiations

Generally, negotiations centre on wages and benefits provisions, hours of work and overtime provisions, work rules, seniority provisions, job and income security provisions, and union security and rights provisions. Preparing for negotiations includes planning the strategy and assembling data to support bargaining proposals. This will permit collective bargaining to be conducted on an orderly, factual, and positive basis with a greater likelihood of achieving desired goals. Negotiators often develop a bargaining book that serves as a cross-reference file to determine which contract clauses would be affected by a demand. The bargaining book also contains a general history of contract terms and their relative importance to management.[3] Assuming that the collective agreement is not the first to be negotiated by the parties, preparation for negotiations ideally should start soon after the current agreement has been signed. This practice will allow negotiators to review and diagnose weaknesses and mistakes made during the previous negotiations while the experience is still current in their minds.

Sources to Consult

Internal data relating to grievances, disciplinary actions, transfers and promotions, layoffs, overtime, former arbitration awards, and wage payments are useful in formulating and supporting the employer's bargaining position. The supervisors and managers who must live with and administer the collective agreement can be very important sources of ideas and suggestions concerning changes that are needed in the next agreement. Their contact with union members and representatives provides them with a firsthand knowledge of the changes that union negotiators are likely to propose.

Data obtained from government sources such as the Bureau of Labour Information and Statistics Canada bulletins and publications can help to support the employer's position during negotiations; information from national newspapers such as *The Globe and Mail* and reports from the Conference Board of Canada can also be of use. Each of these data sources can provide information on general economic conditions, cost-of-living trends, and geographical wage rates covering a wide range of occupations.

Pattern bargaining
Bargaining in which unions negotiate provisions covering wages and other benefits that are similar to those provided in other agreements existing within the industry or region.

Bargaining Patterns

When unions negotiate provisions covering wages and other benefits, they generally seek to achieve increases at least equal to those provided in other agreements existing within the industry or region. For example, the Canadian Auto Workers would negotiate similar contract provisions for workers at Ford, General Motors, and Chrysler. Employers quite naturally try to minimize these increases by citing other employers who are paying lower wages and benefits. Other negotiated collective agreements can establish a pattern that one side or the other may seek to follow in support of its own bargaining position. This practice is known as **pattern bargaining**. In preparing for negotiations, therefore, it is essential for both the union and the employer to be fully aware of established bargaining patterns within the area or the industry.

Academic researchers and managers have widely discussed the decline in pattern bargaining.[4] With periods of low economic growth, combined with increased domestic and global competition, employers have been more willing to resist union demands to "accept the pattern." For employers, profitability and efficiency and comparative labour costs become additional arguments against accepting existing contract terms of other employers. However, pattern bargaining still remains a characteristic of North American collective bargaining.[5] Pattern bargaining allows unions to show their members that they are receiving wages and benefits similar to other employees doing like work (a necessity in avoiding union political problems), and employers are assured that their labour costs are comparable with those of their competitors.[6]

Given the fact that bargaining in the private sector is governed by provincial legislation to a great degree, employers and unions sometimes find it difficult to negotiate on a national basis. Multiprovincial agreements do occur. For example, Steel Company of Canada (Stelco) concluded a multiprovincial contract by involving negotiators from multiple locations.[7]

Bargaining Strategies

Negotiators for an employer should develop a plan covering their bargaining strategy. To ensure adherence to the employer's course of action, this plan should be prepared as a written document. The plan should consider the proposals that the union is likely to submit, based on the most recent agreements with other employers and the demands that remain unsatisfied from previous negotiations. The plan should also consider the goals the union is striving to achieve and the extent to which it may be willing to make concessions or to resort to strike action in order to achieve these goals.

At a minimum, the employer's bargaining strategy must address these points:

- Likely union proposals and management responses to them
- A listing of management demands, limits of concessions, and anticipated union responses
- Development of a data base to support management bargaining proposals and to counteract union demands
- A contingency operating plan should employees strike

Certain elements of strategy are common to both the employer and the union. Generally, the initial demands presented by each side are greater than those it actually may hope to achieve. This is done in order to provide room for concessions. Moreover, each party will usually avoid giving up the maximum it is capable of conceding in order to allow for further concessions that may be needed to break a bargaining deadlock.

Conducting the Negotiations

The economic conditions under which negotiations take place, the experience and personalities of the negotiators on each side, the goals they are seeking to achieve, and the strength of the relative positions are among the factors that tend to make each bargaining situation unique. Some labour agreements can be negotiated informally in a few hours, particularly if the contract is short and the terms are not overly complex. Other agreements, such as those negotiated with large organizations like the National Hockey League and Stelco, required months before settlements were reached.

Bargaining Teams

The composition and size of bargaining teams are often a reflection of industry practice and bargaining history. Normally each side will have four to six representatives at the negotiating table. The chief negotiator for management will be the vice-president or manager for labour relations; the chief negotiator for the union will be the local union president or union business agent. Others making up management's team may include representatives from accounting or finance, operations, employment, legal, or training. The local union president is likely to be supported by the chief steward, various local union vice-presidents, and a representative from the national union.

Many negotiators, over a period of time, acquire the ability "to read their opponents' minds," to anticipate their actions and reactions. Inexperienced negotiators

National Hockey League Players Association President Mike Gartner arriving at NHL headquarters for what would become protracted negotiations with the league on a new collective bargaining agreement.

bargaining for the first time, on the other hand, may misinterpret their opponents' actions and statements and unintentionally cause a deadlock. Furthermore, managers who must bargain with labour officials in a different culture may be unaware of the rules, rituals, and steps to be followed to keep negotiations moving toward a mutually acceptable agreement. In Japan, for example, "saving face" is an important aspect of Japanese culture that often influences the negotiating process.[8]

Opening the Negotiations

The initial meeting of the bargaining teams is a particularly important one because it establishes the climate that will prevail during the negotiations that follow. A cordial attitude, with perhaps the injection of a little humour, can contribute much to a relaxation of tensions and help the negotiations to begin smoothly. This attitudinal structuring is done to change the attitudes of the parties toward each other, often with the objective of persuading one side to accept the other side's demands.[9]

The first meeting is usually devoted to establishing the bargaining authority possessed by the representatives of each side and to determining the rules and procedures to be used during negotiations. If the parties have not submitted their proposals in advance, these may be exchanged and clarified at this time.

Analyzing the Proposals

The negotiation of a collective agreement can have some of the characteristics of a poker game, with each side attempting to determine its opponent's position while not revealing its own. Each party will normally try to avoid disclosing the relative importance that it attaches to a proposal so that it will not be forced to pay a higher price than is necessary to have the proposal accepted.[10] As with sellers who will try to get a higher price for their products if they think the prospective buyer strongly desires them, negotiators will try to get greater concessions in return for granting those their opponents want most.

The proposals that each side submits generally may be divided into those it feels it must achieve, those it would like to achieve, and those it is submitting primarily for trading purposes. Proposals submitted for trading purposes, however, must be realistic in terms of the opponent's ability and willingness to concede them. Unrealistic proposals may serve only to antagonize the opponent and cause a deadlock.

Resolving the Proposals

Regardless of its degree of importance, every proposal submitted must be resolved if an agreement is to be finalized.[11] A proposal may be withdrawn, accepted by the other side in its entirety, or accepted in some compromise form.

For each bargaining issue to be resolved satisfactorily, the point at which agreement is reached must be within limits that the union and the employer are willing to accept. In a frequently cited bargaining model, Ross Stagner and Hjalmar Rosen call the area within these two limits the **bargaining zone**. In some bargaining situations, such as the one illustrated in Figure 16-2, the solution desired by one party may exceed the limits of the other party. Thus that solution is outside the bargaining zone. If that party refuses to modify its demands sufficiently to bring them within the bargaining zone or if the opposing party refuses to extend its limit to accommodate the demands of the other party, a bargaining deadlock will result.[12]

Bargaining zone
Area within which the union and the employer are willing to concede when bargaining.

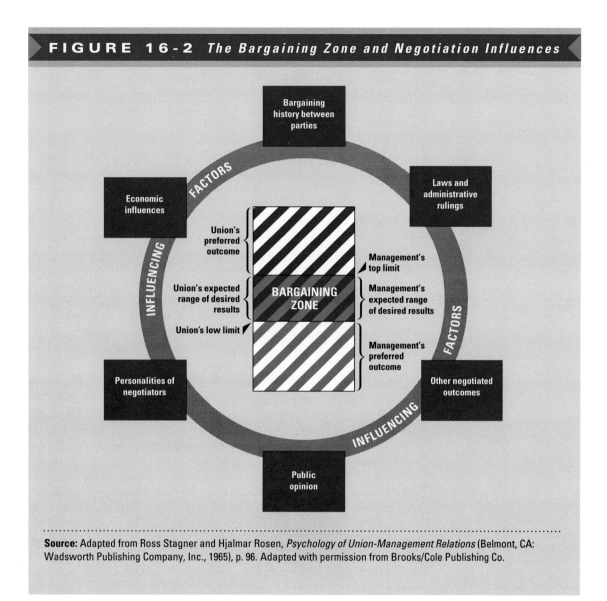

FIGURE 16-2 *The Bargaining Zone and Negotiation Influences*

Source: Adapted from Ross Stagner and Hjalmar Rosen, *Psychology of Union-Management Relations* (Belmont, CA: Wadsworth Publishing Company, Inc., 1965), p. 96. Adapted with permission from Brooks/Cole Publishing Co.

For example, when bargaining a wage increase for employees, if the union's lowest limit is a 4 percent increase and management's top limit is 6 percent, an acceptable range—the bargaining zone—is available to both parties. If management's top limit is only 3 percent, however, a bargaining zone is not available to either side and a deadlock is likely to occur. Figure 16-2, which is based on the original model by Stagner and Rosen, shows that as bargaining takes place, several important variables influence the negotiators and their ability to reach agreement within the bargaining zone.

two

objective

The Union's Power in Collective Bargaining

During negotiations, it is necessary for each party to retreat sufficiently from its original position to permit an agreement to be achieved. If this does not occur, the negotiations will become deadlocked, and the union may resort to the use of economic power to achieve its demands. Otherwise, its only alternative will be to have members continue working without a labour agreement once the old one has expired. The economic power of the union may be exercised by striking, picketing, or boycotting the employer's products and encouraging others to do likewise. As managers well know, the ability to engage or even threaten to engage in such activities also can serve as a form of pressure.

Striking the Employer

A strike is the refusal of a group of employees to perform their jobs. Although strikes account for only a small portion of total workdays lost in industry each year, they are a costly and emotional event for all concerned.[13] Unions usually will seek strike authorization from their members to use as a bargaining ploy to gain concessions that will make a strike unnecessary. A strike vote by the members does not mean they actually want or expect to go out on strike. Rather, it is intended as a vote of confidence to strengthen the position of their leaders at the bargaining table.

Since a strike can have serious effects on the union and its members, the prospects for its success must be analyzed carefully by the union. It is most important for the union to estimate the members' willingness to endure the personal hardships resulting from a strike, particularly if it proves to be a long one.[14] Research has shown clear differences between employees willing to strike and those less certain about crossing a picket line. For example, potential strikers have more seniority, are better paid, have more years of union membership, and express more support for their union than nonstrikers.[15]

Also of critical importance is the extent, if any, to which the employer will be able to continue operating through the use of supervisory and nonstriking personnel and employees hired to replace the strikers. The greater the ability of the employer to continue operating, the less the union's chances of gaining the demands it is attempting to enforce through the strike.[16] Failure to achieve a desired settlement can result in the employees' voting either the union officers out of office or the union out of the organization in a labour relations board conducted decertification election.

The number of work stoppages involving one or more workers fell from 1050 in 1981 to a projected 185 in 1995.[17] Figure 16-3 shows that the percentage of lost time due to work stoppages has declined dramatically in the past two decades. Approximately nine in ten collective agreements are settled without a strike. HRM practitioners conclude that the decline in the use of the strike by unions can be attributed to the decrease in employee support and public tolerance for strikes. The use of replacement workers is illegal in the provinces of Quebec and British Columbia.

Picketing the Employer

When a union goes on strike, it will picket the employer by placing persons at business entrances to advertise the dispute and to discourage people from entering or

> **FIGURE 16-3** *Chronological Perspective on Work Stoppages*

STOPPAGES IN EXISTENCE DURING MONTH OR YEAR

PERIOD	NUMBER BEGINNING DURING MONTH OR YEAR	# OF STOPPAGES	# OF WORKERS INVOLVED	PERSON-DAYS NOT WORKED	% OF ESTIMATED WORKING TIME
1976	920	1,040	1,586,221	11,544,170	0.53
1977	742	806	217,647	3,320,050	0.15
1978	1,003	1,057	400,622	7,357,180	0.32
1979	987	1,049	462,386	7,819,350	0.33
1980	952	1,028	439,003	9,129,960	0.37
1981	943	1,050	341,851	8,850,560	0.35
1982	611	680	464,181	5,712,500	0.23
1983	576	645	329,472	4,440,900	0.18
1984	653	716	186,916	3,883,400	0.15
1985	762	829	162,333	3,125,560	0.12
1986	657	748	484,255	7,151,470	0.27
1987	579	668	582,042	3,810,910	0.14
1988	483	548	206,796	4,901,260	0.17
1989	568	627	444,747	3,701,360	0.13
1990	519	579	270,471	5,079,190	0.17
1991	399	463	253,334	2,516,020	0.09
1992	353	404	149,475	2,108,140	0.07
1993	324	382	101,827	1,519,490	0.05
1994	317	379	81,245	1,617,960	0.06
1995*	135	185	67,620	696,550	0.06

*Preliminary figures.

Source: "Chronological Work Stoppages," Workplace Information Directorate, Labour Branch, Human Resources Development Canada, August 1995. Used with permission.

leaving the premises. Unions cannot picket on any privately owned premise without permission, nor can they block exits and entries to these premises. Even when the strikers represent only a small proportion of the employees within the organization, they can cause the shutdown of an entire organization if a sufficient number of the organization's remaining employees (i.e., sympathy strikers) refuse to cross their picket line. Also, because unions often refuse to cross another union's picket line, the pickets may serve to prevent trucks and railcars from entering the business to deliver and pick up goods. For example, a Teamster truck driver may refuse to deliver produce to a food store whose employees are out on strike with the United Food & Commercial Workers Union.

If a strike fails to stop an employer's operations, the picket line may serve as more than a passive weapon. Employees who attempt to cross the line may be subjected to verbal insults and even physical violence, although this is illegal. Mass picketing, in which large groups of pickets try to block the path of people attempting to enter an organization, may also be used. However, the use of picket lines to exert physical pressure and incite violence is illegal and may harm more than help the union cause.

Boycotting the Employer

Boycott
A union tactic to encourage others to refuse to patronize an employer.

Another economic weapon of unions is the **boycott**, which is a refusal to patronize the employer. This action can hurt an employer if conducted by a large enough segment of organized labour. In contrast to a strike, a boycott may not end completely with the settlement of the dispute. During the boycott, many former customers may have developed either a bias against the employer's products or a change in buying habits that is not easily reversed.

A *primary boycott* occurs where a union asks its members or customers not to patronize a business where there is a labour dispute; for example, production employees on strike against a hand tool manufacturer might picket a retail store that sells the tool made by the employees. Under most circumstances this type of boycott is legal, provided the union advises consumers to boycott the tools and not the neutral store. A union may go a step further, however, and attempt to induce third parties, primarily suppliers of the struck employer, to refrain from business dealings with the employer with whom it has a dispute. A boycott of this type, called a *secondary boycott*, generally is illegal.

objective

The Employer's Power in Collective Bargaining

The employer's power in collective bargaining largely rests in being able to shut down the organization or certain operations within it. The employer can transfer these operations to other locations or can subcontract them to other employers through *outsourcing*. General Motors outsources to foreign manufacturers many parts used in the assembly of North American cars. In exercising their economic freedom, however, employers must be careful that their actions are not interpreted by the labour relations board to be an attempt to avoid bargaining with the union.

Operating during Strikes

When negotiations become deadlocked, typically it is the union that initiates action and the employer that reacts. In reacting, employers must balance the cost of taking a strike against the long- and short-term costs of agreeing to union demands. They must also consider how long operations might be suspended and the length of time that they and the unions will be able to endure a strike. An employer who chooses to accept a strike must then decide whether or not to continue operating if it is possible to do so.

Organizations today seem to be more willing to face a strike than they were in former years. Several reasons have been advanced to explain this change, including:

1. Union members seem less willing to support strike activity. Thus the union is less able to maintain strike unity among its members.
2. Because organizations are forced to reduce labour costs to meet domestic and global competition, unions have no choice but to accept lower wages and benefits.
3. Technological advances enhance the employer's ability to operate during a strike.
4. Organizations are able to obtain favourable, often concessionary, contracts.

Should employees strike the organization, employers in certain jurisdictions are limited in their ability to hire replacement workers. Quebec and British Columbia have passed "anti-scab" laws, forbidding the use of replacement workers during a strike. The use of "scabs" (replacement workers) at Canada Post and Gainers Meats in the 1980s created a great deal of anger among picketing workers. Employers have the right to dismiss workers who engage in sabotage or violence during a strike.

Workers are entitled to return to their jobs, but not necessarily their previous position, once a strike is settled. The right to return to work is often an issue to be negotiated. Although laws vary, in many cases employees must submit, in writing, their intention to return to their job once a strike is finalized.

Using the Lockout

Lockout
Strategy by which the employer denies employees the opportunity to work by closing its operations.

Although not often used, a **lockout** occurs when an employer takes the initiative to close its operations. Under LRB provisions, an employer cannot enforce a lockout within a prescribed number of hours (48 to 72 hours) of a strike vote. Lockouts affect nonstriking workers. For example, when miners at Inco are locked out, administrative work ceases and office personnel are locked out or laid off. Employers may be reluctant to resort to a lockout, however, because of their concern that denying work to regular employees might hurt the organization's image.

objective

Resolving Bargaining Deadlocks

When a strike or a lockout occurs, both parties are soon affected by it. The employer suffers a loss of profits and customers, and possibly of public goodwill. The union members suffer a loss of income that is likely to be only partially offset by strike benefits or outside income. The union's leaders risk the possibility of losing members, of being voted out of office, of losing public support, or of having the members vote to decertify the union as their bargaining agent. As the losses to each side mount, the disputing parties usually feel more pressure to achieve a settlement.

Mediation and Arbitration

When the disputing parties are unable to resolve a deadlock, a third party serving in the capacity of a conciliator, a mediator, or an arbitrator may be called upon to provide assistance. In most jurisdictions, conciliation is compulsory before a legal strike or lockout. The conciliator, appointed by the Ministry of Labour, helps the parties reconcile their differences in an attempt to reach a workable agreement. If the conciliation effort is unsuccessful, a report is filed with the Ministry of Labour, which in rare instances may appoint a conciliation board that accepts presentations from both parties and makes nonbinding formal recommendations. If a settlement cannot be reached at this stage, then a strike is permitted, except in Manitoba, Alberta, Saskatchewan, and Quebec where strikes are permissible during conciliation. This two-stage conciliation process is normally reserved for high-profile cases in which significant social and economic consequences would result from a strike.

Mediation is similar to conciliation except that it is voluntary (the two parties contract a neutral third party to help them) and the mediator assumes a more active role as a negotiator. A **mediator** serves primarily as a fact finder and to open up a channel of communication between the parties. Typically the mediator meets with one party and then the other in order to suggest compromise solutions or to recommend concessions from each side that will lead to an agreement without causing either to lose face. Mediators have no power or authority to force either side toward an agreement. They must use their communication skills and the power of persuasion to help the parties resolve their differences.[18]

Arbitration is the only third-party resolution form that results in binding recommendations. An **arbitrator** assumes the role of a decision maker and determines what the settlement between the two parties should be. In other words, arbitrators write a final contract that the parties must accept. Compared with mediation, arbitration is not often used to settle private-sector bargaining disputes. In those essential-service areas within the public sector where strikes are prohibited, the use of **interest arbitration** is a common method to resolve bargaining deadlocks. Because one or both parties are generally reluctant to give a third party the power to make the settlement for them, a mediator typically is used to break a deadlock and assist the parties in reaching an agreement. Once an agreement is concluded, an arbitrator may be called upon to resolve disputes arising in connection with the administration of the agreement. This is called *rights arbitration* or *grievance arbitration*, which will be discussed shortly.

Mediator
Third party in a labour dispute who meets with one party and then the other in order to suggest compromise solutions or to recommend concessions from each side that will lead to an agreement.

Arbitrator
Third-party neutral who resolves a labour dispute by issuing a final decision in the disagreement.

Interest arbitration
The binding determination of a collective bargaining agreement by an arbitrator.

objective

Trends in Collective Bargaining

Managers continue to see the 1990s as a period of great importance to labour–management relations. Advances in technology and continued competitive pressures have their impact. These conditions affect the attitudes and objectives of both employers and unions in collective bargaining. They also influence the climate in which bargaining occurs and the bargaining power each side is able to exercise.[19]

Changes in Collective Bargaining Relationships

The collective bargaining relationship between an employer and a union has traditionally been an adversarial one. The union has held the position that, while the employer has the responsibility for managing the organization, the union has the right to challenge certain actions of management. Unions also have taken the position that the employer has an obligation to operate the organization in a manner that will provide adequate compensation to employees. Moreover, unions maintain that their members should not be expected to subsidize poor management by accepting less than their full entitlement.

Most unions have been sufficiently enlightened to recognize the danger of making bargaining demands that will create economic adversity for employers.[20] This fact, however, has not stopped unions from bargaining for what they consider to be a fair and equitable agreement for their members. While the goal of organized labour has always been to bargain for improved economic and working conditions, large layoffs caused by economic downturns and domestic and global competition have caused both sides to change their bargaining goals and tactics. We are seeing a gradual movement away from direct conflict and toward more labour–management accommodation.

Facilitating Union–Management Cooperation

Improving union–management cooperation generally requires a restructuring of attitudes by both managers and union officials and members. Robert Frey, president, Cin-Made Corporation, notes, "Key barriers to adopting these new work systems are managers who are more comfortable giving orders with little input and complacent employees who like not having to think. We must understand how difficult the change process is for people and that firm leadership is needed to lead the process."[21]

Furthermore, the crisis of survival has forced unions, their members, and management to make concessions at the bargaining table and to collaborate in finding the solutions that will ensure survival. If cooperation is to continue after the crisis has passed, however, it must rest on a more solid foundation. For example, it has been noted that cooperation lasts only when both sides undertake the endeavour through a systems approach grounded in developmental activities.[22] Also, union–management cooperation programs have a greater chance for success when both parties jointly establish goals and philosophies for mutual gain. Highlights in HRM 1 shows the jointly written statement of purpose and values of the collective agreement developed by Volkswagen Canada and the National Automobile, Aerospace and Agricultural Implement Workers Union of Canada (CAW-Canada).

Additionally, a review of meaningful labour–management cooperative endeavours indicates that success depends on an open and honest style of communication. Furthermore, both supervisors and employees must be trained in participative and problem-solving approaches to problem resolution. At Algoma Steel Inc., located in Sault Ste. Marie, Ontario, hundreds of workers and managers attended problem-solving workshops and have been applying their new skills to reduce the number of grievances from 500 outstanding to three.[23] Finally, a philosophy of trust and respect must underlie the labour–management relationship. It is particularly important that union members believe that management is sincerely interested in their personal well-being. Commenting on the philosophy necessary for successful cooperative programs, one author wrote, "The [successful] philosophy emphasizes the building of trust and mutual understanding between key management and union personnel,

HRM **highlights**

1 LABOUR–MANAGEMENT COOPERATION

**COLLECTIVE AGREEMENT
BETWEEN:
VOLKSWAGEN CANADA INC.
BARRIE, ONTARIO
(hereinafter called "the Company")
AND
NATIONAL AUTOMOBILE, AEROSPACE AND AGRICULTURAL
IMPLEMENT WORKERS UNION OF CANADA (CAW-CANADA)
AND ITS LOCAL 1991
(hereinafter referred to as "the Union")**

PURPOSE AND VALUES OF AGREEMENT

It is the mutual desire of the parties hereto to foster a progressive, equal, just, proactive and harmonious relationship. These principles and goals are consistent with the corporation's mission of becoming the leading organization in Canada measured in terms of customer satisfaction.

The parties recognize that attainment of these goals, coupled with continuing mutual effort, open communication, safe and fair working conditions, should provide the highest degree of job security possible in a market driven economy. To help ensure success, the parties further recognize that:

The field of labour relations is an evolutionary process which can be improved as a result of mutual trust and respect, common purpose, and a positive workplace environment;

A co-operative workplace environment will help provide a strong foundation for achieving high operational efficiency and productivity, and higher product quality, together with employee satisfaction and job security;

By achieving these goals, the Company may enhance and improve its position in the global market, and be better able to continue to provide stable employment, equitable treatment, a congenial working environment, a safe workplace with fair compensation recognizing the employees' contribution to the overall success of the enterprise, and a social commitment to the community.

The culture of the plant will be based on co-operation, mutual trust and respect, and the recognition and preservation of the established values: putting people first; a belief in unparalleled customer care; the fostering of innovation; and a belief in providing real value in everything we do.

The Company and Union agree that if these endeavours are to be a success, labour and management must work together. To attain these goals, all employees share in the common endeavour with the following responsibilities:

- Support and abide by reasonable standards of conduct and attendance policies;
- Promote good housekeeping and maintain a safe work environment;
- Support and promote efficient work processes;
- Strive to achieve quality goals and endeavour to improve quality standards.

In order to develop and maintain flexibility of the workforce, while at the same time developing the ability and interest of the individual employee, the parties are committed to a continuous learning and development process for the employees. This process will include multi-job training, involvement in group decision-making processes to discuss better ways to produce products, and group efforts based on employees' active and voluntary participation and familiarization on matters such as quality, safety, increasing productivity, increasing work efficiency, and enhancement of the work environment. The parties have agreed to co-operate in the implementation of these activities and to encourage employee participation.

Source: Donald McQuirter, Manager, Human Resources, Volkswagen Canada, Inc. August 1995.

including the common definition of problems, the examination of new approaches to those problems, and the sharing of relevant information."[24]

Concessionary Bargaining

To prevent layoffs and plant closures and, it is hoped, put members back to work, enlightened labour leaders recognize the need to help employers reduce operating costs. Getting their members to "give back" wages, benefits, work rules, or any gains received in previous bargaining, however, can prove difficult and politically dangerous for union officers. To reduce this danger, greater emphasis must be placed on educating members regarding the need to cooperate. Members of management often require similar education.

Economic adversity motivates concessionary bargaining and the implementation of cooperative programs.[25] A troubled financial condition, however, may not always bring forth the desired union concessions. While union leaders might recognize an organization's financial crisis, their willingness to make concessions depends on (1) a positive labour–management relationship, and (2) their view of management as credible. Union officers, who tend to question the need for concessions, may consider such management bargaining positions as opportunistic.

Concessions sought by managers have been fairly consistent across industries and are directed toward (1) limiting, freezing, or lowering compensation payments, and (2) increasing employee productivity. To gain wage concessions, employers may offer gainsharing plans (see Chapter 12) that link compensation to productivity or sales. Profit sharing and stock ownership are other plans being offered to motivate employees and reward improvements in performance.

Restrictive work rules are particularly troublesome to employers because, in this age of technology, these rules are detrimental to productivity. Union concessions may include reduction in job classifications or fewer restrictions on work tasks. In return for concessions granted to employers, unions are demanding provisions for greater job security.[26] Unions are also likely to demand provisions restricting the transfer of work, outsourcing (subcontracting), and plant closures by employers. Getting advance notice of shutdowns, as well as severance pay and transfer rights for displaced employees, will be high on the "want lists" of union negotiators. For employees likely to be replaced by technology, unions will bargain for retraining programs as a means to upgrade employee skills.

The Labour Agreement

objective

After an agreement has been reached, it must be put in writing, ratified by the union membership, and signed by the representatives of both parties. The scope of the agreement (and the length of the written document) will vary with the size of the employer and the length of the bargaining relationship. Highlights in HRM 2 shows some of the major articles in the agreement between Volkswagen Canada and CAW. Two important items in any labour agreement pertain to the issue of management rights and the forms of security afforded the union.

The Issue of Management Rights

Management rights have to do with conditions of employment over which management is able to exercise exclusive jurisdiction. Since virtually every management right can and has been challenged successfully by unions, the ultimate determination of these rights will depend on the relative bargaining power of the two parties. Furthermore, to achieve union cooperation or concessions, employers have had to relinquish some of these time-honoured rights.

Residual Rights

In the labour agreement, management rights may be treated as residual rights or as defined rights. The **residual rights** concept holds that

Residual rights
Concept that management's authority is supreme in all matters except those it has expressly conceded to the union in the collective agreement.

> *management's authority is supreme in all matters except those it has expressly conceded in the collective agreement, or in those areas where its authority is restricted by law. Put another way, management does not look to the collective agreement to ascertain its rights; it looks to the agreement to find out which and how much of its rights and powers it has conceded outright or agreed to share with the union."*[27]

Thus anything not specified in the collective agreement is, by default, under the sole authority of management.

Residual rights might include the right of management to determine the product to produce or to select production equipment and procedures. Employers who subscribe to the residual-rights concept prefer not to mention management rights in the labour agreement on the grounds that they possess such rights already. To mention them might create an issue with the union.

> ### HIGHLIGHTS IN HRM

2 LABOUR AGREEMENT BETWEEN VOLKSWAGEN CANADA AND THE CANADIAN AUTO WORKERS (SELECTED ARTICLES)

highlights

ARTICLE NO.
1 Recognition
2 Management Rights
5 Union Membership and Dues Checkoff
6 Administration of Discipline
7 Dispute, Grievance, and Arbitration Procedure
8 Strikes and Lockouts
12 Job Posting
13 New Employee Orientation
14 Total Productive Maintenance Training
15 Technological Change
16 Employee Privileges
17 Maternity, Adoption, and Parental Leave
18 Personal Leave of Absence

ARTICLE NO.
19 Union-related Leave
22 Health and Safety
31 Emergency Callback Pay
32 Injury on the Job
33 Hours of Work
34 Overtime Equalization
35 Overtime
39 Company Benefit Programs
40 Wages
41 Partial or Total Plant Closure
42 Classifications and Job Descriptions

Source: Correspondence with Donald McQuirter, Manager, Human Resources, Volkswagen Canada, Inc. August 1995.

Defined rights

Concept that management's authority should be expressly defined and clarified in the collective agreement.

Defined Rights

The **defined rights** concept, on the other hand, is intended to reinforce and clarify which rights are exclusively those of management. It serves to reduce confusion and misunderstanding and to remind union officers, union stewards, and employees that management never relinquishes its right to operate the organization. For example, a defined right would include the right of management to take disciplinary action against problem employees. The great majority of labour agreements contain provisions covering management rights. The following is an example of a general statement defining management rights in one labour agreement:

> *It is agreed that the company possesses all of the rights, powers, privileges, and authority it had prior to the execution of this agreement; and nothing in this agreement shall be construed to limit the company in any way in the exercise of the regular and customary functions of management and the operation of its*

business, except as it may be specifically relinquished or modified herein by an express provision of this agreement.[28]

Union Security Agreements

When a labour organization is certified by the labour relations board as the exclusive bargaining representative of all employees in a bargaining unit, by law it must represent all employees in the unit, nonunion and union members alike. In exchange for its obligation to represent all employees equally, union officials will seek to negotiate some form of compulsory membership as a condition of employment. Union officials argue that compulsory membership precludes the possibility that some employees will receive the benefits of unionization without paying their share of the costs. Such employees are referred to as "free riders."

A standard union security provision is dues checkoff, which gives the employer the responsibility of withholding union dues from the paycheques of union members who agree to such a deduction. One form of dues checkoff, called the *Rand formula* after Justice Ivan Rand, requires all employees to have the dues deducted. About 47 percent of collective agreements contain a clause with the Rand formula. The second type of duescheck, called the *voluntary revocable checkoff*, permits the employee to revoke the payment of dues at some future date. The final form, the *voluntary irrevocable checkoff*, does not permit this.[29]

Other common forms of union security found in labour agreements include the following:

1. The *closed shop* states that employers will hire only union members.
2. The *union shop* provides that any employee not a union member upon employment must join the union within a specified time period (e.g., three months) or be terminated.
3. The *agency shop* provides for voluntary membership. However, all bargaining unit members must pay union dues and fees.
4. The *maintenance-of-membership shop* requires that employees who voluntarily join a union must maintain membership during the life of the agreement. Membership withdrawal is possible during a designated escape period.
5. The *open shop* allows employees to join the union or not. Nonmembers do not pay union dues.
6. The *modified union shop* requires new workers to join the union and current union members to remain in the union. However, it permits established employees who are nonunion to remain so.

Few issues in collective bargaining are more controversial than the negotiation of these agreements. Though rare, closed-shop clauses are perhaps the most controversial because they require employers to recruit employees from a union hiring hall. The problems associated with closed shops are outlined in Reality Check. The pros and cons of closed-shop arrangements are the subject of Ethics in HRM.

Working in conjunction with the union-shop clause are the various seniority provisions of the labour agreement. Unions prefer that many personnel decisions (promotions, job transfers, shift assignments, vacations) be based on seniority, a criterion that limits the discretion of managers to make such decisions solely on the basis of merit.

> **REALITY CHECK**

COLLECTIVE BARGAINING AT ROGERS COMMUNICATIONS

"Crafting the collective agreement is a most exacting and most challenging process," says Carol Gibson, vice-president, human resources, Western Canada, at Rogers Communications in Vancouver. "I have to manage the tension between what the company wants, what the employees want, and what the employees want as represented by their unions. These words then have to be interpreted by a third party—the arbitrator—who has a different kind of power than a judge. There is no recourse if the arbitrator does not understand the intent of the agreement."

The time frame for the negotiation of a collective agreement varies considerably. "The last one took eighteen months for a four-year agreement," Gibson recalls, "and before it was officially ratified, I had begun preparing for the next round by starting a file. The collective agreement is a living document, always subject to interpretation and potential for conflict and change. A clause can lie dormant for years, because we haven't had to apply it or we have only applied it in one way. Then business circumstances change or a new manager reads it in a different way and there is a desire to test its intent. The result is often a grievance. A number of grievances or difficulties in interpretation will lead us to renegotiate that clause in the next round."

This happened in the most recent round of negotiations. The communications industry is a stable industry, where the average length of employment is sixteen years and the average age is 45. But Rogers was dealing with the International Brotherhood of Electrical Workers (IBEW), a union that traditionally supplied electricians to the construction industry, which is notably unstable. As a result of the instability, all construction companies used union hiring halls to recruit employees. These halls would send two to three employees for a job, selected on the basis of who you know. Gibson felt this had to change:

"We wanted to select on specific criteria, on qualifications such as skills and abilities, because we are a high-tech industry. But this is a big issue for unions, because they get a lot of power from their hiring halls. Employees also liked the union hiring halls, because their children or relatives could get hired. They saw it as security for their children. In addition, employees have a strong commitment to the union, which was responsible for getting them their jobs. The hiring hall was an emotional issue. We wanted to not use the hiring halls, and the union resisted. In the end, we locked them out for nine months and forced them to negotiate."

Administration of the Collective Agreement

Negotiation of the labour agreement, as mentioned earlier, is usually the most publicized and critical aspect of labour relations. Strike deadlines, press conferences, and employee picketing help create this image. Nevertheless, as managers in unionized organizations know, the bulk of labour relations activity comes from the day-to-day

ETHICS IN HRM

UNION SECURITY CLAUSES

Early in the history of labour relations, a yellow dog contract was the employer's way of preventing employees from joining a union. The closed-shop clause in collective agreements is the union's way of requiring employees to join a union. Closed-shop clauses are found in 2 percent of agreements (excluding the construction industry); maintenance of membership clauses in 4 percent; union shops in 23 percent and modified union shops in 21 percent of agreements. Unions argue that compulsory membership is necessary because unions provide an indivisible service in that workers benefit from the agreements whether they pay for them or not. If these free riders could benefit without paying dues, then the union's position would be weakened as other workers chose the same strategy. Also, the union has more control over members than nonmembers during situations such as strikes. Through the use of hiring halls, unions can control the labour supply and ensure that senior employees are not replaced by more junior ones, that laid off workers are rehired, and that pro-union members are rehired.

Employers resist closed-shop arrangements. Although hiring halls could be seen as a free placement service, employers argue that the workers sent may not be the ones they would have chosen. Those workers who can't obtain union membership are prevented from working. In 1988, the owners of a crane rental company challenged this use of closed shops in Ontario. Their grandson was prevented from working for them because not only did the collective agreement require union membership, but the only way to become a member was to take an apprenticeship course. The judge upheld the provision, saying the grandson could work for another crane rental company that did not have this provision. Is it unfair to restrict people's right to work by making them join unions? If workers have the right to join a union, should they also have the right not to join? Alternatively, is it fair that some employees can be free riders?

Source: A.W.J. Craig and N.A. Solomon, *The System of Industrial Relations in Canada*, 4th ed. (Scarborough, ON: Prentice-Hall Canada, 1993).

---

administration of the agreement, since no agreement could possibly anticipate all the forms that disputes may take. In addition, once the agreement is signed, each side will naturally interpret ambiguous clauses to its own advantage. These differences are traditionally resolved through the grievance procedure.

Negotiated Grievance Procedures

Grievance procedure
Formal procedure that provides for the union to represent members and nonmembers in processing a grievance.

objective

The **grievance procedure** typically provides for the union to represent the interests of its members (and nonmembers as well) in processing a grievance. It is considered by some authorities to be the heart of the bargaining agreement, or the safety valve that gives flexibility to the whole system of collective bargaining.[30] There are fundamentally two types of grievances: individual and policy. An individual grievance exists when an employee (or groups of employees) files a grievance for an alleged transgression of rights, such as discipline warnings. A policy grievance is filed by the union over issues that may ultimately affect workers, such as the contracting out of work.

When negotiating a grievance procedure, one important concern for both sides is how effectively the system will serve the needs of labour and management. A well-written grievance procedure will allow grievances to be processed expeditiously and with as little red tape as possible. Furthermore, it should serve to foster cooperation, not conflict, between the employer and the union.

The operation of a grievance procedure is unique to each individual collective bargaining relationship. Grievance procedures are negotiated to address the organization's structure and labour–management philosophy and the specific desires of the parties. Although each procedure is unique, there are common elements among systems.[31] For example, grievance procedures normally specify how the grievance is to be initiated, the number and timing of steps that are to compose the procedure, and the identity of representatives from each side who are to be involved in the hearings at each step (see Figure 16-4). When a grievance cannot be resolved at one of the specified steps, most agreements provide for the grievance to be submitted to a third party—usually an arbitrator—whose decision is final. It is not the function of an arbitrator to help the two parties reach a compromise solution. Rather, it is the arbitrator's job to mandate how the grievance is to be resolved.

Initiating the Formal Grievance

In order for an employee's grievance to be considered formally, it must be expressed orally and/or in writing, ideally to the employee's immediate supervisor. If the employee feels unable to communicate effectively with the supervisor, the grievance may be taken to the union steward, who will discuss it with the supervisor. Since grievances are often the result of an oversight or a misunderstanding, many of them can be resolved at this point. Whether or not it is possible to resolve a grievance at the initial step will depend on the supervisor's ability and willingness to discuss the problem with the employee and the steward. Supervisors should be trained formally in resolving grievances. This training should include familiarization with the terms of the collective agreement and the development of counselling skills to facilitate a problem-solving approach.

In some instances, a satisfactory solution may not be possible at the first step because there are legitimate differences of opinion between the employee and the supervisor or because the supervisor does not have the authority to take the action required to satisfy the grievant.[32] Personality conflicts, prejudices, emotionalism, stubbornness, or other factors may also be barriers to a satisfactory solution at this step.

Preparing the Grievance Statement

Most collective agreements require that grievances carried beyond the initial step must be stated in writing, usually on a form similar to the one shown in Highlights in HRM 3. Requiring a written statement reduces the chance that various versions

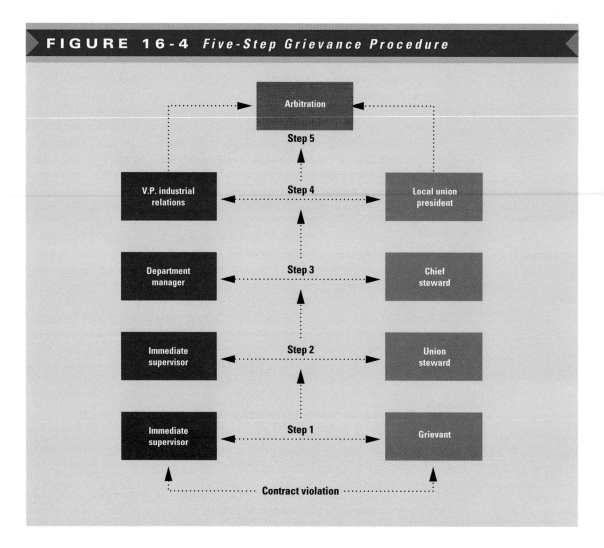

FIGURE 16-4 *Five-Step Grievance Procedure*

of the grievance will appear because of lapses in memory.[33] It also forces employees to think more objectively about their grievances. When this is done, grievances that stem from trivial complaints or feelings of hostility are less likely to be pursued beyond the first step.

Grievance Resolution

If a grievance is to be resolved successfully, representatives of both management and the union must be able to discuss the problem in a rational and objective manner. A grievance should not be viewed as something to be won or lost. Rather, both sides must view the situation as an attempt to solve a human relations problem. If the conflict cannot be resolved, all collective agreements in Canadian jurisdictions contain a provision for arbitration, or **grievance resolution**. Only about 2 percent of grievances reach the arbitration stage.[34] An arbitrator (usually a lawyer or professor

Grievance resolution
A process in which a neutral party assists in the resolution of an employee grievance.

skilled in arbitration) or a board or panel (consisting of a union nominee, a management nominee, and a neutral chair) hears the case and submits a decision, including the rational. The decision is final and the parties are legally bound to accept the decision unless there is a serious concern over the arbitrator's competence or integrity.

One criticism of the arbitration process is that it is slow (up to one year) and costly. One solution is **expedited arbitration,** which is an agreement to bypass some steps in the grievance process when the issue is particularly important or urgent, as in the case of employee dismissals. The United Steelworkers of America and the International Nickel Company of Canada Ltd. use expedited arbitration in their Sudbury and Port Colborne operations.

Grievance Arbitration

The function of **arbitration** is to provide the solution to a grievance that a union and an employer have been unable to resolve by themselves. As mentioned earlier, arbitration is performed by a neutral third party (an arbitrator or impartial umpire). This third party's decision dictates how the grievance is to be settled. Both parties are obligated to comply with the decision. Even if one of the parties believes the arbitrator's award is unfair, unwise, or inconsistent with the labour agreement, that party may have no alternative but to comply with the decision.

Sources of Arbitrators
An arbitrator must be an individual who is acceptable to both disputing parties. An arbitrator who is retained on a permanent basis to resolve all grievances arising under an agreement has the advantage of being familiar with the agreement and the labour–management relationship. Most grievances, however, are resolved by arbitrators who are appointed on an ad hoc basis. If both parties are satisfied with an arbitrator's performance, that person may be called upon to resolve subsequent grievances.[35]

Many collective agreements include a list of mutually acceptable arbitrators. In the absence of such a list, the labour relations board can provide one. If both parties cannot agree on an arbitrator, then the labour relations board may appoint one. Typically, arbitrators are professionals such as professors, lawyers, or retired government labour arbitrators. Because of their professional backgrounds, they tend to be identified with neither labour nor management and are therefore able to occupy a position of neutrality.

The Decision to Arbitrate
If a grievance cannot be resolved through the grievance procedure, each disputing party must decide whether to use arbitration to resolve the case. The alternatives would be for the union to withdraw the grievance or for the employer to agree to union demands.

In deciding whether to use arbitration, each party must weigh the costs involved against the importance of the case and the prospects of gaining a favourable award. It would seem logical that neither party would allow a weak case to go to arbitration if there were little possibility of gaining a favourable award. Logic, however, does not always prevail. For example, it is not unusual for a union to take a weak case

Expedited arbitration
An agreement to bypass some steps in the grievance process.

Arbitration
Arbitration over interpretation of the meaning of contract terms or employee work grievances.

HRM
highlights

3 THE GRIEVANCE PROCEDURE RECORD

GRIEVANCE PROCEDURE RECORD
for
VWC - BARRIE PLANT
and
LOCAL 1991 CANADIAN AUTO WORKERS

LEVEL #1

DATE SUBMITTED TO PSC _____ DEPARTMENT _____

GRIEVOR'S NAME _____ NATURE OF GRIEVANCE _____

_____

_____

_____

_____

_____

ARTICLES GRIEVED _____

REDRESS SOUGHT _____

GRIEVOR'S SIGNATURE _____

COMMITTEE PERSON'S SIGNATURE _____

PSC'S ANSWER TO LEVEL #1

DATE ANSWERED _____

_____

_____

_____

_____

❏ ACCEPTED BY THE UNION   ❏ NOT ACCEPTED BY THE UNION

PSC'S SIGNATURE   _____

GRIEVOR'S SIGNATURE   _____

COMMITTEE PERSON'S SIGNATURE   _____

LEVEL #2

DATE SUBMITTED _____　　DATE ANSWERED _____

MANAGEMENT COMMITTEE RESPONSE _____

_____

_____

_____

_____

_____

❏ ACCEPTED BY THE UNION　　　　　　❏ NOT ACCEPTED BY THE UNION

MANAGEMENT REP'S SIGNATURE　　_____

GRIEVOR'S SIGNATURE　　　　　　_____

COMMITTEE PERSON'S SIGNATURE　_____

DATE　　　　　　_____

_____
_____

LEVEL #3

DATE SUBMITTED _____　　DATE ANSWERED _____

COMPANY'S ANSWER _____

_____

_____

_____

_____

_____

❏ ACCEPTED BY THE UNION　　　　　　❏ NOT ACCEPTED BY THE UNION

_____　　　　　_____

For the Company　　　　　　　　Plant Chairman's Signature

DATE _____

Source: Volkswagen Canada, Inc.

to arbitration in order to demonstrate to the members that the union is willing to exhaust every remedy in looking out for their interests. Union officers also are not likely to refuse to take to arbitration the grievances of members who are popular or politically powerful in the union, even though their cases are weak. Moreover, unions have a legal obligation to provide assistance to members who are pursuing grievances. Because members can bring suit against their unions for failing to process their grievances adequately, many union officers are reluctant to refuse taking even weak grievances to arbitration. The most commonly arbitrated issues relate to discipline, discharge, work assignments, and schedules.

Management, on the other hand, may allow a weak case to go to arbitration to demonstrate to the union officers that management "cannot be pushed around." Also, managers at lower levels may be reluctant to risk the displeasure of top management by stating that a certain HR policy is unworkable or unsound. Stubbornness and mutual antagonism also may force many grievances into arbitration because neither party is willing to make concessions to reach an agreement, even when it may recognize that it is in the wrong.

The Arbitration Process

Submission to arbitrate

Statement that describes the issues to be resolved through arbitration.

The issues to be resolved through arbitration may be described formally in a statement known as a **submission to arbitrate**. Each party makes a joint submission to the arbitrator indicating the rationale for the grievance. The submission to arbitrate must state the nature of the dispute with reference to the section of the collective agreement that has been allegedly breached and the remedy sought. Such a statement might read: "Was the three-day suspension of Alex Hayden for just cause? If not, what is the appropriate remedy?" If this statement is not available, then the arbitrator will attempt to formulate one based on oral presentations from both parties. If minutes and memoranda covering the meetings held at earlier stages of the grievance procedure have been prepared, these are sometimes submitted prior to the formal hearing to acquaint the arbitrator with the issues.

In arbitrating a dispute, it is the responsibility of the arbitrator to ensure that each side receives a fair hearing during which it may present all of the facts it considers pertinent to the case. The procedures for conducting arbitration hearings and the restrictions governing the evidence that may be introduced during these hearings are more flexible than those permitted in a court of law. Hearsay evidence, for example, may be introduced, provided it is considered as such when evaluated with the other evidence presented. The primary purpose of the hearing is to assist the arbitrator in obtaining the facts necessary to resolve a human relations problem rather than a legal one. The arbitrator, therefore, has a right to question witnesses or to request additional facts from either party.

Depending on the importance of the case, the hearings may be conducted in an informal way or in a very formal manner not unlike that of a court trial. If desired by either or both parties, or by the arbitrator, a court reporter may be present during the hearing to prepare a transcript of the proceedings. After conducting the hearing and receiving posthearing briefs (should the parties choose to submit them), the arbitrator customarily has a prescribed period in which to consider the evidence and to prepare a decision. In the majority of labour contracts, the costs of arbitration are shared equally by the parties.

Arbitration award
A final and binding award issued by an arbitrator in a labour–management dispute, arising from the interpretation or administration of the collective agreement.

The Arbitration Award

The **arbitration award** should include not only the arbitrator's decision but also the rationale for it. The reasoning behind the decision can help provide guidance concerning the interpretation of the labour agreement and the resolution of future disputes arising from its administration. In pointing out the merits of each party's position, the reasoning that underlies the award can help lessen the disappointment and protect the self-esteem of those representing the unsuccessful party. In short, tact and objective reasoning can help to reduce disappointment and hard feelings.

The foundation for an arbitrator's decision is the collective agreement and the rights it establishes for each party. In many instances, the decision may hinge upon whether management's actions were justified under the terms of this agreement. Sometimes it may hinge upon the arbitrator's interpretation of the wording of a particular provision. Established HR policies and past practices can also provide the basis for determining the award.

In many grievances, such as those involving employee performance or behaviour on the job, the arbitrator must determine whether the evidence supports the employer's action against the grievant. The evidence must also indicate whether the employee was accorded the right of due process, which is the employee's right to be informed of unsatisfactory performance and to have an opportunity to respond to these charges. Under most collective agreements an employer is required to have just cause (i.e., a good reason) for the action it has taken, and such action should be confirmed by the evidence presented.

If the arbitration hearing indicates that an employee was accorded due process and the disciplinary action was for just cause, the severity of the penalty must then be assessed. Where the evidence supports the discipline imposed by the employer, the arbitrator will probably let the discipline stand intact. However, it is within the arbitrator's power to reduce the penalty. It is not uncommon, for example, for an

Negotiators for both the owners and ballplayers gather in the early stages (August 1994) of the talks to settle the baseball strike.

arbitrator to reduce a discharge to a suspension without pay for the period the grievant has been off the payroll.

Unlike decisions in a court of law, awards—at least in theory—are supposed to be reached on the basis of the facts of the case rather than on the basis of precedents established by previous cases. The reason for this is that no two cases are exactly alike. Each case should therefore be decided on its own merits. In practice, however, precedents do at times have some influence on the decision of an arbitrator, who may seek guidance from decisions of other arbitrators in somewhat similar cases. These decisions are compiled and stored by the labour relations boards in each jurisdiction. Publishing houses such as CCH Canadian Limited have records of these decisions.

How Arbitrators Decide Cases

Because of the importance and magnitude of arbitration in grievance resolution, the process by which arbitrators make decisions and the factors that influence those decisions are of continuing interest to managers. Arbitrators typically use four factors when deciding cases:

1. The wording of the collective agreement
2. The submission to arbitrate as presented to the arbitrator
3. Testimony and evidence offered during the hearing
4. Arbitration criteria or standards (i.e., similar to standards of common law) against which cases are judged

When deciding the case of an employee discharged for absenteeism, for example, the arbitrator would consider these factors separately and/or jointly. Arbitrators are essentially constrained to decide cases on the basis of the wording of the labour agreement and the facts, testimony, and evidence presented at the hearing.

Since discipline and discharge issues generally constitute a majority of all arbitration, it is useful to understand the reasons given by arbitrators when they overturn managers in these cases. This information will help managers when they prepare cases for arbitration. In one study, five reasons accounted for over 70 percent of all reversal cases:

- The evidence did not support the charge of wrongdoing.
- The evidence supported the charge, but there were mitigating circumstances.
- Management committed procedural errors that prejudiced the grievant's rights.
- The rule was fair, but punishment for its infraction was harsh.
- Management was partly at fault in the incident.[36]

In practice, arbitration decision making is not an exact science. In fact, the decisions of arbitrators can be rather subjective. Arbitrators can, and do, interpret contract language differently (e.g., What does "just cause discharge" actually mean?); assign varying degrees of importance to testimony and evidence; judge the truthfulness of witnesses differently; and give arbitration standards greater or lesser weight as they apply to facts of the case. Each of these influences serves to introduce subjectivity into the decision-making process.

Problems with Grievance Arbitration

Grievance arbitration poses several critical problems today. Specifically, arbitration is criticized for taking too much time, becoming too expensive, and often creating frustration for the aggrieved employee and/or the supervisor in the dispute. The busy schedules of the arbitrator and the union and management officers, as well as a backlog of cases, frequently cause long delays in resolving relatively simple disputes. "Creeping legalism" through the increased use of lawyers and legal procedures portends a movement away from the original purposes of labour arbitration.

Furthermore, the judicial system is having to balance the rights of employees to resolve grievances that can arise under both the labour agreement and employment equity legislation. In British Columbia, Ontario, and Quebec, employees who work in a unionized environment can charge discrimination under either the Human Rights Act or provisions of the collective agreement. For example, a worker in Winnipeg who was forced to retire at age 65 lost his case before an arbitration board, but won it under the Manitoba Human Rights Act. Unions in some provinces can lose certification or have their collective agreements rendered void if they are found guilty of discriminating. Female employees have challenged collective agreement provisions that reserve certain jobs exclusively for men, thus adversely affecting the female employee's bumping, layoff, and seniority rights.[37]

SUMMARY

objective

Negotiating a labour agreement is a detailed process. Each side begins by preparing a list of proposals it wishes to achieve while additionally trying to anticipate those proposals desired by the other side. Bargaining teams are then selected and all proposals are analyzed to determine their impact on and cost to the organization. Both employer and union negotiators must be sensitive to current bargaining patterns within the industry, general cost-of-living trends, and geographical wage differentials. Managers establish goals that seek to retain control over operations and to minimize costs, while union negotiators focus their demands on improved wages, hours, and working conditions. An agreement is reached when both sides make compromises with respect to their original positions and final terms fall within the limits of the parties' bargaining zone.

objective

The collective bargaining process includes not only the actual negotiations but also the power tactics used to support negotiating demands. When negotiations become deadlocked, bargaining becomes a power struggle to force from either side the concessions needed to break the deadlock. The union's power in collective bargaining comes from its ability to picket, strike, or boycott the employer. The employer's power during negotiations comes from its ability to lock out employees or to operate during a strike by using managerial or, in some jurisdictions, replacement employees.

objective

Mediation is the principal way of resolving negotiating deadlocks. Mediators seek to assist the negotiators through opening up lines of communication between the parties and offering suggestions to resolve deadlocked proposals. In some situations, interest arbitration is employed to finalize the labour agreement. Interest arbitration is rarely used in the private sector; however, it is used often in those areas within the public sector where unions are prohibited from striking.

During the 1990s, several trends in labour relations have become evident. These include attempts to develop more cooperative labour–management endeavours and attitudes of less adversarial collective bargaining. Management has used concessionary bargaining to minimize or lower labour costs while improving workplace productivity through the reduction of restrictive work rules. Unions have stressed employee retraining and job security when seeking employer concessions.

The typical collective agreement contains numerous provisions governing the employment relationship between labour and management. The major areas of interest concern wages (rates of pay, overtime differentials, holiday pay), hours (shift times, days of work), and working conditions (safety issues, performance standards, retraining). To managers, the issue of management rights is particularly important. These rights hold that management's authority is supreme for all issues except those shared with the union through the collective agreement.

Differences between labour and management are normally resolved through the grievance procedure. Grievance procedures are negotiated and thus reflect the needs and desires of the parties involved. The typical grievance procedure consists of three, four, or five steps—each step having specific filing and reply times. Higher-level managers and union officials become involved in disputes at the higher steps of the grievance procedure. The final step of the grievance procedure may be arbitration. Arbitrators render a final and binding decision when problems are not resolved at lower grievance steps.

The submission agreement is a statement of the issue to be solved through arbitration. It is simply the problem that the parties wish to have settled. The arbitrator must answer the issue by basing the arbitration award on four factors: the contents of the labour agreement, the submission agreement as written, testimony and evidence obtained at the hearing, and various arbitration standards developed over time to assist in the resolution of different types of labour–management disputes. Arbitration is not an exact science in that arbitrators attach varying degrees of importance to the evidence and criteria by which disputes are resolved.

KEY TERMS

arbitration

arbitration award

arbitrator

bargaining zone

boycott

collective bargaining process

defined rights

expedited arbitration

grievance resolution

grievance procedure

interest arbitration

lockout

mediator

pattern bargaining

residual rights

submission to arbitrate

surface bargaining

DISCUSSION QUESTIONS

1. Is collective bargaining the same as negotiating? Explain.
2. Of what significance is the "bargaining zone" in the conduct of negotiations? What are some influences affecting negotiated outcomes?
3. What are some of the possible reasons an employer may be willing to face a strike that could result in a loss of customers and profits?
4. How does mediation differ from arbitration, and in what situations is each of these processes most likely to be used?
5. What are some of the bargaining concessions generally sought by employers and unions in return for the concessions they may grant?
6. What are some of the developments that are posing a threat to union security today?
7. At an election conducted among the twenty employees of the Exclusive Jewellery Store, all but two voted in favour of the Jewellery Workers Union, which subsequently was certified as their bargaining agent. In negotiating its first agreement, the union demanded that it be granted a union shop. The two employees who had voted against the union, however, informed the management that they would quit rather than join. Unfortunately for the store, the two employees were skilled gem cutters who were the most valuable of its employees and would be difficult to replace. What position should the store take with regard to the demand for a union shop?
8. What are some of the reasons a union or an employer may allow a weak grievance to go to arbitration?

....

CASE: # Labour-Management Partnership at Algoma Steel

Employee buyouts of Canadian companies such as Algoma Steel shift the traditional bargaining strategies of labour and management. In 1991, employees at Algoma Steel, Canada's third largest steel maker, concluded the largest worker buyout in the history of North American business. As majority shareholders, the employees directly selected four members of the thirteen-member board of directors, and had an influence in the selection of another seven. The traditional adversarial, competitive stance is being replaced by cooperation, collaboration, and consensus. The experiment at Algoma proves that it is possible to develop cooperative responses to threats from the external environment.

Before 1991, labour relations at Algoma were bitterly adversarial. Union and management officials confronted each other with different issues, beliefs, politics, and desired outcomes. Each side brought to the relationship a confrontational behaviour forged from a long pattern of hostile interactions. The unions viewed management as an autocratic group that cared little for employees and that demanded numerous "givebacks" through bargaining concessions. Management viewed union leaders as antagonistic and solely interested in preserving the status quo by using threats or pressure politics. In the early stages of the new relationship, success was described as being able to sit in the same room without physical violence.

The turnaround in labour relations at Algoma began only when both sides realized the significance of their problems and decided to develop a cooperative labour–management partnership based upon mutual respect and joint collaboration. At Algoma Steel, the cooperative effort is managed by the joint steering committee, on which representatives of both management and labour act as co-chairs. This cooperation extends to the shop floor, where employees are grouped into employee participation units (EPUs). Worker empowerment is based on the idea that workers know best how to run the workplace. Ideas from workers are submitted to these units, where they are evaluated quickly and, if accepted, implemented by the team. Employee suggestions saved the company $1.2 million over one four-month period. Employees share in the profits, and in 1994 pocketed about an extra $400 dollars each.

Workers are involved in the kinds of decisions formally reserved for management, such as work flexibility, hiring, and training. Even major changes, such as quality programs, are proving more successful because the labour–management committees introducing the changes have more credibility than the former managers.

Communication patterns have changed. Workers are hard-wired, sending messages to management directly through e-mail. This enables management to respond to worker queries and to squelch rumours that would have had the potential to disrupt production. Trust has increased to the point where there are now only about 100 grievances, none of which requires arbitration, compared to 1200 annual grievances in one union local (there are seven in all), with 30 going to arbitration.

The national unions are suspicious about the unions cooperating with management, and some supervisors are uncomfortable about the transfer of power to workers. Managers had to learn to respect the workers and realize that being a manager did not confer extra privileges in benefits. As one union spokesperson asked, "Do senior managers need a better dental plan than everyone else? When they become senior managers, do their teeth suddenly fall out?"

Workers had to learn that they were in the best position to identify problems and suggest solutions. As Denis Desjardins, coordinator of the company's employee participation program, says, "It's a fabulous opportunity. Every worker thinks, 'If only I could change things around here.' Now they have the chance."

The magnitude of Algoma's turnaround since the company's near bankruptcy in 1991 is remarkable. All laid-off workers have been recalled, the workforce has increase by about 15 percent, and in 1994 the company was the most profitable steel company in North America (aided by increases in steel prices).

Sources: K. Mark, "Buyout and the Bottom Line," *Human Resources Professional* (April 1995): 17–19; M. Lowe, "Steel Resolve," *The Financial Post Magazine*, April 1995, 20–24; and V. Galt, "Algoma Reinvents Labour Relations," *The Globe and Mail*, April 21, 1995, B1.

Questions

1. What are the key factors involved in maintaining the effectiveness of cooperative labour–management programs?
2. What kinds of training would both management and labour need in order to learn to work in a cooperative relationship?
3. If steel prices drop radically, what will be the impact on the perception of the success of this cooperative effort?

Salary Negotiation Tactics

Although you are unlikely to be involved in the negotiation of a collective agreement, you will be involved in negotiations of other issues of importance to you. Negotiating a salary may be one of the more important ones. Asking for a raise is an emotionally difficult process. However, this process resembles the collective bargaining process in that each party has goals, uses power plays, reads nonverbal cues, but does want to achieve a win-win solution.

Table 1 lists six common negotiating strategies and provides examples of effective and ineffective tactics. Table 2 lists the pattern of negotiation found in a typical pattern of salary negotiation. The dotted line dividing stage IV and Stage V is an indication that subtlety has ended and open conflict begins.

Using the two tables as performance aids, construct a mock interview with your manager in which you ask for a raise in pay. Try role playing the salary negotiation with a friend before attempting the negotiation with your manager.

Table 1
Effective and Ineffective Use of Negotiation Tactics

Tactics Used in Negotiation	Example of Use by Manager	Example of Use by Employee
Reasoning *Effective Tactics* Strong, persuasive statements about reasons for the position taken; Appeal to other party's sense of logic; No dependence on the opinions or practices of others	"The budget is tight and we can all move ahead if we each tighten up our belts for just a little longer"	"I've worked hard, performed very well and I deserve to be equitably compensated for my contribution"
Ineffective Tactics Argumentative; Using weak examples or exaggeration to challenge what the other negotiator says; Justifying position by reliance on the opinions or practices of others	"You are asking for the whole world ... only GOD or the CEO can give you that"	"Supervisor X is giving all his people hefty increases"
Ingratiation *Effective Tactics* Demonstration that person can be relied upon to support the other party; Positive evaluation of other; Friendliness	"No matter what happens here today, you know that I support you"	"No matter what happens here today, you know that I trust you"

Tactics Used in Negotiation	Example of Use by Manager	Example of Use by Employee
Ineffective Tactics Insincere compliments; Superficial offers to support other; Grand, but obviously false plans to work together in the future	"I think of you and me as a team and I have big plans for your future"	"We all think you are the greatest and you are a really snappy dresser"
Creating Alternatives *Effective Tactics* Problem solving; Generating workable possibilities; Suggesting different ways to look at the problem; Action-oriented ideas	"Keep in mind that this is a great place to work, you have excellent benefits, and a wonderful group of people to work with"	"Maybe you could speak to your boss about a special case salary adjustment or a change of job title to justify it"
Ineffective Tactics "Administrative orbiting" by always needing more information to make a decision; Coming up with highly unlikely events which might cause problems for every new idea	"If I only knew what our overhead is going to be, I would know what I can give you. I never know what might come up"	"Before I accept your offer, I have to investigate what other companies are paying someone with my talents"
Coalition Formation *Effective Tactics* Political savvy; Joining forces with superiors, subordinates, or peers to enhance power position; Identifying goals which consolidate units; Sincere willingness to collaborate; Strategic use of secrecy and disclosure of information	"The other managers and I all feel that at this time only rewards for some special type of contribution can be given"	"I have talked with a number of people in other departments and we all agree that it is time for some support from management if we are going to get this done"
Ineffective Tactics Forming ineffective alliances; Unfair stereotypes of those who have opposing views; Wrongly assuming that cohesiveness or consensus exists; Dubious plans for unity; Excessive secrecy or disclosure of info	"You aren't another Kelly are you? Always claiming that this or that is unfair; we don't need any more claims against us"	"I talked with Bob and Kelly and the three of us agreed that we are not going to take this anymore. We don't know what to do yet, but we will do something"

Tactics Used in Negotiation	Example of Use by Manager	Example of Use by Employee
Coercion		
Effective Tactics		
Use of threats that clearly will be backed up with action; Knowing when, where, how, and how much to use force to obtain compliance; Applying the minimal necessary (often implied) threat; Providing a rationale to the coerced party for the necessity of using power	"I am forced to do something that I really don't enjoy: I either must lay some people off or else cut back on salaries this year. We are going to be looking at everyone very carefully to decide who stays and who goes"	"I love my job here and the people are the best. The problem is that I have family obligations: My kids want to go to a good college and that costs a lot of hard-earned money"
Ineffective Tactics		
Use of weak threats; Exerting excessive force to obtain compliance when other tactics could have the same result; Excessive threats that create hostility; Failure to explain why it was necessary to use force	"Who do you think you are? I'm the boss here and I don't have to explain anything to you except this: Do what I say or this place will be no more than a memory for you"	"I'll straighten it out alright, but not with you, with your boss. We'll see who has the last say on this after he/she hears what is really going on here"
Avoidance		
Effective Tactics		
Recognizing when some time and distance between the parties may be necessary to regain perspectives; Removing disruptions or trivial issues from discussion; Knowing when other opinions or information would help to resolve the problem	"Maybe we should think this over some more. I want to reflect on it and I would like you to discuss it with some of your co-workers. See if they agree with you. We will meet at the same time one week from today to resolve this issue"	"Your offer sounds very good but I would like some time to think it over, discuss it with my spouse, and review my options. I just like to be certain before I make a commitment"
Ineffective Tactics		
Non-action; Trying to wear down other party by claiming that other people must act first; False insistence that the proper procedures or channels have not been used; Strategy of "Ignore it and it will go away" while claiming that the issue is "being studied"	"You know that I can't do anything until those snails at headquarters review it, then HR and payroll get a whack at it. My hands are tied but I'll get back to you the minute I hear something"	"If I just do a good job and don't make any waves, the boss will be sure to be grateful and give me the increase that I deserve"

Table 2
Common Tactics Used by Managers and Employees During Salary Negotiation

| Stage | PATTERN OF NEGOTIATION | | BEHAVIOURIAL STYLE | |
	Negotiator	Tactic	Assertiveness	Cooperativeness
STAGE I	Manager	Reasoning	High	High
	Employee	Reasoning	High	High
STAGE II	Manager	Coalition Formation	High	Low
	Employee	Ingratiation	Low	Very High
STAGE III	Manager	Ingratiation	Low	Very High
	Employee	Coalition Formation	High	Low
STAGE IV	Manager	Creative Alternatives	High or Low	High or Low
	Employee	Creative Alternatives	High or Low	High or Low
STAGE V	Manager	Coercion	Very High	Very Low
	Employee	Avoidance	Low	Low
STAGE VI	Manager	Avoidance	Low	Low
	Employee	Coercion	Very High	Very Low

Source: "Negotiating Salaries: Managing Conflict to Achieve Equitable Pay," in G. Kroeck and S. Fraser, *Tactical Experiences in Human Resources Management* (Toronto: Harcourt Brace & Company, 1994), 139–145.

NOTES AND REFERENCES

1. Thomas R. Colosi and Arthur E. Berkeley, *Collective Bargaining: How It Works and Why* (New York: American Arbitration Association, 1992). See also Francisco Hernandez-Senter, Jr., "Closing the Communication Gap in Collective Bargaining," *Labor Law Journal* 41, no. 7 (July 1990): 438–444.

2. J. Godard, *Industrial Relations: The Economy and Society* (Toronto: McGraw-Hill Ryerson, 1994).

3. John A. Fossum, *Labor Relations: Development, Structure, Process*, 6th ed. (Homewood, IL: BPI-Irwin, 1995), 278.

4. Peter Cappelli, "Is Pattern Bargaining Dead? A Discussion," *Industrial and Labor Relations Review* 44, no. 1 (October 1990): 152–155.

5. John W. Budd, "The Determinants and Extent of UAW Pattern Bargaining," *Industrial and Labor Relations Review* 45, no. 3 (April 1992): 523–537.

6. Daniel Q. Mills, *Labor–Management Relations*, 5th ed. (New York: McGraw-Hill, 1994).

7. S. Dolan and R.S. Schuler, *Human Resource Management: The Canadian Dynamic* (Scarborough, ON: Nelson Canada, 1994).

8. Peter H. Corne, "The Complex Art of Negotiation between Different Cultures," *Arbitration Journal* 47, no. 4 (December 1992): 46–50.

9. For the original description of attitudinal structuring, see Richard E. Walton and Robert B. McKersie, *A Behavioral Theory of Labor Negotiations* (New York: McGraw-Hill, 1965). This book is considered a classic in the labour relations field.

10. William Ury, *Getting Past No: Negotiating with Different People* (New York: Bantam Books, 1991).

11. Bruce C. Herniter, Erran Carmel, and Jay F. Nunamaker, Jr., "Computers Improve Efficiency of the Negotiation Process," *Personnel Journal* 72, no. 4 (April 1993): 93–99.

12. Ross Stagner and Hjalmar Rosen, *Psychology of Union–Management Relations* (Belmont, CA: Wadsworth, 1965), 95–97.

13. Rajib H. Sanyal, "The Withering Away of the Strike: The Ross-Hartman Analysis Thirty Years Since," *Labor Studies Journal* 15, no. 4 (Winter 1990), 47–68.

14. Jan I. Ondrich and John F. Schnell, "Strike Duration and the Degree of Disagreement," *Industrial Relations* 32, no. 3 (Fall 1993): 412–431.

15. Michael H. LeRoy, "Multivariate Analysis of Unionized Employees' Propensity to Cross Their Union's Picket Line," *Journal of Labor Research* 13, no. 3 (Summer 1992): 285–291.

16. Brenda Paik Sunoo and Jennifer J. Lambs, "Winning Strategies for Outsourcing Contracts," *Personnel Journal* 13, no. 3 (March 1994): 69. See also Bruce E. Kaufman, "Labor's Inequality of Bargaining Power: Changes over Time and Implications for Public Policy," *Journal of Labor Research* 10, no. 3 (Summer 1989): 285–297; and John G. Kilgor, "Can Unions Strike Anymore? The Impact of Recent Supreme Court Decisions," *Labor Law Journal* 41, no. 5 (May 1990): 259–269.

17. Workplace Information Directorate, Labour Branch, Human Resources Development Canada, "Chronological Work Stoppages," August 1995. Used with permission.

18. Deborah M. Kolb, *When Talk Works: Profiles of Mediators* (San Francisco, CA: Jossey-Bass, 1994). See also Sam Kagel and Kathy Kelly, *The Anatomy of Mediation: What Makes It Work* (Washington, DC: Bureau of National Affairs, 1989).

19. Ernest J. Savoie, "Recognition and Revitalization Fundamentals for Sustaining Change," *Labor Law Journal* 44, no. 8 (August 1993): 486–491.

20. For examples of concessionary bargaining and the development of labour–management cooperative programs, see Keith L. Alexander, "It's Time for USA to Take Labor's Outstretched Hand," *Business Week*, August 16, 1993, 30; "Labor Deals That Offer a Break from Us vs. Them," *Business Week*, August 2, 1993, 30; and Peggy Stuart, "Labor Unions Become Business Partners," *Personnel Journal* 72, no. 8 (August 1993): 54–63.

21. *American Workplace* 1, no. 1 (September 1993): 2.

22. Jill Kriesky and Edwin Brown, "The Union Role in Labor–Management Cooperation: A Case Study at the Boise Cascade Company's Jackson Mill," *Labor Studies Journal* 18, no. 3 (Fall 1993): 17–32.

23. V. Galt, "Algoma Reinvents Labour Relations," *The Globe and Mail*, April 21, 1995, B1.

24. Paula B. Voss, "The Influence of Cooperative Programs on Union–Management Relations, Flexibility, and Other Labor Relations Outcomes," *Journal of Labor Research* 10, no. 1 (Winter 1989): 103.

25. Leslie A. Nay, "The Determinants of Concession Bargaining in the Airline Industry," *Industrial and Labor Relations Review* 44, no. 2 (January 1991): 305–365.

26. Peter Nulty, "Look What the Unions Want Now," *Fortune*, February 1993, 128–135.

27. For an expanded discussion of management's reserved rights, see Paul Prasow and Edward Peters, *Arbitration and Collective Bargaining*, 2nd ed. (New York: McGraw-Hill, 1983), 33–34.

28. Labour agreement, Wabash Fibre Box Company and Paperworkers.

29. Craig and Solomon, *System of Industrial Relations*, 304.

30. Judith L. Carter and Edwin L. Brown, "Union Leaders' Perception of the Grievance Procedure," *Labor Studies Journal* 15, no. 1 (Spring 1990): 54–55. See also Frank Elkouri and Edna Asher Elkouri, *How Arbitration Works*,

4th ed. (Washington, DC: Bureau of National Affairs, 1985): 153.

31. Jeanette A. Davy and George W. Bohlander, "Recent Findings and Practices in Grievance-Arbitration Procedures," *Labor Law Journal* 43, no. 3 (March 1992): 184–190.

32. George W. Bohlander, "Public-Sector Grievance Arbitration: Structure and Administration," *Journal of Collective Negotiations in the Public Sector* 21, no. 4 (Fall 1992): 278.

33. Michael J. Duane, "To Grieve or Not to Grieve: Why Reduce It to Writing?" *Public Personnel Management* 20, no. 1 (Spring 1991): 83–88.

34. J. Gandz and J.D. Whitehead, "Grievances and Their Resolution," in M. Gunderson et al., eds., *Union Management Relations in Canada*, 2nd ed. (Don Mills, ON: Addison-Wesley, 1989).

35. Some labour agreements call for using arbitration boards to resolve employee grievances. Arbitration boards, which may be either temporary or permanent, are composed of one or more members chosen by management and an equal number chosen by labour. A neutral member serves as chair. See Peter A. Veglahn, "Grievance Arbitration by Arbitration Boards: A Survey of the Parties," *Arbitration Journal* 42, no. 2 (July 1987): 47–53.

36. George W. Bohlander, "Why Arbitrators Overturn Managers in Employee Suspension and Discharge Cases," *Journal of Collective Bargaining in the Public Sector* 23, no. 1 (Spring 1994): 73–89.

37. H.C. Jain, "Human Rights: Issues in Employment," in H.C. Jain and P.C. Wright, eds., *Trends and Challenges in Human Resource Management* (Scarborough, ON: Nelson Canada, 1994), 69–88.

Part 6

International Human Resources Management and HR Audits

Part 6 focuses on the topics of HR in multinational companies and the auditing of specific HR functions. Chapter 17 deals with the challenges faced by multinational enterprises when they staff managers and executives in overseas assignments. Special considerations are given to understanding cultural, social, and legal differences of job assignments in foreign countries. In Chapter 18, the effectiveness of HR programs is examined. Included here are HR audit procedures available to both department supervisors and HR specialists. Auditing the many HR functions and programs is a prerequisite to the effective utilization of both monetary and human resources.

After studying this chapter you, should be able to

one
objective

Identify the types of organizational forms used for competing internationally.

two
objective

Explain how domestic and international HRM differ.

Discuss the staffing process for individuals working internationally.
three
objective

Identify the unique training needs for international assignees.
four
objective

five
objective

Reconcile the difficulties of home-country and host-country performance appraisals.

six
objective

Identify the characteristics of a good international compensation plan.

seven
objective

Explain the major differences between Canadian and European labour relations.

Chapter 17

International Human Resources Management

T*he emphasis throughout this book has been on HRM as it is practised in organizations in Canada. But many of these firms also engage in international trade. A large percentage carry on their international business with only limited facilities and representation in foreign countries. Others have extensive facilities and personnel in various countries of the world. Managing these resources effectively, and integrating their activities to achieve global advantage, is a challenge to the leadership of these companies.*

We are quickly moving toward a global economy. While estimates vary widely, approximately 70 to 85 percent of the Canadian economy today is affected by international competition. Recent popular books have suggested that many North American companies need to reassess their approach to doing business overseas, particularly in the area of managing human resources. To a large degree, the challenge of managing across borders boils down to the philosophies and systems we use for managing people.[1] In this chapter, we will observe that much of what is discussed throughout this text can be applied to foreign operations, provided one is sensitive to the requirements of a particular international setting. Canadians have done well internationally, not just because of technology literacy but because of Canada's multicultural and multilingual workforce, combined with skills in transportation, resources development, communications, and financial services.[2] For example, in the information technology sector, Quebeckers are working on Mexico's new tax system, Calgarians are working on information systems in Venezuela, Haligonians are managing the desktop systems technology for a Dallas company, Vancouverites are providing systems integration services in Korea, and people in Waterloo are developing point of sales systems for PepsiFoods around the world.[3]

The first part of this chapter presents a brief introduction to international business firms. In many important respects, the way a company organizes its international operations influences the type of managerial and human resources issues it faces. In addition, we briefly describe some of the environmental factors that also affect the work of managers in a global setting. Just as with domestic operations, the dimensions of the environment form a context in which HRM decisions are made. A major portion of this chapter deals with the various HR activities involved in the recruitment, selection, development, and compensation of employees who work in an international setting. Throughout the discussion the focus will be on Canadian multinational corporations.

Managing Across Borders

objective

International corporation
A domestic firm that uses its existing capabilities to move into overseas markets.

Multinational corporation (MNC)
A firm with independent business units operating in multiple countries.

International business operations can take several different forms. Figure 17-1 shows four basic types of organizations and how they differ in the degree to which international activities are separated to respond to the local regions and integrated to achieve global efficiencies. The **international corporation** is essentially a domestic firm that builds on its existing capabilities to penetrate overseas markets. Companies such as CP, Bombardier, and Magna used this approach to gain access to Europe—they essentially adapted existing products for overseas markets without changing much else about their normal operations.

A **multinational corporation (MNC)** is a more complex form that usually has fully autonomous units operating in multiple countries. Shell, Phillips, and ITT are three typical MNCs. These companies have traditionally given their foreign subsidiaries a great deal of latitude to address local issues such as consumer preferences, political pressures, and economic trends in different regions of the world.

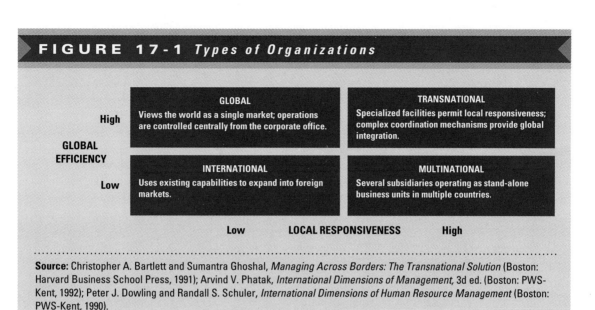

FIGURE 17-1 *Types of Organizations*

	Low LOCAL RESPONSIVENESS **High**	

GLOBAL
Views the world as a single market; operations are controlled centrally from the corporate office.

TRANSNATIONAL
Specialized facilities permit local responsiveness; complex coordination mechanisms provide global integration.

INTERNATIONAL
Uses existing capabilities to expand into foreign markets.

MULTINATIONAL
Several subsidiaries operating as stand-alone business units in multiple countries.

GLOBAL EFFICIENCY — High / Low

LOCAL RESPONSIVENESS — Low / High

Source: Christopher A. Bartlett and Sumantra Ghoshal, *Managing Across Borders: The Transnational Solution* (Boston: Harvard Business School Press, 1991); Arvind V. Phatak, *International Dimensions of Management,* 3d ed. (Boston: PWS-Kent, 1992); Peter J. Dowling and Randall S. Schuler, *International Dimensions of Human Resource Management* (Boston: PWS-Kent, 1990).

Global corporation
A firm that has integrated worldwide operations through a centralized home office.

Transnational corporation
A firm that attempts to balance local responsiveness and global scale via a network of specialized operating units.

Frequently these subsidiaries are run as independent companies, without much integration. The **global corporation**, on the other hand, can be viewed as a multinational firm that maintains control of operations back in the home office. Japanese companies such as Matsushita and NEC, for example, tend to treat the world market as a unified whole and try to combine activities in each country to maximize efficiency on a global scale. These companies operate much like a domestic firm, except that they view the whole world as their marketplace.

Finally, a **transnational corporation** attempts to achieve the local responsiveness of an MNC while also achieving the efficiencies of a global firm. To balance this "global/local" dilemma, a transnational uses a network structure that coordinates specialized facilities positioned around the world. By using this flexible structure, a transnational provides autonomy to independent country operations, but brings these separate activities together into an integrated whole. For most companies, the transnational form represents an ideal, rather than a reality. However, companies such as Ford, Unilever, and British Petroleum have made good progress in restructuring operations to function more transnationally.[4]

Although various forms of organization exist, in this chapter we will generally refer to any company that conducts business outside its home country as an *international business*.

Canada, of course, has no monopoly on international business. International enterprises are found throughout the world. In fact, some European and Pacific Rim companies have been conducting business on an international basis much longer than their North American counterparts.[5] The close proximity of European countries, for example, makes them likely candidates for international trade. Figure 17-2 identifies the world's 50 largest public companies. These companies are in a strong position to affect the world economy in the following ways:

FIGURE 17-2 *The World's 50 Largest Public Companies*

Ranked by market value as of July 31, 1994, as determined by Morgan Stanley Capital International Perspective. (In millions of U.S. dollars; financial data at December 31, 1993, exchange rates.)

COMPANY	MARKET VALUE	COMPANY	MARKET VALUE
1 NTT (Japan)	$130,344	26 British Telecom (U.K.)	35,170
2 Royal Dutch/Shell (Netherlands/U.K.)	97,170	27 British Petroleum (U.K.)	34,576
3 General Electric (U.S.)	86,005	28 Matsushita Electric Industrial (Japan)	34,311
4 Toyota Motor (Japan)	78,788	29 Nestle (Switzerland)	33,564
5 Mitsubishi Bank (Japan)	75,029	30 Mobil (U.S.)	33,396
6 Exxon (U.S.)	73,899	31 Allianz Holding (Germany)	32,009
7 AT&T (U.S.)	73,875	32 Ford Motor (U.S.)	31,811
8 Industrial Bank of Japan (Japan)	70,890	33 Hitachi (Japan)	31,613
9 Fuji Bank (Japan)	65,354	34 Bank of Tokyo (Japan)	31,331
10 Sumitomo Bank (Japan)	63,339	35 HSBC Holdings (U.K.)	31,265
11 Sanwa Bank (Japan)	62,542	36 BellSouth (U.S.)	31,005
12 Dai-Ichi Kangyo Bank (Japan)	59,190	37 GTE (U.S.)	30,345
13 Coca-Cola Co. (U.S.)	57,575	38 Johnson & Johnson (U.S.)	30,220
14 Wal-Mart Stores (U.S.)	57,469	39 American International Group (U.S.)	29,919
15 Philip Morris (U.S.)	48,235	40 Amoco (U.S.)	29,722
16 Sakura Bank (Japan)	46,363	41 Motorola (U.S.)	29,601
17 Nomura Securities (Japan)	43,295	42 Unilever (Netherlands/U.K.)	29,599
18 Tokyo Electric Power (Japan)	40,515	43 Microsoft (U.S.)	29,232
19 Roche Holding (Switzerland)	40,459	44 Chevron (U.S.)	28,909
20 DuPont (U.S.)	40,231	45 Asahi Bank (Japan)	28,496
21 Procter & Gamble (U.S.)	38,008	46 Seven-Eleven (Japan)	28,344
22 Merck (U.S.)	37,148	47 Long-Term Credit Bank (Japan)	27,948
23 General Motors (U.S.)	36,990	48 Bristol-Myers Squibb (U.S.)	27,260
24 IBM (U.S.)	36,018	49 Glaxo Holdings (U.K.)	26,637
25 Singapore Telecom (Singapore)	35,723	50 Tokai Bank (Japan)	26,331

Source: Reprinted by permission of *The Wall Street Journal*, copyright 1994 by Dow Jones & Company, Inc. All rights reserved worldwide.

1. Production and distribution extend beyond national boundaries, making it easier to transfer technology.
2. They have direct investments in many countries, affecting the balance of payments.
3. They have a political impact that leads to cooperation among countries and to the breaking down of barriers of nationalism.

The Environment of International Business

In Chapter 2, the role of environment—both internal and external—in HRM was emphasized. Understanding the external environment is critical to the success of managing any international business. The dramatic changes that have occurred in recent years in Russia and eastern Europe will have their effects on HRM. Of probably even greater influence is the unification of markets in the European Union (EU). In concept, the EU will turn Europe into a unified buying and selling power that will compete as a major economic player with North America and Japan.* Highlights in HRM 1 describes some of the effects that unification may have on HRM practices within Europe. Though there are many obstacles to complete unification, the goal of the EU is for goods, services, capital, and human resources to flow across national borders in Europe in a manner similar to the way they cross provincial lines in Canada.[6] A similar transition will likely occur within North America with the passage of NAFTA (discussed in Chapter 2). In the years ahead we will have a unique opportunity to observe the effects of globalization on HRM.

Certainly the economic environment and the physical environment (population, climate, geography, and so on) are important factors in the making of managerial decisions. Of special importance in international business, however, is the cultural environment (communications, religion, values and ideologies, education, social structure). Figure 17-3 is an overview of the complexity of the **cultural environment** in which HR must be managed. Culture is an integrated phenomenon, and by recognizing and accommodating taboos, rituals, attitudes toward time, social stratification, kinship systems, and the many other components listed in Figure 17-3, managers will pave the way toward greater harmony and achievement in the **host country** (the country in which an international business operates).

Different cultural environments require different managerial behaviours. Strategies, structures, and technologies that are appropriate in one cultural setting may lead to failure in another.[7] Managing relations between an organization and its cultural environment is thus a matter of accurate perception, sound diagnosis, and appropriate adaptation. Several techniques and approaches are available to assist employees in coping with demands imposed by the cultural environment.[8] Interestingly, companies in one location often push aside interorganizational differences to share experiences and to assist each other in resolving conflicts that arise with the host country's culture.

Cultural environment
The language, religion, values, attitudes, education, social organization, technology, politics, and laws of a country.

Host country
The country in which an international corporation operates.

---

*Originally, the EU was composed of twelve nations: Belgium, Denmark, France, Germany, Greece, Ireland, Italy, Luxembourg, Netherlands, Portugal, Spain, and the United Kingdom. Recently, these countries voted to add Sweden, Finland, and Austria to their ranks.

1 HR ISSUES OF A UNIFIED EUROPE

STAFFING

Unification provides workers the right to move freely throughout Europe and opens labour markets on a pan-European basis. However, unemployment rates vary dramatically across countries throughout Europe. For example, Spain's unemployment rate hovers around 25 percent (43 percent for individuals under age 25), whereas the unemployment rates in Norway and Switzerland are less than 10 percent. Many of these differences reflect the existence of hard-core unemployed—more than 40 percent of the 17 million unemployed in the EU have been out of work for at least a year, and a third have never worked at all. These problems are due to many factors, including political systems, sociocultural differences, and worker training. In some cases, unemployment is the result of racial discrimination. Managers must overcome these problems to take advantage of the labour markets that have been opened to them.

Fortunately, the EU prohibits discrimination against workers and unions. However, while member countries are required to interpret national law in light of EU directives, most companies are still trying to reconcile EU policies with laws in their home countries. While legislation provides protection based on race and gender, age discrimination is still not outlawed.

TRAINING AND DEVELOPMENT

Bringing education up to date to prepare Europe's youth and to eliminate the bottlenecks that already exist in many advanced industries will not be simple. Under a unified Europe, every worker is guaranteed access to vocational training. Germany remains a model of apprenticeship programs and worker development.

While the EU provides a path for increasing diversity, countries throughout Europe tend to remain nationalistic. There is a need for "Euroexecutives"—those who speak many languages, are mobile, and are experienced at managing a multicultural workforce.

PRODUCTIVITY

To be competitive in a global economy, Europeans must increase their level of productivity. Europeans on average work fewer hours, take longer vacations, and enjoy far more social entitlements than their counterparts in North America and Asia. For example, in contrast to the ten vacation days that Canadian employees receive, employees in Europe enjoy far more leisure time. In the United Kingdom, France, and the Netherlands workers receive about 25 days of paid vacation, while workers in Sweden and Austria receive 30. In many countries, these periods are established by law and must be reconciled in a unified Europe.

COMPENSATION AND BENEFITS

Wages also differ substantially across countries throughout Europe. For example, workers in industrialized countries such as Germany and Switzerland receive an average hourly wage of about $15 (benefits account for approximately $10 extra). Workers in Greece and Portugal, in contrast, have wages that are down around $3 or $4 (the value of benefits adds only about $2). Market forces are likely to harmonize these differences somewhat. In addition to the wage differences across countries, workers in Europe are more highly paid than workers in other parts of the world. To be competitive, companies will need to exert market forces to bring compensation levels more in line with productivity.

Although pay discrimination is prohibited by law, women workers still tend to be in low-paying jobs. Because of this, the European Commission has proposed "codes of practice on equal pay for work of equal value," similar to comparable value in Canada. Even so, it appears that a freer labour market is eliminating pay differences.

In addition to wage issues, the EU has also addressed issues related to benefits. Under EU mandate, all workers have the right to social security benefits regardless of occupation or employer. In addition, even persons who have been unable to enter the workforce are given basic social assistance. Several directives on occupational safety and health exist to establish minimal standards throughout Europe.

LABOUR RELATIONS

In the past, powerful trade unions have fiercely defended social benefits. In a unified Europe, unions retain collective bargaining rights laid out under the host country's laws and the right to be consulted regarding company decisions.

Stimulating economic growth to create jobs may mean eliminating rigid work rules and softening policies related to social benefits. Union leaders have promised to fight these initiatives.

Sources: "Europe's Unlevel Playing Field," *The Economist*, June 4, 1994, 18; "Europe's Paper Tiger," *The Economist*, July 30, 1994, 42; Jan S. Krulis-Randa, "Strategic Human Resource Management in Europe after 1992," *International Journal of Human Resource Management* 1, no. 2 (Spring 1990): 131–138; Hugh G. Mosley, "The Social Dimension of European Integration," *International Labour Review* 129, no. 2 (1990): 147–164; F.D. Blau and L.M. Kahn, "The Gender Earnings Gap: Learning from International Comparisons," *American Economic Review* 82, no. 2 (May 1992): 533–538; "EU: MNCs Face New Challenges as Frontiers Merge," *Crossborder Monitor* 2, no. 10 (March 16, 1994): 1; Jane Sasseen, "EU Dateline," *International Management* 49, no. 2 (March 1994): 5; Dieter Sadowski, "The Impact of European Integration and German Unification on Industrial Relations in Germany," *British Journal of Industrial Relations* 32, no. 4 (December 1994): 523–537.

objective

Domestic versus International HRM

The internationalization of corporations has grown at a faster pace than the internationalization of HRM. Executives in the very best companies around the world still lament that their HR policies have not kept pace with the demands of global competition.[9] And unfortunately, the academic community has not been a particularly good source for ready-made answers to international HRM problems. While various journals on international business have published articles on HRM over the years, it was not until 1990 that a journal specifically devoted to this area—the *International Journal of Human Resource Management*—was started.

International HRM differs from domestic HRM in several ways. In the first place, it necessarily places a greater emphasis on certain functions. As shown in Figure 17-4, functions and activities of significance to international HRM include relocation, orientation, and translation services to help employees adapt to a new and different environment outside their own country. Assistance with taxation matters, banking, investment management, home rental while on assignment, and coordination of home visits is also usually provided by the HR department.[10]

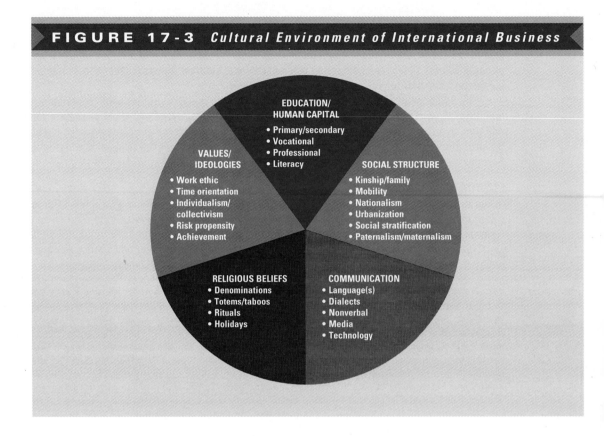

FIGURE 17-3 *Cultural Environment of International Business*

The HR department in an overseas unit must be particularly responsive to the external environment. The human consequences of failure are often more severe in an international business than in a domestic business. International HR managers are also exposed to other risks. Political events may result in risks such as the possibility of terrorist attacks on personnel. There is also the need to change emphasis in HR operations as a foreign subsidiary matures. To ensure their success, most larger corporations have a full-time staff of HR managers devoted solely to assisting globalization. McDonald's, for example, has a team of five HR directors who travel as internal consultants. Their job is to keep local directors in over 50 countries updated on international concerns, policies, and programs. Other companies, such as Dow Chemical, are working rapidly to develop worldwide HR information systems that electronically link personnel records and other forms of information.[11] The issues encountered by one human resources manager who regularly prepares executives for international assignments are outlined in Reality Check.

objective

International Staffing

International management poses many problems in addition to those faced by a domestic operation. Because of geographic distance and a lack of close, day-to-day relationships with headquarters in the home country, problems must often be

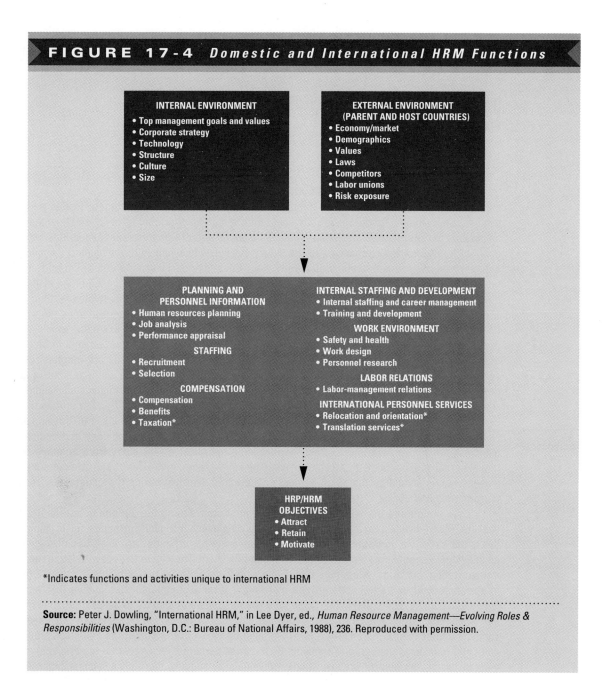

FIGURE 17-4 *Domestic and International HRM Functions*

INTERNAL ENVIRONMENT
- Top management goals and values
- Corporate strategy
- Technology
- Structure
- Culture
- Size

EXTERNAL ENVIRONMENT (PARENT AND HOST COUNTRIES)
- Economy/market
- Demographics
- Values
- Laws
- Competitors
- Labor unions
- Risk exposure

PLANNING AND PERSONNEL INFORMATION
- Human resources planning
- Job analysis
- Performance appraisal

STAFFING
- Recruitment
- Selection

COMPENSATION
- Compensation
- Benefits
- Taxation*

INTERNAL STAFFING AND DEVELOPMENT
- Internal staffing and career management
- Training and development

WORK ENVIRONMENT
- Safety and health
- Work design
- Personnel research

LABOR RELATIONS
- Labor-management relations

INTERNATIONAL PERSONNEL SERVICES
- Relocation and orientation*
- Translation services*

HRP/HRM OBJECTIVES
- Attract
- Retain
- Motivate

*Indicates functions and activities unique to international HRM

Source: Peter J. Dowling, "International HRM," in Lee Dyer, ed., *Human Resource Management—Evolving Roles & Responsibilities* (Washington, D.C.: Bureau of National Affairs, 1988), 236. Reproduced with permission.

Expatriates (home-country nationals)
Employees from the home country who are sent on international assignment.

resolved with little or no counsel or assistance from others. It is essential, therefore, that special attention be given to the staffing practices of overseas units.

There are three sources of employees with whom to staff international operations. First, the company can send people from its home country. These employees are often referred to as **expatriates**, or **home-country nationals**. Second, it can hire

REALITY CHECK

INTERNATIONAL ASSIGNMENTS AT FOUR SEASONS REGENT HOTELS AND RESORTS

John Young, senior vice-president, human resources for Four Seasons Regent Hotels and Resorts, discusses how human resources practices are different on an international level, and how they prepare employees for international movement. Four Seasons is one of Canada's success stories on the international front. Catering exclusively to the luxury market, it has had to move beyond Canadian soil to capitalize on this market strategy. Currently, Four Seasons operates in 19 countries, and in the near future will be expanding in Asia, Europe, the Middle East, and South America. Founded in 1963, it now boasts 22,000 employees worldwide. Ironically, there are only 1500 Canadian employees.

"Some of the differences we have found in terms of human resource practices revolve around labour relations/labour law issues," states Young. "In Indonesia, for example, employment law presumes unionization, just as in Singapore, Hong Kong, Australia, and New Zealand. In Malaysia and the U.S., unionization is not the norm. In Western cultures, individual needs are emphasized, and as such, human resources focuses on employee satisfaction, performance management, and career development. In Asia there is more emphasis on group needs and conformity, thus leading human resources practice to focus more on administration and policing of policy. Training in Asia tends to be highly structured, targeted at non-management employees, and stresses 'rules' and 'dos and don'ts.' In North America the emphasis is on conceptual training, management development, and realistic performance appraisal. In Asia, by contrast, performance appraisal steers away from negative feedback, however realistic, because of the cultural issue of 'saving face.' In the Caribbean, the culture presumes that promotion should be based on seniority, whereas in North America the expectation is based on performance and ability.

"We encourage the movement of management staff among the various countries in which we operate. Much of this activity deals with bringing employees into North America for training because this is our strongest operational base where the learning opportunities are best. Each assignment that an individual accepts creates a different challenge for them. They have to deal with language, housing, transportation, currency, education, diet, climate, politics, religion, etc., which can cause a great deal of stress as well as tremendous growth. For longer term assignments that involve the relocation of family and spouse, we explain clearly the inherent stresses and also try to assess the cohesiveness of the family unit. While we can obtain work permits for our employees, this is not the case for their spouses and/or their children. Therefore, we must be very careful during the selection process to be open and realistic with everyone involved. Based on experience, we know that the first year will be the most stressful. We help to prepare these individuals by sending them on a familiarization trip to the assigned country for a few days; a short 'reality check.' It is extremely important that our employees understand the community and become familiar with local customs and practices. We provide guided reading in the form of materials obtained from the U.S. State Department in Washington. Those who succeed have the ability to accept and tolerate differences—even find them interesting and challenging—rather than comparing the new location with 'home'.

"Whenever human resource professionals become involved in international relocations they must become fully familiar with the various tax treaties that exist between the countries. We typically pay expatriates in U.S. dollars, net of all taxes. Longer term transfers within our chain are geared primarily to our senior employees.

"The issue of women in senior management is becoming increasingly important. We do not want to discriminate, but cannot ignore the huge cultural obstacles faced by women assigned to some parts of Asia or the Middle East. Currently, about 10 percent of our transfers are women and that number is increasing."

Young adds further, "Selection goes well beyond traditional 'diversity' or 'employment equity' considerations since we are staffing a growing global business. Because we are moving people throughout the world we need to ensure that the employees we assign to a given country are not only technically and interpersonally competent, but also able to function within the cultural and linguistic environment. There is not much point in sending managers to build a business in Korea if they can't communicate with the employee group! Even with no significant Korean community in a given Canadian city, Koreans (or other ethnic groups) may be in evidence in our workforce as we prepare for a particular venture. Our continued success may well depend on exactly this kind of proactive selection and development of future management staff."

Source: Interview by Deborah M. Zinni, August 1995.

Host-country nationals
Natives of the host country.

Third-country nationals
Natives of a country other than the home country or the host country.

host-country nationals (natives of the host country) to do the managing. Third, it can hire **third-country nationals**, natives of a country other than the home country or the host country.

Use of each of the three sources of overseas personnel involves certain advantages and disadvantages. Some of the more important advantages are presented in Figure 17-5. Most corporations use all three sources for staffing their multinational operations, although some companies exhibit a distinct bias for one of the three sources.[12] Over the years, and especially as MNCs have evolved, many have steadily shifted to the use of local personnel. There are three reasons for this trend:

1. Hiring local citizens is less costly because the company does not have to worry about the costs of home leaves, transportation, and special schooling allowances.
2. Since local governments usually want good jobs for their citizens, foreign employers may be required to hire them.
3. Using local talent avoids the problem of employees having to adjust to the culture.

At early stages of international expansion, many businesses prefer to use host-country nationals since these individuals can best help the company respond to local customs and concerns. As the company's international presence grows, home-country managers are frequently expatriated to stabilize operational activities (particularly in less developed countries). At later stages of internationalization, different companies use different staffing strategies; however, most employ some combination of host-country, home-country, and third-country nationals in the top-management team.

Recently, there has been a trend away from putting expatriates in top-management positions. In many cases, Canadian companies want to be viewed as true international citizens. To avoid the strong influence of the home country, companies

FIGURE 17-5 *Comparing Sources of Overseas Managers*

HOST-COUNTRY NATIONALS	HOME-COUNTRY NATIONALS (EXPATRIATES)	THIRD-COUNTRY NATIONALS
Less cost	Talent available within company	Broad experience
Preference of host-country governments	Greater control	International outlook
Intimate knowledge of environment and culture	Company experience	Multilingualism
Language facility	Mobility	
	Experience provided to corporate executives	

frequently change staffing policies to replace Canadian expatriates with local managers.[13] Over the years, MNCs have tended to use more third-country expatriates. For example, when Eastman Kodak recently put together a launch team to market its new Photo-CD line, the team members were based in London, but the leader was from Belgium.

It should be recognized that while top managers may have preferences for one source of employees over another, the host country may place pressures on them that restrict their choices. Such pressure takes the form of sophisticated government persuasion through administrative or legislative decrees to employ host-country individuals.

Recruitment

In general, employee recruitment in other countries is subject to more government regulation than it is in Canada. Regulations range from those that cover procedures for recruiting employees to those that govern the employment of foreign labour or require the employment of the physically disabled, war veterans, or displaced persons.[14] Many Central American countries, for example, have stringent regulations about the number of foreigners that can be employed as a percentage of the total workforce. Virtually all countries have work-permit or visa restrictions that apply to foreigners. A **work permit** or **work certificate** is a document issued by a government granting authority to a foreign individual to seek employment in that government's country.

Various methods are used to recruit employees from internal and external sources. In any country, but particularly in the developing countries, a disadvantage of using current employees as recruiters is that considerations of family, similar social status, culture, or language are usually more important than qualifications for the vacant position. More than one manager depending on employees as recruiters has filled a plant with relatives or people from the same home town. In small towns much

Work permit/work certificate
Government document granting a foreign individual the right to seek employment.

of the recruiting is done by word of mouth. Therefore, having locals involved is critical. Churches, unions, and community groups also play a role.

MNCs tend to use the same kinds of external recruitment sources as are used in their home countries. While unskilled labour is readily available in the developing countries, recruitment of skilled workers is more difficult. Many employers have learned that the best way to find workers in these countries is through radio announcements because many people lack sufficient reading or writing skills. The solution is to have a recruiter who uses local methods within the context of the corporation's culture and needs or to put an expatriate in charge of recruiting.

The laws of almost all countries require the employment of local people if adequate numbers of skilled people are available. Thus recruiting is limited to a restricted population. Specific exceptions are granted (officially or unofficially) for contrary cases, as for Jamaican farm workers in Canada and for Italian, Spanish, Greek, and Turkish workers in Germany and the Benelux countries (i.e., Belgium, Netherlands, Luxembourg). Foreign workers invited to come to perform needed labour are usually referred to as **guest workers**. The employment of nonnationals may involve lower direct labour costs, but indirect costs—language training, health services, recruitment, transportation, and so on—may be substantial.[15]

Guest workers
Foreign workers invited in to perform needed labour.

Selection

North American corporations have had a very significant impact on foreign HRM practices. The success of international businesses has caused many local firms and corporations based in other countries to study the methods of the North American firms. Employment selection practices in Canadian corporations emphasize merit, with the best-qualified person getting the job. In other countries, firms have tended to hire on the basis of family ties, social status, language, and common origin. The candidate who satisfies these criteria gets the job even if otherwise unqualified. There has been a growing realization among foreign organizations, however, that greater attention must be given to hiring those most qualified.

In the industrialized countries, most businesses follow standard procedures of requesting employee information, including work experiences, in interviews and on application forms. Prospective employees may be given a physical examination and employment tests. In many European countries, an employer is forbidden to make unfavourable statements about former employees. In Belgium and France, this prohibition was established by legislation; in Germany, by court decision.[16]

The Selection Process

The selection process should emphasize different employment factors, depending on the extent of contact that one would have with the local culture and the degree to which the foreign environment differs from the home environment. For example, if the job involves extensive contacts with the community, as with a chief executive officer, this factor should be given appropriate weight. The magnitude of differences between the political, legal, socioeconomic, and cultural systems of the host country and those of the home country should also be assessed.

If a candidate for expatriation is willing to live and work in a foreign environment, an indication of his or her tolerance of cultural differences should be obtained. On the other hand, if local nationals have the technical competence to carry out the job successfully, they should be carefully considered for the job before the firm launches a search (at home) for a candidate to fill the job. As stated previously, most corporations realize the advantages to be gained by staffing foreign subsidiaries with host-country nationals wherever possible.[17]

Selecting home-country and third-country nationals requires that more factors be considered than in selecting host-country nationals. While the latter must, of course, possess managerial abilities and the necessary technical skills, they have the advantage of familiarity with the physical and cultural environment and the language of the host country. The discussion that follows will focus on the selection of expatriate managers from the home country.

Selecting Expatriates

Estimates suggest that by the year 2000, nearly 15 percent of all employee transfers and relocations will be to an international location. Figure 17-6 shows a list of the most common locations for U.S. expatriate assignment.

Failure rate
Percentage of expatriates who do not perform satisfactorily.

The problem facing many corporations is to find employees who can meet the demands of working in a foreign environment. Unfortunately, the **failure rate** among expatriates has been estimated to range from 25 to 50 percent, with an average cost per failure of $40,000 to $250,000.[18] The most prevalent reasons for failure among expatriates are shown in Highlights in HRM 2. Many of these causes extend beyond technical and managerial capabilities and include personal and social issues as well. Interestingly, one of the biggest causes of failure is a spouse's inability to adjust to his or her new surroundings.[19]

There are no screening devices to identify with certainty who will succeed and who will fail. But there are requirements that one should meet to be considered for a managerial position in an international location. Historically, expatriate selection decisions have been driven by an overriding concern with technical competency. And this is an important criterion for success. However, the ability to adapt to a different type of environment frequently overshadows technical competence in the selection decision. Satisfactory adjustment depends on flexibility, emotional maturity and stability, empathy for the culture, language and communication skills, resourcefulness and initiative, and diplomatic skills. Companies such as Colgate-

---

FIGURE 17-6 *Top 10 U.S. Expatriate Experiments*

1	England	6	Singapore
2	Belgium	7	Germany
3	Austrialia	8	Netherlands
4	France	9	Hungary
5	Mexico	10	Japan

Source: From a survey by PHH Homequity, reported in "Rating the International Relocation Hot Spots," *Personal Journal* (December 1993): 19. Reprinted with permission.

2   RANKING OF CAUSES OF EXPATRIATE FAILURE

	North American Managers	Expatriate Managers*	Asian Managers	Australian Managers
1. Manager's inability to adapt	2	1	1	1
2. Spouse's inability to adapt	1	2	2	2
3. Inability to cope with larger responsibilities	5	4	6	3
4. Other family-related matters	3	5	5	4
5. Manager's personality	4	3	3	5
6. Lack of motivation to work overseas	7	7	4	6
7. Lack of technical expertise	6	6	7	7
8. Other	8	8	8	8

*Expatriates were Americans, British, Canadians, French, New Zealanders, or Australians working outside their home countries.

Sources: R.J. Stone, "Expatriate Selection and Failure," *Human Resource Planning* 14, no. 1 (1991): 9–18; R.L. Tung, "Selection and Training Procedures of U.S., European, and Japanese Multinationals," Copyright 1982 by The Regents of the University of California, reprinted from the *California Management Review* 25, no. 1 (1982) by permission of The Regents.

Core skills
Skills considered critical in an employee's success abroad.

Augmented skills
Skills helpful in facilitating the efforts of expatriate managers.

Palmolive, Whirlpool, and Dow Chemical have identified a set of **core skills** that they view as critical for success abroad and a set of **augmented skills** that help facilitate the efforts of expatriate managers. These skills and their managerial implications are shown in Highlights in HRM 3.[20] It is worth noting that many of these skills are not significantly different from those required for managerial success at home.

Women Going Abroad
Traditionally companies have been hesitant to send women on overseas assignments. Executives may either mistakenly assume that women do not want international assignments, or they assume that host-country nationals are prejudiced against women. The reality is that women frequently do want international assignments—at least at a rate equal to that of men. And while locals may be prejudiced against women in their own country, they view women first as foreigners (*gaijin* in Japanese)

HIGHLIGHTS IN HRM

3   PROFILE OF THE 21ST-CENTURY EXPATRIATE MANAGER

CORE SKILLS	MANAGERIAL IMPLICATIONS
Multidimensional perspective	Extensive multiproduct, multi-industry, multifunctional, multicompany, multicountry, and multienvironment experience
Proficiency in line management	Track record in successfully operating a strategic business unit(s) and/or a series of major overseas projects
Prudent decision-making skills	Competence and proven track record in making the right strategic decisions
Resourcefulness	Skilful in getting himself or herself known and accepted in the host country's political hierarchy
Cultural adaptability	Quick and easy adaptability into the foreign culture—an individual with as much cultural mix, diversity, and experience as possible
Cultural sensitivity	Effective people skills in dealing with a variety of cultures, races, nationalities, genders, religions; also sensitive to cultural difference
Ability as a team builder	Adept in bringing a culturally diverse working group together to accomplish the major mission and objective of the organization
Physical fitness and mental maturity	Endurance for the rigorous demands of an overseas assignment

AUGMENTED SKILLS	MANAGERIAL IMPLICATIONS
Computer literacy	Comfortable exchanging strategic information electronically
Prudent negotiating skills	Proven track record in conducting successful strategic business negotiations in multicultural environment
Ability as a change agent	Proven track record in successfully initiating and implementing strategic organizational changes
Visionary skills	Quick to recognize and respond to strategic business opportunities and potential political and economic upheavals in the host country
Effective delegatory skills	Proven track record in participative management style and ability to delegate

Source: C.G. Howard, "Profile of the 21st-Century Expatriate Manager," *HR Magazine* (June 1992): 93–100. Reprinted with the permission of *HR Magazine*, published by the Society for Human Resource Management, Alexandria, Va.

and only secondly as women. Therefore, cultural barriers that typically constrain the roles of women in a male-dominated society may not totally apply in the case of expatriates.

Importantly, in those cases where women have been given international assignments, they generally have performed quite well. The success rate of female expatriates has been estimated to be about 97 percent—a rate far superior to that of men.[21] Ironically, women expatriates attribute at least part of their success to the fact that they are women. Because locals are aware of how unusual it is for a woman to be given a foreign assignment, they frequently assume that the company would not have sent a woman unless she was the very best. In addition, because women expatriates are novel (particularly in managerial positions), they are very visible and distinctive. In many cases, they may even receive special treatment not given to their male colleagues.[22] The ethical dilemma of sending women to countries in which they might be treated as second-class citizens is discussed in Ethics in HRM.

Staffing Transnational Teams

Transnational teams

Teams composed of members from multiple nationalities working on projects that span multiple countries.

In addition to focusing on individuals, it is also important to note that companies are increasingly using **transnational teams** to conduct international business. Transnational teams are composed of members from multiple nationalities working on projects that span multiple countries.[23] These teams are especially useful for performing tasks that the firm as a whole is not yet designed to accomplish. For example, they may be used to transcend the existing organizational structure in order to customize a strategy for different geographic regions, transfer technology from one part of the world to another, and communicate between headquarters and subsidiaries in different countries.

The fundamental task in forming a transnational team is assembling the right composition of people who can work together effectively to accomplish the goals of the team. Many companies try to build variety into their teams in order to maximize responsiveness to the special needs of different countries. For example, when Heineken formed a transnational team to consolidate production facilities, it made certain that team members were drawn from each major region within Europe. Team members tended to have specialized skills, and additional members were added only if they offered some unique skill that added value to the team.

Selection Methods

The methods of selection most commonly used by corporations operating internationally are interviews, assessment centres, and tests. While some companies interview only the candidate, others interview both the candidate and the spouse, lending support to the fact that companies are becoming increasingly aware of the significance of the spouse's adjustment to a foreign environment and the spouse's contribution to managerial performance abroad. However, despite the potential value of considering a spouse's adjustment, the influence of such a factor over the selection/expatriation decision raises some interesting issues about validity, fairness, and discrimination. For example, if someone is denied an assignment because of concerns about his or her spouse, there may be grounds for legal action.

To ensure validity, selection interviews are best conducted by senior executives who have had managerial experience in foreign countries. For example, at Mobil Oil the manager of international placement and staffing and two assistants with foreign

> ## ETHICS IN HRM

THE GAIJAN SYNDROME

Asian markets represent a tremendous business opportunity for Canadian companies. The four tigers of the Pacific Rim countries—Hong Kong, Korea, Singapore, and Taiwan—represent the fastest-growing economies in the world. The People's Republic of China has attracted international business interest because of the sheer size of its market. Japan continues to dominate international trade.

The other notable fact about Asia is the paucity of women managers. Although women in these countries operate smaller and family-owned businesses, they are invisible within large corporations at the senior levels. One interpretation of this situation is that women are not welcome in management ranks in Asia; another is that they are not perceived as competent, or that the managerial role is regarded as unacceptable for a woman.

Should Canadian companies, then, send women managers to Asia? Most don't. Only 1.3 percent of Canadian expatriate managers are female. Surveys show that, although male and female MBAs are equally interested in international management assignments, almost half of the companies surveyed were hesitant to give women these assignments, believing that foreigners are prejudiced against women managers.

However, a survey of women who had worked overseas indicated advantages such as high visibility leading to easier access to foreigners' time and attention. One result was clear. Women were perceived as *gaijin*—foreigners, not women. Behaviour that would not be condoned among local women was accepted by the host country.

Source: N.J. Adler, "Pacific Basin Managers: A *Gaijan*, Not a Woman," in M. Mendenhall and G. Oddou, eds., *International Human Resource Management* (Boston: PWS-Kent 1991).

experience conduct a four-hour interview with the candidate and the spouse to discuss all phases of the job. Emphasis is placed on the culture and the adaptability demands made on the candidate and the spouse.[24]

Assessment centres typically use individual and group exercises, individual interviews with managers and/or psychologists, and some personality and mental ability tests to evaluate candidates. Exercises that reflect situations characteristic of the potential host culture are usually included. The use of assessment centres has been shown to have high face validity and to be an effective tool for selecting from a large pool of international managerial candidates.[25]

A variety of measures, particularly personality inventories, can be used to determine an individual's ability to adapt to a different cultural environment.[26] Such

Senior executives with experience in foreign countries conduct selection interviews.

inventories as the *Minnesota Multiphasic Personality Inventory (MMPI)*, the *Guilford-Zimmerman Temperament Survey*, and the *California Test* (the Indirect Scale for Ethnocentrism) are among those generally recommended. This third test is probably the most promising of these measures, since data suggest that high ethnocentrism correlates with overseas job failure.[27]

As noted in Chapter 7, the validity of any selection method is likely to be higher when it is based on a thorough job analysis, and personality tests are no exception to this rule. In using personality inventories and other types of personality tests, it is advisable to employ the services of a licensed psychologist. One consulting firm has developed an assessment tool known as the *Overseas Assignment Inventory (OAI)*. Based on twelve years of research involving more than 7000 cases, the *OAI* helps identify characteristics and attitudes that potential international candidates should have.[28] One test, the *Modern Language Aptitude Test*, predicts with considerable accuracy a person's chances of being able to learn a foreign language. Where it is essential that a person learn a foreign language, employers find that it is important to have some assurance that the prognosis is favourable.[29]

Training and Development

Although companies try to recruit and select the very best people for international work, it is often necessary to provide some type of training to achieve the desired level of performance. Over time, given the velocity of change in an international setting, employees may also need to upgrade their skills as they continue on the job. Such training may be provided within the organization or outside in some type of educational setting.

Skills of the Global Manager

If businesses are to be managed effectively in an international setting, managers need to be educated and trained in global management skills. A recent Korn/Ferry study of 1500 CEOs and senior managers found that one of the biggest concerns is that by the year 2000, there will be a critical shortage of managers equipped to run global businesses.[30] In this regard, Levi Strauss has identified the following six attributes of **global managers**: (1) able to seize strategic opportunities, (2) capable of managing highly decentralized organizations, (3) aware of global issues, (4) sensitive to issues of diversity, (5) competent in interpersonal relations, and (6) skilled in building community.[31]

As noted throughout the book, it is particularly important for managers to learn to work with others in teams.[32] Unlike their American counterparts, Canadian managers are frequently at an advantage because they have experience in working with people from different backgrounds. For transnational teams to perform well, team leaders need to perform three primary roles. First, they must act as an *integrator* of the team, bringing people from different functional backgrounds and cultures together. Second, they must be a *catalyst* for the team, encouraging individual team members to initiate and act on their own ideas, often across dispersed geographical areas. Third, team leaders need to be an external *advocate*, representing the team to persons outside the team and outside the organization.

Corporations that are serious about succeeding in global business are tackling these problems head-on by providing intensive training. Companies such as SNC Lavelin and NorTel and others with large international staffs prepare employees for overseas assignments. (These firms and others, including Coca-Cola, Procter & Gamble, and Mattel, also orient employees who deal in international markets.) The biggest mistake managers can make is to assume that people are the same everywhere. An organization that makes a concerted effort to ensure that its employees understand and respect cultural differences will realize the impact of its effort on its sales, costs, and productivity.[33]

Content of Training Programs

There are at least four essential elements of training and development programs that prepare employees for working internationally: (1) language training, (2) cultural training, (3) career development and mentoring, and (4) managing personal and family life.[34]

Language Training

Communication with individuals who have a different language and a different cultural orientation is, most executives agree, the biggest problem for the foreign business traveller. Even with an interpreter, much is missed. While foreign-language fluency is important in all aspects of international business, most Canadians are not skilled in languages other than English and/or French. Students who plan careers in international business should start instruction in one or more foreign languages as early as possible.[35]

Fortunately for most Canadians, English is almost universally accepted as the primary language for international business. Particularly in cases where there are

Global managers
Managers equipped to run global businesses.

many people from different countries working together, English is usually the designated language for meetings and formal discourse.[36] Although English is a required subject in many foreign schools, students may not learn to use it effectively. Many companies provide instruction in English for those who are required to use English in their jobs. Trainers who use English to communicate information and instructions about the job must recognize the discomfort that foreign trainees may experience. Learning job skills in a second language is usually much more difficult than learning them in one's native tongue. In addition, certain concepts may not even exist in the foreign trainees' culture. The word "achievement," for example, doesn't exist in some Asian and African languages.

Several tips for teaching where English is a second language for the trainees are presented in Highlights in HRM 4. Many of the tips may also be applied in interpersonal communication on and off the job with people who have a limited understanding of North American English. By placing oneself in the foreigner's position, one can soon learn how far to go in applying the tips.

Learning the language is only part of communicating in another culture. One must also learn how the people think and act in their relations with others. The following list illustrates the complexities of the communication process in international business.

1. In England, to "table" a subject means to put it on the table for present discussion. In North America, it means to postpone discussion of a subject, perhaps indefinitely.
2. In North America, information flows to a manager. In cultures where authority is centralized (Europe and South America), the manager must take the initiative to seek out the information.
3. Getting straight to the point is uniquely North American. Europeans, Arabians, and many others resent North American directness in communication.
4. In Japan, there are sixteen ways to avoid saying "no."
5. When something is "inconvenient" to the Chinese, it is most likely downright impossible.
6. In most foreign countries, expressions of anger are unacceptable; in some places, public display of anger is taboo.
7. The typical Canadian must learn to treat silences as "communication spaces" and not interrupt them.
8. In general, Canadians must learn to avoid gesturing with the hand.[37]

To understand the communication process, attention must be given to nonverbal communication. Figure 17-7 illustrates that some of our everyday gestures have very different meanings in other cultures. In summary, when one leaves Canada, it is imperative to remember that perfectly appropriate behaviour in one country can lead to an embarrassing situation in another.

Since factors other than language are also important, those working internationally need to know as much as possible about (1) the place where they are going, (2) their own culture, and (3) the history, values, and dynamics of their own organization. Highlights in HRM 5 gives an overview of what one needs to study when preparing for an international assignment.

highlights

**4   TEACHING TIPS WHEN ENGLISH IS A
    SECOND LANGUAGE**

- Speak slowly and enunciate clearly.
- Do not use idioms, jargon, or slang.
- Repeat important ideas expressed in different ways.
- Use short, simple sentences; stop between sentences.
- Use active, not passive, verbs.
- Use visual reinforcement: charts, gestures, demonstrations.
- Have materials duplicated in the local language.
- Pause frequently and give breaks.
- Summarize periodically.
- Check comprehension by having students reiterate material.
- Encourage and reward, as appropriate to the culture.
- Never criticize or tease.

Source: Lennie Copeland and Lewis Griggs, *Going International* (New York: Random House, 1985), 149. Reproduced with permission.

Culture Training

Cross-cultural differences represent one of the most elusive aspects of international business. Generally unaware of their own culture-conditioned behaviour, most people tend to react negatively to tastes and behaviour that deviate from those of their own culture.

Managerial attitudes and behaviours are influenced, in large part, by the society in which managers receive their education and training. Similarly, reactions of employees are the result of cultural conditioning. Each culture has its expectations for the roles of managers and employees. For example, what one culture encourages as participative management another might see as managerial incompetence.[38] It is important to make judgments within the context of the host culture. For example, Delta Hotels Ltd. of Toronto disagrees with the view that Cuban workers are exploited by their government when Delta pays a fee for every worker it hires. Simon Cooper, CEO, explains, "Cuba has a cradle-to-grave socialist country that takes care of all the needs of its people. I wouldn't presume to judge the degree to which the population is or isn't exploited."[39]

> ## FIGURE 17-7 *Nonverbal Communications in Different Cultures*

CALLING A WAITER

In North America, a common way to call a waiter is to point upward with the forefinger. In Asia, a raised forefinger is used to call a dog or other animal. To get the attention of a Japanese waiter, extend  the arm upward, palm down, and flutter the fingers. In Africa, knock on the table. In the Middle East, clap your hands.

INSULTS

In Arab countries, showing the soles of your shoes is an insult. Also, an Arab may insult a person by holding a hand in front of the person's face.

A-OKAY GESTURE

In North America, using the index finger and the thumb to form an "o" while extending the rest of the fingers is a gesture meaning ok or fine. In Japan, however, the same gesture means money. Nodding your head in agreement if a Japanese uses this sign during the discussion could mean you are expected to give him some cash. And in Brazil the same gesture is considered a seductive sign to a woman and an insult to a man.

EYE CONTACT

In Western and Arab cultures, prolonged eye contact with a person is acceptable. In Japan, on the other hand, holding the gaze of another person is considered rude. The Japanese generally focus on a person's neck or tie knot.

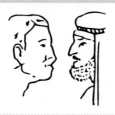

HANDSHAKE AND TOUCHING

In most countries, the handshake is an acceptable form of greeting. In the Middle East and other Islamic countries, however, the left hand is considered the toilet hand and is thought to be unclean. Only the right hand should be used for touching.

SCRATCHING THE HEAD

In most Western countries, scratching the head is inter-preted as lack of understanding or non-comprehension. To the Japanese, it indi-cates anger.

INDICATING "NO"

In most parts of the world, shaking the head left and right is the most common way to say no. But among the Arabias, in parts of Greece, Yugoslavia, Bulgaria, and Turkey, a person says no by tossing the head to the side, sometimes clicking the tongue at the same time. In Japan, no can also be said by moving the right hand back and forth.

AGREEMENT

In addition to saying yes, Africans will hold an open palm perpendicular to the ground and pound it with the other fist to empha-size "agreed." Arabs will clasp their hands together, forefingers pointed outward, to indicate agreement.

Source: S. Hawkins, *International Management* 38, no. 9 (September 1983): 49. Reprinted with permission from *International Management*.

HIGHLIGHTS IN HRM

HRM highlights

5 PREPARING FOR AN INTERNATIONAL ASSIGNMENT

To prepare for an international assignment, study the following subjects:
1. Social and business etiquette
2. History and folklore
3. Current affairs, including relations between the country and Canada
4. The culture's values and priorities
5. Geography, especially the cities
6. Sources of pride: artists, musicians, novelists, sports, great achievements of the culture, including things to see and do
7. Religion and the role of religion in daily life
8. Political structure and current players
9. Practical matters such as currency, transportation, time zones, hours of business
10. The language

Source: Lennie Copeland and Lewis Griggs, *Going International* (New York: Random House, 1985), 216. Reproduced with permission.

Being successful as a manager depends on one's ability to understand the way things are normally done and to recognize that changes cannot be made abruptly without considerable resistance, and possibly antagonism, on the part of local nationals. Some of the areas in which there are often significant variations among the different countries will be examined briefly.

A wealth of data from cross-cultural studies reveals that nations tend to cluster according to similarities in certain cultural dimensions such as work goals, values, needs, and job attitudes. Using data from eight comprehensive studies of cultural differences, Simcha Ronen and Oded Shenkar group countries into the clusters shown in Figure 17-8. Countries having a higher GDP per capita in comparison with other countries are placed close to the centre.

Ronen and Shenkar point out that while evidence for the grouping of countries into Anglo, Germanic, Nordic, Latin European, and Latin American clusters appears to be quite strong, clusters encompassing the Far Eastern and Arab countries are ill defined and require further research, as do clusters of countries classified as independent. Many areas, such as Africa, have not been studied much at all.[40] It should also

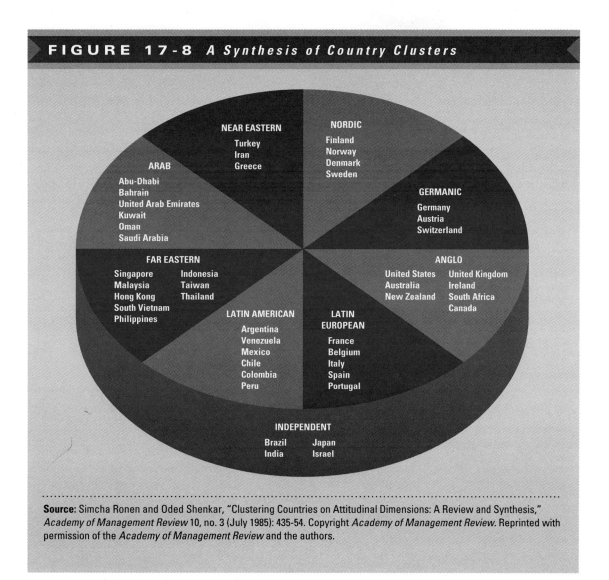

FIGURE 17-8 *A Synthesis of Country Clusters*

Source: Simcha Ronen and Oded Shenkar, "Clustering Countries on Attitudinal Dimensions: A Review and Synthesis," *Academy of Management Review* 10, no. 3 (July 1985): 435-54. Copyright *Academy of Management Review*. Reprinted with permission of the *Academy of Management Review* and the authors.

be noted that the clusters presented in Figure 17-8 do not include Russia and the former satellites of what was the Soviet Union.

Studying cultural differences can be helpful to managers in identifying and understanding differences in work attitudes and motivation in other cultures. In Japan, for example, employees are more likely to feel a strong loyalty to their company, although recent reports show that this may be changing. North Americans, when compared with the Japanese, may feel little loyalty to their organization. On the other hand, the Latin American tends to work not for a company but for an individual manager. Thus managers in Latin American countries can encourage performance only by using personal influence and working through individual members of a group. In North America, competition has been the name of the game; in Japan, Taiwan, and other Asian countries, cooperation is more the underlying philosophy.[41]

One of the important dimensions of leadership is the degree to which managers invite employee participation in decision making. While it is difficult to find hard data on employee participation in various countries, careful observers report that North American managers are about in the middle on a continuum of autocratic to democratic decision-making styles. Scandinavian and Australian managers also appear to be in the middle. South American and European managers, especially those from France, Germany, and Italy, are toward the autocratic end of the continuum; Japanese managers are at the most participatory end. Because Far Eastern cultures and religions tend to emphasize harmony, group decision making predominates there.[42]

Most research on motivation in work settings is about people in industrially advanced nations. Those studies that have been done in Third World countries reveal that work motivation can be attributed to **culture strength** (beliefs, values, and norms that have not been diluted by other cultures) as well as to the level of industrialization. As Western values influence the culture and as industrialization increases, worker motivation changes.[43] Motivation is a dynamic process and requires continued study in any setting. Understanding work motivation in a particular culture is crucial to the overseas manager.

Culture strength
Beliefs, values, and norms undiluted by cross-cultural influences.

Career Development

International assignments provide some definite developmental and career advantages. For example, working abroad tends to increase a person's responsibilities and influence within the corporation. In addition, it provides a person with a set of experiences that are uniquely beneficial to both the individual and the firm.[44] Most people who accept international assignments do so in order to enhance their understanding of the global marketplace and to work on a project they perceive as important to the organization.[45]

However, in many cases, an overseas assignment is more risky for the average employee than staying with the employer in the home country. Far too often, people who have been assigned abroad return home after a few years to find that there is no position for them in the firm and that they no longer know anyone who can help them. In a surprising number of cases, returning expatriates experience reverse culture shock, and may have even more difficulty adjusting to life at home than they did adjusting to their foreign assignment.[46] Even in those cases where employees are successfully repatriated, their companies often do not fully utilize the knowledge, understanding, and skills they developed in overseas experiences. This hurts the employee, of course, but it may hurt equally the firm's chances of using that learning to gain competitive advantage.

To maximize the career benefits of a foreign assignment, two key questions about the employer should be asked before accepting an overseas post: (1) Do the organization's senior executives view the firm's international business as a critical part of their operation?; and (2) Within top management, how many executives have a foreign-service assignment in their background, and do they feel it important for one to have overseas experience? At Dow Chemical, for example, 14 of the firm's 22-member management committee, including the CEO, have had overseas assignments. To ensure appropriate career development, Dow appoints what employees refer to as a "godfather" for those who get overseas assignments. The godfather, usually a high-level manager in the expatriate's particular function, is the home country contact for information about organizational changes, job opportunities, and anything related to salary and compensation. At Exxon, employees are given a general idea of what they can expect after an overseas assignment even before they leave to assume it. With this orientation, they can make a smooth transition and continue to enhance their careers.[47]

Colgate-Palmolive and Ciba-Geigy make a special effort to keep in touch with expatriates during the period that they are abroad. Colgate's division executives and other corporate staff members make frequent visits to international transferees. Ciba-Geigy provides a full repatriation program for returning employees for the purpose of (1) reversing culture shock for the transferee and his or her family and department, (2) smoothing the return to the home organization, and (3) facilitating the readjustment process so that the company can benefit from the expatriate's knowledge and experience.[48]

Not all companies have career development programs designed specifically for repatriating employees. A study of 175 employers who belong to SHRM International reveals that many companies are not aware of the need for such programs. Only 31 percent of those included in the survey had formal programs. The reasons most frequently mentioned for not having a program were (1) lack of expertise in establishing a program (47 percent), (2) cost of the program (36 percent), and (3) no need perceived by top management for such a program (35 percent). It is interesting to note that HR managers also did not perceive the need for training and thus did not alert top managers to the problem.[49]

Managing Personal and Family Life

As noted previously, one of the most frequent causes of an employee's failure to complete an international assignment is personal and family stress. **Culture shock**— a disorientation that causes perpetual stress—is experienced by people who settle overseas for extended periods. The stress is caused by hundreds of jarring and disorienting incidents such as being unable to communicate, having trouble getting the telephone to work, being unable to read the street signs, and a myriad of other everyday matters that are no problem at home. Soon minor frustrations become catastrophic events, and one feels helpless and drained, emotionally and physically.

In Chapter 9, we observed that more and more employers are assisting two-career couples in finding suitable employment in the same location. To accommodate dual-career partnerships, some employers are providing informal job help to the spouses of international transferees. However, other companies are establishing more formal programs to assist ex-patriate couples. These include career- and life-planning counselling, continuing education, intercompany networks to identify job openings in other companies, and job-hunting/fact-finding trips. In some cases, a company may even create a job for the spouse—though this is not widely practised. The available evidence suggests that while a spouse's career may create some problems initially, in the long run it actually may help ease an expatriate's adjustment process.[50]

Culture shock
Perceptual stress experienced by people who settle overseas.

Training Methods

There are a host of training methods available to prepare an individual for an international assignment. Unfortunately, the overwhelming majority of companies provide only superficial preparation for their employees. Lack of training is one of the principal causes of failure among employees working internationally.

In many cases, the employee and his or her family can learn much about the host country through books, lectures, and videotapes about the culture, geography, social and political history, climate, food, and so on. The content is factual and the knowledge gained will at least help the participants to have a better understanding of their assignments. Such minimal exposure, however, does not fully prepare one for a foreign assignment. Training methods such as sensitivity training, which focuses on learning at the affective level, may well be a powerful technique in the reduction of ethnic prejudices.

Companies often send employees on temporary assignments—lasting, say, a few months—to encourage shared learning. Although temporary assignments are probably too brief to allow employees to absorb all the nuances of a culture, companies such as Ferro and Dow use them to help employees learn about new ideas and technologies in other regions.[51] In other instances, employees are transferred for a much longer period of time. For example, in 1985 Fuji-Xerox sent fifteen of its most experienced engineers from Tokyo to a Xerox facility in Webster, New York. Over a five-year period, these engineers worked with a team of American engineers to develop the "world" copier. By working together on an extended basis, the U.S. and Japanese employees learned from each other—both the technical as well as the cultural requirements necessary for a continued joint venture.[52]

Developing Local Resources

Apart from developing talent for overseas assignments, most companies have found that good training programs also help them attract needed employees from the host countries. In less developed countries especially, individuals are quite eager to receive the training they need to improve their work skills. Oftentimes, however, a company's human capital investment does not pay off. It is very common, for example, that locally owned firms hire away those workers who have been trained by the foreign-owned organizations. Managers of North American subsidiaries in Mexico have been heard to complain that "they must be training half the machinists in Mexico."[53]

Apprenticeship Training

A major source of trained labour in European nations is apprenticeship training programs. On the whole, apprenticeship training in Europe is superior to that in Canada. In Europe, the dual-track system of education directs a large number of youths into vocational training. The German system of apprenticeship training, one of the best in Europe, provides training for office and shop jobs under a three-way responsibility contract between the apprentice, his or her parents, and the organization. At the conclusion of their training, apprentices can work for any employer but generally receive seniority credit with the training firm if they remain in it.[54]

Management Development

Foreign nationals have generally welcomed the type of training they have received through management development programs offered by North American organizations. Increasingly, companies such as Motorola and Hewlett-Packard have entered into partnerships with university executive education programs to customize training experiences to the specific needs of expatriate managers and foreign nationals.[55]

Performance Appraisal

As we noted earlier, individuals frequently accept international assignments because they know that they can acquire skills and experiences that will make them more valuable to their companies. Unfortunately, one of the biggest problems with managing these individuals is that it is very difficult to evaluate their performance. Even the notion of performance evaluation is indicative of a Western management style that focuses on the individual, which can cause problems in other countries. For these reasons, performance appraisal problems may be among the biggest reasons why failure rates among expatriates are so high and why international assignments can actually derail an individual's career rather than enhance it.[56]

Who Should Appraise Performance?

In many cases, an individual working internationally has at least two allegiances: one to his or her home country (the office that made the assignment) and the other to the host country in which the employee is currently working. Superiors in each location frequently have different information about the employee's performance and may also have very different expectations about what constitutes good performance.[57]

Home-Country Evaluations

Domestic managers are frequently unable to understand expatriate experiences, value them, or accurately measure their contribution to the organization. Geographical distances pose severe communication problems for expatriates and home-country managers. Instead of touching base regularly, there is a tendency for both expatriates and domestic managers to work on local issues rather than coordinate across time zones and national borders. Information technology has improved this situation, and it is far easier to communicate globally today than just a few years ago.[58] But even when expatriates contact their home-country offices, it is frequently not to converse with their superiors. More likely they talk with peers and others throughout the organization.

Host-Country Evaluations

Although local management may have the most accurate picture of an expatriate's performance—managers are in the best position to observe effective and ineffective behaviour—there are problems with using host-country evaluations. First, local cultures may influence one's perception of how well an individual is performing. As noted earlier in the chapter, participative decision making may be viewed either positively or negatively, depending on the culture. Such cultural biases may not have any bearing on an individual's true level of effectiveness. In addition, local management frequently does not have enough knowledge of the entire organization to know how well an individual is truly contributing to the firm as a whole.

Given the pros and cons of home-country and host-country evaluations, most observers agree that performance evaluations should try to balance the two sources of appraisal information.[59] Although host-country employees are in a good position to view day-to-day activities, in many cases the individual is still formally tied to the home office. Promotions, pay, and other administrative decisions are connected there, and as a consequence, the written evaluation is usually handled by the home-country manager. Nevertheless, the appraisal should be completed only after vital input has been gained from the host-country manager. As discussed in Chapter 10, multiple sources of appraisal information can be extremely valuable for providing independent points of view—especially if someone is working as part of a team. If there is much concern about cultural bias, it may be possible to have persons of the same nationality as the expatriate conduct the appraisal.

Adjusting Performance Criteria

As we discussed at the beginning of this chapter, an individual's success or failure is affected by a host of technical and personal factors (see Highlights in HRM 2). Many of these factors should be considered in developing a broader set of performance criteria.

Augmenting Job Duties

Obviously the goals and responsibilities inherent in the job assignment are among the most important criteria used to evaluate an individual's performance. However, because of the difficulties in observing, documenting, and interpreting performance information in an international setting, superiors often resort to using "easy" criteria such as productivity, profits, and market share. These criteria may be valid but also deficient if they do not capture the full range of an expatriate's responsibility. There are other, more subtle factors that should be considered as well. In many cases, an expatriate is an ambassador for the company, and a significant part of the job is cultivating relationships with citizens of the host country.

Individual Learning

Any foreign assignment involves learning. As one might guess, it is much easier to adjust to similar cultures than to dissimilar ones. A Canadian can usually travel to Australia and work with locals almost immediately. Send that same individual to Malaysia, however, and the learning curve is steeper. The expatriate's adjustment period may be even longer if the company has not yet established a good base of operations in the region. The first individuals transferred to a country have no one to show them the ropes or to explain local customs. Even relatively simple activities such as navigating the rapid transit system can prove to be problematic.

Organizational Learning

It is worth noting that bottom-line measures of performance may not fully convey the level of learning gained from a foreign assignment. Yet learning may be among the very most important reasons for sending an individual overseas, particularly at

Personnel abroad may require training to teach them how to cultivate relationships with citizens of the host country.

early stages of internationalization.[60] Even if superiors do acknowledge the level of learning, they frequently use it only as an excuse for less-than-desired performance, rather than treating it as a valuable outcome in itself. What they fail to recognize is that knowledge gained—if shared—can speed the adjustment process for others. However, if the learning is not shared, then each new employee sent to a region may have to go through the same cycle of adjustment.

Providing Feedback

One of the most interesting things about performance feedback in an international setting is that it is clearly a two-way street. Although the home-country and host-country superiors may tell an expatriate how well he or she is doing, it is also important for expatriates to provide feedback regarding the support they are receiving, the obstacles they face, and the suggestions they have about the assignment. More than those in most any other job, expatriates are in the very best position to evaluate their own performance.

In addition to ongoing feedback, an expatriate should have a debriefing interview immediately upon returning home from an international assignment. These repatriation interviews serve several purposes. First, they help an expatriate re-establish old ties with the home organization and may prove to be important for setting new career paths. Second, the interview can address technical issues related to the job assignment itself. Third, the interview may address general issues regarding the company's overseas commitments, such as how relationships between the home and host countries should be handled. Finally, the interview can be very useful for documenting insights an individual has about the region. These insights can then be incorporated into training programs for future expatriates.

objective

Compensation

One of the most complex areas of international HRM is compensation. Different countries have different norms for employee compensation. Managers should consider carefully the motivational use of incentives and rewards in foreign countries. While nonfinancial incentives such as prestige, independence, and influence may be motivators, money is likely to be the driving force for North Americans. Other cultures are more likely to emphasize respect, family, job security, a satisfying personal life, social acceptance, advancement, or power. Since there are many alternatives to money, the rule is to match the reward with the values of the culture. For example, Figure 17-9 shows how pay plans can differ on the basis of one cultural dimension: individualism. In individualistic cultures such as Canada pay plans often focus on individual performance and achievement. However, in collectively oriented

FIGURE 17-9 *Individualism and Compensation Strategies*

		DOMINANT VALUES	CORPORATE FEATURES	COMPENSATION STRATEGIES	SAMPLE COUNTRIES
INDIVIDUALISM	HIGH	• Personal accomplishment • Selfishness • Independence • Individual attributions • Internal locus of control • Belief in creating one's own destiny • Utilitarian relationship with employee	• Organizations not compelled to care for employees' total well-being • Employees look after individual interests • Explicit systems of control necessary to ensure compliance and prevent wide deviation from organizational norms	• Performance-based pay utilized • Individual achievement rewarded • External equity emphasized • Extrinsic rewards are important indicators of personal success • Attempts made to isolate individual contributions (i.e., who did what) • Emphasis on short-term objectives	• United States • Great Britain • Canada • New Zealand
	LOW	• Team accomplishment • Sacrifice for others • Dependence on social unit • Group attributions • External locus of control • Belief in the hand of fate • Moral relationship	• Organizations committed to a high level of involvement in workers' personal lives • Loyalty to the firm is critical • Normative, rather than formal, systems of control to ensure compliance	• Group-based performance is important criterion • Seniority-based pay utilized • Intrinsic rewards essential • Internal equity key in guiding pay policies • Personal need (e.g., number of children) affects pay received	• Singapore • South Korea • Indonesia • Japan • Taiwan

Source: L.R. Gomez-Mejia and T. Welbourne, "Compensation Strategies in a Global Context," *Human Resources Planning* 14, no. 1 (1991): 29–41.

cultures such as Japan and Taiwan, pay plans focus more on internal equity and personal needs.[61]

In general, a guiding philosophy for designing pay systems might be "think globally and act locally." That is, executives should normally try to create a pay plan that supports the overall strategic intent of the organization but provides enough flexibility to customize particular policies and programs to meet the needs of employees in specific locations.[62] After a brief discussion of compensation practices for host-country employees and managers, we will focus on the problems of compensating expatriates.

Compensation of Host-Country Employees

Host-country employees are generally paid on the basis of productivity, time spent on the job, or a combination of these factors. In industrialized countries, pay is generally by the hour; in developing countries, by the day. The piece-rate method is quite common. In some countries, including Japan, seniority is an important element in determining employees' pay rates. When companies commence operations in a foreign country, they usually set their wage rates at or slightly higher than the prevailing wage for local companies. Eventually, though, they are urged to conform to local practices to avoid "upsetting" local compensation practices.

Employee benefits in other countries are frequently higher than those in Canada. In France, for example, benefits are about 70 percent of wages and in Italy 92 percent, compared with around 44 percent in Canada. Whereas in Canada most benefits are awarded to employees by employers, in other industrialized countries most of them are legislated or ordered by governments.[63]

In Italy, Japan, and some other countries, it is customary to add semi-annual or annual lump-sum payments equal to one or two months' pay. These payments are not considered profit sharing but an integral part of the basic pay package. Profit sharing is legally required for certain categories of industry in Mexico, Peru, Pakistan, India, and Egypt among the developing countries and in France among the industrialized countries.[64] Compensation patterns in eastern Europe are in flux as these countries experiment with capitalistic systems.

Compensation of Host-Country Managers

In the past, remuneration of host-country managers has been ruled by local salary levels. However, increased competition among different companies with subsidiaries in the same country has led to a gradual upgrading of host-country managers' salaries. Overall, international firms are moving toward a narrowing of the salary gap between the host-country manager and the expatriate.

Compensation of Expatriate Managers

Compensation plans for expatriate managers must be competitive, cost-effective, motivating, fair and easy to understand, consistent with international financial management, easy to administer, and simple to communicate. To be effective, an international compensation program must

1. Provide an incentive to leave the home country
2. Allow for the maintenance of an accustomed standard of living

3. Facilitate re-entry into the home country
4. Provide for the education of children
5. Allow for the maintenance of relationships with family, friends, and business associates[65]

Expatriate compensation programs used by most North American based international corporations rest on the **balance-sheet approach**, a system designed to equalize the purchasing power of employees at comparable position levels living overseas and in the home country and to provide incentives to offset qualitative differences between assignment locations. The balance-sheet approach comprises four elements:

1. *Base pay*, which is made essentially equal to pay of domestic counterparts in comparably evaluated jobs
2. *Differentials*, which are given to offset the higher costs of overseas goods, services, housing, and taxes
3. *Incentives*, which compensate the person for separation from family, friends, and domestic support systems, usually 15 percent of base salary
4. *Assistance programs*, which cover added costs such as moving and storage, automobile, and education expenses[66]

The differentials element is intended to correct for the higher costs of overseas goods and services so that, in relation to their domestic peers, expatriates neither gain purchasing power nor lose it. A myriad of calculations must be done to arrive at a total differential figure.

The costs of utilizing expatriate managers are higher today than ever before. Many North American corporations are sending fewer managers overseas, often substituting host-country managers. Others are reducing allowances, benefits, and overseas pay incentives.[67] An increasing number of corporations employ foreign graduates from North American MBA programs. The many foreign graduate students enrolled in business programs at universities are a pool of potential managers who combine the training and acculturation of a North American MBA with their own native background.

Balance-sheet approach
A compensation system designed to match the purchasing power of a person's home country.

seven
objective

International Organizations and Labour Relations

Labour relations in countries outside Canada differ significantly from those in Canada. Differences exist not only in the collective bargaining process but also in the political and legal conditions. A Canadian who works as an executive or as a manager overseas soon learns the differences and learns how to operate effectively under conditions that are quite different from those at home. These executives also learn that there may be no assistance of value from headquarters and that they must rely heavily on local employees with expertise in labour–management relations.

To acquaint the reader with the nature of labour–management relations in an international setting, we will look at the role of unions in different countries, at international labour organizations, and at the extent of labour participation in management.

The Role of Unions

The role of unions varies from country to country and depends on many factors, such as the level of per capita labour income, mobility between management and labour, homogeneity of labour (racial, religious, social class), and level of employment. These and other factors determine whether the union will have the strength it needs to represent labour effectively. In countries with relatively high unemployment, low pay levels, and no union funds for welfare, the union is driven into alliance with other organizations: political party, church, or government. This is in marked contrast to Canada, where the union selected by the majority of employees bargains only with the employer, not with other institutions.

Even in the major industrial countries one finds national differences are great with respect to (1) the level at which bargaining takes place (national, industry, or workplace), (2) the degree of centralization of union–management relations, (3) the scope of bargaining, (4) the degree to which government intervenes, and (5) the degree of unionization.[68]

Labour relations in Europe differ from those in Canada in certain significant characteristics:

1. In Europe, organizations typically negotiate the agreement with the union at the national level through the employer association representing their particular industry, even when there may be local within-company negotiations as well. This agreement establishes certain minimum conditions of employment that frequently are augmented through negotiations with the union at the company level.

2. Unions in many European countries have more political power than those in Canada, with the result that when employers deal with the union they are, in effect, dealing indirectly with the government. As in Canada, unions are often allied with a particular political party, although in some countries these alliances are more complex, with unions having predominant but not sole representation with one party.

3. There is a greater tendency in Europe for salaried employees, including those at the management level, to be unionized, quite often in a union of their own.[69]

Like North American, European countries are facing the reality of a developing global economy. It has been increasingly evident in Europe that workers are less inclined to make constant demands for higher wages. The trend has been to demand compensation in other ways—through a proliferation of benefits, for example, or through greater participation in company decision making.[70] Various approaches to participation will be discussed later.

Collective Bargaining in Other Countries

We saw in Chapter 16 how the collective bargaining process is typically carried out in companies operating in Canada. When we look at other countries, we find that the whole process can vary widely, especially with regard to the role that government plays. In the United Kingdom and France, for example, government intervenes in all aspects of collective bargaining. Government involvement is only natural where parts of industry are nationalized. Also, in countries where there is heavy nationalization there is more likely to be acceptance of government involvement, even in the nonnationalized companies. At Renault, the French government-owned automobile manufacturer, unions make use of political pressures in their bargaining with managers, who are essentially government employees. The resulting terms of agreement then set the standards for other firms. In developing countries, it is common for the government to have representatives present during bargaining sessions to make sure that unions with relatively uneducated leaders are not disadvantaged in bargaining with skilled management representatives.

International Labour Organizations

The fact that international corporations can choose the countries in which they wish to establish subsidiaries generally results in the selection of those countries that have the most to offer. Inexpensive labour is certainly a benefit that most strategists consider. By coordinating their resources, including human resources, and their production facilities, companies operate from a position of strength. International unions, such as the United Auto Workers, have found it difficult to achieve a level of influence anywhere near that found within a particular industrial nation. Those that have been successful operate in countries that are similar, such as the United States and Canada.

The most active of the international union organizations has been the International Confederation of Free Trade Unions (ICFTU), which has its headquarters in Brussels. Cooperating with the ICFTU are some twenty International Trade Secretariats (ITSs), which are really international federations of national trade unions operating in the same or related industries. The significance of the ITSs from the point of view of management lies in the fact that behind local unions may be the expertise and resources of an ITS. Another active and influential organization is the International Labor Organization (ILO), a specialized agency of the United Nations. It does considerable research on an international basis and endorses standards for various working conditions, referred to as the *International Labor Code*. At various times and places, this code may be quoted to management as international labour standards to which employers are expected to conform.

Labour Participation in Management

In many European countries, provisions for employee representation are established by law. An employer may be legally required to provide for employee representation on safety and hygiene committees, worker councils, or even on boards of directors. While their responsibilities vary from country to country, worker councils basically provide a communication channel between employers and workers. The legal codes that set forth the functions of worker councils in France are very detailed. Councils are generally concerned with grievances, problems of individual employees, internal regulations, and matters affecting employee welfare.

A higher form of worker participation in management is found in Germany, where representation of labour on the board of directors of a company is required by law. This arrangement is known as **codetermination** and often by its German word *Mitbestimmung*. Power is generally left with the shareholders, and shareholders are generally assured the position of chair. Other European countries and Japan either have or are considering minority board participation.[71]

Codetermination
Representation of labour on the board of directors of a company.

Each of these differences makes managing human resources in an international context more challenging. But the crux of the issue in designing HR systems is not choosing one approach that will meet all the demands of international business. Instead, organizations facing global competition must balance multiple approaches and make their policies flexible enough to accommodate differences across national borders. Throughout this book, we have noted that different situations call for different approaches to managing people, and nowhere is this point more clearly evident than in international HRM.

SUMMARY

There are four basic ways to organize for global competition: (1) the *international* corporation is essentially a domestic firm that has leveraged its existing capabilities to penetrate overseas markets; (2) the *multinational* corporation has fully autonomous units operating in multiple countries in order to address local issues; (3) the *global* corporation has a world view but controls all international operations from its home office; and (4) the transnational corporation uses a network structure to balance global and local concerns.

International HRM differs from domestic HRM in its emphasis on a number of responsibilities and functions such as relocation, orientation, and translation services to help employees adapt to a new and different environment outside their own country.

Because of the special demands made on managers in international assignments, many factors must be considered in their selection and development. Though hiring host-country nationals or third-country nationals automatically avoids many potential problems, expatriate managers are preferable in some circumstances. The selection of the latter requires careful evaluation of the personal characteristics of the candidate and his or her spouse.

Once an individual is selected, an intensive training and development program is essential to qualify that person for the assignment. Wherever possible, development should extend beyond information and orientation training to include sensitivity training and field experiences that will enable the manager to understand cultural differences better. Those in charge of the international program should provide the help needed to protect managers from career development risks, re-entry problems, culture shock, and terrorism.

Although home-country managers frequently have formal responsibility for individuals on foreign assignment, they may not be able to fully understand expatriate experiences because geographical distances pose severe communication problems. Host-country managers may be in the best position to observe day-to-day performance but may be biased by cultural factors and may not have a view of the organization as a whole. To balance the pros and cons of home-country and host-country evaluations, performance evaluations should combine the two sources of appraisal information.

objective

Compensation systems should support the overall strategic intent of the organization but be customized for local conditions. For expatriates, in particular, compensation plans must provide an incentive to leave the home country, enable maintenance of an equivalent standard of living, facilitate repatriation, provide for the education of children, and make it possible to maintain relationships with family, friends, and business associates.

objective

In many European countries—Germany, for one—employee representation is established by law. Organizations typically negotiate the agreement with the union at a national level, frequently with government intervention. Since European unions have been in existence longer than their Canadian counterparts, they have more legitimacy and much more political power. Salaried employees and managers are more likely to be unionized in Europe than in Canada.

KEY TERMS

augmented skills	global manager
balance-sheet approach	guest workers
codetermination	host country
core skills	host-country nationals
cultural environment	international corporation
culture shock	multinational corporation (MNC)
culture strength	third-country nationals
expatriates/home-country nationals	transnational corporation
failure rate	transnational team
global corporation	work permit/work certificate

DISCUSSION QUESTIONS

1. Describe the effects that different components of the cultural environment can have on HRM in an international firm.
2. In what ways are Canadian managers likely to experience difficulties in their relationships with employees in foreign operations? How can these difficulties be

minimized? Why are expatriate Canadian managers less likely than their U.S. counterparts to experience difficulties when abroad?

3. This chapter places considerable emphasis on the role of the spouse in the success of an overseas manager. What steps should management take to increase the likelihood of a successful experience for all parties involved?

4. What are the major differences between labour–management relations in Europe and those in Canada?

5. The proportion of foreign investment in Canada is relatively high compared to that in other industrialized nations. Given that a foreign national is typically the CEO of the Canadian subsidiary, what are the HRM implications for the subsidiary's employees?

6. What is codetermination? Do you believe that it will ever become popular in Canada? Explain your position.

7. If you were starting now to plan for a career in international HRM, what steps would you take to prepare yourself for overseas assignments?

8. Talk with a foreign student on your campus; ask about his or her experience with culture shock on first arriving in Canada. What did you learn from your discussion?

CASE: Teleco's Expansion within the European Union

Teleco Electronics is heavily involved in sales of computer and electronic equipment in Europe. At this time, Teleco's international sales account for 31 percent of its total volume, and almost half of those sales are in the European Union (EU) countries. Because of the large volume of sales in Europe, Teleco has decided to build a manufacturing operation in one of the EU countries. There are a number of advantages that Teleco can derive from this decision. Currently, because the company must work through numerous intermediaries, sales within Europe are very complicated and expenses are high. By building a manufacturing operation, Teleco can reduce some of these sales expenses. Furthermore, Teleco can take advantage of the Single European Act of 1992 by avoiding the taxes associated with imported products if its products are manufactured within one of the EU countries.

The vice-president of human resources, Chuck Waldo, has stated that an important part of the decision to expand is determining which EU country would provide the best location for the facility. Labour laws still vary widely among EU member countries, and despite the Single European Act, there is disagreement among member countries over which of the labour laws are to become common across countries. Even with considerable commonality, cultures and languages will still affect labour practices to a great extent. In deciding which country to choose for the manufacturing plant, Waldo has charged his staff with considering several important issues associated with the management of human resources in the EU. Among the issues to be considered are the social policies of the countries.

Germany represents one extreme in the area of social policy. It has very strong labour unions and one of the best-protected labour forces among EU member states. Its workers receive a minimum of eighteen days of vacation per year; the maximum hours of work per day are eight, and 48 per week. Spain represents the other extreme in social policy associated with labour protection. Its workforce has much less protection than Germany's in the areas of wages, health, and safety. Unemployment in Spain is about 20 percent, and labour costs are much lower than elsewhere. By contrast with Germany, however, its minimum vacation is longer—2.5 days per month—and while its maximum workday is nine hours, the maximum per week is 40 hours. Ireland represents still another labour environment. Its per capita income is low and unemployment is high, somewhat like Spain's. However, the educational level of its citizens is very high. Minimum vacation is three weeks per year, and there is no maximum on the number of hours that one may work per day or week.

Despite differences among the countries, there is pressure from the labour unions for a common social charter among EU member states. The implementation of common social policy in the form of an EU-mandated social charter has important implications for HR decisions. The charter has the potential to drastically change the way a firm operates in the EU. A common charter would remove the competitive advantages of a given country. For example, Spain would no longer be able to offer the advantage of cheap labour with the implementation of a common wage and salary structure. The likelihood of these social issues being settled soon is still low despite the Single European Act of 1992, and many observers believe that adoption of a common charter prior to the year 2000 is very unlikely.

Questions

1. What considerations led Teleco to decide to expand its manufacturing to Europe?
2. What considerations should Waldo take into account in choosing among EU member states for the location of the manufacturing plant?
3. Besides those mentioned in the case, are there other labour force factors that Teleco should consider when selecting a country?

Culture Quiz

The possibility of an international assignment as part of your career plan may interest you. But are you ready to adapt to a foreign culture? The following quiz provides an assessment of your sensitivity to other cultures.

Inventory of Cross-Cultural Sensitivity

The following questionnaire asks you to rate your agreement or disagreement with a series of statements.

Please circle the number that best corresponds to your level of agreement with each statement below.

1 = Strongly Disagree   7 = Strongly Agree

1. I speak only one language.   1 2 3 4 5 6 7

2. The way other people express themselves is very interesting to me.   1 2 3 4 5 6 7

3. I enjoy being with people from other cultures.   1 2 3 4 5 6 7

4. Foreign influence in our country threatens our national identity.   1 2 3 4 5 6 7

5. Others' feelings rarely influence decisions I make   1 2 3 4 5 6 7

6. I cannot eat with chopsticks.   1 2 3 4 5 6 7

7. I avoid people who are different from me.   1 2 3 4 5 6 7

8. It is better that people from other cultures avoid one another.   1 2 3 4 5 6 7

9. Culturally mixed marriages are wrong.   1 2 3 4 5 6 7

10. I think people are basically alike.   1 2 3 4 5 6 7

11. I have never lived outside my own culture for any great length of time.   1 2 3 4 5 6 7

12. I have foreigners to my home on a regular basis.   1 2 3 4 5 6 7

13. It makes me nervous to talk to people who are different from me.   1 2 3 4 5 6 7

14. I enjoy studying about people from other cultures.   1 2 3 4 5 6 7

15. People from other cultures do things differently because they do not know any other way.   1 2 3 4 5 6 7

16. There is usually more than one good way to get things done.   1 2 3 4 5 6 7

17. I listen to music from another culture on a regular basis.   1 2 3 4 5 6 7

18. I decorate my home or room with artifacts from other countries.   1 2 3 4 5 6 7

19. I feel uncomfortable when in a crowd of people.   1 2 3 4 5 6 7

20. The very existence of humanity depends upon our knowledge about other people.   1 2 3 4 5 6 7

21. Residential neighborhoods should be culturally separated.   1 2 3 4 5 6 7

22. I have many friends.   1 2 3 4 5 6 7

23. I dislike eating foods from other cultures.   1 2 3 4 5 6 7

24. I think about living within another culture in the future.   1 2 3 4 5 6 7

25. Moving into another culture would be easy.   1 2 3 4 5 6 7

26. I like to discuss issues with people from other cultures.   1 2 3 4 5 6 7

27. There should be tighter controls on the number of immigrants allowed into my country.   1 2 3 4 5 6 7

28. The more I know about people, the more I dislike them.   1 2 3 4 5 6 7

29. I read more national news than international news in the daily newspaper.   1 2 3 4 5 6 7

30. Crowds of foreigners frighten me.   1 2 3 4 5 6 7

31. When something newsworthy happens I seek out someone from that part of the world to discuss the issue with.   1 2 3 4 5 6 7

32. I eat ethnic foods at least twice a week.   1 2 3 4 5 6 7

Scoring the Culture Quiz

The QUIZ can be scored by subscales. Simply insert the number circled on the test form in the spaces provided under each subscale heading. Reverse the values for the items maked with an asterisk (*). For instance, reverse scoring results in:

     7 = 1, 6 = 2, 5 = 3, 4 = 4, 3 = 5, 2 = 6, 1 = 7

Then, add the values in each column for the subscale score. A total ICCs score is obtained by adding the various subscale scores together. At the present time, individuals can be ranked relative to others in a particular group. Further studies to expand the 32 items and to assess the predictive ability of the instrument are currently underway.

Scoring Guide

C Scale		B Scale		I Scale		A Scale		E Scale	
item	score	item	score	item	score	item	score	item	score
1*	_____	2	_____	3	_____	4*	_____	5*	_____
6*	_____	7*	_____	8*	_____	9*	_____	10	_____
11*	_____	13*	_____	14	_____	15*	_____	16	_____
12	_____	19*	_____	20	_____	21*	_____	22	_____
17	_____	25*	_____	26	_____	27*	_____	28*	_____
18	_____	30	_____	31	_____				
23*	_____								
24	_____								
29*	_____								
32	_____								

Totals

C Scale = _____
B Scale = _____
I Scale = _____
A Scale = _____
E Scale = _____
Total Score = _____

*Reverse score all items marked with * as these are negatively worded scores.

After taking the cultural sensitivity test, you will be anxious to interpret your scores. Although no published psychometric data is available for score comparisons, the following ranges provide a rough interpretation of scores. The first scale is the "C" or Cultural Integration Scale. This scale measures one's willingness to integrate with other cultures. Scores from 10–30 would be low, 31–50 would be average, and 51–70 would be high.

The "B" or Behavioural Response Scale measures the perception of one's behaviour towards others. Scores from 6–15 would be low, 16–30 would be average, and 31–42 would be high.

The "I" or Intellectual Interaction. Scale measures one's intellectual orientation toward interactions with other cultures. Scores from 6–15 would be low, 16–30 would be average, and 31–42 would be high.

The "A" or Attitudes Towards Others Scale measures one's attitudes toward people from other cultural groups. Scores from 5–14 would be low, 15–24 would be average, and 25–35 would be high.

The "E" or Empathy Scale measures one's ability to emphatize with people from other cultures. Scores from 5–14 would be low, 15–24 would be average, and 25–35 would be high.

The Total Score ICCS Score measures one's overall sensitivity towards people from different cultures. Scores from 32–95 would be low, 96–160 would be average, and 161–224 would be high.

Source: Reprinted by permission from Kenneth Cushner, School of Education, Kent State University, September 1995.

NOTES AND REFERENCES

1. K. Ohmae, *The Borderless World: Power and Strategy in the Interlinked Economy* (New York: Harper Business, 1990); M. Mendenhall and G. Oddou, *International Human Resource Management* (Boston: PWS-Kent, 1991).

2. C.L. Taylor, "Dimensions of Diversity in Canadian Business: Building a Business Case for Valuing Ethnocultural Diversity," *Conference Board of Canada Report 143-95*, April 1995, Toronto.

3. "Small World," *The Globe and Mail*, May 25, 1993, B20.

4. Charles C. Snow, Sue Canney Davison, Donald C. Hambrick, and Scott A. Snell, *Transnational Teams in Global Network Organizations* (Lexington, MA: International Consortium for Executive Development Research, 1993).

5. Arvind V. Phatak, *International Dimensions of Management*, 4th ed. (Cincinnati: South-Western, 1995), Chapter 1. See also Taylor Cox, Jr., "The Multicultural Organization," *Academy of Management Executive* 5, no. 2 (May 1991): 34–47; Noritake Kobayashi, "Comparison of Japanese and Western Multinationals—Part I," *Tokyo Business Today* 58, no. 10 (October 1990): 50.

6. Brian Brooks, Marsh Cameron Haller, Jean Robert Viguie, "EC 92: The Impact on Pay Delivery," *Benefits and Compensation International* 19, no. 8 (February 1990): 20–22. For a comprehensive overview of EC-92 designed to assist managers in planning a strategy for the European market, see Heinz Weihrich, "Europe 1991: What the Future May Hold," *Academy of Management Executive* 4, no. 2 (May 1990): 7–18. See also Robert O'Connor, "Britain Trains to Compete in a Unified Europe," *Personnel Journal* 70, no. 5 (May 1991): 67–70.

7. Stewart J. Black and Lyman W. Porter, "Managerial Behaviors and Job Performance: A Successful Manager in Los Angeles May Not Succeed in Hong Kong," *Journal of International Business Studies* 22, no. 1 (1991): 99–113.

8. Vern Terpstra and Kenneth David, *The Cultural Environment of International Business*, 3rd ed. (Cincinnati: South-Western, 1991).

9. Nancy J. Adler and Susan Bartholomew, "Managing Globally Competent People," *Academy of Management Executive* 6, no. 3 (1992): 52–65. See also Nancy J. Adler and Susan Bartholomew, "Academic and Professional Communities of Discourse: Generating Knowledge of Transnational Human Resource Management," *Journal of International Business Studies* 23, no. 3 (1992): 551–569.

10. Ellen Brandt, "Global HR," *Personnel Journal* (March 1991): 38–44; Peter J. Dowling, "International HRM," in *Human Resource Management—Evolving Roles &*

Responsibilities, ed. Lee Dyer (Washington, DC: Bureau of National Affairs, 1988), 1:228–1:242. See also A.G. Kefalas, *Global Business Strategy—A Systems Approach* (Cincinnati: South-Western, 1990), Chapter 12; and Noel Shumsky, "Keeping Track of Global Managers," *Human Resources Professional* 5, no. 4 (Spring 1993): 6–9.

11. Brandt, "Global HR," 38–44.

12. Phatak, *International Dimensions of Management*, Chapter 6.

13. Peter Coy and Neil Gross, "When the Going Gets Tough, Yanks Get Yanked," *Business Week*, April 26, 1993, 30; Daniel Pruzin, "Location . . . and More," *World Trade* 6, no. 9 (October 1993): 84–92.

14. Herbert J. Chruden and Arthur W. Sherman, Jr., *Personnel Practices of American Companies in Europe* (New York: American Management Association, 1972), 25.

15. Richard D. Robinson, *Internationalization of Business: An Introduction* (New York: Dryden Press, 1984), 104–106.

16. Lennie Copeland, "Cross-Cultural Training: The Competitive Edge," *Training* 22, no. 7 (July 1985): 49–53.

17. Raymond J. Stone, "Expatriate Selection and Failure," *Human Resource Planning* 14, no. 1 (1991): 9–18. See also Rosalie L. Tung, "Selection and Training of Personnel for Overseas Assignments," *Columbia Journal of World Business* 16, no. 1 (Spring 1981): 68–78; and Rosalie L. Tung, *The New Expatriates: Managing Human Resources Abroad* (Cambridge, MA: Ballinger, 1988).

18. Gary W. Hogan and Jane R. Goodson, "The Key to Expatriate Success," *Training and Development Journal* 44, no. 1 (January 1990): 50–52. See also Allan Bird and Roger Dunbar, "Getting the Job Done Over There: Improving Expatriate Productivity," *National Productivity Review* 10, no. 2 (Spring 1991): 145–156.

19. Stone, "Expatriate Selection and Failure," 9–18; Tung, "Selection and Training of Personnel," 68–78.

20. Stewart J. Black and Hal B. Gregersen, "Antecedents to Cross-Cultural Adjustment for Expatriates in Pacific Rim Assignments," *Human Relations* 44, no. 5 (May 1991): 497–515. See also Bruce W. Stening and Mitchell R. Hammer, "Cultural Baggage and the Adaptation of Expatriate American and Japanese Managers," *Management International Review* 32, no. 1 (1992): 77–89.

21. Howard, "Profile of the 21st-Century Expatriate Manager," 93–100.

22. Nancy J. Adler, "Women Managers in a Global Economy," *HR Magazine* 38, no. 9 (September 1993): 52–55. See also Nancy J. Adler, "Pacific Basin Managers: A *Gaijin*, Not a Woman," *Human Resource Management* 26, no. 2 (1987): 169–191; and Hilary

Harris, "Women in International Management: Opportunity or Threat?" *Women in Management Review* 8, no. 5 (1993): 9–14.

23. Snow et al., *Transnational Teams.*

24. Simcha Ronen, *Comparative and Multinational Management* (New York: Wiley, 1986), 184–186.

25. Ibid., 539.

26. R.L. Tung, "Selection and Training Procedures of U.S., European, and Japanese Multinationals," *California Management Review* 25, no. 1 (Fall 1982): 57–71.

27. Tung, "Selection and Training of Personnel," and Ronen, *Comparative and Multinational Management*, 536. See also Robert P. Tett, Douglas N. Jackson, and Mitchell Rothstein, "Personality Measures as Predictors of Job Performance: A Meta-Analytic Review," *Personnel Psychology* 44 (1991): 703–740.

28. Madelyn R. Callahan, "Preparing the New Global Manager," *Training & Development Journal* 43, no. 3 (March 1989): 29–32.

29. Terpstra and David, *Cultural Environment of International Business*, 41.

30. Donald C. Hambrick, James W. Fredrickson, Lester B. Korn, and Richard M. Ferry, "Reinventing the CEO," *21st Century Report* (Korn/Ferry and Columbia Graduate School of Business, 1989).

31. Sheila Rothwell, "Leadership Development and International HRM," *Manager Update* 4, no. 4 (Summer 1993): 20–32. See also Peter Blunt, "Recent Developments in Human Resource Management: The Good, the Bad and the Ugly," *International Journal of Human Resource Management* 1, no. 1 (June 1990): 45–59.

32. Victoria J. Marsick, Ernie Turner, and Lars Cederholm, "International Managers as Team Leaders," *Management Review* 78, no. 3 (March 1989): 46–49; Terpstra and David, *Cultural Environment of International Business*, 5; Spencer Hayden, "Our Foreign Legions Are Faltering," *Personnel* 67, no. 8 (August 1990): 40–44; J.R. Katzenbach and D.K. Smith, *The Wisdom of Teams: Creating the High Performance Team* (Boston: Harvard Business School Press, 1993). See also M. Domsch and B. Lichtenberger, "Managing the Global Manager: Predeparture Training and Development for German Expatriates in China and Brazil," *Journal of Management Development* 10, no. 7 (1991): 41–52.

33. Lennie Copeland, "Cross-Cultural Training: The Competitive Edge," *Training* 22, no. 7 (July 1985): 49–53. See also Mark Mendenhall and Gary Oddou, "The Dimensions of Expatriate Acculturation: A Review," *Academy of Management Review* 19, no. 1 (January 1985): 39–47; "Learning to Accept Cultural Diversity," *The Wall Street Journal*, September 12, 1990; and Barry Rubin, "Europeans Value Diversity," *HR Magazine* 36, no. 1 (January 1991): 38–41, 78.

34. Edward Dunbar and Allan Katcher, "Preparing Managers for Foreign Assignments," *Training and Development Journal* 44, no. 9 (September 1990): 45–47.

See also Paul R. Sullivan, "Training's Role in Global Business," *Executive Excellence* 8, no. 9 (September 1991): 9–10.

35. Lee H. Radebaugh and Janice C. Shields, "A Note on Foreign Language Training and International Business Education in U.S. Colleges and Universities," *Journal of International Business Studies* 15, no. 3 (Winter 1984): 195–199.

36. Snow et al., *Transnational Teams.*

37. Lennie Copeland and Lewis Griggs, *Going International* (New York: Random House, 1985).

38. Dean B. McFarlan, Paul D. Sweeney, and John L. Cotton, "Attitudes toward Employee Participation in Decision-Making: A Comparison of European and American Managers in a United States Multinational Company," *Human Resource Management* 31, no. 4 (Winter 1992): 363–383.

39. P. Knox, "Firms Seek Foothold in Cuba," *The Globe and Mail*, August 14, 1995, B1.

40. Lee Roberts, "HRD in Africa," in Leonard Nadler, ed., *The Handbook of Human Resource Development*, 2nd ed. (New York: Wiley, 1990). See also Merrick L. Jones, "Management Development: An African Focus," in Mark Mendenhall and Gary Oddou, eds., *Readings and Cases in International Human Resource Management*, 2nd ed. (Cincinnati: South-Western, 1995): 250–263.

41. Fred Luthans, Harriette S. McCaul, and Nancy Dodd, "Organizational Commitment: A Comparison of American, Japanese, and Korean Employees," *Academy of Management Journal* 28, no. 1 (March 1985): 213–218. See also Nancy J. Adler, *International Dimensions of Organizational Behavior* (Boston: Kent, 1991).

42. Geert Hofstede, "Cultural Constraints in Management Theories," *Academy of Management Executive* 7, no. 1, (February 1993): 81–94. See also Ronen, *Comparative and Multinational Management*, 184–186.

43. Fons Trompenaars, *Riding the Waves of Culture: Understanding Cultural Diversity in Business* (London: Economist Books, 1993).

44. Gary Oddou and Mark Mendenhall, "Grooming Our Future Business Leaders?" *Business Horizons* 34, no. 1 (January/February 1991): 26–34.

45. Snow et al., *Transnational Teams.*

46. Stewart J. Black, "Returning Expatriates Feel Foreign in Their Native Land," *Personnel* 68, no. 8 (August 1991): 17. See also Hal B. Gregersen, "Commitments to a Parent Company and a Local Work Unit during Repatriation," *Personnel Psychology* 45, no. 1 (Spring 1992): 29–54.

47. Carey W. English, "Weigh the Risks First on That Job Abroad," *U.S. News & World Report* (December 2, 1985): 82. See also Philip R. Harris, "Employees Abroad: Maintain the Corporate Connection," *Personnel Journal* 65, no. 8 (August 1986): 106–110; Paul L. Blocklyn, "Developing the International Executive," *Personnel* 66, no. 3 (March 1989): 44–47;

Mark Mendenhall and Gary Oddou, "The Overseas Assignment: A Practical Look," *Business Horizons* 31, no. 5 (September-October 1988): 78–84.

48. Blocklyn, "Developing the International Executive," 47. See also Susan Carey, "Expatriates Find Long Stints Abroad Can Close Doors to Credit at Home," *The Wall Street Journal*, May 17, 1993, B1.

49. Michael G. Harvey, "Repatriation of Corporate Executives: An Empirical Study," *Journal of International Business Studies* 20, no. 1 (Spring 1989): 131–144; Robert T. Moran, "Corporations Tragically Waste Overseas Experience," *International Management* 43, no. 1 (January 1988): 74.

50. Gregory K. Stephens and Stewart Black, "The Impact of Spouse's Career-Orientation on Managers during International Transfers," *Journal of Management Studies* 28, no. 4 (July 1991): 417–428.

51. Snow et al., *Transnational Teams*.

52. Ibid.

53. Donald A. Ball and Wendell H. McCulloch, Jr., *International Business—Introduction and Essentials*, 4th ed. (Plano, TX: Business Publications, 1990), 628.

54. Chruden and Sherman, *Personnel Practices*, 40–41.

55. Althea Bloom, "The Wide World of Corporate Training," *Hemispheres* (September 1993): 39–43.

56. Gary Oddou and Mark Mendenhall, "Expatriate Performance Appraisal: Problems and Solutions," in Mendenhall and Oddou, *International Human Resource Management*, 399–410.

57. R.S. Schuler, J.R. Fulkerson, and P.J. Dowling, "Strategic Performance Measurement and Management in Multinational Corporations," *Human Resource Management* 30, no. 3 (Fall 1991): 365–392.

58. S.A. Snell, P. Pedigo, and G.M. Krawiec, "Managing the Impact of Information Technology in Human Resource Management," in G.R. Ferris, D. Rosen, and D.T. Marnum, *Handbook of Human Resources Management* (Oxford, UK: Blackwell Publishing, in press).

59. Stewart J. Black and Hal B. Gregersen, "Serving Two Masters: Managing the Dual Allegiance of Expatriate Employees," *Sloan Management Review* 33, no. 4 (Summer 1992): 61–71.

60. Christopher A. Bartlett and Sumantra Ghoshal, *Managing across Borders: The Transnational Solution* (Boston: Harvard Business Press, 1991), 24–25.

61. Richard M. Hodgetts and Fred Luthans, "U.S. Multinationals' Compensation Strategies for Local Management: Cross Cultural Implications," *Compensation and Benefits Review* 25, no. 2 (March-April 1993): 42–48.

62. Douglas J. Carey and Paul D. Howes, "Developing a Global Pay Program," *Journal of International Compensation and Benefits* (July/August, 1992). See also Mariah E. De Forest, "Thinking of a Plant in Mexico?" *Academy of Management Executive* 8, no. 1 (February 1994): 33–40.

63. Ball and McCulloch, *International Business*, 640. "Cost of Individual Employee Benefits Expressed as a Percentage of Gross Annual Payroll," *19th Survey of Employee Benefits Costs in Canada* (Toronto: KPMG, 1994), Tables 9 and 10.

64. Robinson, *Internationalization of Business*, 108–113. See also Lin P. Crandall and Mark I. Phelps, "Pay for a Global Work Force," *Personnel Journal* 70, no. 2 (February 1991): 28–33.

65. Raymond J. Stone, "Pay and Perks for Overseas Executives," *Personnel Journal* 65, no. 1 (January 1986): 64–69. See also Ranae M. Hyer, "Executive Compensation in the International Arena: Back to the Basics," *Compensation and Benefits Review* 25, no. 2 (March-April 1993): 49–54; Peggy Stuart, "Global Payroll—A Taxing Problem," *Personnel Journal* 70, no. 10 (October 1991): 80–90.

66. Calvin Reynolds, "Compensation of Overseas Personnel," in Joseph J. Famularo, ed., *Handbook of Human Resources Administration*, 2nd ed. (New York: McGraw-Hill, 1986), 56-2, 56-3. See also Crandall and Phelps, "Pay for a Global Work Force," 28–33.

67. Joann S. Lublin, "Companies Try to Cut Subsidies for Employees," *The Wall Street Journal*, December 11, 1989, B1. See also Neil B. Krupp, "Overseas Staffing for the New Europe," *Personnel* 67, no. 7 (July 1990): 20–24; Kate Gillespie, "U.S. Multinationals and the Foreign MBA," *Columbia Journal of World Business* 24, no. 2 (Summer 1989): 45–51.

68. Robinson, *Internationalization of Business*, 94–97.

69. Chruden and Sherman, *Personnel Practices*, 116. See also Brooks Tigner, "The Looming Labor Crunch," *International Management* 44, no. 2 (February 1989): 26–31.

70. Reginald Dale, "International Forces Will Prevail, but Will Unions Be Able to Change with New Global Workplace?" *Personnel Administrator* 28, no. 12 (December 1983): 100–104. See also "Looking for Work: In Employment Policy, America and Europe Make a Sharp Contrast," *The Wall Street Journal*, March 14, 1994, A1; and "Payroll Policy: Unlike Rest of Europe, Britain Is Creating Jobs, but They Pay Poorly," *The Wall Street Journal*, March 28, 1994, A1.

71. Robinson, *Internationalization of Business*, 86.

one
objective

*Discuss the contributions
of HR audits to an
organization.*

two
objective

*Identify specific HR areas
to be audited.*

three
objective

*Identify the major
formulas used to evaluate
the work environment.*

four
objective

*Describe employee attitude
surveys and the
information that can be
gained from their use.*

five
objective

*Explain how to analyze
audit findings.*

Chapter 18

Auditing the
Human Resources
Management Program

$\mathbf{W}$*e have completed the discussion of the functions that make up the HR program. Now it seems appropriate to analyze the ways in which the value of this program to an organization may be assessed. Auditing the HR program will be the focus of this chapter.*

Like financial audits, audits of the HR program should be conducted periodically to ensure that its objectives are being accomplished. An HR audit typically involves analyzing data relative to the HR program, including employee turnover, grievances, absences, accidents, employee attitudes, and job satisfaction. The most effective audit is one that provides the maximum amount of valid information concerning the overall effectiveness of the HR program in contributing to the strategic objectives of the organization.

While it typically focuses on the HR department, an HR audit is not restricted to the activities of that department. It involves a study of the functions of HRM throughout the total organization, including those performed by managerial and supervisory personnel. More emphasis, however, should be placed on judging the effectiveness of the HR department at the operating level because of its impact on employee attitudes and behaviours and its services to managers and employees. The decisions and activities of HR managers influence the effectiveness of the HR function as well as overall human resources, and ultimately, organizational effectiveness.

objective

Contributions of the Human Resources Audit

Current emphasis on productivity improvement, pay-for-performance, employee empowerment, and team building has increased the attention given to human resources and their contributions to the achievement of organizational success. The HR audit is a method of ensuring that the human resource potential of the organization is being fulfilled, while providing an opportunity to:

1. Evaluate the effectiveness of HR functions—compensation, training, recruitment, selection, employment equity, health and safety, and so on
2. Benchmark HR activities to ensure continuous improvement
3. Ensure compliance with laws, policies, and regulations
4. Improve the quality of the HR staff
5. Promote change and creativity
6. Focus the HR staff on important issues
7. Bring HR closer to the line functions of the organization[1]

If an organization is to remain competitive, it must undergo continual change. An audit of its HR program can help managers identify variances between actual and expected or desired conditions. The audit becomes a data-based stimulus for change. Not only can the audit expedite change, it can be used as an instrument of change. For example, if it is desirable that an HR manager make changes in the department, an audit can be used as a neutral instrument for the views of superiors, peers, subordinates, and non-HR personnel in the organization. Thus multiple pressures for change are brought upon all managers.

Conducting the Audit

Audits may be conducted by internal or external personnel.[2] There are advantages and disadvantages to each approach. Insiders know more about the organization and are in a better position to determine which aspects require evaluation. They are also less likely to be viewed as a threat by those being audited. How objective the insiders will be, however, is always a question. External auditors are likely to be more objective and have less ego involvement.

The fact that legal and HR considerations have become so complex makes it appropriate for employers to consider using an external auditor who has substantial experience in both HR and employment law.[3] At the present time, however, only about 3 percent of companies surveyed use outside consultants. Corporate or executive management, corporate HR administration, or the HR research department typically performs the audit.[4]

Steps in the Audit Process

Before discussing the various aspects of the HR program that provide the content for an audit, we will first take a look at the steps typically followed in an organizational audit. HR auditing specialists suggest that the audit process should consist of the following six steps:

1. Introduce the idea of the audit and emphasize the benefits to be derived from it. Obtain commitment of top management.
2. Select personnel with a broad range of skills for the audit team and provide training as needed.
3. Gather data from different levels in the organization.
4. Prepare audit reports for line managers and HR department evaluation.
5. Discuss reports with operating managers who then prepare their own evaluation.
6. Incorporate corrective actions into the regular organization objective-setting process.

These managers are being briefed on the objectives of their HR audit.

Since auditing is a form of research, it is important that the findings be based on objective, reliable, and valid data. HR records of all types are available for use in audits. In addition to analyzing records, interviews are usually conducted with managers at different levels, the HR manager, the HR staff, and a selected number of supervisors and nonmanagement personnel.

objective

HR Areas to Be Audited

The most important function of the HR audit is to determine the effectiveness with which the objectives of the HR program are being met. Before starting the audit, the objectives and standards of the program should be stated clearly. An audit should include at least three major approaches: (1) measuring HR's compatibility with organizational goals, (2) determining compliance with laws and regulations, and (3) evaluating the performance of specific HR programs and functions.

Measuring Compatibility with Organizational Goals

The process of setting goals requires close coordination with top management. This ensures that the HR policies and procedures are consistent with top management's goals and objectives. The audit provides an opportunity to assess the extent to which objectives are being met and to revise policies and procedures accordingly.

Benchmarking
A continuous and systematic process for comparing some aspect of organizational performance against data from an organization considered to be superior in that area.

Once HR objectives are established, the HR staff may benchmark different HR activities or functions in order to identify areas for improvement. **Benchmarking**— a part of the total-quality movement—operates as a systematic process for comparing some aspect of an organization with that of an organization recognized as a leader in the particular area under study. The HR practices of Malcolm Baldrige National Quality Award winners in the United States—Cadillac, Globe Metallurgical, and Wallace—provide useful benchmarks for organizations wishing to assess their own HR activities. There is no Canadian equivalent award for companies engaged in outstanding HR practices.

For the HR department to use benchmarking successfully, it must benchmark on the basis of clearly defined measures of competency and performance. The measures must objectively define the current situation and identify areas for improvement.[5] Highlights in HRM 1 shows several aspects of training that can be benchmarked against organizations considered superior in the training function. While no single model exists to benchmark exactly, the simplest models are based on the late Edward Deming's classic four-step process. The four-step process advocates that managers:

- *Plan*. Conduct a self-audit to define internal processes and measurements; decide on areas to be benchmarked and choose the comparison organization.
- *Do*. Collect data through surveys, interviews, site visits, and/or historical records.
- *Check*. Analyze data to discover performance gaps and communicate findings and suggested improvements to management.
- *Act*. Establish goals, implement specific changes, monitor progress, and redefine benchmarks as a continuous improvement process.[6]

Like other quality initiatives, benchmarking and its evaluative component should become part of the regular HR audit process.

1   BENCHMARKING HR TRAINING

MEASUREMENT NAME	MEASUREMENT TYPE	HOW TO CALCULATE	EXAMPLE
Percent of payroll spent on training	Training activity	Total training expenditures ÷ total payroll	U.S. average = 1.4 percent of payroll spent on training per year.
Training dollars spent per employee	Training activity	Total training expenditures ÷ total employees served	Three Baldrige winner spent $1,100 per employee on training in 1990.
Average training hours per employee	Training activity	Total number of training hours (hours x participants) ÷ total employees served	U.S. average for large firms (100 + employees) = 33 hours per employee in 1990.
Percent of employees trained per year	Training activity	Total number of employees receiving training ÷ total employee population	Three Baldrige winners trained an average of 92.5 percent of their workforces in 1990.
HRD staff per 1,000 employees	Training activity	Number of HRD staff ÷ total employee population × 1,000	Three Baldrige winners had an average of 4.1 HRD staff members per 1,000 employees.
Cost savings as a ratio of training expenses	Training results: Bottom line	Total savings in scrap or waste ÷ dollars invested in training	A Baldrige winner reported saving $30 for every $1 spent on TQM training (or an ROI of 30:1).
Profits per employee per year	Training results: Bottom line	Total yearly gross profits ÷ total number of employees	An electronics firm earned average profits per employee of $21,000 in 1990.
Training costs per student hour	Training efficiency	Total costs of training ÷ total number of hours of training	Three Baldrige winners reported $27 in average training costs per hour of training in 1990.

Source: Adapted from Donald J. Ford, "Benchmarking HRD," *Training and Development* 47, no. 6 (June 1993): 36–41 Copyright 1993 by the American Society for Training and Development. Reprinted with permission. All rights reserved. See also Monica Belcourt and Phillip Wright, *Performance Management through Training and Development,* Nelson Canada HRM Series (series editor, M. Belcourt) (Scarborough, ON: Nelson Canada, 1995).

Determining Compliance with Laws and Regulations

As we have noted throughout this book, the number of laws and regulations affecting HRM has increased dramatically over the years. Organizations typically establish programs and procedures for achieving compliance with them. Top management needs to be aware of the manner in which managers at all levels are complying with the laws and regulations.[7] Equal employment opportunity, safety, and pension plans are among the compliance areas often investigated in comprehensive audits. There is no Canadian legislation that deals with reporting requirements by functional area. There are, however, documentation requirements in the areas of pay equity and employment equity, necessitated by the possibility of a program review by a government official.

It is essential that managers anticipate the types of information that will be required by government agencies and establish systems for maintaining such information in a computer file. The collection of data in advance will avoid last-minute crises in data-gathering requests.

Employers should take a proactive approach to compliance with laws and regulations. It is important not only to establish effective policies and procedures but also to make sure that subordinates understand them thoroughly. Sexual harassment, discussed in Chapter 3, is a good example of a problem area. Problems often arise from lack of knowledge of the specific on-the-job behaviours that constitute sexual harassment under the law. Through a questionnaire it is possible to test employee understanding of what is and is not sexual harassment.

Highlights in HRM 2 is a sampling of items that could be used during a sexual-harassment audit. Such an instrument, which is essentially a test, is a valuable tool for determining what employees know and do not know about important areas.

Evaluating Program Performance

Each of the functional areas of HRM should help to meet the overall objectives of an HR program. It is important, therefore, to audit each of these functions to determine how effectively and economically they are being performed. Since it is not possible to discuss in this text all the details involved in the audit of each functional area, we suggest in Figure 18-1 the general types of questions that should be answered in an audit. The sources of in-house information—usually records and reports—that are available for use in the audit are also included in the figure.[8]

Most of the sources of information listed in Figure 18-1 yield statistical data that are readily available in many organizations. Where electronic information systems are being used, such information can be kept current for analysis and reporting. HR professionals predict even greater use of information systems in carrying out the various HR audit functions. One need only turn to the *Human Resources Professionals Magazine*, *Personnel Journal*, or *HR Reporter* to find articles with specific recommendations for the use of computers as well as advertisements of companies specializing in software for HR activities.[9]

As valuable as the information sources listed in Figure 18-1 are in measuring the effectiveness of the major HRM functions, overreliance on quantitative measures may yield conclusions that seem objectively valid but fail to assess whether HR clients are really satisfied with the services they receive. This suggests using periodic studies of clients' perception of services rendered. Clients may include line executives and managers, employees, applicants, or even union officers.[10] User reactions

highlights

2   QUESTIONS USED IN AUDITING SEXUAL HARASSMENT

ACTIVITY	IS THIS SEXUAL HARASSMENT?			ARE YOU AWARE OF THIS BEHAVIOUR IN THE ORGANIZATION?	
• Employees post cartoons on bulletin boards containing sexually related material.	Yes	No	Uncertain	Yes	No
• A male employee says to a female employee that she has beautiful eyes and hair.	Yes	No	Uncertain	Yes	No
• A male manager habitually calls all female employees "sweetie" or "darling."	Yes	No	Uncertain	Yes	No
• A manager fails to promote a female (male) employee for not granting sexual favours.	Yes	No	Uncertain	Yes	No
• Male employees use vulgar language and tell sexual jokes that are overheard by, but not directed at, female employees.	Yes	No	Uncertain	Yes	No
• A male employee leans and peers over the back of a female employee when she wears a low-cut dress.	Yes	No	Uncertain	Yes	No
• A supervisor gives a female (male) subordinate a nice gift on her (his) birthday.	Yes	No	Uncertain	Yes	No
• Two male employees share a sexually explicit magazine while observed by a female employee.	Yes	No	Uncertain	Yes	No

FIGURE 18-1   *Auditing the Major Functions in HRM*

HUMAN RESOURCES FUNCTION	SOURCES OF INFORMATION
Planning and Recruitment	
• Do job specifications contain bona fide occupational qualifications?	• HR budgets
• Are job descriptions accurate, periodically reviewed, and updated?	• Recruitment cost data
• Are there any human resources that are not being fully utilized?	• Job descriptions and specifications
• Is the affirmative action program achieving its goals?	• Hiring rate
• How effective is the recruiting process?	
• How productive are the recruiters?	
Selection	
• How valid are selection techniques?	• Employment interview records
• Is there evidence of discrimination in hiring?	• Applicant rejection records
• Are interviewers familiar with the job requirements?	
• Do interviewers understand what questions are acceptable and unacceptable to ask of job applicants?	• Transfer requests
• Are tests job-related and free from bias?	• Human rights complaints
• How do hiring costs compare with those of other organizations?	
Training and Development	
• How effective are training programs in increasing productivity and improving the quality of employee performance?	• Training costs data
• Are there sufficient opportunities for members of the designated groups to advance into management positions?	• Production records
• What is the cost of training per person-hour of instruction?	• Accident records
• What is the relationship between training costs and accidents?	• Quality-control records
Performance Appraisal	
• Are the performance standards objective and job-related?	• Performance appraisal
• Do the appraisal methods emphasize performance rather than traits?	• Production records
• Are the appraisers adequately trained and thoroughly familiar with the employee's work?	• Scrap loss records
• Are the appraisals documented and reviewed with employees?	• Appraisal interview records
• Are the performance appraisal data assembled in such form that they can be used to validate tests and other selection procedures?	• Attendance records
	• Disciplinary action records
Compensation	
• Does the pay system, including incentive plans, attract employees and motivate them to achieve organizational goals?	• Wages and benefits data
• Do the compensation structure and policies comply with employment equity, pay equity, and Revenue Canada requirements?	• Wage-survey records
	• Unemployment

FIGURE 18-1 *(cont.d)*

HUMAN RESOURCES FUNCTION	SOURCES OF INFORMATION
• Is the choice of weights and factors in job evaluation sound and properly documented? • Do benefits costs compare favourably with those of similar organizations?	compensation insurance • Turnover records • Cost-of-living surveys
Labour Relations • Are supervisors trained to handle grievances effectively? • Is there ongoing preparation for collective bargaining? • What is the record of the number and types of grievances, and what percentage of grievances have gone to arbitration?	• Grievance records • Arbitration award records • Work stoppage records • Unfair labour-practice complaint records

may be obtained through attitude surveys, discussions with employees and focus groups, manager and supervisor comments, and similar approaches.

Measuring Human Resources Costs

Management is typically interested in the costs of the activities that are required to meet the HR objectives. Standard cost-accounting procedures can be applied to all of the HRM functions. Cost savings are easily demonstrated in (1) compensation policies and procedures, (2) benefit programs and insurance premiums, (3) workers compensation (4) recruiting, training, and management development, (5) employment equity, and (6) turnover and outplacement.[11]

In establishing a program for measuring HR costs, it is important to enlist the participation of the HR staff. In addition to gaining understanding and acceptance for the audit process, through participation the staff can identify a large number of measurable activities that can be included in formulas for measuring costs. Costs of orientation, for example, can be computed per employee per department (or HR department orientation expense). The cost of various recruiting and hiring procedures can likewise be computed. For example, the source cost of recruits per hire (SC/H) can be computed by the following formula:

$$SC/H = \frac{AC + AF + RB + NC}{H}$$

where AC = advertising costs, total monthly expenditure (example: $28,000)

AF = agency fees, total for the month (example: $19,000)
RB = referral bonuses, total paid (example: $2300)
NC = no-cost hires, walk-ins, nonprofit agencies, etc. (example: $0)
H = total hires (example: 119)

Substituting the example numbers in the formula:

$$SC/H = \frac{\$28,000 + \$19,000 + \$2300 + \$0}{119}$$

$$= \frac{\$49,300}{119}$$

$$= \$414 \text{ (source cost of recruits per hire)}$$

The basic formula can be changed to include only one group of employees such as engineers or managers. The example of source costs per hire is only one of many formulas available.

Area-Specific Audits

In addition to reviewing the functional activities of the HR department, area-specific audits can evaluate topics of current importance to managers. Two areas of present concern are cultural audits and the glass ceiling.

Cultural Audits

Cultural audit
Audit of the organizational culture and quality of work life in an organization.

Companies such as the Bank of Montreal and CIBC are identified as organizations having an employee-oriented culture. The **cultural audit** essentially involves discussions among top-level managers of how the organization's culture reveals itself and how the culture may be influenced. It requires a serious examination of such questions as:

- What do employees spend their time doing?
- How do they interact with each other?
- Are employees empowered?
- What is the predominant leadership style of managers?
- How do employees advance within the organization?

Conducting in-depth interviews and making observations over a period of time are the ways to learn about the culture. With the increased diversity of the workplace, cultural audits can be used to determine the existence of subcultures. Subcultures within an organization may well have very different views about the nature of work and how work should be done.

Equity Audits

Glass ceiling
The invisible, yet real or perceived, attitudinal or organizational barriers that serve to limit the advancement opportunities of minorities and women.

The **glass ceiling** has been defined as "those artificial barriers or systemic barriers, based on attitudinal or organizational bias, that prevent qualified individuals from advancing upward in their organizations into management-level positions." Equity audits focus on the culture of the organization, including practices that appear to hinder the upward mobility of members of the designated groups. Employees should have equal access to:

The advancement of women to upper-level management is often hindered by the glass ceiling.

- Upper-level management and executive training
- Rotational assignments
- International assignments
- Opportunities for promotion
- Opportunities for executive development programs at universities
- Desirable compensation packages
- Opportunities to participate on high-profile project teams
- Upper-level "special assignments"[12]

Conducting an equity audit prior to government review can help an organization to avoid fines and externally imposed corrective action. As noted by one HR practitioner, "The audit can document any barriers and the reasons they exist."[13] It will be increasingly untenable for an organization to have a diverse workforce and a majority male senior management team. Self-audits are one step to tapping the potentials of a diversified workforce.

objective

Indicators in Evaluating the Work Environment

Throughout this book we have emphasized that the work environment can have a significant effect on the motivation, performance, job satisfaction, and morale of employees. It is possible to assess the quality of the environment within an organization by studying certain indicators. These indicators, which may also be used to assess the HR functions, are widely used in all types and sizes of organizations. They include employee turnover rates, absenteeism rates, injury and illness records, and responses from employee attitude surveys.

Employee Turnover Rates

"Employee turnover" refers to the movement of employees in and out of an organization.

Costs of Turnover

Replacing an employee is time-consuming and expensive. Costs can generally be broken down into three categories: separation costs for the departing employee, replacement costs, and training costs for the new employee. These costs are conservatively estimated at two to three times the monthly salary of the departing employee, and they do not include indirect costs such as low productivity prior to quitting and lower morale and overtime for other employees because of the vacated job. Consequently, reducing turnover could result in significant savings to an organization. Highlights in HRM 3 details one organization's costs associated with the turnover of one computer programmer. Note that the major expense is the cost involved in training a replacement.

Computing the Turnover Rate

Turnover rate
Number of separations during a month divided by the total number of employees at mid-month times 100.

The **turnover rate** for a department or an entire organization is an indicator of how employees respond to their work environment. The following formula can be used for computing turnover rates:

$$\frac{\text{Number of separations during the month}}{\text{Total number of employees at mid-month}} \times 100$$

Thus, if there were 25 separations during a month and the total number of employees at mid-month was 500, the turnover rate would be:

$$\frac{25}{500} \times 100 = 5 \text{ percent}$$

Another method of computing the turnover rate is one in which the rate reflects only the avoidable separations (S). This is accomplished by subtracting unavoidable separations (US), for example, relocation of a spouse, return to school, or death, from all separations. The formula for this method is as follows:

$$\frac{(S - US)}{M} \times 100 = T \text{ (turnover rate)}$$

where M represents the total number of employees at mid-month. For example, if there were 25 separations during a month, 5 of which were US, and the total number of employees at mid-month (M) was 500, the turnover rate would be

$$\frac{25 - 5}{500} \times 100 = 4 \text{ percent}$$

3   COSTS ASSOCIATED WITH THE TURNOVER OF ONE COMPUTER PROGRAMMER

Turnover costs = Separation costs + Replacement costs + Training costs

Separation costs

1. Exit interview = cost for salary and benefits of both interviewer and departing employee during the exit interview = $30 + $30 = $60
2. Administrative and recordkeeping action = $30

     Separation costs = $60 + $30 = $90

Replacement costs

1. Advertising for job opening = $2500
2. Pre-employment administrative functions and recordkeeping action = $100
3. Selection interview = $250
4. Employment tests = $40
5. Meetings to discuss candidates (salary and benefits of managers while participating in meetings) = $250

     Replacement costs = $2500 + $100 + $250 + $40 + $250 = $3140

Training costs

1. Booklets, manuals, and reports = $50
2. Education = $240/day for new employee's salary and benefits X 10 days of workshops, seminars, or courses = $2400
3. One-to-one coaching = ($240/day/new employee + $240/day/staff coach or job expert) X 20 days of one-to-one coaching = $9600
4. Salary and benefits of new employee until he or she gets "up to par" = $240/day for salary and benefits X 20 days = $4800

     Training costs = $50 + $2400 + $9600 + $4800 = $16,850

Total turnover costs = $90 + $3140 + $16,850 = $20,080

Source: Adapted from Michael W. Mercer, *Turning Your Human Resources Department into a Profit Center* (New York: AMACOM, 1993). Copyright 1993 Michael W. Mercer. Reproduced with permission from Michael W. Mercer, Ph.D., Industrial Psychologist, The Mercer Group, Inc., Chicago, Ill.

This method yields what is probably the most significant measure of the effectiveness of the HR program, since it can serve to direct attention to avoidable separations where management has the most opportunity to influence better selection, training, supervisory leadership, improved working conditions, better wages, and opportunities for advancement.

The quantitative rate of turnover is not the only factor to be considered. The quality of personnel who leave an organization is also important.

Determining Causes of Turnover

Exit interview
Interview conducted to determine why employees leave an organization.

To determine why employees leave, many organizations conduct an **exit interview** during the employee's final week of employment. One study of a limited number of organizations found that 83 percent of these interviews are conducted by the HR department. In most cases, the interviewers are employment recruiters. This is advantageous for two reasons: (1) employees are likely to be more open when speaking with someone with whom they have had previous contact, and (2) recruiters are usually experienced interviewers.[14] Topics covered in exit interviews are shown in Figure 18-2.

The validity of the reasons for leaving that employees give during the exit interview has to be questioned. Many employees follow the rule of leaving on good terms and may consider frank discussion detrimental to their interests. Standardizing the interview by asking the same questions, advising exiting employees that information will be used in a constructive, not retaliatory, manner, and checking reasons given with supervisory personnel and co-workers can help to improve the reliability and validity of data.

Absenteeism Rates

Absenteeism rate
Number of worker days lost through job absence during a period divided by the average number of employees times the number of workdays, and the result multiplied by 100.

How frequently employees are absent from their work—the **absenteeism rate**—may also indicate the state of the work environment and the effectiveness of the HR program. A certain amount of absenteeism is, of course, unavoidable. There will always be some who must be absent from work because of sickness, accidents, serious family problems, and other legitimate reasons.

FIGURE 18-2 *Topics Covered during Exit Interviews*

- Reasons for departure
- Relationships with supervisors
- Fairness of performance appraisal reviews
- Evaluation of pay and advancement opportunities
- Rating of working conditions
- Things liked best about job/organization

- Things liked at least about job/organization
- Communication from management
- Evaluation of training received
- Organizational climate
- Suggestions

Costs of Absenteeism

Traditional accounting and personnel information systems often do not generate data that reflect the costs of absenteeism. To call management's attention to the severity of the problem, absenteeism should be translated into dollar costs. A system for computing absenteeism costs for an individual organization is available. Organizations with computerized absence-reporting systems should find this additional information easy and inexpensive to generate. The cost of each person-hour lost to absenteeism is based on the hourly weighted average salary, costs of employee benefits, supervisory costs, and incidental costs.

For example, for a hypothetical company of 1200 employees with 78,000 person-hours lost to absenteeism, the total absence cost is $560,886. When this figure is divided by 1200, the cost is $464.41 per employee for the period covered. (In this example, the absent workers were paid. If absent workers are not paid, their salary figures are omitted from the computation.)

Computing the Absenteeism Rates

It is advisable for management to determine the seriousness of its absenteeism problem by maintaining individual and departmental attendance records and by computing absenteeism rates. Neither a universally accepted definition of absence nor a standard formula for computing absenteeism rates exists.[15] However, one method used by many companies is:

$$\frac{\text{Number of worker days lost through job absence during period}}{\text{Average number of employees} \times \text{number of workdays}} \times 100$$

If 300 worker days are lost through job absence during one month having 25 scheduled working days at an organization that employs 500 workers, the absenteeism rate for that month is:

$$\frac{300}{500 \times 25} \times 100 = 2.4 \text{ percent}$$

Job absence can be defined as the failure of employees to report to work when their schedules require it, whether or not such failure to report is excused. Scheduled vacations, holidays, and prearranged leaves of absence are not counted as job absence.

Computing absenteeism rates permits the identification of problem areas—those industries, occupations, or groups of workers with the highest incidence of absence or with rapidly increasing rates of absence. For example, a Nova Scotia government audit of sick leave established that its employees took an average of 10.8 sick days per year, compared to a national average of 7.3 days for public-sector workers and 6.6 days for all Canadian workers; sick leave costs this province's government about $25 million per year in 1991–1992.[16] (The abuse of sick-leave programs is discussed in Ethics in HRM.) The Conference Board of Canada and Statistics Canada publish absenteeism data that organizations can use for purposes of comparison.

> **ETHICS IN HRM**

SICK-LEAVE ABUSE

Medical reasons represent the largest cause of absenteeism in Canada. Every large organization has a sick-leave policy that allows employees who are sick to be paid. The number of "sick days" permitted ranges from five to twenty days per year. The costs per employee per year range from $200 to $620, depending on the size of the company. Most policies allow unused days to accumulate, so that if an individual has a serious illness he or she can be covered for extended periods.

An audit of sick-leave patterns will tend to indicate that some individuals never take sick leave, some use blocks of sick leave for major illnesses, and others are sick one or two days per month, depending on the policy. Two ethical problems arise from these patterns.

One is the potential for abuse. HR managers feel that a policy of giving a specific number of sick days per year encourages abuse, as employees come to regard sick days as an entitlement like vacation days. For example, air traffic controllers were accused of abusing the system. Two controllers would strike a deal whereby one would call in sick, knowing the other would be called in on double time pay and return the favour later.

When employees can't accumulate or bank sick-leave days, they may use them as "personal leave days." The policy may require a note from a doctor, an easy hurdle to overcome. One reporter faked a flulike illness and obtained notes from nine in ten doctors. Is sick leave an earned right?

Banking sick leave is another issue. One healthy school official, who took only 4.5 sick days in 33 years, received $96,000 upon retirement because the collective agreement allowed him to bank twelve to twenty days per year. Are sick days "owed" to employees?

Sources: "MD Notes a Breeze to Obtain," *Winnipeg Free Press*, April 4, 1993, A1; "School Official Got $96,000 for Sick Leave He Didn't Use," *Vancouver Sun*, December 17, 1992, A1; and G. Rowan, "High Overtime Criticized in Audit, *The Globe and Mail*, December 20, 1993, A1, A2.

Reducing Absenteeism

While an employer may find that absenteeism rates and costs are within an acceptable range, it is advisable to study the statistics and determine exactly where the numbers are rooted. Rarely does absenteeism spread itself evenly across an organization.[17] A fairly high number of workers may have perfect attendance records, while some may be absent frequently. Effective HRM requires that individual attendance records be monitored by supervisors, that incentives be provided for perfect attendance, and that progressive discipline procedures be used with employees who have a record of chronic absenteeism.[18] The direct and continuing involvement of all managers and supervisors is essential.

By establishing a comprehensive absenteeism policy, the Allen-Bradley Company was able to cut absenteeism 83.5 percent in a 25-month period. Part of the company's attendance policy reads:

> It is important to the successful operation of the Motion Control Division that employees be at work each scheduled workday. Each employee is performing an important set of tasks or activities. Excessive and/or avoidable absenteeism places unfair burdens on co-workers and increases the company's cost of doing business by disruption of work schedules, [creating] inefficiency and waste, delays, costly overtime, job pressures and customer complaints.[19]

Occupational Injuries and Illnesses

We noted in Chapter 14 that employers are required by occupational health and safety legislation to maintain a log and summary of occupational injuries and illnesses. Detailed information about accidents and illnesses provides a starting point for analyzing problem areas, making changes in the working environment, and motivating personnel to promote safety and health.

Information about safety records is usually compiled by workers' compensation boards across Canada. The Industrial Association for the Prevention of Accidents (IAPA) uses these records, and others from various government agencies, to publish information about safety statistics. In order to make such comparisons, it is necessary to compute for an individual organization the *incidence rate*, which is the number of injuries and illnesses per 100 full-time employees during a given year. The standard formula for computing the incidence rate is shown by the following equation, where 200,000 equals the base for 100 full-time workers who work 40 hours a week, 50 weeks a year:

$$\text{Incidence rate} = \frac{\text{Number of injuries and illnesses} \times 200{,}00}{\text{Total hours worked by all employees during period covered}}$$

Incidence rates thus provide a basis for making comparisons with other organizations doing similar work. These rates are also useful for making comparisons between work groups, between departments, and between similar units within an organization. Application of this formula to the experience of one organization and the use of a table for comparative purposes are illustrated in the following example.

Shannon's Concrete Company, with an average annual employment of 80 individuals during 1994, experienced fifteen recordable injuries and illnesses in that year. The total number of hours worked by all employees during this period was 127,000 (from payroll or other time records):

$$\frac{15 \times 200{,}000}{127{,}000} = 23.6 \text{ incidence rate}$$

Therefore, Shannon's Concrete experienced an incidence rate for total recordable cases of 23.6 injuries and illnesses per 100 full-time employees during 1994.

objective

Attitude surveys

Employee survey
conducted on an
organization-wide or
department-wide basis to
obtain data for use in
making organizational
changes.

Employee Attitude Surveys

The influence of attitudes and values on employee productivity is well recognized. In assessing attitudes, employers are typically interested in those attitudes that relate to the job; to effectiveness of supervision; and to communication, compensation, training and development, and special organizational concerns.[20] With such information it is possible to make organizational changes that will, it is hoped, increase productivity and job satisfaction. One of the most objective and economical approaches to obtaining data for use in making organizational changes is through **attitude surveys**. These surveys are usually conducted on an organization-wide or plant-wide basis and usually involve the administration of a questionnaire (or inventory) or the use of interviews.

Organization-Specific Attitude Surveys

A central reason for developing an organization-specific attitude survey is the recognition that each organization has distinctive characteristics as a place to work. Surveys that include customized questions produce data on key issues such as quality of training or supervision that are critical to current operations.[21] Furthermore, tailor-made questionnaires can uncover vital information about the progress of newly implemented HR activities while pointing the way to new or improved HR programs.[22]

Organization-specific surveys are best designed when managers and employees participate with the HR staff to develop survey areas and questions. Top managers can identify overall issues for review while employees provide input in concerns relevant to them.[23]

Organization-specific questionnaires are not readily comparable to industry averages. Fortunately, these surveys provide a tool for gauging progress toward attaining an organizational vision. By using your organization as your primary benchmark, you can design a survey to measure progress toward attaining a specific cultural vision, instilling certain values, or achieving organizational goals.[24] CIBC Insurance, in its developmental and rapid growth stages, surveyed employees every six months. The steps in conducting a questionnaire survey are described in Figure 18-3.

Commercial Questionnaires

Organizations can purchase standard survey instruments from national sources. This practice will save the HR staff from the development, tabulation, and analysis of data. It allows for comparison of responses with related industry groups and is considered an economical way to run an employee survey.

One commercially available questionnaire is the *Campbell Organizational Survey* (COS), published by National Computer Systems, Inc. This survey is designed to collect information about employee feelings of satisfaction, or frustration, about various aspects of the working environment such as supervision, support for innovation, and top leadership.[25] The COS asks for responses to statements about working life such as the following:

I have a lot of freedom to decide how to do my work.
Many of my co-workers are under a lot of pressure.
My supervisor keeps me up to date about what is happening.

> **FIGURE 18-3**   *Steps in Conducting an Attitude Survey*
>
> 1. **Planning the survey.** A careful planning of the survey is essential to its success. The objective of the survey should be clearly determined and discussed by representatives of the various groups concerned, namely, managers, supervisors, employees, and the union.
>
> 2. **Designing the questionnaire.** The questionnaire or inventory used in a survey should cover all phases of the employment situation that are believed to be related to employee satisfaction and dissatisfaction. Attitude surveys are better accepted by employees when employees at all levels participate in the development of the questionnaire items.
>
> 3. **Administering the questionnaire.** The conditions under which the attitude questionnaire is administered are of vital importance to the success of the survey and to the morale of the participants. Employees should be fully oriented so that they understand the purpose of the survey. Prepublicity should be given through newsletters, special bulletins, and mailers. The usual procedure is to administer the questionnaire anonymously to large groups during working hours.
>
> 4. **Analyzing the data.** A tabulation of results broken down by departments, male versus female employees, hourly versus managerial personnel, and other meaningful categories is the starting point in analyzing the data. If data are available from previous surveys, comparisons can be made. Comparisons are usually made between departments within the organization.
>
> 5. **Taking appropriate action.** Once problems are identified, appropriate action should be taken. Feedback on survey results and follow-up action that management has planned should be given to employees.

The 44 items in the COS cover the thirteen scales listed in Highlights in HRM 4. According to the developer's research, these scales are related to job satisfaction and productivity.

The COS provides not only summary statistics for an entire working group but also a personal profile of each respondent. Thus the COS can serve as both an attitude survey and a job-satisfaction questionnaire. The manual for the COS contains considerable information about the reliability and validity of the COS, the use of the instrument for one-on-one counselling and in small group discussions, and the implementation of the results.

Getting the most from the answers obtained in a survey requires careful analysis of the data (see step 4 in Figure 18-3). While data on the total population will probably reveal areas of HRM that need improvement, problems of small critical groups of employees can be lost when ratings of all employees are combined and averaged. Ratings of those who are very dissatisfied will be offset by the ratings of those who are extremely satisfied. To obtain a clear picture of the strengths and weaknesses of the organization and provide a guide to solutions, analysis by groups is essential.

In one survey, conducted by one of the authors, the organization specified that results be tabulated according to departments compared against the organizational average for each survey question. Highlights in HRM 5 illustrates how the data for

HIGHLIGHTS IN HRM

HRM
highlights

4   CAMPBELL ORGANIZATIONAL SURVEY SCALES

The categories listed compose the thirteen scales used to measure job satisfaction and productivity in the COS.

The work itself	Benefits
Working conditions	Job security
Freedom from stress	Promotional opportunities
Co-workers	Feedback Communications
Supervision	Organizational planning
Top leadership	Support for innovation
Pay	

Source: David Campbell, *Manual for the Campbell Organizational Survey* (Minneapolis, Minn.: National Computer Systems, 1990), 6. Reproduced with permission.

questions were presented to senior management. Findings from this study clearly indicate that a better understanding of organizational problems can be obtained from a careful analysis of the patterns of ratings for different groups within an organization, however the groups are defined.

Use of Interviews

Another way to learn about employee attitudes is through an interviewing program.[26] Interviewers should make it clear that the object of the interviews is to ascertain how to make the organization a more productive and satisfying place to work. The emphasis is on listening and encouraging participants to speak freely.

A list of items requiring action is maintained, and concrete and prompt feedback to employees on the action taken is essential. Organizations such as Xerox, Kraft Foods, and General Electric have found that the upward communication system utilizing interviews has paid off in terms of reduced absenteeism and turnover, less waste and spoilage, improved safety records, increased productivity, and higher profits.

Regardless of the method used to collect employee opinions, to be useful the data must be evaluated against some comparison group. Figure 18-4 identifies different ways to compare survey data.

HIGHLIGHTS IN HRM

HRM
highlights

5 ATTITUDE RATINGS, DEPARTMENT AND COMPANY AVERAGES—SELECTED QUESTIONS

DIMENSION	DEPARTMENT AVERAGES[1]				COMPANY AVERAGE[2]
	A	B	C	D	
My supervisor gives me timely feedback about my performance.	3.6	3.9	3.8	3.0	3.7
My supervisor is available and willing to discuss issues of concern to me.	4.3	4.2	4.5	3.4	4.2
My supervisor has good human relations skills.	3.5	3.9	3.8	3.3	3.8
I feel well informed about overall company policies and procedures.	3.9	3.3	3.8	3.7	3.5
Communications from managers are complete.	2.5	2.9	3.8	3.3	3.0
Departments cooperate with each other.	3.3	3.3	4.5	3.0	3.3
I believe morale is good in my department.	3.1	3.3	3.7	2.7	3.4
My pay is competitive with other companies within this industry.	2.9	3.2	3.3	3.3	3.4
I am adequately trained to perform my present job.	3.7	4.1	4.3	3.6	4.1
The promotional opportunities in this company are good.	2.3	2.6	3.0	2.4	3.2
This company cares about its employees.	3.3	3.2	4.0	3.3	3.5

1. Averages are based on numbers assigned to each scale choice: Very satisfied = 5, Satisfied = 4, Neutral = 3, Dissatisfied = 2, and Very dissatisfied = 1.
2. Company average is based on nine department averages.

Source: Results taken from an actual attitude survey conducted by George W. Bohlander.

FIGURE 18-4 *Ways to Compare Employee Survey Data*

After data are collected, they must be analyzed—the numbers must be translated into a clear picture. Yet, the meaning of a specific result is not always obvious. For example, if 55 percent of employees say the organization is a good place to work, is this an area of concern? The majority gave favorable ratings, but 45 percent did not. To identify the key strengths and concerns, your data can be compared:

- **Among major topic areas in the survey.** Do employees give favorable ratings to the benefits but unfavorable ratings to pay? How do ratings of training compare to ratings of advancement and opportunity?

- **Among employee subgroups.** Do senior managers differ from middle managers in their perceptions of the organization? Do hourly employees differ from professionals in their sense of pay equity? How do older employees differ in their view of advancement opportunities?

- **To other organizations.** Consulting firms with expertise in employee opinion surveys typically maintain large databases of employee responses to standard questions. Using this information, you can compare your results to what would be expected from other employers in your industry or geographic area.

- **To past surveys in your organization.** Are employee opinions becoming more or less favorable? As important as it is to know where you stand now, it's equally important to know where you are headed.

- **To corporate objectives.** Some employers take the strategy of attracting and retaining employees through superior pay and advancement opportunities. Others prefer to emphasize a rich benefit program and job security. In both cases, it's important to compare how management wants to position the corporation relative to employee perception.

To understand your results and develop appropriate action plans, management needs to look at the information from each of these perspectives.

Source: William E. Wymer and Jeanne M. Carsten, "Alternative Ways to Gather Opinions," *HR Magazine* 37, no. 4 (April 1992): 71–78. Reprinted with the permission of *HR Magazine*, published by the Society for Human Resource Management, Alexandria, Va.

Using Audit Findings

In the preceding discussion, we observed that there are many sources and indicators from which information may be obtained about the overall effectiveness of the HRM program. This information must then be analyzed to identify the types of corrective action needed and the personnel best suited to carry it out.

Methods of Analyzing the Findings

Several approaches may be used in analyzing the information gathered from the various sources that have been described. These approaches include the following:

1. Compare HR programs with those of other organizations, especially the successful ones.
2. Base an audit on some source of authority, such as consultant norms, behavioural science findings, or an HRM textbook.
3. Rely on some ratios or averages, such as the ratio of HR staff to total employees.
4. Use a compliance audit to measure whether the activities of managers and staff in HRM comply with policies, procedures, and rules—an internal audit.
5. Manage the HR department by objectives and use a systems type of audit.[27]

George Odiorne recommends approach 5 of the approaches listed above, for when HR department objectives or goals are supportive of the organizational goals, top management is more likely to recognize the value of the department's functions and provide the support it needs. Where the comparison method is used, figures from outside sources are available. We have seen that comparison data may be obtained from government agencies, reporting services, employer associations, industry trade associations, and consulting firms.

Surveys conducted regularly by various organizations provide information that can be used to compare costs of the total program and its parts. Data on the compensation of HR professionals, department budgets, and personnel staff ratios are reported periodically in journals and in reporting services' publications. The **personnel staff ratio** is the number of persons on the personnel staff per 100 employees on the organization payroll. Surveys report personnel staff ratios ranging from one HR specialist per 571 employees to one per 120 employees. The range is wide because some surveys define an HR employee as a specialist or professional, while others include all HR staff (e.g., receptionists and clerks) in this definition. Larger, more white-collar organizations employ more specialized HR personnel.[28]

> **Personnel staff ratio**
> Number of persons on the HR staff per 100 employees on the organization payroll.

Costs of the Program

We noted earlier in the chapter that it is important to translate audit findings into dollar costs wherever possible. Saying that turnover is "expensive" is not enough. When cost data are available, it is possible to make informed decisions about how much should be spent to improve existing programs or institute new ones, such as a program to reduce turnover. HR specialists should take the lead in preparing cost figures for as many of the HR activities as possible. With such figures the relationship between costs and benefits, and between costs and effectiveness of the proposed activities can be clearly demonstrated. A **cost-benefit analysis** is the analysis of the costs of a particular function—for example, training—in monetary units as compared with nonmonetary benefits such as attitudes, health, and safety. A **cost-effectiveness analysis** is the analysis of the costs of a particular function in monetary units as compared with monetary benefits resulting from increases in production, reductions in waste and downtime, and so on.

> **Cost-benefit analysis**
> A comparison of the monetary costs of a particular function against the nonmonetary benefits received, like improved employee morale.

> **Cost-effectiveness analysis**
> A comparison of the monetary costs of a particular function against the monetary benefits resulting from increased organizational performance.

If HR managers are to be effective and valued as part of the management team, they must have a measurement orientation.[29] According to Jac Fitz-enz, since value in organizations is most often expressed in financial terms, "HR professionals are gradually giving up vague, subjective terms for the more specific, objective language of numbers."[30] Innovative HR departments are increasing their influence within

> ## REALITY CHECK RC

ADDING VALUE THROUGH BENCHMARKING

Brian Orr, senior consultant, Sierra Systems Consultants, is a proponent of benchmarking HR to establish sound business processes in order to contribute to the overall effectiveness of the organization. "Benchmarking is an evolutionary step beyond auditing," Orr says. "Human resources has no established standards from which to compare various HR practices. In financial auditing, auditors have followed GAAP standards on a global basis, providing a type of benchmark. Because of those standards, the financial audit function can contribute to overall business success. In HR, the contribution to business success becomes more difficult. For a majority of companies in Canada, HR is in a transitional phase, moving toward becoming more value added."

There are two aspects to benchmarking. Specifically, HR needs to evaluate where they are now, and where they want to be so that they can develop a road map. According to Orr, "Four areas of HR should be audited. These are policy and strategy; program design, HR administrative practices and procedures, and HR systems. We know from studies conducted that HR professionals are spending 80 percent of their time on administrative functions. If their time could be freed up from labour-intensive tasks, they could become more business-focused and add value."

Orr sees benchmarking as a methodology that leads to a systematic way of learning or researching. He recommends eight steps:

1. Decide what area to benchmark. The scope of HR is too vast, so focus on a smaller area.
2. Audit how you are doing things today. There is usually a variance between what is actually written in policy and what is happening. To understand what is affecting performance, you need to look at the reality.
3. Start to research what companies are doing. This information is usually found in professional journals, association reports, and presentations.
4. Contact successful companies for an appointment to meet with them to discuss and review their practices. There are two aspects— what and why.
5. Analyze the results and determine what your organization needs and what practices will work for you.
6. Determine what tools will be needed to get the job done.
7. Develop an implementation plan
8. Implement and monitor progress.

"Only when things start to change will you know if your benchmark strategy is working," says Orr. "The value in benchmarking is in the results." The success of HR will be measured by how well it can contribute to an organization's success.

Source: Interview by Deborah M. Zinni, August 1995.

their organizations by moving beyond the traditional administrative role and practising "human value management"—helping their organizations to achieve important human, production, and financial objectives by using people's skills and talents to the best advantage. One consultant describes the process of adding value through benchmarking in Reality Check on page 688.

Preparation of Reports and Recommendations

One of the most important activities of the audit team is the preparation of reports of their findings, evaluations, and recommendations. The reports should include everything that is pertinent and useful to the recipients. One report is usually prepared for line managers. A special report is prepared for the HR department manager, who also receives a copy of the report given to line managers.

The value to be derived from information obtained from audits lies in the use made of the information to correct deficiencies in the HR program. An analysis of the data may reveal that procedures for carrying out some of the HR functions need to be revised. It is even possible that certain parts of the total program should undergo a thorough revision if they are to meet the objectives that have been established for them. Finally, the policies for each of the various functions should be examined to determine their adequacy as part of the overall HR policy.

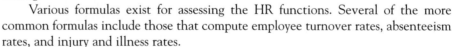

> **SUMMARY**

one
objective

HR audits serve to evaluate various personnel policies, functions, or activities that contribute to organizational success. The audit is a data-based evaluation that can be used to support or change existing HR policies or procedures or to suggest completely new areas for improvement.

two
objective

Comprehensive HR audits will encompass three areas: assessing the HR department's compatibility with overall organizational goals; assessing organizational compliance with all applicable federal, provincial, and municipal laws and regulations; and evaluating the individual HR functions such as recruitment, health and safety, and compensation. Area-specific audits may evaluate topics of current concern to managers such as the culture of the organization or the existence of a glass ceiling.

three
objective

Various formulas exist for assessing the HR functions. Several of the more common formulas include those that compute employee turnover rates, absenteeism rates, and injury and illness rates.

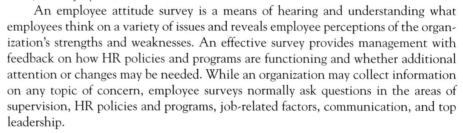
four
objective

An employee attitude survey is a means of hearing and understanding what employees think on a variety of issues and reveals employee perceptions of the organization's strengths and weaknesses. An effective survey provides management with feedback on how HR policies and programs are functioning and whether additional attention or changes may be needed. While an organization may collect information on any topic of concern, employee surveys normally ask questions in the areas of supervision, HR policies and programs, job-related factors, communication, and top leadership.

objective

To be meaningful, audit findings should be compared with some accepted measure of performance. This can be done, for example, by benchmarking against other organizations or by comparison with industry norms or different research findings.

KEY TERMS

absenteeism rate	cultural audit
attitude surveys	exit interview
benchmarking	glass ceiling
cost-benefit analysis	personnel staff ratio
cost-effectiveness analysis	turnover rate

DISCUSSION QUESTIONS

1. Why is it important to audit the HRM program periodically?
2. Some organizations employ specially trained consultants to conduct HR resources audits.
   a. What are the advantages and disadvantages of using consultants for this purpose?
   b. Consultants often compare the audit findings from an organization with those of other organizations with which they are familiar. Of what value are such comparisons?
3. Explain how benchmarking contributes to a successful HR audit.
4. Many organizations have found it necessary to be prepared for compliance audits by government agencies.
   a. How can managers best prepare themselves for such an audit?
   b. How much effort should be devoted to preparing for compliance audits?
5. Describe the type of information available in records and reports that can be used in auditing the major HR functions. Give some examples of data that are easily computerized.
6. Why is it important to compute absenteeism rates? What steps can management take to reduce absenteeism?
7. What are the advantages of conducting periodic employee attitude surveys? Are any problems likely to arise over a survey? Explain.

CASE: Western Cannery's Employee Attitude Survey

The management of Western Cannery, a firm that employs 1500 workers to prepare and can baby foods, decided it was time to survey its employees to determine their attitudes toward their jobs and general working conditions. For about two weeks the operations manager, who had had previous experience with surveys, met with representatives of management and employees to develop areas and questions for the survey. A timetable was established for completion of the survey instrument and for conducting the survey. All employees were given details about the purpose of the survey and how it would be conducted.

On the scheduled day, employees assembled in the company auditorium in groups of 200. After a brief orientation by the operations manager, a questionnaire containing about 100 items was administered. The employees answered the items by checking "Agree," "Disagree," or "Undecided." Provision was also made for employees to write their comments on the form. The only identification required on the questionnaire was the individual's crew number.

After all employees had participated and data were tabulated and summarized, reports were prepared for submission to the department heads and the plant manager. The reports were broken down by each major department and by crews. The comments that employees had written on the form were summarized to facilitate their use by those concerned.

The following is an extract from the company report that was sent to the manager of the preparation department. It concerned a crew of 45 employees (Crew X-31) who prepared meats and vegetables for canning. The crew was under the supervision of a general supervisor who had three lead persons also responsible to him. Crew X-31 employees were paid on the basis of straight time plus incentive bonuses.

Extract of Report

The statistical analysis of the questionnaires for this crew reveals that attitudes toward the company as a whole, top management, and other areas measured are quite favourable. Employee attitudes toward the following areas, however, are quite unfavourable:

- Friendliness and cooperation of fellow employees
- Supervisor and employee interpersonal relations
- Technical competence of supervision

The comments that employees wrote on their answer sheets concerning the three areas viewed unfavourably can be summarized as follows:

- *Friendliness and cooperation of fellow employees.* There are apparently older employees who adopt a bossy and domineering manner regarding those with less seniority. Certain groups in the crew, specifically aboriginals and women, feel underutilized and treated in an inferior manner by their colleagues. Those ordinarily engaged in the preparation of vegetables resent being transferred, when necessary, to the preparation of chicken on the basis that they cannot make a sufficient bonus. They suspect favouritism at such times.

- *Supervisor and employee interpersonal relations.* The general supervisor often bypasses the lead persons in contacts with employees. There are frequent changes in work that come up without warning or explanation, allowing only enough time to give orders to change what is being done and to transfer employees to other types of work where perhaps less bonus is to be made. The lead person, therefore, becomes more often than not the harbinger of bad news rather than the motivator. Scheduling of rest periods is a problem.
- *Technical competence of supervision.* Although there is possibly enough equipment available for the employees to do their jobs, the equipment does not seem to be in the right place at the right time. Food carts are one of the main shortages, and any change in work amplifies this. Employees do their job the same way day after day, but the inspectors can change their minds in interpreting procedure. They then write a note about an employee, giving name and badge number to the plant manager. The employee sometimes gets a written reprimand, and this causes friction. Employees feel that it should be brought to the employee's attention in some other way. There have been times when the employees tried to retaliate by damaging the product.

Questions

1. If you were the manager of the preparation department, what immediate action would you take on the basis of this report? What long-range action would you take?
2. What role should the HR department play in the follow-up of the critical aspects of the attitude survey?
3. Was this survey necessary? Couldn't management obtain the same type of information by just keeping its eyes and ears open? Discuss.

Auditing and Benchmarking the Career Plan

A. Auditing

Each of the eighteen chapters in this text contained an exercise designed to help you formulate a career plan. Review the list of exercise to assess your completion rate.

	Completed ✓
1. Getting Ready	
2. Self-Employment	
3. Wrongs versus Rights	
4. Life Planning	
5. Your Dream Job	
6. Job-Search Strategies	
7. Résumé Preparation	
8. Training Lists	
9. Assessing Values	
10. Performance Feedback	
11. Compensation in Your Career	
12. Assessing Your Incentives	
13. Flexible Benefits	
14. Job Stress Assessment	
15. Conflict Management Styles	
16. Salary Negotiation Tactics	
17. Culture Quiz	
18. Auditing and Benchmarking the Career Plan	

B. Benchmarking

Identify people you admire who have been successful and who are recognized leaders. Define why you think they are successful. To do this, determine the performance measure of success. For example, at 40 Bill Gates was the world's richest individual. Nancy Green was 23 when she won the Olympic Gold Medal for skiing, and 34 when she started a hotel business in Whistler, British Columbia. You may wish to identify measures of success that have meaning for you, such as:

- finish an MBA by 30
- start a home business by 35
- be able to live a comfortable life while working twenty hours per week

Using all the information you have gathered in the Career Counsels, complete your Career Plan, and measure your success against your personal benchmarks.

NOTES AND REFERENCES

1. Mark A. Huselid, "Documenting HR's Effect on Company Performance," *HR Magazine* 39, no. 1 (January 1994): 79–85. See also Anne S. Tsui and Luis R. Gomez-Mejia, "Evaluating Human Resource Effectiveness," in Lee Dyer, ed., *Human Resource Management: Evolving Roles and Responsibilities* (Washington, DC: Bureau of National Affairs, 1988), 1:187–1:198.

2. Vicki S. David, "Self-Audits: First Step in TQM," *HR Magazine* 37, no. 9 (September 1992): 39–41.

3. Johnathan A. Segal and Mary A. Quinn, "How to Audit Your HR Programs," *Personnel Administrator* 34, no. 5 (May 1989): 67–70.

4. Tsui and Gomez-Mejia, "Evaluating Human Resource Effectiveness," 1:198.

5. Donald J. Ford, "Benchmarking HRD," *Training and Development* 47, no. 6 (June 1993): 36–41. See also Michael J. Spendolini, "The Benchmarking Process," *Compensation and Benefits Review* 24, no. 5 (September-October 1992): 21–29.

6. Ford, "Benchmarking," 38.

7. Ronald L. Adler and Francis T. Coleman, *Employment-Labor Law Audit* (Rockville, MD: Bureau of National Affairs, 1994).

8. For an excellent source of information about the types of data that should be gathered within each HR functional area, see G. Rampton, I. Turnbull, and A. Doran, *Human Resources Management Systems*, Nelson Canada HRM Series (series editor, Monica Belcourt) (Scarborough, ON: Nelson Canada, 1996).

9. Joanne Wisniewski, "The Needs-Based HRIS Audit," *HR Magazine* 36, no. 9 (September 1991): 61–82.

10. Tsui and Gomez-Mejia, "Evaluating Human Resource Effectiveness," 1:194, 1:195.

11. Wayne F. Cascio, *Costing Human Resources: The Financial Impact of Behavior in Organizations*, 3rd ed. (Boston: PWS-Kent, 1991): 8–9. See also Eric G. Flamholtz, *Human Resource Accounting: Advances in Concepts, Methods, and Applications*, 2nd ed. (San Francisco: Jossey-Bass, 1985).

12. Cari M. Dominguez, "A Crack in the Glass Ceiling," *HR Magazine* 35, no. 12 (December 1990): 65–66.

13. Patrick Kelly, "Conduct a Glass Ceiling Self-Audit Now," *HR Magazine* 38, no. 10 (October 1993): 76–80.

14. Robert A. Giacalone and Stephen B. Knouse, "Farewell to Fruitless Exit Interviews," *Personnel* 66, no. 9 (September 1989): 60–62. See also Steve Jenkins, "Turnover: Correcting the Causes," *Personnel* 65, no. 12 (December 1988): 43–48.

15. Dan R. Dalton and Debra J. Mesch, "On the Extent and Reduction of Avoidable Absenteeism: An Assessment of Absence Policy Provisions," *Journal of Applied Psychology* 76, no. 6 (December 1991): 810–816.

16. A. Jeffers, "Our Civil Servants Sickest in Country" *Halifax Chronicle Herald*, December 12, 1994, A1, A2; L. Kelly, "Attendance Management: An Issue of the 90's," *Worklife* 8, no. 5 (1992): 12–14.

17. K. Dow Scott and Elizabeth L. McClelland, "Gender Differences in Absenteeism," *Public Personnel Management* 19, no. 2 (Summer 1990): 229–252.

18. Jeff Stinson, "Company Policy Attends to Chronic Absentees," *Personnel Journal* 70, no. 8 (August 1991): 82–85.

19. Allen-Bradley Employee Handbook.

20. Stephen L. Guinn, "Surveys Capture Untold Story," *HR Magazine* 37, no. 9 (September 1990): 64–66.

21. Catherine M. Petrini, "Another Look at Employee Surveys," *Training and Development* 49, no. 7 (July 1993): 15–18.

22. Robert J. Sahl, "Develop Company-Specific Employee Attitude Surveys," *Personnel Journal* 69, no. 5 (May 1990): 46–51.

23. Michael T. Roberson and Eric Sundstrom, "Questionnaire Design, Return Rates, and Response Favorableness in an Employee Attitude Questionnaire," *Journal of Applied Psychology* 75, no. 3 (June 1990): 354–357. See also Thomas Rotondi, "The Anonymity Factor in Questionnaire Surveys," *Personnel Journal* 68, no. 2 (February 1989): 92–101; and Leland G. Verheyen, "How to Develop an Employee Attitude Survey," *Training and Development Journal* 42, no. 8 (August 1988): 72–76.

24. David W. Bracken, "Benchmarking Employee Attitudes," *Training and Development* 46, no. 6 (June 1992): 49–53.

25. Information about the *Campbell Organizational Survey* may be obtained from National Computer Systems, 5606 Green Circle Drive, Minneapolis, MN 55343.

26. William E. Wymer and Jeanne M. Carsten, "Alternative Ways to Gather Opinions," *HR Magazine* 37, no. 4 (April 1992): 17–78.

27. George S. Odiorne, "Evaluating the Human Resources Program," in Joseph J. Famularo, *Handbook of Human Resources Administration*, 2nd ed. (New York: McGraw-Hill, 1986).

28. S. Dolan and R. Schuler, *Human Resource Management: The Canadian Perspective* (Scarborough, ON: Nelson Canada, 1994).

29. Cascio, *Costing Human Resources*, 119–121.

30. Jac Fitz-enz, *Human Value Management* (San Francisco: Jossey-Bass, 1990): 311–312.

NAME INDEX

ORGANIZATION INDEX

SUBJECT INDEX

PHOTO CREDITS

To the owner of this book

We hope that you have enjoyed *Managing Human Resources,* Canadian edition, and we would like to know as much about your experiences with this text as you would care to offer. Only through your comments and those of others can we learn how to make this a better text for future readers.

School _____ Your instructor's name _____

Course _____ Was the text required? _____ Recommended? _____

1. What did you like the most about *Managing Human Resources?*

_____
_____
_____

2. How useful was this text for your course?

_____
_____
_____

3. Do you have any recommendations for ways to improve the next edition of this text?

_____
_____
_____

4. In the space below or in a separate letter, please write any other comments you have about the book. (For example, please feel free to comment on reading level, writing style, terminology, design features, and learning aids.)

_____
_____
_____
_____

Optional

Your name _____ Date _____

May Nelson Canada quote you, either in promotion for *Managing Human Resources* or in future publishing ventures?

Yes _____ No _____

Thanks!

- - - - - - - - - - - FOLD HERE - - - - - - - - - - -

TAPE SHUT

MAIL ⟩⟩ POSTE

Canada Post Corporation / Société canadienne des postes

Postage paid
if mailed in Canada

Port payé
si posté au Canada

Business Reply

Réponse d'affaires

0107077099　　　**01**

0107077099-M1K5G4-BR01

Nelson

TAPE SHUT

Nelson Canada
Market and Product Development
1120 Birchmount Rd.
Scarborough, ON M1K 9Z9

PLEASE TAPE SHUT. DO NOT STAPLE.